Federal Courts

ASPEN PUBLISHERS

EXAMPLES&EXPLANATIONS

Federal Courts

Laura E. Little
Professor of Law and James E. Beasley Chair in Law
Temple University, Beasley School of Law

Wolters Kluwer
Law & Business

AUSTIN   BOSTON   CHICAGO   NEW YORK   THE NETHERLANDS

© 2006 Aspen Publishers, Inc.
a Wolters Kluwer business
http://lawschool.aspenpublishers.com

Aspen Publishers
Attn: Permissions Department
76 Ninth Avenue, 7th Floor
New York, NY 10011-5201

Printed in the United States of America.

1 2 3 4 5 6 7 8 9 0

ISBN 978-0-7355-6146-5

Library of Congress Cataloging-in-Publication Data

Little, Laura E., 1957-
   Federal courts : examples and explanations / Laura Little. – 1st ed.
     p. cm.
   ISBN 978-0-7355-6146-5 (alk. paper)
  1. Courts–United States. 2. Jurisdiction–United States. 3. Judicial power–United States.
4. Procedure (Law)–United States. I. Title.

KF8719.L58 2007
347.73′2–dc22

2007016795

About Wolters Kluwer Law & Business

Wolters Kluwer Law & Business is a leading provider of research information and workflow solutions in key specialty areas. The strengths of the individual brands of Aspen Publishers, CCH, Kluwer Law International and Loislaw are aligned within Wolters Kluwer Law & Business to provide comprehensive, in-depth solutions and expert-authored content for the legal, professional and education markets.

CCH was founded in 1913 and has served more than four generations of business professionals and their clients. The CCH products in the Wolters Kluwer Law & Business group are highly regarded electronic and print resources for legal, securities, antitrust and trade regulation, government contracting, banking, pension, payroll, employment and labor, and healthcare reimbursement and compliance professionals.

Aspen Publishers is a leading information provider for attorneys, business professionals and law students. Written by preeminent authorities, Aspen products offer analytical and practical information in a range of specialty practice areas from securities law and intellectual property to mergers and acquisitions and pension/benefits. Aspen's trusted legal education resources provide professors and students with high-quality, up-to-date and effective resources for successful instruction and study in all areas of the law.

Kluwer Law International supplies the global business community with comprehensive English-language international legal information. Legal practitioners, corporate counsel and business executives around the world rely on the Kluwer Law International journals, loose-leafs, books and electronic products for authoritative information in many areas of international legal practice.

Loislaw is a premier provider of digitized legal content to small law firm practitioners of various specializations. Loislaw provides attorneys with the ability to quickly and efficiently find the necessary legal information they need, when and where they need it, by facilitating access to primary law as well as state-specific law, records, forms and treatises.

Wolters Kluwer Law & Business, a unit of Wolters Kluwer, is headquartered in New York and Riverwoods, Illinois. Wolters Kluwer is a leading multinational publisher and information services company.

For Rich, Cate, and Graham

Summary of Contents

Contents

PART III   LIMITATIONS OF FEDERAL COURT ADJUDICATION   91

Chapter 5   Justiciability Doctrines   93

Chapter 6   Congressional Control over Jurisdiction   115

PART IV THE ROLE OF STATE COURTS IN THE FEDERALIST SYSTEM 219

Chapter 9 State Court Authority to Enforce Federal Law 221

Chapter 10 State Court Responsibility to Enforce Federal Law 229

PART VI FEDERAL COURTS AS SUPERVISORS OF STATE AND LOCAL OFFICIALS

Chapter 13 Eleventh Amendment Restrictions — 333

Chapter 14 Section 1983   371

Contents

PART VII   FEDERAL COURTS AS LAWMAKERS   417

Chapter 15   The *Erie* Mandate   421

Chapter 16   Federal Common Law   443

Acknowledgments

This project was generously supported by Temple University's Beasley School of Law and its fine library staff. I owe special gratitude to Professor Richard Greenstein, Professor Craig Green, and Professor Celestine McConville, who reviewed parts of the manuscript. Professor Mark Rahdert provided inspiration and support, as did my first Federal Courts teacher and colleague, Professor Rob Bartow. Able research assistance came from Brooke Leach, Samantha Evans, Joe Karlan and — especially — Joe Langkamer. Michael Foley provided expert and creative help with the figures. Finally, I am indebted to Shirley Hall, Sehnyoung Lee, and Jennifer Kelly for their help in processing the manuscript.

PART I

Introduction to Federal Courts

1

Strategy for Studying Federal Courts and Jurisdiction

Power. That's what Federal Courts and Jurisdiction is all about. And power struggles are inherently interesting. Should your mind stray from distraction or boredom as you study, remind yourself that underlying the complex web of federal court doctrines is a question of brute force: who gets to control the various aspects of human existence that make their way into our legal systems? These power struggles occur among a variety of actors in U.S. society — but the clashes between Congress and the courts and between the federal and state governments comprise the bulk of federal court disputes.

Like other areas of law, such as Civil Procedure, Federal Courts and Jurisdiction is often abstract, detached from physical boundaries and the realities of daily life outside the legal system. Making matters worse, federal court rules result from complex and seemingly contradictory Supreme Court decisions. Not to worry. Several strategies are available to help you navigate the maze.

A. EYE ON THE BOTTOM LINE

Remember that many, many federal court decisions are fundamentally about whether one of the parties (usually the plaintiff) can get the case into federal court and whether the opposing party can get the case out of federal court. The actual opinion may evaluate a broad array of factors, including precedent, jurisprudence, governmental theory, and hidden ideological motivations. But the bottom-line question most often is: will a federal court get to the merits of this case? Remembering this practical strategy should help you remain mindful of the "forest" while trying to master the "trees." As you focus on the bottom-line question, make sure you understand the plight of the party trying to get the case into federal court.

This focus on the bottom line should help you understand the practical effect of a decision denying or granting a litigant federal court access. To avoid oversimplification, however, you need to remember that some federal jurisdiction doctrines do not turn on federal court access. Examples are those decisions that analyze *how* federal courts must resolve cases (by, for instance, applying state law in a diversity action or creating federal common law) and those decisions that address *whether* and *how* state courts resolve cases with federal components (by, for example, being required to entertain federal causes of action in some instances but being excused from doing so when sovereign immunity precludes the lawsuit). Whether the case concerns the "bottom line" or these other matters, one can generally be assured that the federal jurisdiction issue triggers important ideological stakes.

Example 1-1

The plaintiff is a transgender individual who believes that her employer fired her because she was undergoing a change in gender. She filed her suit in federal district court. Assume that the United States Supreme Court decided that the federal district court lacked subject matter jurisdiction and dismissed the case.

Explanation

The bottom line of the Court's decision in this example is straightforward: the plaintiff is *out* of federal court. In evaluating the practical effect of this bottom line, you might ask, "Does the decision mean that the plaintiff's employment discrimination injuries will go unremedied? Will the plaintiff have substantial difficulty getting redress in another forum, such as state court?" The answers may shed light on the justices' motivations for the decision. Although the Supreme Court decision may have focused expressly on the threshold question of subject matter jurisdiction, the decision's effect may significantly influence substantive rights. For that reason, one might explore the possibility that broad principles of governmental structure or other ideology unrelated to the specifics of subject matter jurisdiction motivated the justices. This chapter discusses these possible ulterior motives.

B. GOVERNMENTAL THEORY

Opinions about federal courts reflect important debates about the optimal structure for government. These debates fall into two broad categories:

federalism and separation of powers. Federalism in this context means the appropriate allocation of authority between the federal and state governments. Which government — federal or state — gets to set and apply the rules for the particular area of life litigated in the case? Separation of powers concerns whether the judicial, legislative, or executive branch has the power to regulate. In the federal courts arena, the most pertinent separation of powers concerns focus on the three branches of the federal government. This is sometimes called horizontal separation of powers, while the relationship between the state and federal governments is sometimes called vertical separation of powers. This book uses the term "separation of powers" as the Supreme Court justices most often do: to refer only to separation within the federal government. Using the term "vertical" to describe separation of powers in federalism is misleading in that it suggests a consistently hierarchical relationship between the state and federal courts. Federal courts doctrine, however, is brimming with instances where federal courts go out of their way to avoid usurping or interfering with state power. Examples include the Anti-Injunction Act, abstention doctrines, the doctrine of independent and adequate state grounds, habeas corpus law, and the Rooker-Feldman doctrine. These doctrines, as well as others that reflect deference to state power, will be covered in the pages that follow.

Figure 1-1 may help you conceptualize the distinction between federalism and separation of powers. In evaluating this diagram be mindful of a concept explored later in this book: the federal government's supremacy (its place "on top") does not mean supremacy for all purposes. After all, the federal government is a government of limited authority, with state and local governments possessing many powers that the federal government does not.

United States Supreme Court opinions often explicitly state that theories of government impel a particular result. In disposing of the case described

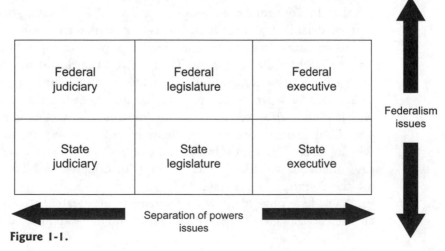

Figure 1-1.

in Example 1-1, the Supreme Court might reason that the United States Congress did not grant the federal courts power to consider discrimination claims of this variety. The Court might conclude that, if a federal district court refused to exercise jurisdiction in the situation in Example 1-1, the district court would illegitimately invade congressional prerogatives in the federal system. In other words, the Court might explain Example 1-1's result in terms of separation of powers.

One way to understand the contrasting or inconsistent results in federal court cases is to appreciate that the various members of the Supreme Court do not embrace the same views on separation of powers or federalism. These different views on governmental theory can explain varying results.

Many theories of government penetrate federal court cases, characterized by both subtle and dramatic variety. Three sets of theories, however, are particularly useful in understanding differences in Supreme Court decisions. The first two sets reflect battling orientations toward government. One set — often revealed in cases presenting separation of powers issues — includes the "functionalist" orientation versus the "formalist" orientation. The second set — often reflected in cases presenting federalism issues — involves the "nationalist" orientation versus the "federalist" orientation. The third is the process model, which proves most useful in resolving federalism questions.

In cases presenting separation of powers issues, the Court's decision whether to analyze the issues using a functionalist or formalist perspective powerfully influences the result. Separation of powers questions concern whether a branch is properly exercising a particular power. In Example 1-1, one might ask whether the federal constitutional scheme gives the federal judiciary power to grant a remedy in a discrimination case. A formalist orientation would likely consider the list of tasks the Constitution assigns to the federal judiciary and ask whether the challenged task is on that list. (As a general matter, formalists tend to focus on order, clarity of notice, and efficiency.) In a separation of powers context, a formalist would likely point out that the Constitution envisions federal courts adjudicating cases arising under federal law, and that Example 1-1 presents such a case.

Functionalists tend to be more open to power sharing and to generally "messy" analysis than formalists. Thus, the functionalist focuses less on the precise list of tasks the Constitution provides for each branch of government in analyzing a separation of powers dispute. Instead, a functionalist asks whether a branch's exercise of power constitutes an incursion on another branch's domain or core functions. In Example 1-1, a functionalist might ask whether a federal court's adjudication of an employment discrimination case interferes with the president's or with Congress's ability to do the job the Constitution describes.

Many have observed how the Supreme Court gyrates between formalist and functionalist approaches without explanation. The approach the Supreme

Court follows powerfully impacts case results. Formalist opinions tend to strike down a grant of power to a particular branch. Functionalist opinions, on the other hand, entertain a balance of factors and almost always justify a grant of power.[1]

The other major set of contrasting concepts related to federal jurisdiction cases are federalism and nationalism. In contemporary parlance, the term "federalist" evokes the image of an individual preferring state power over federal power, and "nationalist" describes one willing to expand federal power. In the context of federal jurisdiction cases, Professor Richard Fallon expounded on this distinction, observing that opinions oriented toward nationalism tend to reflect the view that federal judges have a greater ability and willingness to apply federal law than state judges.[2] Nationalist opinions also often emphasize the Constitution's grant of supremacy to the federal government and the special need for the national government to protect federal rights. Federalist opinions highlight the protection of state sovereignty and equal abilities among federal and state judges in applying federal law. In particular, these opinions often emphasize that state courts have the duty and competence to interpret and to apply federal law, and in fact do so with regularity, especially in the context of criminal cases. On numerous occasions, federalist opinions point out that Article III of the United States Constitution does not actually create lower federal courts. According to these opinions, the possibility of only state courts being available to adjudicate federal matters is an important reason to resist expanded federal jurisdiction.

The factors characterizing federalist or nationalist opinions do not appear in every case. Yet opinions often reflect these factors as part of their reasoning. Thus, for example, the opinion behind the result in Example 1-1 may hold that employment issues are traditionally within the state domain and that state courts are competent to apply any federal laws that may touch on the employer-employee relationship. A dissenting opinion in Example 1-1 might argue that federal courts should intervene in the controversy because an important federal guarantee — equal protection of the laws — hangs in the balance.

The third theory of governmental structure — the process model — is related to the federalist/nationalist dichotomy. The process model presumes that jurisdictional power should be allocated to ensure fair and accurate

---

1. For further discussion of functionalism and formalism in separation of powers cases, *see*, *e.g.*, Laura E. Little, *Envy and Jealousy: A Study of Separation of Powers and Judicial Review*, 52 Hastings L.J. 47, 110-112 (2000).

2. Professor Richard Fallon explains the federalist/nationalist distinction in full in his article *The Ideologies of Federal Courts Law*, 74 Va. L. Rev. 1141 (1988). Many contemporary theorists debate whether state and federal courts are equal in their ability and willingness to apply federal law. *See*, *e.g.*, Michael E. Solimine & James L. Walker, Respecting State Courts: The Inevitability of Judicial Federalism (1999); Burt Neuborne, *The Myth of Parity*, 60 Harv. L. Rev. 1105 (1977); Michael Wells, *Behind the Parity Debate: The Decline of the Legal Process Tradition in the Law of Federal Courts*, 71 B.U. L. Rev. 609 (1991).

litigation results. When a court produces a result that is the product of a well-designed decision-making apparatus, the process model holds that the result is entitled to respect (even if another court could have done a better job). If, however, significant flaws are apparent in the court process, then the parties did not enjoy an opportunity for "full and fair" litigation, and the process model calls for opening the matter afresh.[3]

Federal courts use the process model most often when deciding whether to allow relitigation of a dispute already adjudicated in state court. The model counsels a federal court to evaluate only whether the parties received a sufficiently respectable quality of process and procedure in the earlier litigation. If the federal court concludes that the state forum satisfied this standard, it will not consider the merits of the dispute.

The three sets of models — formalist/functionalist, federalist/nationalist, and process — do not cover all federal jurisdiction cases. They nevertheless provide useful bases of analysis for categorizing federal jurisdiction cases, understanding disagreements among the justices, and explaining inconsistencies among cases.

C. ULTERIOR MOTIVE: WHAT ELSE IS UP THEIR SLEEVE?

One is often tempted to consider the possibility that judges decide Federal Courts and Jurisdiction cases based on ideological agendas, untethered from the constraints of precedent or existing theories of government. Under this view, a decision may result from a motive or belief unrelated to the structure of government, even though the opinion may not describe this motive. So, for example, we might explain the result in Example 1-1 by concluding that the justices who joined the majority opinion were hostile to discrimination claims or to transgender individuals such as the plaintiff.

Many argue that the ulterior-motive approach to understanding federal court cases is accurate and necessary. Ultimately, for the beginning student struggling to understand the complex doctrines actually discussed in decisions, this approach is of limited use. Using ulterior motives to explain decisions, a student frequently leaves many questions unanswered: How are we to identify the true ulterior motives? Are we to ignore all the stated reasons for the decision in favor of the implicit agendas? Are we to abandon traditional common law methodology in explaining factual distinctions in cases? Thus, although recognizing unstated reasons behind decisions is

---

3. Professor Paul Bator is identified as the first to articulate this process model concept. *See* Paul M. Bator, *Finality in Criminal Law and Federal Habeas Corpus for State Prisoners*, 76 Harv. L. Rev. 441 (1963).

essential to deep appreciation and subtle understanding of case law, one is best advised to focus first on the reasoning explicit on the face of the opinion.

D. UNDERSTANDING THE BASIC STRUCTURE OF THE FEDERAL JUDICIARY

1. What the Constitution Says

Article III of the United States Constitution provides first and foremost that the federal courts should decide "cases" or "controversies." Through this language, the Constitution restricts the federal courts' job description to resolving problems that litigants bring to them. While many judges and commentators believe federal courts have an important role in effecting social change, federal courts lack the affirmative power to proactively reach out and identify social problems for resolution. This limitation frequently influences federal jurisdiction decisions, restricting a court from enunciating broad principles or from rendering rulings that extend beyond the parties to the case before the court.

The Constitution provides for nine categories of disputes that federal courts can resolve, but the most common are cases arising under federal law and diversity cases in which federal courts act as umpires, resolving disputes between citizens of different states. Although it mentions these categories, the Constitution does not create lower federal courts. The framers encountered disagreement on the question of whether to create lower federal courts and decided to "punt," giving to each successive Congress the prerogative to decide whether or not to establish lower federal courts. (This is known as the "Madisonian Compromise.") While Congress immediately exercised this prerogative, the framers' decision not to create lower courts through the Constitution is another limitation affecting federal jurisdiction decisions.

Other Article III language crucial to federal jurisdiction provides that federal judges should enjoy life tenure, holding their "Offices during good behaviour" and receiving compensation that may not be diminished "during their Continuance in Office." This quality allows federal judges greater independence than the elected officials of the federal government and elected members of the state judiciary.

Although Article III is the constitutional provision with the strongest influence on federal court power, other constitutional language expands and limits the job description of federal tribunals. Most notably, the Eleventh Amendment — discussed in detail in Chapter 13 — significantly curtails the types of disputes federal courts may hear.

2. The Court System Layout

The federal court system now includes the United States Supreme Court, courts of appeals, district courts, several specialized federal courts, and many administrative agencies. Each court has authority to decide matters included in Article III's list of subject areas. The United States Supreme Court reviews cases coming from the lower federal courts as well as the state court system. Occasionally the Supreme Court exercises original jurisdiction, when cases are begun there. The federal district courts, however, are the primary courts in the federal system where a plaintiff first files her case.

Some federal courts operate under statutes granting them jurisdiction only over specific matters. Congress has also empowered independent administrative bodies and regulatory agencies to decide disputes governed by federal law. Often the judges in these courts lack life tenure or protection from salary diminution. Accordingly, these tribunals do not fall in the branch of government described in Article III. Yet the tribunals perform "court-like" functions because they adjudicate controversies between specific parties. Because they are creatures of Congress, created pursuant to Congress's Article I power, these adjudicative entities are frequently called "legislative courts" or "Article I courts."

In other instances, the executive branch creates federal tribunals, most notably courts-martial and other military tribunals. Controversy surrounding this executive assertion of power has emerged sporadically throughout United States history, making its most recent appearance in the wake of the 9/11 terrorist attacks. Chapter 6 reviews restrictions on the executive in creating tribunals and also outlines the doctrines governing legislative courts.

Authority of Federal Courts to Adjudicate

Doctrines of subject matter jurisdiction govern the authority of federal courts to adjudicate cases. For a lower federal court to possess subject matter jurisdiction, the court needs both the United States Constitution and a United States statute to authorize that power. The Constitution and statutes authorize lower federal courts to hear a broad range of cases. The three most important areas of federal subject matter jurisdiction for lower federal courts are covered in this part: federal question jurisdiction, diversity-of-citizenship jurisdiction, and supplemental jurisdiction. Key concepts pertaining to the United States Supreme Court's jurisdiction appear in Part V.

In reviewing the various requirements and complications, remember that the scope of federal court jurisdiction entails sensitive power struggles. The more power federal courts possess, the more federal courts conflict with other branches of state and federal government and the more work they take away from state courts. These sensitive issues of federalism and separation of powers are particularly important to informing decisions in close cases.

CHAPTER 2

Federal Question Jurisdiction in Lower Federal Courts

Article III of the United States Constitution states that the judicial power of the United States "shall extend to all Cases, in Law and Equity, arising under this Constitution, the Laws of the United States, and Treaties made, or which shall be made, under their Authority." This is known as "arising under" or "federal question" jurisdiction. The federal statute vesting district courts with this power, 28 U.S.C. §1331, provides that the district courts "shall have original jurisdiction of all civil actions arising under the Constitution, laws, or treaties of the United States." Despite the similarity between Article III's language and that of §1331, the Supreme Court has interpreted the two provisions differently, finding that Article III "arising under" jurisdiction is broader than "arising under" jurisdiction established in §1331 (see Figure 2-1). This difference in meaning matters for those circumstances where Congress wishes to authorize jurisdiction based on the Constitution's "arising under" power, yet is legislating in a specific context for which 28 U.S.C. §1331 does not provide the statutory jurisdiction.

A. THE MEANING OF "ARISING UNDER" IN THE CONSTITUTION

The test for constitutional "arising under" power came from the pen of Chief Justice Marshall in *Osborn v. Bank of the United States*, 22 U.S. (9 Wheat.) 738 (1824). Chief Justice Marshall announced that the Constitution allows

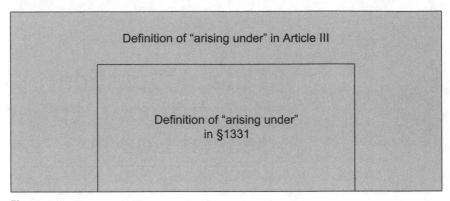

Figure 2-1.

federal courts to hear a case so long as federal law is a potential ingredient in the case. This is a sweeping power: not only does the power include cases where federal law creates the right of action, but it also encompasses lawsuits where federal law — although possibly relevant — never actually enters into the litigation.

Example 2-1

Assume that Congress is concerned about citizens' use of Global Positioning System (GPS) devices. GPS devices receive signals from a network of satellites, a network that was originally developed by the United States military as a part of its navigation system but later was made available to all. Congress believed that GPS devices might prove particularly useful to terrorists and could interfere with national security. In an effort to maintain some degree of federal control over GPS devices, Congress decided to grant federal district courts subject matter jurisdiction over all lawsuits that concern GPS devices (including suits based on state law causes of action). Is this subject matter jurisdiction statute constitutional under Article III?

Explanation

The answer to the specific question of whether the statute is constitutional under Article III is yes. Analysis of the question requires one to evaluate the *Osborn* test. To decide whether the jurisdictional statute passes the *Osborn* test, one should ask, "Is it possible that a question of federal law might arise in the cases authorized by the jurisdictional statute?" It is indeed possible for federal law concerns to arise in the authorized cases because improper use of the Global Positioning System might in fact involve federal issues relating to the national military, foreign relations, and global navigation networks. These issues may potentially arise in every case concerning GPS devices, even though settled legal precedent may render some issues unlikely to arise repeatedly in case after case. *Osborn* requires not that actual federal issues arise in every case, but that they be potential ingredients in the case. Moreover, one might contest federal regulation of GPS devices on the grounds of civil liberties or other constitutional grounds. The potential for these federal constitutional challenges does not, however, undermine the conclusion that the subject matter jurisdiction statute satisfies the *Osborn* Article III test.

In Example 2-1, subject matter jurisdiction comes from the specific jurisdictional statute mentioned in the example. Much more common, however, are cases for which the statutory authorization is the general subject matter jurisdiction statute, 28 U.S.C. §1331. The *statutory* meaning of "arising under" for §1331 is both narrower and more complicated than the constitutional meaning. The statutory meaning therefore arises much more frequently as an issue in litigation, and requires more extensive study.

B. THE MEANING OF "ARISING UNDER" IN 28 U.S.C. §1331

A major question for jurisdiction under §1331 is whether the federal component in a given case is of such a character that the suit actually arises under federal law. One can think of this as an inquiry into the potency or concentration of the federal component. If a case is viewed as a glass of clear water and the "federal" essence comes in the form of a concentrated purple liquid, one might ask how many drops of purple concentrate it takes to make the glass sufficiently tinted that the glass of water can be said to "arise under" federal law. This inquiry into the "purple tint" created by the federal question does not simply ask how "concentrated" the federal component is, but also explores the federal question's "chemistry." As instructions for exploring this "chemistry," the Supreme Court explains that one should evaluate whether the federal question is necessary to the case, actually disputed, and substantial. Even in instances where these three qualities are present, a complication may arise from sensitive concerns of balancing state and federal power. Finally, §1331 also requires that the federal element appear in the right *place* in the case. Interpreting 28 U.S.C. §1331, the Supreme Court has held that a district court has jurisdiction only when the federal question is clear on the face of the plaintiff's complaint. Examples of this rule, known as the "well-pleaded complaint" or *Mottley* rule, follow the discussion of the "necessary," "actually disputed," and "substantiality" requirements as well as the "federal-state balance" concern.

1. The Requirement that the Case Present a Necessary, Disputed, and Substantial Federal Element Under §1331

Example 2-2

Congress passed a statute restricting the times when telemarketing representatives can make telephone solicitations at residences. As part of the statute, Congress authorized private individuals to sue telemarketing companies that have violated the prohibitions in the statute. The statute specifies the proof required for the private individuals to prevail as well as the precise damages that may be awarded in the lawsuits. Does a lawsuit authorized against a telemarketing company pursuant to this statute "arise under" federal law?

Explanation

The answer is an easy yes: federal law not only provides the details of the legal rules being litigated in the case, but also created the cause of action allowing the plaintiff to sue in a private civil action against the defendant. In a situation where federal law is the source of the cause of action sued on, one can normally assume that the case satisfies §1331.

In the 1916 decision *American Well Works Co. v. Layne & Bowler Co.*, 241 U.S. 257 (1916), Justice Holmes sought to restrict "arising under" jurisdiction to situations such as the one in Example 2-2, reasoning that a suit arises under the law that creates the plaintiff's cause of action. But after *American Well Works*, the Supreme Court began to recognize that "arising under" jurisdiction exists in other instances as well. In particular, the Court in *Smith v. Kansas City Title & Trust Co.*, 255 U.S. 180 (1921), upheld "arising under" jurisdiction in a case in which the plaintiff sued on a *state* law cause of action but nonetheless needed to establish a federal legal principle to recover. Challenging a company's purchase of securities as actionable under state corporate law, the plaintiffs argued that the purchase could form the federal basis of their *state* corporate law cause of action because the securities were invalid under *federal* law. Plaintiffs' federal law theory was that the United States statute authorizing the securities was invalid under the federal Constitution. As the plaintiffs framed their case, this federal issue was essential to the resolution of the state-created lawsuit. Holding that the suit arose under federal law, the Supreme Court reasoned, "[T]he controversy concerns the constitutional validity of an act of Congress which is directly drawn in question. The decision depends upon the determination of this issue." *Smith*, 255 U.S. at 201.

The Supreme Court has refined the *Smith* approach. Most recently, the Court reaffirmed that a "federal court ought to be able to hear claims recognized under state law that nonetheless turn on substantial questions of federal law" so as to allow litigants to "resort to the experience, solicitude, and hope of uniformity that a federal forum offers on federal issues." *Grable & Sons Metal Products, Inc. v. Darue Eng'g & Mfg.*, 545 U.S. 308, 312 (2005). For state law claims with an embedded federal issue, *Grable* broke the inquiry into four discrete parts:

- Whether the state law claim "necessarily" raises a federal issue
- Whether the federal issue is "actually disputed"
- Whether the federal issue is "substantial"
- Whether, in adjudicating the dispute, the federal court would disturb "any congressionally approved balance of federal and state judicial responsibilities"

545 U.S. at 312.

The *Grable* Court concluded that these requirements were satisfied in the case, where the plaintiff had brought a state quiet title action, claiming that the record title was invalid because the Internal Revenue Service had not given proper notice of the property's seizure as required by federal statute. Applying the four requirements, the Court reasoned that each was satisfied:

- The *necessary* element was satisfied because the question of proper notice under the statute was an essential element of the quiet title claim.
- The *actually disputed* element was satisfied because the IRS notice issue was the only contested issue in the case.
- The *substantiality* element was satisfied because the United States has a strong interest in collecting taxes, in having tax matters determined by judges who are experienced in federal tax law, and in guiding its actions by clear notice requirements in tax collection proceedings.
- The *federal-state balance* element was satisfied because tax title litigation is a tiny component of the "federal-state division of labor."

545 U.S. at 314-315. The *Grable* Court did not explicitly state that all four elements must be satisfied, but its application of each element to the quiet title claim itself strongly suggests that all four are needed for a federal court to have "arising under" jurisdiction over a state law claim with an embedded federal statutory component. One reading of *Grable* holds that a plaintiff's claim to §1331 jurisdiction is less fragile and factor dependent where the embedded federal component is a constitutional issue.

Moreover, in a case decided the next term, *Empire Healthchoice Assurance, Inc. v. McVeigh*, 126 S. Ct. 2121 (2006), the Supreme Court suggested that a court should apply each element rigorously. The *Empire Healthchoice* Court also described cases that assert a state law cause of action but nonetheless satisfy each of the four *Grable* elements as a "special and small category" of cases arising under federal law. 126 S. Ct. at 2136.

Empire Healthchoice suggests that one should be careful not to read Grable as liberally authorizing federal question jurisdiction. Empire Healthchoice involved a health insurance carrier for federal employees that brought an action against a former federal employee's estate, seeking benefit reimbursement on the ground that the estate recovered damages for injuries in a state court tort action. In distinguishing Grable, the Empire Healthchoice Court observed that the federal issue in Grable was a "pure issue of law" that could be settled "once and for all and thereafter would govern numerous" cases concerning a federal agency. Id. at 2137 (internal quotation marks omitted). By contrast, the Court described the "nonstatutory" reimbursement claim in Empire Healthchoice as "poles apart" from the "slim category" of cases that Grable represented. Id.

Example 2-3

Sally had extensive technical expertise in working with nuclear energy equipment. She entered into an employment contract with a private company to service nuclear equipment that was the same as equipment used in nuclear power plants. Her employment contract required her to enroll in courses and other training necessary to maintain her technical proficiency license with a federal licensing entity that regulates personnel working in public nuclear power plants. The licensing requirements are set forth in a federal statute governing public nuclear power plants and their employees. While recognizing that Sally had satisfied all other provisions in the employment contract, the employer believed that Sally had not complied with the contract's training requirements. Specifically, the employer maintained that, under its reading of the federal regulations, Sally had not done what was necessary to maintain her technical proficiency license. The employer's reading of the regulations is based on a particular interpretation of the words used in the regulations. Sally disagreed with how the employer defined these words. Thus, the dispute is a purely legal question about the meaning of the regulations' terms, and not a factual issue concerning how the regulations apply to Sally's specific circumstances. The employer removed Sally from her regular duties and filed a state law breach of contract suit against her. Does the suit arise under federal law?

Explanation

Although a close case, the employer's suit appears to satisfy all four elements of the Grable test for "arising under" jurisdiction. For the employer to win under the facts presented in the example, the federal court must interpret the federal licensing provisions and conclude that Sally has not taken the steps needed to maintain her license. The meaning of the licensing provisions is therefore necessary to the employer's suit. As described in the example, the parties disagree over the meaning of these provisions, and the provisions are central to the suit. Thus, they are actually disputed. Of course, the employer may fail to make out the other components of the state law breach of contract claim, or Sally might discover a state law defense to this claim. These unsubstantiated, hypothetical possibilities should not preclude the federal question jurisdiction, so long as the parties actually contest the federal issue.[1]

Next, the *substantiality* element appears to be satisfied. The reasoning in *Grable* analyzed *substantiality* from the "macro" viewpoint of the federal system (as opposed the "micro" viewpoint of the parties). From the perspective of the federal system, licensing provisions for nuclear power technicians implicate issues of public safety and the maze of federal regulations pertaining to nuclear power plants. One could easily argue that the federal government has a substantial interest in using federal court expertise to ensure uniform interpretation of the laws governing nuclear power. Admittedly, Example 2-3 arises in a private employment context, not one concerning nuclear power plants, which is the context for which Congress wrote the licensing laws. Yet, unlike the federal question allegedly at issue in *Empire Healthchoice Assurance, Inc. v. McVeigh*, the federal issue here is a question of law concerning the proper construction of the licensing provision terms, and not a "fact-bound and situation-specific" application of the terms to Sally's circumstances. 126 S. Ct. at 2137. Morever, the public safety stakes are high here, entailing important regulatory matters. In contrast to the issue in *Empire Healthchoice*, regarding a health insurer's contract claim for reimbursement — the issue here concerns the qualification of nuclear power plant engineers — arguably a significantly stronger federal interest justifying the use of federal court resources.

---

1. *Broder v. Cablevision Sys. Corp.*, 418 F.3d 187, 193-194 (2d Cir. 2005) (splicing contract claim with embedded federal question into two claims, one requiring federal law and the other not requiring federal law.) *Broder* is consistent with earlier Supreme Court case law. *See Merrell Dow Pharmaceuticals Inc. v. Thompson*, 478 U.S. 804, 817 n.15 (1986) (reasoning that the possibility that a plaintiff may recover on pure state law grounds does not eliminate federal question jurisdiction). Nevertheless, the Court of Appeals for the Ninth Circuit has explicitly taken issue with *Broder*'s application of *Grable*'s "necessarily" prong to the state contract claim. *See, e.g., Armitage v. Deutsche Bank AG*, No. C 05-3998 PJH, 2005 U.S. Dist. LEXIS 30997, at *6-12 (N.D. Cal. Nov. 14, 2005) (arguing where federal issue is necessary only to theory and not whole cause of action itself, federal jurisdiction does not exist, which is consistent with presumption against removal).

Other lower federal courts applying the *Grable* "necessarily" prong have interpreted the decision as requiring a claim that rests on a federal issue. *See, e.g., Collins v. Pontikes*, 447 F. Supp. 2d 895, 900-901 (N.D. Ill. July 17, 2006) (stating federal law regarding loans was one aspect of case, but not enough to allow federal jurisdiction requiring sole dependency on federal issue); *Snook v. Deutsche Bank AG*, 410 F. Supp. 2d 519, 521-523 (S.D. Tex. 2006) (finding validity of federal tax law was but a facet, not the sole contested issue in the case, and thus no federal jurisdiction existed over state law claims); *Pennsylvania v. Tap Pharmaceutical Products, Inc.*, 415 F. Supp. 2d 516, 524-526 (E.D. Pa. 2005) (finding no jurisdiction in state law claim of unfair trade and consumer protection because interpretation of "average wholesale price" was not necessary for plaintiffs to prevail); *Sheridan v. New Vista, LLC*, 406 F. Supp. 2d 789, 794 (W.D. Mich. 2005) (stating federal tax law was not sole issue and did not take "front and center stage in the litigation" as in *Grable*).

Finally, allowing federal court jurisdiction in Example 2-3 would likely not disturb the balance of state and federal judicial responsibilities. State courts generally entertain private employment contract disputes. However, the same can be said for quiet title suits such as *Grable*. In reckoning with this *federal-state balance* factor, the *Grable* Court reasoned that "it is the rare state quiet title action that involves contested issues of federal law." 545 U.S. at 319. Likewise, one could readily conclude that breach of employment suits that turn on a question of nuclear regulatory law are quite rare, and that a federal court would not upset the balance of state and federal power in adjudicating this lawsuit.

Example 2-4

A state social service agency administered a prescription drug program for low-income citizens. The agency purchased the drugs from a group of pharmaceutical manufacturers, which the agency believed improperly inflated the wholesale price of the drugs. In its complaint, the agency asserts that the drug companies' overcharging practices violate state laws that require parties to adhere to fair dealing practices when doing business with state agencies. State law provides that a plaintiff may establish an unfair-practices claim in a variety of ways, including proof of other regulations or proof of business practices in a commercial setting. In view of this, the agency pleaded two bases for alleging that the drug companies were charging unreasonably high wholesale prices. First, the agency averred that the prices it had been paying were far more than the prices drug companies were required to charge federal entities under statutory requirements governing federal prescription drug programs. Second, the agency's complaint stated that the prices it paid were greater than those the drug companies have charged over 100 private hospital pharmacies. The agency filed suit in federal court, arguing that the suit requires the federal court to interpret federal statutory requirements governing drug prices charged to federal entities. Is this component of the case sufficient to confer federal question jurisdiction?

Explanation

No, the embedded federal question regarding drug prices to federal entities is likely not sufficient to establish federal question jurisdiction for this state law cause of action. The state agency may try to establish that it has satisfied *Grable* by arguing that it will prevail if the federal court interprets the federal regulations in the manner that the agency advocates. Accordingly, the agency may assert, its fair-dealing lawsuit under state law "depends" on the meaning of the federal question. Several facts suggest, however, that the state agency will not succeed in satisfying each element of the *Grable* test.

To begin with, the federal question is not *necessary* to the disposition of the lawsuit. As the state law is framed, the state agency may prevail by establishing that lower prices were charged to hospital pharmacies in a private commercial setting. Pursuing this approach, the agency's complaint asserts specific facts to establish overcharging based on commercial pricing. This theory would provide a win for the agency without any litigation on the federal law issue.

Next, even if the agency does rely on the federal statute, the *actually disputed* element may still not be satisfied. Under the facts given, one does not know whether the statute is sufficiently ambiguous to prompt the drug companies to contest the meaning. The price required by the statute may be so clear that the parties will not litigate that issue. For that reason, one cannot conclude definitively that the element is satisfied.

The *substantiality* element is similarly uncertain. On one hand, the element may be satisfied if the agency can convince the judge that interpreting the federal pricing provisions are an integral part of an important federal regulatory program. The facts are unclear as to whether this is so, particularly since the entity being charged here is a state entity and not a federal entity as envisioned in the congressional scheme. Nothing suggests that Congress legislated out of any concern with state entities. The court is therefore likely to conclude that this context is akin to *Empire Healthchoice*, where the Court suggested that it could count on the state court to competently apply any peripheral federal question that arises in the case.

For the *federal-state balance* element, one might make an argument similar to that in Example 2-3. That is, one might acknowledge that state unfair-practices litigation is a very small fraction of state and federal court caseloads, and therefore this element is satisfied. One potential problem with this conclusion, however, arises from the plaintiff's identity: it is a state entity. In another case interpreting 28 U.S.C. §1331, *Franchise Tax Board v. Construction Laborers Vacation Trust*, 463 U.S. 1, 21 (1983), the Supreme Court suggested that "arising under" jurisdiction need not be expanded for state entities, which have at their disposal ample opportunity to pursue their grievances in their own courts. While one cannot be certain of how important this problem may be, it is yet another weakness in establishing jurisdiction in Example 2-4. Together with the difficulty in establishing the other *Grable* elements — particularly the *necessary* and *substantiality* elements — one can be confident that the federal court lacks "arising under" jurisdiction.

2. The Federal-State Balance Element

The fourth element from *Grable & Sons Metal Products, Inc. v. Darue Eng'g & Mfg.*, requiring the federal court to consider whether exercising federal question jurisdiction over state law causes of action would disturb "any congressionally approved balance of federal and state judicial responsibilities," has a revealing history. The element relates to the 1986 case of *Merrell Dow Pharmaceuticals v. Thompson*, 478 U.S. 804, in which the Supreme Court introduced the *federal-state balance* concern into the statutory "arising under" inquiry. Because the precise meaning of *Merrell Dow* has dogged lower courts for several decades, its clarification in *Grable* bears special attention.

In *Merrell Dow*, the Court evaluated whether a state tort case "arose under" federal law. The state tort in the *Merrell Dow* case rested in part on the allegation that the defendant drug company had violated a federal misbranding prohibition and thus was presumptively negligent under state law. Assuming that federal law applied to resolve the state law claim, the Court examined the federal interest at stake and the implications of finding that a federal court could hear the claim. The *Merrell Dow* Court decided that the federal court should not hear the claim, resting its decision on the observation that Congress had created the standard of conduct concerning misbranding but had not created a federal "cause of action" to pursue violations of the misbranding law. Congress had not, in the Supreme Court's view, created for plaintiffs a federal right to sue drug companies for a violation of their federal right to be free from misbranded drugs. Instead, Congress vested the Food and Drug Administration with power to enforce that right through the administrative enforcement process.

The *Merrell Dow* Court reasoned that because Congress had not provided a private federal cause of action for violation of the federal branding requirement, "it would ... flout, or at least undermine, congressional intent to conclude that the federal courts might nevertheless exercise federal-question jurisdiction and provide remedies for violations of that federal statute" within the context of a private action created by state law. 478 U.S. at 812. Clarifying this reasoning in *Grable*, the Court said that the absence of a federal private right of action was not the only thing that mattered in *Merrell Dow*. Other factors, the *Grable* Court explained, influenced the result in *Merrell Dow*, such as " 'sensitive judgments about congressional intent,' " controlling the volume of federal court litigation, the litigants' interest, and the possibility of causing a significant shift of what were traditionally state cases into federal courts. 545 U.S. at 317 (quoting *Merrell Dow*, 478 U.S. at 810).

Grable — in clarifying *Merrell Dow* — thus lays out several considerations for a federal district court evaluating whether it has federal question jurisdiction to adjudicate a dispute involving federal law as a component of a state law cause of action. The federal court not only should look to see whether Congress created a federal cause of action, but should also explore whether Congress intended the case to be heard in federal court. If Congress created a standard of conduct without creating a federal cause of action, that at least suggests Congress's "ambivalence" about allowing federal question jurisdiction. 545 U.S. at 319. In addition to this and any other factors that may reveal congressional intent, the federal court should consider (1) whether allowing federal court jurisdiction in cases of this type would "materially affect, or threaten to affect" the workloads of state and federal courts; (2) whether allowing jurisdiction would impose structural consequences on the institutions of state and federal courts; and (3) whether parties' interest in litigating their disputes in a federal forum weighs in favor of jurisdiction. *Id.* at 319-320.

In *Merrell Dow* (as clarified in *Grable*), the trigger for this detailed inquiry into congressional intent was a situation where Congress created a statutory scheme with a standard of conduct but did not create a private civil action. Because Congress failed to create a federal cause of action, the *Merrell Dow* Court inferred that Congress did not want federal courts to adjudicate the standard of conduct in any private civil action. *Grable* made clear that this conclusion represented too broad an analytical leap. Instead, the *Grable* Court prescribed further analysis before one determines whether Congress intended federal courts to adjudicate a state cause of action that incorporates a federal component.

With this background, one might ask whether there might be extra concern in Examples 2-3 and 2-4 about the federal-state balance element. Indeed, both examples involve a congressionally created standard of conduct but no federal cause of action. But a potentially important distinction exists between *Merrell Dow* and cases such as those depicted in Examples 2-3 and 2-4. In these examples, the federal standards of conduct appear in statutory schemes that do not directly pertain to the context of the litigation. Example 2-3 concerns the qualification of a worker in private industry, but the congressional scheme concerns qualifications of public nuclear power plant employees. Similarly, Example 2-4 concerns drug prices paid by a state entity, but the congressional scheme concerns drug prices paid by a federal entity. The difference in context may help a plaintiff trying to satisfy the *federal-state balance* element. After all, Congress could not be expected to have created a federal cause of action for contexts unrelated to the statutory scheme. Thus, one might not reasonably draw a meaningful inference from the absence of any federal cause of action.[2]

---

2. That being said, the fact that the congressional standard is wrenched out of its federal context for the purpose of the lawsuits in both examples may create problems for the substantiality element. Because the contexts are different from those for which Congress created the standards of conduct, Congress may not view the contexts as important areas in which to regulate. In the new contexts, therefore, the meaning of the standards of conduct might not present a substantial federal question.

Example 2-5

A customer entered into a service contract with a cable television company. The contract provided that the rates would be calculated and charged in accordance with 47 U.S.C. §543, which requires that the company charge uniform rates throughout the geographical area in which the customer is located. This statutory requirement is one of many enforced against cable companies by federal administrative agencies. The statutory scheme containing the uniformity requirement is complex but does not provide for any private causes of action. The customer believes that the cable company has breached the contract by failing to honor the uniformity requirement. The company, however, took the position that the customer was not reading §543's uniformity requirement properly, and is incorrectly defining the terms of the statute. The customer filed a state law breach of contract action in federal court, alleging as the sole basis for the breach the company's failure to charge her a uniform rate as required by the contract. The uniformity provision in the cable television statute is the only federal element in the case. Does the federal court have subject matter jurisdiction over the case?

Explanation

The customer has fashioned a case that resembles the legal structure of the suit rejected in *Merrell Dow*. Nonetheless, the customer has an excellent chance of establishing each *Grable* requirement, including the *federal-state balance* element. To begin with, the breach of contract claim *necessarily* raises an *actually disputed* federal issue, since the customer and cable company disagree on only one possible basis for the breach: noncompliance with the federal law's uniformity requirement. Moreover, because cable television rates are heavily regulated by federal law, one can argue that the federal issue here is a *substantial* one, which would benefit from expert federal court interpretation; a misinterpretation might send unnecessary complications through the complex web of federal regulation. Moreover, unlike the suit in *Empire Healthchoice Assurance, Inc. v. McVeigh*, the dispute over the statutory language appears to involve a pure question of law about the definition of the statutory term, rather than a fact-bound question about the statute's application to specific facts and circumstances.

As to the *federal-state balance* requirement, *Merrell Dow* and *Grable* provide that Congress's failure in Example 2-5 to create a private federal cause of action suggests that Congress may have been ambivalent about allowing federal jurisdiction. The facts, however, reveal no factors suggesting that Congress had decided not to allow "arising under" jurisdiction. One can marshal the other components of the federal-state balance requirement in favor of jurisdiction. For example, one has difficulty conceiving of numerous cable customers bringing breach of contract suits based on §543's uniformity requirement. Since the suit is unlikely to recur often, letting the suit into federal court would neither materially change the work performed by state and federal courts nor impose structural consequences on those courts. Finally, one could argue that both litigants have an interest in expert federal court interpretation of the cable television regulations — particularly the cable company, which is subject to the §543 uniformity requirement. These arguments together make a strong case for satisfying the *federal-state balance* requirement for "arising under" jurisdiction in Example 2-5.

3. The "Well-Pleaded Complaint" Requirement

Examples 2-3, 2-4, and 2-5 raise federal question jurisdiction issues because federal law entered the cause of action at only one place in each case. One important quality of these three examples is that the *place* where the federal law issues entered each case was the proper one: the plaintiff's complaint. Under the rule of *Louisville & Nashville R.R. Co. v. Mottley*, 211 U.S. 149 (1908), the federal question providing the basis for "arising under" jurisdiction must appear on the face of the plaintiff's "well-pleaded" complaint. The *Mottley* or "well-pleaded complaint" rule is not satisfied where the federal issue would be raised only by the defendant in response to the complaint or by the plaintiff in reply to the defense. In other words, the federal district court must determine jurisdiction under §1331 on the basis of the cause of action that the plaintiff is asserting.

Example 2-6

Candid Times published an article stating that Olivia Official accepted a bribe. *Candid Times* then printed a retraction, admitting that the statement was false. Olivia Official filed a state law defamation action against *Candid Times*, stating that the article was false and that it blackened her reputation, causing her great damage. Knowing that *Candid Times* enjoys some First Amendment protection for publishing information about a public official such as herself, Olivia was careful to include in her complaint assertions that this First Amendment privilege did not apply to the article in suit here. Specifically, Olivia Official included statements on the face of her complaint that *Candid Times* published the article with knowledge of its falsity and was therefore outside First Amendment protection. In response, *Candid Times* acknowledged that the article was defamatory but strenuously objected to the suggestion that the First Amendment privilege did not apply. In addition, *Candid Times* argued that the federal court lacked power to hear the case. Accordingly,

Candid Times filed a motion to dismiss for lack of subject matter jurisdiction, asserting that the case did not arise under federal law. Should the court dismiss the case?

Explanation

Even assuming that Olivia Official's First Amendment argument is absolutely right on the facts and law, Olivia's complaint fails the *Mottley* rule. The federal district court should grant *Candid Times'* motion to dismiss for lack of subject matter jurisdiction. Olivia's cause of action is premised entirely on the state law theory of defamation. State law governs each element: whether the statement is "of or concerning" Olivia, whether the statement was communicated to others, whether it is false, and whether it tends to blacken Olivia's reputation in the community or tends to dissuade others from associating with her. The only federal issue concerns the First Amendment, which enters the case only by way of a possible defense. Even though she mentions the issue in her complaint, Olivia can make out her cause of action solely by referring to state law. She cannot create federal question jurisdiction by anticipating *Candid Times'* response to her state law cause of action. *Candid Times* did not cure this defect by actually asserting the First Amendment argument itself.

The result in Example 2-6 may appear quite curious, given that the parties' energy in the case will likely focus on an important issue of constitutional law crucial to our national system of government and federal civil rights. Indeed, the rest of the litigation's issues are largely undisputed, and the court that ultimately adjudicates the case will interpret how the First Amendment applies to the facts presented. Unfortunately, the *Mottley* rule sweeps too broadly at times and excludes from federal district courts cases that would benefit from federal court expertise. The *Mottley* rule focuses simply on the location of the federal question, and not on its importance to the case, to federal regulation, or to society in general.

Despite the *Mottley* rule's flaws, many sound arguments support the rule. Requiring the federal issue to be part of the plaintiff's complaint allows the court to decide the jurisdictional question early, before the court and parties have committed resources that may be wasted if the court should ultimately dismiss the case for lack of subject matter jurisdiction. The rule is consistent with our adversary system, which is based on the assumption that the truth will emerge from the process of opposing parties zealously litigating their own cases. Without the "well-pleaded complaint" rule, plaintiffs would have an incentive to brainstorm possible federal defenses that defendants might raise. Under the rule, jurisdiction derives from the claims and defenses parties actually make, rather than from guesses about what arguments the parties might raise. As such, the "well-pleaded complaint" rule serves sensible principles of judicial administration.

Despite arguments in favor of the "well-pleaded complaint" rule, it presents some of the most complicated problems in federal court jurisdiction. Two "wrinkles" in the doctrine deserve particular mention. The first arises in declaratory judgment actions necessitating additional analysis when one is confronted with a plaintiff seeking declaratory relief. The second appears in the context of preemption and can be considered an exception to the "well-pleaded complaint" rule.

a. Declaratory Judgment

By statute, Congress has empowered federal courts to issue judgments that declare the legal rights of parties to a dispute. The purpose of the Declaratory Judgment Act, 28 U.S.C. §§2201-2202, is to allow parties early access to court so that they can clarify their rights. The device allows either party to seek court clarification early, before the dispute has matured. Thus, one party can file a declaratory complaint anticipating the defense that the opposing party might raise if the dispute were to mature and the plaintiff were to bring a traditional suit for damages or an injunction. For that reason, declaratory judgment suits often invite violations of the "well-pleaded complaint" rule.

The law is clear that Congress did not intend the Declaratory Judgment Act to expand the subject matter jurisdiction of federal courts. Thus, federal courts watch out for plaintiffs using the declaratory judgment mechanism to get a case into federal court that otherwise could not be properly filed there. This concern is especially acute in the context of the *Mottley* rule. Accordingly, federal courts scrutinize declaratory judgment complaints that contain a federal question to ensure that the claim underlying the complaint actually arises under federal law.

To ensure that a case is not in federal court solely by virtue of the declaratory judgment mechanism, one must make sure that the declaratory judgment remedy is not enabling the plaintiff to anticipate what would appear as a defense in a lawsuit for damages or an injunction. To undertake this analysis, one must determine the most likely damages or injunction suit that would arise between the parties and then ask whether the federal question would likely appear in the defense of that suit. If so, the declaratory judgment suit cannot continue. Even though the federal question may appear on the face of the declaratory judgment complaint, the court would dismiss the proceeding as an improper use of the Declaratory Judgment Act. Acknowledging that the act was not intended to get cases into federal court that would otherwise be excluded, the court would conclude that the declaratory judgment proceeding fails for lack of subject matter jurisdiction.

i. Skelly Oil Recognizes the Declaratory Judgment Wrinkle

The Supreme Court first explored the declaratory judgment wrinkle in *Skelly Oil Co. v. Phillips Petroleum Co.*, 339 U.S. 667 (1950). As the Court later explained, *Skelly Oil* established that "if, but for the availability of the declaratory judgment procedure, a federal claim would arise only as a defense to a state created action, jurisdiction is lacking." *Franchise Tax Board v. Construction Laborers Vacation Trust*, 463 U.S. 1, 16 (1983) (quoting 10A CHARLES WRIGHT, ARTHUR MILLER & MARY KANE, FEDERAL PRACTICE AND PROCEDURE §2767 (2d ed. 1983)). The facts of *Skelly Oil* help to illustrate the types of situations in which this concern arises. Skelly Oil contracted with Phillips Petroleum to sell natural gas. The contract was subject to the condition that the Federal Power Commission grant Phillips Petroleum a certificate. In granting the certificate, the Federal Power Commission imposed unanticipated requirements. Skelly Oil then terminated the contract, arguing that the conditional certificate did not satisfy the contract requirement. Phillips Petroleum then brought a declaratory judgment action, seeking a declaration that Skelly Oil had to honor the contract because the Federal Power Commission had issued a valid certificate.

The Supreme Court in *Skelly Oil* held that the suit did not satisfy federal question jurisdiction. The Court reasoned that if the case had arisen outside the declaratory judgment context, it would have been a breach of contract suit by Phillips Petroleum against Skelly Oil. The suit did in fact contain a federal question about the nature of the Federal Power Commission's certificate. But that question, the Court maintained, would arise in Skelly Oil's defense, not in the breach of contract claim itself.

The *Skelly Oil* Court made clear that the Declaratory Judgment Act should not allow a plaintiff such as Phillips to gain access to federal court, when the plaintiff would have been relegated to state court in the absence of the act. Accordingly, the Court required analysis of the plaintiff's options if the plaintiff were unable to bring an action for a declaratory judgment. In that event, the plaintiff and the defendant might resolve their differences or they might ultimately pursue an injunction or damages action. That type of litigation is sometimes called a "coercive suit," the idea being that the injunction or damages remedy "coerces" compliance with the law.

Under the *Skelly Oil* analysis, the Supreme Court suggested that a district court evaluating federal question jurisdiction in a declaratory judgment suit must project the coercive suit that would likely evolve between the parties in the absence of a declaratory remedy. Specifically, the district court should ask whether the case would fall within federal question jurisdiction if the dispute matured and the parties pursued damages or an injunction. What the Court did not establish definitively, however, was whether federal question jurisdiction depends on the existence of a coercive action in which the declaratory judgment plaintiff becomes a coercive plaintiff, with a federal question on the face of her coercive complaint. One might call this an "alignment requirement," under which the coercive plaintiff and the declaratory plaintiff must be the same person or entity.

Courts and commentators have debated whether *Skelly Oil* requires alignment. On one hand is language from *Skelly Oil* suggesting that the declaratory plaintiff must possess a federal claim herself: "'Prior to [the Declaratory Judgment] Act, a federal court would entertain a suit on a contract only if the plaintiff asked for an immediately enforceable remedy like money damages or an injunction. . . . The Declaratory Judgment Act allowed relief to be given by way of recognizing the plaintiff's right even though no immediate enforcement of it was asked.'" *Skelly Oil*, 339 U.S. at 671-672 (quoted in *Textron Lycoming Reciprocating Engine Div. v. UAW*, 523 U.S. 653, 660 (1998)).

Yet another line of thought holds that the case does not require alignment. According to this view, federal question jurisdiction would exist in a declaratory judgment action if either the declaratory judgment plaintiff or the declaratory judgment defendant were to become the coercive action plaintiff with a federal question in her well-pleaded complaint.[3] Further case law adds to, rather than resolving, this controversy.

Example 2-7

Marketing Corporation marketed a product extensively throughout the United States. Complaining Corporation believed the product violated federal safety standards and subjected consumers to risk of injury. Complaining Corporation threatened to send a letter to retailers urging them not to sell the product because it violated federal safety standards. Marketing Corporation believed that such a letter would amount to trade libel, and told Complaining Corporation that it would file a trade libel action if the letter was sent. Trade libel is a state law cause of action for defamation to recover damages to the plaintiff's business. Rather than waiting until Complaining Corporation sent out the letter, Marketing Corporation brought a declaratory judgment suit to have the court declare that Marketing Corporation's product did not violate federal safety standards and that such a letter would therefore be libelous. Does this declaratory judgment action pass the *Skelly Oil* rule?

Explanation

Marketing Corporation's declaratory judgment action does indeed pass the *Skelly Oil* rule. The coercive action that would likely result in the absence of a declaratory judgment suit is the threatened trade libel action. If Marketing

---

3. *See* LARRY W. YACKLE, FEDERAL COURTS 257-270 (2d ed. 2003), for a thorough discussion of these two views of *Skelly Oil*.

Corporation were to file a coercive complaint for damages based on trade libel, the complaint would allege as part of the cause of action that Complaining Corporation's safety standard allegation is false. The question of Complaining Corporation's adherence to federal safety standards arises under federal law. Accordingly, a federal question would be an element of the plaintiff's claim for trade libel.

Skelly Oil predated several federal question jurisdiction cases, including *Grable & Sons Metal Products, Inc. v. Darue Eng'g & Mfg.*, 545 U.S. 308 (2005). Thus, the *Skelly Oil* Court did not discuss matters such as the four *Grable* requirements in evaluating whether the declaratory judgment action satisfied the jurisdictional requirements of §1331. Nevertheless, *Skelly Oil* established that federal court jurisdiction in a declaratory judgment case should depend on whether prevailing jurisdictional rules authorize district courts to adjudicate the case without reference to the declaratory judgment remedy. Thus, analysis of federal question jurisdiction must extend beyond identifying a federal question in the plaintiff's complaint. The federal question must be sufficient to vest the district court with jurisdiction. So, for example, if the complaint would set forth a state law cause of action only, the complaint must satisfy the four elements of *Grable*: the *necessary, actually disputed, substantiality,* and *federal-state balance* requirements.

The safety standard question appears to satisfy the *Grable* requirements. The question appears to be the sole basis for the parties' disagreement and pertains to a crucial element of the plaintiff's cause of action for trade libel. Thus, the cause of action necessarily raises an actually disputed federal component in the litigation. While few facts in Example 2-7 allow one to make a complex argument about substantiality, a question involving human safety is not easily characterized as insubstantial or unimportant. To be forthright, however, one must acknowledge that this requirement may be difficult to establish in the case under the rigorous approach of *Empire Healthchoice Assurance, Inc. v. McVeigh*, 126 S. Ct. 2121 (2006).

As to the *federal-state balance* requirement, no facts in the problem indicate that Congress expressed an intent in the federal safety statute or elsewhere to prevent federal courts from adjudicating this action. Moreover, one would not expect that trade libel suits with an embedded federal question regarding safety standards would be so common as to affect the flow of litigation into state and federal courts. In fact, such suits are likely to amount to a tiny fraction of the work shared between state and federal courts. For the parties, on the other hand, the issue is highly consequential. The plaintiff, Marketing Corporation, has an extremely strong interest in an authoritative federal court determination of whether it is marketing a product that is dangerous under federal safety standards and therefore capable of inflicting harm on consumers and subjecting Marketing Corporation to untold tort liability. For all these reasons, one can easily conclude that the fourth prong of *Grable* is satisfied: allowing a federal district court to hear a state law cause of action with an embedded question of federal safety law is consistent with Congress's judgment as to the appropriate workload balance between state and federal courts.

Finally, the lawsuit complies with any alignment requirement that *Skelly Oil* may have envisioned. Alignment exists because Marketing Corporation is both the declaratory plaintiff and the likely coercive plaintiff (see Figure 2-2). Although we cannot be certain whether *Skelly Oil* sought to require alignment, these facts satisfy that requirement in any event.

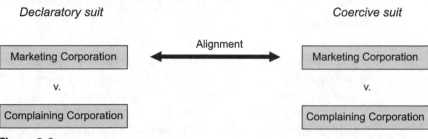

Figure 2-2.

ii. Franchise Tax Board Complicates the Wrinkle

In a subsequent case, *Franchise Tax Board v. Construction Laborers Vacation Trust*, 463 U.S. 1, 23 (1983), the Supreme Court reaffirmed *Skelly Oil* but injected further concerns into the declaratory judgment wrinkle to the "well-pleaded complaint" rule. *Franchise Tax Board* concerned the Construction Laborers Vacation Trust, which administered a fund for construction workers' vacation pay. A federal statute known as ERISA (the Employee Retirement Income Security Act of 1974) regulated this trust. The other party, the California Franchise Tax Board, a state entity responsible for collecting personal income taxes, wanted the trust to pay workers' delinquent taxes from vacation funds. The tax board sought a declaratory judgment that the federal ERISA statute did not prevent it from seeking payment from the trust for these delinquent taxes.

The declaratory suit appeared to run into problems under the *Mottley/Skelly Oil* rule, since the tax board's ultimate goal was to collect taxes by levying on the trust. The most likely coercive suit is therefore a state law collection matter by the tax board against the trust, with the trust raising a federal defense that ERISA preempted the collection suit. But another section of ERISA—§502(a)(3)—complicates this apparently straightforward reading of the likely coercive action between the parties. Section 502(a)(3) specifically grants trustees of entities such as the Construction Laborers Vacation Trust a cause of action for an injunction—governed exclusively by federal law—when their obligations under ERISA are at issue. Thus, it appeared that the federal court could have jurisdiction based on the trust's authority to act as a plaintiff granted under the federal statute. This statutory

2. Federal Question Jurisdiction in Lower Federal Courts

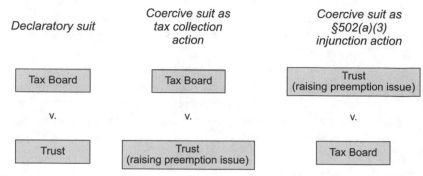

Figure 2-3.

authorization empowered the trust to assert against the Franchise Tax Board an affirmative federal claim that ERISA preempted the Franchise Tax Board's ability to recover taxes from the trust (see Figure 2-3).

The Supreme Court, however, did not view §502(a)(3) as a justification for allowing the declaratory judgment suit to proceed in federal court. The Court observed that this provision did not "go so far" as to provide for federal jurisdiction in suits asserted *against* parties such as the trust. 463 U.S. at 21. Moreover, the Court asserted, "good reasons" suggested that federal courts should not be opened to state entities, such as the trust, that are seeking to litigate local matters such as the "validity of their regulations." Id. The Court observed that state entities have mechanisms to "enforce their own laws in their own courts" and therefore would not be "significantly prejudiced by an inability to come to federal court for a declaratory judgment." Id.

The precise contribution of *Franchise Tax Board* is difficult to pin down. Crucial to the Court's ultimate disposition, however, was the fact that the state entity that had originally brought suit in the case had access to its own state courts to enforce its laws in the face of a federal defense. In emphasizing this, the Court seemed to ignore a procedural quirk in the litigation's history: the tax board had actually filed suit in state court and the trust removed the case to federal court. Thus, it was the *defendant*, Construction Laborers Vacation Trust (a non-state party), that had sought to invoke federal court jurisdiction by removing the case, not the plaintiff, Franchise Tax Board. Nevertheless, the *Franchise Tax Board* Court's emphasis on alternatives for the state party makes clear that any analysis of federal question jurisdiction in a declaratory judgment suit should consider whether the suit involves a state entity with litigation options available in state court. If the plaintiff is such a state entity, *Franchise Tax Board* makes federal jurisdiction far less appropriate.

iii. The Alignment Question Remains

At present, *Franchise Tax Board*'s concern with restricting federal court access for state entities still controls analysis of declaratory judgment cases.

The current status of the alignment requirement is less clear. While *Franchise Tax Board* sent one message on the issue, subsequent case law has given contrary cues.

Franchise Tax Board's language and reasoning imply that the declaratory judgment wrinkle for federal question jurisdiction contains no alignment requirement. In other words, the decision suggests that the declaratory plaintiff and the hypothetical coercive plaintiff need not be the same person or entity. Specifically, *Franchise Tax Board* stated that "[f]ederal courts have regularly taken original jurisdiction over declaratory judgment suits in which, if the declaratory judgment defendant brought a coercive action to enforce its rights, that suit would necessarily present a federal question."[4] Moreover, if alignment had been a concern for the *Franchise Tax Board* Court, the Court could easily have used that as the rationale for rejecting §502(a)(3) as the basis for finding jurisdiction in the declaratory judgment action. As illustrated in Figure 2-3, no alignment existed between the declaratory suit (with the tax board as plaintiff) and a hypothetical coercive suit under §502(a)(3) (with the trust as plaintiff). The Court, however, relied on other reasons for rejecting §502(a)(3) as the basis for federal jurisdiction.

Unfortunately, in a subsequent case, *Textron Lycoming Reciprocating Engine Div. v. UAW*, 523 U.S. 653 (1998), the Supreme Court injected additional uncertainty into the alignment issue. In *Textron*, the UAW sought a federal declaratory judgment that its collective bargaining agreement with Textron was invalid. The UAW argued that the district court had jurisdiction pursuant to the Labor Management Relations Act. The Court rejected this by pointing out that the Labor Management Relations Act provided jurisdiction only to enforce labor contracts, not to declare them invalid. Thus, the UAW simply had a state law claim that a contract was invalid. The UAW maintained that this reasoning was inapplicable because it sought declaratory judgment relief. The UAW reasoned that pursuant to *Skelly Oil*, jurisdiction could rest on the federal claim (such as that illustrated in Figure 2-4) that Textron would have under the Labor Management Relations Act for breach of the collective bargaining agreement.

The *Textron* Court was unpersuaded. Emphasizing the *Skelly Oil* language that appeared to establish an alignment requirement, the Court observed that none of its own decisions have "squarely confronted and explicitly upheld federal-question jurisdiction on the basis of" a claim that the declaratory plaintiff anticipates that the declaratory defendant might bring as a coercive action. *Textron*, 523 U.S. at 659-660. The *Textron* Court noted language in *Franchise Tax Board* observing that federal courts had allowed declaratory

---

4. *Franchise Tax Board v. Construction Laborers Vacation Trust*, 463 U.S. 1, 19 (1983). In making this statement, the *Franchise Tax Board* Court referred to declaratory judgment cases brought by alleged patent infringers.

2. Federal Question Jurisdiction in Lower Federal Courts

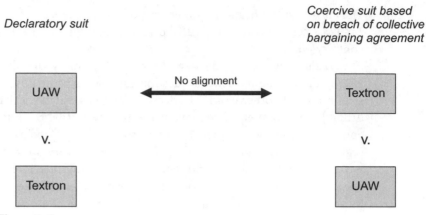

Figure 2-4.

judgment cases to proceed in instances where the case did not satisfy the alignment requirement. Nevertheless, the *Textron* Court minimized this language in *Franchise Tax Board*, suggesting that the supporting cases that *Franchise Tax Board* cited were unique because they arose in the context of patent infringement, an area of exclusive federal court jurisdiction.

Making matters even cloudier, the *Textron* Court's reasoning regarding alignment appears as dictum because the Court ultimately dismissed the suit for lack of a case or controversy. In addressing the "case or controversy" problem, the *Textron* Court stated that it assumed "without deciding" that the alignment problem did not destroy federal question jurisdiction. 523 U.S. at 660. A prudent treatment of this issue, however, requires analysis of alignment and the observation that at least some Supreme Court case law seems to require it.

iv. Synthesizing the Declaratory Judgment Case Law

Although complicated, the case law on federal question jurisdiction in declaratory judgment suits can be synthesized in the form of the following reasoning chain:

Step 1. Identify the federal question in the declaratory judgment suit. For "arising under" jurisdiction, the declaratory judgment complaint needs to reflect a federal question. This is a necessary requirement but is not sufficient to establish federal question jurisdiction.

Step 2. Look at the facts in the declaratory judgment suit to identify the reason the parties are in conflict. Project this conflict into the suit for damages or an injunction that would result if the parties' dispute matured into a traditional lawsuit. This hypothetical suit for damages or an injunction is sometimes called a "coercive" suit.

Step 3. Analyze whether the federal question would be part of the plaintiff's well-pleaded complaint in the hypothetical coercive suit that would likely result between the parties. If so, the declaratory judgment suit may satisfy the "well-pleaded complaint" rule. Because case law suggests that an alignment requirement exists between the declaratory plaintiff and the coercive plaintiff, prudence counsels proceeding to step 4 before concluding definitively that the suit satisfies the "well-pleaded complaint" rule.

Step 4. Analyze whether the suit satisfies the alignment requirement. For this requirement to be satisfied, the plaintiff in the declaratory suit must be the same entity or individual as the plaintiff in the coercive suit.

Step 5. Evaluate whether the federal component of the coercive suit is sufficient for §1331 jurisdiction. If the coercive suit asserts a cause of action created by federal law, "arising under" jurisdiction is clearly present. If the coercive suit asserts a state law cause of action, ask whether the suit satisfies the four elements of *Grable & Sons Metal Products, Inc. v. Darue Eng'g & Mfg.*, 545 U.S. 308 (2005): the *necessary, actually disputed, substantiality,* and *federal-state balance* requirements.

Step 6. Check to see whether the declaratory plaintiff is a state entity that has available mechanisms within its own courts for testing the validity of its regulations. If so, *Franchise Tax Board v. Construction Laborers Vacation Trust*, 463 U.S. 1, 23 (1983), suggests that federal question jurisdiction is not present.

Here's an example for trying out this reasoning chain.

Example 2-8

Peachtree Retirement Houses, Inc., runs several retirement communities in New Jersey and Pennsylvania. Careproviders, Inc., is a group of physicians under contract with Peachtree to provide medical care to the residents of Peachtree's retirement homes. The contract required Peachtree to carry correspondence among Careproviders' physicians, who staffed the various retirement homes. For many years, Peachtree dutifully complied with the contract by picking up and delivering the physicians' mail.

Peachtree found itself in a quandary when a court decision called into question the legality of Peachtree's carriage of the correspondence without payment of postage. If Peachtree continued to fulfill its contractual duty, it could be in violation of the federal statutes (interpreted in the court decision) granting a mail-carrying monopoly to the United States Postal Service.

Careproviders, which relied on Peachtree's mail carriage, became concerned that Peachtree would cease to perform this duty and wanted to settle the issue. Thus, Careproviders planned to institute a declaratory judgment action asking the court to declare the rights of Peachtree and Careproviders and to determine what mailings Peachtree could lawfully carry.

Would a United States district court have subject matter jurisdiction to adjudicate the action?

Explanation

Because this example concerns a plaintiff's request for declaratory relief, its resolution requires analysis under the six steps synthesized from the declaratory judgment case law.

Step 1: Identify the federal question. The federal question in the case concerns whether the mail-carrying monopoly of the United States Postal Service prevents Peachtree from lawfully carrying the correspondence among the physicians.

Step 2: Identify the likely hypothetical coercive suit. The parties are in conflict because they have a contract that may be prohibited under federal law. Peachtree is likely to avoid the risk of violating federal law and therefore to discontinue performing part of the contract. Thus, the coercive suit that immediately comes to mind is a breach of contract action by Careproviders against Peachtree. Peachtree would defend this suit by raising the federal question.

Step 3: Apply the "well-pleaded" complaint rule. The coercive suit outlined in step 2 flunks the "well-pleaded complaint" test. The federal question comes in by way of the defense. For that reason, further analysis is unnecessary and steps 4, 5, and 6 become irrelevant. Careproviders' declaratory action could not be brought in federal court pursuant to §1331 in the absence of the declaratory judgment remedy.

Rewind to step 2. Skelly Oil and Franchise Tax Board were not explicit about the level of creativity allowed one who is envisioning scenarios for supporting a hypothetical coercive suit. The Court's conservative approach to federal jurisdiction, however, implies that one should not conjure new facts, new parties, or outlandish legal theories in conceptualizing the coercive suit. With this constraint, one might consider whether something other than a standard breach of contract suit would unfold between Peachtree and Careproviders — a coercive suit with the federal question in the coercive complaint. Upon reflection and research into contract law, one might find some promise in a suit for anticipatory repudiation. Under this scenario, Peachtree would make a positive statement that it will not perform its mail-carrying responsibilities under the contract. Careproviders would respond that Peachtree is insisting on an incorrect interpretation of federal law in repudiating its obligations under the contract. Based on this chain of events, Careproviders would then file a coercive suit based on anticipatory repudiation.

Revisit step 3. Under this new conceptualization of the coercive suit, the federal question arguably would appear on the face of the well-pleaded complaint. Although contract law varies among jurisdictions, some states

provide that a plaintiff pursuing a cause of action for anticipatory repudiation may prevail upon a showing of the plaintiff's own willingness to
perform a contract and the defendant's positive (yet unjustified) statement
that the defendant will not perform the contract. In order to make out her
case, the plaintiff must assert reasons why the defendant's repudiation is
wrongful. In the context of Example 2-8, this means that Careproviders'
complaint would allege that Peachtree's repudiation is wrongful. To support
this allegation, Careproviders' complaint would include statements establishing why Peachtree's interpretation of federal law governing mail carrying
is incorrect. In other words, Careproviders would properly include a federal
question in its well-pleaded complaint. While the success of this reasoning
may depend on subtleties of state law governing anticipatory repudiation,
the reasoning nevertheless provides Careproviders with a reasonable prospect of satisfying the "well-pleaded complaint" rule.

Step 4. Assuming that it has satisfied the "well-pleaded complaint"
hurdle, Careproviders must next reckon with the alignment requirement.
Fortunately, the alignment requirement is no problem. Under the scenario
in the preceding paragraph, Careproviders is the hypothetical coercive plaintiff. The original facts cast Careproviders as the declaratory plaintiff. In an
instance where the alignment requirement presents a problem, one might
argue that the case law is unclear as to whether the Supreme Court actually
intended to impose an alignment requirement after *Textron.* Given the parties
here, however, that argument is unnecessary.

Step 5. Having satisfied any alignment requirement, Careproviders must
establish that the federal question satisfies the elements of *Grable:* the *necessary,*
actually disputed, substantiality, and *federal-state balance* requirements. Because uncertainty about the scope of federal laws governing mail carrying is the only
reason the parties need litigation, Careproviders can easily establish that the
federal question is a *necessary* component to their *actual dispute.* The *substantiality*
factor is weaker than the first two *Grable* factors, because the case arguably calls
for a fact-specific application of a federal standard, rather than a pure
question of law, a quality that *Empire Healthchoice Assurance, Inc.* suggested
strongly militated against federal jurisdiction. Nonetheless, the question
does implicate important issues about the scope of a federal statutory scheme:
the proper reach of the federal mail-carrying monopoly implicates the power
of the United States Postal Service and other mail delivery institutions crucial
to the well-being of United States citizens and the national economy. For this
reason, one might reasonably assume that the *substantiality* factor is satisfied. As
for the *federal-state balance* concern, nothing in the facts suggests the type of
complex federal statutory scheme lacking a congressionally authorized cause
of action that concerned the court in *Merrell Dow Pharmaceuticals Inc. v. Thompson.*
The parties have reached a stalemate in their relationship, and authoritative
federal court interpretation of the mail-carrying laws is needed so that they
can perform their professional and business obligations. Moreover, similar to

Grable, one can easily conclude that allowing federal jurisdiction over contract disputes concerning the scope of the United States Postal Service's mail-carrying monopoly will not alter the flow of cases into state and federal courts.

b. Complete Preemption

In at least one circumstance, the strictures of the "well-pleaded complaint" rule "bend" to allow federal question jurisdiction for cases that — upon first reading — appear to rest on state law. These cases ultimately "arise under" federal law by force of federal preemption. This wrinkle, known as complete preemption, can appear in suits for declaratory judgments as well as in suits calling for other remedies.

The doctrine of federal preemption provides that state law must yield to federal law in a number of instances, including those where Congress has made a claim to regulate an entire area of human interaction by occupying a field of regulation. The preemption doctrine provides the foundation for the "complete preemption" wrinkle, which may be characterized as an exception to the "well-pleaded complaint" rule.

In an area where Congress has preempted regulation, a state cause of action is not independently enforceable and is controlled by federal law. Where the preemptive force is especially strong, the state cause of action can be viewed — from its inception — to be one arising under federal law. As the Supreme Court has explained, occasionally "the pre-emptive force of a statute is so 'extraordinary' that it 'converts an ordinary state common law complaint into one stating a federal claim for purposes of the well-pleaded complaint rule.' " *Caterpillar Inc. v. Williams,* 482 U.S. 386, 393 (1987) (quoting *Metropolitan Life Ins. Co. v. Taylor,* 481 U.S. 58, 65 (1987)). The Supreme Court has called this circumstance an "independent corollary" to the "well-pleaded complaint" rule, *Caterpillar,* 482 U.S. at 393 (quoting *Franchise Tax Board,* 463 U.S. at 22), and some lower courts call it an "exception," e.g., *Wagner v. Amor 17 Corp.,* 321 F. Supp. 2d 1195, 1203 (D. Nev. 2004).

The trick in identifying complete preemption is accurately concluding that Congress has preempted a state law cause of action with a particular federal statute. The enterprise calls for statutory construction and knowledge of areas where the Supreme Court is likely to find complete preemption. Key areas where the Supreme Court is likely to find extensive preemption are labor law, pension law, Native American land rights, national banking, foreign policy, immigration, and nuclear power. One should be careful, however, before assuming that preemption exists for a particular law within these general subjects. Instead, one should use the complete preemption concept only after researching whether federal courts have determined that Congress preempted the precise legal concept at issue in the litigation, and thereby intended for a state law claim to be converted to a federal law claim. The Supreme Court has found complete preemption for the purpose of federal question jurisdiction in cases regulated by ERISA, *Metropolitan Life Ins. Co. v. Taylor*, 481 U.S. 58 (1987); cases seeking to enforce claims under collective bargaining agreements, *Avco Corp. v. Aero Lodge No. 735*, 390 U.S. 557 (1968), *Caterpillar Inc. v. Williams*, 482 U.S. 386 (1987); and cases concerning usury claims against national banks, *Beneficial National Bank v. Anderson*, 539 U.S. 1 (2003). Courts have also interpreted the Supreme Court decision in *Oneida Indian Nation v. Oneida Cty. of New York* 414 U.S. 661 (1974), as applying the doctrine to a question arising in a Native American rights dispute.

Over a strong dissent by Justice Scalia, the Supreme Court in *Beneficial National Bank* applied the complete preemption doctrine in a removal context, allowing removal of a state court action under 28 U.S.C. §1331. *Beneficial National Bank* held removable a cause of action for a national bank's usury violations. The Court emphasized that Congress both intended the National Bank Act to provide the exclusive cause of action for usury claims and sought to protect the special nature of federally chartered banks. Accordingly, the Court held that the National Bank Act had sufficient preemptive force to establish removal jurisdiction, even though the plaintiffs had framed their case in state law terms only.

Example 2-9

An avid smoker, Grace smoked a cigarette brand known as Coffin Nails. She ultimately developed lung cancer and filed a state law negligence action in federal district court against the manufacturer of Coffin Nails, alleging that the manufacturer had failed to warn her of the dangers of using its product. The Coffin Nails package displayed a warning that was specified by federal statute. Grace alleges in her complaint that the warning was not sufficient to alert her to the product's dangers under state law and that the federal mandate requiring the warning did not preempt her ability to pursue a state tort action for damages.

Explanation

Cigarette warning regulation is not an area where Congress has completely preempted a state law cause of action. Accordingly, the state law cause of action for failure to warn is not "transformed" into one arising under federal law. Grace is correct that the scope of federal regulation of cigarette labels is pertinent to her lawsuit. Unfortunately for her, however, the federal regulation is pertinent only to a defense based on preemption or a defense based on compliance with the federal warning requirement. The federal regulation does not control the elements of her state law cause of action. Thus, her lawsuit does not satisfy the "well-pleaded complaint" rule and does not arise under federal law for the purposes of 28 U.S.C. §1331.

Example 2-10

United Workers Union entered into a collective bargaining agreement with XYZ Company. The agreement provided that the workers would have access to convenient parking spaces. United Workers Union believed that XYZ did not honor that portion of the agreement and has filed suit in state court, alleging a breach of the collective bargaining agreement. XYZ Company sought to remove the case to federal court. Stating that the suit is simply a state law contract dispute about the meaning of "convenient parking spaces," United Workers Union fought the removal and argued that the federal court lacks subject matter jurisdiction. Is the case properly removable?

Explanation

Yes, the case is properly removable because United Workers Union has raised a claim subject to the complete preemptive force of federal labor law. Accordingly, the claim arises under federal law and the federal court has subject matter jurisdiction. The Supreme Court has stated that a claim founded directly on rights created by collective bargaining agreements is "purely a creature of federal law, notwithstanding the fact that state law would provide a cause of action in the absence of [federal law]." *Franchise Tax Board v. Construction Laborers Vacation Trust*, 463 U.S. 1, 23 (1983). In other words, the federal statute governing labor-management relations has so powerful a preemptive force that it eliminates any state cause of action regarding enforcement of the terms of a collective bargaining agreement. *See Avco Corp. v. Aero Lodge No. 735*, 390 U.S. 557 (1968).

Finally, the removal context for this complete preemption question does not change the result. The Supreme Court eliminated any doubt that the complete preemption principle applies in the context of removal in *Beneficial National Bank v. Anderson*, 539 U.S. 1 (2003).

Diversity of Citizenship Jurisdiction in Lower Federal Courts

Article III of the United States Constitution lists many different kinds of diversity cases. The article allows the federal judiciary to exercise power over controversies between two states, between a state and citizens of another state, between citizens of different states, and between a state (or the citizens thereof) and foreign states (or their citizens or subjects). By far, the most common category among them is controversies between citizens of different states. This category is the focus of this chapter.

The framers included diversity of citizenship in the list of powers granted to federal courts as a remedy for interregional bias among the states. The framers intended diversity jurisdiction to position federal courts as neutral forums available to litigants who feared they might suffer bias in out-of-state courts. The reasoning goes like this: unlike many state court judges, federal judges within a state do not face reelection pressures. Life tenure insulates federal judges from state politics and frees them to rule in favor of out-of-staters without fear of losing their jobs in state elections.

Dispute perennially arises in Congress and in academic literature about whether mass communication, readily accessible transportation systems, and the national mindset of Americans have eroded the regionalism that inspired diversity jurisdiction. Many argue that diversity cases unnecessarily distract federal courts from the more pressing duty of interpreting the ever-expanding body of federal law. Not only do diversity cases take up valuable room in the federal court docket, they require federal courts to engage in the difficult task of guessing at the meaning of state law.[1] Despite

---

1. The Erie doctrine requires federal courts to look to state law for rules of decision in diversity cases. See infra Part VII for discussion of the Erie doctrine.

these arguments, most experts predict that Congress is unlikely to abolish diversity of citizenship jurisdiction, particularly given the vigorous lobbying efforts of many in the practicing bar who support diversity jurisdiction. Moreover, eliminating diversity jurisdiction to save federal courts would have the politically unpalatable consequence of overburdening state courts, which already suffer from a crushing caseload.

While not sufficient to doom diversity jurisdiction altogether, the arguments against using federal court resources in diversity cases serve as useful tools for resolving disputes about the scope of diversity jurisdiction. For close cases calling into question whether a federal court should exercise diversity jurisdiction, the arguments present a tiebreaker. This orientation against finding diversity jurisdiction is reflected in many Supreme Court cases, which refer repeatedly to interpreting the scope of the power narrowly.

To understand the jurisdictional grant over disputes between citizens of different states, one must focus on not only Article III, but also on the statute granting diversity jurisdiction to lower federal courts, 28 U.S.C. §1332. Section 1332(a) provides, in part, that the "district courts shall have original jurisdiction of all civil actions where the matter in controversy exceeds the sum or value of $75,000, exclusive of interest and costs, and is between . . . [c]itizens of different States." As with federal question jurisdiction, courts have interpreted the statutory grant more restrictively than the constitutional grant of power to federal courts. The remainder of this chapter will explore crucial components of §1332's language. Starting with the meaning of "different States" in §1332(a), this chapter goes on to review problems of determining citizenship, calculating the "amount in controversy" requirement, and identifying forbidden subject areas. Each of these topics pertains to the general provision for diversity of citizenship jurisdiction in §1332(a). Additionally, the chapter reviews special rules for class actions under §1332(d).

A. DEFINING "DIFFERENT STATES": THE COMPLETE DIVERSITY RULE

In *Strawbridge v. Curtiss*, 7 U.S. (3 Cranch) 267 (1806), the Court held that diversity of citizenship jurisdiction did not exist even though the plaintiffs in the case were from a different state than a defendant. In *Strawbridge*, the plaintiffs were from Massachusetts and only one of the multiple defendants was from Vermont; the rest of the defendants were from Massachusetts. This lineup created "minimal diversity" because at least one defendant was from a different state from at least one of the plaintiffs, but that was not sufficient under the *Strawbridge* Court's reading of the diversity statute. Rather, the Court read the statute as requiring "complete diversity"—a requirement that every plaintiff have a different citizenship from every defendant.

Example 3-1

Linda and Lydia are both from Montana. As plaintiffs, they sue four defendants: Deborah and Donna, who are both from New Mexico, and Monica and Molly, who are both from Arizona. Is there complete diversity between the parties?

Explanation

Yes. Example 3-1 satisfies the complete diversity requirement, because all the plaintiffs and all the defendants are from different states.

Example 3-2

Angela is from Pennsylvania. She sues Bonnie, who is from New Jersey; Carol, who is from Maryland; and Denise, who is from Pennsylvania. Is there complete diversity between the parties?

Explanation

This example does not satisfy the complete diversity requirement because the plaintiff, Angela, shares citizenship with a defendant, Denise. This example does, however, satisfy minimal diversity, because at least one of the defendants is from a different state than the plaintiff.

Courts and commentators agree that the complete diversity requirement is a statutory requirement under the general diversity statute, 28 U.S.C. §1332. Nearly identical language in Article III, §2 of the Constitution, however, requires only minimal diversity.

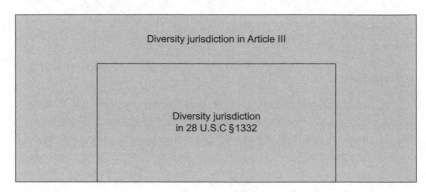

Figure 3.1.

This difference in scope is significant: even though Congress has restricted the reach of diversity under 28 U.S.C. §1332, the Constitution allows Congress to grant federal courts jurisdiction based on minimal diversity only. In fact, Congress has used other statutes to grant jurisdiction based on minimal diversity in specific contexts, such as interpleader, multi-forum litigation, and class actions. For the purposes of §1332, the bottom line is that a case that satisfies the statute's "complete diversity" requirements will also satisfy the less restrictive requirements of Article III, §2.

B. DETERMINING CITIZENSHIP

Rules vary for determining the citizenship of individuals, corporations, unincorporated associations, and class action litigants. This section considers the various rules.

1. Citizenship Rules for Individuals

For an individual to be a citizen of a state, the person must be a citizen of the United States and "domiciled" in that particular state. A person can have only one domicile, which is determined by the individual's subjective intent to make a place her home, and by her physical presence in that place. This "mind and body" test can have significant ramifications when an individual wishes to change her domicile. But, for purposes of §1332, the point of reference is the domicile at the time suit commences. If diversity exists at the time the action is filed, it is not destroyed if one of the parties moves.

Example 3-3

Zelda lived in Maine, which was where she attended all her schooling and owned a house. She planned to move to California someday, wanting to make the state her new home. Even though she had never even visited California, Zelda believed her heart and soul belonged there. Upon her graduation from college in Maine, Zelda mustered the courage to plan the move to California. She lined up a job interview in California, sold her house, told everyone she was moving to California, rented a California apartment over the Internet, closed her Maine bank account, transferred her church membership to a California church, bought a plane ticket to California, and set off to fly there from the airport in Boston, Massachusetts. En route to the airport, she had an automobile accident in Maine and needed to be hospitalized there.

A federal lawsuit concerning the car accident was filed against Zelda while she was still in the hospital. The plaintiff was a Maine resident who alleged damages of over $1,000,000, and sought to invoke the federal court's diversity jurisdiction. The plaintiff asserts that Zelda is a citizen of California. Is the plaintiff correct?

Explanation

No, the plaintiff is not correct. Zelda is not a citizen of California because she is not yet domiciled there. She satisfies the "mind" but not the "body" component of the domicile test. For the mind component, she has demonstrated the intent to make California her new home. Evidence of intent is gleaned from the facts listed in Example 3-3: place of employment, location of property and bank accounts, voting and car registration, personal declarations, and membership in groups. Zelda has not, however, become physically present in California — a fact that cannot be overcome by her manifestations of intent to move there or her planned trip outside of Maine. She has therefore not lost her Maine domicile. That is not to say that once Zelda established a physical presence in California, she would lose her domicile there by simply going on a brief vacation away from the state. She cannot, however, establish domicile in California without having actually gone to the state.

Example 3-4

Consider the same facts as in Example 3-3, except now Zelda is discharged from the Maine hospital and flies to California before the lawsuit is filed. Zelda receives service of process in her California apartment. As in Example 3-3, the lawsuit concerns the car accident in Massachusetts. Can the plaintiff maintain a diversity action in federal court based on Zelda's domicile?

Explanation

Zelda has now satisfied the "body" portion of the domicile test: she is physically present in California. Since she also intends to make California her home, Zelda possesses California citizenship for §1332 purposes. It is no consequence that she had not yet obtained California citizenship at the time of the events giving rise to the lawsuit. Courts determine citizenship for the purposes of §1332 at the time the lawsuit is filed.

2. Citizenship Rules for Corporations

Congress defines the citizenship rules for corporations in §1332(c)(1): "a corporation shall be deemed to be a citizen of any State by which it has been incorporated and of the State where it has its principal place of business. . . ."[2] Note that this language anticipates that a corporation, unlike a flesh-and-blood individual, can have citizenship in more than one jurisdiction. First, the statute provides that the corporation shall be a citizen of *any* state that has incorporated it. In the unlikely event that a corporation chooses to satisfy the incorporation requirements of more than one state, incorporation can provide the corporation with more than one state of citizenship. Next, the statute provides that the corporation is a citizen of "the State" where it has its principal place of business. The words "the State" suggest that a corporation can have only one principal place of business; yet, because this location may be different from the state of incorporation, this language provides another possibility for a corporation to possess more than one citizenship.

Because §1332 envisions that a corporation can have only one principal place of business, one may have to make a close call in choosing among possible locations. If the corporation has activity in more than one state, one should consider all of the corporation's activities and identify where most of them took place. If no state clearly emerges as the "winner," the location of the corporation's home office or nerve center becomes its principal place of business.

Example 3-5

Negligent Corporation is incorporated in the state of California and manufactures products that it markets throughout the western United States. Its home office and manufacturing facilities are in Nevada, where it employs thirty people. Negligent Corporation also owns a storage and distribution facility in Oregon, where it employs twenty-six people. Pamela Plaintiff is a resident of California who was injured by one of Negligent Corporation's products. She planned to sue Negligent Corporation in federal court, invoking the court's diversity jurisdiction. Does the court have diversity jurisdiction?

---

2. Section 1332 provides an exception to this rule for insurance companies: "in any direct action against the insurer of a policy or contract of liability insurance, whether incorporated or unincorporated, to which action the insured is not joined as a party-defendant, such insurer shall be deemed a citizen of the State of which the insured is a citizen, as well as of any State by which the insurer has been incorporated and of the State where it has its principal place of business. . . ."

Explanation

The court lacks diversity jurisdiction. Nevada and Oregon both provide the location for significant parts of Negligent Corporation's activity. A hub of business activity exists in Nevada, where Negligent Corporation focuses its production and administrative work. Because Negligent Corporation has declared its home office is in Nevada, that fact provides a tiebreaker, designating Nevada as its principal place of business and a place of citizenship for purpose of §1332. Pamela's own citizenship, however, overlaps with the place of incorporation of Negligent Corporation — California — so no diversity exists for §1332 purposes.

3. Citizenship Rules for Unincorporated Associations

In §1332, unincorporated associations do not have a separate identity for citizenship purposes. Instead, an unincorporated association is deemed a citizen of every state where one of its members is a citizen. Incorporated associations include entities such as labor unions, partnerships, trade associations, boards of directors for non-corporate institutions, and joint stock companies.[3] In light of this rule, the Supreme Court held in *Carden v. Arkoma Assocs.*, 494 U.S. 185, 195-196 (1990), that diversity among the parties depends on the citizenship of both general and limited partners in a partnership. (General partners usually manage the partnership; limited partners generally invest in the partnership without taking control responsibilities.) In ruling that a court must consider all parties' citizenship, the *Carden* Court reasoned that the current burden on federal court dockets makes the policy of strictly construing the diversity statute especially important. 494 U.S. at 207.

Some confusion has surrounded the citizenship of a limited liability corporation (LLC). This business form is a hybrid, sharing characteristics with standard corporations as well as unincorporated associations. Courts now generally agree that the citizenship of an LLC should be analyzed in the same way as the citizenship of other unincorporated entities: for deciding whether diversity jurisdiction is present, the court must consider the citizenship of all members of the LLC.

Example 3-6

The American Association of Professional Dogwalkers is an unincorporated association, with members in all fifty states, but nowhere else in the world. That means that it can never be a party to a federal court proceeding under §1332, right?

---

3. LARRY L. TEPLY & RALPH U. WHITTEN, CIVIL PROCEDURE 89-90 (3d ed. 2004)

Explanation

Trick question! Under §1332(e), the word "States" is defined to include "the Territories, the District of Columbia, and the Commonwealth of Puerto Rico." Thus, although the American Association of Professional Dogwalkers cannot be a litigant in §1332 suits where the opponent is a citizen of one of the fifty states, the association can be a party in suits where the opposing parties are from one of the nontraditional "States" under §1332(e).

4. Citizenship Rules for Class Actions

a. Basic Rule

In *Supreme Tribe of Ben-Hur v. Cauble*, 255 U.S. 356 (1921), the Supreme Court announced that diversity in class action suits is based on the citizenship of the class representatives. In *Ben-Hur*, class representatives who were not from Indiana sued Indiana defendants. The question arose as to whether the trial court's judgment bound class members who were from Indiana and therefore not diverse from the defendants. The United States Supreme Court ruled that the trial court had possessed diversity of citizenship jurisdiction and that the judgment bound all class members. The Supreme Court has never explained whether this holding derives from principles of supplemental jurisdiction (which are explored next) or from the notion that for citizenship purposes under §1332(a), the class representative is the only entity that matters. Whatever the precise rationale, the Court's interpretation of §1332 (a) in *Ben-Hur* appears undisturbed, despite subsequent changes in class action law.[4]

For class actions satisfying specific requirements, the Class Action Fairness Act of 2005 (CAFA) provides a different rule than *Ben-Hur* and expands the federal court diversity jurisdiction for class actions even further. Codified in 28 U.S.C. §1332(d), CAFA class actions generally include those certified under the federal class action rule (Federal Rule of Civil Procedure 23) or a similar state provision including 100 or more class members and an aggregate of more than $5,000,000 in controversy (exclusive of interest and

---

4. *See, e.g.*, RICHARD D. FREER, INTRODUCTION TO CIVIL PROCEDURE 741 (2006) (stating that the Ben-Hur holding remains "vital to this day"). *See also* Richard D. Freer, *The Cauldron Boils: Supplemental Jurisdiction, Amount in Controversy, and Diversity of Citizenship Class Actions*, 53 EMORY L.J. 55, 60 (2004) (explaining Ben-Hur); Alan B. Morrison, *Straightening Out the Supplemental Jurisdiction Mess: Short and Long Term Fixes*, 74 U.S.L.W. 2179, 2181 (Oct. 4, 2005) (stating that after the Class Action Fairness Act of 2005 became law, "there will now be two sets of rules on diversity class actions"). For a helpful review of CAFA, *see* Edward F. Sherman, *Class Actions After the Class Action Fairness Act of 2005*, 80 TUL.L. REV. 1593 (2006).

costs). The specific requirements for CAFA class actions differ from other contexts.

For example, the citizenship requirement for CAFA class actions mandates minimal diversity only: diversity jurisdiction exists if "any member of a class of plaintiffs is a citizen of a State different from any defendant." 28 U.S.C. §1332(d)(2)(A).[5] Congress intended CAFA to handle situations where two or more plaintiff class actions have been filed. Thus, some CAFA requirements refer to "proposed plaintiff classes," suggesting that a court considering whether to exercise diversity jurisdiction under §1332(d)(2) must sometimes consider class action lawsuits other than the one before the court. The overall purpose of CAFA is to greatly expand federal court jurisdiction over class actions, expressing a strong preference for federal court control over interstate class actions.

Example 3-7

A case was filed under Federal Rule of Civil Procedure 23 and was certified as a class action with more than 100 class members and an aggregate amount in controversy in excess of $5,000,000 (exclusive of interest and costs). The sole class representative, Cary, is from Pennsylvania. Sixty plaintiffs in the class are from New Jersey and sixty-five plaintiffs in the class are from Maryland. There are three defendants: one from Pennsylvania, one from Maryland, and one from New Jersey. Is the citizenship requirement for diversity jurisdiction satisfied?

Explanation

The first step in analyzing facts from a case like Example 3-7 is to determine whether it is a CAFA class action or not. Because the class action is certified under Federal Rule of Civil Procedure 23, with more than 100 members and over $5,000,000 in controversy, the case appears to be covered by CAFA. No facts suggest the presence of any CAFA exceptions (described in detail next). Accordingly, the citizenship standard requires minimal diversity, as provided under 28 U.S.C. §1332(d)(2)(A). This minimal standard is satisfied in Example 3-7: at least one plaintiff is from a different state from at least one defendant.

If the class action in Example 3-7 fell outside the ambit of CAFA, the next step would be to determine whether the class action satisfies the citizenship requirements of §1332(a), as interpreted in *Supreme Tribe of Ben-Hur v. Cauble*. Example 3-7 does not satisfy the *Ben-Hur* rule, which requires the named

---

5. Diversity also exists under CAFA if "any member of a class of plaintiffs is a foreign state or a citizen or subject of a foreign state and any defendant is a citizen of a State" or if "any member of a class of plaintiffs is a citizen of a State and any defendant is a foreign state or a citizen or subject of a foreign state." 28 U.S.C. §§1332(d)(2)(B)-1332(d)(2)(C).

plaintiff to be a citizen of a different state than all the defendants. The named plaintiff here is from the same state as one of the defendants.

b. Discretionary Exception to the Basic Rule: §1332(d)(3)

Despite §1332(d)'s broad approach to defining diversity of citizenship in CAFA class actions, the section identifies several exceptions to the minimal diversity rule. Section 1332(d) contains a discretionary exception — explained in this section — and mandatory exceptions discussed in the next section. Under the discretionary exception, the district court may decline jurisdiction if between one-third and two-thirds of plaintiffs as well as the primary defendants are from the same state where the action was originally filed. 28 U.S.C. §1332(d)(3). Once the court determines that the case satisfies this threshold requirement, the federal court decides whether to decline jurisdiction by asking if jurisdiction is appropriate in "the interests of justice . . . and the totality of the circumstances." 28 U.S.C. §1332(d)(3). To inform its analysis, the district court should consider the following factors:

1. Whether the claims concern matters of national or interstate interest;
2. Whether the claims will be governed by the laws of states other than the forum;
3. Whether the class action is pleaded so as to avoid federal jurisdiction;
4. Whether the action was brought in a forum with a distinct connection with the class members, the alleged harm, or the defendants;
5. Whether the number of class members who are citizens of the forum state (considering all proposed plaintiff classes) is in the aggregate substantially larger than the number of citizens from any other state *and* the other members of the proposed class are spread among a substantial number of states; and
6. Whether, during the three-year period before the class action was filed, one or more other class actions asserting the same or similar claims were filed.

Example 3-8

A case was filed under Federal Rule of Civil Procedure 23, and was certified as a class action. Plaintiffs are building owners in South Carolina and Georgia. There are 1,000 plaintiffs in the class: 335 plaintiffs are from Georgia and 665 plaintiffs are from South Carolina. The defendants are Concrete Company and Quarry Company, both of which are incorporated in South Carolina, where their principal places of business are located. Quarry Corporation sold to Concrete Company a chemical used to produce concrete. Business was conducted as follows: Quarry Corporation sold the chemical to Concrete Company in South Carolina, Concrete Company processed it at a South Carolina plant, and Concrete Company sold the finished product to construction companies that build in South Carolina and Georgia. All of Concrete Company's sales were consummated in South Carolina. The plaintiffs claimed that the chemical was inherently defective and led to structural problems with their buildings. The class was defined to include all entities that purchased the defective chemical and experienced structural problems as a result of the defect.

The plaintiffs filed suit in federal district court in South Carolina. All parties agreed that South Carolina substantive law would govern plaintiffs' claim. The defendants argued that the suit should be dismissed under the discretionary factors in 28 U.S.C. §1332(d)(3). Should the court dismiss the lawsuit?

Explanation

While no definitive answer presents itself, the district court would be well within its discretion in dismissing the lawsuit. The class action in the example satisfies the citizenship requirements of §1332(d)(2) because minimal diversity exists: at least one plaintiff is from a different state from at least one defendant. Nevertheless, defendants are correct that this example falls within the ballpark of §1332(d)(3)'s invitation for federal district courts to decline jurisdiction. Specifically, this is a situation in which "greater than one-third, but less than two-thirds of the members of all the proposed plaintiff classes . . . and the primary defendants are citizens" of the same state where the action was originally filed. 28 U.S.C. §1332(d)(3). Both defendants are from South Carolina, 665 plaintiffs out of 1,000 are from South Carolina (less than two-thirds would be 666 or fewer plaintiffs), and the action was filed in South Carolina. The case therefore satisfies the preliminary threshold for §1332(d)(3) to apply. (In the real world, one may encounter considerable difficulty identifying all the people in the class as well as their citizenship. This information, however, is crucial to the CAFA's operation.)

Since the example satisfies §1332(d)(3)'s preliminary threshold, the district court should consider the section's discretionary factors to decide whether to decline jurisdiction. No definite answer emerges under §1332(d)(3). Nonetheless, many discretionary factors from §1332(d)(3) counsel the district court *not* to exercise its jurisdiction authorized in §1332(d)(2). Based on the following analysis, the court could legitimately choose to dismiss the suit.

Factor 1: Whether the claims concern matters of national or interstate interest. This factor does not weigh in favor of federal jurisdiction in Example 3-8. The transactions and product underlying the controversy are centered in South Carolina. Congressional history explaining this factor admonishes that where "a case presents issues of national or interstate significance, that

[fact] argues in favor of the matter being handled in federal court." Class Action Fairness Act of 2005, S. Rep. 109-14, at 36 (2005), as reprinted in 2005 U.S.C.C.A.N. 3, 35, available at 2005 WL 627977. One may readily conclude that no issues of national or interstate significance exist in this example, thus weighing against federal jurisdiction.

Factor 2: Whether the claims will be governed by the laws of other states. This factor derives from the premise that, although perhaps not formally less respectful of other states' laws compared with their own, state courts are — in practice — more inclined to apply forum state law than federal courts. Where a federal court determines that forum state law will apply to the whole case, this "factor will favor allowing the state court to handle the matter."[6] Because the parties agree that the law of the forum state — South Carolina — will govern here, this factor favors declining federal jurisdiction.

Factor 3: Whether the class action is pleaded so as to avoid federal jurisdiction. This factor seeks to test whether the class is defined in such a way as to avoid federal jurisdiction by omitting certain potential class members or claims that arise under federal law. The class definition and claim in Example 3-8 appear naturally framed. All obvious plaintiffs are included in the class and no pertinent federal claim suggests itself. This factor therefore favors allowing a state court to handle the matter.

Factor 4: Whether the action was brought in a forum with a distinct connection to the class members, the alleged harm, or the defendants. This factor is designed to take into account a concern that lawsuits might be filed in "out-of-the-way" state courts with "no real relationship to the controversy at hand." Sen. Judiciary Comm. Report on Class Action Fairness Act of 2005, S. Rep. No. 109-14, at 37 (2005), as reprinted in 2005 U.S.C.C.A.N. 3, 36, available at 2005 WL 627977. The factor does not weigh in favor of federal court jurisdiction here, given the many strong connections between South Carolina and the case.

Factor 5: Whether the number of class members who are citizens in the State (considering all proposed plaintiff classes) is in the aggregate substantially larger than the number of citizens from any other state and the other members of the proposed class are from a substantial number of states. Upon initial analysis, it appears that this factor might weigh in favor of state court, since a substantially larger portion of the plaintiffs are from South Carolina than from any other state. Ultimately, the factor does not favor state court jurisdiction, since it also requires that the other members of the class must be from a substantial number of other states. This is not the case here, given that all the non–South Carolinian plaintiffs are from only one state: Georgia. Under these circumstances, this factor actually

---

6. Sen. Judiciary Comm. Report on Class Action Fairness Act of 2005, S. Rep. No. 109-14, at 37 (2005), as reprinted in 2005 U.S.C.C.A.N. 3, 36, available at 2005 WL 627977. This report provides extensive guidance on the meaning of these factors. Lower courts have relied on this report. *See, e.g., Schwartz v. Comcast Corp.*, No, 05-2340, 2005 U.S. Dist. LEXIS 15396, at *16 (E.D. Pa. July 29, 2005).

weighs in favor of federal jurisdiction because Georgia (as well as South Carolina) would have a strong interest in the controversy, and presumably the federal court would be in a better position to remain neutral in evaluating competing interests between Georgia and South Carolina.

Factor 6: Whether, during the three-year period before the class action was filed, one or more other class actions asserting the same or similar claims were filed. Nothing in the facts of Example 3-8 indicates that any claims were asserted in any other class action pertaining to the wrongs alleged. Thus, factor 6 also does not favor federal court jurisdiction. Congressional history explains that this factor serves fairness and efficiency by evaluating "whether a matter should be subject to federal jurisdiction so that it can be coordinated with other overlapping or parallel class actions." Sen. Judiciary Comm. Report on Class Action Fairness Act of 2005, S. Rep. 109-14, S. Rep. No. 109-14 (2005), 2005 U.S.C.C.A.N. 3, 36, at 2005 WL 627977.

Although the factors do not unanimously oppose federal jurisdiction for Example 3-8, the bulk of the factors point in that direction. Accordingly, a court could quite reasonably dismiss the action under §1332(d)(3), concluding that the action is essentially a South Carolina action, properly belonging in South Carolina state court.

c. Mandatory Exceptions to the Basic Rule in §1332(d)

Section 1332(d) requires federal courts to decline jurisdiction in CAFA class actions under a number of circumstances. First, §1332(d) details subject matter categories for specific claims that do not get the benefit of the liberal minimal diversity rule. Claims that may not be brought under §1332(d)(2) include claims under the Securities Act of 1933, claims under the Securities Exchange Act of 1934, and claims concerning the internal affairs or governance of a corporation or other form of business enterprise. Next, federal courts must decline §1332(d)(2) jurisdiction over suits with fewer than 100 plaintiffs in total and suits in which the primary defendants are states, state officials, or other governmental entities (against whom the federal court may be foreclosed from ordering relief for reasons such as the Eleventh Amendment, which is discussed in Part VI).

Finally, a complicated provision — §1332(d)(4) — mandates a set of circumstances in which federal courts must decline jurisdiction. Section 1332(d)(4) states that federal courts may not take jurisdiction under §1332(d)(2) in cases where

1. Greater than two-thirds of the members of all proposed plaintiffs are citizens of the forum state;
2. At least one in-state defendant exists from whom members of the class seek significant relief and whose conduct forms a significant basis of the claims;

3. The principal injuries resulting from the alleged conduct (or related conduct) of each defendant were incurred in the state where the action was originally filed; and

4. No other class action asserting the same or similar factual allegations against any of the defendants on behalf of the same or other persons has been filed during the preceding three years.

The purpose of this section is to disqualify from federal court jurisdiction local controversies that "uniquely affect[] a particular locality to the exclusion of all others." Sen. Judiciary Report on Class Action Fairness Act of 2005, S. Rep. No. 109-14, at 39 (2005), as reprinted in 2005 U.S.C.C.A.N. 3, 38, available at 2005 WL 627977.

Example 3-9

A products liability class action was filed in Nebraska federal district court against an out-of-state refrigerator manufacturer and several in-state retailers. The plaintiffs invoked the district court's diversity jurisdiction over class actions pursuant to 28 U.S.C. §1332(d)(2). The complaint alleged that the glass shelving on a particular model of refrigerator was defectively manufactured, would readily shatter, and caused injury to consumers around the country. The plaintiffs brought the suit only on behalf of Nebraska residents, even though this particular refrigerator was marketed throughout the entire United States. The total amount in controversy exceeded $500,000, exclusive of interest and costs. This suit included 500 plaintiffs. No other suits were filed complaining about the glass shelves. The defendants moved to dismiss the suit, arguing that §1332(d)(4) requires the court to do so.[7]

Explanation

The class action in this example satisfies the citizenship requirements of §1332(d)(2) because minimal diversity exists: at least one plaintiff is from a different state from at least one defendant (the refrigerator manufacturer). The defendants nevertheless argue that this case falls into the mandatory exception to §1332(d)(2). Applying this exception, one observes that factors 1 and 4 are satisfied:

Factor 1: Greater than two-thirds of the members of all proposed plaintiffs are citizens of the forum state. This factor is satisfied because all of the plaintiffs are from the forum state, Nebraska.

Factor 4: No other class action asserting the same or similar factual allegations against any of the defendants on behalf of the same or other persons has been filed during the preceding three

---

7. The inspiration for this example can be found in the Senate Report explaining the CAFA. Sen. Judiciary Report on Class Action Fairness Act of 2005, S. Rep. No. 109-14, at 41 (2005), as reprinted in 2005 U.S.C.C.A.N. 3, 39, available at 2005 WL 627977.

years. This factor is satisfied because no other action concerning the defective shelves has ever been filed.

Together, factors 1 and 4 suggest that the case falls into the §1332(d)(4) exception. But Congress listed the factors in §1332(d)(4) using the conjunctive — the factors are tied together with an "and" rather than an "or." Thus, all four factors must be satisfied for the §1332(d)(4) exception to apply. This case does not satisfy the second and third factors.

Factor 2: At least one in-state defendant exists from whom members of the class seek significant relief and whose conduct forms a significant basis of the claims. This factor is not satisfied because the conduct of the in-state retailers does not form a significant basis of the claim. Rather, the claims focus on the negligent manufacture of the glass shelves, an activity attributable to the out-of-state manufacturer.

Factor 3: The principal injuries resulting from the alleged conduct (or related conduct) of each defendant were incurred in the state where the action was originally filed. This factor fails because consumers around the country have incurred injuries from the alleged defect. The complaint focuses on these national injuries. Although this particular suit focuses only on Nebraska plaintiffs, §1332(d)(4) is designed to eliminate suits from federal court jurisdiction where the principal injuries are local only, and in this case, the principal injuries were national. According to the language of the statute, one cannot say that the principal injuries resulting from the alleged conduct of each defendant were incurred in Nebraska. These injuries were incurred in many states. Thus, the district court should not grant the motion to dismiss pursuant to 28 U.S.C. §1332(d)(4).

Even though mandatory dismissal is not justified in Example 3-9, the defendants might attempt to argue that the district court should exercise its discretion to dismiss the action pursuant to §1332(d)(3). In this instance, however, the threshold requirement is unsatisfied: this is not a case where between one-third and two-thirds of plaintiffs as well as the primary defendants are from the same state where the action was originally filed. Greater than two-thirds of the plaintiffs are from the state where the action was originally filed (Nebraska), but the primary defendant (the refrigerator manufacturer) is from a different state.

C. CALCULATING AMOUNT IN CONTROVERSY

I. Timing and Standard for Calculation

Section 1332(a) precludes jurisdiction unless the parties' dispute concerns matters worth *over* $75,000. Congress has increased this "amount in controversy" requirement over the years in order to reduce the volume of diversity actions. The most recent amendment, from $50,000 to $75,000, came in 1996.

One calculates the $75,000 requirement as of the commencement of the action and without including interest and costs. If the relief sought is a non-monetary remedy — such as an injunction — courts need to evaluate whether the value of the remedy exceeds $75,000. Courts take different approaches to this valuation problem. Some identify the cost that the defendant would incur in complying with an order issuing the relief, while other courts value the injury that the defendant's illegality has inflicted or would inflict on the plaintiff. Whether the plaintiff alleges monetary or non-monetary relief, the defendant may challenge the plaintiff's alleged amount in controversy. Once the defendant raises this challenge, burden shifts to the plaintiff to defeat the defendant's suggestion that the plaintiff could not possibly recover the amount alleged. The plaintiff's burden, however, is not onerous: The plaintiff need only show that the defendant is not clearly correct. Specifically, the plaintiff must establish only that it is not "clear to a legal certainty" that the plaintiff could not recover this amount.[8] This proof requirement reflects the liberal approach of §1332(a), which requires only that the parties have a dispute over matters worth more than $75,000, not that the plaintiff actually must prove damages in excess of $75,000.

Example 3-10

Victoria Victim sued Alice Accidentprone for damages arising from an accident in which Victoria broke her arm. The accident occurred in 2007 in a state park in the state of X. Victoria and Alice are domiciled in different states, and Victoria filed the suit in federal district court, invoking the court's diversity of citizenship jurisdiction.

Victoria's complaint asserted that Alice was liable for medical bills totaling $20,000, pain and suffering, and punitive damages. The parties stipulated that the law governing their dispute was the law of the state of X. One month after the suit was filed, the legislature of state X passed a statute preventing any party from recovering pain and suffering damages as well as punitive damages in an action based on accidents occurring in state parks in X. The statute is retroactive to causes of action arising after December 31, 2006. Alice moved to dismiss the case, arguing that Victoria could not prove the "amount in controversy" requirement. Does Alice have a valid argument?

Explanation

Alice is wrong. The court should not dismiss the case. Because the newly enacted statute eliminating pain and suffering damages and punitive damages does apply to this suit, Alice may try to argue that Victoria can recover only the amount of her medical bills ($20,000), an amount far short of the jurisdictional amount. Nonetheless, the court should evaluate the

---

8. *Gibbs v. Buck*, 307 U.S. 66 (1939).

adequacy of the amount in controversy at the time Victoria filed the lawsuit. At that time, no bar to punitive pain and suffering damages existed. Such damages could have increased the total recovery above the $75,000 mark. Thus, *at the time suit was filed*, the parties had a dispute over matters potentially worth more than $75,000. The retroactivity of the damages statute is irrelevant to this analysis.

2. Aggregation Rules

a. Aggregation by One Plaintiff

A single plaintiff suing a single defendant for two or more claims may aggregate her claims to meet the $75,000 jurisdictional threshold. This is true even if the claims are completely unrelated and do not arise out of the same transaction or occurrence.

Example 3-11

As in Example 3-10, Victoria and Alice are from different states, and Victoria broke her arm in an accident caused by Alice. Assume that Victoria sued Alice in federal court to recover the $20,000 in doctor bills incurred in connection with the broken arm but did not assert any other damages arising from the accident. Victoria did, however, assert a $65,000 claim for breach of contract, arguing that Alice owed Victoria for editing work in a project unrelated to the accident. Victoria sought to invoke the court's diversity jurisdiction; may she do so?

Explanation

Yes. Victoria's case satisfies the jurisdictional requirements of §1332(a). She is diverse from the defendant, and her two claims against Alice total more than $75,000.

What is the rule when a single plaintiff sues more than one defendant? Can she add up her claims against all the defendants in order to satisfy the "amount in controversy" requirement? The answer is that it depends on the nature of the claims against the defendants. If they are joint claims — seeking recovery for the same loss — then the plaintiff can add the claims together. If they are separate claims regarding separate injuries, then the plaintiff cannot aggregate.

Example 3-12

Michelle files suit against Elizabeth and Olivia, alleging that they broke into her house and stole her pedigreed dog. She claims damages of $100,000. Does this allegation satisfy the "amount in controversy" requirement?

Explanation

Yes, the "amount in controversy" requirement is satisfied. Michelle's claim against Elizabeth and Olivia is a joint claim because she seeks recovery for one loss: the theft of her pedigreed dog. Accordingly, the court will evaluate the total value of the claim for the purpose of determining the jurisdictional amount. From this perspective, the joint claim is sufficient, since it exceeds $75,000.

b. Aggregation by Multiple Plaintiffs

The general rule that prevailed for many years required that when two or more named plaintiffs brought suit together against a single defendant under Federal Rule of Civil Procedure 20,[9] each plaintiff must individually satisfy the "amount in controversy" requirement of §1332(a). Only one exception to this general rule existed: plaintiffs could combine separate claims against a defendant to satisfy §1332(a)'s jurisdictional amount in the unusual circumstance where the plaintiffs sued under a "common undivided interest" and a "single title or right" — as in the case of jointly held property.[10] The Supreme Court radically changed this approach in *Exxon Mobil Corp. v. Allapattah Servs. Inc.*, 545 U.S. 546 (2005).

The *Exxon Mobil* Court found the basis for this change in the supplemental jurisdictional statute, 28 U.S.C. §1367, which Chapter 4 analyzes in detail. Specifically, the *Exxon Mobil* Court ruled that, where at least one diverse plaintiff in an action satisfies §1332(a)'s "amount in controversy" requirement, §1367 authorizes supplemental jurisdiction over claims of other plaintiffs in the same case, even if the dollar value of those claims is less than the jurisdictional amount. 545 U.S. at 559. The Supreme Court's holding did not purport to undermine the earlier recognized exception for plaintiffs who

---

9. Federal Rule of Civil Procedure 20 allows joinder of claims by multiple parties and is distinguishable from the class action rule, Federal Rule of Civil Procedure 23.
10. *See* CHARLES ALAN WRIGHT & MARY KAY KANE, LAW OF FEDERAL COURTS §36, 211-214 (6th ed. 2002).

combine separate claims to satisfy the jurisdictional amount in a suit under a theory of "common undivided interest" and a "single title or right."

The *Exxon Mobil* holding is conditioned on the requirement that the multiple plaintiffs in the action are properly joined as part of the same case or controversy under Article III. As explored more fully in Chapter 4, this "case or controversy" rule requires that the plaintiffs' claims "derive from a common nucleus of operative fact," which means that the claims must have a common factual foundation. To test whether this requirement is satisfied, one should evaluate whether the two claims have sufficient overlap that a litigant would be expected to try them together in one proceeding. One way of checking whether this rule is satisfied is to ask whether the plaintiffs are properly joined as parties under Federal Rule of Civil Procedure 20(a), which provides that "[a]ll persons may join in one action as plaintiffs if they assert any right to relief jointly, severally, or in the alternative in respect of or arising out of the same transaction, occurrence, or series of transactions or occurrences and if any question of law or fact common to all these persons will arise in the action." The "transaction or occurrence" standard of the Federal Rules of Civil Procedure is viewed as narrower than the Article III "case or controversy" standard.[11] Thus, a litigant who satisfies the joinder requirement of Federal Rule 20(a) will also satisfy the constitutional "case or controversy" requirement of the supplemental jurisdiction statute. (And if the litigant does not satisfy Rule 20 joinder requirements, the court can dismiss the action on that distinct ground).[12]

Example 3-13

As in Example 3-10, Victoria and Alice are from different states, and Victoria broke her arm in an accident caused by Alice. Vera, who is from the same state as Victoria, broke her leg in the same accident caused by Alice. Assume that Victoria sued Alice in federal court to recover the $20,000 in medical bills incurred in connection with the broken arm, but did not assert any other damages arising from the accident. Victoria asserted no other claim against Alice. Joining Victoria's complaint, Vera sued as a plaintiff and sought $80,000 in damages for medical bills and lost wages resulting from her absence from work while she recuperated from the accident. Is there jurisdiction over the *entire* suit under 28 U.S.C. §1332(a)?

---

11. See, e.g., *Sparrow v. Mazda Am. Credit*, 385 F. Supp. 2d 1063, 1067 (E.D. Cal. 2005); Michelle S. Simon, *Defining the Limits of Supplemental Jurisdiction Under 28 U.S.C. §1367: A Hearty Welcome to Permissive Counterclaims*, 9 Lewis & Clark L. Rev. 295, 297, 308 (2005).

12. *Exxon Mobil* did not authorize §1332 jurisdiction where a single plaintiff sues multiple defendants in a pure diversity case but lacks a joint or common claim against the defendants and has the required amount in controversy against only one or some of the defendants. As explained further in Chapter 4, *Exxon Mobil* did not eliminate this "amount in controversy" deficiency even where the plaintiff's claims against the multiple defendants are related closely enough to fall within the same constitutional case for the purposes of §1367(a).

Explanation

Another trick question! No, jurisdiction does not exist over the *entire* suit under §1332(a). The case *does* satisfy the complete diversity rule, since all the plaintiffs are from a different state than the defendant. But the jurisdictional amount is not satisfied for both plaintiffs. The court would need to look to the supplemental jurisdiction statute to justify jurisdiction over Victoria's claim for $20,000. As it turns out, the supplemental jurisdiction statute would support jurisdiction over that claim. The court would have subject matter jurisdiction over the entire case, but the authority derives from the operation of *both* 28 U.S.C. §1332(a) and 28 U.S.C. §1367.

The court may exercise supplemental jurisdiction over Victoria's claim because it has a common factual basis with Vera's claim. The claims arise from the same car accident and the plaintiffs would use the same facts to establish the foundation of Alice's liability. Even though Vera's claim may include more elaborate factual presentations necessary to establish lost wages, those additional facts do not detract from the status of the two claims as being part of the same Article III case or controversy. As further support for this conclusion, one could point out that Vera and Victoria are properly joined as parties under Federal Rule of Civil Procedure 20 because their claims derive from the same occurrence. Since the Rule 20 test is more difficult to satisfy than the "same case or controversy" requirement of the supplemental jurisdiction statute, one can easily conclude that the court has supplemental jurisdiction over Victoria's claim.

Example 3-14

Carol and Cassidy both slipped on grease on the floor of a restaurant owned by Dana. Carol and Cassidy are from the same state, and Dana is from a different state. Carol asserts that she incurred $50,000 damages as a result of the fall and Cassidy asserts that she incurred $26,000 as a result of the fall. They have joined in an action against Dana in federal district court. Can the federal district court exercise subject matter jurisdiction over their suit?

Explanation

No, the federal district court does not have subject matter jurisdiction. Under *Exxon Mobil Corp. v. Allapattah Servs. Inc.*, 545 U.S. 546 (2005), the plaintiffs can aggregate their claims to meet the $75,000 requirement only if one of the plaintiffs' claims exceeds that amount. Neither plaintiff has a claim that meets this jurisdictional amount; thus, the court does not have power to hear the case under either the diversity statute, 28 U.S.C. §1332(a), or the supplemental jurisdiction statute, 28 U.S.C. §1367.

c. Aggregation in Class Actions

The Class Action Fairness Act of 2005 (CAFA) provides unique aggregation rules for class actions that fall within its scope. In particular, the statute provides that the amount in controversy in a CAFA class action must exceed "the sum or value of $5,000,000, exclusive of interest and costs." 28 U.S.C. §1332(d)(2). Section 1332(d)(6) explains that this figure is determined by aggregating the claims of all "individual class members." Thus, CAFA provides a new method of determining the amount in controversy different from the method outlined in *Exxon Mobil Corp. v. Allapattah Servs. Inc.* and prior cases. As the Supreme Court recognized in *Exxon Mobil*, however, CAFA does not provide the exclusive method of getting a class action into federal court, under diversity or supplemental jurisdiction.[13] *Exxon Mobil* and CAFA thus create two independent "sets of rules on diversity class actions."[14] For the CAFA aggregation rules to apply, however, the class action must satisfy the basic threshold requirements for a CAFA class action (discussed in section B.4.a of this chapter) and must avoid the sweep of the discretionary and mandatory exceptions to CAFA (discussed in sections B.4.b and B.4.c of this chapter).

Example 3-15

The facts are identical to those in Example 3-9 (class action filed concerning a product's liability in Nebraska district court).

As stated in Example 3-9, the total amount of controversy for this class action exceeded $5,000,000, exclusive of interest and costs. As it turns out, however, none of the individual class members had an amount in controversy over $30,000. Defendants therefore argued that the federal court lacks subject matter jurisdiction. Should the federal court dismiss for lack of subject matter jurisdiction based on the aggregation rules?

Explanation

The first step in analyzing class action cases is to determine whether the class action is a CAFA action. Example 3-15 appears to be a CAFA class action because it includes more than 100 class members and, as outlined in the explanation for Example 3-9, neither the mandatory nor discretionary exception applies. Accordingly, the CAFA aggregation rule applies. This rule is

---

13. *Exxon Mobil v. Allapattah Servs. Inc.*, 545 U.S. 546, 572 (2005)("[t]he CAFA . . . does not moot the significance of our interpretation of §1367, as many proposed exercises of supplemental jurisdiction, even in the class-action context, might not fall within the CAFA's ambit.")
14. Alan B. Morrison, *Straightening Out the Supplemental Jurisdiction Mess: Short and Long Term Fixes*, 74 U.S.L.W. 2179, 2181(Oct. 4, 2005).

satisfied here, since the amount in controversy exceeds $5,000,000, exclusive of interest and costs, after aggregating the claims of class members.

If, however, the class action did not fall within the ambit of CAFA, the result would be different. As a non-CAFA class action, the jurisdictional amount in the case would be governed by §1332(a) and §1367, as interpreted in *Exxon Mobil*. *Exxon Mobil* requires that at least one diverse plaintiff must satisfy §1332(a)'s requirement that the amount in controversy exceed $75,000. Yet in Example 3-15, no plaintiff has an amount in controversy in excess of $30,000. Moreover, each plaintiff appears to assert a claim for an independent injury to individually owned refrigerators. They cannot, therefore, avail themselves of pre–*Exxon Mobil* case law allowing plaintiffs to combine separate claims to satisfy the jurisdictional amount under a theory of "common undivided interest" and a "single title or right."

D. IDENTIFYING FORBIDDEN SUBJECT AREAS

The diversity of citizenship jurisdiction of federal district courts has two exceptions not explicitly described in the statutory language: domestic relations and probate matters. Even though a case may satisfy all of the statutory requirements of 28 U.S.C. §1332, the district court may lack power to adjudicate the controversy if it characterizes the case as falling within one of these two categories.

1. Domestic Relations

The Supreme Court has long held that "[t]he whole subject of the domestic relations of husband and wife, parent and child, belongs to the laws of the States and not to the laws of the United States." *In re Burrus*, 136 U.S. 586, 593-594 (1890). The Court thus recognizes a domestic relations exception to diversity of citizenship jurisdiction, which it rationalizes by pointing to state court expertise in these matters. Moreover, unlike federal courts, state systems often possess monitoring institutions in which social workers and other state court agents ensure compliance with state custody and support decrees. The existence of these ancillary institutions ensures the efficacy of state court judgments in the domestic relations arena.

The domestic relations exception to diversity jurisdiction does not apply, however, simply because members of the same family are involved in the case or controversy before the court. The Supreme Court recently clarified that the exception applies only in "cases involving the issuance of a divorce, alimony, or child custody decree." *Ankenbrandt v. Richards*, 504 U.S. 689, 704 (1992).

Example 3-16

Sally and Sam were divorced in North Carolina. The state court that issued the divorce judgment also issued a judgment of shared custody in 2005. Immediately thereafter, Sally became a citizen of South Carolina, while Sam continued to be a North Carolina citizen. One day in 2007, Sam pulled into Sally's driveway to drop off the kids, swerved to avoid hitting Sally's dog, and accidently hit Sally's house. The accident caused major structural damage to the house, which cost $80,000. Sam refused to pay anything to Sally on the ground that Sally was negligent in letting the dog out of the house. Sally filed suit in federal district court, invoking the court's diversity-of-citizenship jurisdiction. Sam moved to dismiss on the basis of the domestic relations exception to diversity-of-citizenship jurisdiction. Should the court dismiss the case?

Explanation

The district court should deny Sam's motion. Sam might argue that the accident occurred as he was in the process of fulfilling his obligations under the custody agreement. This peripheral relationship with a domestic relations matter, however, is insufficient to trigger the exception. The parties' dispute does not involve a court's decision to issue the custody decree. The dispute does not involve enforcement of the decree. The parties are simply two individuals with a tort dispute who happen to have at one time been married. The case thus falls squarely into the district court's jurisdiction under §1332(a).

Example 3-17

Plaintiff and defendant obtained a separation agreement and later divorced. The divorce court incorporated this agreement into the divorce decree. Plaintiff brought a contract suit in federal district court, alleging that her husband breached the separation agreement. The contract that she sued on is a separation agreement, which a state court incorporated into a final divorce decree. Under the separation agreement, plaintiff's former husband agreed to put their home on the real estate market. Plaintiff alleged that her former husband failed to put the home on the market in accordance with the terms of the contract, and, for that reason, the home had not sold. The contract states that its terms shall be governed by the law of the Commonwealth of Pennsylvania. Plaintiff argued that the suit would turn on whether defendant had substantially complied with the terms of the contract, which was a question to be answered by reference to the substantive contract law of Pennsylvania.

Plaintiff is from New York, and defendant is from Pennsylvania. The home is worth approximately $800,000. Plaintiff alleged jurisdiction on the basis of §1332(a), and defendant has moved to dismiss for lack of subject matter jurisdiction. Should the court dismiss the case?

Explanation

Since the suit appears to fall squarely within the diversity-of-citizenship jurisdiction of the district court, the district court should dismiss the case only if the suit falls within the domestic relations exception. Plaintiff may seek to avoid the exception by framing the suit as a contract suit. The dispute, however, arises directly out of a divorce decree, which incorporated the separation agreement. Thus, the divorce decree itself — not simply the law of contracts — imposes the obligations of the separation agreement. Accordingly, plaintiff is seeking a declaration of rights and obligations arising from formal marital status. To adjudicate the parties' rights and obligations, the court will need to interpret and apply the divorce decree. For this reason, the suit falls within the domestic relations exception. After all, the final division of the couple's marital assets will depend on resolution of this dispute.

2. Probate Matters

Probate is the process of finalizing the affairs of a deceased person, paying her debts (including taxes) and distributing her assets according to either her will or intestacy laws. Federal courts decline to probate wills and administer the estate of a deceased person. Two reasons explain why federal courts are exempt from these two functions. First, like domestic relations, probate matters have historically fallen within state courts' expertise. Second, exempting these matters from federal court adjudication ensures uniformity and finality: we can be assured that only state courts will involve themselves in probate disputes.

The question arises, however, how close a dispute must be to a probate matter to disqualify the federal court from hearing the case. As it has for domestic relations, the Supreme Court has drawn the probate exception narrowly, stating that the exception exempts federal courts only from two types of matters: "the probate or annulment of a will and the administration of a decedent's estate."[15] In connection with this general statement, the Court clarified that the exception "precludes federal courts from endeavoring to dispose of property that is in the custody of a state

---

15. *Marshall v. Marshall*, 126 S. Ct. 1735 (2006), concerned the possibility of a probate exception to federal bankruptcy jurisdiction. In the course of discussing the scope of such an exception, however, the Court affirmed earlier case law identifying the existence of a probate exception to diversity jurisdiction. *See id.* (discussing *Markham v. Allen*, 326 U.S. 326 U.S. 490 (1946)).

probate court." *Id.* Other matters that may relate to the probate, however, are within the federal court's jurisdiction. Thus, the *Marshall* Court refused to apply the probate exception in that case, where the federal suit asserted libel and tortious interference with a gift. In rejecting the probate exception's application to the suit, the Court emphasized that the suit raised a tort claim, requesting an in personam judgment. These matters, the Court explained, do not fall within any special expertise of the state probate court. Moreover, the Court observed that the case did not involve the probate or annulment of a will, and the parties did not seek to have the federal court attempt to reach a res in the custody of the state court.

Example 3-18

Daniel Decedent died in an accident. Following his death, a trust — the Daniel Decedent Revocable Trust — was established as part of the administration of his estate. The trust owns real property, in which the Invasive Mining Company owns mineral rights. The trust believes that the Invasive Mining Company exceeded the reasonable use of the real property and is guilty of trespass. Thus, the trust brought suit in federal district court, invoking the court's diversity jurisdiction. Although acknowledging that the parties are diverse and the "amount in controversy" requirement is satisfied, the Invasive Mining Company argued that the district court should dismiss the case under the probate exception to diversity-of-citizenship jurisdiction. Should the district court accept this argument?

Explanation

No, the district court should not dismiss the case under the probate exception. Like the lawsuit at issue in *Marshall*, the suit here is a tort action for personal liability of a defendant. For the exception to apply, this lawsuit would have to administer Daniel Decedent's estate, dispose of his property, or seek control over some res in the control of a probate court. This action is far outside the confines of those matters.

CHAPTER 4

Supplemental Jurisdiction in Lower Federal Courts

Imagine that you have been invited to a party. Even though the invitation's envelope bears your name only, you have a relative visiting whom you'd like to bring along. You phone the host and ask, "Can my relative come too?" Your relative is welcomed at the party, but only because you received a formal invitation. So it goes with supplemental jurisdiction,[1] which you might think of as "can my relative come too?" jurisdiction.

For a lawsuit to be welcomed in federal district court, at least one claim must fall within the court's original jurisdiction. In this context, "original jurisdiction" refers to diversity, federal question, or some other standard jurisdictional basis provided by statute.[2] An original jurisdiction claim has a "formal invitation" into federal court. A litigant may assert an additional claim lacking this formal invitation, but only if the claim is sufficiently related to the original jurisdiction claim. The jurisdictional theory behind the additional, tag-along claim is *supplemental jurisdiction*. The claim comes into federal court because of its relationship to the original jurisdiction claim, which is referred to in this chapter as a *foundation claim*, an *anchor claim*, or an *invited claim*.

---

1. "Supplemental jurisdiction" is a modern term that embraces the earlier concepts of pendent jurisdiction and ancillary jurisdiction.
2. Sometimes "original jurisdiction" is used in contrast with "appellate jurisdiction." That is not the meaning intended in the supplemental jurisdiction context. Here, "original" denotes standard jurisdictional power named in Article III and a jurisdictional statute.

A. SUPPLEMENTAL JURISDICTION IS USED ONLY WHEN NECESSARY

A litigant relies on supplemental jurisdiction only if absolutely necessary. If a claim falls within the district court's original jurisdiction, that original jurisdiction provides the court's power. If the claim also satisfies the requirements of supplemental jurisdiction, one may be tempted to argue that supplemental jurisdiction provides the court's power over the claim. But supplemental jurisdiction is limited, as its name suggests: it is only a supplement to be used when no other jurisdictional theory applies.

Example 4-1

Pauline was fired from her job as a result of employment discrimination. Federal and state employment discrimination statutes have identical requirements. Pauline sued her employer, Pam, in federal court, asserting two claims. One claim averred that Pam violated federal law; the other asserted that the same conduct violated state law. Pam and Pauline are citizens of Illinois. Pauline asserted damages of $100,000 for each claim. Under what theories would the district court have jurisdiction over both claims?

Explanation

Pauline's federal claim falls within the original jurisdiction of the district court, since it arises under federal law for the purposes of 28 U.S.C. §1331. This is not true for the state claim. Diversity of citizenship is also not a factor. No independent basis for jurisdiction over the state claim presents itself. Thus, one should analyze whether supplemental jurisdiction justifies the district court hearing the state claim together with the federal claim. Since the two claims arise from the same facts and present nearly identical legal theories, the state claim easily satisfies the requirements of supplemental jurisdiction, explained in more detail next.

Example 4-2

Now assume the same facts as Example 4-1, except that Pauline and Pam are citizens of different states: Pauline is from Illinois and Pam is from Wisconsin. Under what theories would the district court have jurisdiction over both claims?

Explanation

In this example, Pauline and Pam have diverse citizenship and the $100,000 claim for damages satisfies the "amount in controversy" requirement. The court thus has diversity of citizenship jurisdiction over the state law claim. One should therefore not rely on supplemental jurisdiction to justify the court's power over this claim.

B. CONSTITUTIONAL UNDERPINNINGS OF SUPPLEMENTAL JURISDICTION

How is it that a nonfederal claim between nondiverse parties can get into federal court? After all, federal court jurisdiction applies only if the jurisdictional category is included in Article III's grant of power to the federal court. Article III says nothing about adjudicating nonfederal claims between nondiverse parties. The answer comes from the language of Article III, which grants federal courts power over "cases" or "controversies." The Constitution conceives of a federal court's workload in terms of entire cases, not individual claims. Once a claim that lies within a federal court's original jurisdiction has given the federal court subject matter jurisdiction, the court takes power over the whole case.

The problem arises in determining whether two claims fall within the same "case" or "controversy" as the Constitution uses those terms. The Supreme Court provided a test for this problem in *United Mine Workers v. Gibbs*, 383 U.S. 715 (1966). *Gibbs* stated that two claims belong to the same constitutional case or controversy if they "derive from a common nucleus of operative fact." 383 U.S. at 725. Translating this test into practical terms, the Court explained that two claims compose the same constitutional case or controversy if a litigant "would ordinarily . . . [expect] . . . to try . . . [the claims] in one judicial proceeding." *Id.* In applying this test, one looks for overlapping evidence that could be used to prove the common factual foundation for the two claims.

As explained in Chapter 3, one way of testing whether the *Gibbs* rule is satisfied is to ask whether the two claims are part of the same "transaction or occurrence, or series of transactions or occurrences." These terms are used in the Federal Rules of Civil Procedure in reference to joinder of parties and claims. The "transaction or occurrence" standard of the Federal Rules of Civil Procedure is viewed as narrower than the Article III "case or controversy" standard.[3] Thus, a litigant who satisfies the joinder requirements of the Federal Rules will also satisfy the constitutional "case or controversy" requirement of the supplemental jurisdiction statute.

After explaining its "common nucleus of operative fact" rule, the *Gibbs* Court added a series of discretionary factors that influence the ultimate decision of whether a federal court actually exercises supplemental jurisdiction. The question of whether the two claims derive from a common nucleus of operative fact goes to whether the district court has *power* to hear the case. The discretionary factors bear on whether prudence counsels the district court to exercise that power — specifically, whether "judicial economy, convenience, and fairness to the litigants" favor exercising power over the entire case. 383 U.S. at 726. Thus, the *Gibbs* Court explained that a district court may decline to exercise its power over a supplemental claim if, for example, the claim within the district court's original jurisdiction (the "invited" claim) is dismissed early in the litigation, if state law issues dominate the litigation, or if trying the invited claim and the supplemental claim together would confuse the jury.

Example 4-3

Angela was poisoned while using weed killer on her garden. After missing several weeks of work and incurring substantial doctors' bills, Angela recovered. Amy's business manufactured and sold the weed killer. Amy and Angela are from the same state. Angela brought a suit against Amy in federal district court raising three claims. Claim 1 asserted that Amy's weed killer had too high a concentration of poison and therefore violated federal law regulating the toxic content. Claim 2 asserted that Amy's weed killer was toxic and unsafe for human use, and therefore violated state law negligence principles. Finally, claim 3 asserted that on the day Angela purchased the weed killer from Amy, Amy's business had left many obstacles in the parking lot, and as a result Angela incurred substantial damage to her car. State law negligence provides the legal theory behind this claim.

After discovery, this case was set for trial. On the day that the parties were to start picking a jury, Amy made a motion to dismiss the two state law claims for lack of subject matter jurisdiction. Should the court grant the motion?

---

3. *See, e.g., Sparrow v. Mazda Am. Credit*, 385 F. Supp. 2d 1063, 1067 (E.D. Cal. 2005); Michelle S. Simon, *Defining the Limits of Supplemental Jurisdiction Under 28 U.S.C. §1367*, 9 Lewis & Clark L. Rev. 295, 297, 308 (2005).

Explanation

The district court *may* grant the motion as to claim 2 and *must* grant the motion as to claim 3. First, claim 3 flunks the "common nucleus of operative fact" test. The foundation claim in this action — claim 1, regarding violations of federal law regulating poison concentration — will focus on such matters as the percentage of poison in the product, Angela's physical vulnerability to the product's toxins, the amount of the product that Angela used, and the circumstances under which she used it. These facts do not overlap with those needed to establish claim 3, which will turn on evidence related to the parking lot's configuration, the obstacles present, and Angela's driving. Thus, under *Gibbs*, the district court would actually lack power over claim 3 and would act illegitimately in continuing to adjudicate the claim (see Figure 4-1).

The story is different for claim 2, which overlaps significantly with claim 1. To establish claim 2, the trial would adjudicate whether the amount of toxin in the product violated Amy's duty to use reasonable care in producing a product for human use. In litigating the claim, the parties would use the same evidence about the weed killer, Angela's vulnerabilities, and Angela's use of the product introduced for claim 1. Thus, the district court would probably conclude that it has power over claim 2: claims 1 and 2 derive from a common set of facts.

Under the rubric of *Gibbs*, the district court need not exercise this power over claim 2. The district court may decide, for example, that differences between the state and federal law standards governing toxins are too subtle for the jury to distinguish. On the other hand, the district court may note that substantial federal judicial resources — as well as litigant resources — have already been expended in the case. For that reason, concerns of efficiency and fairness favor exercising power, even if the jury might encounter confusion.

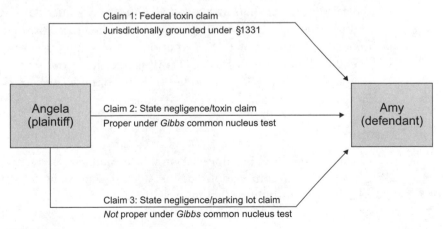

Figure 4-1.

C. THE SUPPLEMENTAL JURISDICTION STATUTE

Part II of this book opens with the statement "For a lower federal court to possess subject matter jurisdiction, the court needs both the United States Constitution and a United States statute to authorize that power." This need for statutory authorization is important for those with a federalist orientation who wish to constrain federal court power and who take solace in the framers' original decision to give Congress the judgment of how much (if any) lower federal court power to allow. These concerns render controversial the Court's decision in *United Mine Workers v. Gibbs*, 383 U.S. 715 (1966). After all, under the premise of interpreting the meaning of the constitutional language "case or controversy," the *Gibbs* Court enabled federal courts to exercise power over a range of claims that Congress had not included in its jurisdictional statutes.

But Congress eventually filled the gap with the supplemental jurisdiction statute, 28 U.S.C. §1367. The statute has three main sections: §1367(a) contains a general grant of supplemental jurisdiction, §1367(b) eliminates some of this supplemental jurisdiction for diversity actions, and §1367(c) lists discretionary factors guiding a district court that is trying to decide whether to exercise the power granted in §1367(a).

1. Section 1367(a): Congress Giveth

a. Codifying *Gibbs*

Section 1367(a) grants jurisdiction in broad terms, stating that "in any civil action of which the district courts have original jurisdiction, the district courts shall have supplemental jurisdiction over all other claims that are so related to claims in the action within such original jurisdiction that they form part of the same case or controversy under Article III of the United States Constitution." The section's reference to a "case or controversy under . . . the United States Constitution" is unambiguous: Congress meant to codify the approach of *United Mine Workers v. Gibbs*. Courts and commentators agree that §1367(a) embodies *Gibbs*'s "common nucleus of operative fact" test.

Example 4-4

Consider the facts of Example 4-1, in which Pauline asserts state and federal employment discrimination claims against Pam. Should Pauline use §1367(a) to justify jurisdiction over this suit?

Explanation

Yes, Pauline needs to invoke §1367(a) for her state law claim. Her federal law claim provides the anchor for original jurisdiction because the claim arises under federal law for §1331 purposes. Since neither "arising under" jurisdiction, diversity of citizenship jurisdiction, nor any other, independent basis for jurisdiction is available for the state law claim, the federal court can exercise power over the claim only under §1367(a). The state law claim easily satisfies the *Gibbs* test because the parties dispute the same conduct using the state law claim as they dispute using the anchor or "invited" claim.

As was true before Congress enacted §1367, one looks to supplemental jurisdiction only if no other jurisdictional theory will support federal court power. Thus, if Pauline and Pam were from different states, §1367(a) would not enter the jurisdictional analysis of this case. Diversity of citizenship jurisdiction would support the district court's power over the state law claim.

b. Joining Additional Parties

Beyond codifying *Gibbs*, §1367(a) establishes that supplemental jurisdiction extends to "claims that involve the joinder or intervention of additional parties." This provision, designed to overrule the result in an earlier Supreme Court case, authorizes supplemental jurisdiction even for claims that are asserted by or against parties not litigating the foundation or "invited" claim within the court's original jurisdiction.

Example 4-5

Pauline was fired from her job as a result of employment discrimination. She filed a federal court complaint against the owner of the company, Pam, and Pauline's immediate supervisor, Juan. Pauline, Pam, and Juan are all from the same state. Pauline's complaint had two claims. Claim 1 was based on federal law and named Pam, the company's owner, as the defendant. Federal law does not, however, authorize liability against Pauline's immediate supervisor, Juan. Thus, in claim 2, Pauline asserted that Juan was liable under state law for the employment discrimination. The same acts of discrimination support both claim 1 and claim 2. Does the district court have power over both claims?

Explanation

The district court has subject matter jurisdiction over both claims. The foundation claim is claim 1 because it arises under federal law. Claim 2

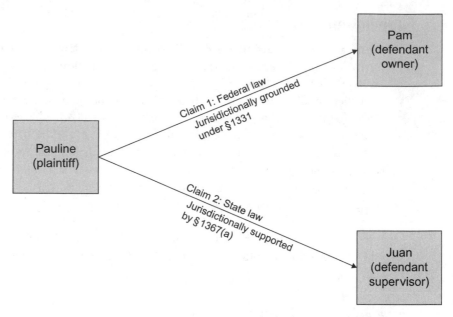

Figure 4-2.

has a common factual foundation with claim 1 and therefore is part of the same constitutional case or controversy for the purposes of §1367(a) (see Figure 4-2). Section 1367(a)'s last sentence makes clear that the difference in the defendant's identity between claims 1 and 2 does not diminish the court's power.

2. Section 1367(b): Congress Taketh Away

The jurisdictional power granted in §1367(a) is not absolute. Section 1367(b) takes away some of the power Congress grants in §1367(a) — but only where the anchor claim is based on diversity of citizenship. To understand Congress's motivation behind §1367(b), one finds guidance in earlier case law.

a. Integrating Supplemental Jurisdiction with the Complete Diversity Requirement

Thus far, the examples in this chapter have illustrated supplemental jurisdiction only where the foundational claim is "invited" into federal court under federal question jurisdiction. Diversity jurisdiction can also anchor a case that has a supplemental claim. Alas, in these cases, however, the law is more complicated than for cases with the federal question anchor. Most of the complications come from complete diversity requirement of *Strawbridge v. Curtiss*, 7 U.S. (3 Cranch) 267 (1806).

Example 4-6

Beth, a citizen of Alabama, sued Bonita, a citizen of Mississippi, for damages that Beth incurred during a car accident involving Bonita and another woman, Bernadette. Beth's claim is based on state law negligence. Bernadette is a citizen of Alabama. Beth also wants to bring a state law negligence claim against Bernadette for damages incurred in the car accident. Can she do so in federal court?

Explanation

No, Beth cannot bring the claim against Bernadette in federal court. Beth's claim against Bonita is founded on diversity of citizenship (see Figure 4-3). Beth's claim against Bernadette is based on the same occurrence as her claim against Bonita, and therefore shares a common nucleus of operative fact. To allow the claim against Bernadette to come into federal court under supplemental jurisdiction, however, would undermine the complete diversity requirement. A plaintiff may not use one claim against a diverse defendant as the foundation claim for another claim against a nondiverse defendant. As made clear in Supreme Court opinions and the relevant jurisdictional statutes, the complete diversity requirement limits the scope of supplemental jurisdiction.

The Supreme Court explored how the complete diversity requirement limits the scope of supplemental jurisdiction in *Owen Equip. & Erection Co. v. Kroger*, 437 U.S. 365 (1978). *Kroger* held that a plaintiff relying solely on

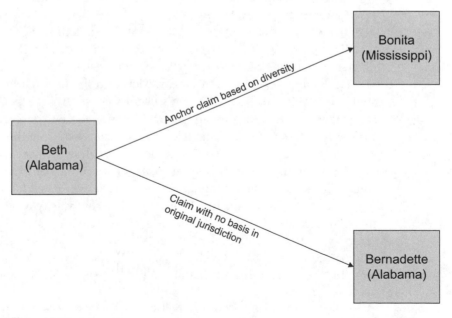

Figure 4-3.

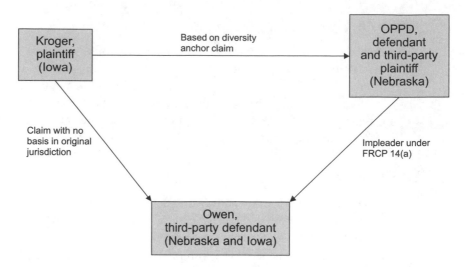

Figure 4-4.

the federal court's diversity jurisdiction may not assert a claim against a nondiverse third-party defendant. The plaintiff, Kroger, was an Iowa resident who sued a power company (OPPD), a Nebraska citizen, for the death of her husband under state law. OPPD impleaded a corporation, Owen, under Federal Rule of Civil Procedure 14(a), which allows impleader only on the theory that Owen was liable for all or part of Kroger's claim against OPPD. (When OPPD did this, it became a third-party plaintiff as well as a defendant.)

Kroger responded to this impleader by amending her complaint to assert a direct claim against Owen for liability arising out of the same accident that was the subject of her claim against Owen. It turned out, however, that Kroger was a citizen of both Nebraska and Iowa and therefore was diverse to neither OPPD nor Owen (see Figure 4-4).

The Supreme Court held that the district court should not have extended supplemental jurisdiction to Kroger's claim against Owen. The Court reasoned that the complete diversity requirement would have prevented Kroger from originally suing Owen, but that Kroger circumvented this limitation by amending her complaint. The Court declined to allow Kroger to do so.

The result in *Kroger* is the logical consequence of the complete diversity rule. What is most interesting about the case, however, is that the Court endorsed OPPD's claim against Owen, even though diversity was lacking for that claim as well.[4] Why was this allowed? In the Court's view, Kroger's claim against Owen was not as closely yoked to the anchor claim in the original complaint as was OPPD's claim against Owen. Kroger asserted two independent bases of liability in suing both OPPD and Owen.

---

4. The Court endorsed supplemental jurisdiction in the diversity context for situations involving cross-claims and counterclaims as well as impleaders. 437 U.S. at 375.

OPPD's third-party claim against Owen, on the other hand, was "logical[ly] dependen[t]" on Kroger's claim against OPPD.[5] Adding to this explanation, the Court observed that Kroger voluntarily chose to bring her state law claim in federal court. By contrast, OPPD was haled into court against its will. If Kroger was unhappy about not being able to consolidate her claims into one federal court action, she was free to do so in state courts.

b. Limiting Supplemental Jurisdiction with §1367(b)

The language of §1367(b) is complicated.[6] Congress imported the spirit of *Owen Equip. & Erection Co. v. Kroger* into §1367. Specifically, Congress provided that where diversity claims establish the foundation for federal jurisdiction, §1367(b) limits the reach of §1367(a)'s grant of supplemental jurisdiction. For §1367(b)'s limitation on supplemental jurisdiction to apply to a claim, all of the following four conditions must be present:

1. The foundation claim in the action must rest solely on 28 U.S.C. §1332 (diversity jurisdiction).
2. The claim must be asserted by a plaintiff, a person proposed to be joined as a plaintiff under Federal Rule of Civil Procedure 19, or a person to intervene as a plaintiff under Rule 24.
3. If the claim is asserted by a plaintiff, it must be against a person made a party under Federal Rule of Civil Procedure 14, 19, 20, or 24.
4. The exercise of supplemental jurisdiction must be "inconsistent with the jurisdictional requirements of section 1332."

28 U.S.C. §1367(b) (2000).

Even without reviewing the joinder requirements of the Federal Rules of Civil Procedure, one can appreciate this section's limited scope. First, the section applies only where the foundation claim is a diversity claim. Second, it applies to claims by plaintiffs (or potential plaintiffs). Third, Congress intended the section to preserve the interpretation of the diversity statute in *Owen Equipment & Erection Co. v. Kroger*.

---

5. Although the Court did not say so, this distinction apparently supported the conclusion that OPPD's claim was more closely tied to the foundation claim and therefore more intimately connected with the same constitutional "case or controversy" than Kroger's claim against Owen.

6. Section 1367(b) provides in full:

> In any civil action of which the district courts have original jurisdiction founded solely on section 1332 of this title, the district courts shall not have supplemental jurisdiction under subsection (a) over claims by plaintiffs against persons made parties under Rule 14, 19, 20, or 24 of the Federal Rules of Civil Procedure, or over claims by persons proposed to be joined as plaintiffs under Rule 19 of such rules, or seeking to intervene as plaintiffs under Rule 24 of such rules, when exercising supplemental jurisdiction over such claims would be inconsistent with the jurisdictional requirements of section 1332.

Example 4-7

Assume that a federal statute governs certain matters dealing with loans between banks and low-income customers. Shark Company lent Linda money to pay medical bills. Linda filled out an application form, and on the basis of the information stated therein, the bank lent her $80,000. Both Linda and Shark Company are from New Mexico. Linda failed to pay on her loan as it came due, and Shark discovered that Linda had lied about her income on the application. Shark filed suit against Linda, raising two claims. Claim 1 stated a state law breach of contract action, asserting that Linda breached her loan agreement with Shark by failing to pay the amount due on the loan and failing to comply with the contract term requiring her to complete the application honestly. Claim 2 asserts a federal law claim that Linda violated a federal statute requiring borrowers on loans such as this to make honest representations on the loan application. Since claim 1 is a state law claim, does the district court need §1367 for jurisdiction? If so, does §1367(b) create a problem?

Explanation

The district court does indeed need §1367 for jurisdiction over claim 1. Nonetheless, given that claim 1 exhibits considerable factual overlap with claim 2, one may conclude that the claims are part of the same constitutional case or controversy. Moreover, §1367(b) does not create any problems because the anchor claim here is a federal question claim, not a diversity claim. One of the conditions for §1367(b) to apply is thus lacking here. Section 1367 therefore authorizes the needed jurisdiction.

Example 4-8

Shark Company lent Linda money. Linda completed an application form, and on the basis of the information stated therein, the bank lent Linda $80,000. For this example, assume that no federal law governs this transaction. Linda is from Arizona and Shark Company is from New Mexico. Linda failed to pay on her loan when it came due, and Shark discovered that Linda had lied about her income on the application. Shark filed suit against Linda, asserting a state law breach of contract claim that Linda breached her loan agreement with Shark by, first, failing to pay the amount on the loan and, second, failing to comply with one of the contract's terms requiring that she complete the application honestly. Linda responded to this complaint by impleading her former husband — Lawrence — under Federal Rule of Civil Procedure 14. Linda claimed that Lawrence defrauded her into entering into the loan contract and is therefore liable for any judgment entered against her. Lawrence is a resident of Arizona. Is there jurisdiction over Linda's claim against Lawrence?

Explanation

No diversity exists between Lawrence and Linda. Thus, if jurisdiction is present, §1367(a) must provide the source. Linda's claim against her former husband concerns the circumstances under which she entered into the contract. The facts of this claim overlap substantially with the facts of the original complaint. The two claims are therefore part of the same constitutional case or controversy and satisfy §1367(a)'s requirements. Nevertheless, because the foundation claim is a diversity claim, §1367(b) might limit jurisdiction. But §1367(b) limits only claims by a plaintiff, a person proposed to be joined as a plaintiff under Federal Rule of Civil Procedure 19, or a person intervening as a plaintiff under Rule 24. Here the claim is pressed by a defendant who became a third-party plaintiff when she filed her claim under Federal Rule of Civil Procedure 14(a). Thus, Linda's third-party claim is outside §1367(b)'s limits.

Example 4-9

Priscilla is a citizen of Montana. She sued Doretta, a citizen of Wyoming, claiming that Doretta breached a contract she had with Priscilla. Priscilla claimed damages, including consequential damages, totaling $100,000. Doretta counterclaimed against Priscilla, asserting that Priscilla breached the contract and is liable to Doretta for $20,000. Is there jurisdiction over both Priscilla's claim and Doretta's counterclaim?

Explanation

28 U.S.C. §1332(a) provides subject matter jurisdiction for Priscilla's claim against Doretta because they have diverse citizenship and the claim exceeds $75,000. Doretta needs §1367(a) for subject matter jurisdiction because the amount of the counterclaim is only $20,000. Doretta's counterclaim satisfies §1367(a) because it arises out of the same contract as Priscilla's claim against Doretta. Because the foundation for jurisdiction in the suit is §1332(a), however, Doretta must consider the limitation of §1367(b). As in the previous example, §1367(b) does not pose an obstacle since the counterclaim is not asserted by a plaintiff, a person proposed to be joined as a plaintiff under Federal Rule of Civil Procedure 19, or a person intervening as a plaintiff under Rule 24.

c. Using §1367(a) to Meet the "Amount in Controversy" Requirement in Diversity Cases

As interpreted by the United States Supreme Court, the diversity jurisdiction statute, 28 U.S.C. §1332(a), is satisfied if the total of a single plaintiff's claims against a single defendant exceeds the $75,000 jurisdictional threshold, even if each of the plaintiff's individual claims falls short of this amount. To meet the jurisdictional requirement of §1332(a), the plaintiff can aggregate two or more claims against a single defendant whether or not the two claims are related, share a common nucleus of fact, or arise out of the same transaction or occurrence. This plaintiff does not need the supplemental jurisdiction statute — §1367(a) — to get into federal court; she has an official invitation from §1332(a).

As explained in Chapter 3, this interpretation of §1332(a) does not prevail when two or more named plaintiffs bring suit together. Under the general interpretation of §1332(a) that governed this situation for many years, each plaintiff had to individually satisfy the "amount in controversy" requirement of §1332(a).[7] But the Supreme Court radically changed this approach in *Exxon Mobil Corp. v. Allapattah Servs. Inc.*, 545 U.S. 546 (2006).

The *Exxon Mobil* Court based this change on supplemental jurisdiction, ruling that where at least one diverse plaintiff in an action satisfied §1332(a)'s "amount in controversy" requirement, §1367 authorizes supplemental jurisdiction over claims of other plaintiffs in the same case, even if the dollar value of those claims is less than the jurisdictional amount. 545 U.S. at 549. This holding requires that multiple plaintiffs in the action satisfy the jurisdictional requisites for §1367(a): the plaintiffs' claims must be part of the same case or controversy under Article III. As explained above, one may test whether this requirement is satisfied by evaluating whether the plaintiffs are properly joined as parties under Federal Rule of Civil Procedure 20(a). Rule 20(a) provides that "[a]ll persons may join in one action as plaintiffs if they assert any right to relief jointly, severally, or in the alternative in respect of or arising out of the same transaction, occurrence, or series of transactions or occurrences and if any question of law or fact common to all these persons will arise in the action." Since the "transaction or occurrence" standard of the Federal Rules of Civil Procedure is narrower than the Article III "case or controversy" standard,[8] a litigant who satisfies the joinder requirement of Federal Rule 20(a) will also satisfy the Article III "case or controversy" standard, adopted in the supplemental jurisdiction statute.

Exxon Mobil rendered considerable changes to the law governing the intersection of §1332 and §1367. One area left unchanged by *Exxon Mobil*,

---

7. As explained in Chapter 3, only one exception to this general rule existed: plaintiffs could combine separate claims against a defendant to satisfy §1332(a)'s jurisdictional amount in the unusual circumstance where the plaintiffs sued under a "common undivided interest" and a "single title or right" — as in jointly held property. *See* CHARLES ALAN WRIGHT & MARY KAY KANE, LAW OF FEDERAL COURTS §36, at 211-214 (6th ed. 2002).

8. *See, e.g., Sparrow v. Mazda Am. Credit*, 385 F. Supp. 2d 1063, 1067 (E.D. Cal. 2005); Michelle S. Simon, *Defining the Limits of Supplemental Jurisdiction Under 28 U.S.C. §1367*, 9 LEWIS & CLARK L. REV. 295, 297, 308 (2005).

however, concerns those cases in which a single plaintiff sues multiple defendants in a pure diversity case, but lacks a joint or common claim against the defendants and has the required "amount in controversy" against only one or some of the defendants. No §1367 jurisdiction would exist in such an instance, even where the plaintiff's claims against the multiple defendants are sufficiently related as to fall within the same constitutional case for the purposes of §1367(a).

Example 4-10

Victoria, a citizen of Maine, sued Ethel, a citizen of Massachusetts, for $100,000 in damages resulting from Ethel's fraudulent behavior. Marina, a citizen of Maine, joined as a plaintiff, also suing Ethel and arguing that she was injured by Ethel's same fraudulent behavior in the amount of $40,000. Marina properly joined Victoria's action under Federal Rule Civil Procedure 20(a) because her claim arises from the same transaction as Victoria's claim, and the suit includes shared questions of fact and law. Does a federal court have subject matter jurisdiction over both Victoria's and Marina's claims?

Explanation

Yes. The federal court has diversity jurisdiction over Victoria's claim against Ethel. This provides the foundation claim for using §1367(a) to justify jurisdiction over Marina's claim. (Marina's claim cannot enter on the basis of diversity-of-citizenship jurisdiction because the amount in controversy is too low.) Section 1367(b) does not change this result, even though §1332(a) provides the foundation for the suit. As reasoned by the *Exxon Mobil* Court, §1332(b) does not block claims by plaintiffs such as Ethel, who permissively joined the action under Federal Rule of Civil Procedure 20. Note, however, that *Exxon Mobil* does not change the requirement that, for supplemental jurisdiction to exist, all plaintiffs must be diverse from all defendants in the original lawsuit.

Example 4-11

Victoria, a citizen of Maine, sued Ethel, a citizen of Massachusetts, for $100,000 in damages resulting from Ethel's fraudulent behavior in connection with a loan transaction. Victoria also sued Rosalina, a citizen of Massachusetts, for damages she negligently caused in processing the loan transaction. According to the complaint, Rosalina's conduct was unrelated to Ethel's conduct, but exacerbated the injury inflicted on Victoria. The complaint alleges that the amount by which Rosalina's conduct exacerbated the injury was $40,000. Does a federal court have subject matter jurisdiction over Victoria's claims against Ethel and Rosalina?

Explanation

The court has jurisdiction only over Victoria's claim against Ethel. Victoria's claim against Rosalina does not satisfy the jurisdictional amount requirement. One cannot avoid this deficiency by arguing that the claims against Ethel and Rosalina are common, undivided, or joint: the claims depend on separate misconduct and caused separate injury. One might make a strong argument that the two claims derive from a common nucleus of operative fact and are therefore part of the same constitutional case for the purposes of §1367(a). The existing law, however, requires that each claim by one plaintiff against separate defendants satisfy the "amount in controversy" requirement. *Exxon Mobil Corp. v. Allapattah Servs. Inc.* did not change that rule. Accordingly, exercise of jurisdiction over the claim against Rosalina would be inconsistent with the jurisdictional requirements of §1332, and the claim falls within the prohibition of §1367(b).

3. Section 1367(c): Congress Delegates

In *United Mine Workers v. Gibbs*, 383 U.S. 715, 726 (1966), the Supreme Court stated that, even though the Constitution endows federal courts with power over all claims within the same constitutional case, a federal district court need not exercise that power when "judicial economy, convenience, and fairness to the litigants" counsel against it. 383 U.S. at 726. In §1367(c), Congress endorsed the wisdom of allowing federal courts to decline supplemental jurisdiction in particular cases. Consequently, even though §1367(a) grants power over supplemental claims, §1367(c) delegates to courts discretion whether to exercise that power.

Section 1367 articulates the discretionary factors governing supplemental jurisdiction differently than *Gibbs*. Section 1367(c) provides that a district court "may," but need not, decline to exercise supplemental jurisdiction over a claim if one of four separate factors is implicated: "(1) the claim raises a novel or complex issue of State law, (2) the claim substantially predominates over the claim or claims over which the district court has original jurisdiction, (3) the district court has dismissed all claims over which it has original jurisdiction, or (4) in exceptional circumstances, there are other compelling reasons for declining jurisdiction." Case law is not consistent on the question of whether the statutory provisions should be read to encompass the discretionary factors that the *Gibbs* Court mentioned for declining jurisdiction, which were "judicial economy, convenience, and fairness." One could quite reasonably argue, however, that a case in which "judicial economy, convenience, and fairness" weigh against exercising jurisdiction is also a case in which, under §1367(c)(4), "exceptional circumstances" provide "compelling reasons to decline jurisdiction." According to this line of argument, §1367(c)(4) incorporates the *Gibbs* standard.

Example 4-12

Consider the facts of Example 4-10, in which Victoria and Marina both sued Ethel. Marina was allowed to join Victoria's action under Federal Rule Civil Procedure 20(a) because her claim arose from the same transaction as Victoria's claim, and there would be shared questions of fact and law. You know from the preceding explanation that the federal court has supplemental jurisdiction, pursuant to §1367(a), over Marina's claim against Ethel. Assume, however, that after eight months of discovery, Ethel filed a motion for summary judgment against Victoria and Marina. Ethel argued that neither plaintiff could establish a genuine issue of material fact as to whether Ethel had engaged in fraudulent conduct. The district court granted summary judgment only against Victoria. Should the court allow Marina to proceed to trial with her claim?

Explanation

Marina's problem is that the foundation for federal jurisdiction — Victoria's claim against Ethel — is now gone. Thus, the "invited guest" is no longer present at the party and Marina's claim remains as an interloper. In *Gibbs*, the Court advised that a district court could reasonably proceed with the case against such an interloper after the trial had begun. If, however, the district court believes that the case would be an unworthy or unwise use of federal resources, the court would be acting within its discretion in dismissing the case pursuant to §1367(c)(3). Such dismissal would be particularly appropriate if Ethel could show that Marina could bring the case to trial in state court easily, efficiently, and without prejudice to the parties.

Example 4-13

Sara asserted two claims against Salil: one for violation of federal securities law and one for violation of state securities law. Each claim arose from the same transaction, although the legal protections under federal securities law vary significantly from the legal protections under state securities law. Salil argued that the court should not exercise jurisdiction in this case because a jury might confuse state and federal law concepts. According to Salil, the district court should dismiss the entire case under §1367(c). Should the court dismiss the case?

Explanation

Salil is at least partially wrong. If a court exercises discretion under §1367(c), the court declines only to exercise supplemental jurisdiction. That is, the court dismisses only the state claim. Although both claims arise from the same constitutional case and the district court would have power under §1367(a), the court might conclude that the possibility of confusion justifies

83

not exercising that power. If the confusion arises from the complexity of the state law, the court may dismiss under §1367(c)(1). Otherwise, the court needs another theory for declining jurisdiction. In *Gibbs*, the Court stated that "the likelihood of jury confusion in treating divergent legal theories of relief . . . would justify separating state and federal claims for trial." 388 U.S. at 726. *Gibbs*, however, has been superseded by statute. The district court may nonetheless develop a theory consistent with both *Gibbs* and §1367(c). For example, the district court might conclude that the confusion would make the litigation cumbersome and inaccurate, thereby undermining the efficiency of the proceedings as well as fairness and convenience for the parties. If so, the court might reason that the confusion renders the case sufficiently extraordinary to merit dismissal under §1367(c)(4).

4. Putting It All Together: A Summary Example

The following set of "rolling" examples provides an opportunity to test how the supplemental jurisdiction rules fit together.

Example 4-14

A tree fell on a car that Yvonne was driving, and she sustained serious injuries. Yvonne is a citizen of Maine. Negligent Corp., the entity responsible for maintaining the tree that fell on the car, is incorporated in New Hampshire and has its principal place of business there. Yvonne brought suit in federal district court against Negligent Corp., asserting three counts. Count 1 alleges that Negligent Corp. acted negligently under state law in failing to maintain the tree and is liable to Yvonne in an amount exceeding $80,000. Count 2 alleges that Negligent Corp. violated a federal statute allowing a private cause of action for individuals injured by trees that may interfere with interstate utility lines. Count 3 alleges that Negligent Corp. owes Yvonne money under a contract unrelated to the accident. The amount of money owed under this contract claim is $30,000. Does the federal court have subject matter jurisdiction over all three claims?

Explanation

The district court has jurisdiction over count 1 pursuant to 28 U.S.C. §1332(a) because the parties are diverse and the amount in controversy exceeds $80,000 (which is greater than the jurisdictional threshold of $75,000). The court has jurisdiction over count 2 pursuant to 28 U.S.C §1331. The federal cause of action is a creature of federal law and thus indisputably arises under federal law for the purposes of §1331. (If the federal statute did not explicitly provide for a federal cause of action, one might need to analyze the case under the principles outlined in Chapter 2 relating to federal question jurisdiction.) Finally, the district court has juris-diction over count 3 pursuant to §1332(a), since a plaintiff may aggregate all her claims against a defendant for the purposes of §1332(a)'s "amount in controversy" requirement. Yvonne need not resort to the supplemental jurisdiction statute: each of her claims falls within the original jurisdiction of the district court.

Example 4-15

After receiving service of Yvonne's complaint, Negligent Corp. filed a third-party complaint against Ted, who is a citizen of Maine. Ted is an independent contractor who has a contract with Negligent Corp., under which he is obligated to maintain the tree that fell on Yvonne's car. Neg-ligent Corp.'s third-party complaint impleaded Ted pursuant to Federal Rule of Civil Procedure 14. According to the third-party complaint, Ted was negligent in maintaining the tree and, as a result, was liable to Negligent Corp. under indemnity principles (see Figure 4-5). Is there subject matter jurisdiction over Negligent Corp.'s third-party complaint?

Explanation

Negligent Corp. may bring this third-party complaint pursuant to §1332(a) because Negligent Corp. has diverse citizenship relative to Ted and the amount in controversy for this third-party complaint exceeds $80,000 (and is therefore greater than the jurisdictional threshold of $75,000). Negligent Corp. is potentially liable to Yvonne under count 1 of her

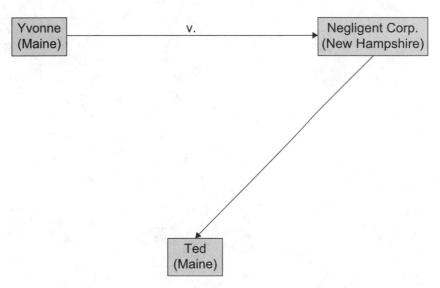

Figure 4-5.

complaint for an amount exceeding $80,000 in damages relating to the accident. Negligent Corp.'s theory is that liability under count 1 may be passed on to Ted under indemnity principles. Like Yvonne in Example 4-14, Negligent Corp. does not resort to the supplemental jurisdiction statute because it does not need to: the third-party complaint falls within the original jurisdiction of the district court.

Example 4-16

Once Negligent Corp. brought Ted into the case, Yvonne sought to assert her own claim against Ted for negligent maintenance of the tree (see Figure 4-6). Her theory of recovery is based on state law. Is there subject matter jurisdiction over this claim?

Explanation

The district court has supplemental jurisdiction over this claim pursuant to 28 U.S.C. §1367. The claim does not fall within the original jurisdiction of the district court because Ted and Yvonne are not diverse and the theory of liability derives from state law. Yvonne's claim against Ted includes no federal question. Thus, Yvonne must append this claim to the counts in her original complaint. Specifically, counts 1 and 2 provide the foundation claims for the supplemental claim against Ted because these counts concern the accident and therefore derive from the same constitutional case or controversy as Yvonne's accident claim against Ted. Count 3 of Yvonne's original complaint against Negligent Corp. does not provide a foundation claim because it is unrelated and is not part of the same constitutional case or

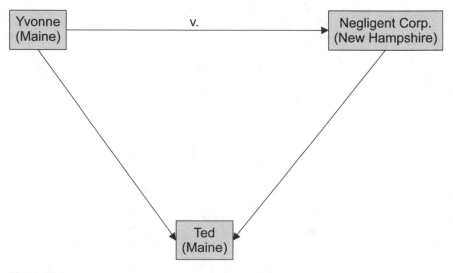

Figure 4-6.

controversy as Yvonne's claim against Ted; it therefore cannot support the supplemental claim under 28 U.S.C. §1367(a).

Having satisfied the standard of §1367(a), Yvonne must turn her attention to §1367(b), but it does not cause difficulty. Why? Section 1367(b) removes supplemental jurisdiction in civil actions "of which the district courts have original jurisdiction founded solely on section 1332." As explained in Example 4-13, counts 1 and 2 of Yvonne's original complaint rest on §1332 *and* §1331. Thus, §1367(b)'s limitations are inapplicable. The final step for Yvonne, then, is to evaluate whether the district court might be inclined to avoid supplemental jurisdiction under any of the discretionary factors in §1367(c). No facts in Example 4-13, 4-14, or 4-15 implicate these factors. Supplemental jurisdiction thus appears certain.

If, for the sake of illustration, one were to assume that Yvonne's original complaint rested only on 28 U.S.C. §1332, Yvonne would need to worry about §1367(b)'s limitations because the action would be "founded solely on section 1332." Under these circumstances, Yvonne's claim against Ted would involve two additional conditions for §1367(b): it is (1) a claim asserted by a plaintiff and (2) a claim against a person made a party under Federal Rule of Civil Procedure 14.

The question remains whether Yvonne's claim against Ted satisfies the final condition of §1367(b), in which exercising supplemental jurisdiction is "inconsistent with the jurisdictional requirements of section 1332." It appears that this language is satisfied, because allowing Yvonne to bring this claim enables her to circumvent the requirements of complete diversity. Like Kroger's claim against Owen in *Owen Equip. & Erection Co. v. Kroger*, 437 U.S. 365 (1978), Yvonne's claim against Ted is not logically dependent on her claim against Negligent Corp. Courts interpret §1367(b) as embodying the restrictions in *Owen Equip. & Erection Co. v. Kroger*. For these reasons, allowing Yvonne's claim against Ted would be inconsistent with the jurisdictional requirements of §1332. If Yvonne's original complaint did not contain a federal question, §1367(b) would prohibit supplemental jurisdiction over her claim against Ted.

Example 4-17

Assume that after the accident, Yvonne told many of Ted's customers that he was negligent in maintaining the tree and that he could not be trusted to perform competent work. As a result, Ted was considering suing Yvonne for slander. Thus, after Negligent Corp. brought Ted into the case, Ted decided to assert a slander claim against Yvonne for her statements in connection with the accident (see Figure 4-7). Is there subject matter jurisdiction over this slander claim?

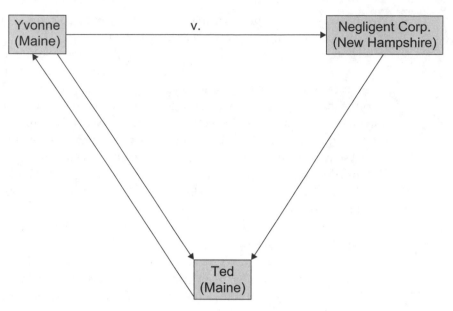

Figure 4-7.

Explanation

The district court probably has supplemental jurisdiction over this claim pursuant to 28 U.S.C. §1367. The claim does not fall within the original jurisdiction of the district court because Ted and Yvonne are not diverse, and Ted's claim rests on state law, with no federal question. Thus, Ted must look to Yvonne's complaint for the foundation of his claim. As was the case for Yvonne's claim against Ted in Example 4-16, counts 1 and 2 of Yvonne's original complaint likely provide the foundation claims for Ted's supplemental claim because counts 1 and 2 concern the accident, and the alleged slander also concerns events surrounding the accident. Ted's slander claim is more removed from the accident itself than is Yvonne's negligence claim against Ted. Indeed, Ted's slander claim requires the introduction of new facts and legal theories not at all relevant to Yvonne's original complaint. Nonetheless, the slander claim *derives* from the accident and therefore shares the same core facts as counts 1 and 2 of Yvonne's original complaint against Negligent Corp. For that reason, the slander claim can be said to be part of the same constitutional case as Yvonne's accident claim against Negligent Corp. Count 3 of Yvonne's original complaint against Negligent Corp. does not provide a foundation claim because it is unrelated and therefore cannot be used to support the supplemental claim under 28 U.S.C. §1367(a).

One might ask whether Ted should have the prerogative of using Yvonne's original complaint for his foundation, as he is not even a party to that complaint. This concern is dispelled by the last sentence of §1367(a), which states that "supplemental jurisdiction shall include claims that involve the joinder or intervention of additional parties." Ted was joined as an additional party, and his claim therefore involves "joinder" of an "additional part[y]" for the purposes of this language. Moreover, as was the case in Example 4-16, Ted need not worry about §1367(b), because original jurisdiction for the action does not rest solely on §1332. Finally, no facts indicate any reason for the district court to decline to exercise supplemental jurisdiction using the discretionary factors of §1367(c).

For the sake of illustration, one might test how Ted would fare under §1367 if the case included no federal question and original jurisdiction rested only on 28 U.S.C. §1332. In that event, Ted would need to confront §1367(b)'s limitations, because the action would be "founded solely on section 1332." He could quickly dispense with §1367(b), however, since that section applies only to claims by a plaintiff, a person proposed to be joined as a plaintiff under Federal Rule of Civil Procedure 19, or a person intervening as a plaintiff under Rule 24. Ted — the person making the claim at issue — does not fall into any of those categories. This result is consistent with the reasoning of *Owen Equip. & Erection Co. v. Kroger*, because Ted was haled into court, did not have the prerogative of choosing the federal forum, and should not be suspected of circumventing the complete diversity requirement.

Limitations on Federal Court Adjudication

Part II outlined power grants to lower federal courts, flowing from the language of Article III and from specific jurisdictional statutes. Every grant of power is circumscribed, however, by limitations, which are the subject of Part III. Some limitations are inextricable elements of constitutional and statutory authority. The best example of these internal limitations are justiciability doctrines, discussed in Chapter 5. Most limitations come from sources outside specific jurisdictional grants. For example, political impulses within Congress press for eliminating certain types of subject matter within general grants of power to federal courts. A variety of these controls (and their possibility of success) are explained in Chapter 6, titled Congresssional Control over Jurisdiction. Chapter 7 discusses how a specific limitation — the Anti-Injunction Act — is tied to federalism concerns and has significant ramifications for civil rights actions. Finally, Chapter 8 examines court-created abstention doctrines, which instruct a federal court to forbear from exercising power granted in the unqualified language of jurisdictional statutes.

CHAPTER 5

Justiciability Doctrines

A. VALUES SERVED BY JUSTICIABILITY DOCTRINES

Article III gives federal courts the power to resolve "cases" or "controversies." These simple words act as potent limits on a federal judge's job description. Following their constitutional mandate, federal courts should not be proactive; they should not reach out to identify social problems and develop potential cures. Rather, federal courts are passive recipients of specific disputes between specific litigants. The Constitution restricts their function to resolving those disputes. The justiciability doctrines add flesh to this basic framework for federal court power.

Developed by the United States Supreme Court, the justiciability doctrines test whether a case is "justiciable" — that is, whether the case is amenable to judicial resolution. As such, the doctrines support values related to governmental structure: federalism and separation of powers. By limiting what federal courts can do, the justiciability doctrines prevent the courts from invading the prerogatives of other branches of the federal government (separation of powers) as well as the prerogatives of state governments (federalism). The doctrines also provide a type of quality assurance for federal court work product. They achieve this quality control by ensuring that federal courts adjudicate only within the context of specific facts litigated by committed adversaries who have an incentive to investigate fully and to litigate vigorously. In this way, the justiciability doctrines foster decisions based on accurate information presented in a context where federal courts can project the likely consequences of their rulings. Work quality is also maintained because the doctrines shield the judiciary from a deluge of cases. Some justiciability doctrines also serve the value of self-determination—the principle that individuals should be able to control their own destiny and seek court intervention to resolve their disputes on their own terms.[1]

These values suggest that justiciability doctrines perform beneficial functions. One may also find considerable defects in the doctrines and criticize the ways in which courts use them. Critics argue that federal courts deploy justiciability doctrines to deliver defeat to plaintiffs without candidly ruling on the merits of their claims; to avoid discussing controversial, yet important, social issues; and to restrict access by deserving citizens to federal court. As in other areas of federal jurisdiction law, critics suggest that federal courts use justiciability doctrines to mask substantive or ideological motivations using the apparently neutral garb of jurisdictional technicalities.

B. OVERVIEW OF THE JUSTICIABILITY DOCTRINES

The justiciability doctrines govern what matters a federal court can handle, when those matters can be brought to federal court, and who can properly bring them to the federal court for resolution. The doctrines break down as follows: The what category includes the prohibition against advisory opinions and the political question doctrine. The when category divides between the ripeness and mootness doctrines. The standing doctrine gives meaning to the who category.

1. The Doctrines Restricting *what* Matters a Court Can Handle

Under the doctrine prohibiting advisory opinions, a court can resolve disputes only between actual parties with opposing positions. This doctrine thus confines federal courts to their constitutionally delineated task: adjudicating "cases" or "controversies." In contemporary times, this doctrine is often relevant when a party asks a court to issue a declaratory judgment pronouncing the party's rights, even though no true controversy with an opposing litigant has emerged.

Example 5-1

The President of the United States was considering issuing an executive order allowing the use of stun guns during interrogation of suspected terrorists. Before issuing the order, he wanted to ensure that it was constitutional. His representative contacted a public interest group dedicated to the civil rights

---

1. Lea Brilmayer, *The Jurisprudence of Article III: Perspectives on the "Case or Controversy" Requirement,* 93 HARV. L. REV. 297, 310-315 (1979) (discussing the value of self-determination).

5. Justiciability Doctrines

of those suspected of international terrorism. The group agreed to bring suit seeking a declaration that the proposed executive order was unconstitutional. Is the case justiciable?

Explanation

The case violates the prohibition against advisory opinions. The parties have no true controversy, but have colluded in order to manufacture a case. Parties may not agree to create federal court power in this way. If the federal court provided the requested declaratory judgment, it would not be eliminating a fight, but merely rendering advice to the executive branch.

Also in the *what* category is the prohibition against federal court intrusion into matters best resolved by the politically accountable branches of the federal government: Congress and the president. Known as the "political question doctrine," this justiciability doctrine contemplates that courts will undertake a case-specific inquiry into whether a dispute turns on a non-justiciable political question. The United States Supreme Court has named six factors for a federal court to analyze in deciding whether a question is political: (1) "a textually demonstrable constitutional commitment of the issue to a coordinate political department"; (2) "a lack of judicially discoverable and manageable standards for resolving it"; (3) "the impossibility of deciding without an initial policy determination of a kind clearly for nonjudicial discretion"; (4) "the impossibility of a court's undertaking independent resolution without expressing lack of the respect due coordinate branches of government"; (5) "an unusual need for unquestioning adherence to a political decision already made"; and (6) "the potentiality of embarrassment from multifarious pronouncements by various departments on one question." *Baker v. Carr*, 369 U.S. 186, 217 (1962).

The Supreme Court most frequently emphasizes the first of these *Baker v. Carr* factors, but the Court has never suggested that any particular combination of the six factors is decisive. In fact, federal court decisions on the political question doctrine have been notoriously difficult to predict. Scholars and other commentators often note that the federal courts may invoke the doctrine in order to manipulate a result on the merits of a particular dispute. Nonetheless, in evaluating fact patterns for possible application of the doctrine, one may find guidance by considering the types of matters that the Supreme Court has found the political question doctrine should govern: cases concerning the ratification of treaties, conduct of war, qualifications of ambassadors, enforcement of the Constitution's "republican form of government clause," internal governance of Congress, and adequacy of National Guard training.

Example 5-2

Assume that before 2007, there existed a country known as the United Republic of Slivovich (URS). In 2005 officials from the URS rented offices in New York City in order to open a consulate there. The consulate represented the official interests of the URS in the United States, granting visas, performing customs functions, and answering questions from the public about travel, study, and work in the URS. URS officials signed a ten-year lease for these New York City offices. In 2007, however, the URS ceased to exist, breaking into two separate sovereignties, and the consulate personnel vacated the rented offices. Nevertheless, the landlord sued the two successor sovereignties, alleging that they succeeded to the interests of the URS and were liable for the rent owed for the remainder of the lease term. Is this case justiciable?

Explanation

Because a party to the lease, the United Republic of Slivovich, has ceased to exist, one might consider whether the controversy between the parties to the lease has in fact become moot. (The death of a party often moots a case.) One must remember, however, that the URS's demise occurred before the lawsuit was filed. The landlord has a colorable legal theory that the two successor nations inherited the URS's liabilities. While the landlord may not ultimately prevail, the controversy involving the two successor states remains a live one.

A significant justiciability problem is nevertheless present: the case turns on a political question. The question of whether the successor nations inherited URS's legal responsibilities implicates many of the six factors from *Baker v. Carr*. First, the case concerns foreign affairs, which the Constitution commits to the president and the Congress, not the courts. Because the case turns on succession and sovereignty questions, the usual judicially manageable standards relating to contract disputes are insufficient to decide the case. Diplomatic questions concerning recognition of successor nations are imbedded in the dispute, and these questions are not generally decided by courts but are handled by the politically accountable branches. Accordingly, the third factor — making a threshold policy determination ill suited for judicial discretion — is implicated.

The fact pattern does not suggest that the United States government has already taken a position on the international and domestic status of the two successor nations. Nevertheless, one can easily imagine that the president or Congress may express a position, leaving open the possibility that the remainder of the *Baker v. Carr* factors might present problems. If the court decided the successor status of these nations, this decision might clash with future political decisions on the subject. For example, the State Department and other departments of the executive branch are likely to encounter issues dealing with intergovernmental relations or immigration matters concerning citizens of the two successor nations. If these departments took a position on the official status of the successor nations that was contrary to that of the court in the landlord dispute, the result would be conflicting positions of the federal government, a state of affairs that could embarrass the United States and undercut the credibility of its diplomatic efforts in other contexts.

2. The Doctrines Restricting *When* a Court Can Adjudicate

A federal court can resolve a dispute only at the right time, neither too early (before the parties are truly adversary or before harm is imminent) nor too late (when the parties no longer have a disagreement for which the federal court can find a remedy). Claims entering a court too early implicate the ripeness doctrine. The doctrine of mootness governs suits where the parties' controversy has disappeared.

The ripeness doctrine prevents courts from adjudicating matters deemed premature because the injury is speculative and may never occur. To determine whether a case is ripe for judicial review, courts consider two factors: (1) "the hardship to the parties of withholding court consideration" and (2) "the fitness of the issues for judicial decision." *Abbott Laboratories v. Gardner*, 387 U.S. 136, 149 (1967). Courts often conclude that the hardship consideration is satisfied if an individual is faced with the choice between subjecting herself to punishment and forgoing activities she believes are lawful. The fitness factor generally concerns whether the parties can develop a factual record enabling a court to evaluate the consequences of a legal ruling.

In contrast to ripeness, the mootness doctrine may apply in cases with a well-developed record documenting a true controversy. Mootness recognizes that a controversy must remain alive throughout the litigation process and that a court may no longer hear a case when the parties cease to be adversaries. Thus, the mootness doctrine prevents unnecessary federal court decisions, limits federal judges' authority, and saves judicial effort for cases where the litigants continue to have a concrete stake in the outcome.

Yet because events can "moot" a case on which the parties and the court system have expended considerable resources, the mootness doctrine includes four significant exceptions. First, a case may survive even if a litigant's main "injury" can no longer be avoided—as long as collateral consequences remain. For example, a defendant's challenge to her criminal conviction is not rendered moot once she finishes serving her sentence, because she may continue to suffer from the mark of a criminal record after she is released from prison. Class actions provide the context for the second exception, under which courts are exempted from the mootness doctrine once a class becomes certified. The third exception allows federal courts to consider claims that, although technically moot, are capable of repetition, yet evade review. For this exception to apply, the plaintiff must be likely to suffer the same injury again, and the injury must be inherently limited in duration such that it disappears before federal litigation is complete. *Roe v. Wade*, 410 U.S. 113 (1973), is a classic example of this exception: unwanted pregnancy is inherently limited in duration, and a state official's preventing a fertile woman from obtaining an abortion is an alleged injury the woman is likely to suffer again.

The fourth exception to the mootness doctrine arises in situations where the defendant voluntarily ceases the conduct that is the subject of the suit. To avoid giving defendants the ability to control the power of federal courts, the Supreme Court has established that a defendant's promise to cease offending behavior will not ordinarily moot a controversy. Only if "it is absolutely clear the allegedly wrongful behavior could not reasonably be expected to recur" will a defendant be able to moot a case. *Friends of the Earth, Inc. v. Laidlaw Environmental Servs., Inc.*, 528 U.S. 167, 189 (2000).

3. The Doctrine Restricting *Who* May Bring a Lawsuit

Federal courts can adjudicate only cases brought by litigants who have "standing." The standing doctrine has proved the most versatile and most extensively used of all the justiciability doctrines. The standing doctrine seeks to confine judicial energy to those cases in which a plaintiff has suffered personal injury that is traceable to the defendant's conduct and capable of being redressed by the federal court.

The standing doctrine's subtleties are explored in greater detail later in this section. First, however, are examples that illustrate the relationship among the justiciability doctrines and the values underlying them. The examples show that the justiciability doctrines overlap and can sometimes be interchanged in analyzing a set of facts.

Example 5-3

Mike is unemployed. He lives off his investments, paying local personal property tax on his securities holdings. He heard that the local government in his township had just passed a tax on wage income. Mike had no definite plans to work for wages in the future. He is nonetheless deeply offended by the legislation and filed suit challenging it. He argued that he may take a job at some time in the future, and in that event the tax would constitute a taking of his property without due process of law. He fashioned his claim as a Fourteenth Amendment challenge under the United States Constitution. Is this case justiciable?

Explanation

Mike's case is non-justiciable. A "rough and ready" test for justiciability is that it takes two to have a fight — or, in the language of Article III, to have a "case or controversy." Both sides to the lawsuit must take some active part in the dispute. Here, true controversy is missing from both sides. Mike's claim is simply hypothetical: he may never work for wages and may never actually be subject to tax liability under the law. On the basis of the skeletal facts offered, one might argue that he is not the proper person to bring the lawsuit or that a court adjudicating the case might violate the prohibition against issuing an advisory opinion. Two other elements suggest a timing problem with the lawsuit: Mike's statement that he may take a wage-paying job sometime in the future, and the uncertainty about how and on whom the government will impose the tax. Ripeness thus emerges as an obvious justiciability problem with the lawsuit. Mike's claim requests what is called "pre-enforcement review" of a statute. One would not be wrong in analyzing this example using the standing doctrine or the prohibition against advisory opinions, but courts generally analyze such pre-enforcement review suits using ripeness rather than other doctrines.[2] Moreover, although it is a timing doctrine like ripeness, mootness is not implicated here. The mootness doctrine applies when a once-live controversy "dies." Here, the parties never had a true fight.

Another doctrine that is inapplicable here is the political question doctrine. Mike is bringing a constitutional challenge to a local government enactment, which is a dispute well within the traditional expertise of the federal courts. The power of judicial review — a court evaluating legislation for compliance with the Constitution — became an explicit part of the federal judiciary's powers in *Marbury v. Madison*, 5 U.S. (1 Cranch) 137 (1803). Judicial standards for adjudicating due process challenges are well established, and nothing in the Constitution grants non-judicial branches of the federal government the power to adjudicate constitutional challenges to local enactments.

Example 5-4

Assume the same facts as in Example 5-3. Now, however, Mike admitted in his lawsuit that he did not work for wages. He nevertheless asserted that the tax violates the due process rights of others who do have wage-paying jobs. Is this case justiciable?

Explanation

Mike has talked his way into a clear standing problem. He has suffered no specific injury from the law and has not alleged any facts suggesting that he

---

2. ERWIN CHEMERINSKY, FEDERAL JURISDICTION 115 (4th ed. 2003) (comparing ripeness and standing in the context of pre-enforcement review).

should be allowed to assert the legal rights of others. A court's decision would not provide Mike redress for a personal injury. As in Example 5-3, the case is also not ripe for review, since no facts reveal whether or how the tax law will be enforced. For the same reasons as in Example 5-3, one could argue that the mootness and political question doctrines are again inapplicable.

Example 5-5

Assume the same facts as in Example 5-3, except that now Mike works for a wage and local authorities instructed his employer to begin withholding wage tax. Mike filed suit challenging the wage tax under the federal Constitution. Convinced that Mike had substantial basis for his challenge, the local government enacted legislation repealing the original wage tax. Legislative statements made at the time of repeal suggested that local officials were convinced that the tax was constitutionally as well as politically ill advised. Mike was only one of many taxpayers who vehemently protested the new wage tax. The legislators said they had no intention of instituting the tax in the future, and that they feared they would not be reelected if they ever tried to do so. Is Mike's case justiciable?

Explanation

Mike's original lawsuit had no justiciability problem. He had a true fight with the local government, which had taken action to enforce the tax against him. Moreover, Mike asserted a direct constitutional injury from the tax. The local government, however, "mooted" the controversy.

Do any exceptions to the mootness doctrine apply? No facts in the example support the collateral consequences or class action exception nor does the "capable of repetition yet evading review" exception appear to be satisfied. Mike allegedly is suffering from an unconstitutional wage tax. As a wage worker, he is subject to this injury continuously; the injury is not inherently limited in duration. The injury disappeared here only because the officials found fault with the tax and repealed it. Nothing inherent in the injury suggests that this would happen repeatedly.

This analysis of the case's factual circumstances suggests that the voluntary cessation exception may apply. Indeed, one might ask whether the local officials repealed the law to avoid Mike's litigation and were planning to reintroduce the legislation once the lawsuit was dismissed. The Supreme Court has stated that defendants have a heavy burden in avoiding the voluntary cessation exception. But several factors suggest that the voluntary repeal of the tax is permanent. First, reenactment of the tax would take substantial effort. Second, the officials admitted constitutional problems with the tax, making it even more difficult for them to reestablish the tax successfully. Their admission would support further litigation if officials ever reintroduced the tax. Perhaps most significant, the political fallout from the original tax brings credibility to the officials' assertion of permanent repeal. Their expressed intent to keep the repeal permanent appears bona fide, given that legislators, by nature, seek to remain in power.

C. MORE DETAILS ABOUT STANDING

Standing, on one hand, appears as a routine threshold doctrine governing whether the requisites for suit are established and, on the other hand, holds fundamental importance for the survival of certain types of litigation. This quality is shared with other federal courts doctrines but takes on special significance for standing because of its frequent, yet inconsistent, appearance in federal case law. Standing decisions sometimes appear as though they are intended to dispose of the merits of a suit.

Example 5-6

Juanita and Cynthia are lesbians who shared a thirty-year commitment. Juanita became terminally ill, and immediately before her death she gave Cynthia instructions about cremation and burial of her ashes. After Juanita's death, her parents asserted the right to control the disposition of her remains. The state coroner expressed the intent to release the body to a funeral home operator, with orders to follow the parents' preferences (which differed from Juanita's instructions to Cynthia). Cynthia filed suit against the coroner and the parents, arguing that she had the right to control the disposition of Juanita's remains. The court concluded that Cynthia lacked standing to sue over the disposition of Juanita's remains because she did not have a sufficiently close familial relationship with Juanita and was never named a legal representative of Juanita. How is standing related to the merits of the case in this example?

Explanation

The court's standing decision appears as a thinly veiled decision on the merits. In fact, the underlying dispute in the case is which party the law recognizes as sufficiently close to the deceased to control the disposition of her remains. By holding that Cynthia lacked standing to sue for control, the court essentially decided the merits question of whether the law allowed her to exert control. In the vernacular, this reasoning is called "putting the rabbit in the hat."

1. Constitutional Requisites

Standing doctrine has two components: Article III standing (which is tied directly to the case or controversy requirement) and prudential standing (which reflects institutional limits federal courts have created to implement decisionmaking policies). In explaining prudential standing, the Supreme Court has stated that prudential limits ensure that courts do not "decide abstract questions of wide public significance," where other governmental institutions are more competent to provide effective guidance. *Warth v. Seldin,* 422 U.S. 490, 500 (1975). The prudential principles supplement the Article III requirements.

Article III standing requires "injury in fact," which (as described previously) requires that the plaintiff has suffered personal injury traceable to the defendant's conduct and capable of being redressed by the court. Even if the court finds the injury real and worthy of the law's protection, the plaintiff must show "causation," which requires that the injury be linked to the defendant's conduct. In addition, the plaintiff must establish "redressability"; that is, she must identify some form of relief that will alleviate the injury the defendant has caused. Each of these three requirements is addressed in turn.

a. Injury in Fact

To satisfy the "injury in fact" requirement, the plaintiff's personal injury must be perceptible and recognized as worthy of the law's protection. Courts are wary of abstract injury, preferring to adjudicate tangible losses flowing from economic or physical harm. Federal courts are nonetheless willing to protect such matters as the character of a neighborhood and environmental quality, so long as the threatened harm is not too speculative or obscure. As an initial matter, however, plaintiffs must show that they are subject to harm.

Example 5-7

Jeffrey and Leo, a same-sex couple, had not taken action to solemnize their union in any state of the United States and had no plans to do so. Jeffrey and Leo have filed a challenge to the federal statute known as the Defense of Marriage Act, which provides that no state of the United States is required to give effect to any law, record, or judicial proceeding of another state that treats a same-sex relationship as a marriage. According to their suit, this provision in the Defense of Marriage Act violates their equal protection and due process rights. Are there any standing problems with this suit?

Explanation

Jeffrey and Leo stumble at the first step of their suit. They have problems with Article III standing. It is not that the law won't recognize that a party might suffer injury by encountering an obstacle to marriage. Rather, Jeffrey and Leo's standing problem stems from their failure to take steps to marry or to make imminent plans to marry. For that reason, Jeffrey and Leo have suffered no "injury in fact." They may sincerely believe that the Defense of Marriage Act is capable of violating their equal protection and due process rights, but unless they attempt to become married, they cannot present the court with a concrete harm to redress. Since Article III standing is not established, the court need not wrestle with the prudential considerations.

This example illustrates a characteristic demonstrated in Example 5-3: the overlap among the justiciability doctrines. From this example, one can see how the standing doctrine "bleeds" into the mootness doctrine. Indeed, one might also argue that Jeffrey and Leo's challenge is not ripe for review because they have no present plans to marry.

i. Types of Injuries Sufficient for the Injury Requirement

Jeffrey and Leo's standing difficulties in Example 5-7 arose because they had not taken steps demonstrating that they suffered actual injury from the challenged laws. Sometimes plaintiffs encounter problems with the actual injury requirement because the quality of the injury itself is not of a character sufficient to confer standing, regardless of whether the plaintiff has taken actions that would subject her to injury. Plaintiffs encounter problems where they assert abstract harms, arguing that the defendant has compromised the quality of their physical environment, general marital happiness, or the esteem with which society views their demographic group.

Several Supreme Court cases delineate the parameters of establishing standing based on abstract harms. These cases demonstrate that the more concrete facts supporting the plaintiff's personal injury, the more likely the plaintiff will be able to establish standing to sue for abstract harms. For example, in *Friends of the Earth, Inc. v. Laidlaw Environmental Servs., Inc.*, 528 U.S. 167 (2000), the Supreme Court explained that environmental plaintiffs must show that they use an affected area and suffer because the "'aesthetic and recreational values of the area'" are lessened by the defendant's activity. 528 U.S. at 183 (quoting *Sierra Club v. Morton*, 405 U.S. 727, 735 (1972)). Moreover, to find Article III standing in an environmental case, courts insist that plaintiffs offer more than "general averments," "conclusory allegations," and "speculative 'some day' intentions" to enjoy a recreational area. *Friends of the Earth, Inc. v. Laidlaw Environmental Servs., Inc.*, 528 U.S. at 184 (internal quotation marks omitted). Even specific factual allegations are sometimes not enough. Thus, in *Lujan v. Defenders of Wildlife*, 504 U.S. 555, 562-563 (1992), the Court acknowledged that "the desire to use or observe an animal species, even for purely esthetic purposes, is undeniably a cognizable interest for purpose of standing." Nonetheless, even though Congress had attempted to confer standing on the plaintiffs, the *Lujan* Court held that the plaintiffs lacked standing because they established only that they had viewed the animal species in the past, and had no specific plans to view them in the future.

Example 5-8

Three individuals who lived near a stream brought suit against a manufacturing company that discharged chemical by-products of the manufacturing process into the stream. Plaintiffs alleged they were entitled to damages under environmental laws for injuries resulting from the pollution. The plaintiffs each averred and established that they previously had used the stream and the area around it at least six times a year to picnic, to fish, and to birdwatch. Because of the pollution, they discontinued these recreational activities along the stream. Two plaintiffs alleged that they celebrated family reunions and summer birthdays along the stream for many years in the past, but that the pollution had stopped them from planning those celebrations along the stream. Another individual alleged that she had considered selling her home until she learned from a realtor that the home had declined in value compared with similar homes in the area because of its proximity to the polluted area. Do the plaintiffs have standing to seek damages from the defendant?

Explanation

The plaintiffs have likely established standing. The injuries of plaintiffs here are sufficient under *Friends of the Earth, Inc. v. Laidlaw Environmental Servs., Inc.*: the plaintiffs have routinely used the affected area and would suffer because they would not be able to picnic, to fish, or to birdwatch as a result of the defendant's activity. In addition, the plaintiff whose home is located near the discharge spot has established economic injury due to the defendant's activities. This concrete fact imparts a tangible quality to the more abstract, aesthetic injuries of the other plaintiffs. Moreover, in contrast to the *Lujan* plaintiffs, the plaintiffs here have provided specific details about future as well as past injuries. Indeed, the plaintiffs here allege that the defendant's discharge will impose future damage to property interests and will curtail their future activities.

Supreme Court case law also establishes specific rules about the standing of associations. "Associational standing" allows an association to sue for its members when "(a) its members would have standing to sue in their own right; (b) the interests it seeks to protect are germane to the organization's purpose; and (c) neither the claim asserted nor the relief requested requires the participation of individual members in the lawsuit." *Hunt v. Washington State Apple Adver. Comm'n*, 432 U.S. 333, 343 (1977).

Example 5-9

Assume the same facts as presented in Example 5-8: the defendant manufacturing company has been polluting a stream with its discharge. However, now accompanying the individual plaintiffs in the suit is an advocacy group—Neighbors to Save the Stream (NSS)—comprising neighbors in the area of the stream who own property and have used the area for recreational purposes. Some of the group's members are not individual plaintiffs in the suit, but all of the group's members live in the vicinity of the stream. The group was formed to seek redress for the same injuries claimed by the individual plaintiffs. In this suit, NSS has requested an injunction preventing the defendant from discharging the pollution in the future. Does NSS have standing?

Explanation

NSS appears to have established the requisites for associational standing. The *Hunt* requirements appear to be satisfied here. As explained in Example 5-8, the individual members have standing to sue. Second, the organizing purpose behind NSS is the same as its motivation for joining the lawsuit: to fight the defendant's pollution. Third, since NSS is not making a claim specific to an individual plaintiff or seeking damages incurred by a specific plaintiff, the members of NSS do not have to participate in the suit. The issue may arise, however, of whether NSS meets the specific requirements of standing to sue for an injunction. Thus, even though NSS has established the requisites for associational standing, the organization must ensure that it has satisfied the requirements for seeking the particular type of relief sought here: an injunction. The next section discusses this additional barrier.

ii. Standing to Seek Particular Remedies

A plaintiff must establish standing for every type of remedy sought. Thus, if a defendant's actions caused physical harm to the plaintiff in the past, the plaintiff may easily establish standing to seek damages for that harm, but must make a separate showing to establish that the court should enjoin the defendant from taking the same actions again. A plaintiff may therefore have standing to seek redress of a past injury through damages, but no standing to seek an injunction against future harm.

The United States Supreme Court outlined the standing requirements for injunctive relief in *City of Los Angeles v. Lyons*, 461 U.S. 95 (1983). In *Lyons*, Los Angeles police stopped an individual for a traffic violation and choked him to the point of unconsciousness. The plaintiff, Lyons, alleged a police department policy of applying unnecessary, life-threatening chokeholds and sought damages as well as injunctive and declaratory relief. Ruling only on Lyons's injunction request, the Court held that Lyons lacked Article III standing to seek an injunction against the chokehold policy. The Court reasoned that Lyons failed to show that the threat of future injury was "real and immediate" rather than "conjectural" or "hypothetical." *Id.* at 102, 105-106.

The *Lyons* Court's standing test for injunctions reflects the "it takes two to have a fight" logic behind justiciability doctrines. The test requires a showing that both sides of the controversy will take action, making likely a recurrence of the events giving rise to the first injury. As the Court explained, to have standing for an injunction against deadly chokeholds, Lyons faced a double-barreled burden. He first would need to allege that "he would have another encounter with the police." *Id.* at 105-106. As for the other side of the fight, Lyons would have "to make the incredible assertion either (1) that *all* police officers in Los Angeles *always* choke any citizen with whom they happen to have an encounter . . . or (2) that the City ordered or authorized police officers to act in such manner." *Id.* at 106. Lower courts have applied this rigorous two-part test not only in injunction cases, but also in cases requesting a declaratory judgment.

Example 5-10

Paula is a high school dropout, twenty-two years old, who has had difficulty keeping a job. When she was nine months pregnant with her first child, she began to experience labor pains and went to the emergency room of a local hospital near her home, Texas General. After initial processing in the emergency room, Paula was sent to the labor and delivery ward, where a staff physician, Dr. Obstetrician, examined her and concluded that she was in active labor. Upon hearing that Paula had no medical insurance, however, Dr. Obstetrician discharged Paula and instructed her to go to a city hospital fifty miles away.

Paula left the local hospital as instructed but had no money for transportation to the city hospital, so she delivered her baby at home. Tragically, the child suffocated during delivery because the umbilical cord was wrapped around its neck. Paula believes that the child would be alive today if trained personnel had assisted the delivery.

Texas General acknowledged that a hospital employee refused care for Paula. The hospital, however, took the position that the economics of health care made the doctor's actions necessary and that the refusal to provide care to Paula was consistent with governing law. Paula's lawyers plan to file a two-count complaint against Texas General, with one count seeking damages and one count seeking an injunction requiring Texas General to develop better procedures for handling indigent maternity patients. Does Paula have standing to pursue both claims?[3]

Explanation

Paula easily has standing to sue for damages. She has a palpable injury — the death of her child — and she has not yet received any sort of remedy to compensate for that loss. Her standing to sue for damages, of course, does not provide her with standing to sue for an injunction. Instead, she must apply the two-part *Lyons* test. Her prior pregnancy demonstrates that she is a fertile, sexually active woman. She lives near Texas General; accordingly, she can demonstrate a significant likelihood that she will use the obstetric services at the hospital again. Because she is indigent and lacks a high school diploma, no facts indicate that she will soon acquire medical care insurance. All of these factors combine to bring her *close* to establishing half of the required showing: she is likely to find herself in the same circumstances again. For the other side of a future controversy, Texas General has provided Paula with an advantage: it has admitted what happened, yet asserted that all its actions were lawful. This admission should enable Paula to establish that Texas General either has a policy of refusing treatment to indigent patients without medical care insurance or instructs its doctors to refuse care under those circumstances.

Paula's standing to sue for an injunction is a close call, particularly if she has no evidence of a formal policy on the part of Texas General and no specific facts about her future reproductive plans. One factor that could influence the court's decision is the status of Texas General. If it is a public hospital operated by a local governmental authority, the federal court may be less likely to recognize standing. Both separation of powers and federalism concerns undergirding the standing doctrine may act as tiebreakers militating against federal court intervention. If, on the other hand, the hospital is a private entity, federalism and separation of powers weigh less heavily against standing, and the federal court is more likely to adjudicate the merits of Paula's injunction request.

---

3. For further discussion of this fact pattern, and the role of remedies principles in resolving it, *see* Laura E. Little, *It's About Time: Unravelling Standing and Equitable Ripeness*, 41 Buff. L. Rev. 933 (1993).

b. Causation and Redressability

Aside from "injury in fact," Article III holds two more requirements for the plaintiff's injury: causation (the defendant must have caused the injury) and redressability (the requested relief must be designed to remedy the injury). A plaintiff may encounter difficulty establishing these two elements when significant factors bearing on the injury and its cure lie outside the parties' control.

Redressability poses a problem for the plaintiff who cannot identify her injury specifically or cannot show that the requested remedy will have a significant impact on her life. Causation frequently poses a problem when the plaintiff's plights results from several complex sources. Often a case that fails the causation requirement fails redressability as well, but this is not always true.

Allen v. Wright, 468 U.S. 737 (1984), provides an example of these two requirements. In *Allen*, parents of black public school children claimed that the Internal Revenue Service had failed to satisfy its obligation to deny tax-exempt status to racially discriminatory private schools. Reasoning that the IRS's actions amounted to government aid to discriminatory private schools, the parents made two arguments: (1) the aid stigmatized them and their children, and (2) the aid diminished their children's chances of receiving an integrated education. The parents maintained that if the IRS enforced the law, the private schools either would have to stop discriminating so they could receive the tax break again or would have to charge more tuition to make up for the lost tax savings. The Court concluded that the first argument failed because "stigma" does not amount to an actual injury in fact. As for the second argument, the Court acknowledged that the relief requested could redress the injury because a change in IRS policy "might have a substantial effect on" desegregating public schools. *Id.* at 753 n.19. Nevertheless, the Court found causation clearly lacking because the parents' injury was " 'highly indirect' " and resulted from " 'the independent action of some third party [i.e., the private schools] not before the court.' " *Id.* at 757 (quoting *Simon v. Eastern Kentucky Welfare Rights Org.*, 426 U.S. 26, 42 (1976)).

Example 5-11

Zelda, an unwed mother, sought child support for her two-year-old child, but the child's father had steadfastly refused to pay anything since the child's birth. Zelda sought to have the state prosecute the child's father for failure to pay support, but the state had a policy of prosecuting only fathers of legitimate children. Zelda brought suit against the state, alleging that its policy unconstitutionally discriminated against illegitimate children. She sought an injunction requiring the state to prosecute fathers of illegitimate children. Does she have standing?

5. Justiciability Doctrines

Explanation

Zelda will have trouble establishing standing to seek the injunction. Interestingly, she is not likely to encounter difficulties with the rule of *City of Los Angeles v. Lyons*. Given that she is raising the young child and the father has consistently maintained that he would not pay support, Zelda will continue to confront an obstacle to recovering the much-needed support. Moreover, the state has an explicit policy of not prosecuting for failure to provide support for illegitimate children, so Zelda will also continue to encounter resistance to prosecution. Thus, both conditions of the *Lyons* test are statisfied.

Zelda's standing problems arise instead from the causation and redressability requirements. First, the father himself is to blame for the nonpayment, not the state. Although the state's willingness to prosecute would add an incentive for payment, the injury results from the failure of a third party — the father — to act. Moreover, in contrast with the black parents in *Allen v. Wright*, Zelda will encounter substantial difficulty demonstrating redressability. If the court were to grant Zelda her requested injunction, this "would result only in the jailing of the child's father," not in Zelda receiving child support. *Linda R. S. v. Richard D.*, 410 U.S. 614, 618 (1973) (making this observation in a similar context). While imprisonment may motivate future payment, payment is not certain.

2. Prudential Considerations

The Supreme Court has resisted creating a finite list of prudential limitations on standing, but notes that prudential standing prohibits the following: (1) " 'a litigant's raising another person's legal rights,' " (2) adjudicating " 'generalized grievances,' " and (3) lawsuits seeking judicial enforcement of rights outside " 'the zone of interests protected by the law invoked.' " *Elk Grove Unified School District v. Newdow*, 542 U.S. 1, 12 (2004) (quoting *Allen v. Wright*, 468 U.S. 737, 751 (1984)). Accordingly, prudential considerations furnish at least three general areas where plaintiffs may encounter pitfalls: third-party claims, generalized grievances, and claims outside a law's intended protection zone. Because the Constitution does not compel a court to apply a prudential limitation, the court may choose not to apply the limitation in a particular case.

a. Third-Party Claims

A plaintiff may not "rest his claim to relief on the legal rights or interests of third parties." *Warth v. Seldin*, 422 U.S. 490, 499 (1975). This prohibition ensures the self-determination of the third party, who may not want her rights or interests litigated. Parties are presumed best positioned to press their own interests. For that reason, limiting standing to those whose own interest is at stake enhances the quality of litigation, the concrete context of the suit, and the court's decisionmaking.

Example 5-12

Victoria is a social worker who works with death row inmates. Her pay rested in part on a determination by the prison warden that she was able to keep the inmates "free from violence" and "cooperative," thus ensuring the smooth functioning of the prison. Victoria was concerned about the practice by prison officials of "advertising" execution dates within the prison. Officials posted a sign visible to all death row prisoners, detailing the dates on which governors signed death warrants and the exhausted avenues for judicial relief for prisoners who had a date set for their execution. Victoria believed that this sign aggravated the prisoners, caused them emotional distress, and made it more likely that they would engage in violence or fail to cooperate with prison officials. She brought suit, challenging the officials' practice of advertising execution dates. Victoria maintained that the practice was barbaric, violating the Eighth Amendment prohibition against cruel and unusual punishment. Does Victoria have standing to assert this claim?

Explanation

Victoria arguably has Article III standing to assert the challenge because she has asserted an injury in fact caused by the prison officials and capable of redress by the court. Victoria's pay depends on her ability to keep prisoners cooperative and free from violence, and she seeks removal of a condition that makes it more difficult for her to succeed in this task.

Victoria is likely to encounter difficulty, however, in asserting the claim under the prudential prohibition against third-party claims. The legal right providing the basis of the claim — the Eighth Amendment protection against cruel and unusual punishment — belongs to the inmates, not to Victoria. To allow Victoria to assert the prisoners' rights may interfere with their own preferences and may require the court to guess at the impact of the practice on the inmates. Invoking the prudential limitation on asserting the claims of a third party, the court is likely to block Victoria.

The United States Supreme Court has relaxed prudential consideration against third-party claims in recent years. The Court has shown willingness to allow exceptions to the rule, particularly when the third party is likely to encounter an obstacle to asserting a claim on her own behalf and the plaintiff has a relationship with that third party. The Supreme Court has also recognized an exception in First Amendment cases where a plaintiff argues that a law is overbroad, infringing the First Amendment rights of others not before the court. Under this exception, a federal court may allow a plaintiff to argue that a law unconstitutionally infringes another's freedom of expression, even though any limitation the law imposes on the plaintiff's speech is constitutional. Motivating this exception is concern that an overbroad law may chill expression, causing those not before the court to silence or suppress protected speech.

Example 5-13

Assume that the state of Wyoming passed a law prohibiting the sale of books instructing home gardeners how to grow plants that yield controlled substances. A state wide retail chain, "How To" Books, Inc., brought suit, arguing that the law is unconstitutional. The book chain had two claims: (1) the legislation reduced its profitability by taking away a portion of its market, and (2) the legislation violated the First Amendment rights of its customers by prohibiting the communication of constitutionally protected information. Should the district court allow "How To" Books to proceed on both claims?

Explanation

"How To" Books, Inc. has Article III standing because the reduction in sales revenue is an injury in fact caused by the law, which the court can redress by granting damages. Although the First Amendment claim is a third-party claim, the court is unlikely to apply the prudential limitation against such claims here. The book chain has a relationship with its customers — even a mere contractual relationship will suffice under the case law. Moreover, a retailer such as "How To" Books, Inc. possesses expertise in the field and superior access to trade information; thus, the retailer is in a better position than customers to identify and to make available books that readers may enjoy. This superior position supports the retailer's role as a third-party claimant asserting customers' rights of information access. Finally, the special status shrouding the First Amendment's freedom of expression weighs heavily in favor of allowing third-party claims. *See Virginia v. Am. Booksellers Ass'n*, 484 U.S. 383 (1988) (allowing the exception for booksellers raising First Amendment claims of book buyers). The First Amendment context of this dispute makes this a particularly easy case for allowing third-party standing. Nonetheless, one should note that the law's special solicitude for First Amendment claims is not necessary for waiving the prohibition against third-party claims. Indeed, the Court has applied similar reasoning in the far less sympathetic context of a retailer selling beer to underage men. *Craig v. Boren*, 429 U.S. 190 (1976).

b. Generalized Grievances

The Supreme Court prohibits standing where a plaintiff asserts a general concern that is "shared in substantially equal measure by all or a large class of citizens." *Warth v. Seldin*, 422 U.S. 490, 499 (1975). This prohibition against asserting generalized grievances applies where the plaintiff is suing simply as a citizen upset that the government is flouting the law or as a taxpayer concerned that the government is expending funds illegally. The Supreme Court has applied this prohibition somewhat inconsistently over the years. On one hand, the Court has allowed plaintiffs to sue as taxpayers claiming that government funding violates the First Amendment's prohibition against establishment of religion (the "establishment clause"). On the other hand, the Court has suggested that the prohibition has rigorous constitutional dimensions, characterizing plaintiffs with generalized grievances as lacking Article III standing. In *Lujan v. Defenders of Wildlife*, 504 U.S. 555, 562-563 (1992), the Court treated as constitutionally mandated the bar to plaintiffs bringing a citizen suit raising general environmental concerns. *Lujan* may be an example of how the prudential concern against generalized grievances is sometimes difficult to distinguish from the Article III "injury in fact" requirement. At the very least, this development signals that courts will not be inclined to waive the prohibition against generalized grievances outside of the establishment clause context.

Example 5-14

Concerned law professor Laura Litigator learned that her township was providing subsidies to local religious schools. Incensed that her tax dollars were being used in this way, she filed suit challenging the practice. Does she have standing to bring the suit?

Explanation

Laura Litigator has standing. She is challenging the local government's expenditure of tax dollars to support a religious institution. This claim is supported by United States Supreme Court case law ruling that the establishment clause prevents the government from forcing citizens to subsidize religion. Because (and only because) this case law focuses on expending tax dollars to foster religion and makes that act illegal, Laura can trace a connection between her taxpayer status and the legal violation alleged. That connection gives her standing. Not all restrictions on government are associated with the government's ability to spend tax dollars. For example, if Laura Litigator brought a suit as a citizen concerned about police brutality toward others, she could not establish a connection between her status as a taxpayer and the legal substance of her allegation. The Court rigorously insists on a nexus between the government's expenditure power and the legal violation, and has even rejected standing for a plaintiff complaining about a government agency's insistence on keeping its budget secret.[4]

c. Zone of Interest

The final prudential rule requires plaintiffs to show that their asserted injuries implicate interests that are "arguably within the zone of interests" protected or regulated by the law they seek to enforce. Courts apply the requirement where the plaintiff seeks to enforce a statutory standard, frequently in the context of an administrative proceeding. Courts apply the test infrequently in constitutional litigation.[5]

Example 5-15

Congress passed a statute designed to regulate school bus safety. Claiming the purpose of ensuring child safety, the statute contained detailed provisions governing the credentials of those who operate school buses, the behavior of bus riders, and the boarding and disembarkation procedures for school buses. A group of school crossing guards sued the school district that employed them, challenging their long hours and other adverse working conditions. The crossing guards premised their suit on the school bus safety statute, arguing that the statute supported their claim. Their complaint asserted that better working conditions would make them more alert and able to protect the safety of children making their way to school. Do the crossing guards have standing?

Explanation

The crossing guards have Article III standing because they have an injury (allegedly poor working conditions) that is capable of court redress and caused by the defendant's work policies. The plaintiffs may encounter difficulty with the zone test, since the relevant statute regulates school buses, not crossing guards. They could avoid dismissal of their suit under this prudential concern if they can show that the statute was intended to protect their interests. They might make this showing by identifying

---

4. In *United States v. Richardson*, 418 U.S. 166 (1974), the Court denied the plaintiff taxpayer standing to challenge the secrecy of the CIA's budget. The plaintiff's challenge was based on a right to statement and accounting of public funds and thus did not rest on a right tied directly to the expenditure power — as is true for the establishment clause cases.
5. Laurence H. Tribe, 1 American Constitutional Law §3-19, at 446-447 (3d ed. 2000) (observing the test applies sporadically in constitutional litigation and is best conceived as part of third-party standing analysis in the administrative law setting).

congressional recognition of a connection between school bus safety and alert crossing guards. In this way, the crossing guards could establish that the statute sought to ensure that crossing guards were able to provide safety for school buses (as well as pedestrians) negotiating intersections near schools.

In several recent cases, the Supreme Court has avoided using the zone test with rigor, stating in one instance that where Congress authorizes citizen suits to enforce a statute, it means to make standing available to the extent permitted by Article III and to override the prudential, "zone of interest" limitation. *Bennett v. Spear*, 520 U.S. 154, 166 (1997). However, the Court has not abandoned the limitation altogether.

Example 5-16

The Postal Express Statute grants the United States Postal Service a mail–carrying monopoly. A provision in the statute allows the postal service to make exceptions to this monopoly if the public interest requires it. The postal service relied on this exception in creating a regulation allowing private mail carriers to handle urgent mail to foreign countries. Alleging that this regulation reduced postal worker jobs, the postal workers' union challenged the regulation, arguing that it was not authorized by the statute. Do the postal workers have standing?

Explanation

Plaintiffs have Article III standing because they have alleged a tangible injury — reducing postal jobs — caused by the defendant's passage of the regulation. If the court agreed that the regulation is invalid, redress would result: more postal workers would be needed for international mail in the future, and previously displaced workers might receive damages. Nevertheless, in the inspiration for this example, *Air Courier Conference of America v. American Postal Workers Union*, 498 U.S. 517 (1991), the Supreme Court held that the plaintiffs failed the "zone of interest" test. According to the Court, Congress intended the Postal Express Act to ensure that public needs were satisfied and that the postal service had adequate revenue to function at a level necessary to serve those needs. The act was not intended to ensure postal worker employment. The plaintiffs are therefore not within the act's intended zone of regulation.

CHAPTER 6

Congressional Control over Jurisdiction

Questions about federal court power should always begin with the constitutional text. In clashes with Congress over court power, federal courts get a helpful opening salvo from Article III. Suggesting no room for negotiation, Article III, §1 says that the "judicial Power . . shall be vested" in federal courts (as opposed to Congress, the president, the states, or nowhere at all). Section 2 of Article III continues the power granting, listing nine specific classes of cases over which federal courts enjoy adjudicatory power. No apparent wiggle room exists here either.

Despite these unqualified power grants to federal courts, Congress has three major sources of constitutional authority over the Supreme Court and other federal courts. Article III, §2, cl. 3 specifies that the appellate jurisdiction of the Supreme Court shall be subject to congressionally created "exceptions" and "regulations." As for the lower courts, Congress enjoys extra latitude: Article III, §1 allows Congress to vest federal judicial power in "one supreme Court, and in such inferior Courts as the Congress may from time to time ordain and establish." Finally, Article I, §8, cl. 9 empowers Congress "to constitute Tribunals inferior to the supreme Court."

Relevant constitutional provisions thus send a mixed message about which branch wields superior power: Congress or the courts. Indeed, if any area of federal court jurisprudence epitomizes the potential for power struggles, this is the one. Throughout history, Congress has taken license to assert itself into controversial topics already adjudicated in federal courts. Congress has, for example, asserted power under the "exceptions and regulations" clause to strip the Supreme Court of appellate jurisdiction over specific subjects. Relying on its authority to create lower federal courts, Congress has also denied the lower courts power to hear specific subject matters. In response, the Court has developed doctrines, outlined here, in an effort to push back: maintaining a delicate balance with Congress by delineating the Court's own ability to control court activities. The doctrines divide into four areas of congressional power: (1) ability to limit Supreme Court jurisdiction; (2) ability to limit lower federal court jurisdiction; (3) ability to control the manner, substance, and result of federal court decisionmaking; and (4) ability to create courts that do not match the description in Article III. While conveniently dividing into these four categories, the doctrines are shrouded in debate.

A. CONGRESSIONAL POWER TO LIMIT SUPREME COURT JURISDICTION

1. The Debate's Parameters

In the power struggle between Congress and federal courts, one finds guidance initially by identifying what is nonnegotiable: Congress cannot touch the Supreme Court's original jurisdiction. A court's original jurisdiction is its power to adjudicate cases filed in that court first, without an earlier court adjudicating the controversy. For the Supreme Court, Article III of the United States Constitution specifies that jurisdiction includes "all Cases affecting Ambassadors, other public Ministers and Consuls, and those in which a State shall be a Party."

Marbury v. Madison, 5 U.S. (1 Cranch) 137 (1803), established that Congress may not *add to* the Court's original jurisdiction. Throughout history, all have assumed that the complementary notion also holds: Congress may not *detract from* the Supreme Court's original jurisdiction. These principles do not keep Congress from requiring the Supreme Court to share its power: Congress may give lower federal courts and state courts concurrent power over matters within the Supreme Court's original jurisdiction. Congress, however, must limit direct regulation of the Supreme Court's original jurisdiction to procedural matters that do not interfere with the Court's jurisdictional power. The Supreme Court has repeatedly said that Congress may not restrict the Court's original jurisdiction granted in Article III. *See, e.g, South Carolina v. Regan*, 465 U.S. 367, 386 (1984) (O'Connor, J., concurring) (reviewing case law and other authorities on Congress's power to control the Supreme Court's original jurisdiction).

Although original jurisdiction issues spawn little debate, complications arise in questions over Congress's power to limit the Supreme Court's *appellate* jurisdiction.[1] The complications derive initially from ambiguities in the following passage in Article III, §2: "the supreme Court shall have appellate Jurisdiction, both as to Law and Fact, with such Exceptions, and under such Regulations as the Congress shall make." Many have debated how to read this language, which is known as the "exceptions clause."

On one end of the spectrum are those who interpret the exceptions clause narrowly, by reading "with such Exceptions, and under such Regulations as the Congress shall make" as modifying *only* the word "Fact." This reading holds that Congress can limit only the Supreme Court's review of facts. At the opposite end of the spectrum are those who read the clause as allowing Congress to axe out whole categories of legal subject areas. History, scholarship, and case law overwhelmingly accept congressional controls that fall within the narrow reading of the exceptions clause. Discomfort arises, however, over extending the clause further, particularly if Congress attempts to take away lower federal review of an Article III subject area. This discomfort arises from recognition that Article III, §1 provides that federal judicial power *shall* extend to nine classes of cases. If a particular subject area is encompassed within one of those nine classes, the argument goes, then at least some federal court should have power to adjudicate it. Otherwise, government fails to fulfill the constitutional mandate providing for federal court power over the listed subject.

Although not universally accepted, one argument holds that Congress is on particularly shaky ground in seeking to exempt from federal court power three of the nine categories of cases described in Article III. For those three categories, the framers wrote that the federal judicial power "shall" extend to "all" cases in that category. The three categories are (1) "all Cases, in Law and Equity, arising under this Constitution, the Laws of the United States, and Treaties made, or which shall be made, under their Authority"; (2) "all Cases affecting Ambassadors, other public Ministers and Consuls"; and (3) "all Cases of admiralty and maritime Jurisdiction." U.S. CONST. art. III, §2. If Congress takes away federal judicial power in these categories, the argument goes, then federal judicial power cannot extend to "all" cases.

Example 6-1

Congress passed a statute providing: "The United States Supreme Court must give substantial deference to state court rulings on the guilt and

---

1. Controversy also extends to Congress's ability to *restrict* (rather than *expand*) appellate jurisdiction. While little direct law on the topic exists, courts and scholars presume that, just as Congress may not expand the Supreme Court's original jurisdiction beyond the limits of Article III, Congress also may not expand the Court's appellate power beyond those limits. *See, e.g., Nat'l Mut. Ins. Co. v. Tidewater Transfer Co.,* 337 U.S. 582 (1949) (in different opinions, six justices agreed that Congress may not enlarge the jurisdiction of federal courts beyond what Article III enumerates).

innocence of criminal defendants. The Supreme Court may not provide relief to a criminal defendant filing a direct appeal from a state court decision unless the state court's decision is based on an unreasonable evaluation of evidence presented in the state court proceeding." Does this statute fall within Congress's power under the Article III exceptions clause?

Explanation

Few, if anyone, would argue that this statute is unconstitutional. By focusing on "evidence" and the determination of "guilt" and "innocence," Congress is making a *regulation* of Supreme Court review of factual decisions and an *exception* to appellate review in criminal cases. If the exceptions clause has any scope at all, that scope includes a prohibition such as this. Significant historical material suggests that the framers were concerned about intrusive appellate review of factual findings and left to Congress the specifics of how and whether to restrict the Supreme Court's authority to relitigate established facts.[2]

Example 6-2

Congress passed a statute stating, "The Supreme Court of the United States shall not exercise appellate jurisdiction over any case that would require the Court to adjudicate any claim based upon equal protection of the laws to the extent that such claim is based on the right to marry without regard to sexual orientation." Does this statute fall within Congress's power under the exceptions clause?

Explanation

Controversy surrounds this question. Those espousing a broad reading of the exceptions clause would uphold the statute because it is an "exception" to the Supreme Court's appellate jurisdiction. To embrace this view, one must read the words "with such Exceptions . . . as the Congress shall make" in Article III as modifying the phrase "the Supreme Court shall have appellate jurisdiction."

Those favoring a narrower reading of the clause would cast a dim view on the statute, since it eliminates from Supreme Court power cases that fall within one of the subject categories Article III grants to federal courts.[3]

---

2. *See, e.g.,* William W. Van Alstyne, *A Critical Guide to* Ex Parte McCardle, 15 ARIZ. L. REV. 228, 260-261 (1973) (explaining that "some (perhaps most)" framers intended the clause as a "safeguard [of] the right to trial by jury insofar as article III itself would authorize de novo redeterminations of fact").

3. Because the Supreme Court's original jurisdiction is limited to matters concerning ambassadors, public ministers, and counsels, and, those in which a state is a party, the Court would

Indeed, cases claiming equal protection of the laws are "Cases, in Law and Equity, arising under this Constitution," as described in Article III, §2. According to this view, Article III envisions that federal court power to hear these cases must be enjoyed to its fullest, particularly since its language grants federal courts authority to hear "all" such cases. This constitutional vision, the argument goes, prevents Congress from creating exceptions beyond such matters as relitigation of facts, procedure, or judicial administration. Finally, a constitutional attack on the statute would be even stronger if the statute prohibited adjudication of the same-sex marriage/equal protection claims in all federal courts, including lower courts. If that were the case, no federal judicial power would be extended to this slice of "arising under" jurisdiction — a result in conflict with the framers' declaration that federal courts should hear "all" cases arising under the Constitution.

History and case law further help resolve this example. Both are surveyed below.

2. History

Appropriate methods for interpreting constitutional language is a matter of great debate. Even the most cautious approach usually advocates evaluating actions taken at the time the states ratified the Constitution and seeing how those actions illuminate the intended meaning of constitutional language. From this viewpoint, actions by Congress to regulate federal court jurisdiction immediately after Article III became law may reveal the exceptions clause's intended meaning.

Soon after the states ratified the Constitution, Congress passed the Judiciary Act of 1789. Under that act, the Supreme Court could review only decisions of a state's highest court that rejected a federal constitutional claim. The act did not give the Court power to review rulings embracing a federal constitutional claim. Of course, these later rulings do "arise under" the Constitution and thus fall within Article III's power grant. Accordingly, the Judiciary Act did not give the Supreme Court all of the judicial power listed in Article III. Nor did the act give lower federal courts the power to hear cases where a state court embraced a federal constitutional claim. In fact, the Judiciary Act did not give lower federal courts general power over cases arising under federal law. By negative inference, then, one might say that Congress "excepted" from all federal court jurisdiction — including the Supreme Court's appellate jurisdiction — cases arising under federal law where the state courts had endorsed a claim of right under the United States Constitution. One can argue, therefore, that those in Congress who enacted

---

not have original jurisdiction over cases falling within the statute. Thus, removing appellate jurisdiction means removing all Supreme Court jurisdiction over this subject area.

the Judiciary Act of 1789 assumed that they could constitutionally exclude whole categories of cases from the Supreme Court's appellate jurisdiction, even if Article III granted federal courts power over those categories.

Those advocating a broad reading of the exceptions clause might argue that the Congress that enacted the Judiciary Act of 1789 reflected the prevailing understanding of the clause's meaning during the period contemporaneous with the clause's ratification. In fact, proponents might even argue that since many in the 1789 Congress participated in the drafting and ratification of the clause, their actions reflect a personal understanding of the clause's meaning (presumably shared by other architects of the constitutional plan).

Whatever persuasive appeal this argument might hold, the argument has not been tested in the United States Supreme Court. The Supreme Court has never ruled on the constitutionality of the portion of the 1789 Judiciary Act that excludes cases upholding a federal right from its appellate jurisdiction. Moreover, Congress has entertained many proposals to limit Supreme Court jurisdiction, including several in the last twenty years. On occasion, Congress has enacted the proposals and court challenges followed. As outlined below, however, the Supreme Court disposed of the challenges without embracing or rejecting historical evidence based on the Judiciary Act of 1789.

Example 6-3

The state of Nevada passed a statute making it illegal for school teachers to promote charities to their students. A group of teachers challenged the law on First Amendment grounds and the Nevada Supreme Court accepted their argument, invalidating the statute. The state of Nevada wished to bring this ruling to the United States Supreme Court for review. Assume that Congress has recently excluded cases of this kind from the United States Supreme Court's appellate jurisdiction. May Congress constitutionally do so?

Explanation

This is the type of case that the Judiciary Act of 1789 excluded from the Supreme Court's appellate jurisdiction — one in which the state court upheld the federal constitutional claim. Yet the case clearly arises under federal law, since the whole reason for the lawsuit is the plaintiffs' claim that the state law violates a federal constitutional provision. Since the Judiciary Act originally excluded this claim from Supreme Court power, one may argue that the Congress that enacted the act presumed that the exceptions clause allowed it to do so. A contemporary statute excluding claims of this type from Supreme Court appellate jurisdiction would be constitutional under this view.

3. Case Law

United States Supreme Court case law on the meaning of the exceptions clause is inconclusive. The leading case is Ex parte McCardle, 74 U.S. (7 Wall.) 506 (1869). To understand McCardle's limitations, one must consider its factual and historical backdrop.

McCardle was a newspaper publisher arrested for articles he published at the end of the Civil War. While awaiting trial before a military commission, McCardle filed a habeas corpus petition in a federal circuit court. The circuit court denied relief, and McCardle then sought review in the United States Supreme Court pursuant to an act dated February 5, 1867, authorizing the habeas corpus remedy. After the Supreme Court argument, Congress amended the February 5 act, adding a specification that the act did not allow appeals to the Supreme Court from a federal circuit court and repealing any previous exercise of such jurisdiction. Citing this repeal, the Supreme Court dismissed the case.

In dismissing McCardle's case, the Court stated that it should exercise only the appellate jurisdiction that Congress has conveyed and thus that it lacked any option but to dismiss the case because Congress had not conferred jurisdiction. Importantly, the Court added that when Congress grants the Court appellate jurisdiction in some cases, the omission of others "impl[ies] a negation" of jurisdiction over those omitted. 74 U.S. (7 Wall.) at 513. In this instance, the Court reasoned, Congress was even more direct, making a specific exception for cases such as McCardle's.

On its face, McCardle appears to establish precedent for the historical argument outlined previously: Congress possesses power under the exceptions clause to withhold appellate jurisdiction over categories of cases falling within the general scope of federal judicial power. Certainly McCardle's broad language supports this view.

One might limit McCardle's precedential value by characterizing the decision as a creature of the politically charged post–Civil War atmosphere — a context with little analogy to other times in our nation's history or to other cases that might arise. While noteworthy, arguments of this type are of limited use in understanding federal courts doctrine. Indeed, many federal court precedents are creatures of unusual historical context. Such is the nature of power struggles — which are the bread and butter of federal courts doctrine.

But there's a doctrinal wrinkle in McCardle as well. Statutes in place at the time provided another vehicle for Supreme Court appellate jurisdiction. In other words, the February 5 act had eliminated only one of two possible routes to the Supreme Court. After Congress repealed the February 5 act, McCardle could have filed a writ of habeas corpus in the Supreme Court under another jurisdictional statute. Thus, one could argue that McCardle simply allowed Congress to limit the routes to appellate review and did not eliminate appellate review altogether. From this perspective, *McCardle* does not authorize Congress to remove completely from appellate jurisdiction a category of cases from the Article III, §2 list.

The Court's subsequent decision in *Ex parte Yerger*, 75 U.S. (8 Wall.) 85 (1869), supports this restrictive reading of *McCardle*. Indeed, the *Ex parte Yerger* Court exercised habeas corpus review, relying on precisely the alternative jurisdictional avenue left in place after the repeal of the February 5 act at issue in *McCardle*.

Encountering a circumstance similar to *Ex parte Yerger* over a hundred years later, the Supreme Court affirmed that decision's approach. In *Felker v. Turpin*, 518 U.S. 651 (1996), Congress had barred the Supreme Court from reviewing court of appeals decisions on whether habeas corpus applicants may file second or successive petitions. In evaluating this attempt to eliminate a portion of the Supreme Court's power, the *Felker* Court concluded that the statute did not deprive the Supreme Court of appellate jurisdiction under Article III. In so ruling, the Supreme Court thus avoided the constitutional question of whether Congress could eliminate all Supreme Court power over habeas corpus.

Finding a portion of its habeas corpus power remaining, the *Felker* Court made a subtle distinction: it treated a habeas corpus petition filed *originally* in the Supreme Court as a matter falling into the Court's *appellate* jurisdiction. Recognizing that this power remained despite Congress's reduction of the Court's habeas corpus powers, the *Felker* Court relied on *Ex parte Yerger*'s admonition against finding an implicit repeal of Supreme Court jurisdictional power. Applying that admonition, the *Felker* Court declined the invitation to find that Congress had attempted to repeal its power to review all habeas corpus matters.

Felker does not answer the constitutional question of whether Congress may eliminate all jurisdiction over specific kinds of cases within the scope of Article III, §2. The case does, however, make clear that the Court will not easily find that Congress has in fact tried to eliminate all of its jurisdiction over a particular kind of case.

Example 6-4

Jane was convicted of aggravated assault and sentenced to life in prison. After she appealed her conviction, the United States Supreme Court denied her request for a writ of certiorari. She then pursued her post-conviction remedies in state court and filed a petition for a writ of habeas corpus in federal court. The federal court denied relief. Later, Jane filed a request to file a second federal habeas petition. In so doing, she complied with the Stop Writ Abuse Act, which required that she request permission from a United States court of appeals to file the second petition. The court of appeals denied this request, and she wishes to ask the United States Supreme Court to review that decision. However, the Stop Writ Abuse Act further provides that court of appeals decisions rendered as part of the act's gatekeeping "shall not be appealable and shall not be the subject of a petition . . . for writ of certiorari in the United States Supreme Court." Jane is considering whether to argue that this provision unconstitutionally divests the United States Supreme Court of jurisdiction over cases that may arise under federal law. Is she likely to succeed with this constitutional challenge?

Explanation

No, Jane is not likely to succeed with her constitutional challenge because the Stop Writ Abuse Act does not eliminate all Supreme Court power over habeas petitions. Researching the current state of Supreme Court jurisdiction over habeas petitions filed by state prisoners, one would discover that the Court possesses power to entertain habeas corpus petitions filed as original matters by state prisoners.[4] Thus, when Congress eliminated the Supreme Court's power to review court of appeals decisions on habeas corpus petitions, it did not seal off all avenues for Supreme Court habeas review of state prisoners' federal claims. Thus, as was the case with the nearly identical statute in *Felker v. Turpin*, the Stop Writ Abuse Act does not deprive the Court of the power to hear habeas petitions filed as original matters. Applying the presumptions against implied repeal announced in *Ex parte Yerger* and applied in *Felker*, the Supreme Court would decline to read the gatekeeping feature of the Stop Writ Abuse Act to deprive the Court of all power over habeas matters.

B. CONGRESSIONAL POWER TO LIMIT LOWER COURT JURISDICTION

As with Supreme Court jurisdiction, the history and case law concerning congressional power over lower federal court jurisdiction is inconclusive. Yet — as with the Supreme Court jurisdiction materials, some threshold principles are firmly established. First, the debate over Congress's power centers on its prerogative to limit lower federal court jurisdiction rather than to *expand* it. Few would suggest that Congress may expand the jurisdiction of lower courts beyond that authorized in Article III.[5] Second, all would likely agree that the Constitution's grant to Congress of discretion on whether to

---

4. 28 U.S.C. §2241(a) provides, "Writs of habeas corpus may be granted by the Supreme Court, any justice thereof, the district courts and any circuit judge within their respective jurisdictions."

5. At least one Supreme Court decision confirms the proposition that Congress may not expand the jurisdiction of lower courts beyond those categories listed in the Constitution. *See, e.g., Nat'l Mut. Insurance Co. v. Tidewater Transfer Co.*, 337 U.S. 582 (1949) (in different

create *any* lower federal courts informs the extent to which Congress may limit the jurisdiction of those courts that it does choose to create. Third, whatever the scope of its prerogative to control lower federal court power, Congress must be mindful not only of Article III's limitations, but also of constitutional restrictions outside of Article III, such as due process and separation of powers concerns. These restrictions, reviewed below, are important harnesses on congressional power over lower courts. First, however, this section defines the term "lower federal court" within the meaning of Article III and then summarizes case law grappling with how much latitude Congress enjoys within the structure of Article III to limit lower court power.

1. What Is a Lower Federal Court?

Article III, §1 vests the "judicial Power of the United States" in the Supreme Court and "in such inferior Courts as the Congress may from time to time ordain and establish."[6] Article III, §1 further provides that those who staff these courts shall hold their jobs "during good Behaviour" and will receive compensation that will not be diminished "during their Continuance in Office." Thus, the framers envisioned that when Congress created "inferior courts" pursuant to Article III, it would also ensure that the judges who staffed the courts would enjoy life tenure and protection from salary diminution, both important protections of judicial independence. Those familiar with territorial courts, federal bankruptcy courts, federal magistrate courts, and similar bodies know that Congress has also created courts with judges who do not enjoy these protections. Because judges of these tribunals lack Article III's protections, the tribunals are deemed "legislative courts," "Article I courts," or "non–Article III courts," to distinguish their treatment from Article III courts.

Example 6-5

Assume that Congress created a court with powers limited to "deciding cases relating to federal taxation." Assume further that Congress provided that the

---

opinions, six justices agreed that Congress may not enlarge the jurisdiction of federal courts beyond what Article III specifies). The Supreme Court has, however, upheld Congress's grant of nonjudicial, specialized powers to lower federal courts in certain areas. *See Mistretta v. United States*, 488 U.S. 361 (1989) (federal judges can engage in rulemaking on the United States Sentencing Commission); *Glidden Co. v. Zdanok*, 370 U.S. 530 (1962) (identifying the Court of Claims and Court of Customs Appeals as Article III courts, even though they perform administrative tasks); *O'Donoghue v. United States*, 289 U.S. 516 (1933) (upholding federal court power to review public utility rates).

6. For a discussion of the relationship between this Article III power and Congress's Article I power to create inferior tribunals, *see* the discussion of non–Article III courts at the end of this chapter.

judges on these courts have a fixed term of fifteen years, subject to renewal at the discretion of Congress. Once the tax court has adjudicated matters, litigants may appeal the decision up through the federal court system, starting with a United States district court, and ultimately can petition the United States Supreme Court for a writ of certiorari. What is the status of these tax courts under Article III?

Explanation

The tribunal that Congress has created has three important characteristics of an Article III court. First, the tribunal performs court-like functions only: it adjudicates cases and does not render advisory opinions or promulgate rules of general application. Second, the tribunal is presumably an "inferior court" within the meaning of Article III because Congress has provided for possible review in the United States Supreme Court. In addition, the tax court exercises power within one of the subject areas listed in Article III, §2: its cases arise under federal law.

But the tax court does not merit the Article III label because its judges do not enjoy life tenure or protection from salary diminution. This deficiency does not mean that the tax courts Congress has created in this example are unconstitutional. Rather, the courts are analyzed as non–Article III courts, created pursuant to other powers of Congress, specifically the Article I power to lay and collect taxes. U.S. Const. art. 1, §8, cl. 1.

The prevailing analysis for evaluating the constitutionality of non–Article III courts appears at the end of this chapter.[7] By contrast, the material immediately following concerns Congress's power to control the workload, process, and output of classic Article III courts: the district courts, the courts of appeals, and the United States Supreme Court. Although, technically speaking, one might call non–Article III courts "lower federal courts," the following material confines that term to Article III district courts and courts of appeals.

2. Congress's Latitude Under Article III

Having identified the characteristics of an inferior Article III tribunal, we next consider how much latitude Article III allows Congress in controlling those tribunals. Must Congress create any inferior Article III tribunals at all?

---

7. The actual United States Tax Court is indeed a non–Article III court. The current thinking is that the Tax Court does, however, meet the constitutional requirements for non–Article III courts. *See, e.g.*, Diane L. Fahey, *The Tax Court's Jurisdiction over Due Process Collection Appeals: Is It Constitutional?*, 55 BAYLOR L. REV. 453 (2003); Deborah A. Geier, *The Tax Court, Article III, and the Proposal Advanced by the Federal Courts Study Committee: A Study of Applied Constitutional Theory*, 76 CORNELL L. REV. 985 (1991).

How many of the judicial powers listed in Article III, §2 must Congress grant to these courts? These questions are particularly important to congressional initiatives to remove controversial constitutional issues, such as abortion and school desegregation, from lower court jurisdiction.

Some controversy surrounds whether Article III's authorization to Congress to create lower federal courts includes discretion to refrain from exercising that power. In an early decision, Justice Story argued that Congress could not refuse to exercise the power to create lower federal courts. Speaking for the Court in *Martin v. Hunter's Lessee*, 14 U.S. (1 Wheat.) 304, 328 (1816), Justice Story observed that Article III's language "is manifestly designed to be mandatory upon the legislature." This language states that the federal judicial power "shall extend to" a list of cases or controversies listed in Article III, §2. Justice Story reasoned that this mandatory language imposed on Congress the "duty to vest the whole judicial power" listed in Article III. *Id.* at 330. In his view, this duty "bound Congress to create some inferior courts." *Id.* at 331. Some commentators agree with the logic of Justice Story's arguments.[8] Others, however, find it inconsistent with the framers' debates — which accepted the possibility that Congress may never create lower federal courts. Language in subsequent Supreme Court decisions discredits Story's approach, rejecting the conclusion that Congress was obligated to create lower federal courts. *See, e.g., Lockerty v. Phillips*, 319 U.S. 182, 187 (1943) (observing that Congress "could have declined to create" lower federal courts).

In addition to the discretion to create *no* lower federal courts, Congress enjoys the prerogative of allowing lower federal courts to hear only some of the cases and controversies listed in Article III. Endorsing this principle in *Sheldon v. Sill*, 49 U.S. (8 How.) 441 (1850), the Supreme Court reasoned that the *greater* power to create lower courts includes the *lesser* power to control what the courts do. As explained in *Sheldon v. Sill*, "Congress, having the power to establish the [lower] courts, . . . may withhold from any court of its creation jurisdiction of any of the enumerated controversies" *Id.* at 448-449. Congress has consistently used the discretion recognized in *Sheldon v. Sill*, withholding some of the Article III powers from lower courts. Indeed, while the first Congress immediately exercised its discretion to create inferior tribunals in the Judiciary Act of 1789, the inferior tribunals that it created lacked many of the powers listed in Article III, §2. Most significantly, the original inferior tribunals did not even possess general federal question jurisdiction.

The Supreme Court has followed the *Sheldon v. Sill* rule in a variety of contexts. Yet debate still rages about how far Congress's discretion truly

---

8. For an example of a lower federal court decision following this position when state courts were also unavailable, *see Eisentrager v. Forrestal*, 174 F.2d 961 (D.C. Cir. 1949), *rev'd, Johnson v. Eisentrager*, 339 U.S. 763 (D.C. Cir. 1949).

extends. None of the cases squarely answers the most controversial question: whether Congress may exclude specific *constitutional* subject areas from lower federal court power. For example, *Sheldon v. Sill* itself concerned whether Congress could take away from lower courts diversity of citizenship jurisdiction where the parties created diversity jurisdiction in the case by assignment of a debt. Another decision in which the Court applied the *Sheldon v. Sill* principle was a diversity action as well.[9] At least three other cases appear outside of the diversity context, dealing with labor law and a federal statute regulating price controls.[10] In the two cases concerning federal price controls,[11] Congress had specified that at least one inferior federal tribunal could still hear the disputes, a fact significant to the Court's ruling that Congress could eliminate power from other lower federal courts. In the third case, *Lauf v. E.G. Shinner & Co.*, 303 U.S. 323 (1938), Congress's restriction focused on preventing lower federal courts from issuing injunctions of certain labor activities. Commentators debate *Lauf's* scope: some say the case allowed Congress to deprive all inferior courts of jurisdiction over certain constitutional claims, and others say that the case should be read as adjudicating only Congress's prerogative to restrict the federal courts' ability to issue a particular remedy.[12] As discussed below, the Constitution allows Congress some discretion to take away remedial powers of lower courts, but that is different from limits on Congress's ability to take away all lower court power over a particular subject area.

Example 6-6

Congress passed a statute stating, "Federal courts of the United States that are inferior to the Supreme Court of United States shall not adjudicate any claim challenging the constitutionality of state or federal laws regulating abortion." Is this statute constitutional under Article III?

---

9. *Kline v. Burke Constr. Co.*, 260 U.S. 226 (1922).

10. *Yakus v. United States*, 321 U.S. 414 (1944) (Emergency Price Control Act); *Lockerty v. Phillips*, 319 U.S. 182 (1943) (Emergency Price Control Act); *Lauf v. E.G. Shinner & Co.*, 303 U.S. 323 (1938) (Norris–La Guardia Act).

11. *Yakus v. United States*, 321 U.S. 414 (1944); *Lockerty v. Phillips*, 319 U.S. 182 (1943).

12. *See, e.g.*, Erwin Chemerinsky, Federal Jurisdiction 196 (4th ed. 2003) (observing that the decision could be limited to whether the federal courts can award a particular remedy); Henry M. Hart, *The Power of Congress to Limit the Jurisdiction of Federal Courts: An Exercise in Dialectic*, 66 Harv. L. Rev. 1362, 1363-1364 (1953) (arguing that *Lauf* establishes that Congress can deny federal courts jurisdiction in a class of constitutional cases so long as state courts are available); Gordon G. Young, *A Critical Reassessment of the Case Law Bearing on Congress's Power to Restrict the Jurisdiction of the Lower Federal Courts*, 54 Md. L. Rev. 132, 165-182 (1995) (debating possible readings of *Lauf*).

Explanation

The Supreme Court is clearly disposed to uphold congressional restrictions on lower federal court jurisdiction. The case law record as well as the broad language of *Sheldon v. Sill* and other Supreme Court cases suggest that this statute is consistent with Article III. Indeed, *Sheldon v. Sill* even suggested that Congress may properly use its Article III discretion in controversial contexts: " 'The political truth is, that the disposal of the judicial power (except in a few specified instances) belongs to Congress: and Congress is not bound to enlarge the jurisdiction of the Federal courts to every subject, in every form which the Constitution might warrant.' " 49 U.S. at 449 (quoting *Turner v. Bank of North America*, 4 U.S. (4 Dall.) 8 (1799)).

Yet one can distinguish each of the Supreme Court cases applying *Sheldon v. Sill* from the statute here, which removes an entire category of federal constitutional rights from lower court power. Given Article III's vision that lower federal courts might exist in order to enforce the guarantees of the United States Constitution, this statute clashes with the spirit, if not the letter, of Article III. One can also read into the statute an intent to reduce the effectiveness of a line of Supreme Court cases, starting with *Roe v. Wade*, 410 U.S. 113 (1973). In so doing, Congress is threatening an important constitutional power implicit in Article III — the power of judicial review recognized in *Marbury v. Madison*, 5 U.S. (1 Cranch) 137 (1803).

Example 6-7

Congress passed a statute stating, "No federal courts of the United States shall adjudicate any claim challenging the constitutionality of state or federal laws regulating abortion." Is this statute constitutional under Article III?

Explanation

How does this statute differ from the statute in Example 6-6? The statute here precludes *all* federal courts — the Supreme Court and inferior tribunals — from adjudicating challenges to abortion laws. Analysis of the statute's constitutionality must consider case law concerning attempts to strip lower federal court jurisdiction as well as case law concerning attempts to strip the Supreme Court's jurisdiction. This example therefore provides an opportunity to synthesize these two strands of cases.

Focusing only on cases that fall into the Supreme Court's original jurisdiction, the analysis is uncomplicated: to the extent that the statute takes away power to adjudicate matters within the Supreme Court's original jurisdiction, the statute is unconstitutional. The Supreme Court has repeatedly said that Congress cannot restrict the Court's original jurisdiction. The statute here is likely to have little or no practical effect on the Supreme

Court's exercise of original power, since few cases challenging the constitutionality of an abortion restriction are likely to fall within the Court's original jurisdiction, and present-day litigants rarely seek to invoke the Supreme Court's original jurisdiction in any type of case. Nevertheless, original jurisdiction does extend to matters in which a state is a party, and one can certainly imagine an instance where a state clashes with another litigant over the validity of the state's abortion regulation.[13]

Although the statute has at least one unconstitutional application, this does not doom the statute for all purposes. One can easily imagine that a court adjudicating the statute's constitutionality might strain its construction a bit, refusing to read the statute as excluding the Supreme Court's original jurisdiction over abortion cases. Consistent with the presumption against jurisdictional preclusion, as well as the principle that courts may sever unconstitutional provisions from an otherwise constitutional statute, this approach would avoid attributing to Congress a clearly unconstitutional intent. According to this analysis, the statute precludes only lower court jurisdiction and Supreme Court appellate jurisdiction.

If the statute's scope is limited to lower court and Supreme Court appellate jurisdiction, its constitutional fate is uncertain. From one perspective, one might argue that the statute is clearly constitutional under Article III: Congress possesses power both to limit the Supreme Court's appellate jurisdiction under Article III's exceptions clause and to restrict lower federal court jurisdiction pursuant to its Article III discretion to decide whether to create lower federal courts at all. From a competing perspective, the statute is problematic under Article III because it eliminates a slice of "arising under" jurisdiction from federal judicial power: cases concerning abortion rights. According to this line of argument, the statute undercuts the promise of Article III, §2 that the federal judicial power shall extend to "all Cases . . . arising under this Constitution." Moreover, the argument continues, Congress clearly meant to strip federal jurisdiction here out of hostility to federal court case law extending protection for abortion rights. Such an intent could unconstitutionally impair the judicial review power implicit in Article III. Indeed, the consequence of the jurisdictional stripping is to take abortion cases out of the federal courts and put them in state courts. Existing Supreme Court precedent will remain frozen, with no opportunity for further clarification or modification in light of changes in society and legal understanding. As explained by state Supreme Court judges in response to another jurisdictional stripping provision, "[w]ithout the unifying

---

13. The question of whether the Supreme Court can actually exercise original jurisdiction over all cases in which states are parties (without regard to sovereign immunity or other principles) is subject to some debate. ROBERT L. STERN, EUGENE GRESSMAN, STEPHEN M. SHAPIRO & KENNETH S. GELLER, SUPREME COURT PRACTICE 559-562 (8th ed. 2002). For the purposes of Example 6-7, one conclusion is certain: the statute is unconstitutional to the extent that it took away the Supreme Court's power over cases that unquestionably fall within the Court's original jurisdiction.

function of . . . [federal court] review, there inevitably will be divergence in state court decisions, and thus the United States Constitution could mean something different in each of the fifty states." Statement of Conference of State Chief Justices, 128 CONG. REC. 689 (1982).

As general Article III interpretations, these competing perspectives appear to cancel each other out. More specific analysis, based on individual cases construing Article III, provides similarly conflicting guidance. On one side is *Felker v. Turpin*, 518 U.S. 651 (1996), which suggests that the possibility that the Supreme Court could still exercise original jurisdiction over some abortion challenges is a factor militating in favor of the statute's constitutionality. *Felker* upheld restrictions on Supreme Court jurisdiction because the restrictions left undisturbed an alternative avenue for Supreme Court review. The *Felker* Court identified the remaining access to Supreme Court review as *appellate* jurisdiction rather than *original* jurisdiction, which would be the case for this example.[14] Nonetheless, the Court suggested that any opportunity for Supreme Court review, even if highly remote, renders a restriction on Supreme Court jurisdiction constitutional.[15]

One could also argue that the cases interpreting lower court restrictions authorize Congress to implement jurisdictional obstacles for lower courts, such as the abortion restriction here. Language in decisions such as *Sheldon v. Sill*, 49 U.S. (8 How.) 441 (1850), supports such broad-ranging restrictions — even in a circumstance where Supreme Court power is restricted as well. On the other side, one could argue that each of the decisions upholding restrictions on lower court jurisdiction avoided the particular question presented in this example: whether Congress can take away the power of lower federal courts to hear a particular category of constitutional question.

At bottom, the Supreme Court case law does not give a definite answer on whether the statute is constitutional under Article III. But the important words here are "under Article III." Other parts of the Constitution — examined next — may provide external restraints on Congress's ability to pass statutes of this kind.

3. Due Process Limitations

Outside of Article III, a significant constitutional limit on Congress's ability to strip lower federal court power appears in the Fifth Amendment due process clause. Due process is relevant to the issue because it embodies

---

14. Note, however, that *Felker* made a subtle distinction: the Court treated a habeas corpus petition filed *originally* in the Supreme Court as a matter falling within the Court's *appellate* jurisdiction.

15. ERWIN CHEMERINSKY, FEDERAL JURISDICTION 182-183 (4th ed. 2003) (stating that "*Felker* seems to stand for the proposition that any continuing basis for Supreme Court review, no matter how unlikely, is sufficient to make a restriction on jurisdiction constitutional").

the core notion that liberty requires litigants to have some access to court to defend their constitutional rights. (The Fifth Amendment provides the due process protections because the federal government, not the states, is the entity implementing the restriction.)

As with other issues pertaining to congressional control over jurisdiction, the precise scope of due process protections here is subject to great uncertainty. Supreme Court case law establishes that litigants enjoy a due process right to have an impartial tribunal adjudicate constitutional claims, but the case law does not establish that the impartial tribunal must be an Article III, lower federal court. Thus, as long as state courts are available, a litigant's due process rights are likely to be satisfied. Significant due process problems emerge, however, if state courts also lack power to adjudicate the subject matter or to issue a meaningful remedy.

Example 6-8

Consider the statute from Example 6-6: "Federal courts of the United States that are inferior to the Supreme Court of United States shall not adjudicate any claim challenging the constitutionality of state or federal laws regulating abortion." Assuming that the statute presents no problem under Article III of the United States Constitution, could one successfully argue that the statute violates the due process rights of individuals seeking to challenge abortion regulations?

Explanation

The answer to this question depends on whether state courts are available to challenge abortion regulations. As explored more fully in Part IV, state courts cannot discriminate against federal claims and are obliged to hear claims that fall within their subject matter jurisdiction. For any particular abortion regulation, one can safely say that some state court of general jurisdiction is likely available to adjudicate the challenge. Thus, state courts appear to be available to adjudicate abortion challenges. Nevertheless, another obstacle to state court review may exist. The Supreme Court has established a rule, also explored in Part IV, that state courts may neither grant habeas corpus petitions brought by federal prisoners nor issue a writ of mandamus against a federal officer. Some lower courts have also held that state courts may not enjoin federal officers from taking action. If a federal officer has responsibility for implementing the challenged abortion regulation, these restrictions may mean that state court review is effectively unavailable for adjudicating the challenge. Under such circumstances, the challenger has a strong due process claim that she was deprived of her right to have a forum for adjudicating her constitutional claim. Cf. *Webster v. Doe*, 486 U.S. 592 (1988) (suggesting that denial of judicial enforcement of constitutional claims would present a serious due process problem).

Rather than grapple with whether Congress has violated litigants' due process right to a tribunal, the Supreme Court has repeatedly avoided the issue by reading avenues for judicial review into challenged legislation. For example, in *Reno v. Catholic Social Serv., Inc.*, 509 U.S. 43 (1993), the Court refused to find that Congress intended to preclude judicial review of decisions regarding illegal immigrants. Noting a presumption in favor of interpreting statutes to allow judicial review, the *Catholic Social Services* Court stated that it would "find an intent to preclude such review only if presented with 'clear and convincing evidence.'" *Id.* at 64 (quoting *Abbott Laboratories v. Gardner*, 387 U.S. 136, 141 (1967). Applying this principle in *INS v. St. Cyr*, 533 U.S. 289, 298 (2001), the Court found that, even though Congress had expressly precluded judicial review of deportation hearings, an individual challenging deportation could still press claims in federal district court by using a petition for a writ of habeas corpus.

These cases illustrate that the Supreme Court vigorously applies the presumption against jurisdictional preclusion. Sometimes this presumption is articulated as a "clear statement" requirement, emphasizing the burden on Congress of making its intent to preclude jurisdiction unambiguous. Notably, the Supreme Court has applied this approach to statutory interpretation in construing several jurisdictional stripping provisions, not just those raising due process concerns. In so doing, the Court was resourceful in identifying alternative avenues for federal court review, such as petitions for writs of habeas corpus and writs of mandamus, that Congress did not identify in the jurisdiction-stripping statute.

Example 6-9

Congress passed a statute providing for an amnesty program for illegal aliens seeking to remain in the United States. The statute provides that the attorney general must decide whether an illegal alien is entitled to an "adjustment of status," allowing her to legally remain in the United States. The statute further states that "if the attorney general rejects an alien's request for an adjustment of status, the alien may obtain judicial review of this denial only in a United States court of appeals as part of a deportation proceeding."

Plaintiffs sought an adjustment of their immigration status. They believe that the attorney general was administering the status adjustment system in an unconstitutional manner. Plaintiffs filed a complaint in federal district court, alleging that the attorney general engaged in a pattern of procedural due process violations in administering the system. The attorney general moved to dismiss the complaint, arguing that the district court lacked jurisdiction. Plaintiffs responded that the district court had general federal question jurisdiction over the case, pursuant to 28 U.S.C. §1331. Plaintiffs maintained that the immigration statute's preclusion of district court jurisdiction was limited to cases where an individual alien sought to reverse the attorney general's specific ruling on the alien's adjustment of status application. Who has the better argument, plaintiffs or the Attorney General?

Explanation

The presumption against jurisdictional preclusion gives plaintiffs the advantage here. One might conclude that the plaintiffs' litigation theory — systematic constitutional violations — attempts an end run around the clear legislative intent to keep status adjustment matters out of district courts. Yet, given the strong inclination to avoid attributing to Congress an intent to eliminate jurisdiction, case law does not support this conclusion.

In a case inspiring this example, *McNary v. Haitian Refugee Center, Inc.*, 498 U.S. 479 (1991), the Supreme Court refused to find that Congress precluded all jurisdiction in the district court. Although Congress had precluded district court review in "adjustment of status" cases, the *McNary* Court presumed that this jurisdictional preclusion did not extend to broad-based constitutional attacks on the attorney general's system. To overcome this presumption, the attorney general had to show clear and convincing evidence that Congress intended to preclude district court jurisdiction over the case. The type of evidence that would satisfy this burden includes statutory language that district courts lack jurisdiction over "all causes" or " 'all questions of law and fact' " pertaining to the "adjustment of status" system. *Id.* at 494 (quoting 8 U.S.C. §1329 (2000) and 38 U.S.C. §211(a)(2000)). In *McNary*, as in this example, the attorney general failed to marshal evidence of this kind.

A litigant wishing to steer clear of Congress's attempt to strip federal court jurisdiction is best advised to make arguments based on the presumption against jurisdiction preclusion. The argument that Congress violates the Fifth Amendment due process clause in failing to provide for federal court review has less support in case law and is likely unavailable if some tribunal is available to hear a challenge. The Fifth Amendment argument falters to the extent that state courts are readily available to adjudicate cases disqualified from federal court. Indeed, the availability of state courts to adjudicate matters forms an important consideration in evaluating all federal court jurisdiction stripping questions.

Aside from the Fifth Amendment, other constitutional challenges to Congress's attempts to control federal courts are available, particularly those based on the Constitution's separation of powers among the branches of the federal government.[16] The contours of separation of powers challenges, which are outlined next, take many forms.

---

16. Yet another theory is based on the argument that legislation restricting court jurisdiction over fundamental rights imposes a discriminatory burden on those rights, and is therefore

C. CONGRESSIONAL POWER TO CONTROL THE MANNER, SUBSTANCE, AND RESULT OF JUDICIAL DECISIONMAKING: SEPARATION OF POWERS CHALLENGES

Although Supreme Court cases may be inconclusive on issues of jurisdictional stripping, the Court has asserted itself more vigorously in protecting the manner, substance, and results of federal court adjudication. Perhaps following the adage "The devil is in the details," the Supreme Court has declared improper Congress's attempts to vest review of federal court decisions in non-judicial branches, to direct particular substantive results in federal court cases, and to open final judgments. Only in the area of remedies has the Court allowed Congress some control over the *details* of what federal courts do. The overarching constitutional principle constraining Congress is separation of powers between the courts and the other two branches of the federal government.

1. Review of Federal Court Decisions

One of the Supreme Court's first attempts to assert itself in the separation of powers area was *Hayburn's Case*, 2 U.S. (2 Dall.) 409 (1792). In *Hayburn*, Congress had authorized the secretary of war to review decisions of the federal courts regarding Revolutionary War veterans' applications for disability pensions. Congress authorized the secretary to ensure that pensions were denied upon a showing of error or impropriety. Finding that this process violated separation of powers, the Court determined that Congress cannot vest in executive branch officials the power to review the decisions of Article III courts.

Example 6-10

Congress passed a statute regulating road building in national parks of the United States. The statute provides that any individual contesting a planned road in a particular park may bring an action in federal district court to test whether the road complies with the statutory conservation standards. The statute provides that, once the district court renders the decision, the losing party in the action may seek review of the decision before the National Park Service, which holds the ultimate responsibility for interpreting the road building statute. Is this procedure constitutional?

---

subject to strict judicial scrutiny; *see* Laurence H. Tribe, *Jurisdictional Gerrymandering: Zoning Disfavored Rights out of the Federal Courts*, 16 Harv. C.R.-C.L. L. Rev. 129, 142-145 (1981).

Explanation

The procedure violates *Hayburn's Case*. The National Park Service is an executive agency, and so cannot enjoy the power to review final judgments of a federal district court. As explained in *Hayburn*, "revision and control" of Article III judgments is "radically inconsistent with the independence of that judicial power which is vested in the courts." 2 U.S. (2 Dall.) at 410 (opinion of Wilson and Blair, JJ. and Peters, D.J.).

2. Mandating the Substance of Judicial Decisions

The Supreme Court announced another separation of powers restriction in *United States v. Klein*, 80 U.S. (13 Wall.) 128 (1872): Congress cannot tell a court what result it must achieve in a particular case. Initially, this restriction may seem confusing; after all, Congress constantly legislates legal standards that control the substantive results in cases. The keys to distinguishing between proper and improper regulation are timing and specificity. Congress may pass general rules that influence the results of a court's adjudication. However, Congress may not interfere with a court's decision in a specific case while the court is adjudicating, unless it changes the law generally. Nor can Congress interfere with a court's decision after the decision has become final.

The facts of *United States v. Klein* help reveal the prohibition's scope. In 1863 Congress enacted a statute allowing individuals whose property was seized during the Civil War to recover the property (or compensation for the property) on proof that they did not assist the enemy during the war. Supreme Court case law allowed litigants to satisfy the requirement that they did not assist the enemy by showing they had received a presidential pardon. Relying on this holding, Klein had sued to recover for seized property and received relief in the lower courts. While the matter was before the United States Supreme Court, Congress adopted a statute providing that a pardon was inadmissible as evidence to aid in the recovery of property. The statute provided instead that the pardon was evidence of disloyalty, and that where pardons were entered into evidence "the jurisdiction of the court in the case shall cease." 80 U.S. (13 Wall.) at 144.

Holding the statute unconstitutional, the Supreme Court emphasized that Congress cannot force a court to enter a result in a particular case. In evaluating whether it should allow the statute to stand, the *Klein* Court queried, "Can we do so without allowing that the legislature may prescribe rules of decision to the Judicial Department of the government in cases pending before it? We think not; . . . We must think that Congress has inadvertently passed the limit which separates the legislative power from the judicial power." *Id.* at 146-147.

The scope of *United States v. Klein* is uncertain. While some emphasize that the Court condemned Congress's attempt to legislate a rule that controlled a pending case, others point out that the *Klein* legislation was suspect because Congress was attempting to control federal court jurisdiction using a statute that interfered with the president's power to grant pardons.[17] Still others point out language in *Klein* noting that the United States was a party to the case and that Congress had developed a rule ensuring that the United States would win the property dispute. *Klein*, 80 U.S. (13 Wall.) at 146 (asking whether Court could uphold Congress's jurisdiction stripping statute "without allowing one party to the controversy to decide it in its own favor"). Despite these battling interpretations, all agree that *Klein* did not purport to undermine Congress's power to develop a new rule that would apply in future cases. Moreover, subsequent Supreme Court cases suggest that it was Congress's change to the litigation process rules (as opposed to the substantive law governing the rights and liabilities of the parties) that rendered its actions particularly problematic in *Klein. See, e.g., Plaut v. Spendthrift Farm, Inc.*, 514 U.S. 211, 218 (1995) (stating that "whatever the precise scope of *Klein* . . . its prohibition does not take hold when Congress 'amend[s] applicable law'" (quoting *Robertson v. Seattle Audubon Society*, 503 U.S. 429, 441 (1992))).

Example 6-11

Assume that Congress passed an anti-discrimination statute regulating schools. The statute provides that schools that discriminate on the basis of sex thereby forfeit their right to receive federal funding. Interpreting this statute, the Supreme Court held that the forfeiture applies only where the school department that discriminated is the same department that receives federal funds. Thus, no forfeiture occurs if federal funding is earmarked for the science department, but the athletic department was the only one engaging in sex discrimination. Displeased with this result, Congress amended the discrimination statute to establish that a school must forfeit all federal funds it receives if *any* of its departments discriminates. Does this amended statute violate *United States v. Klein?*

Explanation

The amended statute is appropriate under *United States v. Klein*. To the extent that *Klein* concerned Congress creating a new decisional principle, the Court did not disapprove of Congress creating new laws for federal courts to apply generally in future cases. The amended discrimination statute in the example appears to govern a broad range of cases and does not attempt to create a

---

17. This position is associated with the classic work by Henry M. Hart, Jr., *The Power of Congress to Limit the Jurisdiction of the Federal Courts: An Exercise in Dialectic*, 66 Harv. L. Rev. 1362 (1953).

special rule to control the result in a pending case. Like the *Klein* statute, the one here favors the United States. Indeed, the amended law makes it easier for the United States to win anti-discrimination suits against educational institutions. Yet one can distinguish *Klein* from this perspective as well. Unlike in this example, Congress in *Klein* secured an advantage for the United States government by stripping federal courts of the power to validate property rights for private individuals. The statute here does not manipulate court procedure in order to "stack the deck" in favor of the United States, but creates a new law of general application that happens to favor the United States.

Example 6-12

The United States Congress enacted a statute making it illegal to kill a member of an endangered species. Assume that an endangered bird species lives in forests administered by the National Forest Service. An environmental group has filed suit, alleging that timber harvesting in these forests is killing the endangered birds, thus violating the Endangered Species Act. While the lawsuit was pending, Congress passed an amendment to the Endangered Species Act stating that if the National Forest Service complied with five conditions before allowing private parties to harvest timber, it would be deemed in compliance with the Endangered Species Act. The five conditions turned out to be easy for the National Forest Service to satisfy, making it obvious that the environmental group would lose its case. Does this statute violate *United States v. Klein*?

Explanation

In this example, Congress appears to be trying to control the result in a particular lawsuit. Its actions may be constitutionally suspect, since *Klein* strongly suggests that Congress may not compel or manipulate case results without changing settled legal principles. Congress can, however, change legal principles, and those changes can modify the results in cases pending at the time of the change. This distinction is clear where Congress implements changes to broad legal standards that apply to a range of lawsuits. Sometimes this distinction is more difficult to navigate where the new standards Congress articulates appear to be tailored to change the result in a particular case. Although presenting a close call, Congress's action in this example falls on the constitutional side of the *Klein* prohibition. Here Congress changed the law by articulating five conditions — not previously part of the law — that are now required under the Endangered Species Act in every instance where a private party wishes to harvest timber in national forests. One can interpret this change, therefore, as sufficiently general as to be constitutional.

This conclusion is supported by the case inspiring this example, *Robertson v. Seattle Audubon Soc'y*, 503 U.S. 429 (1992). In *Robertson*, the Supreme

Court held that Congress did not violate *United States v. Klein* under facts similar to this example, even though Congress had even made explicit reference to pending cases in promulgating the principles that established the legality of the National Park Service's actions. As in the current example, Congress's actions were deemed a change in law, effectively modifying legal principles at issue in the litigation.

3. Reopening Final Judgments

The Supreme Court affirmed a significant separation of powers restraint in *Plaut v. Spendthrift Farm, Inc.*, 514 U.S. 211 (1995). *Plaut* concerned a statutory provision that Congress added to a federal securities law in response to a Supreme Court decision holding that a particular limitations period applied for securities litigation. The Supreme Court had made clear that the limitations period applied to securities claims that were pending, thus ordering that some pending cases be dismissed as time-barred. In response, Congress had enacted a statute reinstating the cases that were dismissed pursuant to the Supreme Court's limitations ruling. This reinstatement statute, the *Plaut* Court held, violated the separation of powers principle that the federal judiciary has "the power, not merely to rule on cases, but to *decide* them, subject" to final review by higher federal courts, not Congress. Id. at 218 (emphasis in original).

Plaut recognized that Congress could influence a federal court ruling by passing a retroactive law. In this circumstance, a trial court must apply the retroactive law pending its decision in the case, and an appellate court must apply the retroactive law to judgments still on appeal when the law was enacted. The statute in *Plaut* differed from these circumstances, however, because the judgments had become final before Congress passed the statute reinstating the federal cases. If all appeals have been exhausted or the time for appeal has expired, a judgment becomes final. In that event, the judicial decision is the last word on the parties' rights and liabilities at issue in the case. Congress may not, the *Plaut* Court reasoned, declare by statute that the specific legal principles binding the parties in the case are something other than what the court has declared.

Example 6-13

A group of newspaper dealers filed suit alleging that a newspaper's distribution methods violated federal antitrust laws. The district court agreed, entering judgment in favor of the plaintiff dealers. The defendant newspaper appealed to the United States Court of Appeals. The court affirmed, agreeing with the district court that the antitrust statutes governed newspaper sales. After the time for filing a petition for a writ of certiorari in the United States Supreme Court had expired in the case, Congress passed a statute exempting newspaper sales from the federal antitrust laws. The statute provided that "this provision shall ensure that all past and future newspaper sales, including those currently subject to litigation, are free from regulation under the federal antitrust laws." Following the statute's passage, the newspaper moved to dismiss the earlier judgment, arguing that Congress's statute established that the federal court acted improperly in applying the antitrust laws against it. Assuming that the newspaper has properly read the statute as applying to cases such as the one against it, should the district court dismiss the earlier judgment?

Explanation

Congress's exemption statute may not constitutionally nullify the effect of the earlier judgment. For that reason, the district court should not dismiss the earlier judgment. The case against the newspaper had become "final" within the meaning of *Plaut*: the court of appeals decision became the last word on the parties' rights and obligations in the case upon the expiration of the time for filing a certiorari petition. "Congress may not declare by retroactive legislation that the law applicable to *that very case* was something other than what [the district court and court of appeals had] said it was." *Plaut*, 514 U.S. at 227 (emphasis in original).

Congress did not avoid *Plaut*'s prohibition by framing its retroactive change to the antitrust laws in general terms. The *Plaut* statute was also framed in class-based terms rather than by reference to specific cases or specific litigants. Noting that a reference to individual cases might suggest that Congress engaged in favoritism, the *Plaut* Court nonetheless reasoned that the *Plaut* statute's application to a whole class of cases did not eliminate its separation of powers flaw. The Court explained that the separation of powers violation, which resulted from Congress's attempt to deprive judicial judgments of their conclusive effect, remained even though the statute applied to a range of cases.

4. Controlling Court Authority to Issue Remedies

Congress has occasionally attempted to control the work of federal courts by limiting the remedies they can use. The Supreme Court's most expansive treatment of this issue appears in *Miller v. French*, 530 U.S. 327 (2000). In *Miller*, the Court provided insight into Congress's power over remedial issues as well as the scope of separation of powers limitations announced in *Hayburn's Case*, 2 U.S. (2 Dall.) 409 (1792), and *Plaut v. Spendthrift Farm, Inc.*, 514 U.S. 211 (1995).

Miller v. French concerned a provision of the Prison Litigation Reform Act (PLRA), a statute declaring new legal standards for injunctions regulating prison conditions. The challenged provision placed an automatic stay on existing injunctions requiring improved prison conditions. According to the provision, a government litigant could file a motion to modify or terminate an injunction pursuant to the PLRA's new legal standards, and that motion operated as a stay of the injunction 30 days after the motion was filed. The effect of Congress's automatic stay, therefore, was to render ineffective a previous federal court decision (the existing prison injunction).

Upholding the automatic stay, the *Miller v. French* Court first concluded that the provision did not violate the prohibition against non-judicial review of judicial orders in *Hayburn's Case*. The Court reasoned that the statute did not authorize Congress or the president to directly review the challenged injunction.

Next the Court grappled with the more complicated question of whether the automatic stay provision violated the *Plaut* prohibition against reopening final judgments. After all, the PLRA appeared to use a revised legal standard to suspend a judicial decision. To avoid the effect of *Plaut*, the Court highlighted the unique nature of injunctions: "Prospective relief under a continuing, executory decree remains subject to alteration due to changes in the underlying law." *Miller*, 530 U.S. at 344. *Miller* thus recognized that Congress possesses more latitude in controlling federal court power to issue prospective relief such as injunctions compared with its power to control retrospective remedies such as damages. Where injunctions have continuing effect and order the parties' relations into the future, they do not enjoy the same immunity from congressional regulation as do final court decisions awarding a damages remedy.

Example 6-14

Bridge Works, Inc. owns a bridge spanning a navigable river. River Cruise, Inc. could not navigate its new cruise ship under the bridge because the bridge was too low. River Cruise, Inc. therefore filed suit against Bridge Works, seeking (1) damages resulting from its inability to navigate the cruise ship under the bridge and (2) an injunction requiring Bridge Works to raise the bridge. Agreeing that the bridge was an unlawful structure, the federal court awarded both types of relief: damages and an order requiring Bridge Works to raise the bridge. This judgment was affirmed by the court of appeals and the United States Supreme Court. Soon thereafter, Congress passed a statute declaring that the bridge in question was a lawful structure and could therefore stand. River Cruise filed another suit, arguing that it is entitled to the earlier remedies because this statute is unconstitutional. Should River Cruise prevail?

Explanation

River Cruise should partly prevail in its second suit. The earlier judgment awarding money damages became final, once reviewed by the United States Supreme Court. Thus, the subsequent statute could not constitutionally alter that final judgment. The injunction, however, provided ongoing, prospective relief that was subject to changes in the underlying law. When Congress changed the law governing whether the bridge was lawful, the injunction against maintaining the bridge was no longer enforceable. River Cruise may still recover its damages but is no longer subject to the benefit of the injunction. This result is supported by the Court's decision in *Pennsylvania v. Wheeling & Belmont Bridge Co.*, 59 U.S. (18 How.) 421, 431 (1856) (distinguishing between damages and an injunction in similar circumstances).

In addition to its power to influence the rules of decision that affect ongoing injunctive relief, Congress possesses power to prevent courts from issuing injunctions altogether. Congress has exercised this power in a statute known as the Anti-Injunction Act, described in the next chapter.

5. Putting It All Together: A Summary Example Exploring Separation of Powers Issues

As a review of the various separation of powers restraints on Congress's ability to control federal court adjudication, consider Congress's reaction to the tragic struggle concerning Theresa Marie Schiavo.

Example 6-15

Terri Schiavo had been in a constant vegetative state for more than ten years. In a proceeding initiated by Schiavo's husband, Florida state courts made a factual finding that, if she were able to express her wishes, she would not want nutrition and hydration provided to maintain her in her current state. The Florida state courts therefore ordered health care personnel to remove her feeding tube. Thereafter, the United States Congress passed an act vesting "the United States District Court for the Middle District of Florida" with jurisdiction to adjudicate any "claim by or on behalf of Theresa Marie Schiavo, for violation of [her] right[s] under the Constitution or laws of the United States relating to the withholding or withdrawal of food, fluids, or medical treatment necessary to sustain her life."[18]

The act, known formally as the "Act for the Relief of the Parents of Theresa Marie Schiavo" and colloquially as "Terri's Law," further provided

---

18. Act for the Relief of the Parents of Theresa Marie Schiavo, Pub. L. 109-3, 119 Stat. 15 (2005).

that "[a]ny parent of Theresa Marie Schiavo shall have standing to bring a suit under this Act." Terri's Law did not stop there, providing that the district court (1) "shall determine de novo any claim ... notwithstanding any prior State court determination"; (2) shall not consider whether the claims were previously "raised, considered, or decided in State court proceedings"; (3) shall not engage in "abstention in favor of State court proceedings"; and (4) shall not decide the case on the basis of whether state court remedies were exhausted.

Are there valid arguments that this statute runs afoul of separation of powers constraints on Congress's ability to control court decisions?

Explanation

Broad-brush arguments show that many components of Terri's Law clash with separation of powers principles. Moreover, a serious argument exists that the act taken as a whole is contrary to the spirit of separation of powers. On a more specific level, one might make a credible argument that Terri's Law runs afoul of *Plaut v. Spendthrift Farm, Inc.*, 514 U.S. 211 (1995). Upon close analysis, however, no part of Terri's Law is clearly unconstitutional under existing separation of powers doctrines.

Starting with a general analysis, one might describe Terri's Law as contrary to Congress's proper legislative function in two ways: the law unabashedly favors particular litigants and commandeers the judicial process. First, the law pinpoints only two persons (Schiavo's parents) with standing to enforce its provisions and vests subject matter jurisdiction in only one federal court, a court convenient for the parents. Next, Terri's Law tailors the applicable standard of review and designates an approach to finality and abstention that allows these litigants to avoid preexisting, unfavorable rulings binding them. Thus, contrary to Congress's constitutional function, the legislation is specifically focused on the plight of certain individuals rather than on broad questions of social policy. As such, Terri's Law violates broad language of *United States v. Klein*, 80 U.S. (13 Wall.) 128, 146 (1872), preventing Congress from prescribing a "rule of decision" for a particular case. Yet, given uncertainties about *Klein*'s scope, one cannot unequivocally conclude that *Klein* invalidates Terri's Law. Unlike *Klein*'s jurisdiction-stripping statute, Terri's law neither interferes with the president's pardon power nor represents an attempt by Congress to protect U.S. property interests by effectively resolving a controversy in favor of the United States.

One may also argue that Terri's Law implements congressional favoritism in a way that unconstitutionally interferes with the judicial function. *See generally Loving v. United States*, 517 U.S. 748, 757 (1996) (separation of powers principles require each branch to avoid impairing another branch's "performance of its constitutional duties"). One may criticize Terri's Law as invading judicial prerogatives to designate standards of review and to develop and apply prudential doctrines governing abstention, waiver, and exhaustion. Taken together, these arguments suggest that Terri's Law is simply too heavy-handed in micro-managing the judicial process to survive separation of powers attack. Specific Supreme Court case law support, however, is generally lacking.[19]

The strongest case supporting an attack on Terri's Law is *Plaut v. Spendthrift Farm, Inc.* One may argue that Congress violated *Plaut's* dictates by effectively directing the federal court to reopen the Florida court's final judgment. Two distinctions, however, may allow this case to avoid *Plaut's* prohibition.

One could first try to distinguish *Plaut* by arguing that the state court's order to remove the feeding tube was a prospective injunction, like the prison injunctions at issue in *Miller v. French*. As such, the state court order could be characterized as "a continuing, executory decree . . . subject to alteration due to changes in the underlying law." *Miller,* 530 U.S. at 344. On the other hand, the order was unlike the prison restructuring injunctions at issue in *Miller* because the order focused on a one-time event — feeding tube removal — that was forestalled only by post-finality lobbying for congressional intervention.

The second way of distinguishing *Plaut v. Spendthrift Farm, Inc.* focuses on the character of the final order Congress is trying to reopen. Unlike the federal court orders subject to reopening in *Plaut,* a *state* court rendered the feeding tube order in the Schiavo litigation. The separation of powers motivations of *Plaut* are therefore clouded in Schiavo by federalism considerations. In at least two circumstances, Congress has allowed for federal courts to review final state judgments.[20] The first circumstance concerns Supreme Court review of the judgments of a state's highest court, a power implicitly authorized in Article III of the Constitution. The second circumstance occurs when lower federal courts review final state criminal judgments during the habeas corpus process. Both circumstances, which are long-standing and deeply entrenched in tradition, suggest greater tolerance in the constitutional scheme for reopening state court judgments compared with federal court judgments. These two circumstances, however, do not wholly dispel the separation of powers problem here. The circumstances involve only general congressional authorization for *federal courts* to reopen state judgments, as opposed to a heavy-handed effort by Congress to force federal courts to reopen a state court judgment (by stripping the federal court of autonomy over standard of review, abstention, waiver, and exhaustion requirements).

---

19. Concurring specially in a challenge to Terri's Law, one judge suggested that this absence of precedent was understandable given the unprecedented nature of Congress's intrusion. *Schiavo ex rel. Schlindler v. Schiavo,* 404 F.3d 1270, 1275 n.4 (11th Cir. 2005) (Birch, J., specially concurring).

20. This observation derives from Steven G. Calabresi, *The Terri Schiavo Case: In Defense of the Special Law Enacted by Congress and President Bush,* 100 Nw. U. L. Rev. 151, 161 (2006).

In short, Terri's Law is open to many separation of powers criticisms. No specific Supreme Court case supports these criticisms directly, although many cases lend indirect or general credence to a separation of powers attack.

D. CONGRESSIONAL POWER TO CREATE NON–ARTICLE III COURTS

When one thinks about literally what constitutes a "federal" court, one might go beyond classic examples such as district courts, courts of appeals, and the United States Supreme Court. Institutions such as magistrate courts, federal administrative agencies, specialized courts such as the Court of Federal Claims, and military tribunals are "federal" institutions that certainly do things that "courts" do, such as adjudicate the rights of parties. Where should one place these institutions within the constitutional mosaic? What is the source of their power?

One might initially look to Article III, which allows Congress to vest judicial power "in such inferior Courts as the Congress may from time to time ordain and establish." And one might also look to the Constitution's laundry list of power grants in Article I, which mentions that Congress may "constitute Tribunals inferior to the supreme Court." Persuasive scholarly arguments notwithstanding, courts have viewed this language from Article I as a reference to the same power as that granted Article III.[21] In other words, the accepted wisdom is that Article I's reference to "Tribunals" is simply a repetition of Congress's Article III power to create lower federal courts with the specific qualities and limitations listed in Article III.

With the language of Article I folded into that of Article III, non–Article III courts are left with no definitive constitutional language to support them. Perhaps for this reason, the principles governing the constitutionality of

---

21. *See, e.g., Glidden Co. v. Zdanok*, 370 U.S. 530, 543 (1962) (plurality opinion) (stating that "[t]he power given to Congress in Art. I, §8, cl. 9 . . . plainly relates to the 'inferior Courts' provided for in Art. II, §1; it has never been relied on for establishment of any other tribunals").

Arguing that the Article I reference provides textual and structural support for alternative tribunals, Professor Pfander maintains that "the Inferior Tribunals Clause [of Article I] can be read to provide a textual predicate for Congress's acknowledged but controversial power to create Article I tribunals outside of Article III." James E. Pfander, *Article I Tribunals, Article III Courts, and the Judicial Power of the United States*, 118 HARV. L. REV. 643, 672-673 (2004). To support this reading, Pfander points to a number of distinctions between the two provisions, such as differences in constitutional language (e.g., Article III's allowance for Congress to "ordain and establish" "inferior Courts" versus Article I's permission for Congress to "constitute tribunals inferior to the supreme Court") as well as differences in surrounding context (Article III contains specific requirements for the courts mentioned, and Article I contains no such specifications). *Id.* at 673-79.

non–Article III courts are murky. Nevertheless, with moderate success, courts and scholars have at least provided an analytical starting point, identifying discrete categories for various types of non–Article III courts.

In delineating these categories, courts and scholars often separate administrative agencies from the other non–Article III courts. Analysts have identified three qualities of administrative agencies that are not always shared by other non–Article III courts: (1) agencies do not enforce judgments, and parties must instead file enforcement suits in an Article III court; (2) agencies may use adjudication as a means to develop policy (thereby blurring the adjudication and rulemaking functions); and (3) agencies are often justified under the rubric of Article III (rather than as an exception to Article III) because full judicial review of administrative action is available in Article III courts.[22] A rich literature has developed regarding administrative agencies, which are often associated with the discipline of administrative law as opposed to federal courts.

The remaining non–Article III courts are sometimes called legislative or Article I courts. One type of legislative court that is justified using analysis similar to that used for administrative agencies is the "adjunct" court. Upholding the constitutionality of adjuncts such as the United States Magistrate Courts, the Supreme Court has observed that such courts are subject to the control and supervision of district courts, which retain (i.e., do not delegate to adjunct courts) "'essential attributes of judicial power,'" such as executing judgments and performing de novo review of adjunct court decisions. *United States v. Raddatz*, 447 U.S. 667, 683 n.10 (1980) (quoting *Crowell v. Benson*, 285 U.S. 22, 51-52 (1932)).

Three other types of non–Article III courts also fall within the category of legislative or Article I courts.[23] First are those that serve specific geographic areas, such as the District of Columbia and federal territories. Next are "public rights" courts, which adjudicate civil disputes between private citizens and the United States. Third are military courts, such as military commissions or courts-martial, which have existed since early American history but have become especially controversial in the era of global terrorism.[24]

---

22. RICHARD H. FALLON, JR., DANIEL J. MELTZER & DAVID L. SHAPIRO, HART AND WECHSLER'S THE FEDERAL COURTS AND THE FEDERAL SYSTEM 379 (5th ed. 2003) (delineating these three characteristics and discussing scholarship analyzing the characteristics).

23. *See, e.g.*, ERWIN CHEMERINSKY, FEDERAL JURISDICTION 29 (4th ed. 2003) (describing four categories of legislative courts, including adjuncts, territorial courts, public rights courts, and military tribunals).

24. Military tribunals are sometimes created by the executive and in those circumstances might more accurately be described as "Article II courts." Perhaps, however, because Congress's role in regulating military tribunals plays prominently in debates about their legitimacy, military tribunals are routinely included under the moniker "Article I" or "legislative courts." Military tribunals are discussed further at the end of this chapter.

Because the judges of adjuncts and other legislative courts lack life tenure and salary protection, the concern arises that they may not provide the same quality of independent justice as judges in Article III courts. Given this concern, and given the vastness of Congress's legislative powers under Article I, the Supreme Court has expressed concern that significant limitations should be imposed on Congress's ability to create adjudicatory tribunals outside of Article III. For that reason, the United States Supreme Court has created doctrines (discussed next) that restrict Congress's ability to create non–Article III tribunals. The Supreme Court has expressed similar concern about executive overreaching in the context of military tribunals. The last part of this chapter discusses that issue further.

I. Legislative Courts: We Don't Want Congress Taking Over the World

Two main constitutional concerns behind Congress creating non–Article III courts are judicial independence and separation of powers. Is Congress attempting an "end run" around Article III's strictures? This concern is lessened in the context of adjunct courts, which render decisions subject to supervision and control by an independent Article III court. In this case, the Article III court eliminates the independence concern and acts as a check on congressional power. In other contexts, the Supreme Court has found that legislative courts do not adequately preserve these constitutional values. Most notably, in *Northern Pipeline Construction Co. v. Marathon Pipe Line Co.*, 458 U.S. 50 (1982), the Supreme Court ruled that bankruptcy courts, created in Congress's 1978 bankruptcy reform, were unconstitutional.

Writing for a plurality of the Court in *Marathon Pipe Line*, Justice Brennan emphasized that, as constituted in the 1978 legislation, bankruptcy courts were not adjunct courts, since they had jurisdiction over all civil matters arising in or related to bankruptcy cases and could enforce their own orders, which were subject to review in the Article III district court only under a deferential "clearly erroneous" standard of review. Moreover, Justice Brennan concluded that bankruptcy courts did not fall within one of the three exceptions for legislative courts: territorial courts, military courts, and "public rights" courts. Obviously, bankruptcy courts are not territorial courts or military tribunals. The plurality reasoned that they also were not "public rights" courts, since bankruptcy court jurisdiction extended beyond public rights into all civil matters, including state law disputes between private parties.

Concurring in the judgment, Justices Rehnquist and O'Connor emphasized the latter concern. In their view, the Constitution prevented Congress from granting bankruptcy courts power to adjudicate state law disputes that are only indirectly related to the adjudication of federal bankruptcy issues.

Why was the state law nature of the claim in *Marathon Pipe Line* so problematic for Justices Rehnquist and O'Connor? At first blush, their focus seems misplaced. Concern with the state law nature of the claim appears tied to *federalism* values. (One might argue, for example, that the bankruptcy courts threaten state sovereignty, which should prevent a federal institution from intruding on the state prerogative of adjudicating a state-created right.) Yet the constitutional values that motivate the restrictions on legislative courts tend to serve *separation of powers* among the branches of the federal government, *not* relations between state and federal governments.

Although the two justices did not fully explain their reasoning, one possible explanation for their concern lies in the assumptions under which the states ratified the Constitution. The Constitution creates a federal government that possesses limited powers, with the states retaining the balance of power. To the extent that the states gave up some of their power under the Constitution's scheme, the argument goes, the power they lost should be specified in the Constitution. Admittedly, the Constitution provides that the federal government may hear cases and controversies for which state law might provide the rule of decision, such as disputes between citizens of different states. But the states ceded that control over state law adjudication only in the context of Article III, where the judges enjoy special protections. The states did not, the argument continues, cede power over state law adjudication in circumstances where the courts do not possess Article III protections. To allow a non–Article III adjudicator to exercise that power thus violates the deal the states made when they ratified the Constitution.

Example 6-16

Assume that Congress created a special tribunal to adjudicate the immigration status of United States residents who are citizens of Spanish-speaking countries. The tribunal is called the Spanish-Speaking Immigrant Court, or SSI Court. The judges staffing the SSI Court are appointed for fifteen year terms at a salary set by congressional budgetary statute each year. The primary job of the SSI Court is to determine whether Spanish-speaking non-citizens may lawfully remain in the United States. However, Congress also provided that non-citizens may use SSI Court proceedings to raise claims against private parties for civil matters — including state law tort and contract claims — that are intertwined with or related to the non-citizen's immigration status. The statute provides that the SSI Court's decisions on immigration status are subject to plenary review by the district court. The SSI Court cannot enter an order requiring non-citizens to be deported; the statute allows only the district court to do that. The SSI Court *can* enter orders enforcing its rulings on the private civil claims; however, the statute provides that these rulings on civil claims are subject to reversal by the district court upon a showing that the rulings are clearly erroneous. Is the SSI Court constitutional under the approach of *Northern Pipeline Construction Co. v. Marathon Pipe Line Co.?*

Explanation

No, the SSI Court is likely not constitutional under *Marathon Pipe Line*. Because the SSI Court is staffed by judges who do not enjoy life tenure or protection from salary diminution, the court is constitutional only if it is either an adjunct or a legislative court falling within one of the three exceptions mentioned in *Marathon Pipe Line*. Taking all of the SSI Court's powers together, none of these characterizations fits.

The most troublesome component of the SSI Court's power is its authority over civil, state law matters between private parties. Given the SSI Court's power to enforce its rulings in these matters, as well as the deferential "clear and convincing evidence" standard of review (which is identical to the standard deemed problematic in *Marathon Pipe Line*), the SSI Court exercises some of the "essential attributes of judicial power." The SSI Court therefore is not an adjunct.

Nor can the SSI Court's power over the civil claims between private parties be justified under one of the three exceptions allowed for non-adjunct, non–Article III courts. The SSI Court's power over civil claims allows adjudication of state law matters that might be only peripherally related to the federal foundation for the court's authority: immigration law. Power over state law civil matters is precisely the quality of bankruptcy courts that troubled Justices Rehnquist and O'Connor, whose concurring votes made possible a ruling that the bankruptcy courts were unconstitutional in *Marathon Pipe Line*. The private nature of the claim in *Marathon Pipe Line* was also key to the Supreme Court's decision to declare bankruptcy courts unconstitutional. These same concerns cast constitutional doubt on the SSI Court in this example.

That is not to suggest, however, that the remaining portion of the SSI Court's power — immigration status adjudication — is constitutionally invalid. Indeed, even under the reasoning of Justice Brennan's relatively doctrinaire plurality opinion in *Marathon Pipe Line*, the SSI Court's authority to rule on immigration status has qualities that might render it constitutional. First, the district court retains key attributes of judicial power over the immigration status rulings, which the SSI Court may not enforce and which the district courts evaluate with a searching "plenary" standard of review. Moreover, the subject matter of the adjudication — immigration status — is easily characterized as a public right, which is historically adjudicated in a non–Article III court. The Supreme Court has also explicitly approved non–Article III tribunals for adjudicating immigration law violations. *See, e.g., Lloyd Sabaudo Societa Anonima Per Azioni v. Elting,* 287 U.S. 329 (1932).

The plurality in *Marathon Pipe Line* was not inclined to sever the clearly unconstitutional part of the bankruptcy court's powers (adjudication of a private state law cause of action) from the remainder of the bankruptcy court's authority to implement federal bankruptcy law. For that reason, the plurality ruled bankruptcy courts unconstitutional as an entity, rather than merely disqualifying them from adjudicating private, state law causes of action. 458 U.S. at 88 n.40. Applying that approach to the SSI Court, one should conclude that the immigration status component of the court's adjudicatory powers does not save the court from being declared unconstitutional under *Marathon Pipe Line.*

Marathon Pipe Line was not the last word on legislative courts. In subsequent cases, the Supreme Court replaced *Marathon Pipe Line*'s formal approach with a more functional balancing approach. Most notably, in *Commodity Futures Trading Comm'n v. Schor,* 478 U.S. 833 (1986), the Supreme Court determined that a non–Article III court's adjudication of a state law cause of action between private parties was not unconstitutional. The adjudicative body involved — the Commodity Futures Trading Commission (CFTC) — possessed the power to adjudicate claims brought against regulated entities for reparations owed as a result of violations of the Commodity Exchange Act, which prohibits fraudulent and manipulative futures transactions. The Commodity Exchange Act also granted the CFTC adjudicative authority over state common law counterclaims that a regulated entity might raise in the same proceeding.

In evaluating whether this scheme violated separation of powers principles, the *Schor* Court spurned "formalistic and unbending rules" in favor a functional, multi-factor analysis. 478 U.S. at 833. The *Schor* Court identified the following factors to consider in evaluating whether a non–Article III court unconstitutionally invades the province of the Article III judiciary:

(1) "the extent to which the 'essential attributes of judicial power' are reserved for Article III courts";

(2) "the extent to which the non–Article III forum exercises the range of jurisdiction and powers normally vested only in Article III courts";

(3) "the origins and importance of the right to be adjudicated, and"

(4) "the concerns that drove Congress to depart from the requirements of Article III."

Id. at 851.

Applying these factors, the *Schor* Court observed that the CFTC scheme left far more of the elements of judicial power to the Article III judiciary than did the bankruptcy scheme at issue in *Marathon Pipe Line.* In particular, the Court noted that the CFTC adjudicated only a narrow area of the law, that the CFTC could not enforce its own orders, and that the district court reviewed CFTC factual rulings under the "weight of the evidence" standard of review and legal rulings using the "de novo" standard of review.

Turning to the next two factors, the *Schor* Court observed that the counterclaims that the CFTC could adjudicate militated *against* finding the scheme constitutional because the counterclaims possessed two problematic qualities: they concerned private rights between private parties (rather than public rights) and state law provided the rule of decision for resolving them. The Court characterized these constitutional difficulties as de minimis, however, given the scope of the power maintained in the district courts as well as the efficiency that resulted from allowing the CFTC to adjudicate the counterclaims together with claims that a regulated entity violated the Commodity Exchange Act. Indeed, for each dispute, the Commodity Exchange Act claim and the counterclaim would arise from the same futures transaction and would thus fit together hand in glove. To prevent the CFTC from adjudicating the counterclaim in that context, the Court explained, would " 'defeat the obvious purpose of the legislation to furnish a prompt, continuous, expert and inexpensive method for dealing with . . . questions of fact' " suited for adjudication by a specialized entity. Id. at 856 (quoting *Crowell v. Benson*, 285 U.S. 22, 46 (1932)).

The contrast between *Marathon Pipe Line* and *Schor* represents a classic illustration of the differences that result from formal and functional analyses of separation of powers questions.[25] In *Marathon Pipe Line*, the plurality reached the unwavering conclusion that the bankruptcy courts were unconstitutional upon observing that — as non-adjuncts — they adjudicated a forbidden type of controversy: state common law claims between private parties. *Schor*, however, did not automatically invalidate the CFTC on that basis, but was willing to consider countervailing factors, such as efficiency and the magnitude of intrusion on Article III prerogatives.

Example 6-17

Consider the Spanish Speaking Immigrant Court or SSI Court described in Example 6-16. Is the SSI Court constitutional under the approach of *Commodity Futures Trading Comm'n v. Schor*?

Explanation

The SSI Court may be unconstitutional under the *Schor* functional, balancing analysis, although it is a closer call than under the *Marathon Pipe Line* analysis. The SSI Court has the same problematic power evaluated in *Schor*: the authority to adjudicate a state common law cause of action between private parties. The SSI Court, however, lacks many of the qualities that protected the Commodity Future Trading Commission in *Schor*. First, the SSI Court

---

25. The jurisprudential approaches of functionalism and formalism are explored further in Chapter 1.

usurps the power of Article III district courts to enforce rulings on the problematic claims. Moreover, the Article III district court cannot readily reverse the SSI Court orders on those claims, since the deferential "clearly erroneous" standard binds the district court's review. Finally, principles of efficiency do not justify the SSI Court's power with the same vigor as in *Schor*. The common law claims available for review in the SSI Court do not necessarily fit intimately with the immigration status adjudication. According to Congress's grant of power to the SSI Court, those claims need only be "intertwined with or related to" the question of immigration status, and thus do not necessarily fall within any special expertise of the tribunal. The SSI Court exercises a broader range of jurisdiction compared with the CFTC in *Schor*, thus invading more of the powers "normally vested in Article III courts." *Schor*, 478 U.S. at 851. Because some claims may not actually concern immigration questions, little evidentiary overlap with immigration questions may exist. Thus, the SSI Court cannot be justified as providing " 'a prompt, continuous, expert and inexpensive method for dealing with . . . questions of fact' " suited for adjudication by a specialized entity. *Id.* at 856 (quoting *Crowell v. Benson*, 285 U.S. 22, 46 (1932)).

The question remains, however, whether the problematic portion of the SSI Court's power can be severed from the court's constitutionally acceptable power over immigration status. Given that the functional approach of *Schor* evinces far more flexibility than the formal approach of *Marathon Pipe Line*, one would expect greater success in making the severability argument under the *Schor* analysis.

2. Military Tribunals: The Executive Does Not Possess a "Blank Check"

Questions about the constitutional legitimacy of military tribunals also focus on the separation of powers among branches of the federal government. For military tribunals, however, the clash concerns the scope of the president's power. Indeed, the issues regarding military tribunals often include the president (to whom the Constitution grants commander-in-chief authority) and the Congress (to which the Constitution gives the power to make rules for the regulation of land and naval forces). But the federal judiciary is also drawn into the fray: the legitimacy of military tribunals also often hinges on whether Article III courts, as opposed to non–Article III military tribunals, are the most appropriate forum to exercise adjudicative power over military members and enemies of the United States.

Case law distinguishes between military tribunals that try members of the United States armed forces and those that try others. United States armed service members may be court-martialed by a non–Article III tribunal because of their status as members of the military. *Solorio v. United States,*

483 U.S. 435 (1987). The tribunals that adjudicate rights of those who are not United States military members are subject to different analysis, which depends on the specific historical circumstances prompting the United States to create the tribunals.

Despite variations in the historical context, certain generalizations emerge from the case law governing tribunals for those who are not members of the United States military. Qualities that tend to render these military tribunals more constitutionally acceptable include (1) powers limited to trying non-citizens of the United States, (2) powers limited to trying military members of nations that are actively hostile toward the United States, (3) extensive procedural protections analogous to those required by the Bill of Rights or to the procedures provided to United States military personnel accused of a crime, (4) adjudication occurring outside the territorial limits of the United States, and (5) adjudicatory powers created as part of a declared war by the United States against another nation or nations. Thus, for example, the Supreme Court has determined that the United States may not constitutionally employ a military tribunal on United States territory against a United States civilian. In Ex parte Milligan, 71 U.S. (4 Wall.) 2 (1866), the Supreme Court held that military courts lacked power to try a civilian charged with aiding the Confederacy during the American Civil War when a federal district court in Indiana was available to adjudicate the defendant's guilt.[26] By contrast, the United States Supreme Court upheld the use of military tribunals during World War II to adjudicate a war crimes prosecution of eight German spies (including one who was a United States citizen) who were captured after arriving in the United States in a German submarine, wearing German uniforms. Ex parte Quirin, 317 U.S. 1 (1942).

As Milligan and Quirin illustrate, the legitimacy of using military tribunals for those who are not United States service members requires a fact-sensitive analysis. Also in this context, however, the Supreme Court has established unqualified principles about overreaching presidential power. Two cases decided in the wake of the terrorist attacks of September 11, 2001, are illustrative: Hamdi v. Rumsfeld, 542 U.S. 507 (2004), and Hamdan v. Rumsfeld, 126 S. Ct. 2749 (2006).

Following the September 11 attacks, Congress passed an Authorization for Use of Military Force. Relying on this authorization, the George W. Bush administration promulgated a November 2001 order asserting the president's authority to designate individuals for criminal trial and punishment as enemy combatants before military commissions. As originally conceived, the military commissions provided minimal procedural protections, which

---

26. The Milligan Court stated that Article III federal courts are "always open to hear criminal accusations and redress grievances; and no usage of war could sanction a military trial there for any offence [sic]whatever of a citizen in civil life, in nowise connected with the military service." 71 U.S. at 121-122.

fell far short not only of protections guaranteed in the Bill of Rights, but also of those protections extended to United States military personnel under the Uniform Code of Military Justice.

Ruling that Congress had granted general authorization to the president to detain enemy combatants after September 11, the *Hamdi* Court invalidated the president's detention scheme as failing to provide detainees with notice and opportunity to be heard sufficient to satisfy due process standards. In so ruling, a plurality of the Court wrote, "[A] state of war is not a blank check for the President when it comes to the rights of the Nation's citizens." *Hamdi v. Rumsfeld*, 542 U.S. 507, 536 (2004). For the jurisprudence of non–Article III tribunals, *Hamdi* is significant because it required creating a federal adjudicative entity to provide due process to detainees in the War on Terrorism.

The Supreme Court's condemnation of the president's scheme for military tribunals was perhaps even more clear in *Hamdan v. Rumsfeld*, 126 S. Ct. 2749 (2006). Despite the president's suggestion that the terrorist threat justifies an inherent unilateral assertion of presidential power to create tribunals of the president's own design, *Hamdan* held that the president must work within a framework of rules already provided by Congress. The Court stated, "Exigency alone, of course, will not justify the establishment and use of penal tribunals not contemplated by Article I, §8 and Article III, §1 of the Constitution unless some other part of that document authorizes a response to a felt need. And that authority, if it exists, can derive only from the powers granted jointly to the President and Congress in time of war." *Hamdan*, 126 S. Ct. at 2773 (citation omitted).

Following *Hamdan*, the president sought authorization from Congress to reconstitute the military commissions. Congress capitulated, passing the Military Commissions Act of 2006. This act embodies a wide range of measures, but most notably authorizes the president to establish military commissions for the prosecution of certain offenses committed by alien unlawful combatants. Another significant provision of the act denies any court or judge jurisdiction to hear or consider an application for a writ of habeas corpus filed by an alien detained by the United States outside the country, where the alien has been determined to be properly detained as an enemy combatant or is awaiting such determination. Litigation will ultimately resolve the impact of the Military Commissions Act of 2006 on *Hamdan* and the precedential effect of the decision.

Example 6-18

Congress was concerned about a rash of property crimes committed against small U.S. military ships on the open seas by pirate vessels manned by citizens of various other countries. Consequently, Congress provided a mechanism to capture the pirates and try them in accordance with the detailed provisions of the Uniform Code of Military Justice. These provisions allow the pirates to be represented by counsel, to confront witnesses against them, and to enjoy protections ensuring the integrity of the evidence used against them.

The President of the United States also was concerned about the pirates. Declaring that the pirates were engaging in acts of war, the president issued an Executive Order establishing military commissions empowered to try the pirates in summary proceedings at sea, without the benefit of counsel or many of the other protections of the Uniform Code of Military Justice. Is this scheme constitutional?

Explanation

The president's scheme for military commissions is likely not constitutional. The appropriate case law for analyzing these commissions are cases such as *Milligan*, *Quirin*, and *Hamdan*, which addressed the legitimacy of military tribunals established to adjudicate the guilt of individuals who are *not* United States military personnel. *Milligan* is perhaps the least analogous precedent, since — unlike the defendant in *Milligan* — the pirates are not United States civilians and the crimes have not taken place within the territory of the United States. The precedent most favorable for the president — *Quirin* — is likewise inapposite because the defendants in that case were either citizens of or working in the interests of a nation engaged in a declared war against the United States. That is not true for the pirates here, who are acting in their own (mercenary) self-interest, independent of any governmental or national interest.

Many aspects of the president's scheme in this example do, however, implicate *Hamdan*. As did the president in *Hamdan*, the president here is attempting to ignore existing mechanisms for the trial of particular enemies. The *Hamdan* Court condemned such an assertion of unilateral presidential power, particularly where, as here, the president is withholding procedural protections guaranteed under Congress's scheme. Moreover, unlike the situation in *Hamdan* and the Military Commissions Act of 2006, nothing in the facts here suggests that Congress endorsed the president's actions by legislatively supporting the decision to provide summary proceedings at sea. Congress's failure to endorse the president's creation of these summary procedure renders the procedures even more constitutionally problematic.

CHAPTER 7

The Anti-Injunction Act

Chapter 6 discusses Congress's power to change legal rules that govern final judgments when those judgments act as prospective injunctions. This chapter discusses another area where Congress has controlled the reach of federal injunctive power: injunctions of state court proceedings. In this context, Congress has eliminated federal court power altogether, with limited exceptions. Indeed, the Anti-Injunction Act, 28 U.S.C. §2283, bars "a court of the United States" from granting "an injunction to stay proceedings in a State court" except in three instances: (1) "as expressly authorized by Act of Congress," (2) "where necessary in aid of its jurisdiction," and (3) "to protect or effectuate its judgments."[1] These provisions significantly limit the actions of federal courts supervising state courts and influence actions of litigants trying to shift litigation from state to federal court or wishing to protect against duplicative litigation.

Exploring these matters, this chapter first outlines the general prohibition against enjoining state court proceedings and then reviews the three exceptions. Convincing a federal court to find one of the three Anti-Injunction Act exceptions applicable is an important step toward an injunction; however, a litigant may encounter further obstacles in the form of abstention doctrines, which are explored in Chapter 8.

---

1. This general prohibition contrasts with a more specific provision, the Tax Injunction Act, 28 U.S.C. §1341, which states that "district courts shall not enjoin, suspend or restrain the assessment, levy or collection of any tax under State law where a plain, speedy and efficient remedy may be had in the courts of such State."

A. THE GENERAL PROHIBITION: NO INJUNCTIONS OF STATE PROCEEDINGS

The Anti-Injunction Act derives from our nation's beginning, in 1793, when Congress enacted a statute mandating that no "injunction be granted to stay proceedings in any court of a state."[2] Why did Congress bother to tie the hands of federal judges wishing to stop state proceedings? The Supreme Court has often said that the prohibition seeks to prevent friction between state and federal courts. And why would friction result? Most assume that federal injunctions would anger state courts. After all, injunctions are an "in your face" remedy, representing the federal judge's personal order forcing the state court to stop adjudicating the case, under penalty of contempt. Others say that hostility may not occur, since a federal injunction may cause little more than a notation on a docket list in the state court clerk's office.[3] Yet in those instances where the state judge actually knows about the injunction, tension may result.

The Anti-Injunction Act may serve other purposes as well, such as avoiding federal interference with a state court's attempt to regulate and honoring state appellate processes that correct state trial court errors. The act also enables issue and claim preclusion laws to serve as the primary vehicle for regulating our nation's system of concurrent jurisdiction, which makes possible duplicative litigation in state and federal systems.[4]

1. Ongoing State Court Proceedings Only

Although the 1793 statute's prohibition evolved over time, the Anti-Injunction Act has remained the same since 1948. The act's current prohibition applies to direct injunctions against state courts and to indirect injunctions against parties who are pursuing state court litigation. The United States Supreme Court has established, however, that the act's prohibition is triggered only if the state court litigation is ongoing.

Example 7-1

Sally wishes to distribute political leaflets at a local shopping mall. She has heard, however, that the state prosecutor believes that handing out such

---

2. Act of Mar. 2, 1793, ch. 22, §5, 1 Stat. 335.
3. See, e.g., ERWIN CHEMERINSKY, FEDERAL JURISDICTION 717 (4th ed. 2003).
4. Another vehicle for regulating duplicative litigation, abstention doctrines, is discussed in Chapter 8.

material violates an anti-terrorism statute recently adopted in the state. Sally filed suit in federal court, seeking an injunction against the prosecutor's instituting criminal charges against her. Desiring to leave open the option of criminal proceedings in the future, the prosecutor argued to the federal court that the Anti-Injunction Act prevents the court from issuing the requested injunctive relief. Is the prosecutor correct?

Explanation

The prosecutor is wrong. The Anti-Injunction Act applies to a request to enjoin a party, such as the prosecutor, from pursuing a state court proceeding. Nevertheless, the act is not applicable before a party initiates state court litigation. In the language of the act, no "proceeding[] in a State court" yet exists to trigger the act's prohibition. *Dombrowski v. Pfister*, 380 U.S. 479, 485 n.2 (1965) (stating that Anti-Injunction Act does not prevent federal court from enjoining a party from starting state court proceedings). Lower courts are in conflict over the question of whether the act prohibits a federal court from issuing an injunction against state court proceedings begun after a party filed for the federal injunction but before the federal court ruled on the injunction request. That circumstance, however, is not applicable here because the prosecutor does not even have specific plans to institute a state prosecution.

2. Declaratory Judgments Too?

The Supreme Court has yet to rule on whether the Anti-Injunction Act's prohibitions apply to requests for declaratory judgments. Declaratory judgments provide an official statement — in the form of a court judgment — of parties' rights and legal relationships. They intrude less on parties' dignity than injunctions because courts cannot enforce declaratory judgments immediately using the contempt power. Instead, the Federal Declaratory Judgment Act, 28 U.S.C. §2202, allows federal courts to enforce the declaratory judgment with "necessary or proper relief," which may include an injunction issued after a hearing. Only if that injunction is not honored may the federal court resort to the contempt power for enforcement. Out of respect for the authority of federal declaratory judgments, however, state courts are expected to honor the judgment's terms and halt proceedings. Thus, a declaratory judgment usually has the same effect as an injunction of a state court proceeding. For that reason, many lower courts have ruled that federal courts are barred from issuing declaratory judgments in cases where the Anti-Injunction Act would prohibit the federal courts from issuing an injunction.

Example 7-2

Salil was injured while working on a dock. Rather than pursue remedies made available to him by a federal statute, the Dockworkers Act, he filed suit in state court, alleging negligence and seeking damages against his employer. The employer then filed suit in federal district court, requesting a declaratory judgment that the state law action was preempted by the Dockworkers Act and that the state court could not validly issue a remedy for the alleged negligence. Salil argued that the federal district court was prohibited from granting this relief under the Anti-Injunction Act. Is Salil correct that the district court should not issue the declaratory judgment?

Explanation

The weight of authority supports Salil. If the district court issues the requested declaratory judgment, that remedy will likely have the same practical effect as a formal injunction: the state court will consider itself obligated to abandon the lawsuit. Even if the state court does not dismiss the suit, the Declaratory Judgment Act authorizes the federal court to issue an injunction as "necessary or proper relief" to enforce the declaratory judgment. Accordingly, the federal declaratory judgment remedy will likely cause the interference with state court processes that the Anti-Injunction Act seeks to prevent.[5]

B. EXCEPTION 1: INJUNCTIONS EXPRESSLY AUTHORIZED BY STATUTE

The Anti-Injunction Act represents a congressionally created bar on federal court injunctions. Just as Congress has the prerogative of creating that bar, it has the prerogative to suspend the bar when it chooses. The Anti-Injunction Act's first exception merely formalizes the latter prerogative: if Congress expressly authorizes federal courts to issue injunctions against state courts in a specific statute, courts assume that Congress meant to nullify the Anti-Injunction Act's bar. Congress has, in fact, authorized injunctions in a number of statutes, including the Bankruptcy Code (allowing an automatic stay of proceedings under 11 U.S.C. §362), the removal statute (allowing an injunction of a state court proceeding under 28 U.S.C. §1446(d) if the state court refuses to relinquish power over a properly removed case), and the Interpleader Act, 28 U.S.C. §2361 (allowing injunctions of state suits to allow federal courts to adjudicate conflicting claims to a limited fund).

---

5. An argument may also be made that the abstention doctrine of *Younger v. Harris*, 401 U.S. 37 (1971), described in detail in Chapter 8, would also preclude the requested remedy.

How "express" must Congress be in order to trigger this exception? The United States Supreme Court provided an answer in *Mitchum v. Foster*, 407 U.S. 225 (1972), which found that the bedrock civil rights statute, 42 U.S.C. §1983, expressly authorizes injunctions of state proceedings. Section 1983 does not specifically say that federal courts may enjoin state proceedings. Instead, the Court found permission for such injunctions from the statute's authorization of equitable remedies (which include injunctions) and in the statute's legislative history and purpose. The Court observed that §1983's goal was to allow federal courts to supervise state instrumentalities, and that the legislative history established state courts as one of those instrumentalities. Accordingly, the Court found §1983 to fall within the expressly authorized exception to the Anti-Injunction Act. A statute falls within this exception, the Court explained, when the statute can be "given its intended scope" only if federal courts have freedom to enjoin state court proceedings.[6]

Example 7-3

Congress has determined that the nation's environment requires uniform regulation and that the federal government should take on that task. Legislative history documents that Congress concluded that state court nuisance actions seeking to regulate pollution interfered with that goal. The legislative history also establishes that Congress viewed these state court actions as a significant source of the problem inspiring federal intervention. Congress ultimately passed a statute stating, "Federal courts should exercise plenary authority to enforce the nation's environmental laws and to avoid contradictory adjudication of rights concerning the environment. To further this end, federal courts should enjoy all remedial powers necessary to ensure uniform enforcement of federal environmental law." Does this statute authorize an exception to the Anti-Injunction Act?

Explanation

Under *Mitchum v. Foster*, 407 U.S. 225 (1972), this statute appears to authorize an exception to the Anti-Injunction Act, even though it does not explicitly state that federal courts may enjoin state court actions. In order to give the environmental statute "its intended scope," federal courts need power to enjoin state proceedings that interfere with uniform enforcement of the environmental laws. The legislative history's reference to state

---

6. *Mitchum*, 407 U.S. at 238. *Mitchum*'s recognition of a §1983 exception to the Anti-Injunction Act is significantly curtailed by the possibility that a federal court may nonetheless decline to issue the injunction pursuant to the doctrine of *Younger v. Harris*, 401 U.S. 37 (1971), described in detail in Chapter 8.

court nuisance actions, as well as the statutory language about avoiding "contradictory adjudication," shows that Congress saw state court actions as an obstacle to that purpose. The statute's grant of "plenary authority" and "all remedial powers" to federal courts encompasses injunctive relief. Both the legislative history and the statutory language make clear that Congress envisioned that the federal interest in uniform environmental laws requires federal courts to interact with state courts by using injunctive powers. Cf. *Vendo Co. v. Lektro-Vend Corp.*, 433 U.S. 623, 640-641 (1977) (opinion for three justices, by Rehnquist, J.) (finding that the Clayton Act did not satisfy the *Mitchum* test because Congress did not envision the "necessary interaction" between federal and state courts to accomplish the act's purpose).

C. EXCEPTION 2: INJUNCTIONS NECESSARY IN AID OF JURISDICTION

The second exception to the Anti-Injunction Act authorizes a federal court to enjoin state court proceedings where necessary in aid of its jurisdiction. One might think of this as the *pre-judgment* exception — an exception that allows federal courts to enjoin state court proceedings while they consider a matter before them for adjudication. While conceivably generous in equipping federal courts with the tools to protect their power, this exception has relatively limited scope. Indeed, the Supreme Court has declared that the exception applies only in two instances: (1) when a state court does not relinquish a properly removed case and (2) when the federal court first exercises power over in rem actions that are later filed in state court as well.[7] The first circumstance for allowing pre-judgment injunctions of state court proceedings — removal — has little consequence, since Congress has already "expressly authorized" an exception in the removal statute, 28 U.S.C. §1446(d), allowing federal courts to enjoin state courts from exercising power over properly removed cases.

The second circumstance — in rem actions — is more significant. In an in rem action, control over a res — such as real property, personal property, or something less tangible, like a fund or trust — provides the foundation for the court's power and ability to render adequate relief. The theory behind in rem actions suggests that when a court exercises power over a disputed res, it must maintain complete control over the res in order to provide full relief. Accordingly, if a federal court entertains the dispute before the state court, the federal court may enjoin state proceedings that

---

7. Lower courts have applied the pre-judgment exception in the context of federal class actions and other complex litigation, but the practice is controversial, and the United States Supreme Court has not endorsed it.

interfere with the federal court's control and disposition of the res. *Toucey v. New York Life Ins. Co.,* 314 U.S. 118, 135-136 (1941).

Example 7-4

Karen, a citizen of California, and Olga, a citizen of Oregon, both asserted that they were the sole owner of a tract of land in Oregon. Karen filed a federal court suit in Oregon, seeking to have the court designate the rightful owner. The federal court attached the land, and the parties began discovery. Olga then filed suit in Oregon state court, seeking to have the state court adjudicate the rightful owner of the property. Karen filed a request to have the federal court enjoin the state proceeding. Olga argued that the injunction was invalid under the Anti-Injunction Act. Does Olga have a valid argument?

Explanation

Olga is wrong. The federal court may enjoin the state court action because (1) the federal court's attachment constitutes the exercise of in rem power over the land, and (2) the federal court action was filed first. The federal court action is explicitly directed at a certain res — the real property — and the federal court cannot proceed effectively without control over the res. For that reason, the federal court may treat its jurisdiction over the res as exclusive.

The Supreme Court has held that the in rem exception applies even though the federal court did not actually seize or take control of property before the state court suit began. The operative event is not actual possession or symbolic seizure of the res, but priority in filing the lawsuit. Moreover, case law establishes that the in rem exception applies in myriad contexts, including those in which the federal courts authorize a receivership, marshal assets, administer trusts, or liquidate estates. *See, e.g., Princess Lida of Thurn & Taxis v. Thompson,* 305 U.S. 456, 466-467 (1939).

Example 7-5

Andrea and several of her friends believe that they were defrauded by Swindler Corporation. They filed a fraud action in federal court, which determined that fraud did occur and that Swindler Corporation lacked current assets sufficient to make Andrea and her friends whole. The federal court further found that Swindler Corporation would quickly dissipate its remaining assets if the court did not assign a receiver to preserve them. The federal court ruled that the receiver should manage the company (and federal court jurisdiction should be retained) until such time as

Swindler Corporation could satisfy its debt to Andrea and her friends. Before the federal court named a receiver to take over the company, another company — Corrupt Corporation — filed an action in state court, asserting that it had entered into a contract with Swindler Corporation to buy all its assets, and requesting that the state court transfer ownership of Swindler Corporation to Corrupt Corporation. Andrea and her friends filed a motion for the federal court to enjoin the state court proceeding, arguing that the federal court needed to establish full control over the assets of Swindler Corporation in order to provide full relief. Corrupt Corporation argued that the Anti-Injunction Act barred the injunction. Is Corrupt correct, or does the injunction fall within an exception to the Anti-Injunction Act?

Explanation

The injunction is likely within the scope of the pre-judgment exception to the Anti-Injunction Act. Although the federal court receiver had not actually taken control of Swindler Corporation at the time the state court suit was filed, the federal court suit is explicitly directed at Swindler Corporation's assets. Equally important, the federal court findings made plain the court cannot provide effective relief to Andrea and her friends without controlling Swindler Corporation. For those reasons, the state court action must yield to the prior federal court action. A contrary argument might prevail if the state court had actually taken possession of Swindler Corporation's assets, in which case the federal court injunction would be harder to justify. *See, e.g., SEC v. Wencke*, 622 F.2d 1363, 1371 (9th Cir. 1980).

The limited circumstances under which federal courts may issue pre-judgment injunctions of ongoing state court proceedings mean that litigants confronting duplicative litigation in two court systems often lack sufficient tools for consolidating the lawsuits. As explored in the next chapter, litigants might find that abstention doctrines help cope with duplicative lawsuits. But those doctrines counsel federal courts to decline the litigation, leaving state courts with power to adjudicate the dispute. Confronted with the mandate of the Anti-Injunction Act, a litigant who wishes to pursue a federal court action usually must tolerate the parallel litigation unless the litigant can convince the state court to halt the action under a state law theory, such as malicious prosecution or a state law analogue to Federal Rule of Civil Procedure 11.

Example 7-6

Prudence is a citizen of state P. She brought a breach of contract action in federal court against Dolly, who is a citizen of state D. Prudence then brought an action in state court against Dolly, seeking the same remedy for breach of the same contract that was the subject of the federal court suit. Dolly was not pleased that Prudence was suing her, and was particularly displeased at being sued twice. Dolly resolved that if she had to defend this lawsuit, she wanted to defend it in federal court. For that reason, she did not want to ask the federal court to dismiss or to stay the federal court suit. Instead, she filed a motion for the federal court to enjoin the state court action, arguing that the injunction was necessary in aid of the federal court's jurisdiction. Is the federal court allowed to enjoin the parallel state action?

Explanation

No, the Anti-Injunction Act bars the requested injunction. Prudence's lawsuit does not fall within any of the circumstances where a federal court may enjoin a state court action "in aid of its jurisdiction" under exception 2 to the Anti-Injunction Act. The action here is simply an in personam action against Dolly and does not involve removal. At this point in the litigation, Dolly must tolerate litigating the dispute in both court systems unless she can convince the state court to dismiss the lawsuit or the federal court to abstain. Otherwise, Dolly must simply hope that the federal court will reach judgment first. If that happens, she can ask the state court to cease litigation pursuant to preclusion principles. If Dolly has difficulty convincing the state court to cease at that point, she can avail herself of exception 3 of the Anti-Injunction Act.

D. EXCEPTION 3: INJUNCTIONS TO PROTECT OR EFFECTUATE JUDGMENTS

Just as exception 2 can be called the pre-judgment exception, exception 3 may be called the post-judgment exception. The post-judgment exception has been applied in a wider range of circumstances than the pre-judgment exception. Generally, the post-judgment exception allows a federal court that has decided an issue to prevent a party from relitigating the issue in state court under circumstances where the issue would have a preclusive effect under principles of res judicata or collateral estoppel. Given this context, the post-judgment exception is also called the "relitigation exception."

Example 7-7

The facts are the same as in Example 7-6, where Prudence sued Dolly in state and federal court. After trial, the federal court entered judgment against Prudence. The court found that Dolly had complied with the contract and that Prudence had no legal foundation for suing her for breach of contract. With that finding, the federal court issued a final judgment. Dolly then filed a motion in the state court action, asking the state court to dismiss the suit. The state court refused even to consider the motion and scheduled the lawsuit for trial on the merits. Dolly returned to federal court, asking the federal court to enjoin the state court proceeding. Should the federal court issue the injunction under the relitigation exception?

Explanation

Yes, the federal court should enjoin the state court proceeding. This is precisely the type of circumstance that the relitigation exception is designed to cover: the federal court disposed of the case on the merits, and the state court refused to give preclusive effect to the final judgment. Interestingly, the state court's failure actually to rule on the preclusion issue makes the case even stronger for Dolly. If the state court had explicitly ruled that the federal court judgment did not preclude the state court from continuing with the litigation, that state court ruling on preclusion would likely be binding on the federal court. Consider how this might work in Example 7-8.

Example 7-8

The facts are again the same as in Example 7-6, with Prudence bringing state and federal court suits against Dolly. After trial, the federal court entered judgment against Prudence. The court found that Dolly had complied with the contract and that Prudence had no legal foundation for suing her for breach of contract. With that finding, the federal court issued a final judgment. Dolly then filed a motion in the state court action, raising the defense of res judicata and asking the state court to dismiss the suit. The state court held that the res judicata doctrine does not preclude the state court from proceeding, and entered a large damages judgment in favor of Prudence. After this damages judgment, Dolly filed a motion in federal court seeking an injunction against enforcement of the judgment. Should the federal court issue this injunction under the relitigation exception?

Explanation

The federal court should not issue the injunction. Under circumstances similar to this example, the United States Supreme Court in *Parsons Steel, Inc. v. First Alabama Bank*, 474 U.S. 518, 524 (1986), ruled that the post-judgment exception to the Anti-Injunction Act is limited "to those situations in which the state court has not yet ruled on the merits of the res judicata issue." Here, the defendant raised the res judicata defense, and the state court rejected it; the federal court must therefore accept the state court's ruling that the state court action is not precluded. Accordingly, the verdict in state court undermines Dolly's victory in federal court.

Although dramatic, this disposition is unusual and unlikely to happen often. In most circumstances, the state court will grant preclusive effect to the federal court judgment under "full faith and credit" principles and preclusion law. In that event, the winning party from the federal court need not seek an injunction of the state court proceedings.[8]

The relitigation exception applies only where federal courts have issued "judgments." But the exception does not apply to every judgment. For example, if a federal court decides that it would be inappropriate for it to hear the case, that determination is not necessarily binding on a state court that is later asked to adjudicate the same dispute. Problems arise, however, because courts can encounter difficulty in determining the precise basis for the federal court judgment: does it concern only the propriety of the federal court's exercising power in the case, or does it rest on some other reasoning?

An example of this ambiguity occurred in *Atlantic Coast Line Railroad Co. v. Brotherhood of Locomotive Engineers*, 398 U.S. 281 (1970). In that case, a federal court had adjudicated a labor dispute between a union and a railroad. The federal court ruled for the union, refusing to stop the union's picketing, but state court later halted the labor activity. The union then returned to the federal court, asking for an injunction to stay the state court decision. In deciding whether the union's injunction request should have been granted, the United States Supreme Court had to ascertain the basis for the first federal court decision in favor of the union. If the first federal court had determined that it simply lacked subject matter jurisdiction over the labor dispute, that ruling did not bind the state court, because it had different subject matter jurisdiction constraints from those of the federal court. Alternatively, if the federal court had decided that federal law protected the picketing, then the state court could be enjoined from disregarding this federal court ruling about substantive rights. The Supreme Court ultimately decided that the federal court's ruling was premised solely on federal subject matter jurisdiction and therefore concluded that the relitigation exception did not apply.

The Supreme Court applied *Atlantic Coast Line Railroad Co.* in a subsequent decision concerning forum non conveniens, *Chick Kam Choo v. Exxon Corp.*, 486 U.S. 140 (1988). According to the *Chick Kam Choo* Court, a forum non conveniens dismissal means only that the law of the forum where litigation is pending deems the forum an inappropriate place to litigate. Thus, a forum non conveniens ruling by a federal court is not binding on another forum, such as a state court.

---

8. On the other hand, Judge Diane Wood suggests that this faith in the state court may be imprudent, arguing that the safest strategy is for the federal court winner to refrain from presenting the preclusion issue in state court and immediately ask the federal court for an injunction. *See* Diane P. Wood, *Fine-Tuning Judicial Federalism: A Proposal for Reform of the Anti-Injunction Act*, 1990 BYU L. Rev. 289, 318-320 (1990).

Example 7-9

Plaintiff filed a wrongful death action in federal district court in Texas. Applying conflict-of-laws principles, the Texas district court concluded that Singapore law would govern the controversy and that the doctrine of forum non conveniens called for dismissal of the suit. After the dismissal, plaintiff filed the same suit in Texas state court. Plaintiff asserted a claim based on Singapore law, and the state court entertained the controversy. Defendants returned to federal district court, seeking an injunction of the state court action. Defendants argued that the injunction was necessary to protect and effectuate the federal court decision not to adjudicate the suit in Texas. Does the Anti-Injunction Act's post-judgment exception apply to the requested injunction?

Explanation

No, this circumstance does not satisfy the Anti-Injunction Act's relitigation exception. As in *Chick Kam Choo*, the relitigation exception to the Anti-Injunction Act is inapplicable here. According to the reasoning of *Chick Kam Choo*, the Texas state court would not necessarily relitigate the federal court's forum non conveniens ruling, because state and federal forum non conveniens law might differ. In this example — as in *Chick Kam Choo* — the earlier federal court ruling concluded that the federal forum was inappropriate for litigating the suit. The ruling did not determine whether a state forum would be appropriate; therefore, the state court should be free to make that determination.

Synthesizing *Chick Kam Choo* and *Atlantic Coast Line Railroad Co.*, one might argue that the relitigation exception applies only when the earlier federal court ruled on "the merits" of a controversy, and not when the federal court dismissed a case on "procedural grounds."[9] Many lower federal courts, however, have not recognized this distinction between "the merits" and "procedural grounds." Instead, the courts have scrutinized whether the federal court's disposition bears on the propriety of a state court's later adjudicating the controversy. One common approach holds that "the relitigation exception may apply even if the merits of the case were never reached, provided that a critical issue concerning the case has been adjudicated properly." *Canady v. Allstate Ins. Co.*, 282 F.3d 1005, 1015 (8th Cir. 2002). This view gives the relitigation exception broader scope than does the

---

9. *See, e.g.*, ERWIN CHEMERINSKY, FEDERAL JURISDICTION 730 (4th ed. 2003) (explaining that "[i]f the federal court ruled on the merits, then its decision should be upheld by an injunction if necessary; but if the federal court dismissed the case on procedural grounds, then the state court should be free to hear the matter").

approach of distinguishing between federal court decisions on "the merits" and those based on "procedural grounds."

Example 7-10

Top Dog Enterprises wanted to buy a basketball team and move the team to a different city. The National Basketball Association (NBA) wanted to stop the purchase and prevent the team transfer. The NBA filed suit in federal court, which issued a preliminary injunction preventing the sale until it could issue a final order on the legality of Top Dog's attempted purchase. As part of its decision to issue the preliminary injunction, the federal district court weighed the public interest, the possibility of irreparable harm, and the likelihood that the NBA would ultimately prevail after trial in the district court. Relying on the preliminary injunction, the NBA finalized the schedule for the next year on the assumption that Top Dog would not be able to make the purchase and move the team. Concerned with the NBA's actions, Top Dog filed suit in state court, asking that court to clear the way for the sale. The state court began adjudicating pretrial motions in the case. The NBA then asked the federal court to enjoin the state court proceeding, arguing that the injunction was necessary to protect and effectuate the preliminary injunction order. Is the NBA correct that the preliminary injunction is covered by the relitigation exception?

Explanation

The NBA's assertion is subject to debate. First, one might argue that the preliminary injunction order is not covered by the relitigation exception because it is not a decision "on the merits." Instead, the preliminary injunction ruling is merely a threshold order designed to preserve the status quo until the district court is able to adjudicate the controversy and issue a final judgment. Yet, in NBA v. Minnesota Professional Basketball, L.P., 56 F.3d 866 (8th Cir. 1995), the court determined that such an order was eligible for protection under the relitigation exception. According to the Minnesota Professional Basketball court, the exception should apply to preliminary injunctions because such injunctions grant "important rights and finally adjudicate[] the issue of preserving the status quo until the district court reaches the case's merits." Id. at 871-872.

There's another difficulty with the NBA's assertion: the relitigation exception applies only to "judgments" of federal courts. One might argue that, as temporary measures protecting the status quo pending trial, preliminary injunction rulings are not "judgments" within the meaning of the relitigation exception. Substantial authority, however, supports the view that preliminary injunctions can be "judgments" under the exception. This view observes that Federal Rule of Civil Procedure 54 defines a judgment as "a decree and any order from which an appeal lies" — a definition that encompasses interlocutory orders subject to immediate appeal.[10] This approach has special force in the context of preliminary injunctions, which are "immediately appealable to prevent irreparable harm." *Minnesota Professional Basketball*, 56 F.3d at 872.

One might limit the approach in cases such as *Minnesota Professional Basketball* by pointing to the extraordinary qualities of preliminary injunctions. After all, preliminary injunctions are issued only upon a showing of threatened irreparable harm, thus justifying their treatment as worthy of special respect and protection.[11] Although one could interpret *Minnesota Professional Basketball* narrowly, other courts have applied its approach broadly. Indeed, courts have applied *Minnesota Professional Basketball* outside of the preliminary injunction context, finding the relitigation exception applicable to a variety of threshold, procedural rulings. *See, e.g., Canady v. Allstate Ins. Co.*, 282 F.3d 1005 (8th Cir. 2002) (applying the exception where an earlier federal court had disposed of the case on grounds of lack of standing); *Baker v. Gotz*, 415 F. Supp. 1243, 1250 (D. Del.), *aff'd*, 546 F.2d 415 (3d Cir. 1976) (applying the exception in the context of earlier federal court decision vacating sequestration orders).

Example 7-11

Viola is from Massachusetts and Vera is from New Hampshire. They were in a car accident in Connecticut. Hearing that New York juries are particularly generous, Viola filed a diversity action against Vera in New York. Vera moved to dismiss the suit for lack of personal jurisdiction because she had no contacts in New York. The federal court dismissed the case on this ground, holding that Vera had insufficient contacts with New York to allow a New York federal court to exercise power over her in a manner consistent with federal due process principles. Viola then filed the exact same suit against Vera in New Hampshire state court, and the state court scheduled the case for trial. Vera asked the federal court to enjoin the state

---

10. *See, e.g.,* Charles Alan Wright, Arthur R. Miller, Edward H. Cooper & Vikram David Amar, 17 Federal Practice and Procedure §4226, at 550 (West 2d ed. 2005) (arguing that this view applies to preliminary injunctions, partial summary judgment motions, and orders subject to the collateral order doctrine, but should not apply to orders appealable only through a discretionary interloctory appeal procedure).

11. In the particular context of *Minnesota Professional Basketball*, one could also justify the ruling by citing the second exception to the Anti-Injunction Act: the pre-judgment exception. The *Minnesota Professional Basketball* court effectively treated the basketball team as akin to a res for the purpose of the second exception to the Anti-Injunction Act, the pre-judgment exception. Even though the federal court nominally relied on the relitigation exception, the court used the state court injunction to maintain federal court power before final judgment over the centerpiece of the suit: the basketball team. Under this reading of *Minnesota Professional Basketball*, the case has limited reach.

court suit, citing the relitigation exception. Does the relitigation exception apply here?

Explanation

Even under a broad reading of the relitigation exception, the federal court should not grant the injunction. The question of whether a federal court in New York may constitutionally exercise personal jurisdiction differs from the question of whether a New Hampshire state court can exercise personal jurisdiction; thus, the New Hampshire state court is not prevented from exercising power because the New York federal court lacked personal jurisdiction over Vera. The New York federal court's ruling was not only a threshold procedural matter, but was also a matter that did not reflect on the propriety of a state court in New Hampshire hearing the case. A Reviser's Note explaining the relitigation exception suggests that the exception applies to matters that the federal court has "fully adjudicated." 28 U.S.C. §2283 (2000) (Reviser's Note). The New York federal court here did not "fully adjudicate[]" the issue of whether a New Hampshire state court may assert personal jurisdiction over the defendant.

Example 7-12

Assume the same facts as Example 7-11 with the federal district court in New York granting the motion to dismiss on personal jurisdiction grounds, citing federal due process principles. Now, however, rather than filing suit in New Hampshire state court, Viola filed suit in New York state court. As before, Vera asked the New York federal court to enjoin the state court suit, relying on the relitigation exception. Should the federal court grant the injunction request?

Explanation

The proper disposition of the injunction request is subject to debate. On one hand, this example is similar to *Chick Kam Choo v. Exxon Corp.*, 486 U.S. 140 (1988), discussed in Example 7-9. The similarity exists because the federal court dismissed the action as filed in an improper forum, and the state court within the same jurisdiction later exercised power over the case. On the other hand, the precise issue decided by the federal court here differs from that in *Chick Kam Choo*: the federal court in this example decided that exercise of personal jurisdiction in New York was inconsistent with due process principles. Thus, the federal court made a constitutional ruling based on Vera's minimal contacts in the geographical territory of New York. One can readily argue that this ruling applies with full force regardless of whether the court exercising personal jurisdiction in New York is a state or a federal court.[12] From this perspective, one might conclude that the relitigation exception applies, and the injunction should issue to protect or effectuate the federal court's judgment regarding personal jurisdiction. Cf. *Bordelon v. Jefferson Feed & Garden Supply, Inc.*, 703 F. Supp. 25 (E.D. La. 1988) (reaching a similar conclusion for an analogous personal jurisdiction issue).

---

12. Technically, different due process clauses bind state and federal courts. The due process clause of the Fifth Amendment controls federal authority, while the due process clause of the Fourteenth Amendment restricts state power. Courts have generally treated precedent under the two clauses, however, as interchangeable. Thus, one may argue that a state court interpreting Fourteenth Amendment due process constraints on personal jurisdiction is bound by an earlier interpretation of Fifth Amendment due process constraints in a case concerning the same persons in the same controversy.

CHAPTER 8

Abstention Doctrines

American school children studying the Constitution learn about the checks and balances among the three branches of the federal government. One of the "checks" they discover in the Constitution's Article III is Congress's control over the job description of lower federal courts. As Chapter 6 explored, Congress has great latitude in delineating the subject matter jurisdiction of the district courts and courts of appeals. So it is not surprising that Congress might decide to restrict broad jurisdictional grants with a specific statutory constraint such as the Anti-Injunction Act. Far more remarkable are constraints that federal courts develop to restrict their own power. These court-made restrictions generally take the form of abstention doctrines,[1] which govern when federal courts can abstain from exercising the powers that Congress granted them in subject matter jurisdiction statutes.

Acquiring their names from the cases in which the Supreme Court first developed them, the abstention doctrines derive from the Supreme Court's views on the wisdom and constitutional propriety of adjudicating particular categories of disputes. The doctrines are animated by principles governing the proper allocation of power between federal and state governments, as well as prudential considerations governing decisionmaking. The abstention doctrines are available in limited circumstances, because the Supreme Court has often said that federal courts have a "virtually unflagging obligation . . . to exercise the jurisdiction" Congress has given them. *Colorado River Water*

---

1. Although grounded in the Constitution's "case or controversy" requirement, justiciability doctrines can also be described as "court-made restrictions" on federal court jurisdiction. These doctrines are described in Chapter 5.

Conservation Dist. v. United States, 424 U.S. 800, 817 (1976). Accordingly, one urging a federal court to abstain confronts a strong presumption that the federal court will not do so. Moreover, one must remember that the abstention doctrines supplement (not displace) congressionally created restrictions on federal court power, such as the Anti-Injunction Act.

Abstention doctrines divide roughly into two categories: those that apply in federal court cases presenting issues of unclear or complicated state law, and those that apply where duplicate proceedings are pending in state and federal courts. This chapter explores these categories in turn.

A. UNCLEAR STATE LAW DOCTRINES: *PULLMAN, THIBODAUX,* AND *BURFORD*

When a case presents a legal issue that is governed by state law or could be resolved by state administrative proceedings, federal courts may consider whether exercising federal power interferes with the state's attempt to regulate the dispute's subject matter. The initial trigger for considering this area of abstention is an unclear state law issue in the case or a complicated network of state laws relevant to the controversy. If one of these triggers is present, then one should look for other qualities: (1) if the case includes a federal constitutional claim, *Pullman* abstention may be appropriate; (2) if the case presents an unclear state law concerning a particularly sensitive and important area in a diversity action, *Thibodaux* abstention may be appropriate; and (3) if the state has an administrative framework or network of regulations for handling the controversy, *Burford* abstention may be appropriate.

Nearly all states have a statute that permits federal courts to request clarification of a particular state law issue by "certifying" questions to state courts. The availability of certification is an important factor that bears on whether (and how) a federal court will employ these abstention doctrines. Certification can sometimes preclude the need for abstention altogether and can simplify or hasten the procedures followed when a federal court decides to abstain.

1. *Pullman* Abstention: Avoiding Unnecessary Constitutional Issues

In *Railroad Comm'n of Texas v. Pullman Co.*, 312 U.S. 496 (1941), the Texas Railroad Commission ordered trains operated in Texas to be supervised by conductors rather than porters. At the time, this order had racial ramifications because conductors were generally white while porters were generally black. The Pullman Company and railroads affected by the order sued in federal court to enjoin the railroad commission's order, arguing that the order violated federal constitutional principles and exceeded the Railroad Commission's authority under state law. If a court were to hold that the commission lacked authority to issue the order, the court need not reach the federal constitutional claim. Under these circumstances, the United States Supreme Court held that where a case presents state law and federal constitutional issues that are each capable of resolving the case, a federal court should decline to decide the federal constitutional claim. In so holding, the Court affirmed the maxim requiring a federal court to avoid constitutional rulings whenever possible. The Pullman Court also observed that, in adjudicating unsettled state law questions, federal courts may misconceive state law and consequently may interfere with sensitive state policies. Thus, if the parties possess "easy and ample means" of getting state courts to adjudicate the state law issue, federal courts should abstain to allow the parties to seek an authoritative ruling of the state tribunal. 312 U.S. at 499-501.

a. Prerequisites for *Pullman* Abstention

The precise prerequisites for Pullman abstention are subject to debate, although authorities agree abstention is appropriate only if three circumstances are present

1. The case presents both state grounds and federal constitutional grounds for relief.
2. The proper resolution of the state ground for the decision is uncertain.
3. The state ground is capable of resolving the controversy.[2]

Some authorities state that to justify Pullman abstention, the district court must also conclude that the federal court's construction of state law would disrupt sensitive or important state policies.[3]

---

2. *See, e.g., Kusper v. Pontikes*, 414 U.S. 51, 54-55 (1973) (quoted in *Southeast Booksellers Ass'n. v. McMaster*, 282 F. Supp. 2d 389, 396 (D.S.C. 2003)); ERWIN CHEMERINSKY, FEDERAL JURISDICTION 787 (4th ed. 2003); 17A JAMES WM. MOORE ET AL., MOORE'S FEDERAL PRACTICE §120 (2005).

3. *See, e.g., Word of Faith World Outreach Ctr. Church, Inc. v. Morales*, 986 F.2d 962, 967, 969 (5th Cir. 1993) (federal court may abstain if one of several factors is present, including the possibility that federal court review risks substantial friction with state regulation); *Chez Sez III Corp. v. Twp. of Union*, 945 F.2d 628, 631 (3d Cir. 1991) (abstention appropriate if federal court's erroneous construction of state law "would disrupt important state policies"); *Ripplinger v. Collins*, 868 F.2d 1043, 1048 (9th Cir. 1989) (to abstain, federal court must find that "the complaint touches a sensitive area of social policy upon which the federal courts ought not to enter unless no alternative to its adjudication is open").

Example 8-1

Deedee Developer wanted to develop a site located in Caramel City. The site was occupied by a historically significant building. Deedee applied for a permit to demolish the building, but the director of the Caramel City Historical Commission denied her request under the newly enacted Historic Properties Ordinance. Deedee filed suit in federal court raising two claims regarding the manner in which the director had denied the permit: (1) the director violated her federal procedural due process rights and (2) the director failed to comply with procedures envisioned by the Historic Properties Ordinance. Deedee asked for an injunction requiring the director to provide procedures that would allow her to litigate her permit request.

The director argued to the district court that the Historic Properties Ordinance is unclear as to what, if any, procedures it requires. Thus, the director argued that this case is perfect for *Pullman* abstention and that the federal court should allow a state tribunal to adjudicate the state law procedure claim. Are the prerequisites for *Pullman* abstention present?

Explanation

The director correctly suggests that the three *Pullman* abstention prerequisites are present in this example:

1. The case contains both a federal constitutional claim and a state law process claim.

2. Uncertainty exists about the meaning of the state law underlying the state claim, since the parties disagree about the procedures mandated by the Historic Properties Ordinance.

3. Disposition of the state procedure claim could obviate the need for adjudication of the federal due process claim. Indeed, if the state law provides for procedures that were not followed, Deedee would get an opportunity to avail herself of those procedures, which may ultimately yield a permit. In other words, she may prevail on state law grounds.

To the extent that *Pullman* abstention requires that the state issue be sensitive or important, that prerequisite is satisfied as well. Issues of property development entail balancing competing concerns: tradition, sense of community, history, economic well-being, and profit motives. This balance is frequently delicate and evokes strong reactions among the state populace.

Example 8-2

Steven's neighbor, April, recently built a large addition to her house. As part of the construction, April instructed her contractors to run a pipe from her downspouts to the edge of the property line near Steven's house. Steven filed suit against April, arguing that channeling water onto his property was a trespass under state common law and a violation of federal environmental law governing storm water management. Steven sought an injunction requiring April to divert the water from his property line (to avoid the trespass) and to comply with the storm water management guidelines (set out in the federal environment laws). April argued that *Pullman* abstention applies. Is April correct?

Explanation

April is wrong. Although Steven's case includes a federal and a state claim, the claims are independent of each other: if he prevails on the state law claim, the injunction he requests would not necessarily remedy his objection under federal environmental laws. Accordingly, resolution of the state law claim will not obviate the need to adjudicate his federal law claim.

Perhaps more fundamentally, the weight of authority holds that *Pullman* abstention applies only where the federal claim is a constitutional claim.[4] Indeed, the motivating principle behind *Pullman* is avoidance of unnecessary constitutional adjudication. Interpreting the Constitution and imposing constitutional rulings on state authority stresses federal-state relations and enhances judicial power at the expense of the democratically elected branches. Thus, the principle of constitutional avoidance keeps federal judicial power within bounds, ensuring that federal judges deploy their judicial review power only when necessary. The concern with restricting judicial power, however, reduces if the federal authority at issue in the case is a federal statute, which is the product of the democratic process and is created by representatives drawn from the states.

Example 8-3

Over the past few years, several consumers have been killed or badly injured using consumer products manufactured and sold in state X. In response to this string of accidents, state X passed a law requiring the state X attorney general to levy fines on any manufacturer of a "dangerous product" within the state. Bianca manufactured and sold several types of widgets in state X and noticed that the state X attorney general began to levy fines on

---

4. *See, e.g., Propper v. Clark*, 337 U.S. 472, 490 (1949). *But see* DAVID P. CURRIE, FEDERAL JURISDICTION 176 (4th ed. 1999) (categorizing *Thibodaux* abstention as a form of *Pullman* abstention for non-constitutional, diversity claims).

manufacturers with businesses similar to Bianca's. In addition, the attorney general has served notice of intention to investigate Bianca's business. Bianca filed a federal declaratory judgment action against the state X attorney general, arguing that the state X statute's prohibition is unconstitutionally vague and that she did not know which, if any, of her product lines was subject to the statutory prohibition. She argued that the statute is so vague as to deprive her of property without due process in violation of the due process clause of the United States Constitution's Fourteenth Amendment. The attorney general argued that the federal district court should abstain under *Pullman* and certify the case to the supreme court of state X for a clarifying interpretation of the "dangerous product" statute. Is the attorney general correct?

Explanation

The attorney general's position is debatable. Bianca's lawsuit is not a typical candidate for *Pullman* abstention because she does not actually assert a state law claim that could provide her with relief. Moreover, the United States Supreme Court has ruled that a mere assertion of constitutional vagueness does not justify *Pullman* abstention. Instead, the district court must examine the challenged statute to determine whether any construction of the statute "would avoid or fundamentally alter the constitutional issue raised in this litigation." *Baggett v. Bullitt*, 377 U.S. 360, 375-376 (1964). Abstention is not required in circumstances where individuals bring a vagueness challenge because they cannot understand what the statute requires of them and do not want to avoid all activity arguably within the statute's scope.

To justify abstention, the attorney general needs to establish that the state issue in the case could be resolved if the state supreme court chooses between one of just a few competing interpretations of the "dangerous product" statute.[5] In other words, the attorney general must also show that Bianca might avoid problems under the "dangerous product" statute if it were construed as not applying to businesses such as hers. To make a final decision on whether the court should abstain, one needs more facts about the statute's terms and how the state supreme court may construe those terms.

If the federal court concludes that resolving the state law issue might obviate the need to decide the federal constitutional question, the court might also consider whether the issue involves sensitive or important concerns — the *Pullman* prerequisite that some authorities require. Product liability may be reasonably described as "important," particularly where — as here — a legislative initiative resulted from a series of injuries in a community. In addition, the court might note that, in a close case, the balance

---

5. If, on the other hand, the statute is subject to an indefinite number of interpretations, abstention is not warranted. *See Baggett*, 377 U.S. at 378.

can tip in favor of abstention where a state has implemented a certification procedure such as here. The Supreme Court has suggested that the certification's availability favors abstention in cases involving "novel" or "unsettled" questions of state law. *Arizonans for Official English v. Arizona*, 520 U.S. 43, 76, 79 (1997).

b. Procedure for *Pullman* Abstention

The procedures generally followed with *Pullman* abstention are for (1) the federal court to retain jurisdiction while it certifies the state law question pursuant to the state court procedure, or (2) the federal court to retain jurisdiction of the matter while the plaintiff takes the state law question to the state court. Under either approach, the plaintiff reserves the right to return to federal court for resolution of the federal constitutional issue, provided the state court does not rule in such a way as to give the plaintiff full relief.

The plaintiff may choose to present both the state and federal issues to the state court. In that event, she will be bound by the state court's disposition on both issues. Alternatively, the case law is clear that a party need not unwillingly relinquish her right to litigate a federal constitutional question in federal court. *England v. Louisiana State Board of Medical Examiners*, 375 U.S. 411, 417 (1964). Prudence counsels, however, that she tell the district court that she wishes to reserve her right to return to federal court to litigate the federal constitutional question if the state court disposition does not resolve the matter.

The plaintiff's prerogative to return to federal court after litigating in state court generally allows her to avoid the res judicata principle that a plaintiff may not split her cause of action.[6] By contrast, collateral estoppel may bind the federal court regarding issues that the state court resolved as a result of the plaintiff's strategy in the state court litigation. Thus, the Supreme Court held in *San Remo Hotel, L.P. v. San Francisco*, 545 U.S. 323, 341 (2005), that *Pullman* abstention's insulation from traditional preclusion principles does not apply where the plaintiff chooses "to advance broader issues than" the specific state law matter from which the federal court abstained. *Id.* at 2503.

Example 8-4

The facts are the same as in Example 8-1: Deedee Developer filed a federal court suit against the Director of the Caramel City Historical Commission, who urged the federal court to abstain. For the reasons stated in the explanation to Example 8-1, the federal court honored the director's request, and abstained from adjudicating the lawsuit.

---

6. ERWIN CHEMERINSKY, FEDERAL JURISDICTION 787 (4th ed. 2003) (because "trying state law issues in state court . . . will not preclude later litigation of federal issues in federal court . . . the traditional res judicata rule against splitting claims is inapplicable").

Assume that Deedee then filed a suit in state court, asking for review of the state procedure claim. Deedee informed the state court that she was reserving her federal due process challenge for federal court. Nonetheless, the state court not only held that the director provided her with all the process anticipated by the Historic Properties Ordinance, but also concluded that both the director's actions and the ordinance complied with federal due process requirements.

Deedee returned to federal court seeking to litigate her federal due process claim. The director argued that the federal court was foreclosed from litigating this matter, because the state court had already decided it. Should the district court adjudicate the federal due process issue?

Explanation

Yes, the district court should litigate the federal due process issue. This example presents a typical case in which a party presents a federal constitutional challenge to a state law. Because the state law may be construed in such a way as to avoid the constitutional challenge, the state law is "antecedent" to federal constitutional challenge. Deedee made clear to the state court that she wished the court to adjudicate only her antecedent state law claim, and took no action to broaden the scope of the state action beyond that state law claim. The state court's decision to reach beyond that does not bind Deedee or the district court.

Example 8-5

Sandy owned a hotel and wanted to market the rooms to tourists in her California town. The town had a problem with homelessness and passed a law known as the Homeless Shelter Act. That act required hotel owners to open 60% of all rooms to provide shelter for the homeless. Sandy filed suit in federal court against the housing chief of her town, arguing that the Homeless Shelter Act was unconstitutional *on its face* under the takings clause of the Fifth Amendment to the United States Constitution. Sandy also argued that the act violated the takings clause of the California Constitution.

The federal court invoked *Pullman* abstention, stating that Sandy was free to raise her federal claim in California state court, but that she could reserve the federal claim for the federal court to adjudicate later if necessary. Sandy filed suit in state court, stating that she wished to reserve her federal claim. In litigating the state law claim, Sandy argued to the California court that the California takings clause and the United States Constitution's takings clause were identical and coextensive. She argued that under both state and federal precedent, the Homeless Shelter Act amounted to a taking of her property without just compensation. The California court agreed that the California takings clause and the United States Constitution's takings clause were identical and coextensive, but ruled that the Homeless Shelter Act did not constitute a taking. Accordingly, the California court decided that the Homeless Shelter Act did not violate the California takings clause, resting its decision on an extensive discussion of federal takings jurisprudence.

After the unfavorable state court decision, Sandy returned to federal court for a ruling on the federal takings claim. The housing chief argued that the federal court was not free to adjudicate this issue, since the state court effectively decided the issue itself. Is the housing chief's argument valid?

Explanation

Under *San Remo Hotel, L.P. v. San Francisco*, 545 U.S. 323 (2005), the housing chief is apparently correct. *San Remo* limited *Pullman* abstention's insulation from traditional res judicata principles, holding that the usual rules of preclusion apply where a plaintiff chooses "to advance broader issues than" the precise state law issues for which the federal court abstained. 545 U.S. at 341. Here, the plaintiff effectively invited the state court to rule on the meaning of federal law as it governs her Fifth Amendment takings claim. Having done so, the plaintiff must live with the consequent state court rulings on the meaning of the Fifth Amendment as it applies to this case.

c. Discretionary Elements of *Pullman* Abstention

Although the United States Supreme Court has at least once treated *Pullman* abstention as mandatory,[7] the Court more frequently treats the abstention doctrine as subject to discretionary factors. In part, this inconsistency is likely a function of the Court's lack of specificity as to the actual prerequisites for *Pullman* abstention. Whatever its source, the Supreme Court's recognition of discretionary concerns spans an array of issues. For example, the Court has stated that abstention is more appropriate if the litigants have access to a state procedure for quickly adjudicating the state law claim, such as a certification procedure.[8] This concern suggests that abstention's effect on the litigants is a factor to consider in deciding whether to abstain. Abstention may impose additional costs on litigants along with a delay before a court finally provides redress for injuries. Sometimes the case's circumstances, as well as available state procedures, can minimize any hardship, making abstention more appropriate.

---

7. See *City of Meridian v. S. Bell Tel. & Tel. Co.*, 358 U.S. 639, 640 (1959).
8. *Arizonans for Official English v. Arizona*, 520 U.S. 43, 76 (1997).

The delay resulting from *Pullman* abstention raises another possible discretionary factor suggested in Supreme Court case law: the importance of the federal constitutional right asserted. Thus, where the plaintiff asserts a First Amendment claim, the Court has expressed concern that delay may impose an unacceptable chilling effect on speech. The Court has also ruled that voting rights claims are poor candidates for *Pullman* abstention because of voting's indispensable role in a properly functioning democracy. Finally, a related discretionary concern arises where the importance of a federal interest in a particular subject area is reflected in a jurisdictional statute that vests federal courts with exclusive jurisdiction. In that context, the plaintiff has no choice but to file the federal component of the case in federal court. Forcing the litigant to seek clarification of the state law issue in state court requires litigation in dual court systems, because the state court cannot reach the federal claim even if the parties want the state court to hear the entire case.

Example 8-6

Ruth has taught photography to public high school students for the last twenty years. Perceiving a problem with teachers improperly influencing students on controversial political issues, the state legislature recently passed a statute preventing public school teachers from participating in local elections. The superintendent of Ruth's school district informed all teachers that they were subject to this prohibition immediately. Ruth refused to comply, noting that her sister was running for mayor and that she had already agreed to help. Ruth had promised to canvass door-to-door and to act as the official photographer for the campaign.

When the superintendent threatened to fire her for refusing to comply with the prohibition, Ruth filed suit in federal court raising two claims: (1) the superintendent erred in applying the prohibition to her, because the state legislature intended the prohibition to apply prospectively to future teachers hired, not retroactively to teachers already employed; and (2) the prohibition violated her rights under the First and Fourteenth Amendments to the United States Constitution to speak freely and to participate in political activities. After she filed suit, Ruth and the superintendent agreed that she could both keep her job and continue to work on her sister's campaign pending the suit's disposition.

The superintendent asked the district court to abstain under *Pullman*. She argued to the district court that it would be appropriate to certify to the state supreme court the following question: "Is the prohibition against political activities intended to apply to teachers who were employed in the state at the time the prohibition became effective?" Should the district court follow the superintendent's advice and abstain under *Pullman*?

Explanation

The district court must make a close call. The prerequisites for *Pullman* abstention appear to be present. The case includes an antecedent state law claim and a federal constitutional claim. The state law claim is antecedent because the district court can avoid adjudicating the constitutionality of the political activity prohibition if that prohibition should not even apply to Ruth. Moreover, even the state official responsible for implementing the prohibition seems to admit to uncertainties about its scope. *Pullman* abstention requires an important and sensitive area of state concern, and political lobbying of school children easily qualifies for that characterization: the statute implicates not only local political issues but education as well. Education enjoys the designation of a state prerogative.

As to possible discretionary factors, the availability of certification does not guarantee *Pullman* abstention, but certainly makes it less cumbersome and possibly less burdensome on the parties. *See Lehman Bros. v. Schein*, 416 U.S. 386, 390 (1974) (endorsing certification procedures, yet stating that "the mere difficulty in ascertaining local law is no excuse for remitting the parties to a state tribunal for the start of another lawsuit"). The agreement between Ruth and the superintendent allowing her to continue both her teaching job and her political activity also makes the abstention less burdensome, because Ruth will not suffer any apparent loss during the period when the state supreme court is clarifying the statute.

On the other hand, the subject matter of the federal constitutional claim strongly weighs against abstention. Not only does the federal claim fall within a specially protected category — First Amendment rights of free expression — but it also concerns political speech. Political speech is perhaps the most valued type of speech, given its role in fostering debate essential to a functioning democracy.

The statute's political context touches yet another area where the Supreme Court has found abstention undesirable: voting rights. Ultimately, this connection will not disqualify abstention, because the statute does not directly implicate voting rights and because the Supreme Court has shown that *Pullman* abstention is sometimes appropriate in litigation over election regulations. Where a challenged state regulation concerns a local issue with which the state has begun to grapple (such as educational policy), the Supreme Court has held that abstention is appropriate even though the regulation affects voting. *See Growe v. Emison*, 507 U.S. 25, 33-34 (1993) (even though case included a voting rights challenge to reapportionment, district court should have abstained under *Pullman* where the state had already taken action to handle the highly politicized reapportionment process).

The obstacle to abstention is the statute's impact on free expression. The superintendent may argue her way around this obstacle by pointing to an important concern motivating the Supreme Court's First Amendment abstention jurisprudence: the concern that speech may be chilled while the case is pending in state court. The chilling effect is reduced here because the superintendent has let the plaintiff continue her political campaigning and her job during the pendency of the suit. While important, this accommodation to Ruth does not wholly dispose of the chilling effect concern. To allow abstention, the district court would also need to discount the possibility that other school teachers will forbear from political speech as a consequence of the state statute and the superintendent's demonstrated intent to apply it to all teachers. If the district court does not weigh this possibility heavily, the court may indeed decide to invoke *Pullman* abstention.

2. *Thibodaux* Abstention: Unclear State Law on an Important Matter

In *Louisiana Power & Light Co. v. Thibodaux*, 360 U.S. 25 (1959), the United States Supreme Court held that a district court exercising diversity jurisdiction should abstain from adjudicating an unclear state law issue to avoid friction between the state and federal governments over the sensitive (and unusually important) matter of the state's eminent domain power. The elements of *Thibodaux* abstention are therefore (1) an unclear state law and (2) a sensitive matter of great importance to a state. Though worthy of note, *Thibodaux* abstention is not frequently invoked by courts, and thus is less important than other abstention doctrines.

Example 8-7

Carl owns property in a township that has experienced enormous growth during the last five years. In response to this growth, the township developed a series of ordinances in an attempt to slow the pace and to zone the community in an appropriate way. Carl wished to build a 500-unit apartment building on a plot of ground in the township. The township denied him the necessary permit for construction. He filed an action in federal district court, invoking the court's diversity of citizenship jurisdiction and asking the court to issue an injunction requiring the township to grant the permit. He claimed that he had complied with the seven land use regulations and the three zoning ordinances that apply to his project. The township argued that the state court had expertise with these provisions and would be in a better position to dispose of this case. The township suggested that the district court should dismiss the case under *Thibodaux* abstention. Should the district court dismiss the case?

Explanation

The Supreme Court has established that a district court exercising diversity of citizenship jurisdiction should not abstain simply because the case presents difficult or uncertain questions of state law.[9] Nonetheless, this example is an excellent candidate for abstention. Like *Thibodaux* itself, the example involves land use, which the *Thibodaux* Court identified as a special context concerning a sensitive local issue. Like eminent domain, zoning and land use planning are exercises of a state's "sovereign prerogative." 360 U.S. at 28. Given the web of complex state laws on the matter, deference to the power balance between the state and federal government favors state court resolution of the matter.

3. *Burford* Abstention: Avoiding Interference with State Administrative Process

a. Initial Articulation of the Doctrine

The United States Supreme Court first announced the *Burford* doctrine in a suit seeking to enjoin a state agency's grant of permission to drill oil wells. *Burford v. Sun Oil Co.*, 319 U.S. 315 (1943). *Burford* was based on diversity of citizenship and federal question jurisdiction. The Court held, however, that whatever a case's jurisdictional foundation, federal courts should exercise "their discretionary power with proper regard for the rightful independence of state governments in carrying out their domestic policy." *Id.* at 318. Although the state law issues were regarded as neither unsettled nor capable of fully resolving the dispute, the Court reasoned that the case concerned a coordinated state system for regulating and conserving oil and gas, and that abstention was appropriate to avoid "needless friction with state policies." *Id.* at 331. In justifying abstention, the Court highlighted the complex state administrative scheme already established for handling the dispute. Unlike the case for the *Pullman* and *Thibodaux* decisions, the Court did not suggest postponing federal court jurisdiction, but advocated dismissing the case instead.

The Court applied *Burford* again in *Alabama Public Service Comm'n v. Southern Railway Co.*, 341 U.S. 341 (1951). In that case, a railway challenged a state commission's denial of its request to discontinue local train service. Although the state had established procedures for challenging the commission's decision, the railway filed the challenge in federal court, arguing that operating the train service would lose money and that the commission's denial amounted to an unconstitutional deprivation of property without due process of law. Emphasizing that the case implicated both an important

---

9. *See, e.g., Meredith v. Winter Haven*, 320 U.S. 228, 236 (1943).

local interest and a state regulatory scheme, the Court found *Burford* abstention appropriate.

Example 8-8

Cindi was divorced, and her ex-husband, James, had custody of the children. The family court had ordered Cindi to pay $100 per week in child support. Cindi wanted to marry Chuck. State law, however, prevented Cindi and Chuck from getting a marriage license because Cindi was not current with her child support payments. The state law required that anyone subject to court-ordered child support obligations must gain permission to remarry from the family court that imposed the obligations. The law provided that the family court should deny permission for individuals in arrears on their support obligations. Cindi filed a federal court suit against the state official responsible for issuing marriage licenses, arguing that the official's failure to issue the license without the family court's permission amounted to an equal protection violation under the United States Constitution. The official argued that the federal court should abstain under *Burford*. Should the district court abstain?

Explanation

The district court should not abstain. Ruling on a state scheme similar to this example, the Supreme Court held in *Zablocki v. Redhail*, 434 U.S. 374 (1978), that abstention was inappropriate because the case lacked a complex state law issue, the resolution of which "would be 'disruptive of state efforts to establish a coherent policy with respect to a matter of substantial public concern.'" *Id.* at 380 (quoting *Colorado River Water Conservation Dist. v. United States*, 424 U.S. 800, 814-815 (1976)). The *Zablocki* Court determined that the state system's terms and procedures were clear, thus presenting a straightforward opportunity for federal constitutional adjudication.

b. Refinement of the Doctrine: Prerequisites

As Example 8-8 illustrates, the Supreme Court has established that mere existence of a state policy and an administrative mechanism for implementing that policy does not justify abstention. Rather, one may consider a case to be a serious candidate for *Burford* abstention only if the case concerns a sensitive or important state policy or implicates a coordinated state regulatory mechanism that a federal court could disrupt.

The Court refined these prerequisites in *New Orleans Public Service, Inc. v. Council of the City of New Orleans*, 491 U.S. 350, 362 (1989), explaining that although *Burford* abstention may be appropriate where "complex state administrative processes" are present, more is required to justify the abstention.

As a threshold matter, the Court explained that a district court may invoke Burford abstention only when "timely and adequate state-court review is available." Id. at 361. Even more restrictively, the Court added, Burford allows a federal court to dismiss a case only if one of the following conditions is met:

- Condition 1: The case presents "difficult questions of state law bearing on policy problems of substantial public import whose importance transcends the result in the case then at bar;" or
- Condition 2: The adjudication of the case in a federal forum "would be disruptive of state efforts to establish a coherent policy with respect to a matter of substantial public concern."

Id. at 361 (quoted in Quackenbush v. Allstate Ins. Co., 517 U.S. 706, 727 (1996)). As interpreted by subsequent courts, this language establishes that Burford abstention is appropriate if either of the two conditions is satisfied.

Example 8-9

Fanny Farmer owned farm land that she wanted to develop into an apartment complex. Fanny entered into an agreement with Drew Developer under which Fanny would lease the land to Drew, who would obtain the necessary permits for the development, build the apartments according to local specifications, and lease the apartments. To gain permission for the development, Drew filed permit requests with the County Office of Land Management, an administrative entity responsible for monitoring land development and compliance with zoning restrictions. Before granting permission to develop, the County Office of Land Management required Drew to provide detailed plans for a storm water drainage system that complied with the local zoning ordinance. Both the zoning ordinance and the plan presented were technical and highly complicated. The county has an established adjudicative system for handling disputes over zoning matters, with an appeal as of right in state court.

After the apartments were built, the complex experienced considerable storm flooding. The County Office of Land Management investigated and discovered that Drew had not built the water management system as specified. The County Office demanded that Fanny Farmer — as owner of the land — make the improvements necessary to bring the development into compliance with zoning regulations. Invoking diversity of citizenship jurisdiction, Fanny filed a federal court suit against Drew for breach of contract, alleging that Drew breached the portion of the contract requiring that the apartments be built according to local specifications. Fanny asked the court to order specific performance of this contractual term by enjoining Drew to build a storm water management system in compliance with the zoning code. Drew argued that the district court should dismiss the case under *Burford* abstention. Should the district court accept Drew's argument?

Explanation

This is a close case, whose disposition depends largely on how the district court characterizes the controversy. One could argue that this is simply a "bread and butter" contract suit, which neither depends on a difficult state law question transcending the suit nor disrupts state attempts to regulate. *See, e.g., Transdulles Center, Inc. v. USX Corp.,* 976 F.2d 219, 223-224 (4th Cir. 1992) (finding *Burford* abstention inappropriate under similar circumstances). As the Court explained in *New Orleans Public Service, Inc.,* the mere presence of a complicated state issue (such as proper storm water management) does not itself justify *Burford* abstention. Arguably, the district court need only interpret the contract and decide whether it has been breached.

On the other hand, numerous factors counsel in favor of *Burford* abstention. Of course, the initial trigger for considering *Burford* is present: a state administrative scheme relevant to the subject matter of the suit. Moreover, the threshold requirement of "timely and adequate state court review" is satisfied in the form of state judicial review of the administrative zoning decisions. Also important to justify abstention is the subject matter of the controversy: storm water management involves zoning and land use regulation — matters often characterized as primarily local — not a federal concern. One could also describe storm water management as a subject of substantial public concern. Although the district court will likely decide the case simply by interpreting a contract between private parties, the interpretation may require the court to make decisions about zoning and land use. In so doing, the federal court could conceivably contradict the state regulators' intent on these exclusively local matters.

Ultimately, the private nature of the dispute suggests that neither of the two *Burford* conditions clarified in *New Orleans Public Service, Inc.* is present. Since the dispute is private, the court's decision will not directly bind the public officials and may not transcend the case at bar, thus failing to meet a component of condition 1. Moreover, the private nature of the dispute may limit the ramifications of the court's decision. This suggests that a component of condition 2 is not satisfied: the federal adjudication may not disrupt state efforts to establish a coherent state policy.

Although one can only speculate about precisely how the federal adjudication would influence local governance, the factors favoring abstention are not robust in this example. Because the Supreme Court has specified that a court should use *Burford* only in extraordinary circumstances, prudence argues against the district court abstaining. *See, e.g., Transdulles Center, Inc. v. USX Corp.,* 976 F.2d 219, 223-224 (4th Cir. 1992) (refusing

Burford abstention in the context of a breach of contract suit involving zoning regulations).

Example 8-10

In an effort to control skyrocketing damage awards in car accident cases, the New Hampshire legislature amended the state's auto insurance statute. The new statute restructured the state's method of providing no-fault insurance benefits. In addition, the statute empowered the state insurance commissioner to regulate the type of care that chiropractors provide to car accident victims, by restricting payment to certain treatments. The insurance commission regulations specify detailed conditions that chiropractors must satisfy to justify compensation for various treatment regimes. The regulations authorize victims to petition the insurance commission, requesting payment for additional care (not described in the regulations), but only upon a showing of necessity by a treating chiropractor. Upon denial of the additional payment, victims may seek review by appeal to the state courts.

A group of chiropractors and victims brought suit against the insurance commissioner in federal district court, arguing that the medical specifications were ill conceived and that the overall scheme violated their equal protection and due process rights under the United States Constitution. The insurance commissioner argued that the federal court should abstain under Burford. Is the insurance commissioner correct?

Explanation

The insurance commissioner is correct: this is a good candidate for Burford abstention. First, "timely and adequate state-court review," is available because the victim may take an appeal as of right from decisions of the insurance commission to the state courts. Moreover, both of the two alternative conditions appear to be satisfied. See Chiropractic America v. LaVecchia, 180 F.3d 99 (3d Cir. 1999) (finding Burford abstention appropriate for a constitutional challenge to similar state insurance regulations).

Condition 1: The case contains "difficult questions of state law bearing on policy problems of substantial public import whose importance transcends the result in the case then at bar." The insurance regulations are steeped in details about medical injuries and chiropractic remedies, which qualify as difficult and complicated subject areas. One could easily conclude that the balance between providing a remedy for accident victims and controlling verdicts in automobile cases presents a problem of substantial public import. Finally, the plaintiffs' challenge is broadly framed, based on the regulation's constitutionality and wisdom in light of medical science. The federal court's disposition could therefore have ramifications that transcend this particular case.

Condition 2: Federal adjudication "would be disruptive of state efforts to establish a coherent policy with respect to a matter of substantial public concern." Automobile insurance is a matter of primarily local concern; the federal government has largely deferred to the states for insurance regulations. New Hampshire here has sought to establish a coordinated scheme that monitors compensation for all aspects of chiropractic treatment. Should the federal court entertain this challenge, it may upset the sensitive balance struck by the state between remedying harm and controlling verdicts.

c. Limiting the Doctrine in Damage Actions

Abstention essentially vetoes Congress's judgment that a federal court should exercise power over a controversy. Separation of powers concerns therefore arise. In *Burford* itself, the Court reckoned with these concerns by repeatedly emphasizing that the federal court's discretion to abstain derived from the court's equitable powers. The *Burford* plaintiff sought an injunction, a remedy traditionally restricted to courts of equity. Equity courts enjoy a flexible jurisprudence and fashion just dispositions tailored to requirements in the particular cases before them. After *Burford*, courts struggled with whether the abstention doctrine was available for federal courts adjudicating cases with non-equitable ("legal") remedies such as damages.

The Court resolved this uncertainty in *Quackenbush v. Allstate Ins. Co.*, 517 U.S. 706, 731 (1996), holding that a district court adjudicating a damage action inappropriately remanded a case to state court using *Burford* abstention. *Quackenbush* did not hold that *Burford* abstention was altogether inappropriate in the damages case. Rather, a federal court in a damage action may simply not use the abstention doctrine to remand or dismiss the case. By dismissing the case, the federal court would displace Congress's decision too dramatically for the court to exercise power over the subject matter. Instead *Quackenbush* suggests that a federal court may stay the damage action, pending further proceedings in the state tribunal. 517 U.S. at 730-731 (stating that "we have only permitted a federal court [in damage actions] to 'withhold action until the state proceedings have concluded'" and that "*Burford* might support a federal court's decision to postpone adjudication of a damages action pending the resolution by state courts" (quoting *Growe v. Emison*, 507 U.S. 25, 32 (1993))).

Example 8-11

An environmental group sued state and private entities, alleging that the usage of water from an aquifer resulted in damage to an endangered species, in violation of the federal Endangered Species Act. The group sought to have the federal court enjoin the defendants from using the water. As it turned out, however, the defendants were using the water in accordance with permits issued as part of the state's Aquifer Act, which regulated the type and amount of water usage, as well as the time and the place the plaintiffs could use the water. The state also has an Aquifer Authority, which adjudicates claims related to the Aquifer Act. The Aquifer Act provides for an appeal as of right to state courts from the Aquifer Authority's adjudication. The district court concluded that it should abstain in the case but did not know what procedural options were available to it. Is a stay the only option?

Explanation

Because this is a suit for an injunction, the district court need not confine itself to a stay of the federal action. *Quackenbush* stated that a federal court in a suit for an injunction or other discretionary remedy (such as a declaratory judgment) may stay the action or decline adjudication altogether by dismissing the case or remanding it to a state tribunal.[10] If the district court chooses to dismiss the suit, the environmental group may pursue relief in "timely and adequate" state proceedings before the Aquifer Authority and state court. If, on the other hand, the district court merely stays the action, the parties may ultimately return to the district court for further proceedings. In many instances, the state proceedings may fully dispose of the case, which will likely bind the federal court to the state ruling under "full faith and credit" and preclusion principles.

B. DUPLICATIVE PROCEEDING DOCTRINES: *YOUNGER* AND *COLORADO RIVER*

Because the United States has overlapping judicial systems, litigants may find their disputes pending in more than one forum. Two abstention doctrines enable litigants to avoid litigating issues in both state and federal court. The most prominent doctrine, *Younger* abstention, protects against federal court interference with ongoing state proceedings where the focus of the federal court suit is the state court proceeding itself. *Younger* abstention has two theoretical foundations: (1) the traditional, equitable reluctance for a court to enjoin criminal proceedings and (2) principles of federalism. The other

---

10. See, e.g., Metro Riverboat Associates, Inc. v. Bally's Louisiana, Inc., 142 F. Supp. 2d 765 (E.D. La. 2001) (staying federal court action for injunction pursuant to Burford abstention); Hartung v. Sebelius, 40 F. Supp. 2d 1257 (D. Kan. 1999) (stating that the court has discretion to stay or dismiss action when abstaining under Burford); LINDA MULLENIX, MARTIN REDISH & GEORGENE VAIRO, UNDERSTANDING FEDERAL COURTS AND JURISDICTION 450-451 (Matthew Bender 1998) (stating that stay option is available in suits for discretionary review). But see ERWIN CHEMERINSKY, FEDERAL JURISDICTION 785 (4th ed. 2003) (stating that Burford "requires the federal court to dismiss the case").

doctrine, *Colorado River* abstention, provides a mechanism for federal courts to relinquish jurisdiction over cases pending simultaneously in state court.

1. *Younger* Abstention: Avoiding Interference with Ongoing State Proceedings

The United States Supreme Court ruled in *Younger v. Harris*, 401 U.S. 37 (1971), that federal courts may not enjoin ongoing state criminal proceedings, except in limited circumstances. John Harris had brought his federal court suit after the district attorney, Younger, instituted a state criminal prosecution against him for violating a state criminal statute. Harris requested that the district court enjoin Younger from continuing the state prosecution, alleging that the state statute violated Harris's First and Fourteenth Amendment rights. The Supreme Court held that because Harris could press his constitutional challenge in defending the criminal action, the federal court should not allow him to pursue his objections in federal court.

Because Harris asked for an injunction of pending state proceedings, one might think the Supreme Court's decision was motivated by the Anti-Injunction Act. But the Court explicitly avoided the Anti-Injunction Act, instead resting its ruling on judicially enforced principles of equity and federalism.

The equitable basis for the case derived from the rule restricting injunctions to circumstances where a plaintiff lacks an adequate remedy at law. Harris, the *Younger* Court reasoned, had an adequate remedy at law because he could raise his constitutional objections in the criminal proceeding. Thus, the criminal proceeding provided Harris with a mechanism for avoiding irreparable harm.

Even stronger, however, was *Younger's* federalism rationale. The Court reasoned that a federal court should avoid interfering with state criminal prosecutions out of "a proper respect for state functions." 401 U.S. at 44. The Court reckoned that abstention was required in order to serve "the belief that the National Government will fare best if the States and their institutions are left free to perform their separate functions in their separate ways." *Id.*

The Court recognized extraordinary instances where principles of equity and federalism might justify a federal court enjoining an ongoing state criminal prosecution, such as (1) where the prosecutor is motivated by "bad faith" or "harassment"; (2) where the state statute is "'flagrantly and patently violative of express constitutional prohibitions in every clause, sentence and paragraph'"; and (3) where "other unusual circumstances . . . would call for equitable relief." *Id.* at 53-54 (quoting *Watsa v. Buck*, 313 U.S. 387, 402 (1941)). Over time, the Supreme Court has clarified — although not expanded — the type of facts that may satisfy these exceptions; however, the Supreme Court *has* expanded the circumstances under which *Younger* abstention applies. Indeed, the Court has enlarged each component of the *Younger* holding that a federal court may not *enjoin* an *ongoing* state *criminal proceeding*. This section reviews how the Supreme Court has expanded these components.

1. *Enjoin:* How far does *Younger* apply beyond injunction requests?
2. *Ongoing:* When does *Younger* apply if the state proceeding is not yet ongoing?
3. *Criminal proceeding:* When does *Younger* apply outside the criminal context?

After reviewing each of these components, this section discusses the *Younger* exceptions: (1) bad faith and harassment, (2) a patently unconstitutional state law, and (3) other exceptional circumstances.

a. *Enjoin:* How Far Does *Younger* Apply Beyond Injunction Requests?

On the same day the Court decided *Younger*, it also decided *Samuels v. Mackell*, 401 U.S. 66 (1971), extending the *Younger* doctrine to requests for declaratory judgments. The Court has not, however, extended the *Younger* doctrine to actions for damages or other remedies, and has noted several times that it has not decided whether *Younger* applies in damage actions.

Declaratory judgments provide an official statement, in the form of a court judgment, of parties' rights and legal relationships. They are viewed as intruding less on parties' dignity than injunctions because courts cannot enforce declaratory judgments immediately with the contempt power. Instead, the Federal Declaratory Judgment Act, 28 U.S.C. §2202, allows federal courts to enforce declaratory judgments with "necessary or proper relief," which may include an injunction issued after a hearing. The federal court may resort to the contempt power only if the defendant does not honor that injunction. Out of respect for the authority of federal declaratory judgments, however, state courts normally would be expected to honor the judgment's terms and to halt the state court proceedings. For that reason, the *Samuels* Court held that a declaratory judgment would "result in precisely the same interference with" state proceedings as an injunction. 401 U.S. at 72. The Court did acknowledge that unique circumstances might exist where the district court should withhold an injunction because of its "intrusive or offensive" effect, but "a declaratory judgment might be appropriate." Id. at 73.

The Court's recognition of possible distinctions between injunctions and declaratory judgments appears in subsequent case law interpreting the *Younger* doctrine. In fact, the justices have taken somewhat contradictory positions on the precise effect of a declaratory judgment. Thus, one must be careful before applying precedent for injunctions to declaratory judgments — and vice versa.

Example 8-12

Courtney is a practicing gynecologist who provides abortion services to her patients. The town's district attorney began to prosecute her for violating a state statute that makes it a crime to perform certain types of abortions. Courtney defended herself in the state criminal proceeding by arguing that the state statute is unconstitutional. She also brought a federal court action against the local prosecutor, arguing that she lost income as a result of the prosecutor's unconstitutional reading of the abortion statute. Courtney therefore sought damages for her lost income. The district attorney argued that the federal court should invoke *Younger* abstention. Should the district court accept the district attorney's argument?

Explanation

The district attorney's argument is reasonable but probably not correct. Technically speaking, the argument is likely incorrect because the Supreme Court has not extended *Younger* abstention beyond requests for injunctions or declaratory judgments. Courtney requests only damages in her lawsuit. Indeed, the Supreme Court's limitation of *Younger* abstention to injunctions and declaratory judgments renders those remedies "triggers" or "issue spotting cues" for considering the possibility that a district court should abstain under the *Younger* doctrine.

Even though the suit requests only damages, the district attorney's argument is reasonable because the federal court action comes at a time when a related state criminal proceeding is pending. Should the federal court rule that the district attorney violated Courtney's constitutional rights by prosecuting her under the statute, that ruling would likely interfere with the state proceeding, because the state criminal court would likely consider itself bound by the federal decision under principles of collateral estoppel and full faith and credit.[11] The lower federal courts are split on whether a district court can provide damage remedies when a related state court criminal proceeding is pending.[12] Nonetheless, to hold that *Younger* abstention applies

---

11. For further sources on the preclusive effect of a federal declaratory judgment, *see* RICHARD H. FALLON, JR., DANIEL J. MELTZER & DAVID L. SHAPIRO, HART & WECHSLER'S THE FEDERAL COURTS AND THE FEDERAL SYSTEM 1240 (Foundation Press 5th ed. 2003).

12. *Compare D.L. v. Unified School District*, 392 F.3d 1223, 1228 (10th Cir. 2004) (applying *Younger* to stay damages action when judgment for plaintiff would have preclusive effect on pending state court proceeding), *Gilbertson v. Albright*, 381 F.3d 965, 978-980 (9th Cir. 2004) (en banc) (applying *Younger* to stay damages action when judgment for plaintiff would have preclusive effect on pending state court proceeding), *Mann v. Jett*, 781 F.2d 1448, 1449 (9th Cir. 1986)

in this case would require embracing some lower court positions and rejecting others.

b. *Ongoing:* What Is an Ongoing Proceeding for *Younger* Purposes?

The *Younger* Court emphasized the ongoing nature of the state criminal proceedings in enunciating its prohibition. Indeed, because the defendant, Harris, could have raised his constitutional objections as a defense to the criminal charge, the *Younger* Court was able to conclude that the defendant had an adequate remedy without the injunctive relief. After *Younger*, however, the Court handed down a series of decisions blurring the line on when a federal court may issue an injunction. The Court's reasoning in subsequent cases relies heavily on the facts of each — making proper understanding of the doctrine dependent on fact-specific analysis of the timing of certain events: criminal activity, criminal prosecution, and the filing of the federal action.

i. *Steffel v. Thompson*

The first decision after *Younger* to speak to the timing question, *Steffel v. Thompson*, 415 U.S. 452 (1974), actually clarified the pending proceeding requirement. In *Steffel*, the plaintiff and his companion were threatened with arrest for violating state trespass laws by distributing handbills at a shopping center. After departing, the plaintiff and his companion returned and were told to leave or the police would be called. The plaintiff left, but his companion stayed and was arrested. The plaintiff then filed a suit in federal court, raising a constitutional challenge to the state trespass law.

The *Steffel* Court held that the federal court *could* issue a declaratory judgment in the plaintiff's case because no state prosecution was pending against him. Reasoning that federal intervention would not disrupt the state criminal justice system, the Court held that allowing the federal action to proceed would not reflect "negatively upon the state court's ability" to protect federal constitutional rights. *Id.* at 462. Moreover, to disqualify the declaratory remedy for potential plaintiffs would put them in the difficult position of either forbearing from desired conduct or engaging in the

---

(holding that federal courts should dismiss damages action if it will have "a substantially disruptive effect" on the pending state prosecution), *and Monaghan v. Deakins*, 798 F.2d 632, 635 (3d Cir. 1986) (holding that federal courts should stay, not dismiss, suits for monetary relief under instances where *Younger* would prohibit injunction), *aff'd in part and vacated in part*, 484 U.S. 193 (1988), *with Lewis v. Beddingfield*, 20 F.3d 123, 125 (5th Cir. 1994) (holding the *Younger* abstention doctrine is not applicable to a claim for damages), *Rivers v. McLeod*, 252 F.3d 99, 101-102 (2d Cir. 2001) (holding the *Younger* abstention doctrine is not applicable to a claim for damages), *and Giulini v. Blessing*, 654 F.2d 189, 193 (2d Cir. 1981) (holding that federal courts generally may adjudicate damage suits, even though related criminal prosecutions are pending in state court).

conduct and risking criminal conviction if they were wrong in believing their conduct was constitutionally protected. The *Steffel* Court invoked a mushroom-toadstool analogy: allowing the declaratory remedy enabled plaintiffs to test whether their desired conduct was a delicious mushroom (i.e., constitutionally protected) or a poisonous toadstool (i.e., unprotected conduct for which they could be punished).

Example 8-13

State law required those who wished to distribute leaflets to voters to file a registration statement with the state board of elections. The law stated that failure to do so would subject violators to substantial criminal fines. Since the law was enacted, the state board of elections had vigilantly monitored leafleting practice and reported violations to the local prosecutor's office, which vigorously pursued all prosecutions. A civil rights group wanted to distribute door to door an information leaflet detailing the civil rights records of candidates in an upcoming election. They had circulated such leaflets in past elections and were warned by the state board of elections that future distributions would be reported to the state prosecutor's office.

Wishing to distribute the leaflet before the election, the civil rights group prepared the leaflet. The election board heard about the leaflet and threatened to notify the local prosecutor if the group distributed it without registering with the board. The civil rights group became concerned about censorship possibilities related to this type of registration requirement, and they filed suit in federal court, seeking an injunction against the registration requirement as a violation of the First Amendment of the United States Constitution. The election board argued that the district court should dismiss the case for two reasons: (1) the case was not ripe for review and was therefore not justiciable, and (2) the *Younger* doctrine prohibited the injunction. Is either argument likely to prevail?

Explanation

Although the election board's first argument would likely fail, the second one is reasonable under the case law, and may prevail. As the board's first argument suggests, this example illustrates that ripeness is frequently an issue in cases implicating the *Younger* doctrine. The doctrine requires a litigant to invoke federal jurisdiction before the state authorities commence the criminal process, so a plaintiff seeking pre-enforcement review of a criminal law has a narrow window of time in which to seek federal redress. Because the plaintiff files suit early in the dispute, cases may arise where the plaintiff files too early — before the parties develop a true controversy.[13]

---

13. For further discussion of the ripeness doctrine, see Chapter 5, section B.

The civil rights group here, however, is not too early. Like the *Steffel* plaintiff, the group has outwardly manifested — by leafletting in the past and creating the leaflet now — an intent to engage in the challenged conduct. Like the *Steffel* authorities, the board of elections and the local prosecutor have demonstrated that they will apply the criminal statute to the plaintiff's actions. It takes two to make a controversy, which is a requirement satisfied here.

The election board's second argument is a closer call. *Steffel* allowed a federal action to proceed because, as in this example, a state prosecution had not begun. Unlike the situation in *Steffel*, however, the civil rights group here requested an injunction, not a declaratory judgment. In fact, the *Steffel* Court explicitly left open the question of whether federal courts could enjoin state prosecutions before they began, and then–Justice Rehnquist argued in his *Steffel* dissent that the declaratory judgment holding did not apply to injunction requests. One might argue that injunctions should be allowed because the federal court is not interfering with the state criminal process if it has not begun. Nonetheless, the *Steffel* Court left open the possibility of distinguishing its ruling on declaratory judgments from one on injunctions, since declaratory judgments "have a less intrusive effect on the administration of state criminal laws" than do injunctions. 415 U.S. at 469. For that reason, the election board may convince the federal court to dismiss the injunction request.

ii. *Hicks v. Miranda*

Viewing *Younger* and *Steffel* together, one might conclude that the *Younger* doctrine prevents a plaintiff from filing a federal court challenge any time after state officials have begun criminal proceedings. An important question, then, is: when do criminal proceedings begin? Several lower courts have treated arrest as the beginning of state criminal proceedings.[14] The circuits appear split, however, on the question of whether state criminal proceedings are ongoing once state officials have begun grand jury proceedings and have issued grand jury subpoenas.[15] Even more important, however, the

---

14. *See, e.g., Rialto Theatre Co. v. City of Wilmington*, 440 F.2d 1326 (3d Cir. 1971); *Eve Prods., Inc. v. Shannon*, 439 F.2d 1073 (8th Cir. 1971). But *see Agriesti v. MGM Grand Hotels, Inc.*, 53 F.3d 1000 (9th Cir. 1995) (holding that under Nevada state law criminal proceedings begin when charge is filed, not upon arrest). Cf. *Redner v. Citrus County*, 919 F.2d 646 (11th Cir. 1990) (stating that criminal proceedings had begun when plaintiff had been twice arrested and twice released on bond).

15. *Compare Texas Ass'n of Bus. v. Earle*, 388 F.3d 515, 519–20 (5th Cir. 2004) (holding that a grand jury proceeding is an ongoing criminal proceeding), *Kaylor v. Fields*, 661 F.2d 1177, 1182 (8th Cir. 1981) (holding that a grand jury proceeding is an ongoing criminal proceeding), *and Craig v. Barney*, 678 F.2d 1200, 1202 (4th Cir. 1982) (holding that a grand jury proceeding is an ongoing criminal proceeding), *with Monaghan v. Deakins*, 798 F.2d 632, 637 (3d Cir. 1986) (holding that a grand jury proceeding is not an ongoing state criminal proceeding, *aff'd in part and vacated in part*, 484 U.S. 193 (1988)), *Voicenet Communications, Inc.*

Supreme Court has moved the trigger for *Younger* abstention even earlier than the beginning of criminal proceedings. *Hicks v. Miranda*, 422 U.S. 332, 349 (1975), held that the federal court must dismiss a suit under *Younger* even if the federal court suit begins *before* state proceedings are instituted if the state proceedings begin before proceedings of "substance on the merits" occur in federal court.

In *Hicks*, police seized copies of an allegedly obscene film from a movie theater and arrested two of the theater's employees. State officials had also begun civil proceedings, which required the theater owner to show cause why the film was not obscene. When the state court declared the film obscene, rather than appeal, the theater owners (who were not defendants in the criminal proceedings against the employees) filed a federal court suit seeking an injunction against the state criminal statute and a declaratory judgment that the statute violated the Constitution. After the district court denied a temporary restraining order, the theater owners moved for a preliminary injunction. The next day, state authorities filed criminal charges against the theater owners, but the district court adjudicated the controversy by issuing both a declaratory judgment and an injunction.

The Supreme Court reversed, holding that the district court should have abstained once the state filed criminal charges against the theater owners. In so holding, the Court noted a fact-specific wrinkle in the case: the theater owners' interests were intertwined with those of the employees, who were already being prosecuted at the time the owners began the federal action. Despite this possible limitation to the *Hicks* ruling, the Court broadly stated its holding: "[W]here state criminal proceedings are begun against the federal plaintiffs after the federal complaint is filed but before any proceedings of substance on the merits have taken place in the federal court, the principles of *Younger v. Harris* should apply in full force." 422 U.S. at 349.

An important question about *Hicks* concerns the meaning of "proceedings of substance on the merits." The Supreme Court has not ventured a definition of the standard, although its cases give some clues. The Court seems to distinguish between adjudication of temporary restraining orders and that of preliminary injunctions. Temporary restraining orders are threshold remedies typically requested on an emergency basis by a party seeking to preserve the status quo immediately after filing a complaint. They generally last for ten days or less, during which time a party may move for a

---

v. *Pappert*, No. 04-1318, 2004 U.S. Dist. LEXIS 15283 at *1 (E.D. Pa. Aug. 5, 2004) (ruling that a pending Pennsylvania investigating grand jury is not an ongoing proceeding), *aff'd* No. 04-2911 2005 U.S. App. LEXIS 3969 (3d Cir. 2005), *and Brennick v. Hynes*, 471 F. Supp. 863, 867 (N.D.N.Y. 1979) (ruling that *Younger* doctrine "does not apply to state grand jury proceedings where the target for investigation has no immediate recourse to state courts").

The United States Supreme Court granted certiorari on this question, but the issue became moot before the Court rendered the decision. *Deakins v. Monaghan*, 484 U.S. 193 (1988).

preliminary injunction. Preliminary injunctions are designed to last during the pendency of the case, until the court enters a final judgment.[16]

From *Hicks* itself, one knows that a federal court's denial of a motion for a temporary restraining order does not satisfy the standard of "proceedings of substance on the merits." The Supreme Court has also stated that a federal court's grant of a preliminary injunction *does* satisfy the standard. Thus, where state proceedings begin after the federal court grants a preliminary injunction, *Younger* abstention does not prevent the federal court from moving forward (see Figure 8-1).[17]

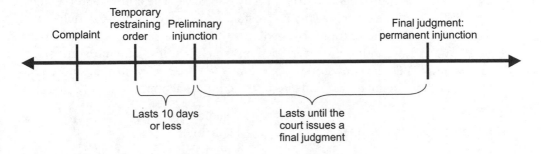

Figure 8-1. Timeline for Injunctive Relief.

Example 8-14

Eleanor sat as a judge in attorney disciplinary proceedings. During the course of a disciplinary action against Sara, Eleanor encountered evidence that Sara's friend was planning to commit a homicide imminently. This evidence provided Eleanor with a dilemma because the disciplinary rules prevented her from disclosing any evidence before the disciplinary action was completed. Despite the possibility of criminal prosecution and punishment, Eleanor believed that she was morally obligated to report the information to the police to prevent the loss of a life. She disclosed the information and thereafter filed an action against the local prosecutor in federal district court. Eleanor sought an injunction and a declaratory judgment; the injunction would prevent the prosecutor from prosecuting her, and the declaratory judgment would establish that the prohibition was void, because it was against public policy to prevent disclosure that would preserve a human life. She moved for a temporary restraining order against prosecuting authorities, but the district court denied this motion. The next day, the prosecutor ordered her arrest and filed charges against her for violating the

---

16. The final judgment can be in the form of a permanent injunction, which is permanent in the sense that it is a final judgment of the court, but is not necessarily perpetual.
17. *Hawaii Hous. Auth. v. Midkiff*, 467 U.S. 229, 238 (1984).

confidentiality provision. The prosecutor then moved for the district court to dismiss the federal case under *Younger*. Is the prosecutor likely to prevail?

Explanation

Under the authority of *Hicks*, the prosecutor will likely win the motion, because "proceedings of substance on the merits" had not yet occurred in the federal action. For this reason, the prosecutor is able to exercise what has been called "reverse removal power," essentially moving the proceedings from federal to state court by instituting state criminal proceedings. The rationale for this ruling is threefold: (1) the federal action would interfere with state criminal proceedings; (2) judicial resources would not be wasted by halting the federal action, which is still in an embryonic stage; and (3) Eleanor now has an opportunity to raise her "void as against public policy" argument as a defense to the criminal action.

iii. Doran v. Salem Inn, Inc.

The Supreme Court further complicated the question of whether *Younger* applies if a federal action is begun before state proceedings in *Doran v. Salem Inn, Inc.*, 422 U.S. 922 (1975). In *Doran*, three bar owners brought a federal action challenging the constitutionality of a new ordinance prohibiting them from continuing to feature topless dancing. The bars sought declaratory relief and a preliminary injunction preventing the authorities from enforcing the ordinance. After the district court denied a temporary restraining order, one of the bars began to feature topless dancing. Authorities started criminal proceedings against the "noncompliant" bar owner and employees. The other two bars remained compliant, and the district court eventually granted a preliminary injunction for all three bar owners.

The Supreme Court affirmed the preliminary injunction only for the two compliant bar owners. The Court reasoned that the compliant owners would otherwise have no means of raising their constitutional challenge, and the federal litigation would not disrupt any pending state proceeding. As for the noncompliant owner, however, the Court reversed the grant of the preliminary injunction, invoking *Hicks* as precedent for denying that owner access to a federal remedy (see Figure 8-2).

Example 8-15

Lisa and Amy distributed flyers at the local grocery store, protesting a plan to put a bike path through their neighborhood. The grocery store called the police, who told Lisa and Amy that leafleting was a violation of the criminal trespass ordinance. Lisa and Amy stopped, and they filed a federal court action challenging the constitutionality of the ordinance. They requested a

8. Abstention Doctrines

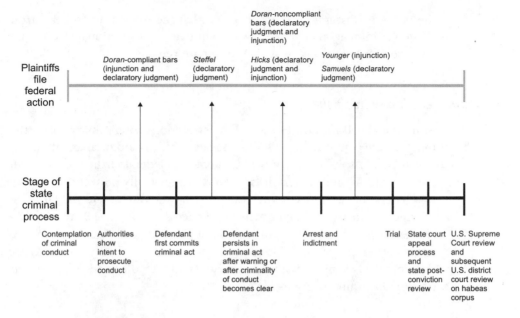

Figure 8-2. When Can State Criminal Defendants Access Federal Court Under the *Younger* Doctrine?

declaratory judgment as well as an injunction that would prevent police from arresting them for leafleting in the grocery store. The district court denied Lisa and Amy's motion for a temporary restraining order. Both women filed a motion for a preliminary injunction, and Amy then began distributing leaflets at the local grocery store. The police arrested Amy, and the prosecutor filed charges against her. Amy argued that the district court could issue a preliminary injunction to benefit both Lisa and her. She maintained that the state proceedings would be no more disrupted by a preliminary injunction favoring both Lisa and herself than they would if the preliminary injunction benefited Lisa only. Is Amy's argument correct?

Explanation

Amy is not correct; both *Hicks* and *Doran* undercut her argument. Because the federal court action did not extend beyond the filing of a preliminary injunction action at the time criminal proceedings began, "proceedings of substance on the merits" had not occurred in federal court, and *Younger* abstention is therefore appropriate.

Amy does have a point that a preliminary injunction favoring Lisa may impact the criminal proceeding against Amy, since the state court may find that the injunction shows the criminal action to be unconstitutional. In distinguishing relief for the noncompliant and for the compliant bars in *Doran*, however, the Supreme Court made clear that it was willing to allow the potential disruption to occur, given that the party who forbears from alleged criminality may have no way to litigate a constitutional claim in the absence of a federal action with appropriate remedies.

iv. Permanent Injunctive Relief

Although the *Doran* Court was willing to endorse preliminary injunctive relief for the compliant bars, it was less favorable toward permanent injunctive relief: "At the conclusion of a successful federal challenge to a state statute or local ordinance, a district court can generally protect the interests of a federal plaintiff by entering a declaratory judgment, and therefore the stronger injunctive medicine will be unnecessary." 422 U.S. at 931. The Supreme Court has repeated this admonition, stating that permanent injunctive relief is appropriate in "'exceptional circumstances'" only upon "'a clear showing that an injunction is necessary in order to afford adequate protection of constitutional rights.'"[18]

Example 8-16

Kathy, a resident of Missouri, found the slogan on the state's license plate ("Show-Me State") offensive to her religious beliefs. In violation of Missouri's motor vehicle code, she covered up the slogan twice, and was twice prosecuted for doing so. After the second prosecution was completed, she filed a federal action arguing that the application of the criminal provisions of the state vehicle code in this instance violated her First Amendment rights. After discovery and during trial in the case, the state officials prosecuted Kathy a third time for covering up the slogan. The trial court then entered judgment in favor of Kathy. She requested that the district court enter a permanent injunction against her further prosecution for covering up the license plate slogan. May the district court issue a permanent injunction here?

Explanation

Supreme Court case law authorizes the district court to issue a permanent injunction in this context. Under similar circumstances, the Supreme Court found that three prosecutions in a short period of time amounted to "exceptional circumstances." *Wooley v. Maynard*, 430 U.S. 705, 712 (1977). Moreover, *Younger* abstention is inappropriate given that

---

18. *Wooley v. Maynard*, 430 U.S. 705, 712 (1977) (quoting *Spielman Motor Sales Co. v. Dodge*, 295 U.S. 89, 95 (1935)).

"proceedings of substance on the merits" had occurred in the federal case. One may also claim that the repeated prosecution amounted to harassment, thus introducing an exception to the *Younger* doctrine that is explored next.[19]

c. Criminal Proceedings: When Does *Younger* Apply Outside the Criminal Context?

The *Younger* holding confined the limitation on federal courts to injunctions against ongoing state *criminal* proceedings. The Supreme Court quickly expanded the holding's scope to civil actions brought by a state "in aid of and closely related to criminal statutes." This expansion started in *Huffman v. Pursue, Ltd.*, 420 U.S. 592, 604 (1975), a case where state officials instituted a civil nuisance proceeding against an adult movie theater for violating a state statute prohibiting exhibition of obscene films. This context was well suited to expanding the *Younger* doctrine, given that the state nuisance proceeding was "akin to a criminal prosecution" and operated to reinforce a criminal prohibition. *Id.* The potential precedent set in *Huffman*, however, was not lost on the dissenters, who saw the decision as a dangerous assault on federally enforced civil rights and as a toehold toward expanding *Younger* into myriad civil contexts.

The *Huffman* dissenters' prediction proved accurate. In short order, the Supreme Court expanded the *Younger* doctrine in a civil action brought by a state to recover fraudulently obtained welfare payments. *Trainor v. Hernandez*, 431 U.S. 434, 444 (1977). Like earlier applications of *Younger*, the *Trainor* litigation included the state — acting in a sovereign capacity — as a party to the action.

Even more expansive than *Trainor* were the Court's decisions in *Juidice v. Vail*, 430 U.S. 327 (1977), and *Pennzoil Co. v. Texaco Inc.*, 481 U.S. 1 (1987), in which the Court applied the abstention doctrine in private civil suits where the state was not a party. The Court's justification for *Younger* abstention in each case was the presence of an important state interest at issue in the litigation: the efficacy of the contempt process in *Juidice v. Vail*, and the enforcement of an appeal bond requirement in *Pennzoil Co. v. Texaco, Inc.*

Similarly, the Court expanded *Younger* abstention into administrative proceedings in *Middlesex County Ethics Comm. v. Garden State Bar Ass'n*, 457 U.S. 423 (1982). The state process in *Middlesex* was a state bar disciplinary proceeding, which the Supreme Court described as judicial in nature and involving the "extremely important" state interest in maintaining the "professional conduct" of attorneys (see Figure 8-3). *Id.* at 434.

---

19. *See* MARTIN REDISH, FEDERAL JURISDICTION: TENSIONS IN THE ALLOCATION OF JUDICIAL POWER 361 (2d ed. 1990).

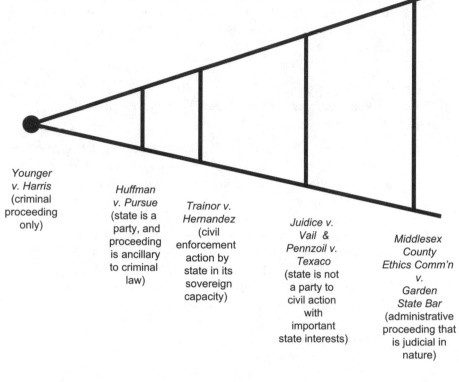

Figure 8-3. Expansion of the Doctrine of *Younger v. Harris* into Civil and Administrative Proceedings.

The Supreme Court has made clear that a district court should evaluate the importance of the state interest by considering its significance broadly, not by focusing merely on the resolution of the particular case. *New Orleans Public Service, Inc. v. Council of City of New Orleans* (NOPSI), 491 U.S. 350 (1989). In so holding, the Supreme Court appeared to halt the expansion of *Younger* into different varieties of civil actions. The NOPSI Court explained that even though *Younger* abstention extended to "civil proceedings involving certain orders that are uniquely in furtherance of the state courts' ability to perform their judicial functions," the abstention doctrine does not require a federal court to abstain for "a state judicial proceeding reviewing legislative or executive action." *Id.* at 367-368.

Example 8-17

Susie Lee wished to construct a commercial building on her property. She applied for permission before the state zoning commission, which told her that she could build only if she designated space for a future road. Susie Lee did not want to designate this space, so she started to develop the property without the necessary permission. The zoning commissioner initiated administrative proceedings and filed a petition to prevent Susie Lee from continuing with the development. An administrative law judge would adjudicate the matter after Susie Lee responded to the petition. Rather than file a response, however, Susie Lee filed a federal court suit seeking to enjoin the attempt to halt her development as contrary to her substantive and procedural due process rights. Susie Lee argued that the district court should continue to adjudicate the lawsuit, which is not the type of proceeding to which *Younger* abstention should apply. Is Susie Lee correct that *Younger* abstention should not apply for state administrative proceedings such as these?

Explanation

Although the ongoing state proceedings here are not classic criminal proceedings, *Younger* will probably apply — Susie Lee is likely wrong. To begin with, the administrative nature of the state proceedings here should not preclude the *Younger* doctrine. As in *Middlesex County Ethics Comm. v. Garden State Bar Ass'n*, 457 U.S. 423 (1982), the zoning proceedings here are judicial in nature, since a judge will adjudicate the controversy after hearing from both sides. Also similar to the attorney discipline proceedings in *Middlesex County*, the proceedings here concern a broad area of sensitive and important social policy: land use planning.

In fact, the proceedings here may present an even stronger case for *Younger* abstention than those in *Middlesex County*, because they are enforcement proceedings and are therefore key to an effective state scheme. These proceedings are also akin to the contempt proceeding in *Juidice v. Vail*, 430 U.S. 327 (1977), because they ensure that citizens comply with official orders and therefore are necessary to maintaining citizens' respect for state authority. The law enforcement quality of the *Juidice* proceedings convinced the Court to expand *Younger* beyond lawsuits in which the state is a party. Here, the proceedings not only possess a law enforcement character, but also include the state as a party in its sovereign capacity. Accordingly, this example provides a strong candidate for *Younger* abstention.

d. Exceptions

In *Younger*, the Court stated that even where the prerequisites for *Younger* abstention are satisfied, the district court may choose not to abstain in three different circumstances: (1) cases in which state court proceedings amount to "bad faith or harassment"; (2) cases in which the state statute involved is not only arguably invalid on its face but "flagrantly and patently violative of express constitutional prohibitions in every clause, sentence and paragraph, and in whatever manner and against whomever an effort might be made to apply it"; and (3) cases involving "[o]ther unusual situations calling for federal intervention."[20] These exceptions derive from *Younger's* equitable roots — the notion that a federal injunction is not necessary if the federal plaintiff is subject to adequate redress in the state court proceedings. The presence of one exception gives sufficient reason to doubt whether the state proceedings provide a full and fair opportunity to adjudicate the federal claim.[21]

i. Bad Faith or Harassment

The idea behind the bad faith or harassment exception is to allow a federal court to issue an injunction or a declaratory judgment if state court procedures are not adequate to protect federal rights. Where a prosecutor or other state official is motivated by bad faith or an intent to harass, the state process cannot be trusted. The Supreme Court has explained that bad faith or an intent to harass are present if "a prosecution has been brought without a reasonable expectation of obtaining a valid conviction." *Kugler v. Helfant*, 421 U.S. 117, 126 n.6 (1975). In evaluating whether this exception is triggered, lower courts have looked for evidence of the official's subjective intent.

Example 8-18

Jane is an outspoken critic of the local police department. After getting a tip from a reliable informant, the police obtained a warrant from a neutral magistrate and searched her home. They found stolen goods and therefore arrested Jane for larceny. As part of the investigation, police officials dusted her car for fingerprints. They did not take adequate steps to save the fingerprint samples and therefore needed to repeat the work. Next, Jane's criminal case was set for a preliminary hearing. On the day of the preliminary hearing, Jane appeared with her attorney, but the prosecutor missed the proceeding because of a scheduling error by her department. Jane sued in federal court, arguing that the criminal suit was filed in retaliation for her criticism of the police department, and thus violated her First Amendment rights. She maintained that the *Younger* doctrine should not apply because the bungled fingerprinting and scheduling error demonstrate that the officials are motivated by bad faith and an intent to harass. Should the district court accept this argument?

---

20. 401 U.S. at 50, 53-54.
21. For the second exception regarding flagrantly unconstitutional statutes, the reasoning is that a state authority that would enforce such an obviously unconstitutional statute would likely be operating in bad faith, giving reason to doubt the integrity of the state process and its ability to provide adequate redress. *See* LARRY W. YACKLE, FEDERAL COURTS 467 (2d ed. 2003).

Explanation

The district court will probably find Jane's evidence of bad faith and harassment insufficient. The bungled fingerprinting and scheduling error may reflect negligence (or even incompetence), but not animus or ill will. Although she has a theory as to *why* the officials might be motivated by subjective bad intent, Jane has no actual evidence of such a motive. Moreover, the reliable informant and the stolen goods in Jane's house are, no doubt, sufficient to make out a prima facie case of larceny. The officials therefore have a reasonable expectation of obtaining a valid conviction. For that reason, the court will likely not impute to them actual ill will or bad faith.

ii. Patently Unconstitutional State Law

The Supreme Court regularly cites the exception that *Younger* abstention should not apply if a criminal statute is "flagrantly and patently" unconstitutional. The Court has not, however, used it to rule out *Younger* abstention in any particular case. To the contrary, the Court's rejecting the exception under certain circumstances suggests that it reads the exception narrowly.[22]

iii. Other Extraordinary Circumstances

The *Younger* decision did not specify what types of other extraordinary circumstances would justify federal intervention in the face of ongoing proceedings, but did explain that pending state proceedings should be used to raise federal claims "unless it plainly appears that this course would not afford adequate protection." *Younger*, 401 U.S. at 45. After *Younger*, the Court clarified that a state tribunal does not provide adequate protection of federal rights where the tribunal's adjudicator has a direct financial interest in the outcome of the proceedings and is therefore fairly charged with bias.[23]

Example 8-19

A state trial judge was indicted for misdeeds allegedly arising out of testimony that the judge had given before a grand jury investigating corruption in the state court system. She filed suit in federal court seeking to enjoin the state criminal proceedings against her, claiming that she had been coerced to give the testimony by members of the state supreme court. She alleged that this significant involvement of the state supreme court rendered it impossible for state courts to provide her with a fair trial. The defendant in federal

---

22. *Trainor v. Hernandez*, 431 U.S. 434 (1977) (rejecting the possibility that the exception may apply to proceedings under a state attachment statute to recover fraudulently obtained welfare payments).
23. *Gibson v. Berryhill*, 411 U.S. 564, 577-578 (1973).

court — the state prosecutor — argued that the district court should abstain under *Younger*. The plaintiff responded that her federal suit was an appropriate case for the extraordinary circumstances exception. The plaintiff argued that, given the state supreme court's supervisory and administrative power over the state judiciary, the state courts lacked the competence to adjudicate her coercion defense because of their bias and their professional stake in the outcome. In response, the prosecutor noted that, should the case ever come before the state supreme court, interested justices were duty bound to recuse themselves if they had a personal interest in the matter. Does the extraordinary circumstances exception apply here?

Explanation

The extraordinary circumstances exception will likely not apply here. To accept plaintiff's argument, one would need to conclude that her allegations about state supreme court justices impeach the integrity of the entire state court system. The plaintiff has no specific direct evidence that the trial and appellate judges are biased against her or predisposed against her defense to the criminal charges. Moreover, the recusal provisions offer a mechanism for disqualifying state supreme court justices who may be directly interested in her suit but fail to recuse themselves automatically. *See Kugler v. Helfant*, 421 U.S. 117 (1975).

e. Relation with Anti-Injunction Act

The *Younger* Court said that its decision did not rest on the Anti-Injunction Act but instead derived from federalism and equitable principles. A year after the Court decided *Younger*, the Court held in *Mitchum v. Foster*, 407 U.S. 225 (1972), that 42 U.S.C §1983, which authorizes civil actions against state and local governments for violations of federal law, provide an express statutory exception to the Anti-Injunction Act. This means that a federal court could issue an injunction against state court proceedings in a §1983 action, without concern for the bar against such injunctions in the Anti-Injunction Act. Accordingly, under *Mitchum*'s reading of §1983 and the Anti-Injunction Act, *Younger* could *not* have rested on the Anti-Injunction Act because the federal suit in that case was based on §1983.

One might reasonably conclude that *Younger* and *Mitchum* are in tension with one another. After all, *Mitchum* allows injunctions of state court proceedings and *Younger* prohibits such injunctions. Technically, however, the two decisions are consistent: *Mitchum* relies on the premise that a federal court may enjoin state court proceedings as a general matter in §1983 actions, and *Younger* carves out circumstances where that option is not available. Because *Younger* covers only state criminal cases and civil cases that implicate an important state interest, *Mitchum* endorses some injunctions against state court proceedings not prohibited under *Younger*.

While technically reconcilable, the two cases illustrate how competing models of federal court jurisdiction can yield disparate results. *Younger* reflects a federalist orientation toward federal jurisdiction issues: the case gave prominence to the view that state courts should be left to perform their functions and could be trusted to provide a full and fair opportunity to litigate challenges based on federal law. By contrast, *Mitchum* reflects a nationalist orientation, emphasizing both the need for a federal forum to enforce federal rights and Congress's skepticism about the ability of state courts to respect those rights. As the *Mitchum* Court explained, "[T]he very purpose of §1983 was to interpose the federal courts between the States and the people, as guardians of the people's federal rights — to protect the people from unconstitutional action under color of state law."[24]

Example 8-20

The town of Hopeful regulates electrical rates. The energy provider for the town requested a rate hike by filing a request with the Hopeful town council. The council granted the request, but a community group filed a statutorily authorized appeal of the decision in the state trial court. After the state trial court began to consider this appeal, the energy provider filed a federal suit under 42 U.S.C. §1983, arguing that the appeal procedure was invalid on federal due process and federal preemption grounds. The energy provider sought two orders: one enjoining the state court proceeding and one endorsing its request for a rate hike. The town of Hopeful argued that the federal court should abstain. How should the district court analyze *Mitchum v. Foster* and *Younger v. Harris* in evaluating this abstention request?

Explanation

The district court might want to start with the question of whether Congress has created a statutory obstacle to the requested injunction. The Anti-Injunction Act is such an obstacle, but this suit falls within one of the exceptions: as held in *Mitchum v. Foster*, Congress expressly authorized an exception to the Anti-Injunction Act for §1983 suits. Even though the Anti-Injunction Act does not create an obstacle here, the district court must also consider whether the federalism and equitable concerns explored in the doctrine of *Younger v. Harris* preclude the requested injunction.

---

24. 407 U.S at 242. For further discussion of the federalist and nationalist models, see Chapter 1 and Richard H. Fallon, Jr., *The Ideologies of Federal Courts Law*, 74 VA. L. REV. 1141 (1988).

Although the state proceeding is ongoing, it is not the type of state court proceeding to which *Younger* abstention applies. The proceeding is civil, is not ancillary to the criminal law, and does not clearly concern the type of important, broad-based state interest at issue in cases like *Juidice v. Vail* or *Pennzoil Co. v. Texaco, Inc.* Unlike those cases, this example does not involve enforcement of state orders or the administration of the state judicial system. In a proceeding similar to this example (*NOPSI*), the Supreme Court rejected *Younger* abstention, stating that it had *never* "suggested that *Younger* requires abstention in deference to a state judicial proceeding reviewing legislative or executive action." *See New Orleans Pub. Serv., Inc. v. Council of City of New Orleans (NOPSI)*, 491 U.S. 350, 368 (1989).

f. Procedure

The *Younger* Court established a clear procedure for lower courts with regard to this abstention doctrine: dismissal of the action. Unlike the case for other abstention doctrines, district courts generally do not have the option of staying the matter.[25] Moreover, in contrast to abstention doctrines such as *Pullman* or *Burford*, courts entertain no confusion about how much discretion they possess to invoke *Younger* abstention; once they determine that all factors triggering *Younger* are present, the district court must abstain. The equitable and federalism underpinnings of *Younger* seem to compel this result.

2. *Colorado River* Abstention: Avoiding Piecemeal Litigation

Like the other abstention doctrines, the *Colorado River* doctrine derives from a specific case. The case concerned parallel lawsuits pending in both state and federal courts involving the same dispute and the same parties. This phenomenon — duplicate lawsuits in different forums — is a classic problem inherent in any system with multiple courts that have concurrent jurisdiction. In the United States federalist system, few tools are available for litigants facing this problem, and many tools — such as Federal Rule of Civil Procedure 11, the cause of action for malicious prosecution, and preclusion principles — are available only in limited circumstances. *Colorado River* abstention

---

25. *See, e.g., Gibson v. Berryhill*, 411 U.S. 564, 577 (1973) (stating that *Younger* "contemplates the outright dismissal of the federal suit, and the presentation of all claims, both state and federal, to the state courts"); *but cf. Deakins v. Monaghan*, 484 U.S. 193, 202 (1988) (holding that where a state criminal defendant requests monetary relief (not injunctive relief) in a related federal action, the federal court may stay rather than dismiss the lawsuit).

provides a mechanism for fighting duplicative, parallel litigation — but, like the other tools, also has limited usefulness.

a. Basic Elements

To appreciate the limits of *Colorado River* abstention, one must understand the unusual circumstances that inspired the doctrine. In *Colorado River Water Conservation Dist. v. United States*, 424 U.S. 800 (1976), the United States filed a federal court suit against more than one thousand defendants, seeking a declaration of water rights on federal lands. One defendant then moved to join the United States as a party in a previously filed state proceeding concerning the same water rights. A litigant may generally not sue the United States in state court without its consent, but Congress has provided such consent for water rights actions.

In response to a motion of the parties, the district court abstained. In holding that the district court had properly abstained, the Supreme Court noted that a federal court may not abstain simply because parallel litigation is pending in state court. The *Colorado River* Court recognized, however, that extraordinary circumstances may sometimes justify abstention "for reasons of wise judicial administration." 424 U.S. at 818. The Court listed factors to consider in evaluating whether extraordinary circumstances are present:

1. The presence of a res (such as water) over which both state and federal courts have asserted jurisdiction
2. The relative "inconvenience of the federal forum"
3. The need to avoid "piecemeal litigation"
4. The order of filing of the federal and state actions

Id. Although observing that no single factor determined whether a district court should abstain, the *Colorado River* Court found that each factor militated in favor of abstention in the case before it, emphasizing that Congress had expressed a strong policy against piecemeal litigation in water rights adjudication by consenting to a suit in state court.

Importantly, in a subsequent case, *Moses H. Cone Memorial Hosp. v. Mercury Constr. Corp.*, 460 U.S. 1 23-27 (1983), the Court added a fifth and a sixth factor for district courts to consider in evaluating whether to abstain:

5. The presence of a federal question in the case
6. The adequacy of state procedures to protect the rights of all parties[26]

---

26. Not all sources list the sixth factor as a consideration, but several lower courts have interpreted *Moses H. Cone* as injecting this factor into the analysis. *See, e.g, Blue Cross & Blue Shield v. Cruz*, 396 F. 3d 793 (7th Cir. 2005); *Moorer v. Demopolis Waterworks & Sewer Bd.*, 374 F.3d 994 (11th Cir. 2004); *Woodford v. Cmty. Action Agency of Greene County*, 239 F.3d 517 (2d Cir. 2001).

Explaining that a district court should apply all of the factors in a flexible and pragmatic way, the *Moses H. Cone* Court clarified that the presence of a federal question would militate against abstention and that inadequate state procedures also weigh heavily against abstention.

Example 8-21

Cheryl held a party at her beach house, and her third-floor deck collapsed under the weight of thirty guests. All guests were injured, and all pursued a state law tort action against Cheryl and the carpenter who built the deck. Seventeen guests were from different states than Cheryl and the carpenter. The out-of-state guests filed a diversity action in federal court, asserting their state tort claims. Thereafter, the thirteen other guests from the same state as Cheryl and the carpenter filed suit in state court. These thirteen plaintiffs raised the same claims as were raised in the federal court action. The state and federal courts are in the same location close to the accident, and the state court procedures are well developed for adjudicating tort claims of this kind. While she is not poor, Cheryl's personal resources for paying judgments are limited — as are the liability provisions in her homeowner's policy.

Cheryl and the carpenter argued that the federal court should abstain under *Colorado River*. Should the federal court accept this argument?

Explanation

This example does not present a sufficiently extraordinary case for *Colorado River* abstention. The federal court should not accept the defendants' arguments, even though the example demonstrates one particularly strong factor favoring abstention: parallel, duplicative lawsuits pending in state and federal courts.[27] Magnifying this factor's significance are Cheryl's limited insurance and financial resources, which suggest that each plaintiff may not receive a full remedy for the harm done. With lawsuits pending in two forums, the courts are likely to disperse this limited pool resource in an unequal manner: the first set of plaintiffs to prevail may receive full recovery and thereby deplete the assets available to pay a second judgment. Abstention would force the litigation to be consolidated in state court, making a just distribution of the limited recovery resource pool more likely.

While deserving of weight, the "limited resources" argument does not itself justify abstention. Courts have ruled that parallel litigation alone is insufficient to justify abstention absent a congressionally imposed policy against duplicative litigation, such as in *Colorado River* itself. *See Ryan v. Johnson,*

---

27. In fact, this factor is a threshold requirement. Without parallel proceedings, some courts have held that *Colorado River* abstention is simply unavailable. *See, e.g., Ryan v. Johnson,* 115 F.3d 193, 196 (3d Cir. 1997).

115 F.3d 193, 200 (3d Cir. 1997) (holding *Colorado River* abstention inapplicable under similar circumstances).

Examination of the other factors reveals that parallel, duplicative litigation is the only factor favoring abstention in this example. First, the state and federal courts have not exercised jurisdiction over any res such as land, water, another natural resource, or the corpus of a trust fund. The second factor — convenience of the federal forum — does not favor abstention because the federal forum is equally convenient to the state court. Likewise, the fourth factor weighs against abstention, since the federal lawsuit preceded the state suit. The fifth factor — presence of a federal question — is also of no help in this state law action. Finally, the sixth factor does not support abstention because state procedures are fully adequate for adjudicating the state case.

Example 8-22

The state of Georgia filed a state court action alleging that a local water and sewer board violated state and federal water pollution control statutes. A private plaintiff, who was specifically injured by the local board's decisions respecting water quality, intervened as a co-plaintiff, and the state court entered an order stating that the water and sewer board should make no decisions respecting water quality pending completion of the state litigation. The private plaintiff then filed a federal court action against the water and sewer board, raising the same state and federal claims as raised in the state suit. The state and federal courts are in the same location, and the state court procedures are well developed for litigating cases of this kind. The local board argued that the district court should invoke *Colorado River* abstention. Should the district court do so?

Explanation

The district court would not abuse its discretion if it abstained. *See Moorer v. Dempolis Waterworks & Sewer Board*, 374 F.3d 994 (11th Cir. 2004) (invoking "abuse of discretion" standard to uphold a district court's decision to abstain under similar circumstances). It is perhaps no accident that the *Moorer* court upheld the abstention decision, given that the dispute involved an important resource — water. This example would be a close call if it did not also concern water, since only some of the *Colorado River* factors favor abstention: the state court litigation and state control over the water occurred first, and piecemeal litigation is likely. The presence of some federal law bearing on the dispute argues against abstention, although that factor may not weigh heavily since federal law does not control the entire case. Two factors, however, weigh heavily against abstention: the state court is no less convenient than federal court, and the federal court has every reason to believe that the state of Georgia and the private plaintiff will vigorously prosecute the case using adequate state court procedures.

Counseling district courts in evaluating whether to abstain, the Supreme Court explained in *Moses H. Cone*, "[T]he task is to ascertain whether there exist 'exceptional' circumstances, the 'clearest of justifications,' that can suffice under *Colorado River* to justify the *surrender* of . . . jurisdiction." *Moses H. Cone*, 460 U.S. at 25-26. This language is aimed at demonstrating how truly extraordinary the circumstances must be for a federal court to decline the congressionally granted power to adjudicate a lawsuit. For that reason, one might argue that few, if any, cases unequivocally point toward *Colorado River* abstention. The best one can usually say is that a strong case like the one in this example falls within the discretionary realm where a district court is acting properly in choosing to abstain.

b. Procedure

When a federal court decides to invoke *Colorado River* abstention, the question arises whether the court should dismiss or stay the action. As a practical matter, the choice is usually inconsequential because a state court decision would have a preclusive effect in federal court, preventing the federal court from adjudicating claims stayed in federal court during the pendency of the state court action. In some instances, however, the state court proceedings may not fully resolve all issues; the federal court may then litigate remaining issues after the state proceedings have ended. For this reason, most lower courts have held that a district court should stay, rather than dismiss, the lawsuit; in such a case a litigant can easily return to federal court after the state proceedings, if necessary. This policy is consistent with the Supreme Court's announcement, stated in the context of *Burford* abstention, that federal courts possess the power to dismiss an action properly within their jurisdiction only for discretionary remedies, such as injunctions. *Quackenbush v. Allstate Insurance Company*, 517 U.S. 706 (1996). The *Quackenbush* reasoning suggests that dismissal is not even an option for district courts invoking *Colorado River* abstention in damages actions.

Example 8-23

Mariah filed a state court action asserting her right to mine for gold in Alaska, and the state court issued an order suspending all mining until the court decided the mining rights dispute. Mariah sought an injunction under state law governing the controversy. Invoking diversity of citizenship jurisdiction, Mariah then filed a federal court action raising the same claim against the defendant named in the state action and also seeking injunctive relief. Although the state court is located near the mining area, the federal court is located 200 miles away. The defendant filed a motion asking the federal court to abstain under *Colorado River*. What should the district court do?

Explanation

This is an appropriate case for *Colorado River* abstention: (1) the state court first exercised power over a res (the gold mine), (2) the federal forum is inconvenient, (3) without abstention, piecemeal litigation over an indivisible resource (gold) would result, (4) the state action was filed first, (5) state law provides the rule of decision in the case, and (6) state procedures appear adequate to dispose of the controversy. Given that Mariah requests injunctive relief, the district court may dismiss the federal action. Nevertheless, the lower courts have shown a marked preference for staying the federal court action in a situation such as this. Staying the action will allow the district court to dispose of any residual matters that might remain concerning mining rights after the state court has ruled.

c. Declaratory Judgment Actions Exempted

In *Wilton v. Seven Falls Co.*, 515 U.S. 277 (1995), the Supreme Court made clear that declaratory judgment actions were exempt from the rigorous requirements of *Colorado River* abstention. Instead, the Court recognized, Congress granted federal courts considerable discretion over whether to issue declaratory judgments, allowing federal courts to defer to parallel state proceedings even in the absence of the extraordinary circumstances required under *Colorado River*.

C. STATUTORY AND JUDICIALLY CREATED RESTRICTIONS OPERATING IN TANDEM: THE ANTI-INJUNCTION ACT AND THE ABSTENTION DOCTRINES CONSIDERED TOGETHER

Perhaps the trickiest part of the abstention doctrines is distinguishing them from statutory restrictions and from each other. Another challenge is identifying which factual circumstances are most appropriate for each of the various doctrines. This section provides a strategy for analyzing a given factual scenario.

For separation of powers reasons, statutory restrictions should provide the starting point for analysis. If Congress has mandated in a statute such as the Anti-Injunction Act that a federal court should not exercise power in a particular case, that restriction should govern. If no statutory restriction exists, then the court should consider the judicially created abstention doctrines.

While complex criteria distinguish the abstention doctrines, each one possesses a key factor that triggers its potential application. While not conclusive as to the final abstention decision, these triggers provide issue-spotting cues for analyzing whether a set of facts presents an occasion to apply a particular abstention doctrine. Here is a list of triggers:

- *Pullman* abstention: a federal constitutional claim with an interwoven state law question
- *Thibodaux* abstention: a federal court deciding unclear, sensitive, and important questions of state law
- *Burford* abstention: a state administrative or regulatory framework that could govern the controversy
- *Younger* abstention: a request for an injunction or declaratory judgment that pertains to a state proceeding
- *Colorado River* abstention: parallel state and federal proceedings that would involve litigating the same issues twice

After identifying the trigger, one can then analyze whether the other criteria for the abstention doctrine are present in a particular case. The abstention doctrines are not mutually exclusive: more than one doctrine may govern a federal court dispute.

Example 8-24

Lolly and Dora were landowners in Utah. They were both Utah residents and owned parcels of land adjacent to federal park lands. Lolly and Dora both made claim to a specific portion of these parcels. This contested portion was contiguous to federal land. The dispute over this land arose from an interpretation of a deed drafted by a representative of the United States government conveying to Lolly and Dora the two parcels. State law governs the construction of the deed and the ultimate question of who owns the contested land. State law also directs that the intent of the grantor in a land transaction governs the interpretation of a deed. In this instance, the grantor is the United States government.

Concerned that property disputes near federal land may adversely affect interests of the United States, Congress had passed the following Disputed Property Jurisdictional Statute:

> Where two or more adverse claimants assert an interest in land adjacent to federal land, a federal district court has subject matter jurisdiction over their claims regardless of the identity of the claimants, the citizenship of the parties, or the amount in controversy. The federal court may employ both legal and

equitable remedies in order to give full, swift, and effective relief to all the claimants.

Invoking this statute, Lolly filed a federal court suit to settle the question of who owns the contested land. The federal court issued a writ attaching the land in question. Immediately thereafter, however, Dora filed an action asking the state court to settle the same ownership dispute and to attach the property for the pendency of the state court action. The state and federal courts are in the same location. Lolly then requested that the federal court enjoin the state court action and determine the ownership question itself. Dora argued that restrictions on federal court power rendered it unlawful and inappropriate for the federal district court to grant this request. How should the district court evaluate Dora's argument?

Explanation

The district court should start by considering whether Congress has imposed a statutory restriction on the requested exercise of jurisdiction. Because Lolly has asked the district court to enjoin an ongoing state court proceeding, the Anti-Injunction Act may provide such a restriction. If the Anti-Injunction Act precludes Lolly's requested relief, then the court need not even consider the abstention doctrines.

Two exceptions to the Anti-Injunction Act appear to be present in this case. First, because the federal suit is in the nature of an in rem action over a res — real property — the injunction is "necessary in aid of" the federal court's jurisdiction. The theory behind this pre-judgment exception is that the federal court needs to maintain control over the res in order to give effective relief. Second, the injunction appears to be expressly authorized by Congress through the Disputed Property Jurisdictional Statute. That statute expressly authorizes the federal court to issue injunctive relief in land dispute cases. Moreover, Congress appears to have contemplated that injunctions issued in cases under that statute may focus on state courts that adjudicate property disputes without properly protecting the interests of the United States. Accordingly, one might argue that the Disputed Property Jurisdictional Statute can be "given its intended scope" only if a federal court has freedom to enjoin ongoing state proceedings. *Mitchum v. Foster*, 407 U.S. 225, 238 (1972).[28]

Since the Anti-Injunction Act does not present an obstacle to the federal court adjudicating the merits of Lolly's case, the court must next consider the various abstention doctrines. The court might first identify whether the case contains any trigger or issue-spotting cue.

---

28. For more detailed discussion of the Anti-Injunction Act, see Chapter 7.

Pullman abstention: Lolly is not asserting a federal constitutional claim. Nor does her land contest implicate any constitutional issues. The trigger for *Pullman* abstention is therefore missing. The purpose of *Pullman* is to provide a mechanism for federal courts to avoid constitutional adjudication, and that purpose is not present here.

Thibodaux abstention: The example mentions state law in an area that arguably could be characterized as important and sensitive: land ownership. But the facts nowhere suggest uncertainty in the state law. Accordingly, the example does not present the unusual circumstances required for *Thibodaux* abstention. Notably, Lolly and Dora are citizens of the same state, and the district court is not exercising diversity of citizenship jurisdiction — a typical component of a *Thibodaux* abstention case. Instead, the court is exercising jurisdiction that Congress deemed particularly important in this type of case. The district court should therefore be careful before choosing to reject Congress's judgment by extending *Thibodaux* abstention to this context.

Burford abstention: The example mentions state law but does not present a special state regulatory or administrative scheme for handling property disputes of this kind. The *Burford* cue is thus not triggered.

Younger abstention: The trigger for *Younger* abstention is directly implicated: Lolly requests an injunction of a state court proceeding. Accordingly, the district court should evaluate whether the abstention doctrine applies. Upon analysis, the district court will discover that a significant prerequisite is missing: the state court proceeding is neither criminal nor does it involve the type of important state interest that the Supreme Court has found sufficient for applying the abstention doctrine in civil cases. Thus, *Younger* abstention does not apply.

Colorado River abstention: The cue for *Colorado River* abstention is present: parallel state and federal proceedings that would involve litigating the same issue twice. The district court should look further, therefore, into whether the *Colorado River* doctrine advises the court to abstain from the case altogether. Several other factors favor *Colorado River*: the federal and state courts have asserted power over a res (the land), the federal action was filed first, and the state procedures appear adequate to dispose of the dispute. In addition, although the case has federal elements, state law provides the rule of decision.

On the other side of the balance, the district court might observe that the inconvenience factor points away from *Colorado River* abstention: the federal and state courts are in the same location. That, however, is unlikely to be determinative. Instead, the truly problematic *Colorado River* factor is "the need to avoid piecemeal litigation." In this example, piecemeal litigation is threatened because Dora and Lolly are pursuing their ownership claims in two separate forums. By mandating in the Disputed Property Jurisdictional Statute that federal courts should provide "full, swift, and effective relief to all claimants," Congress has, in fact, evinced a desire to avoid piecemeal litigation.

The difficulty for *Colorado River* abstention, however, is that Congress's strategy was to authorize *federal* courts to control the disputes. Therefore, Congress gave precisely the opposite cue as in the *Colorado River* case itself, which provided consent to sue the United States in *state* court. Accordingly, despite the formal presence of most of the *Colorado River* factors, the example here lacks the type of extraordinary circumstances justifying abstention.

Having exhausted its analysis of statutory and court-created restrictions on the requested federal court injunction, the federal court is free to dismiss Dora's argument that principles governing federal court power render it unlawful and inappropriate for federal district court to grant the request to enjoin the state court proceeding. The federal court may reach the merits of the dispute and issue the injunction if it concludes that the ordinary prerequisites for injunctive relief are satisfied.

PART IV

The Role of State Courts in the Federalist System

A frequently overlooked yet essential component of overlapping jurisdictional powers in the United States federalist system is the role of state courts in enforcing federal law. This state court role impacts federal courts significantly: to the extent that state courts lack authority over federal law, work must fall exclusively to federal courts. Moreover, many statutes and doctrines reviewed in this volume restrict access to federal court and are therefore based on the assumption that state courts stand ready to adjudicate legal rights violations. Thus, the availability of state courts influences the principles that regulate federal court access. The role of state courts is crucial no matter whether one approaches federal court access questions with a federalist orientation or a nationalist orientation: for the federalist analyst, state courts are the presumptively appropriate forums for adjudication; for the nationalist, state courts act as an important backstop, available for adjudication where federal courts are not.[1]

The authority of state courts has significant practical ramifications for litigants. Litigants who find themselves in state court will likely discover they are stuck there — unable to switch their cases to federal court unless they can avail themselves of removal jurisdiction, United States Supreme Court review, or habeas corpus relief in lower federal courts. The litigants'

1. Chapter 1 describes further the federalist and nationalist orientations to federal court issues.

219

confinement to state court thus raises "the stakes for battles" over access to federal court at the beginning of litigation.[2] As the material in the following two chapters illustrates, the principles governing state court power are intertwined with power questions concerning the federal government, including the federal courts as well as Congress.

Chapter 9 reviews rules governing state court authority to enforce federal law. The chapter explains concurrent jurisdiction by state and federal courts and describes limitations on state courts' ability to employ certain remedies against federal officers. Chapter 10 turns to state courts' obligation to enforce federal law. This material not only explains the general notion that state courts are constitutionally obligated to hear federal claims, but also discusses Congress's power to influence state court workload.

---

2. LARRY YACKLE, FEDERAL COURTS 117 (2d ed. 2003).

State Court Authority to Enforce Federal Law

The framers of the United States Constitution seem to have assumed that state courts may adjudicate matters that appear in the list of federal judicial powers in Article III. The framers did not even create lower federal courts, but included in Article III a description of the United States Supreme Court's "appellate jurisdiction." If Congress had not created lower federal courts, from which tribunals would these appeals come? State courts, presumably. Thus, implicit in the framers' reference to appellate jurisdiction is the assumption that state courts might be hearing matters appealed ultimately to the United States Supreme Court.

Alexander Hamilton explained this assumption in *Federalist Papers* No. 82, positing that state courts retained their preexisting authority to hear the types of cases and controversies listed in Article III. Stated differently, after the Constitution created "the federal judicial power," the state courts retained the power they had before the Constitution was ratified. Unlike the limited powers of the federal courts, the state courts had general jurisdiction. As courts of general jurisdiction, state courts possess power unless specifically limited by a superior source. Although a superior source, the Constitution contains no such limitation. Accordingly, state courts are presumed to have concurrent jurisdiction with federal courts by virtue of their preexisting general jurisdiction powers, not because the Constitution actually gives them any power.[3]

---

3. For discussion of possible historical evidence supporting a different view of state court jurisdiction, *see* Michael G. Collins, *Article III Cases, State Court Duties, and the Madisonian Compromise*, 1995 WIS. L. REV. 39, 46-135.

The federalist system does circumscribe state court power in one important respect: state courts do not possess plenary remedial powers over officers of the superior authority — the federal government. Thus, the Supreme Court has ruled that the presumption of concurrent jurisdiction does not include certain state court remedies against federal officers. After reviewing the presumption of concurrent jurisdiction, this chapter outlines these remedial limitations.

A. THE PRESUMPTION OF CONCURRENT JURISDICTION: EFFECT ON STATE COURTS

As a starting point, state courts are presumed to share with federal courts all the powers listed in Article III. But Congress can change that presumption and, in so doing, make federal court jurisdiction exclusive over a particular subject area.

If Congress wants to override the presumption of concurrent jurisdiction, it must be plain about it. State court power is deemed to exist unless foreclosed by (1) "an explicit statutory directive," (2) "unmistakable implication from legislative history," or (3) "clear incompatibility between state-court jurisdiction and federal interests."[4] The Supreme Court applies these requirements with a strong bias against exclusivity. For example, the Court found concurrent jurisdiction, even under a statutory scheme that would lead to state court interpretations of federal criminal offenses, to be a task easily characterized as inviting state court interference with a strong federal interest in uniformity.[5]

Example 9-1

Congress passed a statute governing labor-management relations. The statute states that "United States District Courts shall have jurisdiction to adjudicate disputes concerning the rights of parties under collective bargaining agreements pursuant to this statute." The federal policy governing national labor relations reflected in the statute is so potent that the United States Supreme Court has held that the statute authorizes federal courts to fashion a body of federal common law for enforcing agreements within the statute's scope. The legislative history does not directly determine whether state courts should be allowed to adjudicate disputes arising under the statute. History establishes instead that the overarching purpose of the statute is to promote good relations among labor and management through the collective bargaining process. Should a state court be allowed to adjudicate disputes under the statute?

---

4. *Gulf Offshore Co. v. Mobil Oil Corp.*, 453 U.S. 473, 478 (1981).
5. *Tafflin v. Levitt*, 493 U.S. 455, 467 (1990) (ruling that state courts could hear civil RICO claims because there is "[n]othing in the language, structure, legislative history, or underlying policies of RICO" precluding state court jurisdiction).

Explanation

Applying the presumption of concurrent jurisdiction, state courts should be allowed to adjudicate claims arising from the labor-management relations statute. No express language divests state courts of jurisdiction. The jurisdictional grant to district courts does not negate state court jurisdiction; more than a power grant to district courts is needed to overcome the bias against exclusive federal court jurisdiction. Allowing state courts to adjudicate collective bargaining disputes is also entirely consistent with the statute's purpose as explained in the legislative history: taking labor strife out of the realm of violence and into the orderly procedures of court. The legislative history actually supports state court jurisdiction.

The statute's authorization for federal common law does not clash with state court jurisdiction. State courts are competent to create federal common law, and the United States Supreme Court is available to resolve conflicts in legal interpretations that result from enabling state courts to participate in the common law process. *See, e.g., Charles Dowd Box Co. v. Courtney,* 368 U.S. 502, 507-514 (1962) (making a similar argument in ruling that state courts have concurrent jurisdiction under the Labor Management Relations Act).

Example 9-2

Julian invented a machine that he believed was covered by patent protection. He entered into a contract with a production company under which the company agreed to produce and market the machine and to pay his royalties as long as the machine was properly patented. The company failed to pay Julian any royalties, and he filed suit for breach of contract in a state trial court of general jurisdiction. The company argued that the suit should be dismissed because the state court lacked subject matter jurisdiction. According to the company, the case could not be decided without a ruling as to whether a valid patent protected the machine. Given that federal courts have original exclusive jurisdiction over patents, should the state court accept this argument and dismiss the lawsuit?

Explanation

The state court need not dismiss the lawsuit. The Supreme Court has established that even if federal courts have exclusive jurisdiction over a cause of action arising under a particular statute, a state court may decide federal issues that pertain to the statute and that are embedded in a cause of action within the state court's jurisdiction. Julian's case is a breach of contract cause of action, which falls within the state court's general jurisdiction. The state court may resolve the incidental patent issue in order to dispose of the case. *See Lear, Inc. v. Adkins,* 395 U.S. 653, 675-676 (1969) (state court may adjudicate contract disputes that depend on patent validity).

B. THE PRESUMPTION OF CONCURRENT JURISDICTION: EFFECT ON FEDERAL COURTS

The presumption of concurrent jurisdiction holds that in circumstances where Congress has not explicitly disqualified state courts from exercising jurisdiction, the state courts may exercise power over a federal case (so long, of course, as they have subject matter jurisdiction under state law). The question arises, however, how the presumption operates in the other direction: where Congress explicitly grants *state* courts jurisdiction, are *federal* courts also presumed to possess jurisdiction? The lower courts are in disagreement about this.

Example 9-3

Congress passed the Telephone Consumer Protection Act (TCPA), making it unlawful to use a telephone facsimile (fax) machine to send an unsolicited advertisement. The statute creates a private cause of action to enforce the prohibition. The TCPA also states, "A person or entity may, if otherwise permitted by the laws or rules of court of a State, bring" a private cause of action for violation of the TCPA's ban on unsolicited fax advertisements "in an appropriate court of that State." The statute does not mention federal court jurisdiction, except in one instance: the TCPA provides that state attorneys general may bring public actions to enforce the statute, but requires the attorneys general to bring those actions *only* in federal court.

Monique owns a large company with many fax machines. She filed a private suit under the TCPA in federal court against Deborah, who has been sending unsolicited faxes to Monique's company. May the federal court entertain this action under its federal question jurisdiction set forth in the general "arising under" statute, 28 U.S.C. §1331?

Explanation

The lower courts have reached different results on this question, although the weight of authority has held against federal jurisdiction. These courts reason that concurrent jurisdiction does not operate in parallel fashion for state and federal courts: while state courts are presumed capable of hearing federal cases because they are "courts of general jurisdiction," federal courts are "courts of limited jurisdiction" and thus do not enjoy the same latitude. In fact, a presumption exists *against* federal court jurisdiction: in cases of ambiguity, federal courts are deemed to lack power.[6]

---

6. *See Kokkonen v. Guardian Life Ins. Co. of Am.,* 511 U.S. 375, 377 (1994).

Lower federal courts are creatures of Congress and possess power only when Congress has granted it to them. Thus, where a federal statute evinces the intent for federal courts not to hear a cause of action, a federal court should be presumed to lack jurisdiction. The presumption of concurrent jurisdiction means that Congress need not expressly grant state courts power over a cause of action. When, as with the TCPA, Congress expressly grants state courts power, it must have intended to express the intent that only state courts should hear the private cause of action. Otherwise, its words would be superfluous, since the presumption in favor of state court concurrent jurisdiction implies that state court power is already in place.

Adopting reasoning similar to this, nearly all courts that have considered whether the TCPA meant to divest federal courts of federal question jurisdiction have held that it did.[7] These courts would hold that the federal court should dismiss Monique's lawsuit for lack of subject matter jurisdiction.

At least one court has rejected this line of reasoning, and would entertain Monique's lawsuit. This court concludes that, because the TCPA does not explicitly declare that state court jurisdiction is exclusive, one should not read it as overriding Congress's broad grants of subject matter jurisdiction to federal courts, such as in the federal question jurisdiction statute, removal statute, and Class Action Fairness Act.[8] The court reckoned that reading the TCPA in this way does not render superfluous the language stating that state courts possess jurisdiction. This language helps, the court reasoned, to reinforce "an established norm" and to "avoid[] any argument that . . . federal jurisdiction is exclusive."[9] The court found further support in the explicit TCPA statement that federal courts have exclusive jurisdiction over actions brought by state attorneys general. The natural inference from this, the court argued, is that Congress knew how to make jurisdiction exclusive in any court and explicitly said so when it wanted exclusivity to be the rule. Where it was silent about exclusivity, one should not infer it.

Each of these competing approaches to reading the TCPA's jurisdictional language is valid. Such is the dizzying uncertainty inherent in federal jurisdiction: a range of answers is acceptable. An answer is meritorious if it

---

7. See, e.g., Dun-Rite Constr. , Inc. v. Amazing Tickets, Inc., No. 04-3216, 2004 WL 3239533, at *2 (6th Cir. Dec. 16, 2004); Murphey v. Lanier, 204 F.3d 911, 915 (9th Cir. 2000); Erienet, Inc. v. Velocity Net, Inc., 156 F.3d 513, 520 (3d Cir. 1998); Nicholson v. Hooters of Augusta, Inc., 136 F.3d 1287, 1289 (11th Cir. 1998); Chair King, Inc. v. Houston Cellular Corp., 131 F.3d 507, 514 (5th Cir. 1997); Int'l Sci. & Tech. Inst., Inc. v. Inacom Commc'ns, Inc., 106 F.3d 1146, 1150 (4th Cir. 1997); Brodeur v. Swan Financial Corp., No. 4:05 CV 2418 DDN, 2006 U.S. Dist. LEXIS 21792, at *13 (E.D. Mo. Apr. 11, 2006).
8. See Brill v. Countrywide Home Loans, Inc., 427 F.3d 446, 450 (7th Cir. 2005). The United States Court of Appeals for the Second Circuit has accepted this approach for diversity of citizenship jurisdiction, but not for federal question jurisdiction. See, e.g., Gottlieb v. Carnival Corporation, 436 F.3d 335, 337-339 (2d Cir. 2006).
9. Brill, 427 F.3d at 451.

reasonably and creatively incorporates the relevant legal text, history, and the presumptions that underlie the dual system of United States government.

C. REMEDIAL LIMITATIONS FOR STATE COURT SUITS AGAINST FEDERAL OFFICERS

Principles of general jurisdiction generally vest state courts with power to hear suits against federal officers. The United States Supreme Court, however, has recognized that federalism limits the state court's power to issue coercive orders against officers. Perhaps the most famous decision on this topic is *Tarble's Case*, 80 U.S. (1.3 Wall.) 397, 402 (1872), in which the Court entertained the question of whether a state court could issue a writ of habeas corpus against a federal army commander "to inquire into the validity of the enlistment of soldiers into the military service . . . , and to discharge them . . . when, in [the court's] judgment, their enlistment has not been made in conformity with the laws of the United States."

Given the date of the decision (immediately following the Civil War), the result in *Tarble's Case* is no surprise: the state courts could not control federal military commanders.[10] The Court remarked that the habeas corpus power might be used "to the great detriment of the public service." *Id.* at 409. The rationale for the ruling was much broader, however, with the Court invoking constitutional principles of federalism. The *Tarble's* Court first explained that the Constitution recognized that state and federal governments operate in independent "spheres of action." Despite this independence, however, the federal government's "supremacy" imposed restrictions on state courts, placing the federal government "far beyond the reach of the judicial process issued by a State judge." *Id.* at 406-408.

Example 9-4

Federal authorities arrested and convicted Emerson for a federal crime. The judge sentenced him to five years imprisonment, and he was confined at a federal prison. State authorities discovered that Emerson was involved in a notorious murder; they wanted to have him testify at the homicide trial and possibly prosecute him as a co-conspirator in the homicide. To ensure unfettered access to Emerson for the purpose of this homicide investigation, they asked a state judge to issue a writ of habeas corpus directed at the

---

10. The result in *Tarble's* case was also foreshadowed by *Ableman v. Booth*, 62 U.S. (21 How.) 506 (1859), in which a federal court had convicted an antislavery activist for a violation of the Fugitive Slave Act. The Supreme Court in *Ableman v. Booth* held that a state court's subsequent grant of habeas corpus interfered with federal judicial authority.

Director of Federal Prisons, requiring the director to deliver Emerson to state control. Believing the state prosecution to be extremely important, the state court wishes to issue the writ of habeas corpus. Does it have authority to do so?

Explanation

The state court does not have authority to issue the writ of habeas corpus against the Director of Federal Prisons. While scholars debate the genesis and reach of *Tarble's Case*, a straightforward application of its holding yields the following conclusion: the supremacy clause of the United States Constitution precludes the state court from exercising habeas corpus authority over a federal officer, such as the director.

While the prohibition against state courts issuing writs of habeas corpus is unequivocal, uncertainty surrounds how far the prohibition against coercive relief extends. The Supreme Court has established that the prohibition extends to writs of mandamus. *M'Clung v. Silliman*, 19 U.S. (6 Wheat.) 598 (1821) (state court may not issue a writ of mandamus to the official who acts as registrar in federal land office). The Court has not ruled, however, whether state courts may issue injunctions against federal officials.[11] Lower courts have reached inconsistent results, although the weight of authority denies state courts this power.[12] Interestingly, the Supreme Court has shown no hesitation to allow state courts to issue damage awards in actions against federal officers.

Example 9-5

Antoinette is an attorney who represented clients before a federal immigration agency. She alleged that during several immigration hearings, representatives of the agency defamed her, thereby interfering with her relationships with her clients and injuring her business reputation. Antoinette filed suit in state court against these federal representatives seeking damages and an injunction preventing them from further defamation. May the state court issue the requested relief?

---

11. In dictum, the Supreme Court expressed disapproval: "[N]o state court could, by injunction or otherwise, prevent federal officers from collecting Federal taxes." *Keely v. Sanders*, 99 U.S. (9 Otto) 441, 443 (1879).

12. *Compare, e.g., Pennsylvania Turnpike Commission v. McGinnes*, 179 F. Supp. 578 (E.D. Pa. 1959) (state court cannot enjoin District Director of Internal Revenue Service from paying a tax refund to entity that obtained state turnpike commission funds fraudulently), *aff'd*, 278 F.2d 330 (3d Cir. 1960), *with Perez v. Rhiddlehoover*, 247 F. Supp. 65 (E.D. La. 1965) (state court allowed to enjoin federal voting examiners from registering persons who did not comply with state law voting requirements).

Explanation

The answer is probably no for the requested injunction and yes for the requested damages. The weight of lower federal court authority disfavors the power of state courts to issue the requested injunctive relief. Lower federal courts generally reason that injunctions — like writs of mandamus and writs of habeas corpus — are remedies that can undermine the discretion of federal officers; under this reasoning, state courts should be prohibited from issuing injunctions under the authority of *Tarble's Case* and *M'Clung v. Silliman*. Despite the lower courts' disagreement over injunctions, authorities are uniform in holding that state courts have power to award damages against federal officials for committing tortious acts without authority. Antoinette's ultimate success in obtaining a damage award, however, will depend on whether or not the suit is barred by sovereign immunity or official immunity defenses.[13]

---

13. See Chapters 13 and 14 for further discussion of immunity doctrines.

State Court Responsibility to Enforce Federal Law

The flip side of the question of whether state courts *can* decide federal issues is whether they *must* do so. Does a state court have the discretion to decline to adjudicate a federal issue? In part, the answer is a simple no. If a federal issue is relevant to the deciding of any claim — including state claims — the supremacy clause of the United States Constitution requires the state court to consider the issue and give force to any implicated federal law that disposes of all or part of the case. But matters become more complicated if one asks whether state courts must adjudicate an entire federal cause of action or whether they may simply refuse to take jurisdiction, leaving the litigants with redress in federal (or other state) courts. This chapter first explores that question and then turns to a related matter — for which the case law provides surprisingly little guidance: what, if anything, constrains Congress from controlling state courts, either by manipulating their jurisdiction or creating federal causes of action that the state courts are obligated to adjudicate? First, however, is an illustration of the least controversial state court obligation.

Example 10-1

Bridget filed suit in state court against a cigarette company, claiming that her mother's death was caused by the company's failure to warn her mother of cigarette smoking's dangers. This "failure to warn" cause of action derived from a state tort statute granting the state court subject matter jurisdiction over the cause of action. The defendant cigarette company argued that this cause of action is preempted by the federal act mandating the warnings that companies must place on cigarette package labels. Is the state court obliged to entertain this defense?

Explanation

Yes, the supremacy clause of the United States Constitution requires the state court to consider this defense and — if the defendant is correct about the federal statute's preemptive effect — to dismiss the case. As the Supreme Court has explained, state courts must enforce federal law "because the Constitution and laws passed pursuant to it are as much laws in the States as laws passed by the state legislature." *Howlett v. Rose*, 496 U.S. 356, 367 (1990). The supremacy clause renders the federal cigarette labeling act a " 'supreme Law of the Land,' and charges state courts with a coordinate responsibility to enforce that law according to their regular modes of procedure." *Id.*

A. STATE COURT OBLIGATION TO HEAR A FEDERAL CAUSE OF ACTION

Along with a state court's obligation to adjudicate federal issues that arise as part of a state law cause of action comes the general responsibility to hear federal causes of action. This is not to say that the federal government may force states to create tribunals to hear federal claims. "The general rule, 'bottomed deeply in belief in the importance of state control of state judicial procedure, is that federal law takes the state courts as it finds them.'"[1] Thus, state courts may decline to adjudicate a federal claim — but only if they have "a valid excuse" for doing so. *Howlett*, 496 U.S. at 370.

In the classic case on the valid excuse doctrine, *Testa v. Katt*, 330 U.S. 386 (1947), the Supreme Court of Rhode Island ruled that a state court need not adjudicate a congressionally created federal cause of action that required courts to award treble damages for the injury proven. According to the Rhode Island court, the treble damages authorization rendered the federal claim "a penal law[] . . . in the international sense," which Rhode Island conflict-of-laws principles excused the state court from enforcing. No government, the Rhode Island court reasoned, bears the obligation of enforcing the penal laws of a foreign government. The United States Supreme Court in *Testa v. Katt* vigorously rejected this reasoning, pointing out that the supremacy clause transformed the federal statute's policy into the policy of the state itself. Accordingly, a state cannot properly characterize a federal act as foreign and cannot refuse to enforce a cause of action arising

---

1. *Howlett v. Rose*, 496 U.S. 356, 372 (1990) (quoting Henry M. Hart, Jr., *The Relations Between State and Federal Law*, 54 COLUM. L. REV. 489, 508 (1954)).

from the federal statute on that ground. Rhode Island's conflict-of-laws policy against enforcement of other jurisdictions' penal law was thus not a "valid excuse" for refusing to hear the federal cause of action. *Id.* at 392.

The crucial question is: what is a valid excuse for the *Testa v. Katt* rule? Generally, valid excuses are neutral rules regarding court administration. "Neutral" means nondiscriminatory — in the sense that the rules apply to state and federal laws alike. Enforcing the valid excuse doctrine, the Supreme Court has repeatedly stated that the existence of state court jurisdiction implies a duty to use it to enforce a federal cause of action. The types of neutral state procedural rules that have excused state courts from this duty include (1) a rule allowing dismissal of all claims where neither the plaintiff nor the defendant was a resident of the forum state, (2) a rule allowing dismissal of claims arising outside the forum state's territory, and (3) a rule dismissing a case based on the doctrine of forum non conveniens.[2]

Example 10-2

Congress created a federal statute allowing employees to sue for violations of a federal wage and hour law. Katia had a claim that her employer failed to comply with the overtime provisions, and therefore owed her $20,000. Katia filed suit against her employer in state small claims court. The state court dismissed the suit, explaining that its statutory jurisdiction was limited to claims under $10,000. Did the state court violate *Testa v. Katt*?

Explanation

No, the state court did not violate *Testa v. Katt*. As a claimant under a federal cause of action, Katia must take the state courts as she finds them. The small claims court had a preexisting statutory threshold that applied regardless of claim type. The state court thus had a valid excuse for dismissing the cause of action.

Example 10-3

Elsa was a Florida resident who sued her employer under the Federal Employers Liability Act for injuries she sustained in Georgia. She filed suit in Louisiana state court, which had subject matter jurisdiction over the claim. The Louisiana court, however, dismissed the suit under a Louisiana statute authorizing it to invoke the doctrine of forum non conveniens

---

2. *See, e.g., Missouri ex rel. Southern R. Co. v. Mayfield*, 340 U.S. 1 (1950) (forum non conveniens); *Herb v. Pitcairn*, 324 U.S. 117 (1945) (cause of action outside the jurisdiction); *Douglas v. New York, N.H. & H.R. Co.*, 279 U.S. 377 (1929) (nonresident parties).

in order to dismiss federal claims brought by nonresidents and arising from events that occurred outside of Louisiana. Did the Louisiana court violate *Testa v. Katt*?

Explanation

Yes, the Louisiana court violated *Testa v. Katt*. The forum non conveniens doctrine derives from principles of efficient and fair judicial administration. In a nondiscriminatory context, a state court might have a valid excuse for invoking the doctrine in a case with many out-of-state elements, such as the one in this example. Nevertheless, the Louisiana statute here does not operate in a neutral manner; it authorizes the dismissal of federal claims only and therefore cannot constitute a nondiscriminatory excuse for avoiding the action. *See Russell v. CSX Transportation, Inc.*, 689 So. 2d 1354 (La. 1997) (invalidating a similar statute).

In *Testa v. Katt*, the state court had stated directly that it declined to hear the federal cause of action. State courts may not always be so overt. The Supreme Court, in *Felder v. Casey*, 487 U.S. 131 (1988), found that an apparently neutral state procedural rule had a discriminatory impact on civil rights actions brought pursuant to 42 U.S.C. §1983. *Felder v. Casey* concerned a state requirement that individuals challenging a governmental action must notify the defendant of their claim within 120 days of their alleged injuries. Although the notice-of-claim requirement applied to state and federal causes of action equally, the Supreme Court reasoned that the requirement discriminated against precisely the type of civil rights claim that §1983 was designed to remedy.

Example 10-4

State taxing authorities are seeking to collect taxes from Holly, who believes the taxes are invalid under the equal protection clause of the United States Constitution. She filed a civil rights suit in a state trial court of general jurisdiction pursuant to 42 U.S.C. §1983. The state court dismissed the action, pointing out that the state legislature had made jurisdiction over all state tax matters exclusive to the state tax court. Did the state trial court of general jurisdiction violate *Testa v. Katt*?

Explanation

The trial court does not appear to have violated *Testa v. Katt*. The statute giving exclusive jurisdiction to the state tax court appears to be a preexisting rule of judicial administration that does not discriminate against federal claims. To justify the conclusion that the trial court acted properly, however, one must distinguish the decision in *Felder v. Casey*, 487 U.S. 131 (1988). The Supreme Court in *Felder v. Casey* was not persuaded to uphold the notice-of-claim requirement in that case, even though it applied to state and federal causes of action equally. Instead, the Supreme Court found that the requirement discriminated against federal civil rights claims, because it shut out the civil rights claims completely. The exclusive jurisdiction rule here, by contrast, does not have a disproportionate impact on federal claims: Holly can cure the defect simply by filing her suit in the state tax court. Because the exclusive jurisdiction rule does not impose a harsh impact on federal claims, the trial court's action in declining the federal cause of action likely constitutes a valid excuse.

B. CONSTRAINTS ON CONGRESS'S AUTHORITY OVER STATE COURTS

Structural principles of federalism significantly curtail Congress's authority to regulate non-judicial functions of state and local governments. Using such vehicles as sovereign immunity, the Tenth Amendment, and the Eleventh Amendment, the Supreme Court has vigorously protected state legislatures and executives from congressional incursion. The precedent used for interpreting limitations concerning legislative and executive branches also influences the scope of Congress's authority to impose on state judicial branches the responsibility of adjudicating federal claims. Yet the Supreme Court's jurisprudence is asymmetrical. The Court has alluded to parallel protections for the state courts but has not invested effort in mapping the boundaries on Congress's power. In fact, the Court has several times suggested that Congress's authority over state courts is much broader than its authority over other parts of state government.

In a series of cases from the 1990s, the Supreme Court held that Congress may not "commandeer" state legislatures or executive officials to enforce federal regulatory schemes. The Court held that the Constitution's Tenth Amendment prohibits Congress from (1) obligating state legislatures to enact particular state laws and (2) obligating state executive officials to administer federal regulatory schemes.[3] These holdings are in tension with Testa v. Katt, 330 U.S. 386 (1947), since requiring state courts to entertain federal causes of action obliges states to deploy their governmental apparatus to enforce a federal regulatory program. Nonetheless, the Supreme Court emphasized in these anti-commandeering cases that Congress does not

---

3. Printz v. United States, 521 U.S. 898, 929 (1997) (holding that Congress may not commandeer state officials to administer federal regulatory program); New York v. United States, 505 U.S. 144, 149 (1992) (striking down Congress's attempt to impose on state a duty to legislate regarding disposal of nuclear waste).

violate the Constitution when it requires state courts to enforce certain rights of action that it created.[4]

The 1990s also brought a series of Eleventh Amendment cases establishing that Congress cannot use its Article I power to subject states to suit in federal or state court. That Article I power, the Supreme Court maintained, does not enable Congress to abrogate states' sovereign immunity. To the extent that this case law directly involved state courts' obligation to entertain federal causes of action, the Supreme Court distinguished (albeit inartfully) *Testa v. Katt*.[5] Nonetheless, these sovereign immunity cases starkly contrast with the broad latitude Congress enjoys in imposing on states the burden of adjudicating federal causes of action. After all, sovereign immunity and Eleventh Amendment principles are so important because they protect state autonomy, dignity, and fiscal integrity. Those same concerns hang in the balance when states divert their scarce court resources away from state law concerns in order to satisfy their obligation to adjudicate legal norms of the federal government.

Despite the apparent relevance of the Tenth Amendment, Eleventh Amendment, and sovereign immunity cases to state courts, these cases do not expressly limit Congress's authority over state courts. Indeed, the only express restriction on Congress's authority derives from the valid excuse doctrine itself. As *Testa v. Katt* explained, state courts can refuse to hear a federal cause of action if they have a valid excuse in the form of a neutral principle of judicial administration. Although no direct holding on the issue yet exists, cases suggest that the excuse — if valid — remains within the state domain, and Congress may not take it away. For example, the Supreme Court has implied that Congress may impose the obligation to entertain federal claims only on courts of "adequate and appropriate [jurisdiction] under established local law."[6] The Court has also hinted that Congress should not "enlarge or regulate the jurisdiction of state courts"[7] while enlisting them "'to enforce federal prescriptions.'"[8]

---

4. *See* Anthony J. Bellia, Jr., *Congressional Power and State Court Jurisdiction*, 94 Geo. L.J. 949, 950 (2006) (Supreme Court went "out of its way" to make clear that *Testa v. Katt* survived anticommandeering principle).

5. In *Alden v. Maine*, 527 U.S. 706, 754 (1999), the Supreme Court held that Congress may not subject states to suit in state courts under its Article I powers. The state in the case was effectively discriminating against federal claims under the scheme upheld by the Supreme Court. Accordingly, the Supreme Court reached its holding by reasoning that the state was excused for discriminating because of the importance of the state's sovereign immunity. *See* James E. Pfander, Principles of Federal Jurisdiction 303-304 (2006) (arguing that the Court's attempt in *Alden v. Maine* "to distinguish *Testa* was particularly undistinguished").

6. *Testa*, 330 U.S. at 394; *accord Alden*, 527 U.S. at 752.

7. *Mondou v. New York*, 223 U.S. 1, 56 (1912).

8. *Alden*, 527 U.S. at 752 (quoting *Printz v. United States*, 521 U.S. 898, 907 (1997)).

Example 10-5

Assume that Congress passed a statute, titled the Telemarketing Control Act (TCA), that protects consumers from annoying interruptions by telephone solicitors. Congress did not vest power to enforce the TCA in any administrative agency, but instead created a private cause of action allowing private plaintiffs to bring suit for civil remedies against entities violating the TCA. The statute further provides that "state courts have exclusive jurisdiction over private actions brought under this statute."

According to the TCA legislative history, Congress believed that federal law (rather than state law) was the most appropriate means of regulation in this area because so many soliciting calls are made in interstate commerce. This history explains Congress's thinking in assigning state courts exclusive jurisdiction over this federal law: given the litigation explosion suffered by federal courts and budgetary pressures on the federal government, Congress did not wish to add to the federal government workload. Also according to the legislative history, "[t]he TCA does not dictate which state courts would be the appropriate place for TCA lawsuits. It is the wish of the Congress, however, that the states will ensure that plaintiffs do not encounter burdens in pursuing TCA suits. In particular, states are encouraged to allow TCA suits in small claims courts."

Pam Private filed suit in state court against telemarketer Nancy Nuisance, alleging that Nancy violated the TCA. The state statute governing the state court's jurisdiction does not specifically mention the TCA, but gives the state court general jurisdiction, which it has traditionally exercised in federal question suits as well as in state law trespass and nuisance suits analogous to this one. At Nancy Nuisance's urging, however, the state court concluded that prudence counseled against hearing the suit, for fear that a flood of similar suits would deluge the state court system. The state court reasoned that its docket was already overburdened and its budget already in deficit: the court system simply could not afford to divert precious time and resources from more pressing state law matters, such as state tax collection, tort actions to redress severe physical injuries, and violent crime prosecution. Under such circumstances, the court concluded that Congress could not require it take TCA cases. Did the state court act appropriately?

Explanation

The most pertinent case law does not support the state court's action. The arguments on both sides are strong, however, based on subtle reasoning drawn from analogous Supreme Court case law and the structure of the federalist system.

Starting with the most directly applicable case law, one would first analyze the state court's decision under *Testa v. Katt*, which condemns the state court's refusal to take the suit unless it has a valid excuse. Case law interpreting the valid excuse principle has upheld state court restrictions that are nondiscriminatory and based on judicial administration policies. The state court's decision was based on judicial administration policy: administrative concerns about providing state judicial resources for the most serious of state law matters motivated the state court. The problem, however, is that the state court did not apply a general restriction, but instead created one solely for this context. Where a court develops a restriction for a particular context only, discrimination suspicions arise. And, alas, one easily concludes that the present restriction discriminates against federal law, since the state court reasoned it needed to save court resources for state law matters.

Perhaps most significantly for the *Testa v. Katt* test, the restriction in this example has a severe impact on federal law, thus implicating *Felder v. Casey,* 487 U.S. 131 (1988), which found that an apparently neutral state procedural rule had a discriminatory impact on federal law. The state procedural rule in *Felder v. Casey* imposed a significant burden on potential plaintiffs, who might therefore never receive redress for their federal claims. The impact is even more dramatic here: if all state courts took the court's position in this example, plaintiffs would have *no* tribunal in which to bring TCA violations. Thus, Congress's mandate that only state courts may adjudicate TCA suits magnifies the consequences of a state court's decision not to adjudicate a suit.

So far, things are not looking good for the state court and Nancy Nuisance: the state court's decision does not fall within traditional valid excuses identified in Supreme Court case law and, in fact, looks quite discriminatory. Nonetheless, one might argue that the state court's concern with governmental effectiveness and the state court system's fiscal integrity should be treated as a valid excuse. Enhancing the sympathy for and common sense behind this argument are the types of state law cases that TCA cases might displace (state tax collection, tort actions to redress severe physical injuries, and violent crime prosecution). One could also strengthen the argument by pointing to language from *Testa v. Katt* and related cases suggesting that Congress should not "enlarge or regulate the jurisdiction of state courts"[9] while enlisting them "to enforce federal prescriptions."[10] Congress here came close to violating this suggestion: in its heavy-handed legislative history, Congress admonished state courts not to impose burdens on plaintiffs and urged states to open their small claims courts to TCA claims. *Testa v. Katt* did not envision that Congress could micro-manage state court systems in this way.

---

9. Mondou, 223 U.S. at 56.
10. *Alden*, 527 U.S. at 752 (quoting *Printz v. United States*, 521 U.S. 898, 907 (1997)).

While not definitive, the Supreme Court's Tenth Amendment and Eleventh Amendment case law supports the conclusion that Congress overstepped its bounds here. Indeed, the Tenth and Eleventh Amendment case law derives from precisely the same concerns that motivated the state court here in refusing Pam's TCA suit: state governmental effectiveness and fiscal integrity.

The Tenth Amendment anti-commandeering jurisprudence is particularly helpful to Nancy Nuisance and the state court. The anti-commandeering principle helps to ensure that when Congress enlists the help of state governments, it generally does so by offering funding to encourage states to cooperate with federal programs. Otherwise, in a time of budget deficits, Congress may be tempted to shift federal regulatory and enforcement duties to state government in an effort to save federal money. That is, in fact, what Congress did in this example. Thus, if the Tenth Amendment cases do not protect state courts as well as legislatures and executives, Congress can shift to states enforcement costs associated with litigation. Again, that would be the result here if the state court were to honor Congress's intent.

Despite these strong arguments in favor of Nancy Nuisance and the state court, one "trump card" may tilt the scale in favor of Congress's allocation of TCA jurisdiction to state courts: under the Madisonian compromise, the framers did not create lower federal courts and Congress may have never done so itself. In that event, state courts would — as a practical matter — have been forced to hear all federal causes of action that did not fall within the original jurisdiction of the United States Supreme Court. Accordingly, the Constitution's structure presumes that state courts may have borne a heavy burden in service of federal law. For that reason, the Tenth Amendment case law protecting state legislatures and executives is not directly applicable to state courts, which were structurally more important to federal regulation than the other departments of state government. This observation, together with the direct authority of *Testa v. Katt*, suggests that Pam Private is in luck: the state court must hear her TCA case.

Example 10-6

A federal statute, 18 U.S.C. §3231, vests exclusive subject matter jurisdiction over federal crimes in the federal courts. The precise words of the statute are "The district courts of the United States shall have original jurisdiction, exclusive of the courts of the States, of all offenses against the laws of the United States." Assume that Congress is considering repealing this statute in order to give state courts concurrent jurisdiction over federal crimes.[11] What legal problems should Congress consider before implementing this change?

11. The Committee on Long Range Planning of the Judicial Conference of the United States actually proposed statutory changes to permit prosecutors to file certain categories of federal criminal cases in state court nearly exclusively. *See* The Long Range Plan for the Federal Courts, 166 F.R.D. 49 (1996).

Explanation

This example raises several of the constitutional problems discussed in the immediately preceding example, as well as issues unique to the criminal nature of the proposal. Since the end of the twentieth century, federal courts have experienced a flood of litigation. In this example, Congress appears to address this problem by enlisting state courts for assistance. Many state courts, however, are experiencing an even greater flood of cases. Critics of using state courts to adjudicate federal criminal cases suggest that the practice would save the federal courts by, metaphorically speaking, throwing state courts out of the lifeboat. By imposing on state courts in this way, Congress would raise the concerns regarding financial stability and governmental autonomy reflected in the Tenth and Eleventh Amendments. Yet, as with the exclusive jurisdiction statute in Example 10-5, these cases did not directly protect state courts, focusing instead on legislative or executive branches as well as state officials. For that reason, Tenth and Eleventh Amendment case law does not conclusively doom the proposal.

Case law more directly on point is inconclusive. On one hand, *Testa v. Katt* arguably suggests that no constitutional problem exists. In *Testa v. Katt*, the Rhode Island Supreme Court refused to adjudicate the federal cause of action authorizing treble damages, characterizing it as a "penal law." In sweeping language, the *Testa* Court suggested that state courts must enforce a federal penal action: "we cannot accept the basic premise [that] the Rhode Island Supreme Court . . . has no . . . obligation to enforce a valid penal law of the United States." 330 U.S. at 389. One might distinguish *Testa v. Katt* by pointing out that it concerned a civil case, not a criminal case. Scholars disagree on the significance of the distinction, with some suggesting that *Testa v. Katt* should not be expanded to require state courts to adjudicate federal criminal prosecutions. All, however, would likely concede that the issue is worthy of serious analysis.[12]

Criminal law and its enforcement goes to the core of how a sovereign defines itself. Accordingly, the notion of one sovereign enforcing another's criminal law can inspire strong reactions. This is exemplified by a South Carolina Supreme Court justice, who declared in 1835 that state court enforcement of federal criminal law "would invest [federal law] with a mongrel character wholly irreconcilable with its dignity and that of the State from which it derives its appointment."[13] For apparently similar reasons, individual United States Supreme Court justices have stated at various times that the United States Constitution does not allow Congress to delegate

---

12. *See* Anthony J. Bellia, Jr., *Congressional Power and State Court Jurisdiction*, 94 Geo. L.J. 949, 981 (2006), for a helpful review of the case law and scholarship on this issue.
13. *State v. Wells*, 20 S.C.L. (2 Hill) 687 (S.C. Ct. App. 1835) (circuit court opinion of Earle, J.).

federal criminal adjudication to state courts,[14] a viewpoint that supports confining *Testa v. Katt* to civil cases. Yet no Supreme Court holding on the issue exists, and some historical practice supports granting the states federal criminal jurisdiction.

Although no definitive answer exists as to whether Congress's proposal is constitutional under existing case law, the proposal would spawn many practical problems. Unsettled questions include: Which sovereign would enforce a criminal conviction? To which sovereign should financial penalties be paid? Would offenders be imprisoned in state or federal facilities? Which rules of criminal procedure would govern? Which sovereign would exercise the pardon power? Many of these practical problems themselves have serious constitutional implications. For example, the Supreme Court has held that the president's pardon power should be unfettered by legislative restriction. Would Congress's scheme interfere with that prerogative? Likewise, the Supreme Court has held in the anti-commandeering cases that Congress may not enlist state executive departments to enforce federal law. Isn't that precisely what Congress would be doing if it required states to follow through with the federal crime convictions rendered in state courts?

Each of these practical problems argues against a broad reading of *Testa v. Katt*, a reading that not only would endorse Congress's proposal but would also allow state courts to avoid federal criminal jurisdiction only in limited circumstances. At best, however, one can only conclude that the question remains open as to whether the Constitution would allow the proposal to become law.

---

14. *See* Anthony J. Bellia, Jr., *Congressional Power and State Court Jurisdiction*, 94 Geo. L.J. 949, 978-979 (2006).

PART V

Federal Courts as Supervisors of State Courts

One of the most important functions that federal courts perform is to review the products of state court adjudication. This federal court review promotes an accurate and uniform body of federal law and ensures that litigants are treated justly. The United States Supreme Court satisfies this supervisory function by examining state court decisions that come to it through the appellate process. Lower federal courts generally have only the writ of habeas corpus as a vehicle for supervising state court decisions.

Both the Supreme Court and lower courts, however, are circumscribed by principles that seek to maintain the delicate power balance between state and federal governments. Chapter 11 explores restrictions on the United States Supreme Court, and Chapter 12 canvasses the principles governing lower federal court review within the habeas corpus context and otherwise.

Role of the United States Supreme Court

The Supreme Court's structure and power are governed by constitutional provisions, statutes, and — in substantial part — doctrines the Court itself has refined. The basic architecture for the Court's power to adjudicate cases and controversies comes from constitutionally and congressionally defined jurisdiction grants. The Supreme Court has embossed on that architecture its own principles that both enlarge and restrict its power. For example, the Court ensured vastly expanded authority in *Marbury v. Madison*, 5 U.S. (1 Cranch) 137 (1803), when it enunciated the power of judicial review, which positions the Court as the final arbiter of the Constitution's meaning. For over two centuries the Court has exercised most of its authority in two basic ways: (1) review of state court decisions concerning federal law and (2) review of judgments of certain lower federal courts. The Court sometimes exercises its power by adjudicating motions concerning lower court matters or requests for stays. The vast majority of the Court's power, however, resides in its disposition of entire controversies brought to the Court by a petition for a writ of certiorari or by a jurisdictional statement filed on appeal, as opposed to the more limited matters presented in motions or stay applications. This chapter confines its discussion to the Court's power over entire controversies, first reviewing the general constitutional and statutory provisions pertaining to the Supreme Court, and then detailing principles governing the Court's review of state decisions. The chapter ends with a brief discussion of the Court's power over lower federal courts.

A. CONSTITUTIONAL AND STATUTORY GRANTS

The Supreme Court of the United States is the only court actually created by the Constitution. The Constitution, nonetheless, says little about the Court's composition. On the issue of staffing, the Constitution states only that the justices hold their offices "during good behavior" and that they are protected from salary diminution. U.S. CONST. art. III, §1. It is Congress that controls the number of justices, which at present is set at one chief justice and eight associate justices. That number has not remained constant. The Judiciary Act of 1789 provided for a membership of six. The number then bounced up and down for a century or so: from seven to nine to ten, and back to nine in 1869. After a political backlash in response to a plan by President Roosevelt to pack the Court with his supporters, the number of justices has held fast at nine. The statutory provisions authorize the Supreme Court to do its work as a unitary body, with only a narrow range of circumstances where individual justices act alone on matters arising from individual circuits to which they are assigned.

In contrast to the dearth of language regarding staffing, the Constitution provides substantial detail about the Supreme Court's job description. Fundamentally, the Constitution first requires that the Court hear only cases and controversies, rather than issuing advisory opinions, enacting general laws, or performing other governmental acts. The Constitution divides Congress's power to adjudicate into two categories: original jurisdiction and appellate jurisdiction.

Original jurisdiction is the power to hear cases when first brought to court. The Constitution states that the Court has original jurisdiction over cases affecting "Ambassadors, other public Ministers and Consuls, and those in which a State shall be a Party." U.S. CONST. art. III, §2. Congress has established, however, that the Court's original jurisdiction is exclusive only for "controversies between two or more states" and that the remaining original jurisdiction is shared with other courts.

Appellate jurisdiction is the power to review cases already decided in another court. The Constitution establishes the Court's appellate jurisdiction over each of the nine classes of cases or controversies listed in Article III, including — most importantly — cases arising under federal law. The Constitution tempers this grant, however, stating that the Court's appellate jurisdiction is subject to "such Exceptions, and under such Regulations as the Congress shall make." U.S. CONST. art. III, §2. The term "appellate jurisdiction" can be confusing because it includes the power to hear mandatory appeals (sometimes called "appeal jurisdiction") as well as the power to hear cases within the Supreme Court's discretionary review jurisdiction (sometimes called "certiorari jurisdiction").

As detailed in Chapter 6, controversy surrounds the scope of Congress's power to restrict the categories of cases for which the Court may exercise appellate jurisdiction. Less controversial is Congress's control over the *process* by which the Court exercises its appellate jurisdiction. While at one time Congress imposed on the Court only mandatory appellate jurisdiction, through vehicles called appeals or writs of error, Congress has eliminated nearly all of the Court's mandatory jurisdiction. With few exceptions, the Court now has full discretion over which cases it reviews. Congress retained a very small fraction of cases for the Supreme Court's mandatory appeal jurisdiction, including certain civil rights cases and other matters that Congress deemed sufficiently important to *require* Supreme Court supervision. Otherwise, litigants must apply for review via a petition for writ of certiorari, and if the Court deems the case "certworthy," it will issue the writ; the parties then submit briefs on the merits of their dispute.

Example 11-1

Lorraine lost her case in the state supreme court and told her lawyer that she wants to take her case to the United States Supreme Court for reversal. The lawyer does not want Lorraine to develop unrealistic hopes. What should the lawyer tell Lorraine to provide her with a realistic view of her chances of success in the United States Supreme Court?

Explanation

The lawyer should explain to Lorraine that she can file a request for review with the Supreme Court, but that such a request merely asks the Court to make room on its docket so that it can scrutinize the controversy. The Supreme Court has nearly complete discretion over whether to grant this request for full review. In the highly likely event that the case does not fall within the Court's mandatory appeal jurisdiction, Lorraine must rely on the Supreme Court to exercise its discretion, and the chances of this are extremely slim. In recent years, the Supreme Court has granted review in less than 1% of the cases for which a litigant has filed a request for review.[1]

---

1. The percentages range from 1.0% to 1.4% of cases reviewed each year for the ten-year period from 1995 to 2005. *See* John G. Roberts, *Chief Justice's 2005 Year-End Report on the Federal Judiciary*, THIRD BRANCH, Jan. 2006; William H. Rehnquist, *Chief Justice's 2004 Year-End Report on the Federal Judiciary*, THIRD BRANCH, Jan. 2005; William H. Rehnquist, *Chief Justice's 2003 Year-End Report on the Federal Judiciary*, THIRD BRANCH, Jan. 2004; William H. Rehnquist, *Chief Justice's 2002 Year-End Report on the Federal Judiciary*, THIRD BRANCH, Jan. 2003; William H. Rehnquist, *Chief Justice's 2001 Year-End Report on the Federal Judiciary*, THIRD BRANCH, Jan. 2002; William H. Rehnquist, *Chief Justice's 2000 Year-End Report on the Federal Judiciary*, THIRD BRANCH, Jan. 2001; William H. Rehnquist, *Chief Justice's 1999 Year-End Report on the Federal Judiciary*, THIRD BRANCH, Jan. 2000; William H. Rehnquist, *Chief Justice's 1998 Year-End Report on the Federal Judiciary*, THIRD BRANCH, Jan. 1999; William H. Rehnquist, *Chief Justice's 1997 Year-End Report on the Federal Judiciary*, THIRD BRANCH, Jan. 1998; LEE EPSTEIN, JEFFREY A. SEGAL, HAROLD J. SPAETH & THOMAS G. WALKER, THE SUPREME COURT COMPENDIUM: DATA, DECISIONS, AND DEVELOPMENTS 82-83 (2d ed., Congressional Quarterly Inc. 1996).

Thus, even if Lorraine's case possesses qualities that render it worthy of the Supreme Court's close attention,[2] her chances of getting the Court to give the case that attention are minimal. Finally, even if the Court does grant Lorraine's request for a writ of certiorari and thereby agrees to hear the case, Lorraine has no guarantee that the Supreme Court will reverse the state supreme court. It takes votes by four of the justices to grant a request for review, but five votes to reverse a lower court's disposition. Wishful thinking might suggest that the decision to take a closer look at the case suggests a belief on the justices' part that the lower court's ruling might be wrong. But even if that is true, the decision to review the case may be one vote shy of that required to change the result of the lower court.

While the discretionary concerns governing whether the Supreme Court grants review in a case are key to the litigation strategy in getting a case before the Court, a litigant first must consider whether the case falls within the parameters of the statutory grants of jurisdiction. The Supreme Court's power to review state and federal court judgments is governed primarily by two separate statutes: 28 U.S.C. §1257 for state court judgments and 28 U.S.C. §1254 for federal court of appeals judgments. The litigant must also consider the Court's own interpretation of what those statutory requirements provide. The following considers both — the statutory language and the Court's interpretive gloss on that language.

B. PRINCIPLES GOVERNING REVIEW OF STATE COURT DECISIONS

Congress has given the Supreme Court power to review state court judgments for errors in *federal* law. The Supreme Court has interpreted Congress's grant of jurisdiction over state court decisions as precluding power over state law claims. *Murdock v. City of Memphis*, 87 U.S. (20 Wall.) 590 (1875). Jurisdiction extends to final judgments rendered by "the highest court of a State in which a decision could be had," but is limited to three categories of cases:

1. Cases "where the validity of a treaty or statute of the United States is drawn in question"
2. Cases "where the validity of a statute of any State is drawn in question on the ground of its being repugnant" to federal law

---

2. Some of these factors listed in United States Supreme Court Rule 10 include conflicts over a legal issue in the lower courts, conflicts between the decision and a United States Supreme Court decision, and the importance of the issue presented in the case.

3. Cases "where any title, right, privilege, or immunity is specially set up or claimed under the Constitution or the treaties or statutes of, or any commission held or authority exercised under, the United States"

28 U.S.C. §1257(a). Jurisdiction will lie whether or not the state courts upheld the federal law involved. Thus, §1257's basic requirements include: (1) whether the state court decision is final, (2) whether the highest state court that would hear the case rendered the decision, and (3) whether the subject matter of the decision falls within one of the three listed categories of cases.

Example 11-2

Donna filed a civil rights suit under 42 U.S.C. §1983 in the Court of Common Pleas for the state of X, alleging that her federal statutory rights were violated. The Court of Common Pleas held that the type of injury Donna alleged did not fall within the ambit of §1983 and entered a judgment dismissing the case. The Superior Court of the state of X affirmed this judgment in a written opinion. Under the laws of state X, the state X Supreme Court (which is the highest court in the state) has discretionary jurisdiction to hear the case. Donna followed all the applicable rules for filing a petition for review to the state X Supreme Court, but that court denied her petition. Does the United States Supreme Court now have jurisdiction over the case?

Explanation

Yes, the United States Supreme Court has jurisdiction. The state court's judgment is final, since no issues remain for litigation. In addition, the decision was rendered in the highest state court "in which a decision could be had." The state X Supreme Court does not need to have ruled on the case in order for the United States Supreme Court to have jurisdiction. Donna need only establish that she sought review in the highest state court available (even if review was available only on a discretionary basis), and that she did so properly. Since she did all that was necessary to seek review in the state X Supreme Court, the judgment of the state X Superior Court became reviewable in the United States Supreme Court after the state X Supreme Court refused to hear Donna's case. The case also falls into one of the §1257(a) categories. In the language of the final part of §1257(a), Donna's civil rights suit "claimed" a "right" under a "statute[] of . . . the United States."

Since the jurisdictional elements are present, the Supreme Court can take the case if it chooses. Given the Supreme Court's supervisory role over state courts, one might argue that the state court's decision to reject Donna's claim of federal right should render the case more worthy of United States Supreme Court intervention. While the state court's rejection of a federal right may be a factor bearing on the Court's exercise of discretion, it is irrelevant for jurisdiction. For the Supreme Court to have jurisdiction, the state court need not have decided the state issue in a certain way.

Section 1257(a) establishes that the Supreme Court has jurisdiction over only final judgments of state courts that disposed of federal law issues. Applying these requirements, the Supreme Court has developed three relatively complex doctrines: (1) the doctrine requiring litigants to preserve the federal issue during the state litigation, (2) the doctrine of adequate and independent state grounds, and (3) the doctrine of finality. The following discussion examines each of these doctrines.

1. Preservation Requirement

As a prerequisite to exercising jurisdiction, the Supreme Court requires that one of the parties properly raise a substantial federal question during the state proceedings. The requirement that the federal question be substantial ensures that the question is not frivolous or merely formal. The "proper" procedure for raising the federal question is mandated by state practice, so long as that practice provides the litigant with a reasonable opportunity to have the state court adjudicate the issue.

The Court imposes the preservation requirement to ensure that (1) the record is adequate for informed decision making, (2) state courts are given the first chance to adjudicate constitutional challenges to state statutes "since the statutes may be construed in a way which saves their constitutionality," and (3) the federal issue is not "blocked" by a state issue that may be adequate to support the judgment. *Cardinale v. Louisiana*, 394 U.S. 437, 439 (1969).

Example 11-3

Harry was convicted of drug possession in state court. The state intermediate appellate court affirmed his conviction in a published opinion, and the state supreme court denied discretionary review. Harry filed a petition for a writ of certiorari that included the following question presented: Did the state trial court violate the Fifth Amendment to the United States Constitution in admitting the petitioner's confession at his trial? The intermediate appellate court's opinion said nothing about a Fifth Amendment claim, and the prosecutor argued in the state's response to Harry's certiorari petition that Harry did not properly preserve the claim. Does the Supreme Court have jurisdiction to review the claim?

Explanation

The Supreme Court will likely not treat the claim as though it has jurisdiction to review it. Because the state court was silent on the federal question brought to the United States Supreme Court, the Supreme Court will assume that the issue was not properly presented. *Board of Directors of Rotary Int'l v. Rotary Club of Duarte*, 481 U.S. 537, 550 (1987). Harry bears the burden of defeating that presumption by establishing that he presented the issue to the state court, thereby providing the court with "a fair opportunity to address the federal question." *Webb v. Webb*, 451 U.S. 493, 501 (1981). Harry must show that he complied with the state's requirements for presenting his Fifth Amendment claim, by establishing, for example, that he briefed the issue before the superior court and included the issue as part of his request for review before the state supreme court. Harry would probably not meet this burden by showing that his briefs before the appellate courts mentioned the United States Constitution generally. Instead, he must point to specific reference to the particular clause of the Constitution (the Fifth Amendment) that he now invokes.[3]

The United States Supreme Court created the preservation doctrine, in large part, out of concern that the state court consideration of claims enhances the quality of its own decisionmaking. Yet the preservation doctrine is also derived from principles of comity and federalism, taking its cues from state procedural rules concerning the proper presentation of legal claims. In this way, the preservation doctrine is related to, and in some cases is a subset of, the doctrine of adequate and independent state grounds.

2. Adequate and Independent State Grounds

We know from Article III of the United States Constitution and jurisdictional statutes that the Supreme Court may review state cases containing federal claims. Interpreting those provisions, the Court's decision in *Murdock v. City of Memphis*, 87 U.S. (20 Wall.) 590 (1875), adds that, in reviewing cases from state courts, the United States Supreme Court does not have power to hear state law claims.[4] The question then arises as to what the Court can do in a "mixed" case, containing both state and federal law issues. *Murdock* provides guidance for mixed cases: if the state law issue controls the judgment in the case, the Supreme Court will not review the case, and the case is said to rest on "adequate" and "independent" state grounds. *Murdock* instructs that the

---

3. *See, e.g., Herndon v. Georgia*, 295 U.S. 441, 442-443 (1935).
4. In other words, for appellate review of state cases, the United States Supreme Court does not enjoy any type of supplemental jurisdiction, such as that used in lower federal courts.

Supreme Court cannot review the federal component of the case if the state legal ground is capable of supporting the state court's decision in the case.

Often, state courts are not clear about the precise grounds upon which their decisions rest. A state court's opinion may discuss both state and federal cases and provide an ambiguous holding referring to both state and federal materials. In other words, the state court opinion may not specify whether the state ground is independent of the federal ground for the decision. The United States Supreme Court has developed strategies for handling these ambiguous situations.

The main purpose of the "adequate and independent state grounds" doctrine is to avoid advisory opinions. Like lower federal courts, the United States Supreme Court hears only cases and controversies. In accordance with this restriction, the "adequate and independent state grounds" doctrine requires that where the United States Supreme Court reviews a federal issue, its review actually makes a difference in the parties' fortunes. Where the federal claim is constitutional, the doctrine also ensures that the Supreme Court complies with the avoidance principle: the notion that federal courts should avoid adjudicating constitutional issues whenever possible. Finally, the "adequate and independent state grounds" doctrine promotes respect for state sovereignty and prerogatives, fostering support for state procedural rules and allowing federal intervention in parties' affairs only where state law has not provided full relief.

This section first reviews the various circumstances in which state issues may be adequate to support a judgment and then describes strategies for evaluating whether an apparently adequate state ground is actually independent of federal law.

a. What Is an Adequate State Ground?

The circumstances under which the state ground for a decision is adequate to support the judgment fall roughly into two categories: logical adequacy based on an analysis of the case's substantive "bottom line" and procedural adequacy based on a state procedural rule relevant to the litigation. The concept of logical adequacy comes from *Murdock* itself, where the Court explained that the it cannot review a case with state and federal claims if the disposition of the state claim is capable of supporting the outcome of the case. Procedural adequacy generally arises where the state ground for the decision concerns a litigant's failure to comply with a state procedural rule. Usually, the litigant asserts a federal theory for winning the case, but the state procedural rule shields the state court's consideration of the federal issue on the merits. The "adequate and independent state grounds" doctrine provides a means to evaluate whether to allow the procedural default to preclude United States Supreme Court review as well.

i. Logical Adequacy

To test whether a state ground is logically adequate to support the judgment, one first identifies precisely what the state court ruled. The next step is to evaluate which issues the United States Supreme Court is capable of reviewing in the case. If—in ruling on those issues—the United States Supreme Court is not capable of changing the result, then an adequate state ground supports the judgment. Moreover, if the state and federal grounds for the state court's decision were separate and unambiguous, then they are independent of one another as well. One may ultimately conclude, therefore, that the Supreme Court lacks jurisdiction because the case rests on adequate and independent state grounds.

Example 11-4

Katherine is a lawyer. While she was out of town, someone broke into her house and stole her briefcase. She suspected that opposing counsel in a hotly contested lawsuit authorized the burglary. Katherine filed suit in state court against the opposing counsel, raising two claims: (1) the opposing counsel violated a federal statute designed to protect the privacy rights of lawyers and (2) the opposing counsel violated a state trespass law and is therefore liable to her under state tort principles. The parties stipulated that the maximum injury that Katherine suffered was valued at $5,000.

After trial on both the state and federal law claims, the trial court submitted the case to the jury with special interrogatories. The jury returned a verdict for Katherine, answering the special interrogatories as follows:

Question 1: Does plaintiff have a right to relief on the basis of her claim under the United States statute?

Answer: Yes

Question 2: If the answer to Question 1 is "yes," what is the amount of damages that the federal statutory violation can support?

Answer: $5,000

Question 3: Does plaintiff have a right to relief on the basis of her claim under state tort law?

Answer: Yes

Question 4: If the answer to Question 3 is "yes," what is the amount of damages that the state tort law violation can support?

Answer: $5,000

Question 5: If the answer to Question 1 or 3 is "yes," what is the maximum amount of judgment the court should enter in favor of plaintiff?

Answer: $5,000, as stipulated by the parties.

In accordance with the jury's decision and the parties' stipulation, the trial court entered judgment in favor of the plaintiff for $5,000. On appeal, the state intermediate and supreme courts both affirmed, endorsing the jury's verdict. The defendants filed a petition for a writ of certiorari in the United States Supreme Court. Does the Supreme Court have subject matter jurisdiction?

Explanation

No, the Supreme Court does not have jurisdiction because the state courts' decision rests on adequate and independent state grounds. This case is an example of "logical adequacy" of the state ground because the relation between the state and federal claims is such that it is logically not possible for the Supreme Court to change the "bottom-line" result. If the Court were to take the case, it would lack power to review the state claim. Thus, even if it were to reverse the decision on the federal statutory claim, Katherine would still be able to recover the same amount of money. The state claim alone is capable of supporting the $5,000 award. If the Supreme Court were to decide the federal law issue, its decision would be advisory only and, thus, a violation of the Article III requirement that the Supreme Court decide cases and controversies only.

Example 11-5

Assume the same set of facts as in Example 11-4, except that the jury rendered a different verdict. This time, the jury answered "no" to the question of whether Katherine has a right to relief under state tort law. The jury decided in Katherine's favor for $5,000 on the basis of the federal statutory claim. As before, the state appellate courts endorsed the result. Does the United States Supreme Court have subject matter jurisdiction over the case?

Explanation

Yes, the United States Supreme Court has subject matter jurisdiction. The state ground for the decision is not sufficient to support the judgment. At present, Katherine has a $5,000 verdict in her favor, but the Supreme Court will change that result if it reverses the state court decision that she has a right to relief under federal law.

Example 11-6

Now assume the same set of facts as in Example 11-4, except this time the jury answered "no" to both the question of whether judgment should be entered in Katherine's favor on the state tort law claim and the question of whether judgment should be entered in her favor on the federal statutory claim. The state appellate courts endorsed the result. Does the United States Supreme Court have subject matter jurisdiction over the case?

Explanation

Yes, the United States Supreme Court has subject matter jurisdiction. At present, Katherine has no verdict in her favor. The Supreme Court can change this result if it reverses the decision that she has no right to relief under federal law.

Example 11-7

Now for the final permutation: assume the same set of facts as in Example 11-4, except this time the jury answered "yes" to the question of whether Katherine had a right to relief under state tort law (awarding $5,000 in damages on that basis), and "no" to the question of whether she had a right to relief under federal law. The state appellate courts endorsed the result. Does the United States Supreme Court have subject matter jurisdiction over the case?

Explanation

No, the United States Supreme Court does not have subject jurisdiction. At present, state law supports a $5,000 verdict in Katherine's favor, and the Supreme Court cannot modify that result. The Court can reverse the decision that she has no right to relief under federal law, but that would not change the amount that Katherine gets. Again, the Supreme Court's decision on the federal claim would merely be an advisory opinion, and the case rests on an adequate and independent state ground.

The Supreme Court has identified instances when, even though the state ground appears logically adequate to support the judgment, the Court will not treat it as such. For example, if the Court decides that the state ground for a decision is unconstitutional, then the state ground is invalid and incapable of supporting the judgment. Likewise, a state ground that appears fabricated—that lacks "any fair or substantial support" in the record—also will not constitute an adequate state ground for decision. *Ward v. Board of County Commissioners of Love County, Oklahoma*, 253 U.S. 17, 23 (1920).

Example 11-8

Anton was arrested for violating a state law prohibiting individuals from soliciting membership in an organization without satisfying certain conditions, including obtaining a state permit from an official before soliciting. (State law provides that the official's decision is entirely discretionary and unreviewable.) Anton defended the criminal charges by arguing that the restriction on solicitation was overbroad and violated the First Amendment to the United States Constitution. He was convicted, the appellate court affirmed his conviction, and he petitioned the United States Supreme Court for a writ of certiorari. The prosecutor argued in response that the Supreme Court lacks jurisdiction. According to the prosecutor, the case rests on independent and adequate state grounds because Anton failed to comply with state law by failing to obtain a state permit before soliciting members. The prosecutor reasons that this ground alone is capable of supporting the judgment and that the Supreme Court may therefore not reach the merits of the First Amendment overbreadth claim. Is the prosecutor correct?

Explanation

No, the prosecution is not correct. The prosecutor's proffered state ground for the decision—Anton's failure to obtain a permit before soliciting—is premised on a law that itself violates the First Amendment: the permit requirement. *See Staub v. City of Baxley*, 355 U.S. 313, 325 (1958) (finding that a permit requirement is unconstitutional and therefore could not be an adequate and independent state ground under similar circumstances). Because the state law makes "enjoyment of speech contingent on" the official's unreviewable decision of whether to issue the permit, the law violates the First Amendment. *Id.* Accordingly, the state ground for the decision is invalid and cannot support the judgment. The Supreme Court can therefore review the overbreadth challenge if it desires to do so.

Example 11-9

Ethel is a news photographer and wishes to photograph the New Year's Day parade from the roof of city hall, which provides the best vantage point in the city for viewing the festivities. The city refuses individuals access to the roof unless they purchase insurance that would compensate the city for any harm resulting to the roof structure. Ethel and her employer—a news organization—protested the requirement, but the city would not relent.

Fearing that the news organization would lose readership if it did not run adequately compelling photographs of this highly celebrated parade, the employer reluctantly purchased the insurance to enable Ethel to gain access to the roof. Ethel and her employer then brought a challenge to the insurance requirement in state court, arguing that it reduced access to news and violated the First Amendment of the United States Constitution. Although Ethel and her employer fully briefed the First Amendment challenge, the state trial and appellate courts refused to address the challenge, reasoning that state courts do not entertain claims of this kind if a contesting party "freely and voluntarily" purchased the required insurance. Ethel and her employer filed a petition for a writ of certiorari in the United States Supreme Court, raising the First Amendment challenge. Her opponent argued that the state decision rested on an adequate and independent state ground. Does the United States Supreme Court have jurisdiction to review the case?

Explanation

The United States Supreme Court likely has jurisdiction to review the case. The state court's conclusion that Ethel's employer "freely and voluntarily" purchased the insurance is dubious. While the city did not force payment of the insurance by pointing a gun to the employer's head, the employer made the payment under protest and out of concern for losing readership. Accordingly, the record lacks "fair and substantial support" for the decision's state ground: the record does not suggest that the employer freely and voluntarily paid for the insurance. Moreover, given the First Amendment protection for news gathering, the United States Supreme Court might deem the insurance requirement to be an unconstitutional obstacle to news access. In that event, the state ground would be unconstitutional and thus incapable of supporting the judgment.

ii. Procedural Adequacy

A litigant's failure to comply with state procedural rules frequently represents an adequate and independent state ground. The litigant's "procedural bar" or "procedural default" stands as an obstacle to the state court's considering the underlying federal claim, and — the argument goes — should likewise shield the United States Supreme Court from reviewing the federal claim. If the United States Supreme Court were to ignore state procedural defaults, it would fail to accord sufficient respect to the orderly operation of state litigation systems.

The Court does not, however, uncritically defer to state procedural grounds for a decision. Instead, the Court imposes several requirements before treating the state procedural ground as adequate to support the judgment:

- The state court must actually apply the procedural bar in order for the bar to act as an adequate state ground.

- The state procedural ground may not be novel and previously unknown to the litigant seeking Supreme Court review.[5]
- The state procedural ground must be " 'strictly or regularly followed.' "[6]
- The state procedural ground must not impose an unreasonable burden on the litigant.

The protection against unreasonably burdensome rules governs even in cases where the state court applies "a generally sound rule" in an unreasonable or "exorbitant" manner.[7]

In a controversial decision, *Henry v. Mississippi*, 379 U.S. 443, 447 (1965), the Supreme Court ruled that a procedural rule cannot bar Supreme Court review unless the rule serves a "legitimate state interest." The Court has not, however, consistently applied this standard as a requirement to Supreme Court review, and subsequent rulings cast doubt on the extent to which it imposes a rigorous restriction on state courts.[8] One must be careful to note, however, that the Court has not explicitly abandoned the standard, and has in fact followed the standard in at least one decision handed down well after *Henry v. Mississippi*.[9] The Court seems to pay greatest attention to a state rule's purposes where other factors suggest that the rule should not preclude Supreme Court review. At the very least, then, one should be mindful of the purposes of a procedural rule in evaluating whether the rule can act as an adequate and independent state ground.

Example 11-10

Connie was prosecuted for burglary and decided not to take the stand at trial. The United States Supreme Court has ruled that if the defendant requests that the court do so, the Constitution requires the court to tell the jury not to draw a negative inference from the defendant's failure to testify. At the close of the trial, Connie's attorney requested that the judge "admonish" the jury not to draw a negative inference from her failure to testify. The judge did not mention anything to the jury. During post-trial motions in the trial court and on appeal in the state courts, Connie argued that the state courts' failure to

---

5. As the Supreme Court has explained, "Novelty in procedural requirements cannot be permitted to thwart review in this Court applied for by those who, in justified reliance upon prior decisions, seek vindication in state courts of their federal constitutional rights." *NAACP v. Alabama ex rel. Patterson*, 357 U.S. 449, 457-458 (1958).

6. *Hathorn v. Lovorn*, 457 U.S. 255, 263 (1982) (quoting *Barr v. City of Columbia*, 378 U.S. 146, 149 (1964)).

7. *Lee v. Kemna*, 534 U.S. 362, 376 (2002).

8. Robert L. Stern, Eugene Gressman, Stephen M. Shapiro & Kenneth S. Geller, Supreme Court Practice 212-214 (8th ed. 2002) (noting that the Supreme Court has applied the legitimate state interest test from *Henry v. Mississippi* only sporadically and that subsequent cases leave "the status of *Henry* quite uncertain").

9. *See, e.g., Lee*, 534 U.S. at 376.

give the cautionary instruction violated her right to remain silent, protected by the United States Constitution. The state courts each determined that the trial judge's failure to provide the instruction was appropriate, since Connie had asked only for an "admonition," not an "instruction." State law, the courts reasoned, required a defendant to specifically request an "instruction" about failure to testify, and Connie's lawyer did not comply with that requirement. The state courts did not, however, cite any prior case law distinguishing between an admonition and a jury instruction.

Connie filed a petition for a writ of certiorari before the United States Supreme Court, arguing that her right to remain silent was compromised by the trial court's failure to caution the jury against drawing a negative inference from her failure to testify. In response, the prosecution argued that the state court's decision rests on an adequate and independent state procedural ground that should preclude the Supreme Court from hearing the federal issue. Is the prosecutor correct?

Explanation

No, the prosecutor is not correct. First, the state in the example does not seem to consistently follow the "rule" requiring a request for an instruction rather than an admonition. Moreover, in a similar case, the Supreme Court held that the state court's distinction between a request for a jury instruction and a request for an admonition did not create a procedural ground worthy of supporting the verdict. *James v. Kentucky*, 466 U.S. 341 (1984). As the *James* Court reasoned, "[t]o insist on a particular label for this statement would 'force resort to an arid ritual of meaningless form.'" *Id.* at 349 (quoting *Staub v. City of Baxley*, 355 U.S. 313, 320 (1958)). To the extent that Supreme Court case law requires state procedural grounds to serve a "legitimate state interest," this one seems to flunk the test. Accordingly, the purported procedural bar was not only lacking in purpose, novel, and unknown to the defendant, but was also not consistently applied by the state courts. It therefore does not constitute an adequate and independent state ground for the decision.

Example 11-11

Charlotte owns a home, and Nicole is her next-door neighbor. Nicole negligently destroyed trees on the federal forest land adjacent to both of their properties. Charlotte filed suit in state court, arguing that Nicole violated federal environmental laws in destroying the trees and that Charlotte was damaged as a consequence. Nicole introduced a witness at trial who testified that Charlotte's own negligence contributed to the destruction of the trees. Charlotte had argued to the judge during a pretrial motion in limine that federal environmental laws precluded use of this type of testimony, but the judge rejected her argument. Charlotte renewed her objection at the time the witness took the stand, but she did not object after every question asked.

257

The jury returned a verdict in favor of Nicole. Charlotte argued during post-trial motions and to the state appellate courts that the trial court violated federal law in admitting the testimony. The state courts all ruled, however, that Charlotte failed to preserve this argument, since she did not object after every question that Nicole asked the witness. Charlotte explained to the state courts that she thought the jury would be annoyed if she objected after every question to the witness, and that she concluded that disrupting the questions in that way would be strategically harmful for her case. The state courts were unimpressed. Charlotte pressed her federal law argument in a petition for a writ of certiorari in the United States Supreme Court. Nicole responded that the United States Supreme Court lacks jurisdiction because the state court's decision rests on an adequate and independent state ground. Is Nicole right?

Explanation

Nicole is wrong. The United States Supreme Court is unlikely to treat the procedural default as an adequate and independent state ground. The Court has determined that a state procedural rule requiring that an attorney repeat an objection after every question put to a witness is unacceptably burdensome, where an objector makes her challenge known to the court and concludes that repeating the objection would be futile and strategically damaging. *Douglas v. Alabama*, 380 U.S. 415, 422-423 (1965). In several instances the Supreme Court has evaluated state procedural rules requiring litigants to object to evidence at the time it is introduced at trial (the so-called contemporaneous objection rule). Although the Supreme Court has concluded that the contemporaneous objection rule serves legitimate and important state interests, the Court would be unlikely to find that the rule deserves enforcement as specifically required by the state courts in this case, because Charlotte brought her objections to the trial judge's attention twice before the challenged testimony occurred.

iii. Summing Up: Circumstances Under Which a State Ground Will Not Be Adequate

As demonstrated in Example 11-10, an individual case may trigger more than one basis for finding state grounds inadequate to support a judgment. At the same time, only one basis is needed to disqualify a state ground from precluding United States Supreme Court review. The following checklist combines reasons — substantive and procedural — that the Supreme Court has invoked consistently to label state grounds as inadequate to support a state court judgment.

1. The state ground is logically not capable of supporting the bottom-line decision.

2. The state ground is unconstitutional.

3. The state ground does not have fair or substantial support in the record.

4. The state ground is a valid procedural rule, but the state court did not actually apply it to bar review of the federal issue.

5. The state procedural ground is novel and not previously known to the litigant seeking Supreme Court review.

6. The state procedural ground is irregularly followed by state courts.

7. The state procedural ground imposes an unreasonable burden on the litigant.

Example 11-12

A long-standing state rule requires that challenges to the composition of a grand jury take place before indictment. In a series of cases state courts have not applied the rule and have allowed defendants to raise challenges before indictment. The state trial court did, however, apply the rule "to the letter" in the case of Salvatore, who was indicted for aggravated assault two days after his arrest. Salvatore was indigent and therefore entitled to a court-appointed lawyer. His lawyer was not appointed, however, until after the indictment. Once appointed, the lawyer filed a motion challenging the composition of Salvatore's grand jury under the equal protection clause of the United States Constitution, but the state court refused to hear the challenge because Salvatore did not raise the claim before he was indicted. Salvatore was then convicted, and he raised no other basis for challenging his conviction. All of the state appellate courts agreed that they were foreclosed from reviewing the equal protection challenge and affirmed his conviction. Would the Supreme Court also consider itself constrained from reviewing the equal protection challenge?

Explanation

This case triggers several factors on the inadequacy checklist: First, as applied to a litigant who did not have a lawyer appointed in a serious case until after indictment, the procedural rule here is unconstitutional as a violation of due process. *See Reece v. Georgia*, 350 U.S. 85, 90 (1955). In addition, the rule has been irregularly followed and imposes an unreasonable burden on an indigent defendant who lacked counsel until after the indictment. Since only one of these factors is necessary to render the state procedural bar inadequate to support the judgment, the United States Supreme Court would likely not invoke the "adequate and independent state ground" doctrine to preclude review of the equal protection challenge.

These factors alone are sufficient to render the case inappropriate for Supreme Court review. For the sake of thorough analysis one might note that the remaining items on the checklist are *not* triggered. The state procedural bar is fully capable of supporting the bottom-line decision, because Salvatore has no other basis for challenging his conviction. The state ground has substantial support in the record, since the evidence is plain that Salvatore's lawyer did not file the challenge until after Salvatore's indictment. Finally, the state procedural rule is long-standing and does not appear to be novel or fabricated for the purpose of Salvatore's case.

b. Is the State Ground Independent of Federal Law?

As noted earlier, state courts are frequently vague about the precise grounds for their decisions. Where a state court discusses both state and federal cases but does not specify which set of cases provides the basis for the decision, one cannot tell if the state ground is "independent" of the federal ground for the decision. In that event, one need not even try to apply the "inadequacy" checklist to ascertain whether the Supreme Court has jurisdiction.

Over the years, the Supreme Court has developed a number of techniques for coping with the problem. Each technique can be encapsulated in one verb:

Avoid: In some instances, the Supreme Court avoids the case altogether, since it cannot tell whether it has jurisdiction. This approach is problematic because it empowers state courts to insulate their decisions from review and to avoid the United States Supreme Court's supervision.

Ask: At other times, the Supreme Court remands the case to the state court for clarification. This approach can be time-consuming for the litigants and burdensome for state courts with crowded dockets.

Call: The Supreme Court sometimes calls for the record in the case from the state courts to evaluate briefs and hearing transcripts. This process of searching for clues as to whether the state ground is independent of the federal ground is cumbersome and, in some cases, is complicated by state practices governing certified record filing requirements.

Tell: Occasionally, the Supreme Court simply does its best to interpret what the state court intended. This strategy is problematic not only because it is heavy-handed, but also because the Supreme Court might be incorrect in ascertaining what the state court intended; additionally, it sometimes puts the Court in the position of rendering advisory opinions about the meaning of state law.

After inconsistently employing these various approaches to handling ambiguous state court decisions, the Supreme Court developed a new strategy:

Presume: In *Michigan v. Long*, 463 U.S. 1032, 1040-1041 (1983), the Supreme Court announced that it will presume that a case rests on federal grounds in those circumstances "when . . . a state court decision fairly appears to rest primarily on federal law, or to be interwoven with the federal law, and when the adequacy and independence of any possible state law ground is not clear from the face of the opinion."

While at first blush this approach appears to be as heavy-handed as "telling" state courts what their decisions meant, the Supreme Court created an escape hatch for state courts to avoid the effects of the presumption. Through a "plain statement" a state court may insulate itself from Supreme Court review by establishing that the state court refers to federal decisions for "guidance" only, establishing that federal decisions "do not themselves compel" the state court's decision. *Id.* at 1041. In that event, the Supreme Court will not review the decision, but will treat it as though it rests on an adequate and independent state ground.

The *Michigan v. Long* Court did add a footnote recognizing that circumstances may call for using the *ask* approach in place of the *presume* approach. The Court stated, "There may be certain circumstances in which clarification is necessary or desirable, and we will not be foreclosed from taking the appropriate action." *Id.* at 1041 n.6. The Court used this reservation of prerogative in *Bush v. Palm Beach County Canvassing Bd.*, 531 U.S. 70 (2000), when it remanded the case to the Florida Supreme Court for clarification of the state law basis for the opinion, as well as of the relation between the state and federal issues in the case. *Bush* was one of the two Supreme Court opinions concerning the 2000 presidential election. One might distinguish *Bush* from the usual *Michigan v. Long* circumstance because the uncertainties in *Bush* were concerned more with lack of clarity over the scope of state law itself than with the interweaving of state and federal law. Nonetheless, the context for the case — a presidential election that turned on recount procedures in one state — is so extraordinary that one should be cautious about drawing much precedential value from the decision. One would stay on safer ground by assuming that the Court will use the *presume* approach in the event of uncertainty as to the independence of state grounds.

Example 11-13

Grace filed suit challenging her treatment by the state licenses and inspections board, which denied her a building permit without a hearing. Her lawsuit asserted two claims, one based on the United States Constitution's Fourteenth Amendment due process clause and the other based on an identical provision in the state constitution. The trial court entered judgment against Grace, and she appealed all the way up to the state supreme court. The state supreme court mentioned how the language of the state and federal constitutions is identical and how state courts generally look to both state and federal cases in interpreting the meaning of the words "due process of law." The state supreme court analyzed only federal cases in detail, noting that the law of due process was more developed in federal courts than in state courts. Then the state supreme court ended the opinion abruptly, stating "[t]he license and inspections board did not deny Grace due process of law." Grace has filed a petition for a writ of certiorari in the United States

Supreme Court. How will the Court handle the question of whether the case rests on adequate and independent state grounds?

Explanation

The Court will presume that the case rests on federal grounds. This is a classic case for the *Michigan v. Long* presumption, which governs if the state court treated the decision as primarily resting on federal law or if state and federal law are interwoven. Both conditions are satisfied here: the state supreme court satisfied the "interwoven" test by noting that the clauses of the two constitutions are identical and that state courts considered state and federal precedent. The state supreme court also satisfied the "primarily resting on federal law requirement" by citing federal cases more extensively.

If the state supreme court had wished to avoid Supreme Court review of its decision, it should have added the following plain statement to its decision: "This case is decided on separate and independent state grounds. Federal authorities are mentioned for the purpose of guidance only and do not compel this court's decision."

Example 11-14

Jillian was prosecuted in state court for conspiracy to commit felonious assault. At trial, neither she nor her lawyer objected to the jury instructions. On appeal, however, Jillian argued that the jury instructions on conspiracy violated her federal constitutional rights. The state supreme court included in its opinion extensive discussion of the federal constitutional theory behind Jillian's challenge but ultimately affirmed her conviction, stating that she failed to object contemporaneously to the instructions and was therefore barred from pursuing the claim on appeal. Jillian has filed a petition for a writ of certiorari in the United States Supreme Court, arguing to the Court that it should apply the *Michigan v. Long* presumption in order to review her constitutional challenge to the jury instructions. Is this an appropriate case for that presumption?

Explanation

No, this is not an appropriate case to presume that the state supreme court's decision rests on federal law. In order for the *Michigan v. Long* presumption to apply, the case must primarily rest on federal law or the state and federal grounds must be interwoven. Here the discussion of federal constitutional law appears to be dicta — separate from the foundation for the state supreme court's disposition of the case, Jillian's state procedural default. *See, e.g., Gulertekin v. Tinnelman-Cooper*, 340 F.3d 415 (6th Cir. 2003) (holding that state procedural default is not interwoven with defaulted federal claim).

3. Finality

a. Basic Finality Principle

The jurisdictional statute governing Supreme Court review over state cases, 28 U.S.C. §1257, directs the Court to review final decisions only. A final decision is one that "ends the litigation on the merits and leaves nothing for the court to do but execute the judgment."[10] The trigger for a potential finality problem is a state appellate court's decision to remand the case to the trial court, rather than merely affirming or reversing the lower court's judgment. The rationales for the finality principle are similar to those for the doctrine of adequate and independent state grounds: to ensure that the Supreme Court's decisions on federal issues do not unnecessarily invade state prerogatives, that they are based on a fully developed record, and that they are certain to make a difference in the ultimate disposition of the case. The doctrine also protects against piecemeal litigation.

Example 11-15

Maybella filed a securities fraud complaint in state court. The defendant responded to the complaint by arguing that the suit was barred by the statute of limitations. The state trial court accepted the statute of limitations defense and dismissed the case. Maybella appealed this ruling up through the state court system. The state supreme court reversed, holding that the trial court had applied the wrong federal limitations period. The state supreme court remanded the case to the trial court, with instructions for the trial court to reinstate the case and for the defendant to answer the complaint. The defendant would like to take the case to the United States Supreme Court. Does the Supreme Court have subject matter jurisdiction over the case?

Explanation

Because the state supreme court remanded for reinstatement of the complaint, the case does not appear to be final. In that event, the United States Supreme Court does not have jurisdiction. The question then becomes whether the case falls within one of the circumstances in which the Supreme Court has recognized that it still may take power over a case, even though much more is left to do in the case than execute on the judgment. The Court usually does not call these circumstances "exceptions" but, rather, circumstances calling for a "pragmatic approach" to finality.[11] Such situations — detailed below — allow review even though

---

10. *Catlin v. United States*, 324 U.S. 229, 233 (1945).
11. *Bradley v. Richmond School Bd.*, 416 U.S. 696, 723 n.28 (1974) (observing Supreme Court's inclination to follow a " 'pragmatic approach' " to the question of finality (quoting *Brown Shoe Co. v. United States*, 370 U.S. 294, 306 (1962))).

further proceedings (sometimes entire trials) are yet to occur in the state court. After reviewing these circumstances, we will return to this set of facts in Example 11-20.

b. *Cox Broadcasting:* Summary of Categories Under the Pragmatic Approach to Finality

Over a series of cases, summarized in *Cox Broadcasting Corp. v. Cohn*, 420 U.S. 469 (1975), the Supreme Court recognized the following four categories in which the "pragmatic approach" to finality authorizes jurisdiction. In each of these categories, the Supreme Court may take the case, even though substantial proceedings are yet to occur in state court.

- *Preordained cases:* The Supreme Court may review a case in which the federal issue has been decided and, as a consequence, the result of further state court proceedings is preordained; that is, no doubt exists about the outcome of remaining state proceedings.
- *Separated federal issue cases:* The Supreme Court may review state court decisions for which the federal law issues are separable from that part of the case that is yet to occur and will survive the further state proceedings.
- *"Seize It Now" cases:* The Supreme Court may review state court decisions where its only opportunity for reviewing the decision's federal law component occurs prior to the state proceedings on remand.
- *Important federal issue cases:* The Supreme Court may review state court decisions that reflect the following four components:
    1. The state court finally decided the federal issue.
    2. The party seeking review in the Supreme Court may win on the merits during remand proceedings on state grounds.
    3. The federal issue is capable of ending the lawsuit.
    4. An important federal policy might suffer serious harm without immediate review of the federal issue.

Overlap exists between the four categories, and a case will sometimes fit into more than one.

c. Preordained Cases

For cases in the "preordained" category, the federal issue is so significant to the case as to be "conclusive" of the litigation, even though "entire trials" may be yet to occur. In this category, "the case is for all practical purposes concluded" upon decision of the federal issue. *Cox*, 420 U.S. at 479.

Example 11-16

Arielle organized a protest on the lawn in front of an abortion clinic. The police arrested her for criminal trespass and conspiracy. During pretrial proceedings in state criminal court, Arielle filed a motion to dismiss the prosecution. She conceded that she committed the offenses but argued that the prosecution violated her First Amendment rights. The trial court rejected the challenge, and she took an interlocutory appeal through the state court system. Ultimately, the state supreme court affirmed the dismissal of her First Amendment defense and remanded the case for further proceedings. May the United States Supreme Court take the case at this juncture?

Explanation

Yes, the United States Supreme Court may take the case. Arielle's only defense to the charges was the First Amendment defense, which the state courts rejected. One can predict the result on remand with certainty: Arielle has effectively pleaded guilty to the crimes. Without a doubt, the Supreme Court can make a difference in the prosecution if it endorses the First Amendment defense. The Court would not be rendering an advisory opinion. Moreover, Arielle is likely to bring the case to the Court after the remand in any event. Thus, the Supreme Court would serve the interests of judicial efficiency by taking the case now, which could obviate further state court proceedings.

d. "Separated Federal Issue" Cases

In "separated federal issue" cases "the federal issue, finally decided by the highest court in the State, will survive and require decision regardless of the outcome of future state court proceedings." *Cox*, 420 U.S. at 480. This category applies when state proceedings are ancillary to and separate from the federal issue, so that they will not change or dilute the prior resolution of the federal issue. The Supreme Court has invoked this category in cases where the state court still needed to sentence a state criminal defendant or to perform some kind of accounting in a civil case.

Example 11-17

Rupa owned property in a coastal region. The state passed a statute requiring Rupa to take action to mitigate the effects of erosion and to allow the public access to her shoreline. She brought suit in state court, arguing that the statute amounted to a taking of her property under the Fifth Amendment of the United States Constitution, entitling her to just compensation. The state trial court ruled that the regulation was not a taking, but the state supreme court disagreed, and remanded the case for determination of what would be "just compensation" under the circumstances. May the United States Supreme Court take the case at this juncture to consider whether the regulation is indeed a "taking"?

Explanation

Yes, the United States Supreme Court may take the case. The proceedings on remand will not affect the core federal decision in the case: the regulation constitutes a compensable taking. This federal issue will survive and remain unaffected by the amount of compensation ultimately awarded. If the Supreme Court does not take the issue now, the state may ask the Court to take the case after the compensation hearing. In any event, the federal issue will remain the same, and the state court may be spared the effort of ascertaining just compensation if the Supreme Court concludes that the regulation is not a "taking."

e. "Seize It Now" Cases

"Seize it now" cases arise from a combination of factors that would eliminate the federal issue from the case after remand. These cases generally have three components: (1) the state court has finally decided the federal issue, (2) on remand, the state court will entertain the merits of the controversy, and (3) the federal issue will not be available for later Supreme Court review, no matter what happens on remand. As *Cox* explains, "[i]f the party seeking interim review [in the Supreme Court] ultimately prevails on the merits, the federal issue will be mooted; if he were to lose on the merits, however, the governing [laws] would not permit him again to present his federal claims for review." 420 U.S. at 481.

Example 11-18

A state supreme court reversed a criminal conviction on federal constitutional grounds, finding that the prosecution improperly relied on a coerced confession in establishing Deirdra Defendant's guilt at trial. The state supreme court remanded the case for retrial in the state trial court. The prosecution seeks review in the United States Supreme Court, arguing that the state supreme court misapplied the federal constitutional principles governing the admissibility of the confession. Does the Supreme Court have subject matter jurisdiction over the case?

Explanation

Yes, the Supreme Court has jurisdiction. In fact, the only opportunity for the Court to hear the federal issue is now. If, on remand, Deirdra is convicted, she may appeal the conviction but would not raise the confession issue, which had been decided in her favor. On the other hand, if Deirdra is acquitted on remand, the prosecutor will be unable to appeal under the United States Constitution's double jeopardy clause, which protects Deirdra from being tried twice for the same crime.

f. Important Federal Interest Cases

The fourth category of cases within the "pragmatic approach" of finality occurred in *Cox* itself. The category is complicated and relies on four criteria: (1) the state court has finally decided the federal issue, (2) the party seeking review in the Supreme Court might win on the merits in the remand proceedings on state grounds, (3) the federal issue is capable of ending the lawsuit, and (4) an important federal policy might be seriously compromised without immediate review of the federal issue. These factors are extremely subjective and malleable, making this a particularly controversial area of finality doctrine.

Cox concerned a state law invasion of privacy action against a newspaper for publishing a rape victim's name. The state supreme court held that the First Amendment did not prohibit the rape victim's father from pursuing a civil action against the newspaper. The state supreme court remanded the case, however, for a trial on the state law issue of whether the defendant had invaded the plaintiff's zone of privacy.

Articulating the four-factor test, the Supreme Court concluded that each factor weighed in favor of its taking the case at that time. First, the state courts would not be considering the First Amendment issue any further. As for the second factor, the Court reasoned that the newspaper, which was seeking Supreme Court review, might succeed at trial in demonstrating that it did not invade the plaintiff's zone of privacy. If so, the newspaper would have no reason to bring the First Amendment issue to the Supreme Court in the future. Of course, the plaintiff would have no incentive to do so either, since the plaintiff won on that issue. Applying the third factor, the Court concluded that the First Amendment issue could invalidate the state tort action, thus stopping the lawsuit immediately. Finding the fourth factor applicable, the Supreme Court observed that the case included "'an important question of freedom of the press under the First Amendment.'"[12] Without immediate review, the press would have suffered a chilling effect

---

12. 420 U.S. at 485-486 (quoting *Miami Herald Pub'g Co. v. Tornillo*, 418 U.S. 241, 247 n.6 (1974)).

by fearing liability for printing matters of this sort. Thus, the Supreme Court concluded that it should decide the First Amendment issue before the state tort trial was completed.[13]

Example 11-19

Sharon, a disgruntled shareholder, filed a state law shareholder's derivative suit against Dolly, who is the director of a corporation in which Sharon holds stock. The corporation is incorporated in Delaware, where the lawsuit was filed. To obtain jurisdiction over Dolly, Sharon had the Delaware state court sequester Dolly's stock in the corporation by placing a "stop transfer" order on the stock records located in Delaware. Before answering the complaint, Dolly entered a "special appearance" in the action and filed a motion to dissolve the sequestration order on the basis of lack of personal jurisdiction. Although Dolly made a solid argument that the Delaware courts' assertion of jurisdiction over her violated the due process clause of the United States Constitution, the Delaware courts all denied Dolly's requested relief. The Delaware Supreme Court remanded the case, ordering Dolly to answer the complaint. Dolly then filed a petition for a writ of certiorari in the United States Supreme Court. Does the Supreme Court have jurisdiction over the case?

Explanation

Even though the remand to the Delaware trial court suggests a finality problem, the United States Supreme Court would likely conclude that it has jurisdiction. Among the four *Cox* categories of cases, the case most closely fits in the "important federal issue" category. The "preordained" category does not apply because one cannot predict who will prevail on the merits of the derivative claim. Nor is this a "separate federal issue" case because the upcoming litigation and the federal due process issue are intertwined. If in fact the state court cannot constitutionally exercise jurisdiction over Dolly, it cannot fairly litigate the derivative claim. This is not a situation where a state proceeding that has yet to occur — such as a valuation or sentencing — is ancillary to the federal issue. Finally, this example does not present a "seize it now" circumstance. The personal jurisdiction issue could survive the state court litigation if Dolly loses at trial and brings an appeal in which she includes her personal jurisdiction challenge.

In a case similar to this example, *Shaffer v. Heitner*, 433 U.S. 186 (1977), the Supreme Court analogized the case to *Cox*, apparently concluding that *Shaffer* satisfied the "important federal interest" category. As for the first three components, the *Shaffer* Court observed that (1) the state courts had

---

13. *Id.* at 485.

finally decided the personal jurisdiction issue, (2) the party seeking review could prevail on nonfederal grounds, and (3) the personal jurisdiction issue was capable of eliminating the Delaware court's power—thus ending the lawsuit. Regarding the fourth factor, the *Shaffer* Court reasoned that the defendants whose stock was sequestered had the choice of "suffering a default judgment or entering a general appearance and defending on the merits" if the judgment on the due process claim was not considered final and Supreme Court review made available. 433 U.S. at 195 n.12. The Court's solicitude for the defendants' plight suggested a willingness to designate a due process issue as implicating an important federal interest. This is significant given the suggestion in *Cox* that the special problem of a First Amendment chilling effect—although perhaps only temporary—was crucial to the Court's decision to allow review. *Shaffer* shows that the Court is willing to extend the fourth category beyond the First Amendment context.

Example 11-20

The facts are the same as in Example 11-15, concerning a state supreme court that remanded a securities fraud action to the state trial court. In light of the "pragmatic approach" to finality synthesized in *Cox*, does it now look like the Supreme Court has subject matter jurisdiction over the case?

Explanation

The case does not appear to fall within the Supreme Court's jurisdiction. An entire trial is yet to occur in the state court, and the case does not fall into any of the *Cox* categories. The first three categories are clearly inappropriate: (1) the outcome of the state proceedings is not preordained, (2) the federal statute of limitations issue is not separate, because it is entwined with the underlying cause of action, and (3) no obstacle prevents the Court from hearing the statute of limitations issue after trial on the underlying claim.

The most applicable category is the "important federal interest" one. Two components of the example, however, do not correlate with the factors for this category. First, *Cox* asserted that the "important federal interest" category requires the possibility that the party seeking review may prevail on "nonfederal grounds" on remand. This category generally envisions that the issue for which the party seeks review is separate from the merits of the claim that could provide the basis for relief on remand. Although this quality is satisfied in this example, the proceedings on remand will adjudicate a federal law claim. Thus, the defendant could not prevail on "nonfederal grounds," as stipulated in *Cox*. Even if the Supreme Court does not weigh this distinction as being material to this category of finality cases, a potentially dispositive problem does exist with the character of the federal interest.

The statute of limitations issue likely falls short of implicating an important federal interest. Although statute of limitations questions are not trivial, their importance to society generally manifests on an aggregate level, through consideration of a large volume of litigation, rather than within the context of an individual case. Moreover, they are not constitutional issues and do not implicate the type of fundamental values as do the First Amendment and due process questions that have inspired the Court to use this category to justify its "pragmatic approach" to finality.

4. The Three Doctrines Considered Together

The doctrines of federal issue preservation, adequate and independent state grounds, and finality are all discrete but may intersect to create obstacles to Supreme Court review in individual cases. Because federalism and principles of prudent judicial administration inform all three doctrines, however, they tend to complement rather than work against one another.

Example 11-21

In 2007 the California legislature passed a law repealing the provisions governing tenure for public school teachers in the state. The 2007 law stated that tenure for public school teachers was abolished as of December 31, 2007. In January 2008 Hannah, a public school teacher in San Francisco, was fired from her job. Hannah had been granted tenure in 2004, and she brought suit in California state court, alleging that she was fired in violation of the tenure provisions. Hannah's complaint set forth two claims:

1. The California legislature intended the 2007 statute to abolish tenure only for those teachers who had not been tenured prior to December 31, 2007.

2. A contrary interpretation of the 2007 statute would violate the due process clause of the United States Constitution and the due process clause of the California Constitution.

The state trial court did not rule on claim 1. It found for Hannah solely on the basis of claim 2. The trial court reasoned that it need not resolve the legislative intent issue presented in claim 1 because the 2007 statute could be constitutional only if it applied to teachers who had not been tenured prior to December 31, 2007. The California intermediate appellate court affirmed in a judgment issued without opinion.

The California Supreme Court reversed in a cursory opinion, holding that "tenure is not a property right to which the requirements of due process attach." According to the California Supreme Court, the "requirements of due process impose no limitation in this case on the will of the California legislature." For these reasons, the court remanded the case to the trial court with instructions to rule on the legislative intent question presented in claim 1.

At this point in the proceedings, is review available in the United States Supreme Court?

Explanation

When the California Supreme Court ruled, it did not specifically mention the due process clause of the United States Constitution. For that reason, the question may arise of whether Hannah presented the federal claim properly to that Court, thereby implicating the preservation doctrine. Hannah's case contains state and federal claims and therefore also calls for analysis of the doctrine of adequate and independent state grounds. The California Supreme Court remanded the case back to the trial court, so the finality doctrine is an issue. One may analyze the three doctrines in any order. After analyzing each one, however, one would likely conclude that the United States Supreme Court would in fact have jurisdiction in the case.

Preservation: The California Supreme Court mentioned due process in its decision. For this reason, the United States Supreme Court may assume that Hannah has adequately preserved her federal claim. Nevertheless, the California Supreme Court did not mention the United States Constitution, and for that reason the United States Supreme Court will be open to an argument from Hannah's opponent that she did not properly present her federal claim throughout the state court litigation. In that event, Hannah may bear the burden of pointing out to the Supreme Court that she consistently presented the federal claim in briefs and at oral argument. If she can make this showing, the preservation doctrine will not provide an obstacle to Supreme Court review.

Adequate and independent state grounds: Regarding the "adequate and independent state grounds" doctrine, we note that Hannah has framed her case as two claims: a statutory interpretation claim and a due process claim. *Murdock v. City of Memphis*, 87 U.S. (20 Wall.) 590 (1875), says that one should begin analyzing the United States Supreme Court's power to hear the claims by separating the state law issues from the federal law issues. Two state law issues emerge: the statutory interpretation issue and the due process issue based on the California Constitution. *Murdock* says that the United States Supreme Court does not have power to hear any state law issues. But if either of these state law issues is capable of supporting the California Supreme Court's judgment, then the United States Supreme Court cannot decide the federal due process issue. Because the state courts did not even rule on the statutory interpretation claim, that claim can give no support for the state court's judgment.

The state due process claim is more puzzling because one cannot discern whether the California Supreme Court meant to refer to the state due process claim, the federal due process claim, or both when it stated that "tenure is not a property to right to which the requirements of due process attach." The California Supreme Court could also have been declaring that tenure is not a property right under state property law. This declaration about tenure and state property law could be appropriate under due process analysis, but one simply cannot tell what the California Supreme Court intended. *Michigan v. Long*, 463 U.S. 1032 (1983), provides a tool for handling these ambiguities: a presumption that the case rests on federal law. Under this presumption, one can assume that the California Supreme Court did not mean for state law to control either the due process concept or the property law concept.

The case presents a close call in terms of applying the *Michigan v. Long* presumption, because the California Supreme Court's opinion does not mention federal law. Accordingly, the case may not satisfy the requirement that, for the presumption to apply, the state court decision must "fairly appear[ ] to rest primarily on federal law, or to be interwoven with the federal law." *Id.* at 1040. Hannah's efforts to show preservation may be relevant here. If state and federal law were briefed and fully debated during hearings before the state courts, one can argue that the state court decision is "interwoven with federal law." At the least, one can readily conclude that "the adequacy and independence of any possible state law ground is not clear from the face of the opinion." *Id.* at 1040–1041. If Hannah briefed and argued the federal due process issue, the Supreme Court may be inclined to apply the *Michigan v. Long* presumption. Otherwise, the Supreme Court would empower state supreme courts to avoid the presumption by mere silence in the face of vigorous federal law arguments by litigants. Accordingly, the chances are good that the "adequate and independent state grounds" doctrine will not prevent the Supreme Court from ruling on the federal due process issue.

Finality: Even though the "adequate and independent state grounds" doctrine is not likely a problem, Hannah still must clear the finality hurdle. Because the California Supreme Court remanded the case, United States Supreme Court review is not available unless Hannah's case falls into one of Cox's four categories. The "preordained" category does not help Hannah because one cannot predict what will happen on remand. Hannah could either win or lose on the statutory interpretation claim. If she wins the statutory interpretation claim, she would not need the Supreme Court to review any other question. Thus, the Supreme Court could waste its effort by ruling on the federal due process claim.

Cox's "separate federal issue" category is also not applicable here. The remaining litigation in state court is not ancillary to the rest of the case, but is intermingled. If Hannah wins on the state statutory interpretation ground during the remand proceedings, she will have no incentive to seek Supreme Court review of the federal due process question. That question may therefore not survive the proceeding on remand, and is therefore not separate from the rest of the case.

Likewise, the "seize it now" category does not help Hannah. If Hannah loses on the state statutory claim, she would have an incentive to bring the due process claim to the United States Supreme Court again. Thus, the possibility exists that the due process issue may survive the proceedings on remand.

The "important federal issue" category provides Hannah's only hope for clearing the finality hurdle. Each of the four components is arguably satisfied. First, the state court has finally decided the due process question. Second, Hannah may prevail on the state statutory interpretation question, and the federal question will thus go unreviewed. Third, the federal due process question is capable of ending the lawsuit: if federal due process mandates that Hannah retain tenure, then state remand proceedings would be ineffective and unnecessary. Finally, due process of law is certainly an important federal issue, since fair procedure enjoys the status of a "bedrock" principle in our justice system. The Supreme Court showed its willingness to accept this characterization in applying this finality category to federal due process cases in *Shaffer v. Heitner*, 433 U.S. 186 (1977). Moreover, by focusing on the chilling effect resulting from delay in deciding the First Amendment issue in *Cox*, the Supreme Court suggested that the analysis of whether the federal issue is compelling may include a timing component. To take account of this suggestion, one could point out here that other tenured employees in California may suffer without fair procedures if the Supreme Court does not settle the due process issue now. Each of these arguments favors the conclusion that Hannah should benefit from the "important federal interest" category.

With some effort, one may be able to argue around each of the three doctrines standing as obstacles to Supreme Court review of state decisions. The United States Supreme Court may therefore have jurisdiction to hear Hannah's case at this point.

C. PRINCIPLES GOVERNING REVIEW OF FEDERAL DECISIONS

Congress has provided that the Supreme Court may review cases from the federal courts of appeals by "writ of certiorari granted upon the petition of any party to any civil or criminal case, before or after rendition of judgment or decree." 28 U.S.C. §1254(1). The Court's review powers over the courts of appeals fall completely within its discretion to issue a writ of certiorari.

The Supreme Court can review judgments directly appealed from United States district courts, although Congress has limited mandatory direct appeals to a few special circumstances.[14]

Given reduced federalism concerns in reviewing cases from the federal courts, the Supreme Court has substantially more latitude in asserting jurisdiction over federal cases than those from the state courts. From the vantage point of federalism, the Court's role in reviewing decisions of the federal courts is functionally less important than its role in supervising state courts. In its appellate power over lower federal courts, the Court has nevertheless imported doctrines it developed in reviewing state court decisions — most notably, the finality doctrine and the preservation doctrine. Indeed, Congress specifically gave the Supreme Court power over interlocutory (i.e., nonfinal) judgments, but the Supreme Court ordinarily declines to handle these judgments when exercising its discretionary supervisory power.

An additional dimension to the Supreme Court's review power over federal decisions is the Court's position as the institutional "boss" of the federal judiciary. Thus, the intensity of the Supreme Court's concern with the proper functioning of the federal judicial system and the federal judiciary is not paralleled in its approach to reviewing state court opinions. The Supreme Court has shown in its considerations governing the grant of certiorari that it may grant review if a lower federal court "has so far departed from the accepted and usual course of judicial proceedings, or sanctioned such a departure by a lower court, as to call for an exercise of this Court's supervisory power."[15] The Supreme Court has invoked this power in a myriad of contexts, using it often to justify review of evidentiary rulings as well as decisions concerning civil procedure rules and the criminal process.

Example 11-22

Assume that Congress, in an attempt to regulate traffic on the Internet, now requires employers to report e-mail addresses of all employees to the federal government. Morris is a state employee who was forced by the department where he works to register his e-mail address with the federal government. He filed suit in federal district court, raising two claims: (1) the federal statute was not meant to govern state governments, and his employer therefore erred in applying the statute to him; and (2) the statute is an unconstitutional invasion of privacy under the Fourteenth Amendment of the United States Constitution.

---

14. For a review of these circumstances, *see* Robert L. Stern, Eugene Gressman, Stephen M. Shapiro & Kenneth S. Geller, Supreme Court Practice 81-112 (8th ed. 2002).
15. Sup. Ct. R. 10(a).

Although it did not rule on the statutory claim, the district court did rule in Morris's favor on the constitutional claim. The court of appeals affirmed. The state employer petitioned the United States Supreme Court, arguing that the case calls for an exercise of the Court's supervisory powers. Is this the type of case where the Court may invoke those powers?

Explanation

Yes, this example presents the type of circumstance where the Court might invoke its supervisory powers. The federal courts follow a strict principle of adjudication, requiring them to first decide any statutory basis for the case and resolve a constitutional challenge only if absolutely necessary.[16] Here the lower courts reversed the order: adjudicating the constitutional challenge first and avoiding a statutory claim that could have disposed of the case. In granting review in *New York City Transit Authority v. Beazer*, 440 U.S. 568 (1979), the Supreme Court cited such a departure from normal decisionmaking practice. The Court explained that the lower courts' deviation "from the procedure normally followed in addressing statutory and constitutional questions in the same case, as well as [our] concern that the merits of these important questions had been decided erroneously, led us to grant certiorari." *Id.* at 570.

---

16. *Ashwander v. Tn. Valley Auth.*, 297 U.S. 288, 346 (1936) (Brandeis, J., concurring) (articulating the principle of avoiding constitutional questions).

Role of Lower Federal Courts

The lower federal courts have a limited role in directly supervising state courts. In reviewing state court judgments, lower federal courts are generally confined to habeas corpus review of criminal judgments. While lower federal courts may *indirectly* supervise the work products of state courts by entertaining civil rights actions against state judges and other officials, the *Rooker-Feldman* doctrine prohibits lower courts from direct review of state court judgments. These two principles — habeas corpus review and the *Rooker-Feldman* doctrine inform district court power and thus are usefully considered in tandem. The two concepts nevertheless differ remarkably in form, limitation, and requirements. This chapter first explores the often tortuous rules of habeas corpus review in detail and then turns to the more straightforward terms of the *Rooker-Feldman* doctrine. A discussion of civil rights actions and their role in monitoring state courts and other state officials appears in Chapter 14.

A. PRINCIPLES GOVERNING HABEAS CORPUS REVIEW

The Great Writ of Habeas Corpus. Perhaps no other legal concept governing federal courts stands out so prominently as a lightning rod for controversy. Habeas cases stimulate debate over the role of criminal law, constitutional principles, and courts in society as well as controversy over the competence of state courts, conflicting governmental theories, and the ability of judges (including Supreme Court justices) to adjudicate without ulterior motive or an unprincipled desire to achieve an ultimate result. These are the forces at work in the war over the writ of habeas corpus. The war, however, is fought in small battles, and the battlefields are characterized by seemingly arcane rules of access to the writ. The rules are so complicated and abstract that one wonders whether those who create them are avoiding frank talk about the true values at stake, as though these values were "an elephant in the room" that participants are uncomfortable discussing directly.[1] Although such speculation about psychological motivation is rarely the key to approaching legal understanding, mindful appreciation of the values at stake in habeas corpus decisions will help in negotiating the labyrinth of often inconsistent rules.

This review of habeas corpus law is organized according to the main battlefields on which participants have fought out the details of legal doctrine. After an overview of the constitutional and statutory background for habeas corpus, this section focuses on the following battlefields in detail: cognizable claims and procedural bar rules. These topics provide a filter with which to interpret the dialogue among Supreme Court justices, members of Congress, and the public about which values will dominate in shaping habeas corpus law. A brief description of less complex battlefields — the exhaustion requirement, deference to factual findings, statutes of limitations, and limitations on successive petitions — appears at the end of this section. Discussion is largely limited to habeas challenges filed in federal court by state prisoners.

1. Constitutional, Statutory, and Historical Background

A habeas corpus action is a civil action filed by a prisoner and directed at her custodian. The name habeas corpus — meaning "you have the body" — captures its essence: requiring the custodian to justify the prisoner's continued confinement or otherwise release her. The action tests whether the present detention is lawful. Often cases refer to the defendant as "the state" or "the government."

The writ of habeas corpus is premised on the view that, in a free society, the government should always be ready to justify the detention of a human being. When used to the fullest extent, the writ is available even if the prisoner has already benefited from a long series of trial and appellate proceedings. Those who argue for restricting the habeas remedy often point out its cost in terms of finality: the writ allows many "bites at the apple." As a result, the writ promotes inefficiency and institutional instability,

---

1. For an empirical study of whether the Supreme Court uses obfuscatory language to shield the values at stake in federal courts cases, *see* Laura E. Little, *Hiding with Words: Obfuscation, Avoidance, and Federal Jurisdiction Opinions*, 46 UCLA L. REV. 75 (1988).

sometimes upsetting the expectations of society, law enforcement, and other officials who relied fully on settled legal interpretations in existence at the time imprisonment began. By contrast, those who argue that the writ should be always available emphasize its function of protecting liberty, honoring federal constitutional values, ensuring against the imprisonment of the innocent, promoting accuracy in adjudication, and constraining official abuse of power.

The habeas corpus remedy is available to an array of prisoners. For example, state and federal criminal defendants file habeas petitions for post-conviction relief after criminal proceedings, immigrants file habeas petitions to challenge the basis for their deportation, and, at least at one time, enemy combatants captured during a war (including the War on Terrorism) filed habeas petitions to challenge their detentions at military facilities such as the one at Guantanamo Bay, Cuba.[2]

Although currently available to state and federal prisoners, the writ constrained only federal officials. Tracking this early focus on federal officials, the Constitution's suspension clause bars only the federal government from suspending the privilege of the writ of habeas corpus. Moreover, the Judiciary Act of 1789 limited federal court power to issue the writ to prisoners in custody of the federal government, making the writ explicitly unavailable to challenge state officials. Although the Judiciary Act of 1789 allowed the Supreme Court to review state criminal convictions under certain circumstances, Congress did not grant any federal court power to issue writs of habeas corpus to state prisoners until after the Civil War. In 1867 Congress granted state prisoners access to federal courts for claims that they were deprived of liberty in violation of federal law. The modern derivatives of this habeas power over state prisoner claims require that the prisoners be "in custody" for habeas jurisdiction to apply.

The scope of the Constitution's suspension clause, authorizing the federal government to suspend the writ of habeas corpus, is subject to significant debate. Three qualifications, however, clearly constrain the clause's operation. First, the suspension clause allows the federal government to suspend the writ only when "in Cases of Rebellion or Invasion the public Safety may require it." U.S. CONST. art. I, §9. Second, the clause appears in that part of the Constitution pertaining to Congress's power (Article I), not the president's or the judiciary's power. Thus, attempts by presidents to suspend the writ without congressional authorization have been rebuffed. For example, the Supreme Court originally condemned President Lincoln's suspension of the writ, with a showdown averted when Congress subsequently ratified Lincoln's action. Finally, the Supreme

---

2. Congress purported to suspend the privilege of filing for habeas relief in civilian courts for enemy combatants in the Military Commissions Act of 2006.

Court established that the suspension clause protects the writ of habeas corpus "as it exists today, rather than as it existed in 1789."[3]

Throughout history, Congress has endorsed suspending the writ of habeas corpus a handful of times. The most recent context — in the Military Commissions Act of 2006 — is unusual because Congress purported to suspend the writ on its own, rather than authorizing an earlier executive decision to suspend it. Further litigation is needed to resolve whether an act of Congress alone can effectively suspend the writ of habeas corpus and whether the Military Commissions Act of 2006 is a constitutional attempt to do so.

Example 12-1

Celia was convicted of larceny and sentenced to three years imprisonment in a state penitentiary. While in prison, she completed the state court appeals on her conviction, unsuccessfully sought her available post-conviction remedies in state court, and thereafter filed a petition for a writ of habeas corpus in a United States district court. Her petition challenged the use of her confession at trial. Before the federal district court could rule, however, Celia was released on parole. The terms of her release required her to report weekly to her parole officer and to remain within the state. Should the district court dismiss the petition because the "in custody" requirement is not satisfied?

Explanation

No, the district court should not dismiss the petition on that basis. The Supreme Court has interpreted the "in custody" requirement to encompass parole. *Jones v. Cunningham*, 371 U.S. 236 (1963). As demonstrated by Celia's obligation to visit the officer each week and to confine her travel to the state where she lives, parole — like incarceration — includes restrictions on liberty.

Example 12-2

Ted was convicted in state court and is serving his five-year sentence in a state facility characterized by horrific conditions. During his detention, he filed a petition for a writ of habeas corpus in a United States district court, challenging the conditions of his custody. The defendant (who was the warden of the prison) moved to dismiss the habeas petition. Should the district court grant the motion?

---

3. *Felker v. Turpin*, 518 U.S. 651 (1996).

Explanation

Yes, the district court should dismiss the petition. Although Ted satisfies the "in custody" requirement, his petition is flawed because it does not challenge the *fact* of his custody, only the *conditions* of his custody.[4] The appropriate vehicle for asking a federal court to evaluate the conditions of custody is 42 U.S.C. §1983 — which, moreover, is not the appropriate vehicle for a prisoner trying to secure release from custody.[5]

Federal habeas review of state prisoners began slowly at first but grew dramatically in the 1960s. Since the 1970s, Congress and the federal courts have struggled to manage a burgeoning volume of petitions, debating the competing values at play in the decision of whether to make the writ widely available. For petitions from state prisoners, contrasting views of federalism are injected into the debate. Those advocating a nationalist orientation generally highlight the importance of the writ of habeas to clarify and to enforce federal constitutional values, to check abuses of state official power, and to correct state court mistakes in interpreting federal law. Those embracing a federalist orientation emphasize state autonomy and parity with federal courts in their ability and willingness to enforce federal law. These contrasting views of federalism weigh in with the other values that form the historic debate over the availability of the Great Writ.

As one navigates the thicket of ever-changing rules governing habeas review, the dueling values underlying the writ provide beacons for understanding. Whatever manifestation the rules ultimately take, one can be assured that they result from choices over which values should dominate and which should yield (see Figure 12-1).

Though not as consistently present as the values discussed above, separation of powers concerns occasionally mark debates about habeas corpus. In particular, separation of powers dynamics between Congress and the Supreme Court can influence habeas doctrine. For example, in *United States v. Hayman*, 342 U.S. 205 (1952), the Supreme Court rejected a constitutional challenge to 28 U.S.C. §2255, which substituted new habeas procedures for federal (as opposed to state) prisoners. The Supreme Court acquiesced in the procedural innovations, which the Court interpreted as preserving the liberty-guarding goal of the habeas remedy. The Supreme Court has also largely supported the extensive statutory change in the Anti-Terrorism and Effective Death Penalty Act of 1996 (AEDPA).

---

4. *Nelson v. Campbell*, 541 U.S. 637, 643 (2004). *See also* Hill v. McDonough, 126 S. Ct. 2096 (2006) (holding that prisoner may frame a challenge to the manner in which lethal injection is accomplished as an action under 42 U.S.C. §1983).
5. *Preiser v. Rodriguez*, 411 U.S. 475, 499 (1973).

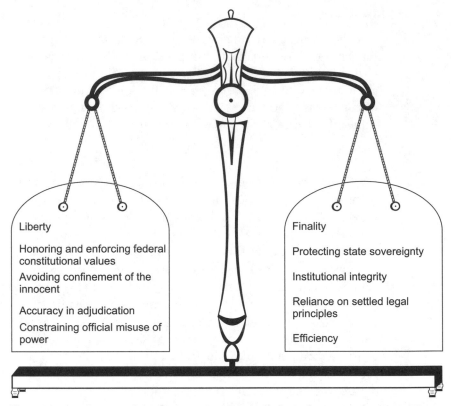

Figure 12-1. The Interplay of Competing Values in the Debate over the Great Writ

The Supreme Court has, however, remained vigilant of Congress's attempts to strip the federal courts of power to issue habeas corpus relief for both state and federal prisoners. Indeed, habeas corpus cases are often emblematic of the power struggles between the Court and Congress. In evaluating attempts by Congress to streamline post-conviction review or to implement policy judgments such as restricting immigration challenges or fighting the war on terror, the Supreme Court has been careful to protect federal court prerogatives to issue habeas writs.[6]

---

6. See, e.g., Rasul v. Bush, 542 U.S. 466 (2004) (holding that a non-citizen held at Guantanamo Bay could challenge his detention by military authorities by petition for writ of habeas corpus filed in federal court in the District of Columbia); INS v. St. Cyr, 533 U.S. 289 (2001) (reading immigration statute restrictively so as to preserve habeas remedy and avoid declaring the statute unconstitutional); Felker v. Turpin, 518 U.S. 651 (1996) (upholding restriction on state prisoners bringing successive petitions by reading statute as preserving the original jurisdiction of the Supreme Court over petitions). See also Hamdan v. Rumsfield, 126 S. Ct. 2749, 2764-69 (2006) (applying statutory construction principles in order to avoid reading the Detainee Treatment Act of 2005 as an attempt to suspend the Supreme Court's appellate jurisdiction in certain habeas cases).

For further discussion of the separation of powers issues implicating congressional control over federal court habeas corpus jurisdiction, see Chapter 6.

2. Cognizable Claims : What Is the Substantive Scope of Inquiry on Habeas?

The general statute governing habeas review for state prisoners has for many years authorized federal district courts to determine whether the prisoner's custody violates "the Constitution or laws or treaties of the United States." 28 U.S.C. §2254. Prisoners who assert nonconstitutional federal claims have tended to encounter resistance. District courts may review such claims only if they expose "fundamental defects" that "inherently" result in "a complete miscarriage of justice"[7] — a standard essentially suggesting that nonconstitutional claims must expose errors of constitutional dimension. For constitutional claims, the Supreme Court and Congress have issued fluctuating edicts regarding what character constitutional claims must possess in order to fall within the district court's scope of review on habeas.

The Supreme Court, in particular, has used a variety of angles for defining the appropriate substantive scope of inquiry on habeas. First, the Court has attempted to identify claims that are "cognizable" on habeas according to the quality of process provided by the state courts. Taking a different tack, the Supreme Court has also disqualified an entire class of claims according to the particular clause of the Constitution supporting the claim. Third, the Court has withheld habeas relief according to the character of "error" committed by the state court. Fourth — approaching the disqualification enterprise from an entirely different theoretical perspective — the Supreme Court has used retroactivity doctrine to eliminate new rules of constitutional law from the district court's scope of inquiry. Finally, contributing to restrictions on cognizable claims, Congress followed the Supreme Court's strategy of focusing on the quality of the state court's "work product" and has apparently endorsed the Court's decision to disqualify new rules of constitutional law from habeas review.

a. The Ends of the Spectrum: *Frank v. Mangum* and *Brown v. Allen*

The decisions in *Frank v. Mangum*, 237 U.S. 309 (1915), and *Brown v. Allen*, 344 U.S. 443 (1953), serve as bookends for the spectrum of habeas review allowed district courts (see Figure 12-2). *Frank v. Mangum* dramatically restricts review, while *Brown v. Allen* reflects broad habeas powers allowing federal courts to exercise their judgment independent of earlier state proceedings.

Frank v. Mangum held that the petitioner could not obtain relief by simply pointing out federal errors committed by the state court. Instead, the district court could grant habeas relief only if the petitioner could show that his conviction was void because the state court that rendered it lacked

---

7. *Reed v. Farley*, 512 U.S. 339 (1994) (quoting *Hill v. United States*, 368 U.S. 424, 428 (1962)).

jurisdiction. The state court lacked jurisdiction if its proceedings denied the petitioner due process — defined as failing to provide the petitioner with the process guaranteed by "established" procedure under *state* laws. 237 U.S. at 326. But a state's failure to provide these procedures at trial was not even enough to trigger meaningful habeas corpus review by the district court. If the state compensated for its deficient process by providing adequate procedures on appeal, then the district court lacked authority to issue habeas relief.

Frank v. Magnum accorded uncompromising respect to the finality of state court adjudication. The 1953 decision in *Brown v. Allen*, on the other hand, set aside principles such as res judicata and collateral estoppel, allowing federal district courts on habeas to adjudicate federal constitutional claims that had been fully litigated and decided in state courts. While not giving district courts license to fully ignore all that happened before the habeas petition, *Brown* nonetheless allowed the courts to conduct "de novo" review of petitioners' claims.[8] The *Brown* Court gave prominence to the notion that a state prisoner should have the opportunity to have any federal constitutional question heard in *federal* court. The Court equated accuracy in adjudication and liberty with federal court review of constitutional claims, jettisoning finality as the governing value in mapping the scope of habeas review.

The history of habeas corpus jurisprudence since *Brown v. Allen* has been a process of moving back across the spectrum toward *Frank v. Mangum*. Concept by concept, the Supreme Court and Congress have chipped away at the "all constitutional claims are welcome here" approach to habeas embraced in *Brown v. Allen*. Yet the Court has never overruled *Brown v. Allen*, declining an opportunity to do so in 1992.[9]

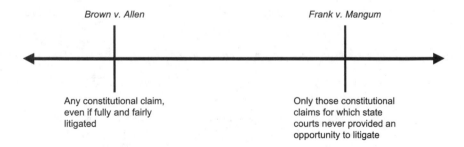

Figure 12-2. Representative Extremes on the Spectrum of Cognizable Claims on Habeus Corpus

---

8. Brown, 344 U.S. at 546 (Jackson, J., concurring).
9. *See Wright v. West*, 505 U.S. 277 (1992) (declining to eliminate de novo review on habeas, although three justices expressed their desire to do so).

Example 12-3

DeLinda was convicted of arson and sentenced to prison. At trial, she objected to the prosecutor's statements made during oral argument, which she contends amounted to a comment on her failure to testify, in violation of the Fifth Amendment. The trial court rejected her challenge. On appeal, she argued the claim at every level, but the state appellate courts rejected her arguments. She raised the issue on post-conviction review in the state courts, all of which rejected the claim on its merits. DeLinda has filed a petition for a writ of habeas corpus with a United States district court. Under the models of Brown v. Allen and Frank v. Magnum, should the district court hear the claim?

Explanation

Brown v. Allen would authorize the district court to entertain the claim on its merits, and Frank v. Magnum would not. For Brown v. Allen, the state courts' rulings on DeLinda's Fifth Amendment claim does not in any way foreclose the district court's review. Frank v. Magnum, however, would allow review only if the state court refused to follow established procedures in the case and the state appellate courts failed to provide corrective process. This type of dereliction of process is not present here, since DeLinda was able to litigate the claim at the trial and on appeal.

b. Eliminating Fourth Amendment Claims: *Stone v. Powell*

One of the first steps in chipping away at Brown v. Allen came with Stone v. Powell, 428 U.S. 465 (1976), when the Supreme Court held that Fourth Amendment claims generally could not be heard on federal habeas. Specifically, the Court ruled that "where the State has provided an opportunity for full and fair litigation of a Fourth Amendment claim, a state prisoner may not be granted federal habeas corpus relief on the ground that evidence obtained in an unconstitutional search or seizure was introduced at his trial." Id. at 494. In reaching this decision, Stone v. Powell focused on the exclusionary rule, which provides that evidence obtained in violation of the Fourth Amendment should be excluded from trial. Minimizing the importance of the exclusionary rule, Stone v. Powell touched on many of the competing values at play in the debate over habeas corpus:

- *Honoring federal constitutional values.* The Court reasoned that the exclusionary rule is not a personal right, but rather an enforcement mechanism to deter police misconduct.
- *Accuracy of adjudication and avoiding confinement of the innocent.* The Court emphasized that the accuracy of evidence obtained in violation of

the Fourth Amendment is not inherently suspect. Thus, adjudication of Fourth Amendment claims is not crucial to testing the innocence of the prisoners.

- *Constraining official abuse of power.* The Court reasoned that the exclusionary rule need be enforced only at trial and on direct review to provide adequate incentive for police to comply with the Fourth Amendment. The chance that valid convictions may be lost on habeas review, the Court reasoned, is marginal and comes too late to impose an additional deterrent effect.

- *State sovereignty.* Heralding the expertise of state judges in routinely adjudicating Fourth Amendment claims, the Court expressed unwillingness "to assume that there now exists a general lack of appropriate sensitivity to constitutional rights in the trial and appellate courts of the several States." 428 U.S. at 494 n.35.

- *Institutional integrity.* In reasoning related to its state sovereignty concerns, the Court emphasized that adjudication of Fourth Amendment claims can lead to freedom for guilty petitioners. Accordingly, the Court suggested that allowing petitioners to litigate these claims on habeas is not worth the cost in terms of lost respect for the criminal justice system.

Example 12-4

Police entered the apartment of Will's uncle and found the uncle dead from stab wounds. They then went to Will's home and convinced Will's father to allow them to enter. Upon entering, they saw Will and noticed he was covered in cuts. Unsatisfied with his explanation for the cuts, they immediately searched him, arrested him, and took him into custody. At Will's trial for homicide, Will's lawyer argued that the police entered the home unlawfully and that his arrest violated the Fourth Amendment. The lawyer maintained that the police tricked Will's father into letting them into the home and that he did not give his consent freely for them to enter. The trial judge held a quick hearing at which Will and the police testified. Will's lawyer cross-examined the police officer. The trial judge credited the police's testimony that Will's father knowingly and freely consented to their entering the apartment. Through direct appeals in state court and state postconviction proceedings, Will maintained that the trial judge made a hasty judgment about the consent issue and that Will would litigate the issue differently had he been given more opportunity to prepare for the hearing. At every stage of the process, the state courts considered the claim on the merits, but dismissed it in a cursory manner, stating that they credited the trial judge's factual findings.

On federal habeas corpus, Will argued that the federal district court should entertain his Fourth Amendment claim because the state trial judge made an inaccurate factual finding, and the other state courts did not give him an adequate opportunity to challenge the factual finding or otherwise litigate the Fourth Amendment challenge. Should the district court consider the merits of Will's Fourth Amendment claim?

Explanation

No, the federal district court should not entertain the merits of the Fourth Amendment claim. To justify federal habeas review, Will must show that the state courts did not provide him with a full and fair opportunity to litigate the Fourth Amendment claim. He has not made this showing. In applying "the full and fair opportunity to litigate" standard, the lower courts have stated that a federal habeas court can entertain a Fourth Amendment claim if the petitioner carries the burden of establishing "an irretrievable breakdown in the process provided by the state."[10] Here, no such breakdown occurred: the state courts provided an opportunity for Will to be heard on the Fourth Amendment issue, an opportunity for him to cross-examine witnesses against him on that issue, and an opportunity for appellate review. Standing alone, a trial court error will not render a Fourth Amendment claim cognizable on habeas.[11] Moreover, the state appellate court's deference to the trial court's factual findings is standard appellate practice, and arguably serves the purpose of fairness because the trial court was in the best position to evaluate the witnesses' demeanor. In any event, respect for state sovereignty suggests that the federal court should approach these matters with a light touch. Finally, Will's assertion that he would litigate the Fourth Amendment issue differently if he had the chance is arguably irrelevant. It is not the manner in which the habeas petitioner availed himself of procedures that matters, but the fact that the state provided adequate procedures at all.[12]

---

10. *Sanna v. DiPaolo*, 265 F.3d 1, 9 (1st Cir. 2001). *See also Moreno v. Dretke*, 450 F.3d 158, 167 (5th Cir. 2006) (stating that *Stone* bars review absent a showing that state procedure is "'routinely or systematically applied'" to deny the petitioner of litigating his Fourth Amendment claim) (quoting *Williams v. Brown*, 609 F.2d 216, 220 (5th Cir. 1980)); *Peoples v. Campbell*, 377 F.3d 1208, 1224-1226 (11th Cir. 2004) (focusing on the availability of appellate review and dismissing the argument that inconsistent state court analyses undermines the *Stone* bar); *Marshall v. Hendricks*, 307 F.3d 36, 82 (3d Cir. 2002) (acknowledging that "structural defect in the system itself" would prevent the *Stone* bar); *Gates v. Henderson*, 568 F.2d 830, 840 (2d Cir. 1977) (holding that ensuring full and fair opportunity to litigate involves inquiring whether the state has provided a process in the first place and if so, whether the defendant is deprived due to an "unconscionable breakdown" in procedure). *But see Cannon v. Gibson*, 259 F.3d 1253, 1260-1261 (10th Cir. 2001) (interpreting "full and fair" as a procedural opportunity to raise the claim as well as a "'colorable application'" of accurate "'constitutional standards'") (quoting *Gamble v. Oklahoma*, 583 F.2d 1161, 1165 (10th Cir. 1978)).
11. *United States ex rel. Petillo v. New Jersey*, 562 F.2d 903, 906 (3d Cir. 1977).
12. *Caver v. Alabama*, 577 F.2d 1188, 1192 (5th Cir. 1978) (ruling that habeas review is unavailable if state provided appropriate process for full and fair opportunity to litigate, even if petitioner did not employ the process).

Example 12-5

Patricia lives in a very small town. Her next-door neighbors had a violent argument, and someone in her neighborhood called the police. The police went to her house with the stated purpose of finding out what she knew about the argument. Long suspecting that Patricia was a "bad seed," however, the police officers decided to break down the front door to search the house. They discovered illegal drugs. Patricia was tried for drug possession in a local court and convicted. At trial her lawyer made a motion to suppress the evidence of the drugs found at the house. At the suppression hearing, the police officers who searched the house testified that a neighbor had tipped them off that Patricia had drugs in the house, that the house smelled of marijuana, and that they heard quick footsteps moving about the house and toilets flushing when Patricia was speaking to them at her front door. Patricia testified that the police were lying and that she was alone in the house that night: no one could have been scurrying around making "let's get rid of the drugs" noises when she stood at the front door. Assume that if Patricia's testimony were credited as true, it would establish that the police violated the Fourth Amendment, even as that provision is narrowly interpreted by the United States Supreme Court and other courts.[13]

The trial judge, who was up for reelection on a "tough-on-crime" platform, denied the motion to suppress. In her opinion denying the motion, the judge stated that the police officers' testimony was credible and Patricia's was not. Patricia renewed her Fourth Amendment challenge at every stage of the appeals process, but the appellate judges all stated that they respected the trial judge's credibility determination and rejected Patricia's argument that the trial judge misunderstood the law of the Fourth Amendment as set forth in Supreme Court opinions. During state collateral proceedings (also known as state post-conviction proceedings), Patricia also failed to get relief on the basis of her Fourth Amendment claim.

Patricia knows that Fourth Amendment claims are not within the scope of review on federal habeas. Although she knows that her strategy is a "long shot," she wants to make the case that *Stone v. Powell* should be overruled, hoping that the Supreme Court will take her case in order to do so. What types of arguments should she make?

---

13. *See, e.g., Hudson v. Michigan*, 126 S. Ct. 2159 (2006) (holding that violation of "knock and announce" rule did not require suppressing evidence found in subsequent search).

Explanation

Patricia can make counter-arguments using the same values discussed by the majority in *Stone v. Powell*, weaving in some observations about her own case:

- *Honoring federal constitutional values.* By not allowing federal habeas courts to entertain Fourth Amendment claims, *Stone v. Powell* did not give adequate deference to constitutional values. Without the exclusionary rule, the Fourth Amendment would be a right without a remedy. To suspend the operation of the exclusionary rule on habeas is to expand the possibility that a prisoner will serve punishment for a conviction obtained in violation of the Constitution. Adequate respect for the meaning of our Constitution therefore demands that courts be able to hear constitutional challenges at every stage of the process.

- *Accuracy of adjudication and avoiding confinement of the innocent.* Although accuracy and avoiding the confinement of innocent people are noble reasons for the writ of habeas corpus, these purposes should not blind the Court to other important individual rights concerns, such as ensuring individuals' privacy and dignity from government abuse. As Justice Brennan said in his dissent in *Stone v. Powell*, "[S]afe-guards . . . are not admonitions to be tolerated only to the extent they serve functional purposes that ensure that the 'guilty' are punished and the 'innocent' freed." 428 U.S. at 524.

- *Constraining official abuse of power.* In some cases, *Stone v. Powell* may be correct in its claim that eliminating the exclusionary rule from habeas review may have little effect on police misconduct. That assumption, however, is inaccurate in the common circumstance where police enjoy a sort of "home team advantage" in state court that does not extend to federal court. Here, the police may well have known that they might be able to get their warrantless search of Patricia's house past the state court judges — many of whom were friends and all of whom were running for reelection. A rhetorical question: Is it a coincidence that the police chief shared the same political party as the state judges in Patricia's town? Whatever the answer, a life-tenured federal judge may be less accommodating to the police than were the state courts.

- *State sovereignty.* The *Stone v. Powell* Court was wrong in assuming that state courts are on parity with federal courts in their ability and willingness to apply federal law. Federal courts are well suited to enforcing constitutional guarantees, particularly where, as here, the state court judges are susceptible to political pressures and share both friendship and ambitions with the police.

- *Institutional integrity.* In reasoning about institutional integrity, *Stone v. Powell* focused on respect for the criminal justice system. But doesn't

respect for the criminal justice system demand that participants —
such as police and prosecutors — not benefit from tainted evidence?
If citizens are to respect the products of the criminal justice system
(convictions), then these products should not result from unconstitutional conduct, such as an illegal search and seizure protected by the
Fourth Amendment.

Critics of *Stone v. Powell* vociferously pressed arguments such as those made
by Patricia in Example 12-5. While not responsive to these critics, the
Supreme Court has resisted extending the decision to other constitutional
rights.

Example 12-6

Annabelle is a government official. Police officers appeared at her office one
day with the intention of arresting her and questioned her about extorting
favors from contractors. At the time they questioned Annabelle, the police
did not advise her of her right to remain silent, protected by the Fifth
Amendment, or her right to consult a lawyer, protected by the Sixth Amendment. She gave a confession at that time, which the prosecution used during
her trial for extortion. At trial, she argued that the trial court should exclude
the confession under *Miranda v. Arizona*, 384 U.S. 436 (1966).

Annabelle was convicted and pressed the *Miranda* issue throughout the
state court proceedings (including state post-conviction proceedings),
asserting that the trial court should have excluded the confession from
her trial. Annabelle raised the *Miranda* claim on federal habeas, and her
opponent, the State, argued that federal courts should extend *Stone v. Powell*'s
prohibition to *Miranda* claims. Is the United States Supreme Court likely to
accept this invitation to extend *Stone v. Powell*?

Explanation

No, the United States Supreme Court in *Withrow v. Williams*, 507 U.S. 680
(1993), actually declined the opportunity to expand *Stone v. Powell* to *Miranda*
cases. In so doing, the Court cited many of the values discussed in *Stone v. Powell*:

- *Honoring federal constitutional values.* The *Withrow v. Williams* Court could
  have followed *Stone v. Powell* by characterizing *Miranda* warnings as
  prophylactic, not based on an individual right explicitly secured by
  the Constitution, and therefore outside the purposes of the habeas
  writ. The Court declined this tack, instead describing *Miranda* as "safeguard[ing] 'a fundamental trial right.'" 507 U.S. at 691 (quoting *United
  States v. Verdugo-Urquidez*, 494 U.S. 259, 264 (1990) (emphasis added in
  Withrow v. Williams)).

- *Accuracy of adjudication and avoiding confinement of the innocent.* The *Withrow v. Williams* Court reasoned that *Miranda* was designed in part to ensure that confessions were freely given and thus more likely to be reliable. The Court therefore also reasoned that *Miranda* claims were more closely linked to ensuring accuracy of convictions and avoiding imprisonment of innocent individuals than are Fourth Amendment claims.
- *State sovereignty.* The Court also reasoned that even if *Miranda* claims were disqualified, petitioners would likely frame their challenges as due process claims that their confessions were unfairly obtained. Under such circumstances, the Court reasoned, convictions could still be overturned on the basis of improperly introduced confessions, and the cause of promoting deference to the state criminal process would not be materially advanced by excluding *Miranda* claims from habeas.

This reasoning related to another value in the Court's habeas calculus:

- Efficiency. The *Withrow v. Williams* Court suggested that due process claims are fact laden, requiring a federal habeas court to undertake detailed analysis of the totality of circumstances under which prisoners make confessions. *Miranda v. Arizona*, however, provides a bright-line test based on whether authorities give proper warnings. *Miranda* claims are therefore more quickly and easily processed. For that reason, the Court deemed it unwise to channel confession challenges on habeas into due process claims.

Withrow v. Williams is not the only case in which the Court declined to extend *Stone v. Powell*. Other contexts include the Sixth Amendment right to effective assistance of counsel,[14] challenges to the racial composition of grand juries,[15] and the standard-of-proof components of jury instructions.[16]

c. Eliminating Claims that Amount to Harmless Error

As part of the movement back toward a restrictive orientation to habeas corpus, the Supreme Court in *Brecht v. Abrahamson*, 507 U.S. 619 (1993), eased the harmless error standard for habeas proceedings. This allows district courts to withhold habeas relief in more cases, even if the district court finds that the state courts actually did commit error.

The harmless error inquiry is a two-step process: (1) the district court evaluates whether a petitioner's claim has merit and (2) if the claim has

---

14. *Kimmelman v. Morrison*, 477 U.S. 365 (1986).
15. *Rose v. Mitchell*, 443 U.S. 545 (1979).
16. *Jackson v. Virginia*, 443 U.S. 307 (1979).

merit, the district court evaluates whether the error was harmless.[17] Concluding that the error is harmless allows the district court to deny the petition for a writ of habeas corpus.

The two-step approach gives the harmless error doctrine a weaker effect on the federal jurisprudence compared with many other doctrines restricting habeas relief. The harmless error doctrine allows the federal court to consider federal claims in full, thereby performing the important role of clarifying federal law.[18] This contrasts with doctrines such as those announced in *Stone v. Powell* (discussed above) and *Teague v. Lane*, 489 U.S. 288 (1989) (discussed below), which effectively take claims "off the table" altogether, preventing habeas courts from considering their merits. From a structural perspective, this distinction is important because the federal courts' governmental function is preserved. For the habeas petitioner, however, the distinction is academic: the petitioner gets no relief from a harmless error, even if the district court gets a chance to clarify a federal right!

The United States Supreme Court applies the harmless error doctrine on direct review, and will ignore error only if the government demonstrates that the error was harmless "beyond a reasonable doubt."[19] In *Brecht v. Abrahamson*, however, the Court ruled that on habeas, district courts should consider a trial error not harmless only if "the error 'had substantial and injurious effect or influence' " on the outcome of petitioner's trial. 507 U.S. at 637 (quoting *Kotteakos v. United States*, 328 U.S. 750, 776 (1946)). The reasons advanced in *Brecht* invoke familiar values:

- *Honoring federal constitutional values.* *Brecht* maintained that state courts will enforce constitutional rights even if the harmless error standard on habeas becomes "less onerous." *Id.*
- *State sovereignty, finality, and efficiency.* *Brecht* reasoned that a more exacting harmless error standard would not be worth the cost in terms of upsetting state judgments and necessitating remedial state court proceedings that follow successful habeas corpus petitions.
- *Accuracy of adjudication.* According to *Brecht*, concern with freeing guilty prisoners militates against a stringent harmless error standard. On retrial after a district court grants habeas relief, evidence may have become stale and inadequate to convict the guilty.[20]

---

17. *See Lockhart v. Fretwell*, 506 U.S. 364 (1993) (explaining that a court evaluates whether error is harmless only after concluding that error occurred).

18. *See* Sam Kamin, *Harmless Error and the Rights/Remedies Split*, 88 Va. L. Rev. 1, 77 (2002) (observing that the harmless error doctrine allows courts to continue to declare the content of federal rights).

19. *Chapman v. California*, 386 U.S. 18, 24 (1967).

20. After the Supreme Court decided *Brecht v. Abrahamson*, Congress passed the Anti-Terrorism and Effective Death Penalty Act of 1996, which affected the standard that federal courts use in

Example 12-7

Ashley was arrested for homicide. After her arrest, Ashley's husband went to the police station, where he was interviewed. His interview, which was taped, established that Ashley had no alibi for the time period when the homicide occurred. Ashley's fingerprints were found at the murder scene, and a bloody hammer containing the victim's blood was found in Ashley's backyard. Both pieces of evidence were admitted at Ashley's trial. In addition, an inmate of the prison where Ashley was confined pending her arraignment testified at trial that Ashley offered to pay her $1,000 if she would corroborate an alibi for Ashley. Also at trial, Ashley's husband invoked the marital privilege so that he could not be called to testify or be cross-examined. The prosecution did, however, introduce the taped interview of Ashley's husband into evidence. Ashley's defense contained no mention of an alibi.

The jury returned a guilty verdict, and Ashley brought direct appeals and post-conviction proceedings in state court. During every proceeding, Ashley challenged the judge's decision to admit the taped interview on the ground that using the tape violated her right to confront witnesses against her, guaranteed by the Sixth Amendment. The state courts all rejected the challenge, and Ashley included this Sixth Amendment confrontation clause claim in her habeas petition. As it turns out, the claim had merit under United States Supreme Court case law. The government contended, however, that the error was harmless. Should the United States district court grant Ashley's habeas petition on the basis of her confrontation clause claim?

Explanation

Under the *Brecht v. Abrahamson* standard, the district court probably should not grant the habeas petition. The district court would have difficulty concluding "beyond a reasonable doubt" that the harmful testimony of Ashley's husband did not affect the trial result. But "beyond a reasonable doubt" is not the standard on habeas. Instead, the district court may grant relief only if it concludes that the confrontation clause challenge — although valid on its merits — had a "substantial and injurious effect or influence" on Ashley's conviction. Given other aspects of the case, the tape recording did not necessarily influence the jury's verdict and was therefore harmless error.

---

evaluating state court determinations regarding clearly established federal law. Some lower courts have held that this statute supersedes *Brecht v. Abrahamson*, at least in the limited circumstance where the state court had ruled on whether a particular error was harmless. *See, e.g., Zappulla v. New York*, 391 F.3d 462 (2d Cir. 2004); *Hale v. Gibson*, 227 F.3d 1298 (10th Cir. 2000). The Supreme Court, however, has cited *Brecht v. Abrahamson* often since Congress passed the statute, suggesting that the case still amounts to robust precedent.

The types of factors that a court might consider in determining whether a confrontation clause error is harmless include the importance of the testimony in the prosecution's case, whether other evidence corroborates or contradicts the witness's testimony, the extent of cross-examination permitted, and the overall strength of the prosecution's case. *See Delaware v. Van Arsdall*, 475 U.S. 673 (1986). Here, the prosecutor's case was filled with abundant inculpatory evidence, such as the fingerprints and the bloody weapon. Moreover, the prison inmate's testimony buttresses the accuracy of the husband's interview by corroborating Ashley's lack of alibi. Although no cross-examination was permitted, the interview ultimately had limited importance in the case because Ashley did not even use an alibi defense and had a disincentive to do so by the inmate's testimony on that topic. Thus, Ashley has little basis on which to complain that the introduction of the tape dissuaded her from using an alibi defense, which would have lacked credibility anyway.

d. Eliminating New Rules of Constitutional Law: *Teague v. Lane*

i. The Basics

Every time the Supreme Court discovers a new constitutional protection for the criminally accused, the Court also creates another issue: to whom does this protection extend? Options include (1) everyone who has been processed in the criminal justice system, (2) all those who will be processed in the future, (3) all those currently serving sentences, (4) all those whose convictions are not yet final on direct appeal, and (5) all those who are fighting for relief under state post-conviction review or federal habeas. Resolving this issue requires grappling with the puzzle of retroactivity: when should a court apply new rules retroactively?

The Supreme Court for many years toyed with different approaches to retroactivity but became attracted in the 1980s to a bright-line approach advocated by Justice Harlan[21] in a series of concurrences. In essence, Justice Harlan suggested that the Court divide criminal defendants into two categories for retroactivity purposes: those whose convictions were pending on direct appeal at the time the Supreme Court announced a new rule, and those whose convictions had become final upon Supreme Court direct review of their case or denial of Supreme Court review before the Court announced the new rule. In Justice Harlan's view, the first category of prisoners should get the benefit of the new rule (if, of course, it is relevant to their conviction) and the second category should not.

---

21. That's the second Justice Harlan. And actually, the Supreme Court generally responds favorably to *anything* that this Justice Harlan propounded.

The Supreme Court adopted the first (and more generous) part of Justice Harlan's bright-line approach in 1987.[22] So when the Court granted certiorari in *Teague v. Lane*, 489 U.S. 288 (1989), suspense was heightened: was the Court willing to adopt the harsher part of the Harlan test, denying habeas petitioners the benefit of newly discovered criminal protections? The answer, it turns out, was yes, with limited exceptions cobbled together from Justice Harlan's opinions.

Teague v. Lane set forth the following formulation: a habeas petitioner does not receive the benefit of the recognition of a new rule of constitutional law after the petitioner's conviction became final except in two instances: (1) if the rule "places 'certain kinds of primary, private individual conduct beyond the power of the criminal law-making authority to proscribe' "; or (2) if the rule is a "watershed rule[] of criminal procedure" that adopts a procedure " 'implicit in the concept of ordered liberty.' " Id. at 307, 311 (quoting *Mackey v. United States*, 401 U.S. 667, 692, 693 (1971)).

In a subsequent case, the Supreme Court broke down the *Teague* inquiry into a series of three steps. To decide whether a habeas petitioner should get the benefit of a claim, a district court should follow all three steps:

1. Determine the date on which the petitioner's conviction became final.
2. Ascertain whether " 'a state court considering [the petitioner's] claim at the time his conviction became final would have felt compelled by existing precedent to conclude that the rule . . . was required by the Constitution.' "[23] If not, the rule is "new" and one must proceed to step 3.
3. Analyze whether the rule falls within one of the exceptions described in *Teague*.[24] If the new rule does not fall within one of the two exceptions, the petitioner does not get the benefit of the new rule. If the rule is not new but was dictated by prior precedent, then the habeas court gives the petitioner the benefit of the rule if it is appropriate to do so under other constraints on habeas relief, such as those reflected in 28 U.S.C. §2254(d)(1) and procedural bar rules.

In evaluating who gets the benefit of a new rule, one must be mindful of another important characteristic of the *Teague* doctrine: the *Teague* prohibition applies both to petitioners trying to get the benefit of a previously announced new rule from another person's case and to petitioners who themselves advocate a particular new rule.

---

22. *Griffith v. Kentucky*, 479 U.S. 314 (1987).
23. *O'Dell v. Netherland*, 521 U.S. 151, 156 (1997) (quoting *Lambrix v. Singletary*, 520 U.S. 518, 527 (1997)).
24. Id. at 156-157.

Example 12-8

Enya, serving a sentence for first-degree murder, appealed her conviction through the state court system, and the United States Supreme Court denied certiorari in 2004. Assume that in 2005 the Supreme Court decided *State v. Joy*, holding that jury instructions violated a defendant's due process rights if the instructions did not offer jurors the option of convicting on a lesser charge based on mitigating evidence. At the time the Court announced this ruling, it acknowledged that it marked a clear break from prior cases. After exhausting post-conviction proceedings in state court, Enya filed a federal habeas petition, arguing that, under *State v. Joy*, the trial court erred in failing to instruct the jury on the possibility of convicting her on second-degree homicide based on mitigating evidence in the case. Should the district court consider her *State v. Joy* claim?

Explanation

No, the trial court should not consider the *State v. Joy* claim. Applying the three-step test, the court should first determine when Enya's conviction became final (2004) and then ask whether a state court adjudicating Enya's suit before that time would have been compelled to give the alternative instruction mandated by *State v. Joy*. The answer to this second question is no, since the Supreme Court itself acknowledged that *State v. Joy* was a break from prior precedent. Thus, *State v. Joy* establishes a new rule and Enya should not get the benefit of it, unless it falls within one of the two exceptions.

The first exception deals with instances where the new rule redefines what is and what is not criminal and subject to a particular punishment. So, for example, a rule announcing that the Constitution prohibits a state from punishing certain conduct — such as private homosexual sodomy — would decriminalize such sexual activity and would therefore be a rule that places " 'primary, private individual conduct beyond the power of the criminal law-making authority to prescribe.' " *Teague*, 489 U.S. at 307 (quoting *Mackey v. United States*, 401 U.S. 667, 692 (1971)). *State v. Joy* does not announce such a rule. *State v. Joy* does not redefine punishable conduct or appropriate sentences, but rather concerns only the conviction options offered to juries. As such, *State v. Joy* enunciates an "in-court rule" about what happens during the litigation process. By contrast, the first *Teague* exception focuses on out-of-court concerns: what type of out-of-court behavior ("primary, private individual conduct") is criminal and subject to particular punishment?[25]

---

25. Outside the area of crime definition, the Supreme Court has applied this exception to the "rules prohibiting a certain category of punishment for a class of defendants because of their status or offense." *Penry v. Lynaugh*, 492 U.S. 302, 330 (1989) (applying the exception to the claim that execution of a prisoner with mental capacity of a child violated the Constitution).

The second *Teague* exception is closer but still not applicable. This exception derives from the values of improving the accuracy of adjudication, avoiding punishment of the innocent, and honoring constitutional values. As for accuracy and innocence, a rule qualifying for this exception should be connected to the goal of improving factfinding and protecting innocence. *State v. Joy* is relevant to this goal, since providing a jury with alternative crime definitions might enable convictions that more closely match the precise conduct committed and thereby punish defendants only for what they actually did (rather than convicting them of crimes of which they are actually innocent).

But *State v. Joy* does not satisfy that portion of the second exception tied to honoring constitutional values. *Teague* set an extremely high bar for this concern, stating the exception is satisfied only for those rules that "implicate the fundamental fairness of the trial, . . . without which the likelihood of an accurate conviction is seriously diminished." 489 U.S. at 312, 313. Tipping its hand as to how it would handle this exception in the future, the Court added, "[W]e believe it unlikely that many such components of basic due process have yet to emerge." *Id.* at 313. Given that the Supreme Court has never yet found this exception satisfied, Enya is unlikely to convince a court that *State v. Joy* presents such an extraordinary rule. Indeed, like the rule of *State v. Joy*, the rule advocated in *Teague* itself concerned the integrity of the jury process. The *Teague* petitioner urged the Court to require the particular jury that decides guilt or innocence to be composed of a fair cross-section of the community (rather than, for example, solely of individuals of a race different from the defendants' race). In dismissing the second exception, the *Teague* Court declared that this fair cross-section claim is a "far cry from the kind of absolute prerequisite to fundamental fairness." *Id.* at 314. *See Gilmore v. Taylor*, 508 U.S. 333, 345 (1993) (finding that a similar rule regarding jury instructions does not fall within the "small core of rules requiring 'observance of those procedures that . . . are implicit in the concept of ordered liberty,'" (quoting *Graham v. Collins*, 506 U.S. 461, 478 (1993))).

Example 12-9

Consider the circumstances of Enya in Example 12-8, where the Supreme Court denied her certiorari petition on direct appeal in 2004. For the purposes of this example, however, the Supreme Court had not decided *State v. Joy* when it evaluates her certiorari petition. Instead, assume that it was Enya herself who urged in her habeas petition that the *State v. Joy* rule be adopted. Does this fact change how the district court, court of appeals, or United States Supreme Court handles the question of whether Enya should get the benefit of this rule regarding providing juries with alternative instructions?

Explanation

No, the three-step analysis is the same regardless of whether the petitioner is pressing a new rule herself or is trying to receive the benefit of a new rule announced in an earlier case. Thus, if Enya advocated the alternative instruction rule herself, she would fare no better than she did in Example 12-8. In fact, she need not even try to advocate the new rule, since the Supreme Court has established that *Teague* is a threshold doctrine: once a court determines that a petitioner will not get the benefit of the rule, the court should not consider whether the rule is meritorious. For that reason, the *Teague* doctrine stifles the development of constitutional law by disqualifying an entire category of cases from serving as vehicles for adjudication of federal rights. In this way, the *Teague* doctrine contrasts with the harmless error doctrine and to some extent, with the mandate of §2254(d)(1), discussed below.

ii. What Is a New Rule?

As case law developed, the Supreme Court embraced a broad approach to defining what constitutes a new rule. For those justices interested in restricting the availability of federal habeas relief, the incentive for this is great: the more claims that are read as presenting new rules, the fewer claims there are to review on the merits and to provide the basis for relief. Presumably, taking the incentive out of creative advocacy on habeas may ultimately diminish the number of petitions that federal courts must process as well.

The *Teague v. Lane* Court acknowledged the difficulty of determining "when a case announces a new rule." As an initial matter, the Court explained, "[A] case announces a new rule when it breaks new ground or imposes a new obligation. . . . To put it differently, a case announces a new rule if the result was not *dictated* by precedent existing at the time the defendant's conviction became final." *Id.* at 301 (emphasis in original). In a subsequent case, the Court stated that unless precedent "compelled"[26] a particular holding, then that holding presents a new rule. Coming at the issue from another perspective, the Court has also explained that if reasonable minds can differ as to whether a decision requires a particular result, a subsequent ruling that locks in the meaning of that decision and requires that particular result is a new rule.[27] Finally, the Court has stated that the application of an established rule in "a novel setting" can constitute a new rule as well.[28]

---

26. *Sawyer v. Smith*, 497 U.S. 227, 237 (1990).
27. *Butler v. McKellar*, 494 U.S. 407, 414 (1990).
28. *Stringer v. Black*, 503 U.S. 222, 228 (1992).

Example 12-10

Briana was convicted, and her conviction became final on direct appeal in 2005. She made a Sixth Amendment challenge throughout her direct appeal proceedings, based on an interpretation of a 1999 decision of the United States Supreme Court. Several federal courts of appeals had interpreted the 1999 decision and come to different conclusions about its meaning. In Briana's case, the state courts all decided to align with the court of appeals in the circuit where they were located, which had adopted an interpretation of the 1999 decision that supported denying relief for the Sixth Amendment claim.

In 2006 the United States Supreme Court sought to resolve the circuit conflict and took a case dealing with this precise Sixth Amendment issue. The 2006 Supreme Court ruled that the claim was supported by the Sixth Amendment and that criminal defendants challenging their convictions on this basis were entitled to new trials. Briana would like to include the claim in her federal habeas corpus petition, seeking the benefit of the 2006 Supreme Court case. Does this case announce a new rule of constitutional law?

Explanation

Yes, Briana's claim relies on a new rule. The circuit conflict over the meaning of the 1999 decision suggests that reasonable minds could differ about the Sixth Amendment issue and that the 1999 decision did not dictate a particular result. In 2006 the Supreme Court did lock in the 1999 decision's meaning, compelling lower courts to follow that meaning in subsequent cases. In so doing, the Supreme Court created a new rule, not compelled by its precedent before that point.[29] Since Briana's conviction became final before the Supreme Court created the new rule, she cannot get the benefit of it.

iii. Understanding Teague in Light of the Habeas Values

One way to remember and understand the components of *Teague* doctrine is to analyze the case in terms of the values it chose to promote:

- *Finality.* Had the Court drawn the retroactivity line differently, it might have had difficulty identifying a category of former criminal defendants who should *not* have a claim to some kind of relief. The result in terms of reversing final criminal judgments would have been enormous.

---

29. Professor Linda Meyer makes the insightful observation that in adopting this approach to a new rule, the Supreme Court is using a legislative model in which new rules are created by votes in the Court's own conference, rather than a common law model in which law develops from case to case when courts apply established principles to new facts. Linda Meyer, "*Nothing We Say Matters*": Teague and New Rules, 61 U. CHI. L. REV. 423, 444, 462-463 (1994).

- *State sovereignty, reliance on legal principles, institutional integrity, and constraining official abuse of power.* According to the definition of a new rule, state officials and state courts could not have anticipated the rule's change in the law. Thus, the courts and officials properly relied on the law as it was understood when they acted, and were not abusing power in failing to follow the new rule. The *Teague* doctrine is thus premised on the view that applying new rules on habeas attacks state sovereignty and institutional integrity by undermining law enforcement efforts many years after the officials reasonably relied on the law.
- *Avoiding confinement of innocents.* The first *Teague* exception attempts to integrate this value by allowing habeas petitioners the benefits of new rules that decriminalize conduct and thereby transform "the guilty" into "the innocent."
- *Honoring constitutional values and accuracy of adjudication.* The second *Teague* exception "tips its hat" to these values by allowing review of "watershed" constitutional principles concerning factfinding accuracy.

e. Eliminating Decisions Based on Clearly Established Federal Law

Congress passed the Anti-Terrorism and Effective Death Penalty Act of 1996 (AEDPA) to address abuse and delay in the federal habeas corpus process. AEDPA altered existing habeas corpus law in a number of ways, introducing dramatic changes to claims capable of yielding habeas relief. In eliminating a category of potentially successful claims, Congress created a more deferential standard for federal courts of habeas in according respect for state judgments. Accordingly, it was *finality* and *state sovereignty* that served as Congress's dominant values in moving habeas doctrine yet one step closer to the approach reflected in *Frank v. Mangum*. The particular AEDPA decision reflecting deference to state court judgments is 28 U.S.C. §2254(d)(1). Not only is this provision complicated on its own terms, but it is also difficult to read together with the doctrine of *Teague v. Lane*. Both angles on the provision are explored next.

i. Dismantling and Reconstructing 28 U.S.C §2254(d)(1)

One can approach 28 U.S.C. §2254(d)(1) as one would a construction project, dismantling it and then putting it back together. To undertake this task effectively, one must start with the whole provision:

> An application for a writ of habeas corpus on behalf of a person in custody pursuant to the judgment of a State court shall not be granted with respect to any claim that was adjudicated on the merits in State court proceedings unless the adjudication of the claim —

> (1) resulted in a decision that was contrary to, or involved an unreasonable application of, clearly established Federal law, as determined by the Supreme Court of the United States

Dismantling the provision, we have the following crucial construction pieces to decipher and reassemble:

- writ of habeas corpus . . . shall not be granted
- claim that was adjudicated on the merits in State court proceedings
- was contrary to . . . clearly established Federal law, as determined by the Supreme Court of the United States
- involved an unreasonable application of clearly established Federal law, as determined by the Supreme Court of the United States

To analyze and understand what each piece of the construction project means, our primary instructions come from the statutory language and the Supreme Court's decision in *Williams v. Taylor*, 529 U.S. 362 (2000).

The First Piece: "writ of habeas corpus . . . shall not be granted"

At first blush, this does not seem to be mysteriously worded. The language is obviously important because it frames the statute in the negative. The language tips off the reader that what follows defines claims that will not provide the basis for habeas review. Accordingly, the section defines yet another category of claims that are removed from the plenary scope of review first announced in *Brown v. Allen*, 344 U.S. 443 (1953).

But what is uncertain is whether this language seeks to take claims completely "off the table" or whether the language allows federal courts to review them. The phrase "shall not be granted" suggests the latter, the idea being that the federal court takes a look at the claim, evaluates whether it falls within one of the categories described in §2254(d)(1), and if so, refuses to grant the writ. The Supreme Court has implicitly agreed with this view by referring to §2254(d)(1) as providing a "standard of review."[30] In this way, §2254(d)(1) differs from the approach of *Stone v. Powell* and *Teague v. Lane*, which completely removes claims from habeas review unless they fall within certain exceptions.

The Second Piece: "claim that was adjudicated on the merits in state court proceedings"

This piece is actually one of the more crucial components of the provision because it specifies what is subject to §2254(d)(1) restrictions: only claims that the state court discussed on the merits and actually decided. Thus, §2254(d)(1) does not apply to claims that the state court concluded

---

30. Larry W. Yackle, Federal Courts: Habeas Corpus 96 n.6 (Foundation Turning Point Series 2003) (citing *Lockyer v. Andrade*, 538 U.S. 63, 71 (2003), and *Woodford v. Garceau*, 538 U.S. 202, 206 (2003)).

were barred or procedurally defaulted, or claims that the petitioner forgot or did not anticipate at the time of state proceedings.

The Third Piece: "was contrary to . . . clearly established Federal law, as determined by the Supreme Court of the United States"

This piece actually has two subparts: "contrary to" and "clearly established federal law."

"Contrary to"

The Court in *Williams v. Taylor*, 529 U.S. 362 (2000), determined that "contrary to" could mean mangling the legal principle invoked or applying a particular legal principle to the wrong set of facts. Under this reading, a state court decision is contrary to the United States Supreme Court's clearly established precedents if it "arrives at a conclusion opposite to that reached by [the Supreme Court] on a question of law or if the state court decides a case differently than [the Supreme Court] has on a set of materially indistinguishable facts." 529 U.S. at 413.

"Clearly established Federal law"

Writing for three other justices, Justice Stevens in *Williams v. Taylor*, 529 U.S. 362 (2000), asserted that the "clearly established federal law" language evoked the "new rule" concept from *Teague v. Lane*, 489 U.S. 288 (1989), and assumed that Congress had "congruent concepts in mind." 529 U.S. at 379-380. But Justice Stevens did not write for the majority of the Court in interpreting this portion of §2254(d)(1). Justice O'Connor did. She largely agreed, however, with Justice Stevens on the relationship with *Teague*. For Justice O'Connor, a "clearly established federal law" meant the opposite of a new rule — that is, an old rule. As she explained, "With one caveat, whatever would qualify as an old rule under our *Teague* jurisprudence will constitute 'clearly established Federal law, as determined by the Supreme Court of the United States' under §2254(d)(1). . . . The one caveat, as the statutory language makes clear, is that §2254(d)(1) restricts the source of clearly established law to this Court's jurisprudence." *Id.* at 412 (citations omitted). (More on the relationship between *Teague* and §2254(d)(1) follows.)

The Supreme Court thus made plain that a claim is not eliminated from habeas review unless one can identify a United States Supreme Court case that specifically establishes the law governing the claim. By limiting the relevant federal law to that "determined by the Supreme Court of the United States," Congress reinforced the Supreme Court's supremacy and also provided greater opportunity for deference to state courts. The Supreme Court reinforced this deference in *Williams* by narrowly reading the word "determined" to include only holdings of the United States Supreme Court.

Under *Williams*, stray language or dicta do not count toward providing the requisite Supreme Court authority for the claim excluded.

The Fourth Piece: "involved an unreasonable application of clearly established Federal law, as determined by the supreme court of the United States"

After nailing down the meaning of the third piece of §2254(d)(1), one has little difficulty deciphering the fourth piece. The only words yet to be defined are "unreasonable application."

"Unreasonable application"

Justice O'Connor's majority decision in *Williams v. Taylor* held that "unreasonable" means objectively unreasonable, not just wrong or incorrect. Moreover, the reference to "unreasonable application" means that a state court might correctly identify a legal principle but make an inexcusable mistake in analyzing how it governs a particular case. As the Court explained, "[A] federal habeas court may not issue the writ simply because that court concludes in its independent judgment that the relevant state-court decision applied clearly established federal law erroneously or incorrectly. Rather, that application must also be unreasonable." 529 U.S. at 411.

Example 12-11

Toni was charged with felony possession of a firearm as well as a lesser, included offense — misdemeanor possession of a firearm. Toni pleaded guilty to the misdemeanor, and the felony charged was dismissed. Before sentencing on the misdemeanor charge, the trial judge vacated the guilty plea and reinstated the felony charge. Toni was then prosecuted and convicted on the felony charge. She argued at the time and throughout state court proceedings that the trial court violated her rights under the double jeopardy clause of the United States Constitution. The state courts rejected that challenge, proceeding under the assumption that under the governing Supreme Court case law, double jeopardy does not attach until after sentencing on a guilty plea. Accordingly, the state courts reasoned that no double jeopardy problem was raised by her felony prosecution because the felony charge was reinstated before she was sentenced on the misdemeanor guilty plea. It turns out, however, that the United States Supreme Court has long adhered to the following three holdings, which appear in three separate cases: (1) a guilty plea is a conviction, (2) double jeopardy attaches once a conviction occurs, and (3) double jeopardy protection is violated if a defendant is prosecuted for a greater offense after being convicted of a lesser included offense. Toni maintained that these holdings establish that double jeopardy attaches to a guilty plea on a lesser included offense before sentencing, proving that the state trial court violated her right against double jeopardy. The state courts identified these three Supreme Court holdings, but concluded that they did not necessarily mandate finding a double jeopardy problem in Toni's case.

Toni has filed a writ of habeas corpus in federal district court arguing for relief on the basis of this double jeopardy violation. She argues that her claim is not disqualified from relief under §2254(d)(1). Is she correct?

Explanation

Toni is probably correct, although good arguments could be made that §2254(d)(1) precludes the district court from issuing habeas relief on the basis of this claim. The threshold question is whether the claim was adjudicated on the merits in state court proceedings (the second piece of the §2254(d)(1) construction project). The answer is a straightforward yes, since Toni raised the claim throughout the state court proceedings, and the state courts considered the terms of the claim and entered judgments rejecting it.

The next question is whether this case implicates the third piece of §2254(d)(1) — the "contrary to" category — or the fourth piece of §2254(d)(1) — the "unreasonable application of" issue. This choice is significant because "contrary to" effectively means "wrong," but "unreasonable" means more than just "wrong." Sound arguments exist on both sides. The "contrary to" category applies to questions of law or to decisions that are opposite those of the Supreme Court in cases with nearly identical facts. Here, none of the relevant Supreme Court cases has this type of factual connection (since it takes all three to come up with a legal principle specific enough to cover the circumstances of Toni's case). But Toni's case *does* entail questions of law resolved in the three Supreme Court opinions dealing with double jeopardy. The logical reading of these three cases together is that double jeopardy attaches to a guilty plea on a lesser included offense prior to sentencing. *See Morris v. Reynolds*, 264 F.3d 38, 51 (2d Cir. 2001) (holding that the three Supreme Court opinions read together establish governing law that the double jeopardy bar arises after a guilty plea to a lesser included offense but before sentencing on that plea). According to this view, the state court ruling opposes the principle derived from the three Supreme Court cases and can therefore be described as adjudicating a claim contrary to clearly established law.

On the other hand, no one Supreme Court case provided a holding that precisely governs the facts of Toni's case. One can therefore argue that while each of the three Supreme Court holdings constitutes "clearly established Federal law," the resolution of Toni's case requires an application of law to fact. Here, the argument continues, the state court's application of the holdings may have been wrong, but was not unreasonable. For example, one might conclude that the state court reasonably (but incorrectly) emphasized certain factual components of Toni's case. Alternatively, one might argue that the state courts reasonably concluded that the three Supreme Court cases were not meant to be read in tandem for the purposes of disposing of other disputes. For either of these possible arguments, the standard of §2254(d)(1) is not violated and no habeas relief should issue. Cf. *Brown v. Payton*, 544 U.S. 133, 147 (2005) (analyzing a state court's decision under the "unreasonable application of" category and concluding that the state court's decision was not unreasonable, even "assum[ing] the 'relevant state-court decision applied clearly established federal law erroneously or incorrectly'" (quoting *Lockyer v. Andrade*, 538 U.S. 63, 76 (2003))).

The choice between the "contrary to" category and the "unreasonable application of" category presumably depends on a judgment about the three Supreme Court holdings: how obvious is it that they combine to create established law? In a case nearly on point, the United States Court of Appeals for the Second Circuit treated the three holdings as naturally combining to create governing law for the purposes of §2254(d)(1). *Morris v. Reynolds*, 264 F.3d at 51. Yet in a subsequent case concerning a different criminal procedure protection, the United States Supreme Court tended to show a preference toward using "unreasonable application" analysis where the "contrary to" category might apply as well. *Brown v. Payton*, 544 U.S. 133, 141-147 (2005) (citing both categories as relevant, yet repeatedly analyzing whether the state court acted unreasonably). That tendency reflects trends in the Supreme Court to defer to state sovereignty, including state court interpretation of federal law.

At present, §2254(d)(1) represents the last chunk out of habeas review to be removed since *Brown v. Allen*. As demonstrated in Figure 12-3, the process of chipping away at *Brown v. Allen* and moving back to the approach of *Frank v. Mangum* has indeed been dramatic.

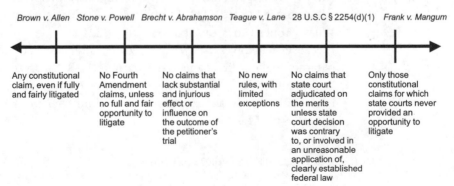

Figure 12-3. The Law Moves Back to *Frank v. Mangum*

ii. The Relationship Between Teague v. Lane and 28 U.S.C. §2254(d)(1)

As noted, Justice O'Connor wrote for the majority in *Williams v. Taylor*, 529 U.S. 362, 412 (2000), that "[w]ith one caveat . . . an old rule under [*Teague v. Lane*, 489 U.S. 288 (1989), constitutes] 'clearly established Federal law.'" 529 U.S. at 412. Likewise, Justice Stevens noted that the concepts from *Teague* and §2254(d)(1) were "congruent." *Id.* at 379-380. These comments suggest that *Teague* and §2254(d)(1) are flip sides: §2254(d)(1) forecloses from habeas relief that which *Teague* leaves alone. From this point of view, one might be tempted to analyze the two concepts sequentially, as if they were mutually exclusive.

Alas, the relationship between the two concepts is not so neat. Although related, the two concepts come at habeas review from different angles: they have different definitions of old and new rules, different approaches to deference to state courts, different cutoff dates for defining new and old rules, and exceptions that do not overlap. In cases subsequent to *Williams v. Taylor*, the Supreme Court has recognized as much, describing *Teague* and §2254(d)(1) as "distinct" from one another.[31]

Whatever confusion results from trying to map the relationship between *Teague* and §2254(d)(1), one important point emerges from these Supreme Court discussions: *Teague* does survive §2254(d)(1). The Court did not necessarily have to take that position; one could reasonably read §2254(d)(1) as preventing habeas relief except in the situation where state courts ruled on an issue involving settled law, but either got the law wrong or applied the law unreasonably to the particular case. By discussing the continuing relevance of *Teague*, however, the Court established that the sweep of §2254(d)(1) is not so great. Moreover, the Court's decisions suggest that a district court should first entertain the *Teague* inquiry and then entertain the §2254(d)(1) analysis if necessary.[32]

The following three questions help in exploring the uncertainties about the relationship between *Teague* and §2254(d)(1):

1. What happens to a case that appears to overcome the *Teague* obstacle (because it does not implicate a new rule) but does not unequivocally fall within §2254(d)(1)? (Example 12-12 addresses this question.)
2. What happens to a case that satisfies §2254(d)(1) but not *Teague* (because it involves a new rule decided after the petitioner's case became final on direct appeal)? (Example 12-13 analyzes this one.)
3. What happens to a case that gets past the *Teague* obstacle (because it satisfies the *Teague* exceptions) but flunks §2254(d)(1)? (See Example 12-14.)

---

31. *Horn v. Banks*, 536 U.S. 266 (2002) (per curiam).
32. *See* LARRY W. YACKLE, FEDERAL COURTS: HABEAS CORPUS 135-138 (Foundation Turning Point Series 2003) (citing as an example *Horn v. Banks*, 536 U.S. 266, 271 n.5 (2002) (per curiam)). Professor Yackle's treatment of the relationship between *Teague* and §2254(d)(1) in his book is thorough, thoughtful, and helpful.

Example 12-12

Lorna was convicted in 2005. She raised a Fifth Amendment claim during her trial, appeal, and state post-conviction review, but the state courts rejected the claim on the basis of a United States Supreme Court holding that had not been applied or cited by any court (including the Supreme Court) since it was decided in 2004. She raises the claim on federal habeas. How should the federal district court analyze *Teague* and §2254(d)(1) in this context?

Explanation

The *Teague* analysis appears to be easy: the claim is not based on a new rule because (1) it is premised on precedent already established at the time of Lorna's conviction, (2) nothing in the example suggests that the state courts needed to change or even infer anything about the Supreme Court precedent before applying it, and (3) the fact pattern does not suggest that reasonable minds could differ as to the meaning of the precedent. Since the claim is not based on a new rule, *Teague* does not eliminate it from the scope of inquiry on habeas.

The §2254(d)(1) analysis is less certain. Given the different contexts for §2254(d)(1) and *Teague*, a petitioner such as Lorna could possibly have a claim that is not a new rule, but is also not clearly established law for §2254(d)(1). In this case, for example, Lorna's claim is not based on a new rule and no court has interpreted or used the 2004 precedent, raising the possibility that the claim is not based on "clearly established" federal court law. In that event, Lorna's claim — since it was adjudicated by the state court — is probably not cognizable on habeas because §2254(d)(1) seeks to restrict relief to adjudicated claims for which the state court made a decision that is contrary to clearly established law or is an unreasonable application of clearly established federal law. This reading of §2254(d)(1) is consistent with Congress's intent to give state court leeway in interpreting and applying federal decisions.

At least two facts strongly suggest, however, that one would err by concluding that the 2004 decision is not "clearly established Federal law," as determined by the United States Supreme Court. First, nothing in the statute suggests that a determination by the United States Supreme Court needs to be interpreted or applied in order to be "clearly established." Moreover, the Supreme Court in *Williams v. Taylor*, 529 U.S. 362 (2000), made plain that it intended to treat rules that are not new rules under *Teague* as clearly established federal law so long as they result from holdings of Supreme Court opinions. Under this reasoning, Lorna's claim is based on "clearly established Federal law," and she can receive habeas relief only if she establishes that the state courts' decision was contrary to the 2004

Supreme Court decision or was an unreasonable application of that decision. Nothing in the example suggests that she could succeed in either of these showings. Thus, §2254(d)(1) will likely prevent Lorna from getting habeas relief.

Example 12-13

Jean's conviction became final when the United States Supreme Court denied certiorari in her case in 2004. In 2005 the Supreme Court announced a decision that it described as marking a break from prior precedent. This 2005 Supreme Court decision was soon interpreted and applied in many cases. In 2007 Jean filed state post-conviction proceedings and argued that the 2005 decision should apply in her case. The state courts concluded on post-conviction review that the 2005 decision was factually distinguishable from Jean's case and should therefore not provide the basis for relief. Jean then filed for federal habeas arguing — correctly — that the state courts' decisions on collateral review were "contrary to . . . clearly established Federal law, as determined by the Supreme Court of the United States" under §2254(d)(1) and that the district court should therefore grant her habeas relief on the basis of her claim premised on the 2005 Supreme Court opinion. Is Jean correct that the district court should grant her habeas relief?

Explanation

No, Jean is not correct. Her argument is accurate in that §2254(d)(1) supports granting her relief, but *Teague v. Lane* prevents this from happening. First, the §2254(d)(1) part of the story: the example provides that the state court's failure to apply the 2005 decision to Jean's case was "contrary to . . . clearly established Federal law." The "contrary to . . ." label applies if the facts of Jean's case were "materially indistinguishable" from the facts of the 2005 Supreme Court decision. *Williams v. Taylor*, 529 U.S. at 413. The fact that the state court adjudication on the 2005 Supreme Court decision occurred during post-conviction review does not make a difference. The 2005 Supreme Court decision was "clearly established Federal law" and the post-conviction proceedings amounted to an adjudication "on the merits in State court proceedings" under the language of §2254(d)(1).

But Jean encounters a problem with *Teague v. Lane*: her conviction had become final at the time the 2005 Supreme Court decision was announced. The Supreme Court's description of the decision as a break from prior law establishes the 2005 holding as a new rule, and nothing in the example suggests that the case falls within any of the exceptions to the *Teague* doctrine. Accordingly, the claim is outside the scope of federal habeas. Since the Court has made clear that the *Teague v. Lane* analysis comes before the §2254(d)(1) analysis, Jean is out of luck even before the district court gets a chance to consider her §2254(d)(1) argument.

Example 12-14

Bethany's conviction became final when the United States Supreme Court denied certiorari in her case in 2004. In 2005 the Supreme Court announced a decision that it described as constituting a break from prior precedent. The decision concerned an extraordinarily important due process protection safeguarding the accuracy of factfinding. This 2005 Supreme Court decision was soon interpreted and applied in many cases. In 2007 Bethany filed state post-conviction proceedings and argued that the 2005 decision should apply in her case. The state courts concluded on post-conviction review that the 2005 decision was relevant to Bethany's case but — after careful consideration of all competing arguments — concluded that the decision should not provide the basis for relief in the case. Bethany then filed for federal habeas arguing that she should get habeas relief under the 2005 Supreme Court decision. Is she correct?

Explanation

Although Bethany may correctly suggest that the 2005 decision set forth a new rule that could apply on habeas, she does not necessarily benefit from it. Because the 2005 decision was a break from prior law, it is likely classified as a new rule that would normally not extend to habeas petitioners whose convictions became final before the rule was announced. Nevertheless, this new rule concerns the accuracy of factfinding and could possibly be characterized as a watershed rule of procedure, thus satisfying an exception to the *Teague* doctrine. Also to Bethany's benefit, the Supreme Court has suggested that the *Teague* exceptions survive the enactment of §2254(d)(1).

But the survival of the *Teague* exceptions as a general matter does not preclude §2254(d)(1) from disqualifying an individual petitioner who otherwise could benefit from a new rule. In this case, the state courts evaluated whether to apply the new rule to Bethany at a point when the new rule had been interpreted and applied in subsequent cases. Thus, as explained in Example 12-13, the new rule no doubt qualified as "clearly established Federal law, as determined by the Supreme Court of the United States," under §2254(d)(1). The state courts denied Bethany relief only after carefully analyzing whether Bethany should get the benefit of the new rule. Since the new rule constituted "clearly established Federal law" and the state courts adjudicated the claim concerning the new rule on its merits, the district court must honor the state courts' decisions to deny relief unless the decisions fall within one of the conditions in §2254(d)(1). Nothing in the example suggests that the state courts' decisions were "contrary to" or amounted to an "unreasonable application of" the 2005 decision. Accordingly, the district court should deny relief to Bethany.

As Examples 12-12, 12-13, and 12-14 show, the relationship between *Teague v. Lane* and §2254(d)(1) is both complicated and critical to the fortunes of individual federal habeas petitioners. The relationship is also key to identifying what broad categories of matters provide the basis for federal habeas relief after considering both *Teague v. Lane* and §2254(d)(1). Specifically, in terms of Figure 12-3, one needs to identify what type of habeas relief might survive in the gap between 28 U.S.C §2254(d)(1) and *Frank v. Mangum*.

What Remains in the Gap Between §2254(d)(1) and Frank v. Mangum?

- *Teague exceptions for new rules.* If a claim presents a new rule under *Teague*, then it might fall within one of the exceptions. If a claim does fall within an exception and is not excluded by §2254(d)(1), then the district court may provide relief on the basis of the claim.
- *Matters satisfying the conditions in* §2254(d)(1). If a claim is based on "clearly established Federal law" as announced by the United States Supreme Court and has been adjudicated by a state court, then a district court can issue habeas relief if the state court decision was "contrary to, or an unreasonable application of" that federal law.
- *Matters relating to old rules (non-new rules) that are not adjudicated by the state court.* Because the *Teague* doctrine applies only to claims based on new rules and §2254(d)(1) applies only to claims adjudicated by a state court, a claim that falls within neither *Teague* nor §2254(d)(1) may be within a district court's substantive scope of inquiry on habeas. In other words, a petitioner may be successful in getting federal habeas review of an old rule that was not adjudicated in state court. This suggests that the current state of the law preserves the notion from *Frank v. Mangum* that federal habeas review should be available if the state court system failed to provide an opportunity to litigate. But as demonstrated in the following section, the failure of the petitioner to litigate a claim in state court suggests that she may have defaulted on her opportunity to do so, thereby raising the question of procedural bar. Thus, although claims may be "in" for the purposes of the district court's substantive review, they are "out" for the purposes of the district court's approach to procedural default.

3. Procedural Bar: Under What Circumstances Will the Federal Court Excuse State Procedural Default?

As the United States Supreme Court does in reviewing state court judgments on direct appeal, federal district courts must consider whether they will allow state procedural rules to stand as obstacles to enforcing federal constitutional rights. If honored, a state procedural rule can act as an independent and adequate state ground supporting a conviction, shielding scrutiny of federal constitutional errors both on direct review in the United States Supreme Court and on habeas in the United States district courts. Defaults occur often, such as when a lawyer fails to object contemporaneously to introduction of evidence or fails to file a brief or a notice of appeal by a particular deadline. State courts may choose to forgive these errors, but if they don't, a defendant may not be able to get habeas review of her underlying federal claim.

In a line of cases parallel to those governing substantive scope of inquiry of cognizable claims, the United States Supreme Court has issued fluctuating edicts about the effect on federal habeas review of a petitioner's failure to comply with state procedural rules. While the procedural bar area similarly has case law representing the extremes of the spectrum, the movement in between these extremes has been less dynamic than in the area of cognizable claims.

a. The Ends of the Spectrum: *Daniels v. Allen* and *Fay v. Noia*

The bookends marking the extreme approaches to state procedural default are *Daniels v. Allen*, 344 U.S. 443 (1953), and *Fay v. Noia*, 372 U.S. 391 (1963). *Daniels v. Allen* issued a restrictive standard for federal habeas courts, while *Fay v. Noia* considerably widened the prerogative of district courts to ignore state procedural default.

In a relatively straightforward ruling, the Supreme Court in *Daniels v. Allen* directed federal district courts to honor a state court's finding of procedural default and to allow state procedural bars to shield habeas review. The Court explained that "[a] failure to use a state's available remedy, in the absence of some interference or incapacity . . . bars federal habeas corpus." 344 U.S. at 487. *Daniels* parallels the restrictive approach to substantive scope of inquiry reflected in *Frank v. Mangum*, 237 U.S. 309 (1915), by precluding federal review unless something is seriously wrong with the state process. *Daniels* focused on procedural flaws in the form of improper interference with the defendant's enjoyment of procedural rights or the defendant's incapacity.

Fay v. Noia concluded that constitutional claims should not remain insulated from federal court review on habeas simply because the defendant forfeited a state remedy by failing to comply with a state procedural rule. *Fay v. Noia* maintained that only where the defendant knowingly participated in the strategic decision not to pursue the state remedy should the procedural bar act as a shield to federal habeas review. As the Court explained, a habeas petitioner should be foreclosed from pursuing a federal claim not raised in state proceedings only if the petitioner "deliberately

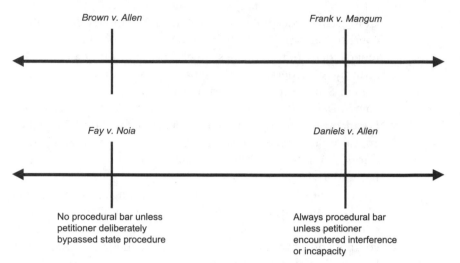

Figure 12-4. Parallel Spectrums for Procedural Bar and Cognizable Claims on Habeus Corpus.

by-passed the orderly procedure of the state courts." Fay, 372 U.S. at 438. (See Figure 12-4.)

b. Requiring Cause and Prejudice (or Actual Innocence): Wainwright v. Sykes

In *Wainwright v. Sykes*, 433 U.S. 72 (1977), the Court dramatically changed *Fay v. Noia*'s "deliberate bypass" standard, substantially narrowing the circumstances under which procedural default would be excused to allow for federal habeas review of constitutional claims. In *Sykes*, the Supreme Court noted that the particular procedural rule involved in the case — the contemporaneous objection rule — served important state interests, which were inadequately protected by the "deliberate bypass" standard. Accordingly, the *Sykes* Court required that a petitioner must live with the consequences of failure to comply with a state procedural rule unless she shows "cause" for having failed to raise the claim properly in state court and actual "prejudice" resulting from the default (see Figure 12-5).

The Court's reasoning in support of abandoning the "deliberate bypass" standard demonstrates the habeas corpus values that *Sykes* chose to serve:

- *Finality, accuracy of adjudication, and efficiency.* The Court reasoned that rules requiring defendants to raise their objections promptly ensure that all parties take stock of the strength of their cases, provide incentives to bring their full resources to bear at the time of trial, and allow the trial judge to cure mistakes during trial. The rules prevent conviction reversal and retrial — at which time the evidence may have grown stale and less probative compared with the initial trial. The "cause and prejudice" standard is therefore designed to make the product of the first trial more likely to remain final and intact.

- *State sovereignty.* The Court expressed concern that the "deliberate bypass" standard did not embody sufficient respect for state procedural systems. The "cause and prejudice" standard, on the other hand, ensures that state systems are honored unless the petitioner provides an adequate excuse for failing to follow the rules that keep the systems running effectively.[33]
- *Institutional integrity.* The *Sykes* Court expressed concern that the "deliberate bypass" standard inspired a "gaming" approach to criminal defense, demonstrating disrespect for the criminal justice institution. Specifically, the Court reasoned, the "deliberate bypass" standard "may encourage 'sandbagging' on the part of defense lawyers, who may take their chances on a verdict of not guilty in a state trial court with the intent to raise their constitutional claims in a federal habeas court if their initial gamble does not pay off."[34]

As illustrated in Figure 12-1, other values are relevant to habeas corpus relief that the *Sykes* court did integrate into its calculus. On the same day that it decided *Sykes*, however, the Court decided related cases that injected another habeas value into the procedural bar equation: *avoiding confinement of the innocent.* These cases, *Murray v. Carrier*, 477 U.S. 478 (1986), and *Smith v. Murray*, 477 U.S. 527 (1986), are discussed next.

i. Defining Actual Innocence

When it decided *Sykes*, the Supreme Court in *Murray v. Carrier*, 477 U.S. 478 (1986), and *Smith v. Murray*, 477 U.S. 527 (1986), established another avenue that a federal habeas court could use to excuse a state procedural default: the petitioner's innocence. These cases established that the federal habeas court can review a defaulted federal claim if the petitioner shows that the federal error that went uncorrected in state court "probably resulted in the conviction of one who is actually innocent." *Carrier*, 477 U.S. at 496. The Court explained that comity and federalism " 'must yield to the imperative of correcting a fundamentally unjust incarceration.' " *Id.* at 495 (quoting *Engle v. Isaac*, 456 U.S. 107, 135 (1982)). Implementing this general principle, the Court has "held that prisoners asserting innocence as a gateway to defaulted claims must establish that, in light of new evidence, 'it is more likely than not that no reasonable juror would have found petitioner

---

33. In *Lambrix v. Singletary*, 520 U.S. 518, 523 (1997), the Court explained that the "cause and prejudice" standard applies in the interests of "federalism and comity."
34. 433 U.S. at 89.

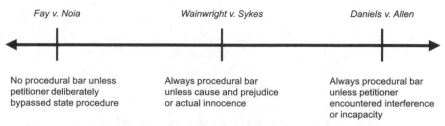

Figure 12-5. Standards for Honoring Procedural Bar on Habeus Corpus

guilty beyond a reasonable doubt.'" *House v. Bell*, 126 S. Ct. 2064, 2076-77 (2006) (quoting *Schulp v. Delo*, 513 U.S. 298, 327 (1995)). The Court found this standard to be satisfied in *House v. Bell*, where the petitioner found new DNA evidence that contradicted evidence at trial and helped support the inference that another suspect committed the crime. The *House v. Bell* Court did not require that the new evidence conclusively exonerate the prisoner, only that it tip the balance of conflicting evidence toward making it "more likely than not that no reasonable juror viewing the record as a whole would lack reasonable doubt." 126 S. Ct. at 2086.

Example 12-15

Delia knew that her friend Sandra was being sexually abused by her (Sandra's) father and that he had threatened to kill Sandra if she ever told anyone. Delia wanted to protect her friend from further abuse, but feared that the police would not believe her or would stall if she merely called them, thus raising the possibility that Sandra's father would make good on his threat. Delia therefore trapped the father, bound him in duct tape, dropped him at the woods, and called the police to give them his location and relate the details of his sexual assaults. The police identified Delia and arrested her for aggravated kidnapping. At trial, she raised the defense of necessity, arguing that the kidnapping was necessary to protect her friend. The prosecutor argued that there was "no way" that Sandra's father posed a threat to his daughter on the day Delia kidnapped him. The jury convicted Delia, and she appealed through the state court system.

On post-conviction review in the state courts, Delia argued that she was entitled to a new trial on the basis of exculpatory evidence that the prosecutor failed to turn over to her: the day after she kidnapped Sandra's father, the very same prosecutor who prosecuted Delia had secured a restraining order against the father to prevent further sexual assault. In obtaining the restraining order, the prosecutor averred that Sandra's father posed an imminent threat to the safety and security of Sandra. As the basis for her new trial request, Delia argues that the prosecutor's failure to turn over this evidence violated her Fourteenth Amendment due process rights under *Brady v. Maryland*, 373 U.S. 83 (1963). The state courts refused her request for a new trial, stating that the claim was procedurally barred.

Delia filed a habeas corpus petition, asserting that her failure to raise the *Brady v. Maryland* claim earlier should be excused because the withheld evidence established that she was actually innocent of the crime convicted. Delia argued that although she committed the physical act of kidnapping, she did not have the mental state required to establish the crime of kidnapping. Should the district court accept her argument?

Explanation

Yes, the district court should probably accept this argument. The evidence of the restraining order is highly probative of Delia's necessity defense. While the evidence does not make Delia's acquittal a foregone conclusion, that type of certainty is not required. The evidence would have significantly bolstered Delia's necessity defense and prevented the prosecutor from arguing that there was "no way" the father would harm his daughter on the day Delia kidnapped him. In addition, the jury may have been more dubious of the prosecutor's kidnapping case against Delia had they known that the very same prosecutor had credited Delia's assertion of danger to Sandra. As such, the withheld evidence makes it "more likely than not that no reasonable juror would have found petitioner guilty beyond a reasonable doubt." *Schulp v. Delo*, 513 U.S. 298, 327 (1995). *See Finley v. Johnson*, 243 F.3d 215 (5th Cir. 2001).

Meeting the standard for actual innocence, however, does not entitle Delia to instant freedom; she has simply used the actual innocence claim as a "gateway"[35] to habeas consideration of her defaulted *Brady* claim. The habeas court may ultimately deny her *Brady* claim on the merits.

ii. Defining Cause

To establish "cause" for failure to comply with a state procedural rule, the habeas petitioner must show that "some objective factor external to the defense impeded counsel's efforts to comply with the State's procedural rule." *Carrier*, 477 U.S. at 488. A petitioner may satisfy this standard by showing that counsel's inability to comply with a procedural rule (1) resulted from official interference, making compliance impracticable; (2) resulted from counsel's lacking reasonable access to legal or factual basis for a claim; or (3) resulted from legal representation that was so fundamentally incompetent and prejudicial as to constitute ineffective assistance of counsel.

Example 12-16

Recall the facts of Example 12-15, in which Delia was convicted for kidnapping Sandra's abusive father. For the purposes of this example, it

---

35. *House*, 126 S. Ct. at 2076-77.

was on post-conviction review in the state courts that Delia argued that she was entitled to a new trial on the basis of exculpatory evidence that the prosecutor failed to turn over to her. As in Example 12-15, the exculpatory evidence consisted of a restraining order that the prosecutor procured the day after the kidnapping. As the basis for her new trial request, Delia argues that the prosecutor's failure to turn over this evidence violated her Fourteenth Amendment due process rights under *Brady v. Maryland*, 373 U.S. 83 (1963). The state courts refused her request, stating that the *Brady* claim was procedurally barred.

In Example 12-15, Delia asserted a compelling argument that her failure to raise the claim before should be excused because the evidence of the restraining order significantly bolstered Delia's necessity defense and prevented the prosecutor from arguing that there was "no way" the father would harm his daughter on the day Delia kidnapped him. Delia used this theory to support her "actual innocence" as a reason for the federal court to forgive the default. Rather than invoking "actual innocence," could Delia have relied on the "cause" standard to excuse her failure to bring the *Brady* claim earlier?

Explanation

Yes, Delia might have relied on the "cause" standard to justify her failure to bring the *Brady* claim earlier. To use the "cause" standard, however, Delia would have to demonstrate that she could not have reasonably known of the restraining order at the time of her procedural default. (This obligation makes the "cause" standard more onerous to satisfy under the circumstances of this case than the "actual innocence" standard.) If Delia can show that she did not know of the protective order at the time of her procedural default, and could not have reasonably known of it, she has likely established cause for the failure to make her *Brady* claim earlier. Delia could strengthen this "cause" argument by pointing out the prosecutor apparently withheld evidence of the protective order, which suggests official interference with Delia's defense. *See Strickler v. Greene*, 527 U.S. 263, 296 (1999) (finding "cause" established where prosecutor's concealment of evidence constituted external impediment to compliance with state procedural rule); *Paradis v. Arave*, 130 F.3d 385, 394 (9th Cir. 1997) (finding that where outside factors prevented petitioner from bringing *Brady* claim in kidnapping case, "cause" standard was satisfied).

By relying on "cause" rather than "actual innocence," Delia has another element to prove before she can satisfy the federal court's criteria for excusing her procedural default. Before the federal court reaches the merits of her *Brady* claim, Delia must demonstrate that she suffered prejudice from the default. The requirements of this "prejudice" standard are discussed below.

When relying on an unavailable legal foundation as an excuse, petitioners often argue that their counsel did not raise particular claims because they did not anticipate changes in the law. While popular, this argument is far from an automatic ticket to habeas relief. First, the Supreme Court has stated that defense attorneys must use available legal "tools" to identify claims and are not excused from raising them simply because precedent suggests they will not succeed. *Engle v. Isaac*, 456 U.S. 107, 131-133 (1982). Moreover, the Supreme Court has ruled that the mere fact that a claim relies on new Supreme Court authority is not sufficient to excuse procedural default, unless the claim " 'is so novel that its legal basis [was] not reasonably available to counsel' " at the time it should have been raised. *Bousley v. United States*, 523 U.S. 614, 622 (1998) (quoting *Reed v. Ross*, 468 U.S. 1, 16 (1984)). Finally—and perhaps most significant—petitioners are often tempted to argue that the law changed unexpectedly and that they could not anticipate a novel claim. In doing so, however, they create problems for themselves under *Teague v. Lane*, 489 U.S. 288 (1989).

Example 12-17

Isabella was convicted in 2004. Her conviction became final when the United States Supreme Court denied her petition for a writ of certiorari in her case in 2005. She began post-conviction proceedings in state court in 2006. While these proceedings were pending, the Supreme Court decided a case that interpreted prior precedent to cover different factual circumstances than those previously recognized. In her post-conviction proceedings in state court, Isabella included a claim based on this 2006 Supreme Court decision. The state courts, however, all ruled that the claim was procedurally barred under state law because of Isabella's failure to raise the claim earlier.

In 2007 Isabella filed a federal habeas corpus petition including the claim based on the 2006 Supreme Court decision. She argued that the district court should excuse her procedural default because the claim is novel and her counsel would have had to be extraordinarily prescient to have anticipated the 2006 decision. Will this argument make it more likely that Isabella will obtain habeas relief on the basis of the claim?

Explanation

This argument will not necessarily enhance Isabella's chances of obtaining habeas relief. She is correct in suggesting that the argument will help her establish cause for her procedural default. The problem, however, is that—in arguing that the claim is novel—she is setting up a *Teague v. Lane* problem. Thus, she may succeed in navigating the procedural bar obstacles to habeas relief, only to talk her way into another problem: a district court decision that she does not get the benefit of the claim because the 2006 Supreme Court decision announced a new rule after her conviction became final on direct review.

iii. Defining Prejudice

To establish the "prejudice" prong of the "cause and prejudice" standard, the petitioner must show that the default worked to "his *actual* and substantial disadvantage, infecting his entire trial with error of constitutional dimensions." *United States v. Frady*, 456 U.S. 152, 170 (1982) (emphasis in original). This suggests that the mere possibility of prejudice is not sufficient, and that the petitioner must generally show that the alleged constitutional error influenced the outcome of the state proceedings.

Example 12-18

Consider again the facts of Example 12-15 and Example 12-16, concerning Delia's kidnapping conviction. As in Example 12-16, on post-conviction review in the state courts Delia argued that she was entitled to a new trial on the basis of exculpatory evidence that the prosecutor failed to turn over to her. As before, the exculpatory evidence consisted of a restraining order that the prosecutor procured the day after the kidnapping. As the basis for her new trial request, Delia argues that the prosecutor's failure to turn over this evidence violated her Fourteenth Amendment due process rights under *Brady v. Maryland*, 373 U.S. 83 (1963). The state courts refused her request, stating that the *Brady* claim was procedurally barred.

The explanation for Example 12-16 concluded that Delia had established "cause" for her failure to raise the claim before. If she relies on this "cause" theory to excuse her failure to raise the claim earlier, Delia also must satisfy the "prejudice" standard. Will she satisfy the "prejudice" standard?

Explanation

Delia may in fact succeed in satisfying the "prejudice" standard, although she carries a heavy burden: she must demonstrate that the prosecutor's failure to turn over the restraining order evidence infected her trial with error of constitutional dimension. Moreover, in the specific context of establishing prejudice from failing to raise a *Brady* claim, the Supreme Court has held that the petitioner must convince the district court that " 'a reasonable probability' " exists "that the result of the trial would have been different if the suppressed [evidence] had been disclosed to the defense. . . . 'The question is not whether the defendant would more likely than not have received a different verdict with the evidence, but whether in its absence he received a fair trial, understood as a trial resulting in a verdict worthy of confidence.'" *Strickler v. Greene*, 527 U.S. 263, 289-290 (1999) (quoting *Kyles v. Whitley*, 514 U.S. 419, 434 (1995)).

As demonstrated in the Example 12-15 discussion of "actual innocence," Delia can make a salient argument as to why she would have been acquitted had the jury heard evidence of the restraining order: the evidence would have significantly bolstered Delia's necessity defense, would have prevented the prosecutor from arguing that there was "no way" the father would harm his daughter on the day Delia kidnapped him, and would have generally undercut the credibility of the prosecutor's case. The Supreme Court has framed the standard for "prejudice" in the procedural bar context differently than the standard for "actual innocence." Nonetheless, Delia has a strong foundation for establishing prejudice, particularly given the Supreme Court's emphasis on the fairness of the trial. The prosecutor's failure to disclose the restraining order was duplicitous conduct that could threaten the district court's faith in the integrity of the trial process and the accuracy of the verdict.

iv. Procedural Default under the AEDPA

Courts and scholars generally agree that the *Sykes* "cause and prejudice" standard survived the enactment of the Anti-Terrorism and Effective Death Penalty Act of 1996 (AEDPA). The statute does provide special rules for death penalty cases in states that establish a sufficient system for providing indigent death row prisoners with adequate counsel in state post-conviction proceedings. These special procedural default rules are similar to the *Sykes* standard, essentially codifying various circumstances where the Supreme Court has found sufficient "cause" for a procedural default. Not all states, however, have been deemed qualified to apply the special rules for capital defendants.

4. Other Limitations on Habeas Review

Although they serve as the main battlefields for federal habeas corpus, substantive scope of review and procedural bar rules are not the only habeas requirements stimulating debate and litigation. Among the other important limitations for federal habeas are the exhaustion requirement, restrictions on reexamining factual findings, statutes of limitations, and the prohibition on successive petitions.

a. Exhaustion Requirements

A long-standing rule designed to ensure proper deference for state sovereignty, the exhaustion rule requires that a habeas petitioner avail herself of state remedies before pursuing federal habeas relief. This ensures that state courts are given the opportunity to correct errors before federal courts "interfere" with the case.

The exhaustion requirement means that many state prisoners will have litigated through the state system twice, once on direct review and once on collateral attack, before initiating federal habeas proceedings. To satisfy the exhaustion requirement for a claim, petitioners must have fairly identified the nature of the federal claim in litigating before the state courts, giving them a genuine opportunity to dispose of the claim. A key to the exhaustion rule, however, is that the petitioner need only exhaust state remedies still available. Thus, if a particular state remedy is foreclosed for failure to comply with state procedure, the petitioner may have a procedural bar problem but not an exhaustion problem.

Among the myriad complexities governing exhaustion is the "mixed petition" rule: federal district courts must dismiss petitions containing claims for which the petitioner has exhausted her state remedies as well as "unexhausted" claims. If the petitioner does not wish to risk abandoning her "unexhausted" claims for all purposes, she must return to state court to litigate them.[36]

The Anti-Terrorism and Effective Death Penalty Act of 1996 (AEDPA) provided some exceptions to the exhaustion requirement, stating that district courts may ignore failure to exhaust and in fact should treat certain unexhausted claims as properly before the court in death penalty cases. In addition, AEDPA allows state attorneys to waive the exhaustion requirement if they do so expressly. While these provisions are helpful to habeas petitioners, the exhaustion requirement continues to impose a considerable burden on them.

Example 12-19

Luke was convicted. At trial and throughout his direct appeal proceedings, he argued that a confession introduced at trial was coerced in violation of his Fifth Amendment rights. Luke missed the filing dates for his appeal to the state supreme court. Under state law, his failure to pursue this appeal foreclosed all further opportunity to pursue a state court remedy on this claim. Luke subsequently discovered, however, exculpatory evidence unrelated to the confession, which he would have introduced at trial to establish his innocence. Although state law allows him to test the newly discovered evidence claim in collateral proceedings before state court, Luke chose instead to combine the newly discovered evidence claim with the Fifth

---

36. See *infra* the following section on statutes of limitations for discussion of a practice for dealing with mixed petitions known as "stay and abey."

Amendment coerced-confession claim in a habeas corpus petition filed in federal district court. Does the district court have power to hear both claims?

Explanation

Technically speaking, the district court has *jurisdiction* to hear both claims. Nevertheless, Luke's petition has problems with exhaustion, a strict requirement binding federal district courts on habeas.

Luke's Fifth Amendment claim is exhausted. His failure to file the appeal on time may present a serious procedural default problem but not an exhaustion problem. Luke has not, however, exhausted all available state remedies on his newly discovered evidence claim. Accordingly, the claim is not exhausted, and Luke's petition is "mixed." Luke therefore has a dilemma: he can proceed in federal court on his Fifth Amendment claim, but if he does so, he risks being barred from subsequently pursuing his "newly discovered evidence" claim. His other alternative is to delay pursuing his Fifth Amendment claim until he exhausts his state court remedies on his "newly discovered evidence" claim.

b. Limitations on Reexamining Factual Findings

The claims brought by state prisoners do not usually arrive as questions of law. They are often fact-specific, sometimes turning on facts discovered subsequent to trial and appeal. The Supreme Court weeds out so-called fact-bound cases when it chooses what to take on direct review or beyond, but district courts evaluating habeas petitions do not have that prerogative. Moreover, habeas petitioners often take issue with the factual finding of state courts. In struggling to instruct district courts grappling with the fact-laden habeas claims, the Supreme Court and Congress have balanced the habeas values of *honoring constitutional values, accuracy of adjudication,* and *avoiding confinement of the innocent* on one hand; and *finality, efficiency,* and *state sovereignty* on the other.

The Supreme Court in *Townsend v. Sain,* 372 U.S. 293 (1963), authorized federal habeas courts to engage in independent factual determinations in several specific instances. AEDPA narrowed the range of circumstances calling for federal habeas courts to scrutinize state court factual findings. First, 28 U.S.C. §2254(e)(1) provides that "a determination of a factual issue made by a State shall be presumed to be correct." The provision adds that a petitioner may rebut the presumption, but only "by clear and convincing evidence." Another provision, 28 U.S.C. §2254(d)(2), allows federal courts to award habeas relief if a prior state court adjudication "resulted in a decision that was based on an unreasonable determination of the facts in light of the evidence presented in the State court proceeding." In applying this standard, the Supreme Court made clear that it does not allow habeas courts to make an independent judgment about credibility, even where the record suggests that "reasonable minds" could "disagree" about the credibility determination.[37]

The decision to defer to state court judgments concerning witness credibility reflects a consistent view of habeas policy to avoid waste and insult to state courts. As illustrated in Example 12-20, however, the balance of habeas values shifts for mixed questions of law and fact.

Example 12-20

Lydia was arrested for homicide, taken to the police station, and questioned without a lawyer. She ultimately confessed to the crime. At trial, she argued to the state trial court that the confession should not be introduced because it was involuntary and therefore invalid under the Fourteenth Amendment. The state trial court held a hearing to determine whether the confession was voluntary. Lydia testified at the hearing that she was questioned for eight hours without being offered food or drink, but the police said the questioning lasted only three hours and that she was repeatedly offered refreshments. The trial court determined that Lydia's testimony was not credible because she likely lost track of time during the questioning, and she had a self-serving reason to exaggerate or lie about whether she was offered food or drink.

On appeal and on post-conviction proceedings in state court, the state courts rejected Lydia's involuntariness claim. On federal habeas, she again challenged the determination that she gave her confession voluntarily. She maintained that the trial court erred in crediting the police officers' testimony over her own, since the police officers themselves had a self-serving reason to exaggerate or lie about how they conducted the questioning. The state argued that the federal district court should defer to the state court's determination that the confession was given freely, using the presumption of correctness from §2254(e)(1). Is the state correct?

Explanation

No, the state is not correct that the court should treat the question of voluntariness to be a question of fact, subject to the presumption of correctness in the habeas statute. The Supreme Court rejected that position in *Miller v. Fenton*, 474 U.S. 104 (1985), holding that a state court's determination that a confession was voluntarily given is subject to plenary review on

---

37. *Rice v. Collins*, 126 S. Ct. 969, 974 (2006) (rejecting federal habeas court's decision to reject credibility of prosecutor's race-neutral explanation for striking African-American juror). The term before it decided *Rice v. Collins*, the Supreme Court handed down a decision authorizing a more searching approach to a credibility determination in the same context. *Miller-El v. Dretke*, 545 U.S. 231 (2005).

federal habeas. That does not necessarily mean, however, that the district court will revisit the credibility determinations as Lydia would like.

In *Miller v. Fenton*, the Court emphasized that confessions are generally crucial evidence of guilt for the prosecutor, and at the same time implicate fundamental protections for the accused. Emphasizing the role of habeas in ensuring that the innocent are not confined and the importance of honoring constitutional guarantees, the Supreme Court noted state court judges' "inevitable and understandable reluctance to exclude an otherwise reliable admission of guilt" as well as the elevated "risk that erroneous resolution of the voluntariness question might inadvertently frustrate the protection of the federal right." 474 U.S. at 117.

The *Miller v. Fenton* Court nonetheless recognized that, although the ultimate issue of voluntariness should be treated as a legal determination, underlying questions about precisely what happened at the interrogation are questions of fact to which the habeas court must accord a presumption of correctness. As illustrations of such "subsidiary questions," the Court listed "the length and circumstances of the interrogation, the defendant's prior experience with the legal process, and familiarity with the *Miranda* warnings." *Id.*

The Supreme Court has not suggested that AEDPA's changes in the law call for abandoning the practice of treating subsidiary matters as "facts" subject to the presumption of correctness. Nor have the lower federal courts.[38] Indeed, AEDPA injected an even stricter approach to deference to state court factfinding than previously prevailed.[39] This is not good news for Lydia, whose basis for challenging the voluntariness determination turns on an underlying credibility question about what happened during the interrogation. Given the Supreme Court's emphasis on discouraging habeas courts from second-guessing credibility determinations under AEDPA,

---

38. Lower federal courts have consistently adhered to the guidelines set forth in *Miller v. Fenton* after AEDPA was enacted. *See Lambert v. Blodgett*, 393 F.3d 943, 976-977 (9th Cir. 2004) (discussing that state factual findings in mixed questions of law and fact are presumed correct); *Coombs v. Maine*, 202 F.3d 14, 18 (1st Cir. 2000) (applying strong deference to state court's credibility determination involving petitioner's confession); *Brown v. Phillips*, No. 03-CV-0361, 2006 U.S. Dist. LEXIS 14018, at *10-17 (E.D.N.Y. Feb. 17, 2006) (deferring to state factfinding and undergoing independent analysis of voluntariness issue); *Duran v. Miller*, 322 F. Supp. 2d 251, 255-257 (E.D.N.Y. 2004) (noting that petitioner did not challenge the voluntariness of his confession in Spanish, only the accuracy of the translation of his confession, and thus there was a presumption of correctness of state court's factual findings); *Crenshaw v. Renico*, 261 F. Supp. 2d 826, 836 (E.D. Mich. 2003) (stating that voluntariness of a confession is a mixed question of law and fact, and reviewing state court record for totality of circumstances); *Kirk v. Carroll*, 243 F. Supp. 2d 125, 134-135 (D. Del. 2003) (presuming correctness of state court factual findings but reviewing de novo the voluntariness of confession).
39. *Gachot v. Stadler*, 298 F.3d 414, 418 n.1 (5th Cir. 2002) (asserting that AEDPA requires an even stronger deference to state court factfinding).

Lydia will likely not convince the habeas court to grant relief by arguing that the state court erred in crediting the police testimony over her own.

c. Statutes of Limitations

An innovation of AEDPA is the creation of formal statutes of limitation for filing federal habeas claims. Codified in 28 U.S.C. §2244, the statute requires state prisoners to file habeas corpus petitions within one year of completing direct review.[40] The statute contains a number of exceptions to this one-year limit, including (1) a tolling provision for the time the petitioner properly pursues state post-conviction proceedings, (2) a tolling provision for the time during which prisoners have encountered an unlawful impediment to asserting their rights, and (3) extra time to file a petition if the United States Supreme Court makes a new constitutional right retroactive for habeas petitioners.

The statute of limitations is motivated by efficiency and institutional integrity concerns and is designed in part to discourage delay tactics and "eleventh hour" habeas petitions filed on behalf of prisoners facing imminent execution. The provisions threaten forfeiture of claims for all prisoners. The Supreme Court, however, has taken a relatively strict approach to interpreting the statute of limitations. For example, the Court has instructed district courts to inquire into the timeliness of petitions on their own initiative[41] and has applied forgiveness rules for late petitions narrowly.[42]

An important area where the Court has taken a middle ground concerns "mixed" petitions with exhausted and unexhausted claims. For petitioners who choose to return to state court to litigate unexhausted claims identified by federal habeas courts, the one-year statute of limitations provision might threaten to extinguish exhausted claims pending the state court proceedings. The Supreme Court endorsed a practice developed by lower federal courts of staying petitions with mixed claims and holding the petitions in abeyance (thereby tolling the statute of limitations) while petitioners litigate the unexhausted claims in state court.[43] The Supreme Court made clear, however, that the district courts should use this power to "stay and abey" sparingly.

d. Limitations on Successive Petitions

For those who hold out habeas as an instrument to ensure that government must always stand ready to justify the continuation of a prisoner's detention,

---

40. AEDPA provides separate statute of limitations periods for federal prisoners (28 U.S.C. §2255) and for state prisoners under a death penalty in states that have been deemed to comply with certain requirements for counsel in post-conviction proceedings.
41. *See Day v. McDonough*, 126 S. Ct. 1675 (2006).
42. *See Pace v. DiGuglielmo*, 544 U.S. 408 (2005).
43. *Rhines v. Weber*, 544 U.S. 269 (2005).

preclusion rules that restrict multiple filings have no place in federal habeas law. This view has not, however, carried the day. With the values of *efficiency* and *finality* dominating the analysis, case law and statutory law restrict second or successive federal petitions. The Supreme Court has come to view multiple petitions as "abuse of the writ," mandating that a district court should dismiss claims in successive petitions unless the petitioner satisfies the standard of "cause and prejudice" under *Wainwright v. Sykes*, 433 U.S. 72 (1977), justifying failure to raise the claims earlier on federal habeas.[44]

AEDPA narrows the circumstances in which a habeas court may hear successive petitions to more specific situations, thus strengthening the prohibition. Under §2244(b)(2) a claim raised for the first time in a second or later petition may be considered only if (1) the claim rests "on a new rule of constitutional law, made retroactive" on habeas or (2) the following two conditions are met: (a) "the factual predicate for the claim could not have been discovered" earlier by "the exercise of due diligence" and (b) "the factual predicate, . . . if proven and viewed in light of the evidence as a whole, would be sufficient to establish by clear and convincing evidence that, but for constitutional error, no reasonable factfinder would have found the applicant guilty of the underlying offense."

What is perhaps more significant, AEDPA creates a detailed procedure whereby a petitioner wishing to file a subsequent petition must first seek leave to file from a court of appeals. Thus, the petitioner may not follow the usual course of filing the petition in district court. The statute is apparently designed to make the court of appeals ruling final on whether the petitioner can proceed with the claim. Nevertheless, the United States Supreme Court, in an important case concerning congressional control of its jurisdiction, held that a habeas petitioner could seek the Court's review.[45]

B. THE *ROOKER-FELDMAN* DOCTRINE: PROTECTING THE SUPREME COURT'S REVIEW POWER

In terms of district court power, habeas corpus is an exception. The structure of our dual system of litigation presumes generally that the United States Supreme Court — and only the United States Supreme Court — directly reviews state court judgments. And the Supreme Court has kept it that way, setting off habeas corpus as the only context in which United States district courts directly review state court judgments.

---

44. *McCleskey v. Zant*, 499 U.S. 467 (1991).
45. See the discussion of *Felker v. Turpin*, 518 U.S 651 (1996), in Chapter 6.

The principle that district courts may not perform appellate review of state court decisions — known as the *Rooker-Feldman* doctrine — derives from two Supreme Court cases. In *Rooker v. Fidelity Trust Co.*, 263 U.S. 413 (1923), plaintiffs asked the district court to declare a state court judgment "null and void." The Supreme Court prohibited this, ruling that federal district courts have no jurisdiction to "entertain a proceeding to reverse or modify" a state court judgment. *Id.* at 416. Reinforcing this position in *District of Columbia Court of Appeals v. Feldman*, 460 U.S. 462, 482 (1983), the Supreme Court held that a district court lacks "authority to review final judgments of a state court in judicial proceedings." This holding established that the state proceedings must be judicial in nature — not legislative — for the doctrine's prohibition on district courts to apply. The *Feldman* Court also stated that the prohibition extends to circumstances where the lower federal court is asked to adjudicate a claim that is not identical to the claim litigated in state court, but is "inextricably intertwined" with a state court judgment. *Id.* at 483 n.16. Significantly, the *Rooker-Feldman* doctrine addresses the district court's subject matter jurisdiction, and therefore can be raised by the court on its own motion.

For many years after the Supreme Court announced the *Rooker-Feldman* doctrine, critics argued that the doctrine duplicates the law governing the "full faith and credit" and preclusion doctrines. Indeed, the "full faith and credit" statute, 28 U.S.C. §1738, commands federal courts to accord a state court judgment the same force and effect that the state court would accord the judgment. Where litigants institute federal proceedings while a state court action is pending, preclusion principles provide the appropriate tool for analyzing the effect on the federal court litigation of a judgment ultimately rendered in the state court action. This requires the lower federal courts to apply preclusion principles at the behest of a party, and foreclose litigation, if the state court would do so.

The Supreme Court helped to separate the *Rooker-Feldman* doctrine and preclusion principles in *Exxon Mobil Corp. v. Saudi Basic Indus. Corp.*, 544 U.S. 280 (2005). The holding of *Exxon Mobil* was narrow: the *Rooker-Feldman* doctrine is confined to instances where the state court rendered a final judgment *before* the federal action commenced. As stated by the *Exxon Mobil* Court, the doctrine applies only to "cases brought by state-court losers complaining of injuries caused by state-court judgments rendered before the district court proceedings commenced and inviting district court review and rejection of those judgments." 544 U.S. at 284.[46]

---

46. The Supreme Court continued the process of separating preclusion principles in *Lance v. Dennis*, 126 S. Ct. 1198, 1202 (2006), holding that the *Rooker-Feldman* doctrine does not bar federal actions "by nonparties to the earlier state-court judgment simply because, for purposes of preclusion law, they could be considered in privity with a party to the judgment."

Example 12-21

Yoko filed suit in state court, alleging a state fraud claim against Margaret. Yoko then filed suit in federal court, alleging that Margaret's fraudulent actions constituted a violation of federal securities fraud statutes. Yoko then moved to amend her state court complaint to add the federal securities fraud claim. The state court denied the motion to amend, stating that the claim lacked merit. The state court action on the state law fraud claim continued.

Margaret filed a motion to dismiss the federal court complaint on the basis of the *Rooker-Feldman* doctrine. She argued that Yoko will be using the federal action as a means to get immediate review of the state court decision that the federal securities claim lacks merit. That task, Margaret maintained, is only for the United States Supreme Court, which is empowered to review a direct appeal of the final judgment rendered by the state trial court and appealed through the state system. Is Margaret correct that the district court should dismiss the lawsuit on the basis of the *Rooker-Feldman* doctrine?

Explanation

No, Margaret is not correct. As explained in *Exxon Mobil*, the *Rooker-Feldman* doctrine does not apply simply because the state court has entered a judgment of some kind when state and federal litigation is pending. Rather, under the *Exxon Mobil* holding, the *Rooker-Feldman* doctrine requires that four conditions be met: (1) the federal action is brought by the state court loser, (2) the loser is complaining about the state court judgment, (3) the state court judgment was rendered before federal proceedings commenced, and (4) the federal action requests the district court to review and reject the state court judgment. 544 U.S. at 284. Because the state action is not complete, a question exists as to whether the state court's ruling constitutes a "judgment" for the purpose of the *Rooker-Feldman*. That issue need not be settled in this example,[47] however, since the third element of the *Exxon Mobil* holding is clearly missing here: the federal action began before the state court ruled on the securities claim. Thus, to the extent that Margaret can preclude federal litigation, her tools are the preclusion and "full faith and credit" doctrines, not the jurisdictional provisions of *Rooker-Feldman*.

Example 12-22

As in Example 12-21, Yoko filed suit in state court, presenting a state fraud claim against Margaret. In this example, however, Yoko next moved to amend her state court complaint to add a securities fraud claim under

---

47. See Example 12-22 for a discussion of this issue.

federal law. The state court denied the motion to amend, ruling that the claim lacked merit. The state court action continued to proceed on the state fraud claim. It was then that Yoko filed suit in federal court, alleging that Margaret's fraudulent actions constituted a violation of federal securities fraud statutes. As in Example 12-21, Margaret filed a motion to dismiss the federal court complaint on the basis of the *Rooker-Feldman* doctrine.

This example differs from Example 12-21 because Yoko filed the federal action after the state court ruled on the motion to amend. Does this difference in timing for filing the federal action change the disposition of Margaret's argument?

Explanation

The weight of authority suggests that the later filing of the federal action does not change the disposition of Margaret's argument: she still loses and the federal court action continues. The issue of whether *Rooker-Feldman* divests the federal district court of jurisdiction, however, is not an easy one.

As for the four conditions of the *Exxon Mobil* holding, the first condition is met: Yoko was the loser in state court for the purpose of the federal securities claim. The second and third conditions may not be met: the state court proceedings were still pending when the federal action was brought, and the dismissal of the complaint was arguably only an interlocutory order. It is true that the state court dismissed the federal claim before the federal action was filed, but the state court order is not necessarily a "judgment" within the meaning of *Exxon Mobil*. In evaluating this concern, however, one should note that *Exxon Mobil* does not specify that the state judgment needs to be "final." Moreover, before *Exxon Mobil*, several courts had held that the *Rooker-Feldman* doctrine bars federal court review of state court interlocutory orders.[48] At least one analogous case after *Exxon Mobil*, however, holds otherwise, ruling that *Rooker-Feldman* does not bar the federal litigation under circumstances similar to those of this example.[49]

The final *Exxon Mobil* condition may not be met here as well. That condition requires that the federal action request the district court to

---

48. *See, e.g., Brown & Root, Inc. v. Breckenridge*, 211 F.3d 194, 199 (4th Cir. 2000) (stating that Congress has empowered federal district courts to exercise only original jurisdiction. "'[I]t cannot be the meaning of *Rooker-Feldman* that, while inferior courts are barred from reviewing final decisions of state courts, they are free to review interlocutory orders'" (quoting *Doctor's Assocs., Inc. v. Distajo*, 107 F.3d 126, 138 (2d Cir. 1997))).

49. *RegScan, Inc. v. Brewer*, No. Cv. A. 04-6043, 2005 U.S. Dist. LEXIS 6510, at *6-8 (E.D. Pa. Apr. 13, 2005) (holding that state court's denial of a motion to amend complaint to add the federal claim did not support the *Rooker-Feldman* doctrine in the parallel federal suit because the state court had not entered a "judgment"). *See, e.g.,* Thomas D. Rowe, Jr. & Edward L. Baskauskas, "*Inextricably Intertwined*" Explicable at Last? Rooker-Feldman *Analysis After the Supreme Court's* Exxon Mobil *Decision*," 2006 FED. CTS. L. REV. 1 (arguing in favor of the *Rooker-Feldman* doctrine applying to interlocutory orders).

review and reject the state court judgment. Assuming that the state court's interlocutory order dismissing the complaint constitutes a "state court judgment" for the purpose of this condition, one might still doubt whether the federal action actually "requests" the district court to review and reject the state court judgment. This doubt raises the question of how far — after *Exxon Mobil* — the *Rooker-Feldman* doctrine extends to bar claims that are "inextricably intertwined" with state court judgments. Commentators conclude that the "inextricably intertwined" concept survives *Exxon Mobil*.[50] Nevertheless, *Exxon Mobil's* attempt to narrow *Rooker-Feldman* suggests that the concept should not be read expansively. Here, the state court dismissed the federal claim in the context of refusing a motion to amend a *state court* complaint. Although the state court may have disapproved the federal claim in the process of denying the motion, factors bearing on state pleading law and concerns unique to state court litigation likely influenced the court's decision. Thus, although the state court's ruling is directly relevant to the federal lawsuit, one cannot say with certainty that the state court decision was designed to reach the very task asked of the federal district court in Yoko's lawsuit: adjudicate a federal law claim in federal court. For that reason, the fourth condition from the *Exxon Mobil* holding is not satisfied, and *Rooker-Feldman* should not bar jurisdiction in Yoko's federal suit.

Uncertainties about the scope of the *Rooker-Feldman* doctrine remain after *Exxon Mobil*. The tone of the case, however, suggests that one should avoid creative use of the doctrine, reading it to limit district court jurisdiction only in cases clearly governed by the *Exxon Mobil* holding. For more complicated issues, other principles relating to parallel litigation — including "full faith and credit" and abstention doctrines — provide tools to avoid injustice and interference with state prerogatives.[51]

---

50. *See, e.g.,* Thomas J. Rowe, Jr. & Edward L. Baskauskas, *"Inextricably Intertwined" Explicable at Last? Rooker-Feldman Analysis After the Supreme Court's* Exxon Mobil *Decision,* 2006 FED. CTS. L. REV. 1, 12 (stating that "Exxon-Mobil did not repudiate or expressly limit" the "inextricably intertwined" concept).

51. One can argue that Congress attempted an end run around the *Rooker-Feldman* doctrine in the Act for the Relief of the Parents of Theresa Marie Schiavo, Pub. L. 109-3, 119 Stat. 15 (2005) ("Terri's Law"), which explicitly tried to strip specific state court determinations of preclusive effect. Concurring specially to a challenge to Terri's Law, one judge suggested that Terri's Law violated the *Rooker-Feldman* doctrine, which should have prevented lower federal courts from exercising jurisdiction to review Florida state court judgments deciding the fate of Terri Schiavo. *Schiavo v. Schiavo,* 404 F.3d 1270, 1272 n.3, 1276 (11th Cir. 2005) (Birch, J., specially concurring). Terri's law is discussed *supra,* in greater detail in Chapter 6.

Federal Courts as Supervisors of State and Local Officials

At one time in its history, during the Civil War, the United States almost stopped working. The federal courts contributed mightily to putting the country back together again, standing ready to hear civil actions challenging the activities of state and local governmental officials and agencies. This important federal court function came into its own during the 1960s and 1970s but derives from events, decisions, and enactments from far earlier in the nation's history.

Article III and other constitutional provisions enable federal courts' supervisory role over state officials and agencies, although the Constitution carefully circumscribes that role. This part traces that tension, beginning in Chapter 13 with a provision limiting the federal courts' supervisory power over states — the Eleventh Amendment. Chapter 14 turns to the bedrock civil rights statute, 42 U.S.C. §1983, which makes possible civil suits by citizens against state and local officials and agencies.

Eleventh Amendment Restrictions

One needs to approach the Eleventh Amendment with the right frame of mind; otherwise it may seem like a bad joke. Why? First, the Amendment simply does not mean what is says. In interpreting the Eleventh Amendment, the Supreme Court has deviated from the Amendment's actual language possibly in more ways than it has for any other part of the Constitution. The Court usually justifies such a course as a faithful effort to reflect what the Eleventh Amendment's framers likely had in mind, even if their language doesn't reflect that intent. Yet the Court abandons this apparent pragmatism in other parts of Eleventh Amendment jurisprudence, often privileging form over substance.

The enterprise of understanding how the Eleventh Amendment operates is deeply important, because the Amendment acts as gatekeeper to the enforcement of federal law against state actors. If the Supreme Court had read the Amendment extremely broadly, there would have been no *Brown v. Board of Education*, no *Roe v. Wade*, no *Lawrence v. Texas* — and the list could go on. The more narrowly the Court reads the Eleventh Amendment bar to suit, the more leeway federal courts have to recognize, clarify, and enforce federal civil rights for citizens against incursion by state government.

As with any constitutional provision, the best place to begin is with the words themselves. But this time, one must remain mindful that the language gives only a hint of the provision's meaning. Here are the words of the Eleventh Amendment:

> The Judicial power of the United States shall not be construed to extend to any suit in law or equity, commenced or prosecuted against one of the United States by Citizens of another State, or by Citizens or Subjects of any Foreign State.

The first step in deciphering this language is to explore the events that precipitated the Amendment. Following a review of that history, this chapter traces the Amendment's interpretations, organized by chronology and the language itself:

- "[A]ny suit . . . against one of the United States by Citizens of another State, or by Citizens or Subjects of any Foreign State"
- "[A]ny suit in law or equity . . . against one of the United States"
- "The Judicial power of the United States"

After this survey of the language, the chapter discusses Congress's power to abrogate the Eleventh Amendment bar and the states' power to waive the bar. Foreshadowing the §1983 material in Chapter 14, this chapter ends by recapping ways that a citizen may get around the Eleventh Amendment and thereby enlist federal courts' aid in challenging state official action.

A. HISTORY: THE LANGUAGE OF ARTICLE III AND *CHISHOLM V. GEORGIA*

Recall that federal courts have limited jurisdiction, and Article III lists nine categories of cases within the federal judicial power. To get into federal court, a case must fall into one of these subject matter jurisdiction categories. Three categories specifically mention the prospect that a state may be a litigant in a federal suit. Most relevant are two provisions triggered by the diverse status of the parties, which provide that the federal judicial power extends to controversies filed (1) "between a State and Citizens of another State" and (2) "between a State . . . and . . . Citizens or Subjects" of "foreign States." U.S. CONST., art. III, §2, cl. 1.

Soon after the states ratified the Constitution, they found themselves defendants in federal court. One early suit, *Chisholm v. Georgia*, 2 U.S. (2 Dall.) 419 (1793), was filed in the Supreme Court by a South Carolina merchant against the state of Georgia to recover under a contract. The Supreme Court held in *Chisholm* that the suit could continue in federal court, rejecting Georgia's assertion that federal courts could not assert jurisdiction over a sovereign state. Reaction to *Chisholm v. Georgia* was dramatic. The Georgia legislature adopted a statute declaring that any person who took action to enforce the judgment in *Chisholm v. Georgia* was " 'guilty of felony and shall suffer death, without benefit of clergy, by being hanged.' "[1] Members of Congress immediately proposed constitutional amendments to overturn

---

1. Robert N. Clinton, *A Mandatory View of Federal Court Jurisdiction: Early Implementation of and Departures from the Constitutional Plan*, 86 COLUM. L. REV. 1515, 1620 n.155 (1986) (quoting 1 CHARLES

the result in the case, and within a short time, the Eleventh Amendment became law.

The Eleventh Amendment was thus a direct (and precipitous) reaction to *Chisholm v. Georgia*, embodying specific language to overturn the result in that case. Once the deed was done, and the Eleventh Amendment's language had obliterated the result in *Chisholm v. Georgia*, opponents were satisfied. For many years, the Amendment enjoyed little attention. In fact, the Supreme Court adjudicated cases in which a state was accused of violating federal law for decades after the Eleventh Amendment was ratified. *See, e.g., Cohens v. Virginia*, 19 U.S. (6 Wheat.) 264, 411-412 (1821) (ruling that the Eleventh Amendment was concerned only with original jurisdiction in an Article III court).

B. "ANY SUIT . . . AGAINST ONE OF THE UNITED STATES BY CITIZENS OF ANOTHER STATE, OR BY CITIZENS OR SUBJECTS OF ANY FOREIGN STATES": *HANS V. LOUISIANA*

Not until a century after the states ratified the Eleventh Amendment did the Supreme Court undertake serious analysis of its meaning. That analysis came in *Hans v. Louisiana*, 134 U.S. 1 (1890), a suit by a Louisiana resident against the state of Louisiana, arguing that the state had unconstitutionally impaired the obligation of contracts by refusing to pay interest owed on bonds it had issued. The *Hans v. Louisiana* Court held that the Eleventh Amendment prohibits suits against a state by its own citizens as well as by citizens of other states and foreign countries. While the terms of the Eleventh Amendment prohibit only suits by citizens of another state, the *Hans v. Louisiana* Court reasoned that to allow a state to be sued by its own citizens would be "anomalous." *Id.* at 18.

Hans v. Louisiana has excited tremendous debate over the years, providing the focus for dueling interpretations of the Eleventh Amendment. Although thinkers have proposed a variety of alternatives, three interpretations dominate: the "sovereign immunity" theory, the "diversity" theory, and the "literalist" theory.[2]

WARREN, THE SUPREME COURT IN UNITED STATES HISTORY 100-101 (1922) and noting that Professor Warren reported that this statute never became law).

2. *See generally* JAMES E. PFANDER, PRINCIPLES OF FEDERAL JURISDICTION 18 (2006) (describing "literalist" and "diversity" views of the Eleventh Amendment); ERWIN CHEMERINSKY, FEDERAL JURISDICTION 404-407 (4th ed. 2003) (describing "diversity" view and the reasoning behind the "sovereign immunity" concept of the Eleventh Amendment).

The sovereign immunity theory proposes that the Eleventh Amendment embodies a wide-ranging constitutional notion of sovereign immunity, shielding states from a vast array of federal suits. This view endorses the result in *Hans v. Louisiana*, 134 U.S. 1, 18 (1890), and likely commands the allegiance of a majority of the United States Supreme Court justices. The idea is that the framers structured the balance between state and federal power with the assumption that the states would enjoy immunity from federal suits, and that *Chisholm v. Georgia* erred in failing to defer to that original assumption of sovereign immunity. The Eleventh Amendment is limited in scope, the argument continues, because it needed only to correct the *Chisholm v. Georgia*'s mistake — to put back into the Constitution what *Chisholm v. Georgia* had taken away. The remainder of states' sovereign immunity remained undisturbed by the decision, and the Eleventh Amendment did not, therefore, need to describe that immunity.

The sovereign immunity theory is often associated with the notion that the Eleventh Amendment is a bar on subject matter jurisdiction, and that invoking "the fundamental principle of sovereign immunity limits the grant of judicial authority in Art. III."[3] Indeed, the Eleventh Amendment is framed in subject matter jurisdiction terms: "The Judicial power of the United States shall not be construed to extend to. . . ." This characterization breaks down, however, because Eleventh Amendment doctrine makes plain that states may waive the Eleventh Amendment bar to suit. Moreover, the Supreme Court treats the Eleventh Amendment bar with less solemnity than it generally approaches matters implicating subject matter jurisdiction, stating that courts may, but need not, raise Eleventh Amendment problems on their own motion.[4]

The diversity interpretation notes that Article III permits subject matter jurisdiction based on either the content of litigation (such as federal question jurisdiction or admiralty jurisdiction) or the parties' identities (such as suits involving governmental entities or citizens of different states). Observing that the language of the Eleventh Amendment focuses only on diversity suits against states by citizens of another state, the diversity theory concludes that the Eleventh Amendment constrains suits in federal court only by virtue of the diverse identities of the parties. From this premise, the diversity theory reasons as follows:

1. The Eleventh Amendment is designed to eliminate only that part of Article III jurisdiction authorizing federal courts to adjudicate

---

3. *Pennhurst State School & Hosp. v. Halderman*, 465 U.S. 89, 98 (1984).
4. *See Wisconsin Dep't of Corr. v. Schacht*, 524 U.S. 381, 389 (1998) (stating that a court need not raise an Eleventh Amendment issue "on its own" and "can ignore it" except if "the state raises the matter"); *Patsy v. Board of Regents*, 457 U.S. 496, 515 n.19 (1982) (stating that "we have never held that [the Eleventh Amendment] is jurisdictional in the sense that it must be raised and decided by this Court on its own motion").

(a) suits by citizens of one state against another state and (b) suits by citizens or subjects of any foreign nation against a state.

2. If a suit has another basis for satisfying Article III jurisdiction — such as the content of the suit — then the Eleventh Amendment does not remove the suit from the federal judicial power.

3. Thus, the Eleventh Amendment does not disqualify federal question or admiralty suits from federal court, even where the parties fall within the prohibited categories that the Amendment describes.

The literalist theory takes the language of the Eleventh Amendment at face value, noting that the Amendment's prohibition is not confined to particular subject areas. Accordingly, the literalist interpretation would disqualify all suits against states by the particular plaintiffs listed in the Eleventh Amendment ("Citizens of another State, or by Citizens or Subjects of any Foreign State") regardless of the content of the suit: state common law, federal question, admiralty, or other subject matter.[5]

Example 13-1

Richard is a Pennsylvania citizen who believes that Pennsylvania has infringed his right to religious freedom in his day-to-day activities. He filed suit in federal court, seeking a remedy for this First Amendment violation. How will he fare under the sovereign immunity interpretation, the diversity interpretation, and literalist interpretation of the Eleventh Amendment?

Explanation

The Eleventh Amendment impose a bar to Richard's federal court suit only under the sovereign immunity interpretation. The sovereign immunity interpretation takes note that Richard is suing the same state where he has citizenship, and it seeks to protect that state's sovereign immunity pre-rogative. Neither the diversity nor the literalist interpretation would find the Eleventh Amendment bar applicable, because Richard is a citizen of the state he names as defendant. The fact that his suit raises a federal question is of no importance for the literalist theory, which holds that the Eleventh Amendment is concerned only with the identities of the parties and applies only if the proper party alignment occurs. The diversity theory does focus on the content of a suit, so the federal law content of Richard's suit would matter for the diversity theory if Richard were not from the state that he is suing.

---

5. For an articulation of this view, see, e.g., Lawrence C. Marshall, *Fighting the Words of the Eleventh Amendment*, 102 HARV. L. REV. 1342 (1989).

Citizens like Richard, most often encounter the policies and practices of the state where they reside, rather than those of other states. Thus, citizens are likely to be aggrieved by their own states' policies and practices. Accordingly, the literalist and the diversity views would significantly restrict the practical effect of the Eleventh Amendment if either theory were adopted by the Supreme Court.

Despite the Court's generous reading of the Eleventh Amendment's language in *Hans v. Louisiana*, and its embrace of implicit sovereign immunity protection for states, the Court has recognized a number of instances where the Eleventh Amendment does not apply, even though one could characterize the suit as directed against a state. Some of these circumstances track the plain language of the Amendment. For example, the Supreme Court has held that a state can be forced to defend a federal court action brought by another state. After all, a state is not a *citizen* or a *subject* and, therefore, is not within the category of the Eleventh Amendment's forbidden plaintiffs. In addition, the Court has read the Amendment's reference to "state" as not including "political subdivisions such as counties and municipalities, even though such entities exercise a 'slice of state power.' "[6] Perhaps even more important for federal law's regulatory potential, the Supreme Court has repeatedly recognized that the United States itself may sue a state in federal or state court. As a superior sovereign, the United States may sue states "where there has been 'a surrender of this immunity in the plan of the convention.' "[7]

Example 13-2

Gary operates a farm in Louisiana. The state of Mississippi diverted part of the Mississippi River and, as a consequence, flooded Gary's farm. Gary requested that Louisiana seek reparations from Mississippi, and Louisiana has filed suit in federal court to do so. Is this action barred by the Eleventh Amendment?

Explanation

Yes, the action is probably barred by the Eleventh Amendment because Louisiana is attempting to help a particular citizen only. To avoid the Eleventh Amendment's force, the state must proceed as a sovereign representing its citizenry generally, not simply the interests of identified persons. In this circumstance, the federal court will likely identify Gary as the real party in interest and prevent the state from using its status to circumvent

---

6. *Lake Country Estates, Inc. v. Tahoe Regional Planning Agency*, 440 U.S. 391, 401 (1979).
7. *Principality of Monaco v. Mississippi*, 292 U.S. 313, 322-323 (1934) (quoting The Federalist No. 81).

Eleventh Amendment protections. *See North Dakota v. Minnesota*, 263 U.S. 365, 375-376 (1923).

Example 13-3

A state imposed motor vehicle excise taxes on members of a Native American tribe living on a reservation. The tribe members believed that the state lacked jurisdiction to do so, and convinced the United States to bring suit in federal court to declare that the state cannot impose the taxes. Does the Eleventh Amendment bar this suit?

Explanation

No, the Eleventh Amendment does not bar this suit. While it is true that the Native American tribe could not have brought suit directly in federal court, the United States can bring a suit on the tribe's behalf. In this way, the United States may avail itself of the principle that, when the state joined the union, it ceded its immunity in suits brought by the United States. This example is the inverse of Example 13-2, and one might expect that a court would look to the Native American tribe as the real party in interest in resolving the Eleventh Amendment issue. Nevertheless, since the reservation is federal territory, the United States has sufficient interest in the controversy to possess the identity of a genuine litigant, not simply a representative. *See United States v. South Dakota*, 105 F.3d 1552, 1560 (8th Cir. 1997) (allowing suit to proceed against state under similar circumstances).

Example 13-4

Jan sued the City of Los Angeles in federal court, challenging the constitutionality of the Los Angeles policy of authorizing police officers to use deadly chokeholds where police have no suspicion of danger. She noted that the Los Angeles Police Department receives substantial funds for its police training from the State of California. The City of Los Angeles moved to dismiss the suit, arguing that the suit was barred by the Eleventh Amendment. Should the district court grant this motion?

Explanation

No, the district court should not dismiss the case on Eleventh Amendment grounds. By accepting funding from California, the City of Los Angeles does not transform itself into a state for the purposes of the Eleventh Amendment. To prevail in such an argument, the City of Los Angeles would need to demonstrate that it was actually acting as an arm of the state. It has not done so here. Accordingly, this is not a suit against "one of the United States" for the purpose of the Eleventh Amendment bar.

Yet another, even more important instance where the Court has declined to read the words "one of the United States" expansively concerns suits against state officers. This topic, known as the Ex parte Young fiction or the "stripping" doctrine, is discussed next.

C. "ANY SUIT IN LAW OR IN EQUITY . . . AGAINST ONE OF THE UNITED STATES": EX PARTE YOUNG AND ITS PROGENY

The Eleventh Amendment says that its bar to suit extends to "any suit in law or equity . . . against one of the United States." As discussed above, this prohibition does not extend to admiralty or maritime suits, which are technically not suits "in law or equity." More remarkable, however, is the Supreme Court's reading of "one of the United States" in this clause: the Court has interpreted the words to exclude suits seeking to stop representatives of a state, acting essentially on behalf of the state, in an unconstitutional manner. That is the rule of Ex parte Young, 209 U.S. 123 (1908).

1. The Logic Behind the Ex Parte Young Fiction

Ex parte Young concerned Minnesota legislation that fixed railroad rates and threatened stiff criminal penalties for railroads that did not comply with the rate structure. Believing that the legislation violated Fourteenth Amendment due process and other federal constitutional guarantees, railroad shareholders brought suit against the Minnesota Attorney General, Young, seeking to enjoin him from enforcing the law. The United States Supreme Court allowed the litigation to proceed—and allowed the injunction to bind Young—on the theory that the suit was not against "one of the United States" for the purpose of the Eleventh Amendment. In the Court's conception, Young's actions were not even attributable to the state of Minnesota.

The Court's theory derived from the following steps of logic:

1. Young was accused of violating the United States Constitution.
2. In ratifying the Constitution, the states ceded to federal power by operation of the supremacy clause.
3. As a consequence of the supremacy clause, states are without authority to violate the Constitution, and therefore cannot lawfully authorize anyone to violate the Constitution.
4. Where an official is violating the Constitution, the official must therefore not be acting under authority of a state.

Thus, Young was not acting under state authority. But why was he named as defendant? Was he a "bad apple" in state government? A "loose cannon" without adequate control or supervision? Of course not.

Young was sued precisely because he was acting on behalf of the state. As attorney general, he had authority to enforce state laws, including the law regulating railroads that was at issue in the litigation. The injunction that the plaintiffs sought purported to bind him from taking official action in enforcing the state legislation. Therein lies the irony: even though he was identified because of his official position, he was deemed to be "stripped" of his affiliation with the state and treated as a private citizen for the purposes of the Eleventh Amendment bar.

The "fictional" quality of this reasoning emerges when one considers what is required to trigger Fourteenth Amendment protection. Individuals can be state actors for purposes of the Fourteenth Amendment only if their actions are attributable to the state. But for the purposes of the Eleventh Amendment bar, the actors' constitutional violations strip them of official status. Constitutional doctrine thus "has it both ways": an individual effectively is the state for the purposes of the Fourteenth Amendment, but is not the state for the purposes of the Eleventh Amendment.[8]

Example 13-5

Assume that during the last election, the secretary of elections for the state of Iowa enforced state regulations that had the effect of preventing certain population groups from voting, in violation of their constitutional rights. Assume further that the secretary of elections is the head of the state board of elections, which is an executive agency under the supervision of Iowa's governor. The board of elections is funded by the state, and the secretary of elections is appointed by the governor.

A group of disenfranchised voters filed a federal court suit after the last election alleging that the secretary of elections denied their right to vote, protected by the United States Constitution; the voters requested that the federal court enjoin enforcement of the state regulations in the next election. As defendants, the disenfranchised voters named the state of Iowa, the board of elections, and the secretary of elections. Is this suit barred by the Eleventh Amendment?

---

8. *Home Telephone & Telegraph Co. v. City of Los Angeles,* 227 U.S. 278 (1913), explicitly endorsed this result, holding that an officer's conduct not subject to Eleventh Amendment protection can constitute state action for Fourteenth Amendment purposes.

Explanation

The Eleventh Amendment bars the suit to the extent that it names the state of Iowa as a defendant, because courts honor the Amendment's explicit protection of "one of the United States."

The Eleventh Amendment also bars the suit to the extent that it names the board of elections as a defendant. Courts treat an action against an agency as an action against the state if a judgment against the agency would have the same practical consequence as a judgment against the state itself.[9] Because the agency is acting as an arm of the state under the control of the executive branch, one can be virtually certain that the state would respond to any judgment against the agency as it would to a judgment against itself. More significantly, the state would satisfy the judgment from the state treasury.

The Eleventh Amendment does not, however, bar the portion of the suit against the secretary of elections. Under the Ex parte Young fiction, the district court may entertain the constitutional challenge and issue an injunction preventing the secretary from enforcing the regulations in the next election. Pursuant to the Ex parte Young fiction, the suit against the secretary of elections is not deemed a suit against the state. Because Iowa is subject to the supreme authority of the United States, the state lacks authority to authorize its secretary of elections to do anything that violates the United States Constitution. The secretary is deemed to be acting on her own.

2. The Prospective/Retroactive Distinction

a. *Edelman v. Jordan*: **The Basic Concept**

After establishing the Ex parte Young fiction, the Supreme Court clarified an important limitation: the fiction suspends the Eleventh Amendment bar only for suits seeking forward-looking relief, such as injunctions. Specifically, the Court ruled that the Eleventh Amendment prevents an award of money damages paid from the state treasury, even if the suit names only a state officer as a defendant.

In *Edelman v. Jordan*, 415 U.S. 651 (1974), the Court clarified the distinction between prospective relief and retroactive relief. In that case, the plaintiffs sued administrators of the Illinois welfare department, arguing that the department was not processing claims with sufficient speed. The lower court ordered the administrators to speed claims processing in the future and to provide "equitable restitution" of the past benefits rightly owed to the recipients. Given that the Supreme Court had earlier ruled that a federal court may not award money damages to be paid from a state's treasury, the plaintiffs' request for equitable restitution presumably sought to align the

---

9. *Lake Country Estates, Inc. v. Tahoe Regional Planning Agency*, 440 U.S. 391, 400-401 (1979).

remedy with injunctive relief, as opposed to a damages remedy. The Supreme Court, however, was unpersuaded by the distinction. The Court upheld the lower court's injunction as prospective relief appropriate under the Eleventh Amendment, but concluded that the equitable restitution was improper because it was the functional equivalent of damages: it would operate retroactively and would "to a virtual certainty be paid from state funds, and not from the pockets of the individual state officials who were the defendants in the action." Id. at 668.

The *Edelman* Court appeared to be motivated by the desire to draw a clear line between prospective and retrospective relief. Yet the Court stumbled on the difficulty — if not the impossibility — of drawing such a line, forthrightly recognizing that the difference between the two types of relief is not "day and night." Id. at 667. Moreover, the *Edelman* Court acknowledged that the "necessary result of compliance" with prospective relief could substantially burden the state treasury — an effect normally associated with retrospective relief. Id. The Court reasoned, however, that "[s]uch an *ancillary* effect on the state treasury is a permissible and often an inevitable consequence" of the *Ex parte Young* fiction. Id. (emphasis added). However, the Court's usage of this concept of "ancillary" has changed over the years.

Example 13-6

Plaintiffs brought a federal suit against the state officials who implement the state's Medicaid program, claiming that they have not provided for sufficient dental care for the last year, as required by federal law. The plaintiffs knew that the Medicaid program would end in the year following judgment in the case, and they therefore requested an injunction requiring the state officials to provide dental benefits for the next year. Experts issued reports stating that this one-year compliance would cost $1,000,000. The plaintiffs also sought payment for the dental benefits not paid for the past year. Based on the experts' reports, costs would total $1,000,000 for these past benefits as well. Are both types of relief allowable under the Eleventh Amendment? Does the retroactive/prospective distinction make sense?

Explanation

The Eleventh Amendment allows the injunction as prospective relief and prohibits reimbursement of the past benefits as retroactive relief. Yet the amount of money from the treasury required for either type of relief is the same: $1,000,000 for a year's worth of benefits. This encourages the notion that distinctions in the Eleventh Amendment sometimes exalt form over substance. Nevertheless, analysis of the retroactive/prospective distinctions using the values underlying the Eleventh Amendment enables one to approach the distinction in a more meaningful fashion.

In part, the Eleventh Amendment implements the sovereign immunity concept of protecting the state treasury. But this is more than simply a matter of preserving stacks of money. Rather, Eleventh Amendment jurisprudence recognizes that state finances require (1) making difficult decisions about which categories of social need deserve public money and (2) budgeting. Budgeting requires state governments to allocate predetermined amounts to the particular categories of need chosen through the political process. With retroactive relief, the money demanded from the state treasury is for a prior time: the policy choices regarding resource allocation and budgeting for that time period have already been made. Retroactive relief, therefore, requires administrators to reevaluate resource allocations to resolve this (presumably) unanticipated expense of damages. With future relief, the administrators have more leeway in the budgeting process. The prospective order gives them notice of a future cost, and they can plan accordingly.

State sovereignty and autonomy are other values underlying the Eleventh Amendment. It is for this reason that Eleventh Amendment jurisprudence exhibits distaste for specific orders, even if they are prospective. The prospective order in this example could come in many forms, such as

- Option 1: "You are not in compliance with the Medicaid dental provisions. You are hereby ordered to be in compliance for the next year."
- Option 2: "You are not in compliance with the Medicaid dental provisions. To bring you into compliance, you are hereby ordered to pay $1,000,000 in dental benefits over the next year."

Although Eleventh Amendment case law exists that would uphold either option, Option 2 is more offensive to Eleventh Amendment values. Option 1 respects the autonomy of state decisionmakers, giving them the latitude (and room for creativity) to comply with the federal law in a way that best accommodates competing state concerns.

An increase in social problems and a decrease in state revenues raise the stakes for allowing states to comply creatively with federal law while accommodating competing social concerns. Those who propose strong Eleventh Amendment jurisprudence sometimes highlight the democratic nature of state budgeting. The difficult process of allocating scarce state resources is vested in democratically elected representatives in state government, who are charged with making political decisions about how to divide a limited pot of money. Federal courts, applying federal law, can substantially hinder that decisionmaking by imposing nonnegotiable orders that effectively funnel money away from other important needs.

States must comply with federal law. But, the argument goes, respect for state autonomy and the processes of democratic state government counsel in favor of allowing states to decide how to comply without unnecessarily earmarking state funds for honoring federal court injunctions and diverting money from other pressing matters.

All this is a complicated way of saying that the Eleventh Amendment preference for the first option not only is based on the idea of leaving states alone, but is also rooted in a preference for allowing democratically elected officials (not life-tenured federal judges) to make tough decisions about who gets society's resources.

These rationales may not convince everyone that *Edelman*'s distinction between prospective and retroactive remedies is the best approach. Indeed, the reasoning breaks down even further in the instances (more common than this example) where prospective relief extends indefinitely into the future. If concern about depleting state treasuries animates the Eleventh Amendment, then requiring states to pay out $1,000,000 each year for the indefinite future is surely more problematic than a one-time, retroactive "hit" on the treasury of $1,000,000. Despite these difficulties, Eleventh Amendment values do demonstrate that the retroactive/prospective distinction is not wholly lacking in rationality: functional differences exist between paying $1,000,000 for a past harm and figuring out how to finance a $1,000,000 benefit for the future.

b. Further Refinement of Retroactive Relief and Ancillary Remedies

The explanation for Example 13-6 illustrates a number of goals underlying contemporary Eleventh Amendment jurisprudence: safeguarding funds in state treasuries, honoring state sovereignty and autonomy, and preserving the democratic decisionmaking processes of state government. To varying degrees, those values guided the Supreme Court as it expounded on two concepts introduced in *Edelman v. Jordan*: retroactive relief and ancillary remedies.

i. Refining "Retroactive"

In *Milliken v. Bradley*, 433 U.S. 267 (1977), the Supreme Court evaluated a remedy to desegregate schools that required the schools to implement a series of programs, including providing remedial education for pupils, hiring counselors, and training school employees. In upholding the remedies, the Supreme Court reasoned that they were designed to "wipe out continuing conditions of inequality produced by the inherently unequal dual school system long maintained by Detroit." *Id.* at 290.

On one level, these remedies were retrospective: they identified the results of a past wrong and tried using the remedies to put the plaintiffs in the position they would have been in but for that wrong. But that does not render the remedies retroactive for purposes of the *Ex parte Young* fiction.

In mapping the distinction between retroactive and prospective remedies, the Court focused on what the remedies actually required the state to do. Because the remedies required the state to take prospective action, they were permissible, even though they were compensatory in nature. Presumably, the remedies were also sufficiently deferential to the state and its budgetary planning to pass Eleventh Amendment scrutiny. In applying these concepts, however, courts have made clear that they will examine remedies to ensure that they truly require the state to take future action. Thus, even declaratory judgments might be deemed retroactive if they serve only to establish an entitlement to damages.[10]

Example 13-7

Consider the facts of Example 13-6, in which plaintiffs sued officials over adequate dental care. Now assume that the plaintiffs knew that they could not ask for payment for the dental benefits that were not paid for the past year. However, many of them had suffered damage as a result of not having received past benefits, and they wanted treatment that would reduce or eliminate the effects of their inadequate dental benefits for the past year, such as treatment for cavities, gum disease, and root canal therapy. They therefore asked the district court for an order requiring the defendant officials "to ensure that plaintiffs receive appropriate treatments to reverse the ill effect of dental neglect to the extent practicable." Is that remedy permissible?

Explanation

The remedy is probably permissible under *Milliken v. Bradley*. The treatment remedies are retroactive in the sense that they are concerned with a past harm, but the remedies actually focus on the future effects of the past harm and are therefore forward looking in the same way as the "catch-up" programs in *Milliken*. The distinction between retroactive, compensatory damages and prospective remedies of this kind, however, is elusive. Both seek to compensate for a past wrong, and both require expenditure of treasury funds. Nevertheless, the treatment remedies in this example are prospective in the sense that they allow budgetary planning and also enable the state to decide how to cure the effects of the past harm. The state officials can use state employees to provide the treatment, contract out the treatments to other dentists, or reimburse patients for treatments they personally arranged. In this way, the remedy respects state autonomy.

---

10. *See, e.g., Green v. Mansour*, 474 U.S. 64, 71-73 (1985) (refusing declaratory judgment, which would provide a first step toward a state court damage remedy and therefore would act as an impermissible "end run" around *Edelman v. Jordan*).

As an additional check to ensure that a suit seeks prospective relief, case law following *Milliken* stated that the *Ex parte Young* fiction requires the state official's federal law violation to be "ongoing."[11] In this example, the officials' unfulfilled obligation to provide adequate dental benefits extended over a period in the past and promised (without federal court intervention) to extend into the future. One may reasonably argue, therefore, that the officials' failure to comply with Medicaid requirements is "ongoing."

ii. Refining "Ancillary" Effects on the Treasury

In *Edelman v. Jordan*, the Court found acceptable the injunction's effect on the treasury because it was "ancillary." The *Edelman* Court seemed satisfied that the effect of the remedy on the treasury was less intrusive than money damages because the effect was indirect. During the era immediately following *Edelman v. Jordan*, the Court took a different, more flexible approach to the concept of "ancillary." One case, *Hutto v. Finney*, 437 U.S. 678 (1978), concerned injunctive relief requiring state officials to raise the conditions in prison to constitutional standards. The *Hutto* Court approved a contempt order for violating the prison injunctions that required the state to pay a fine "out of Department of Correction funds." This order did not have an indirect effect on the state treasury: it required a direct payment of funds from the treasury. In other words, to comply with this contempt order, the officials had to take action indistinguishable from that required for satisfying a compensatory damage remedy — they had to write a check on a government fund. Although a compensatory remedy was forbidden under the Eleventh Amendment, the Court approved the fine, reasoning that the "power to impose a fine is properly treated as *ancillary* to the federal court's power to impose injunctive relief." The Court also observed that the fine was not so large that it interfered with the state's budgeting process. *Id.* at 691, 692 n.18 (emphasis added).

Using similar reasoning, the Court upheld a federal order requiring a state to issue an explanatory order to members of a plaintiff class, advising them of their legal rights regarding welfare benefits.[12] Endorsing this result in a subsequent case, the Court explained that "a request for a limited notice order will escape the Eleventh Amendment bar if the notice is *ancillary* to the grant of some other appropriate relief that can be noticed."[13]

---

11. *See, e.g., Verizon Md., Inc. v. Public Serv. Comm'n of Md.*, 535 U.S. 635, 645-648 (2002) (stating that *Ex parte Young* doctrine requires an inquiry into whether the complaint alleges "an ongoing violation of federal law"); *Idaho v. Coeur D'Alene Tribe of Idaho*, 521 U.S. 261, 281 (1997) (stating that plaintiffs' averment that defendant engaged in ongoing federal law violation is usually sufficient to satisfy *Ex parte Young* doctrine, although finding the doctrine inapplicable under the circumstances of this particular case).

12. *Quern v. Jordan*, 440 U.S. 332 (1979).

13. *Green v. Mansour*, 474 U.S. 64, 71 (1985) (emphasis added).

These cases thus use the term "ancillary" in different ways. *Edelman* used the concept to suggest approval for relief that had an indirect effect on the treasury (which could in fact be a substantial effect). *Hutto* used the concept to suggest that a direct effect on the treasury was acceptable, so long as the relief was insubstantial (a small dollar value) and supported the main prospective relief. Finally, the notice cases reinforced the notion that the Eleventh Amendment allowed relief that was relevant, although tangential, to the main prospective relief.

Example 13-8

Consider the dental care lawsuit from Example 13-6 and Example 13-7. As explained in Example 13-7, many plaintiffs suffered permanent damage as a result of not having received past benefits and therefore wanted treatment that would reduce or eliminate the effects of the inadequate benefits for the past year. This time plaintiffs asked the district court for an order requiring the defendant officials to provide them with a sum of money that would enable them to pursue the appropriate remedial treatment. Is such a remedy permissible under *Edelman*, *Milliken*, *Hutto*, and the notice cases?

Explanation

No, the remedy is not permissible because it (1) falls on the retroactive side of the *Edelman* line and (2) is not saved by the construction of "ancillary" in *Hutto* or the notice cases. The first and most significant problem with this remedy is that it orders a direct payment of money from the state treasury. While *Hutto* endorsed a remedy that required direct payment, the remedy in that case was subsidiary to an indisputably prospective order concerning prison conditions. In this example, the remedy is not subsidiary: it's the only remedy. Second, the remedy does not give the officials leeway in determining how they will comply with federal law; they have no option but to pay a fixed sum of money. Finally, the amount required for compliance promises to be substantial.

Thus, the remedy here is clearly distinguishable from those allowed in *Milliken*, *Hutto*, and the notice cases. What is not so clear is whether, from the defendants' viewpoint, the impermissible remedy is functionally different from the permissible remedy in Example 13-6, which gave the defendant officials options as to how to provide the "catch-up" dental care. In the end, each of the two approaches would probably require about the same resources from the treasury. But again, the Eleventh Amendment result turns on what some might call a formality.

3. *Ex Parte Young* for State Law Claims: The Fiction Breaks Down

When plaintiffs are aggrieved by official action of the state, their claims are not always confined to federal law violations. Plaintiffs often complain that officials violate both state and federal law. For efficiency, they could bring state and federal claims together in one action; *Pennhurst State School & Hosp. v. Halderman*, 465 U.S. 89 (1984), however, prevents plaintiffs from doing that. *Pennhurst* held that the Eleventh Amendment bars federal court plaintiffs from asserting claims based on state law violations, even if the suit names only state officials.

From one point of view, the distinction appears artificial and unjustifiable under Eleventh Amendment values. Is the impact on state sovereignty, autonomy, and financial resources dramatically different where the theory of liability derives from state law rather than federal law? Not really. One could argue that states might be especially insulted when plaintiffs use federal courts to punish them for their violating their own rules, on the theory that there's something particularly undignified about "being shot with your own gun." But that humiliation may not fully justify the outright prohibition against state law claims in federal court. It is not pragmatic goals but formal reasoning that explains the Eleventh Amendment result in *Pennhurst*.

As reviewed earlier in this chapter, the *Ex parte Young* fiction derives from a series of logical steps. The linchpin of the reasoning chain is the supremacy clause: since states are subject to superior federal authority under the Constitution, they are incapable of authorizing officials to violate the Constitution, and officials who violate the Constitution, therefore, cannot be doing so on behalf of the state. Where the violation alleged is one of state law, the supremacy clause drops out of the equation and the fiction collapses. Without the supremacy clause restricting the range of actions the state can authorize, an official violating the law could theoretically be acting on behalf of the state.

Pennhurst can have a harsh effect on individual litigants by removing the option of supplemental jurisdiction and sometimes eliminating the possibility of pursuing relief in *any* forum for state law violations. The decision also has ramifications for the administration of justice by making unavailable the constitutional avoidance principle[14] and the *Pullman* abstention doctrine. These consequences are illustrated in Example 13-9.

---

14. *See Siler v. Louisville & Nashville R.R. Co.*, 213 U.S. 175 (1909) (prescribing method of decisionmaking whereby the federal court must attempt to dispose of case on state law grounds before reaching constitutional challenge). *See also* the discussion of the avoidance principle in Chapters 8 and 10.

Example 13-9

Jill Jockey worked for the New York State Racing Commission. The commission is a state entity with a regulation stating that pregnant women may not work as jockeys. Jill became pregnant and soon thereafter was threatened with dismissal pursuant to the pregnancy regulation. She then filed suit against the head of the commission in federal district court, raising two claims: (1) the commission acted outside its authority because the state statute creating the commission did not authorize it to promulgate regulations such as the one on pregnancy regulation, and (2) the regulation violates the equal protection clause of the Fourteenth Amendment to the United States Constitution. Jill Jockey seeks an injunction preventing the head of the commission from enforcing the pregnancy regulation. Is this suit permissible under the Eleventh Amendment?

Explanation

Jill Jockey may pursue only her *federal* claim in federal court. *Pennhurst* prevents her from including her *state* law claim in the federal suit. If Jill wishes to litigate both claims together, she must do so in state court. She cannot avail herself of supplemental jurisdiction under 28 U.S.C. §1367. Thus, she must give up the right to adjudicate her federal claim in a federal forum if logistically (or financially) she cannot litigate her case "on two fronts" and must therefore file both claims in state court. Moreover, she may discover that sovereign immunity bars her suit in state court, in which case she would have no forum to litigate her state law claim. In that event, her state law injury would go unremedied.

Of more significance to principles of federalism and jurisprudence, preventing Jill from bringing her state claim in federal court may force the federal court to decide her constitutional question based on the equal protection clause. This would deprive the federal court of the opportunity to dispose of Jill's case on non-constitutional grounds as the constitutional avoidance principle recommends.[15] In addition, the mechanisms established under the *Pullman* abstention doctrines would likewise be unavailable,[16] since the district court would not have a state law claim needing clarification by the state court. For these reasons, the rule of *Pennhurst* may not serve state sovereignty and judicial restraint to the extent that the *Pennhurst* Court intended.

Cases in the 1990s suggest that the Supreme Court may have been poised to restrict use of the *Ex parte Young* fiction considerably, far beyond

---

15. *Siler v. Louisville & Nashville R.R. Co.*, 213 U.S. 175 (1909) (prescribing method of decision-making whereby the federal court must attempt to dispose of case on state law grounds before reaching constitutional challenge).
16. *See* Chapter 8 for further discussion of the abstention doctrines.

the *Pennhurst* limitation. For example, in *Seminole Tribe of Florida v. Florida*, 517 U.S. 44 (1996), the Court refused to allow the *Ex parte Young* fiction to operate in an instance where Congress had created an elaborate scheme imposing limited liability on the state itself. While reaffirming the result in *Seminole Tribe*, the Supreme Court in a subsequent case, *Verizon Md., Inc. v. Public Service Comm'n of Md.*, 535 U.S. 635 (2002), eliminated any doubt that the Court would no longer view the doctrine of *Ex parte Young* as settled law.[17] In *Verizon* Justice Scalia, writing for a unanimous Court, explained, "In determining whether the doctrine of *Ex parte Young* avoids an Eleventh Amendment bar to suit, a court need only conduct a 'straightforward inquiry into whether [the] complaint alleges an ongoing violation of federal law and seeks relief properly characterized as prospective.'" *Id.* at 645 (quoting *Idaho v. Coeur d'Alene Tribe of Idaho*, 521 U.S. 261, 296 (1997)).

4. The "Official Capacity"/"Individual Capacity" Distinction

Now for the confusing part. The *Ex parte Young* fiction operates only against officials, the theory being that the state cannot authorize them to violate the Constitution. Therefore, one would think that the officials named as defendants pursuant to the *Ex parte Young* fiction would be sued in their "individual capacity." But that's not the case. Recall, for example, that Attorney General Young in *Ex parte Young* was named as a defendant because he was acting as an official, not because he was a "loose cannon" or a "bad apple" acting on his own and far outside his authority. For that reason, the *Ex parte Young* fiction is precisely that — a fiction — and the Supreme Court disqualified retroactive relief from its scope of operation. Thus, cases like *Ex parte Young* and *Edelman* are "official capacity" suits, in which it is clear that the state itself would pay for any judgment directly from the state treasury.

A litigant may choose to sue an official in her individual capacity, as the litigant would do in an ordinary tort suit against a private tortfeasor. In that event, the plaintiff may seek retroactive relief, and any damages would at least theoretically come from the official's "own pocket." At least two complications emerge, however, that distinguish "individual capacity" suits from ordinary tort actions. First, the official may claim protection from common law immunity doctrines, which are separate and different in scope from sovereign immunity. The immunity doctrines vary depending on the function an official performs, in some cases shrouding the official in absolute protection. More often, these doctrines shield an official from

---

17. *See also Idaho v. Coeur d'Alene Tribe of Idaho*, 521 U.S. 261 (1997); *Seminole Tribe of Fla. v. Florida*, 517 U.S. 44, 73-76 (1996).

liability if she acted in an objectively reasonable manner, given the facts known and the state of clearly established legal principles.[18]

The second complication comes in the form of indemnification policies, under which the state decides to act as an insurer for the officer. Indemnification protection extends farther than immunity protection. An official held liable in her individual capacity might fail to show that she is entitled to common law immunity, but nonetheless may be protected under a state's indemnification policy, which would pay the judgment. States cannot claim sovereign immunity or Eleventh Amendment protection against paying such judgments, because their decisions to indemnify officials are voluntary. Indemnity is essentially a matter between the state and the official, although a plaintiff actually trying to satisfy a judgment may encounter a cumbersome bureaucracy when trying to obtain payment from an indemnification fund.[19]

Another tricky aspect of suing officials is distinguishing between "individual capacity" suits and "official capacity" suits. The Supreme Court established that in distinguishing the two, the point of reference is "the capacity in which the state officer is sued, not the capacity in which the officer inflicts the alleged injury."[20] In other words, the determination does not depend on whether the officer performed official functions at the time the alleged harm occurred. Rather, the determination depends on the plaintiff's intent: if she seeks damages against the officer personally, then the suit is an "individual capacity" suit.

Example 13-10

Ben sued the state secretary of education for failure to provide a proper education for Ben's hearing-impaired child. Ben's suit alleged that the secretary of education had made a series of decisions restricting services for hearing-impaired children and that Ben was forced to expend $50,000 for special services for his child. In his complaint, Ben sued only the secretary of education, asking for damages in the amount of $50,000. The complaint did not state whether Ben was suing the secretary in her official or individual capacity. In response to the complaint, the secretary of education pleaded that she was protected under the common law doctrine of qualified immunity. Ben then sought discovery of information regarding state indemnification policies promising the secretary reimbursement for judgments against her.

The secretary of education moved to dismiss the suit on Eleventh Amendment grounds, asserting that it seeks retroactive relief in violation

---

18. *See Hope v. Pelzer*, 536 U.S. 730 (2002); *Anderson v. Creighton*, 483 U.S. 635 (1987). Immunity doctrines are discussed in detail in connection with 42 U.S.C. §1983 in Chapter 14.
19. *See* Chapter 14 for further discussion of indemnity doctrines.
20. *Hafer v. Melo*, 502 U.S. 21, 26 (1991).

of *Ex parte Young* and *Edelman v. Jordan*. Should the district court dismiss the complaint?

Explanation

The decision of whether to dismiss the complaint depends on the federal circuit in which the complaint is pending. The issue is whether the court should treat Ben's complaint as an "official capacity" complaint because it fails to specify that the secretary is being sued in her individual capacity. Some circuits presume that a suit is an "official capacity" suit unless the complaint states otherwise.[21] Under this approach, the district court would treat the complaint as a suit brought under the *Ex parte Young* fiction, which would make available only prospective relief. Since Ben asks only for damages, his suit seeks retroactive relief exclusively and is therefore improper under *Ex parte Young* and *Edelman*. In that event, the district court should dismiss the suit.

Some circuits, however, impose no presumption on an ambiguous complaint, but take a holistic approach to the capacity issue by evaluating the course of proceedings in the case.[22] The courts look at how the parties' litigation decisions reflect their assumptions about the capacity in which the defendant is being sued — official or individual. If the plaintiff maintains she is suing the defendant in her individual capacity, the court may ask whether the defendant received adequate notice that she was being sued personally.

Applying the "course of proceedings" approach here, the district court would likely conclude that the secretary of education had notice that this is an "individual capacity" case. The parties appear to be litigating the case with that assumption. First, Ben asks only for relief that is impermissible in an "official capacity" case, suggesting that he wants to sue the secretary individually. Second, the secretary apparently is operating on the understanding that her personal liability is on the line by raising a common law immunity defense, which would be irrelevant to an "official capacity" suit. Finally, by seeking discovery about another matter irrelevant to "official capacity" suits — indemnification — Ben is giving the secretary further notice that she is exposed to personal liability. Ben's request for

---

21. *See, e.g., Johnson v. Outboard Marine Corp.*, 172 F.3d 531, 535 (8th Cir. 1999) (explaining that suit is presumed an "official capacity" suit unless parties make an express statement to the contrary).

22. *See, e.g., Moore v. City of Harriman*, 272 F.3d 769, 772-773 (6th Cir. 2001) (following a holistic "course of proceedings" approach); *Biggs v. Meadows*, 66 F.3d 56, 60-61 (4th Cir. 1995) (applying "course of proceedings" approach, which court describes as the dominant approach among circuits). *See generally Kentucky v. Graham*, 473 U.S. 159 (1985) (explaining that course of proceedings typically shows nature of liability sought).

indemnification information also shows his own assumption about how he intends to win a remedy for injuries.

D. "THE JUDICIAL POWER OF THE UNITED STATES": *ALDEN V. MAINE* AND OTHERS

The Eleventh Amendment disqualifies certain cases from adjudication, but the disqualification is confined to "the Judicial power of the United States." The Amendment contains no language restricting this clause, suggesting that the language in fact pertains to *all* of the judicial power of the United States. Nor does the Amendment mention any judicial power other than that of the United States, suggesting that the language restricts *only* the judicial power of the United States. These inferences are wrong on all counts! Instead, the Supreme Court has interpreted (or ignored) the words "[t]he Judicial power of the United States" as follows:

- The language *does not* restrict the United States Supreme Court, which clearly possesses the judicial power of the United States, as that term is used elsewhere in the Constitution: Article III.
- The language *does not* eliminate state courts from restrictions based on Eleventh Amendment concepts.
- The language *does* restrict federal administrative agencies, which are not courts under Article III.

1. The United States Supreme Court *Is Not* Restricted

History testifies that Chief Justice John Marshall took opportunities provided to him (and a few that he provided for himself) to ensure plenary power for the United States Supreme Court. The Eleventh Amendment is no exception. In the wake of the Amendment's ratification, he wrote that the Eleventh Amendment addressed only instances where a federal court exercised original jurisdiction.[23] Accordingly, when a case reached the United States Supreme Court on appeal from a state court, Chief Justice Marshall ruled that the United States Supreme Court was not restricted by the Eleventh Amendment. He declined to embrace a reading of the Amendment that would describe the suit as a prohibited one "against one of the United States," even though the state in the suit was fighting to defend a state court judgment in the United States Supreme Court. Marshall's understanding of the

---

23. *Cohens v. Virginia*, 19 U.S. (6 Wheat.) 264, 411-412 (1821).

Supreme Court's power, untouched by Eleventh Amendment limitations, survives today.

Example 13-11

Assume that a New Mexico agency in charge of enforcing health standards in places of employment, the Department of Workplace Safety, imposes fines on violators. Assume further that the New Mexico legislature passed a statute providing that employers who wish to contest the fine "may initiate refund actions against the state of New Mexico in New Mexico state courts." Accordingly, the statute waives New Mexico's sovereign immunity for state court actions in this context.

Bridget is a citizen of Nevada who runs a New Mexico restaurant that was fined. She filed suit in New Mexico state court contesting the fine and argued the state scheme violated federal due process principles. The state trial court upheld the fine and rejected the constitutional challenge. All state appellate courts affirmed this judgment. Bridget filed a petition for a writ of certiorari in the United States Supreme Court, pressing the due process claim. She named as the respondent in this action "the State of New Mexico," which was the same party named as a defendant in the state court action. Does the Eleventh Amendment bar the United States Supreme Court from hearing the suit?

Explanation

No, the Eleventh Amendment does not bar this suit. One might argue that the language of the New Mexico statute shows that the state legislature intended to waive the state's sovereign immunity only for state court actions. Moreover, the action appears to fall squarely within the language of the Eleventh Amendment: New Mexico is "one of the United States," Bridget is a "Citizen[] of another State" suing New Mexico, and the United States Supreme Court exercises "[t]he Judicial power of the United States." Yet the United States Supreme Court recently reaffirmed its "long-established and uniform practice of reviewing state-court decisions on federal matters, regardless of whether the State was the plaintiff or the defendant in the trial court." *South Central Bell Telephone Co. v. Alabama*, 526 U.S. 160, 166 (1999).

2. States Courts *Are* Restricted

In *Alden v. Maine*, 527 U.S. 706 (1999), the Court grappled with the question of whether Congress, in the exercise of one of its Article I powers, can subject a nonconsenting state to a suit brought by private plaintiffs in the state's own courts. In concluding that Congress could not, the Court relied on the sovereign immunity principles reflected in the Eleventh Amendment. The Eleventh Amendment speaks only of a restriction on "[t]he Judicial power of the United States," and *Alden v. Maine* did not suggest that state courts are literally encompassed in that phrase. Thus, it is not precisely true that the Court ruled that the Eleventh Amendment applies in state court. That, however, is the practical effect of the Court's ruling, because the Court determined that the Eleventh Amendment reflects an understanding that states should not be subjected to liability for violating federal law in any forum — including state courts.

In *Alden v. Maine*, state probation officers sued for overtime pay, alleging that the state had failed to comply with a federal statute, the Fair Labor Standards Act. The state agreed to make a prospective change in wage payments, but refused to pay retroactive overtime. The probation officers sought those retroactive payments in state court, and the state asserted sovereign immunity.

In upholding the federal sovereign immunity defense, the Supreme Court held that the United States Constitution anchors the states' sovereign immunity, which is not "defeasible by federal statute." 527 U.S. at 733. Also, the Court explained that state immunity from private lawsuits was "so well established" at the time the states ratified the Constitution "that no one conceived it would be altered by the new Constitution." *Id.* at 741.

Example 13-12

Carmella brought suit against a part of the state government, the state board of education, in state court. She alleged that she suffered emotional harm from the sexually harassing environment in her school. She also alleged that the board of education violated a federal statute preventing sexual harassment in schools and was liable to her for compensatory damages. The board of education argued that it was immune from suit under state sovereign immunity principles and that the state court should dismiss the suit. Should the state court grant the motion to dismiss?

Explanation

Alden v. Maine should provide authority for dismissing the lawsuit, so long as one fact is established: Congress passed the federal statute that Carmella relied on pursuant to one of its Article I powers, such as the commerce clause. If Congress indeed passed the statute under Article I, then the action is barred, given that the board of education is an arm of the state.

An important component of *Alden v. Maine*'s reasoning concerned original understanding of the Constitution's meaning at the time the states ratified it. Congress's Article I powers were framed during that period and thus were subject to the assumptions and understandings that were inherent in the original document. Congressional powers added later, such as the Fourteenth Amendment, stand on a different footing. The interrelationship between the Eleventh Amendment and Congress's Fourteenth Amendment powers is explored next in the context of abrogation.

3. Federal Administrative Agencies *Are* Restricted

The Eleventh Amendment's prohibition extends to "[t]he Judicial power of the United States," language that tracks Article III, which sets the parameters for the federal judiciary. Yet, as explored briefly in Part I of this book, some federal courts exist that do not fall within Article III's scope and are not staffed with judges who possess life tenure. Some of those courts are known as legislative courts or Article I courts.

Given that the Eleventh Amendment language tracks Article III, one might logically argue that the Eleventh Amendment restricts only Article III courts. "Not so," said the Supreme Court in *Federal Maritime Commission v. South Carolina State Ports Auth.*, 535 U.S. 743 (2002). Specifically, the *Federal Maritime* Court held that private plaintiffs cannot sue states in federal administrative agency proceedings. Recognizing that the agency did not exercise the judicial power of the United States, the Court nevertheless determined that the state's autonomy and dignity would be improperly assaulted by forcing the state to defend an action against it in "court-like administrative tribunals." *Id.* at 760-761.

Example 13-13

The Rhode Island Department of Environmental Management (RIDEM) fired employees for reporting the department's failure to comply with the federal Solid Waste Disposal Act. The employees filed an administrative complaint with the United States Department of Labor, which investigated and found cause for the employees' complaint. The employees then began an administrative proceeding against the State of Rhode Island and RIDEM, seeking damages for RIDEM's violation of the whistleblower protections of the federal Solid Waste Disposal Act. According to the rules of procedure, this proceeding would be litigated before an administrative law judge and would follow rules of evidence and procedure nearly identical to those followed in federal district court. The tribunal is capable of recommending remedies such as damages and injunctions, which are subject to review in the district court, but are generally enforced without significant scrutiny.

Before the administrative tribunal, the state of Rhode Island argued that this administrative proceeding violated its sovereign immunity.

The argument was ignored. Accordingly, Rhode Island filed a suit in district court seeking to enjoin the federal administrative proceeding. Should the district court grant the motion?

Explanation

Under the authority of *Federal Maritime*, the district court should grant the motion. The proceeding in the administrative agency is the functional equivalent of an action in an Article III tribunal, with analogous rules regarding discovery, pleadings, and presentation of evidence. All that is missing is an Article III judge. But that omission is not sufficient to allow the proceedings to avoid the characterization that it "'walks, talks, and squawks very much like a lawsuit,'" a test cited with approval by the Supreme Court in *Federal Maritime*. 535 U.S. at 757 (quoting *South Carolina State Ports Auth. v. FMC*, 243 F.3d 165, 174 (4th Cir. 2001)). Accordingly, forcing an arm of the state of Rhode Island to defend this administrative proceeding brought by private plaintiffs improperly invades the state's sovereign immunity. *See Rhode Island Dep't of Environmental Mgmt. v. United States*, 304 F.3d 31 (1st Cir. 2002) (applying *Federal Maritime* under similar circumstances).

E. CONGRESS'S POWER TO ABROGATE

In the considerable time that has passed since *Hans v. Louisiana*, 134 U.S. 1 (1890), Congress has changed the Eleventh Amendment landscape by enacting explicit rights of action allowing private plaintiffs to sue states in federal court. In this array of legislation, Congress has regulated not only aspects of the national economy, but parts of social life as well. In particular, Congress has created schemes designed to eradicate institutional discrimination on the basis of disability, religion, race, and sex. The notion is that Congress not only has identified a federal right that needs to be protected with specific legislation, but has also determined that a private enforcement mechanism is needed to ensure that the rights are meaningful. In Congress's view, civil actions between private citizens and states are needed to supplement whatever enforcement the federal government can afford.

In the wake of these legislative initiatives, a question has arisen: when Congress creates these rights of action, what force does the Eleventh Amendment possess? Can Congress instruct that the Eleventh Amendment is inapplicable in the private suits that it authorizes? The term of art in this area is "abrogate" — when evaluating whether Congress "abrogated" the Eleventh Amendment, one inquires as to whether Congress intended to suspend the Eleventh Amendment, overriding the Amendment's bar to suit.

The Supreme Court has now determined that Congress may abrogate the Eleventh Amendment, but only when it legislates pursuant to §5 of the Fourteenth Amendment. The Court had previously suggested that Congress could abrogate when it legislates pursuant to its commerce clause power under Article I, but it changed its position. Even the Fourteenth Amendment ruling is weakened by another strand of case law scrutinizing Congress's exercise of Fourteenth Amendment enforcement power. This section first reviews preliminary principles dealing with Fourteenth Amendment abrogation and then turns to the commerce clause case law. The section ends by exploring the interaction of Eleventh Amendment jurisprudence and Fourteenth Amendment jurisprudence.

I. Fourteenth Amendment

The Fourteenth Amendment, which was added as part of a package of constitutional changes after the Civil War, regulates the relationship between states and the federal government. By its terms, the Fourteenth Amendment restricts state power. Section 5 of the Fourteenth Amendment gives Congress some "muscle" to fulfill the Amendment's promise to protect citizens from abusive state power, stating that "[t]he Congress shall have the power to enforce, by appropriate legislation, the provisions of this article."

The Supreme Court, in *Fitzpatrick v. Bitzer*, 427 U.S. 445 (1976), ruled that Congress may abrogate the Eleventh Amendment bar when it legislates to enforce the provisions of the Fourteenth Amendment pursuant to the power granted in §5. The Court reasoned that because the Fourteenth Amendment was intended to limit state sovereignty, Congress possessed power in fashioning "'appropriate legislation'" under §5 to "provide for private suits against States or state officials which are constitutionally impermissible in other contexts." *Id.* at 456.

While acknowledging that the abrogation power exists, the Supreme Court has insisted that Congress make very clear its intent to abrogate. Therefore, the Court has imposed a heightened "clear statement" requirement, ruling that Congress must express its intent to abrogate in unmistakable terms. Designed to protect states, the clarity requirement seeks to ensure that representatives in Congress are on notice when legislation intends to authorize private suits for damages against states in federal court. In that event, political safeguards will ensure that the abrogation was well considered.

Example 13-14

Andy filed an action in federal court under 42 U.S.C. §1983 against the state of Oregon. He argued that the state discriminated against him on the basis of race, and he seeks compensatory damages for the violation. The state filed a motion to dismiss based on the Eleventh Amendment. Andy responded to this motion by arguing that Congress clearly meant to abrogate the Eleventh Amendment bar when it passed the bedrock civil rights statute, 42 U.S.C. §1983. He explained that the statute authorized a private civil action against states in order to cast federal courts in the role of supervising the relationship between states and their citizens. Moreover, he argued, §1983 even provides that infringing states sued "shall be liable to the party injured in an action at law, suit in equity, or other proper proceeding for redress." Since an action at law includes retroactive monetary remedies, Andy insists, Congress made explicit its intent to use the Fourteenth Amendment §5 power to suspend any protection states may enjoy from compensatory damages in private civil actions. Is Andy correct that Congress abrogated the Eleventh Amendment bar in this context?

Explanation

No, Andy is not correct. In *Quern v. Jordan*, 440 U.S. 332 (1979), the Supreme Court ruled that Congress did not show sufficiently clear intent to abrogate the Eleventh Amendment in passing §1983. Over strong dissent, the Court concluded that §1983 possessed neither sufficiently clear language of abrogation nor "a history which focuses directly on the question of state liability and which shows that Congress considered and firmly decided to abrogate the Eleventh Amendment immunity of the States." *Id.* at 345.

Given the importance of §1983 in providing a vehicle for enforcing federal rights against state incursion, the Court's refusal to find that Congress suppressed the Eleventh Amendment bar in passing §1983 significantly limits plaintiffs seeking to redress state-imposed injuries. If the Court had decided *Quern v. Jordan* differently, §1983 litigation may have increased substantially. Perhaps for that reason, the justices in the *Quern v. Jordan* majority were particularly strict in applying the "clear intent to abrogate" standard.

Example 13-15

Congress passed a statute under its Fourteenth Amendment enforcement power, seeking to regulate the circumstances under which employers provide family and medical leave. The text of the statute grants an employee the right to sue his employer for money damages if the employer does not provide the leave mandated by federal law. State governments are listed among the types of employers covered by the federal statute. In addition, the statute's legislative history reflected Congress's knowledge of state-based discrimination against women in employee benefit plans. Does this statute abrogate the Eleventh Amendment bar?

Explanation

Yes, Congress has made its intent sufficiently clear to abrogate the Eleventh Amendment bar. The text of the statute reflects this intent by referring to state employers, civil actions, and money damages. Legislative history reveals that Congress acted with the knowledge that the statute would apply against states by documenting problems with state employers, which provided part of the impetus for the statute's enactment into law. *See Nevada Dep't of Human Resources v. Hibbs*, 538 U.S. 721 (2003). If Congress had wanted to make its intent to abrogate plain on the face of the statute alone, it could have adopted language similar to the following wording, which was found sufficient in *United States v. Georgia*, 126 S. Ct. 877 (2006): "A State shall not be immune under the eleventh amendment to the Constitution of the United States from an action in [a] Federal or State court of competent jurisdiction for a violation of this chapter." *Id.* at 879 (quoting 42 U.S.C. §12202).

2. Commerce Clause

In *Pennsylvania v. Union Gas Co.*, 491 U.S. 1 (1989), a fragile alliance of justices concluded that Congress had the power to abrogate the Eleventh Amendment bar when it legislated under the commerce clause. The Court switched its position, however, in *Seminole Tribe of Florida v. Florida*, 517 U.S. 44 (1996). *Seminole Tribe* is founded on the sovereign immunity theory of the Eleventh Amendment—the notion that sovereign immunity is implicit in the framers' constitutional vision and, thus, reflected in provisions native to the original document, such as the commerce clause in Article I.

The commerce clause is on a different footing than the Fourteenth Amendment, the *Seminole Tribe* Court reasoned, since the Fourteenth Amendment could be read as modifying the assumptions reflected in the Eleventh Amendment. Moreover, since the Fourteenth Amendment realigned state and federal relations, the Amendment is not part of the original constitutional scheme guaranteeing the states protection from involuntary private lawsuits for damages.

Example 13-16

A Native American tribe sued the state of Texas in federal court over a real property dispute. The basis for their suit is a statute passed for the first time in 1790, called the Indian Nonintercourse Act. Congress reenacted the act several times, most of them occurring after the Eleventh Amendment became law. The Native Americans claim that the act was passed pursuant to Congress's war powers in Article I, §8 of the Constitution and that

Congress abrogated the states' Eleventh Amendment protection in the act. Are the Native Americans correct that Congress may use its war powers listed in Article I to abrogate the Eleventh Amendment bar?

Explanation

No, the Native Americans are probably not correct. Under the *Seminole Tribe* rubric, the Supreme Court has provided what appears — at least for the present — to be a bright-line approach: Congress possesses no authority to abrogate using powers that predated the Eleventh Amendment. For that reason, the Court in *Ysleta Del Sur Pueblo v. Raney*, 199 F.3d 281 (5th Cir. 2000), rejected a claim that Congress could abrogate the Eleventh Amendment bar when legislating pursuant to its Article I war powers.

One must be careful, however, in presuming that the Court will not change its position or that all pre–Eleventh Amendment powers listed in the Constitution are off-limits for the purpose of requiring states to answer to private civil lawsuits. For example, in 2006 the Supreme Court issued a surprising announcement concerning the bankruptcy clause in Article I, §8 of the Constitution. In *Central Virginia Community College v. Katz*, 126 S. Ct. 990 (2006), the Supreme Court concluded that under the original constitutional plan, the states surrendered their sovereign immunity in bankruptcy. The *Katz* Court made plain that the case turned not on an abrogation question, but on a specific understanding of the role of bankruptcy law. Thus, *Katz*'s ramifications may be limited to special considerations concerning the bankruptcy power. The decision is nonetheless notable for recognizing that a provision other than the Fourteenth Amendment may eliminate or qualify the states' sovereign immunity in private civil actions.

3. Interaction Between the Eleventh and Fourteenth Amendments: The *Boerne–Seminole Tribe* Squeeze

Although the precise scope of *Seminole Tribe* remains for future cases to clarify, the decision has had one certain ramification: it heightened the importance of the Fourteenth Amendment as a power base for Congress to authorize federal courts to supervise states and state officers. Concomitant with this development, however, the Supreme Court made it more difficult for Congress to justify appropriate legislation under the Eleventh Amendment. This trend began with *City of Boerne v. Flores*, 521 U.S. 507 (1997).

In *City of Boerne*, the Supreme Court condemned Congress for extending legal rights beyond those defined by the Supreme Court in constitutional litigation. *City of Boerne* also declared that Congress must narrowly tailor its laws to eliminate identified constitutional violations: in the Court's view,

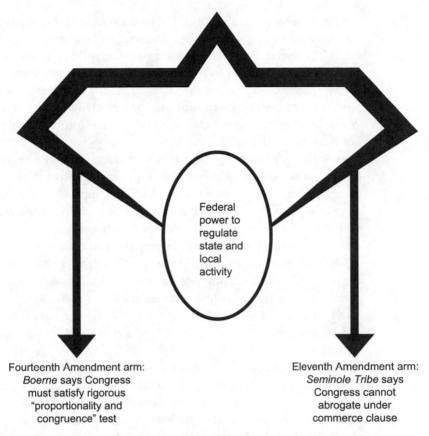

Federal power to regulate state and local activity

Fourteenth Amendment arm:
Boerne says Congress
must satisfy rigorous
"proportionality and
congruence" test

Eleventh Amendment arm:
Seminole Tribe says
Congress cannot
abrogate under
commerce clause

The Pincer Squeezes: *Boerne* and *Seminole Tribe* Interact to
Reduce Federal Power

Figure 13-1. The Pincer Squeezes: *Boerne* and *Seminole Tribe* Interact to Reduce Federal
Power

laws must reflect "congruence" and "proportionality." Literally parsing the
Court's language, one can define the two terms as follows: "congruence"
means that Congress must identify specific constitutional violations that
laws remedy, and "proportionality" means that Congress must carefully
tailor the laws to remedy the violations identified. In application, courts
tend to conflate the two terms, focusing primarily on whether Congress has
sufficiently tailored its statute to remedy specific violations.

After *City of Boerne*, Congress carried a heavy burden in justifying Fourteenth Amendment legislation. Thus, just as *Seminole Tribe* channeled Congress's efforts into Fourteenth Amendment legislation, *City of Boerne*
effectively sabotaged those efforts. The result, one might say, is a *Boerne–
Seminole Tribe* squeeze: a severe reduction of the circumstances in which
Congress can regulate the states using private civil actions (see Figure 13-1).

Since *Seminole Tribe* and *City of Boerne*, the squeeze created by the decisions has demolished many abrogation statutes. In case after case, the Supreme Court has found that, although Congress may have intended to use the Fourteenth Amendment to abrogate the Eleventh Amendment bar, the legislation nonetheless flunked the "congruence and proportionality" test and was therefore inadequate to authorize private civil lawsuits in federal court. When legislation violated the "congruence and proportionality" test, the Court repeatedly found that the legislative records did not reflect a pattern of state violations justifying federal intervention. In those instances where Congress extended legal protections beyond the constitutional protections recognized by the Supreme Court, the Court applied the "congruence and proportionality" test with particular vigor. In *Kimel v. Florida Board of Regents*, 528 U.S. 62 (2000), for example, the Court evaluated whether Congress acted appropriately in applying the Age Discrimination in Employment Act (ADEA) to state and local governments. Concluding that "the substantive requirements the ADEA imposes on state and local governments are disproportionate to any unconstitutional conduct that conceivably could be targeted," the *Kimel* Court found that the ADEA did not pass the "congruence and proportionality" test. *Id.* at 83. Specifically, the Court declared that Congress's extension of the ADEA to "the States was an unwarranted response to a perhaps inconsequential problem." *Id.* at 89.

Pursuing a similarly vigorous scrutiny of congressional findings in *Board of Trustees of the University of Alabama v. Garrett*, 531 U.S. 356 (2001), the Court invalidated portions of the Americans with Disabilities Act (ADA) that empowered disabled persons to sue states for employment discrimination. In considering Congress's abrogation of state immunity from suit, the Court observed that the disabled do not constitute a suspect class for the purposes of strict scrutiny under Fourteenth Amendment equal protection analysis. To justify the abrogation, the Court reasoned, Congress would have had to conclude that states engaged in an irrational pattern of discrimination against disabled individuals that was so pervasive as to justify remedial legislation under the Fourteenth Amendment. The *Garrett* Court determined that Congress had identified no such pattern.

Although the *Boerne–Seminole Tribe* squeeze has invalidated several legislative schemes, the Supreme Court has upheld abrogation legislation in limited circumstances. In one case, the Court upheld an abrogation scheme even where Congress had prohibited more conduct than the United States Constitution condemned. In that case, *Nevada Dep't of Human Resources v. Hibbs*, 538 U.S. 721 (2003), the Supreme Court upheld the federal Family and Medical Leave Act's application to a state employer. The Court noted that the issue of family leave was linked to the Fourteenth Amendment's prohibition against sex discrimination, thereby identifying a constitutional toehold for the act's abrogation of the Eleventh Amendment protection. While the act protected more discrimination than the Constitution, the *Hibbs* Court regarded this as appropriate prophylactic legislation protecting both men and women.

The Court continued the trend begun in *Hibbs* in subsequent cases. First, in *Tennessee v. Lane*, 541 U.S. 509 (2004), the Supreme Court upheld Congress's abrogation of the Eleventh Amendment in Title II of the ADA where the state's misconduct also violated the Constitution. In a subsequent ADA case brought by a prisoner, *United States v. Georgia*, 126 S. Ct. 877, 882 (2006), the Court explained that the determination of whether the abrogation is effective must be evaluated "on a claim-by-claim basis". The Court stated that "insofar as Title II [of the ADA] creates a private cause of action . . . for conduct that *actually* violates the Fourteenth Amendment, Title II validly abrogates state sovereign immunity." 126 S. Ct. at 882. The Court suggested that the abrogation could possibly be valid even if the misconduct violated the ADA but did not violate the Fourteenth Amendment. The Court did not, however, provide standards for analyzing that situation.

These cases suggest that the Court's scrutiny of legislation is less rigorous where the terms of Congress's prohibitions are coextensive with those of the Constitution. While the Court has shown willingness to allow abrogation in other instances, it has been much more inclined to uphold abrogation where Congress's legislation provides a remedy for violations that are already recognized in or consistent with the Supreme Court's constitutional jurisprudence.

Example 13-17

Mira suffers from severe hearing impairment and was imprisoned in a facility run by the state of Illinois. Her hearing impairment is obvious to anyone who interacts with her. Prison officials confiscated her hearing aid and destroyed it. Although she had documented her medical condition and her need for the hearing aid, the prison officials told her that "she would just have to suffer in silence," refusing to allow her to obtain a replacement. She filed a federal court suit against the state of Illinois, alleging that the state violated a federal statute designed to protect individuals with disabilities. The statute applies to individuals in state prison custody and requires the state to take reasonable steps to satisfy the serious medical needs of disabled prisoners, so as to avoid violations of the Eighth Amendment proscription against "cruel and unusual punishment." The statute further provides that where the state is or should be aware of those needs, but nonetheless fails to satisfy them, the prisoner may sue the state in federal court.

The state of Illinois moved to dismiss the complaint, arguing that Congress's attempt to abrogate was invalid in this instance. Should the district court grant the motion to dismiss?

Explanation

No, the district court should not grant the motion to dismiss. Mira appears to have made the showing necessary to establish that Congress effectively abrogated the Eleventh Amendment bar in the context of this case. To come to this conclusion, one might ask the following questions:

Q.   Has Congress made its intent to abrogate the Eleventh Amendment bar clear?

A.   Yes. Congress has left no doubt that the statute binds the state and that the state is subject to suit in federal court.

Q.   Does Congress have the power to abrogate the Eleventh Amendment in this context?

A.   Yes. Case law establishes that Congress may abrogate when it legislates pursuant to the Fourteenth Amendment. Here, Congress is attempting to provide a remedy for Eighth Amendment violations. The Eighth Amendment is incorporated and applied against the states through the vehicle of the Fourteenth Amendment.

Q.   Does the statute satisfy the "congruence" component of *Boerne*?

A.   Yes. The statute is congruent with a constitutional standard. The deprivation suffered by Mira violates the protection against cruel and unusual punishment of the Eighth Amendment. Her allegations establish that the officials demonstrated "deliberate indifference to [her] serious medical needs," the Eighth Amendment standard for this context.[24] In fact, the statute hews close to the constitutional standard and, for that reason, is well poised to survive the *Boerne–Seminole Tribe* pincer.

Q.   Does the statute satisfy the "proportionality" component of *Boerne*?

A.   Yes. The statute satisfies this component because it requires states to take action that closely mirrors the requirements of the constitutional standard enunciated by courts interpreting the Eighth Amendment.

For all these reasons, Congress effectively abrogated the Eleventh Amendment, and Mira's suit may proceed. This conclusion does not, however, mean that all suits prisoners might bring under the statute are valid. *See United States v. Georgia*, 126 S. Ct. 877, 882 (2006) (explaining in a suit by a prisoner filed under the Americans with Disabilities Act that the determination of whether the abrogation is effective must be evaluated on a "claim-by-claim" basis). One cannot be assured of how rigorous the Supreme Court

---

24. *See Degrafinreid v. Ricks*, 417 F. Supp. 2d 403, 411-412 (S.D.N.Y. 2006) (finding an Eighth Amendment violation under similar facts).

would be in applying this claim-by-claim requirement for every statute passed pursuant to the Fourteenth Amendment.

F. STATES' PREROGATIVE TO WAIVE

Unlike most concepts that regulate "[t]he Judicial power of the United States," the Eleventh Amendment may be waived. In this way, the Eleventh Amendment bar is different from traditional subject matter jurisdiction restrictions. The Supreme Court has tailored a rigorous standard for waiver, however, that protects states from unintended or unconsidered waiver. The Court insists that waiver is accomplished only "'by the most express language or by such overwhelming implications from the text as [will] leave no room for any other reasonable construction.'" *Edelman v. Jordan*, 415 U.S. 651, 673 (1974) (quoting *Murray v. Wilson Distilling Co.*, 213 U.S. 151, 171 (1909)). This standard is similar to the obligation of clarity imposed on Congress when it desires to abrogate the Eleventh Amendment bar.

The Supreme Court has assured states that their decision to waive "sovereign immunity in its own courts is not a waiver of the Eleventh Amendment immunity in the federal courts." *Pennhurst State School & Hosp. v. Halderman*, 465 U.S. 89, 100 n.9 (1984). Where a state expressly waives sovereign immunity over a state law claim in state courts and then removes the case to federal court, the removal amounts to waiver of protection in the federal court as well.[25] A state may also expressly waive Eleventh Amendment protection in the context of litigation filed in federal court in the first instance or by state statute.

Perhaps the most common context where courts find that waiver occurs is when states agree to receive federal funds subject to the condition that they consent to suit. Generally, this occurs when Congress creates a federal program and grants funds to states under its spending power, but requires states to consent to suit for alleged violations of the program's requirements. In this context, Congress acts pursuant to the Constitution's spending clause in Article I, §8, which provides that the "[t]he Congress shall have Power . . . to pay the Debts and provide for the common Defence and general Welfare of the United States." The Supreme Court has said that Congress's decision that spending promotes "the general welfare" is entitled to substantial deference. Nevertheless, where Congress qualifies the grant of funds to states upon compliance with certain conditions, such as consent to federal suit, the Supreme Court has established that (1) Congress must express the conditions unambiguously and (2) the conditions must relate

---

25. *Lapides v. Bd. of Regents*, 535 U.S. 613 (2002).

to the purpose of the federal program being funded.[26] Lower courts have developed an implied waiver theory on the basis of this precedent.

Example 13-18

Nuala has a child with a learning disability, which the local public schools in Maine failed to address. Accordingly, she sent her child to private school and has filed an action in federal court to recover the tuition paid. She named as a defendant the state of Maine, which claimed that the suit against it is barred under the Eleventh Amendment. Nuala argued to the contrary. She maintained that Maine waived the Eleventh Amendment protection by accepting federal educational grants, which it passed on to school districts like those in Nuala's community.

The state had accepted numerous grants under a federal statute known as the Individuals with Disabilities Education Act (IDEA), which specifies the accommodations that schools should provide to disabled students. Congress passed IDEA under its spending power set forth in Article I of the Constitution. IDEA specifies that "[a] State shall not be immune under the 11th amendment to the Constitution of the United States from suit in Federal court for a violation of this chapter." 20 U.S.C. §1403(a).

The state of Maine responded that Congress's attempt to make federal courts available to private plaintiffs was ineffective, because Congress passed IDEA under its Article I powers. Maine reasoned that *Seminole Tribe of Florida v. Florida*, 517 U.S. 44 (1996), prevents Congress from removing Eleventh Amendment protection using a pre–Eleventh Amendment power such as one listed in Article I. Is the state of Maine correct that Nuala's action against it is barred by the Eleventh Amendment?

Explanation

Based on significant lower court precedent, Nuala's action would not be not barred, at least to the extent that she proceeds against the state on the theory that it has violated IDEA. This precedent is based on an implied waiver theory, under which Congress's decision to pass IDEA pursuant to an Article I power (the spending clause) would not present a problem pursuant to *Seminole Tribe of Florida v. Florida*, 517 U.S. 44 (1996). *Seminole Tribe* concerned Congress's power under Article I, but only in the context of Congress's attempt to abrogate the Eleventh Amendment bar. No issue of abrogation is presented here. Rather, this example presents a question of waiver.

Courts have held that Congress satisfied the clear statement requirement for waiver in IDEA. Although the quoted provision does not use the words "waiver" or "consent to suit," the provision makes plain that Congress

---

26. *South Dakota v. Dole*, 483 U.S. 203 (1987).

conditioned the receipt of federal funds on the states agreement to appear in federal court for suits alleging violations of IDEA.[27] But that is as far as the waiver extends. Nuala cannot attempt to exploit the waiver by asserting a claim against the state based on a theory of liability other than IDEA.

G. TEN WAYS INTO FEDERAL COURT: A SUMMARY OF EXCEPTIONS TO OR "WAYS AROUND" THE ELEVENTH AMENDMENT

Consider a hypothetical victim: Vera. The government is acting in a way that is causing Vera damage. She needs to file a lawsuit, and she believes that she would get the fairest reception in federal court. Vera believes that the governmental entity causing most of the problem is a state, so she knows that the Eleventh Amendment could be a significant obstacle. What options, alternatives, or exceptions should Vera consider in order to avoid the Eleventh Amendment bar to suit? Here are ten ideas for getting her case into federal court (and keeping it there):

1. She can sue a governmental entity other than the state, such as the city or a political subdivision that is not an arm of the state.
2. She can orchestrate a suit by the United States acting as plaintiff that might provide her with some benefit (without appearing to benefit herself only).
3. She can orchestrate a suit by another state acting as plaintiff that might provide her with some benefit.
4. She could file the suit in state court (if she can do so under the state's sovereign immunity doctrines) with knowledge that she might be able to get the case ultimately into the United States Supreme Court, which is not subject to Eleventh Amendment restrictions.
5. She could file the suit in state court (if she can do so under the state's sovereign immunity doctrines) and create circumstances where the state would be tempted to remove the case to federal court (thus waiving the Eleventh Amendment bar).
6. She could name a state official as a defendant, assert a violation of federal law, and ask for injunctive relief for a federal law violation.
7. She could name a state official as a defendant, ensure that the defendant is named in his "individual capacity," and try to get around common law immunity doctrines in order to recover damages.
8. She can brainstorm a cause of action under a federal statute where Congress has effectively abrogated the Eleventh Amendment bar.

---

27. See, e.g., Litman v. George Mason, 186 F.3d 544, 553 (4th Cir. 1999); Board of Educ. v. Kelly E., 207 F.3d 931, 932-935 (7th Cir. 2000).

9. She can brainstorm a cause of action under a federal statute where the state has waived the Eleventh Amendment bar.

10. She can file suit against the state under circumstances prompting the state to waive the Eleventh Amendment for the purposes of this particular case.

For some of these techniques, Vera has a choice of cause of action in which to frame her suit. Perhaps 42 U.S.C. §1983, the subject of the next chapter, will serve her needs.

14

CHAPTER

Section 1983

A. INTRODUCTION AND HISTORY

The discipline of Federal Courts and Jurisdiction concerns doctrines regulating access to federal court, as well as the rules of federal court procedure. The provisions of 42 U.S.C. §1983 are not about federal court access and procedure. Instead, §1983 is a "cause of action" statute, which allows plaintiffs to seek remedies for federal wrongs in state or federal court.

Then why is §1983 reliably included in Federal Courts and Jurisdiction materials? As it turns out, §1983 is key to a crucial federal court function: review of alleged state and local violations of federal law. The Supreme Court has declared that Congress enacted §1983 in order to "interpose the federal courts between the States and the people, as guardians of the people's federal rights."[1] As such, §1983 works in tandem with the Eleventh Amendment in governing the manner in which federal courts may supervise state officials. The Eleventh Amendment does not restrict suits against local governments and local officials. Thus, for plaintiffs suffering injury at the hands of local governments and officials, the main obstacle to relief comes in the form of restrictive interpretations of §1983's components.

Section 1983 provides the vehicle for an overwhelming number of federal court rulings on constitutional issues that arise as a result of state or local official action. Suits brought under the statute also account for a huge portion of the federal court docket. Thus, the statute is central to the

---

1. *Mitchum v. Foster*, 407 U.S. 225, 242 (1972).

371

daily workload of the federal judiciary as well as to its role in our governmental system. In other words, to the extent that the statute is read expansively, the federal courts have more to do, and the balance of power shifts away from state and local governments. To the extent that courts narrow §1983's reach, the federal court docket becomes lighter, and power shifts back to state and local governments.

Section 1983 was part of a package of legislative enactments Congress passed into law following the Civil War. Enacted in 1871, the act was a response to a campaign of violence directed at black citizens in the South. Part of a law formally entitled "An Act to enforce the Provisions of the Fourteenth Amendment to the Constitution, and for other Purposes," §1983 is also known as "the Ku Klux Klan Act" — in recognition of the central source of the violence against citizens in 1871. The statute reflected Congress's belief that state and local government could not be trusted to ensure that all citizens enjoyed the rights and privileges that the Fourteenth Amendment promised.

Section 1983 is composed of discrete snippets of language that the Supreme Court has interpreted with alternating expansive and restrictive orientations. Understanding §1983 requires a systematic review of these discrete packets of statutory language. Accordingly, a chapter on §1983 organizes itself and calls for a review of the major portions of the statutory language. This chapter proceeds on that journey.

Section 1983 provides,

> Every person who, under color of any statute, ordinance, regulation, custom, or usage, of any State or Territory or the District of Columbia, subjects, or causes to be subjected, any citizen of the United States or other person within the jurisdiction thereof to the deprivation of any rights, privileges, or immunities secured by the Constitution and laws, shall be liable to the party injured in an action at law, suit in equity, or other proper proceeding for redress. . . .

The most significant (and most litigated) words and clauses in this passage are

- "person"
- "under color of"
- "deprivation of any rights, privileges, or immunities secured by the Constitution and laws"
- "action at law, suit in equity, or other proper proceeding for redress"

Interpreting these words, the Supreme Court has drawn on values present in other portions of federal courts jurisprudence. The Court has also used the §1983 cases to debate conflicting models of government, with differing views of state sovereignty and protection of federal rights featured prominently in justifying divergent approaches. Another governmental matter dominant in the Court's §1983 interpretations is the question of parity between state and federal courts. Those justices who believe that the state and federal courts are equal in their willingness and ability to apply federal law tend to read §1983 restrictively. Those who view federal courts as more inclined to interpret federal law carefully and to apply it vigorously tend to champion the importance of the statute, reading it broadly.

Of the significant words and clauses listed above, the clause that initially proved central to the success of §1983 was "under color of." To these words the chapter now turns.

B. "UNDER COLOR OF": *MONROE V. PAPE*

After its enactment, §1983 was not used for many years. It was not until the early 1960s that civil rights plaintiffs began to file §1983 suits with frequency. An important spark that prompted this new interest in §1983 was the Court's decision in *Monroe v. Pape*, 365 U.S. 167 (1961)). *Monroe v. Pape* interpreted §1983 so as to make its cause of action available to a wide range of plaintiffs injured by officials. The Court did this through an expansive reading of the words "*under color of* any statute, ordinance, regulation, custom, or usage, of any State or Territory. . . ."

The facts recited in the *Monroe v. Pape* complaint were dramatic:

> [Thirteen] Chicago police officers broke into [the Monroe] home in the early morning, routed them from bed, made them stand naked in the living room, and ransacked every room, emptying drawers and ripping mattress covers. . . . Mr. Monroe was then taken to the police station and detained on "open" charges for 10 hours, while he was interrogated about a two-day-old murder. . . . [H]e was not taken before a magistrate, though one was accessible, . . . not permitted to call his family or attorney, [and] . . . was subsequently released without criminal charges being preferred against him.

Id. at 169. With facts this egregious, one would assume that the officers were not acting pursuant to official department policy and that in fact Mr. Monroe might have found that state law itself condemned the officers' conduct. And that, indeed, was the case. As the Court explained, "[T]he courts of Illinois are available to give petitioners that full redress which the common law affords for violence done to a person." Id. at 172.

This observation established that the Court believed Congress wanted §1983 to provide a supplementary remedy—available even if state law provided a means of redress. But does the role of §1983 as a supplementary remedy have anything to do with the meaning of the phrase "under color of"? Yes, the supplementary nature of §1983 is in fact crucial to the phrase's meaning.

To understand the connection between the two, consider that one might read "acting under color of state law" to mean "acting in an officially sanctioned way." From this premise, one might pursue the following chain of reasoning:

1. If a state law remedy exists to "punish" an official's conduct, then the conduct could not have been officially sanctioned.
2. The state remedy would not exist to punish the conduct if the conduct were consistent with official state policy.
3. An official would therefore be acting "under color of" only if a state remedy did not exist.

But the *Monroe v. Pape* Court rejected such a narrow reading of "under color of." The Court's interpretation derives from an alternative reasoning chain:

1. An official can be acting "under color of" state law, even though state law disapproves the official's action and provides a remedy to redress injuries resulting from the action.
2. The official thus can act "under color of" whether or not state law condemns the action.
3. The existence of a state remedy — which renders §1983 a supplementary remedy — does not disqualify an official's actions from being characterized as "under color of."

From this reasoning chain, the following questions emerge: Does the "under color of" requirement have limits? Are officers always acting "under color of" simply because they are employed by the state? As it turns out, the requirement does have limits. *Monroe v. Pape* provided a narrower definition than one based on an official's status as a state employee.

The *Monroe v. Pape* Court defined "under color of" as follows: "'Misuse of power, possessed by virtue of state law and made possible only because the wrongdoer is clothed with the authority of state law.'" *Id.* at 184 (quoting *United States v. Classic*, 313 U.S. 299, 326 (1941)). This standard includes within its scope actions by officers that cross the line of legitimate authority possessed by the officer. The standard does not, however, include conduct that occurs in the context of "purely personal pursuits."[2] *Monroe v. Pape*'s definition of "under color of" tracks the concept of state action used for triggering Fourteenth Amendment protection. The definition is also

---

2. *Martinez v. Colon*, 54 F.3d 980, 987 (1st Cir. 1995).

reminiscent of the approach to "official capacity" suits under the *Ex parte Young* fiction used in Eleventh Amendment case law.[3]

Justice Frankfurter wrote a strong dissent in *Monroe v. Pape*. He argued that Congress intended §1983 not to be supplementary, but available only when federal courts are *really* needed. When is that? Federal courts are *really* needed when states are either endorsing or turning a blind eye to misconduct. In his words, §1983 "created a civil liability enforceable in the federal courts only in instances of injury for which redress was barred in the state courts because some 'statute, ordinance, regulation, custom, or usage' sanctioned the grievance complained of." 365 U.S. at 237. Although the conduct did not need to be officially endorsed to merit federal intervention, Justice Frankfurter would require that the plaintiff at least make a showing that the conduct occurred as part of a state settled practice — or, in the words that are often invoked in this context, some "custom or policy."

Justice Frankfurter's position reflects his view of state courts: they should be trusted to handle illegality. Federal courts should be called in only where some evidence exists that state courts are not adequately guarding principles of justice. This view therefore takes a position on the parity debate, which runs prominently throughout federal courts and jurisdiction doctrine. For Justice Frankfurter, the doctrine should presume state courts to be willing and able to protect rights unless a litigant can show the contrary. The majority in *Monroe v. Pape*, by contrast, emphasized legislative history evincing distrust of state courts in concluding that federal courts should always be available where a plaintiff is able to frame her injuries from official misconduct in terms of a federal law violation.

Justice Frankfurter obviously lost his battle over the "under color of" requirement. His position is significant, however, because it has informed subsequent interpretations of other §1983 clauses. In fact, one might say that although he lost the battle to define "under color of," his position has paved the way for effective inroads into "winning the war" of restricting §1983 to circumstances where officials act pursuant to a specific law or a custom or policy of the governmental body the official represents.

Example 14-1

Assume that the state of North Carolina is having a hotly contested election and that a minority party, the Progression Party, has a strong candidate that may unseat the incumbent governor, Lauren. One night at around 10:30 p.m., Margot was driving a truck for the Progression Party in the center of a major town. The truck carried a lighted sign that advertised the Progression Party. As she drove the truck past a noisy and chaotic crowd,

---

3. See Chapter 13, discussing the Eleventh Amendment, for further explanation of the *Ex parte Young* fiction.

someone from a crowd threw a rock at the truck. She stopped the truck to examine the damage. At that point, a uniformed state trooper approached Margot and asked her whether a problem existed. Margot was explaining to the state trooper what had happened when the trooper told her she was causing trouble and started beating Margot with a billy club. At that point, the incumbent governor, Lauren, stepped out of the crowd and told the trooper, "Step away. I'll handle this." Recognizing Lauren as the governor, the trooper stopped the beating and stepped away. Next, Lauren took off her shoe and started beating Margot. Lauren was wearing casual clothes at the time, and never identified herself as the governor.

Margot brought a §1983 action against Lauren for violating her constitutional rights. Lauren moved to dismiss the suit on the ground that the facts failed to establish that she was acting "under color of" state law. Should the district court dismiss the suit?

Explanation

Lauren is correct that the suit should be dismissed for failure to state a claim if the conduct alleged did not occur "under color of" state law. The "under color of" requirement is a component of the §1983 cause of action, without which the action cannot succeed. The question of whether the requirement is satisfied usually entails a highly fact-specific inquiry into the circumstances under which the officer exhibited the challenged conduct. The circumstances here present a close case because Lauren's conduct possesses both personal and official qualities. On balance, however, the conduct probably does not satisfy the *Monroe v. Pape* standard.

The context for the violence in this example suggests that Lauren, as the governor, may have been nervous about losing the next election and was unhappy with Margot's prominent work for the opposing candidate. This observation does not necessarily help establish that Lauren was acting "under color of." While "being the governor" is part of Lauren's official duties, "running for governor" is not. Running for governor is a personal pursuit. Thus, any suggestion that Lauren approached Margot in her capacity as a candidate for reelection does not shroud Lauren's actions with official character.

What *does* raise the specter of official authority, however, is the possibility that Lauren may be using her position as governor to leverage or to enhance her reelection campaign. In this regard, a salient fact in the example is the state trooper's immediate respect for Lauren's instruction, "Step away. I'll handle this." Were Lauren acting as a private citizen only, she would not have possessed the power to order a uniformed police officer to withdraw from a scuffle. Nor would the officer be likely to yield to a private citizen's instruction to withdraw. Although the officer's response does not rise to the level of establishing a "conspiracy" between the state trooper and Lauren, it does suggest that Lauren was interacting with the trooper in her official capacity. The trooper's actions imply awareness that Lauren possessed authority exceeding the trooper's. This is also manifest in the suggestion that the trooper stood by while Lauren continued the beating. A private individual would likely not enjoy such deference from the trooper.

Clearly, the trooper was acting "under color of" state law: the trooper was wearing a uniform, used a department-issued weapon (the billy club), and was purporting to perform law enforcement duties in connection with a disturbance. Thus, Lauren may have been using her official power over the officer toward achieving the unofficial, personal goal of impeding a campaign worker for Lauren's opponent. (A separate, successful §1983 action may be brought against the trooper.)

The argument in favor of liability on the basis of Lauren's official status, however, falters at this point in the facts. Arguably, Lauren's use of her official power ended at the point where she "called off" the officer. From that point in time, Lauren's actions appear personal and nonofficial. And it is those actions — the beating of Margot — that are the basis for the §1983 liability against Lauren.

For guidance in handling this ambiguity, one can turn to the precise language of the *Monroe v. Pape* standard, which states that for the challenged action — beating Margot — to be "under color of" state law, the action must have been "made possible only because [Lauren was] clothed with the authority of state law." 365 U.S. at 184 (quoting *United States v. Classic*, 313 U.S. 299, 325-326 (1941)). In applying this standard, one can ask either of two possible questions: (1) Was the beating possible only because Lauren had the authority to require the officer to withdraw from the scuffle? (2) Was the beating possible only because Lauren summoned the strength as a private citizen to brutalize another human being? Only if the first question reflects the more accurate perspective would Lauren be deemed to be acting "under color of" state law.

Other factors in the case help in choosing between the two alternatives, pointing away from the conclusion that Lauren was acting "under color of." First is the time of the incident: 11:30 p.m. is generally not an hour when a governor performs official functions. Although governors do make public appearances, they generally do not do so late at night in a chaotic setting. Lauren never identified herself as governor and was not dressed in professional attire. Moreover, while a violent action might attend a police officer's dispatch of her official duties, violence is far outside the range of appropriate actions for the chief executive of a major state. If Lauren had been using her authority (or, rather, misusing her authority) to accomplish the beating, she would be more likely to have ordered the trooper to continue. Lauren's act of using her own shoe to perform the beating suggests that the action was performed personally, and not at all within the umbrella of official authority. On balance, then, the facts favor the conclusion that

Lauren was not acting "under color of" when she performed the beating. *See Rodriguez-Rodriguez v. Ortiz-Velez*, 405 F. Supp. 2d 162 (D.P.R. 2005) (concluding that mayor was not acting "under color of" when he physically beat a political party worker).

Example 14-2

Marianne was a middle school teacher for a school district run under the authority of the state of South Dakota. During her probationary period, the principal of Marianne's school evaluated her performance as required under school district regulations. The principal wrote a report about Marianne that could only be described as vicious. The report included comments on Marianne's hygiene ("Marianne is a walking health hazard to all"), her taste in clothes ("Godzilla has better fashion sense than Marianne"), the condition of her car ("Marianne drives a wreck on wheels, which looks like a junk pile in the teachers' parking lot"), and her lack of friends ("Marianne repulses all around her, making it impossible for her to maintain meaningful personal relationships"). The report also said that Marianne's teaching was ineffective. In what appeared to be an unnecessary and mean-spirited gesture, the principal delivered a copy of the report to Marianne at her home before sending it by mail to the school district office.

On the basis of this report, the school district denied tenure to Marianne. She filed a §1983 action against the principal, arguing that the principal's actions denied her due process of law. The principal argued that she is not subject to §1983 liability because the actions described did not occur "under color of" state authority. Should the district court dismiss the complaint?

Explanation

No, the district court should not dismiss the complaint. The principal possesses supervisory power by virtue of state law. Each of the principal's actions that provide the basis for suit — evaluating Marianne, writing a report, and delivering a report — is within the scope of the principal's supervisory duties. Some of the topics discussed in the report are peripheral to the official function of the report: to evaluate Marianne's teaching performance. Nonetheless, the topics may be justified by the observation that, as a teacher, Marianne needs to provide a role model to students. The off-color tone of the comments is not enough to remove the comments from the official's shroud of authority.

The delivery of the report is somewhat problematic, since the manner of delivery was unusual for a professional relationship. But the fact of delivery was not unusual. Indeed, as a supervisor, the principal acted well within her official capacity — indeed, appropriately — in giving Marianne notice of the contents of the report. The context of delivery — outside of the workplace—makes the action less official but does not make it a personal act outside the scope of the principal's duties under state law.

C. EXHAUSTION OF STATE REMEDIES

Monroe v. Pape established that §1983 is available even if state remedies may also be effective in remedying the federal law violation. Thus, the decision stands for the proposition that a civil rights plaintiff need not exhaust state court remedies before filing a §1983 action in federal court. The Supreme Court has several times stated that this principle applies to state administrative remedies as well, although the issue has inspired controversy and debate over which governmental values should dominate decisions about §1983's reach.

In a prominent reaffirmation of the non-exhaustion rule, *Patsy v. Board of Regents of Florida*, 457 U.S. 496, 503-506 (1982), the majority revisited the legislative history of §1983, noting that the congressional debates preceding its enactment reflect three themes: (1) "Congress assigned to the federal courts a paramount role in protecting constitutional rights"; (2) Congress believed that "state authorities had been unable or unwilling to protect the constitutional rights of individuals or to punish those who violated these rights"; (3) "many legislators interpreted the bill to provide dual or concurrent forums in the state and federal system, enabling the plaintiff to choose the forum in which to seek relief." Id. at 503-506. The majority cited each of these themes as evidence that Congress did not want to impose on plaintiffs the burden of first petitioning what may be an unsympathetic state tribunal.

On the other side of the balance are those values emphasized by the dissent. The dissent argued that an exhaustion requirement demonstrates respect for states by allowing them to correct their own mistakes, and in fact encourages states to develop procedures to eliminate the effect of federal law violations. The dissent also urged that the exhaustion rule, being "highly relevant to the effective functioning of the overburdened federal court system, . . . conserves and supplements scarce judicial resources" by screening frivolous claims. Id. at 533.

Patsy v. Board of Regents appeared to settle the question of whether §1983 should have an exhaustion requirement. But, as with many issues in the area of federal courts, the game is not over! Indeed, the tension between the majority and dissent in *Patsy* continues to inform the exhaustion debate. And the dissenting position has gained ground—first in the Supreme Court and then in Congress.

In *Heck v. Humphrey*, 512 U.S. 477 (1994), the Court created an exhaustion requirement for criminal defendants trying to recover damages for an unconstitutional conviction or imprisonment. *Heck* declared that the plaintiff must obtain an executive pardon or reversal of the conviction or sentence on appeal before pursuing a §1983 action. Next, the Supreme Court extended *Heck* to a prisoner's §1983 challenge to prison discipline procedures in *Edwards v. Balisok*, 520 U.S. 641 (1997). *Edwards* required an extension of *Heck*'s exhaustion requirement because the plaintiff in *Edwards* did not attempt to collaterally attack his conviction and sentence, but rather claimed that the discipline system within the prison violated fundamental fairness. Congress embraced this restrictive review of prison litigation in the Prison Litigation Reform Act, 42 U.S.C. §1997e(a), which creates an exhaustion requirement for prisoners who bring lawsuits challenging prison conditions.

Example 14-3

Arno was an office worker for the Arizona State Department on Aging. He repeatedly showed up for work late and was fired as a consequence. He believed that he was fired because of his ethnic background. Rather than file a grievance with the administrative tribunal responsible for adjudicating personnel matters for the state, Arno filed a §1983 action in federal court. Arno named the chief commissioner of the Department on Aging as a defendant. The chief commissioner argued that Arno's suit was premature because Arno had not exhausted his state administrative remedies. Is the chief commissioner correct?

Explanation

No, the chief commissioner is not correct. Arno's suit falls within the general rule of *Patsy v. Board of Regents*, and he therefore does not need to exhaust his state administrative remedies. The exceptions to the *Patsy* rule are subject matter dependent, and apply for prisoner litigation, takings clause litigation, and state tax challenges. The subject matter of Arno's suit does not fall within any of these categories.

Example 14-4

Priscilla is an inmate in a state prison. She is in a work release program under which she is allowed to leave prison every day in order to work in outside employment. One day, after leaving prison grounds, the guard who drives the work release van asked her to have sex with him in the van. When she refused, he beat her brutally. She filed a §1983 suit, arguing that the guard and the warden violated her constitutional rights by subjecting her to this violence. Although the prison has an internal procedure for processing grievances, she did not avail herself of that procedure, fearing even more harassment from other prison guards.

The defendants moved to dismiss the suit, arguing that she failed to exhaust her administrative remedies as required by the Prison Litigation Reform Act (PLRA), which states, "No action shall be brought with respect to prison conditions under section 1983 of this title, or any other Federal law, by a prisoner confined in any jail, prison, or other correctional facility until such administrative remedies as are available are exhausted." 42 U.S.C. §1997e(a). Priscilla responded that this requirement applied only to challenges to general prison conditions, not to complaints focusing on a particular harm done to one inmate. In addition, Priscilla maintained that the sexual harassment and the excessive force she experienced outside the prison walls did not fall within the ambit of the words "prison conditions" in 42 U.S.C. §1997e(a). Is Priscilla correct?

Explanation

No, Priscilla is not correct. For Priscilla to prevail, the court would have to read the PLRA narrowly, hewing close to the precise language. But the Supreme Court has in fact suggested that the contrary approach — a broad reading of the exhaustion requirement — is more consistent with Congress's intent. See, e.g., Booth v. Churner, 532 U.S. 731 (2001) (applying the exhaustion requirement to a prisoner seeking only money damages, despite the unavailability of monetary relief in the administrative forum). Moreover, the Supreme Court has specifically rejected a similar argument by a prisoner subjected to excessive force. In Porter v. Nussle, 534 U.S. 516 (2002), the Court held that the PLRA exhaustion requirement applies to all inmate suits based on conditions of prison life, including excessive-force complaints and complaints about egregious acts done to particular inmates.

Priscilla's case is stronger than the prisoner's case in Porter v. Nussle because the injury to Priscilla took place outside the prison and was therefore not literally a "prison condition." Yet, as Porter v. Nussle explained, Congress's concern in the PLRA was focused less on prison conditions per se than on the problem of prisoner lawsuits that were clogging the federal courts and distracting them from pressing matters. Since Priscilla is a prisoner and her injury occurred as part of her status as a prisoner, her claim falls within the ambit of claims that Congress meant to subject to an exhaustion requirement. Moreover, accepting Priscilla's argument might require the bifurcation of lawsuits into those directly pertaining to general conditions in prisons and those pertaining to more individualized grievances that arose outside the prison walls. This would complicate the procedural rules governing prison litigation, contrary to the intent of Congress to allow tribunals to process prisoner suits more efficiently. In passing the PLRA, Congress sought to keep problems of prison administration out of the complex processes of adversarial litigation, leaving them in the hands of those who are the experts: the state officials who run the prisons.

Aside from the PLRA and judicially created rules for prison litigation, three other subject matter–specific concerns relating to exhaustion deserve note. First, the Supreme Court has applied an exhaustion requirement in the state taxation context. In two cases, the Court has ruled that federal courts should decline to hear requests for damages or injunctive remedies in state tax cases where state law provides an adequate remedy.[4] Next, the demand for "finality" in Fifth Amendment takings clause cases can also compel one to resort to administrative remedies before pursuing a constitutional challenge.[5] Although distinguishable from an exhaustion requirement, the finality barrier for takings claims has the same practical effect as an exhaustion requirement for the §1983 plaintiff. Third, substantive law governing adequate due process can also bear on whether a §1983 plaintiff will succeed in litigating a due process challenge. This matter (which is only peripherally related to exhaustion of state administrative remedies) is discussed later in this chapter, in connection with *Parratt v. Taylor*, 451 U.S. 527 (1981), and its progeny.

D. "PERSON"

Section 1983 provides a cause of action against "[e]very person" who violates federal constitutional rights and statutory rights under color of state law. Despite this apparently broad language, the Supreme Court has been very specific about who qualifies as a "person" — even defining particular circumstances under which a court can deem an entity a "person" for the purpose of §1983 liability. Viewed in a vacuum, the decisions interpreting the "person" requirement appear to be oddly tortuous and complicated. One key to deciphering their mysteries, however, is to remember that the Supreme Court has interpreted §1983's scope against the background of the Eleventh Amendment, which prevents courts from entertaining suits against governments and governmental officials under many circumstances. Since §1983 provides a vehicle for challenging governmental action, the Court is appropriately coordinating two lines of doctrine, interweaving Eleventh Amendment concepts with §1983. Chapter 13 discusses the Eleventh Amendment in detail, and its requirements are reviewed below as necessary.

---

4. *Nat'l Private Truck Council, Inc. v. Okla. Tax Comm'n*, 515 U.S. 582 (1995); *Fair Assessment in Real Estate Ass'n Inc. v. McNary*, 454 U.S. 100 (1981).
5. *See, e.g., Williamson County Regional Planning Comm'n v. Hamilton Bank of Johnson City*, 473 U.S. 172 (1985) (ruling that plaintiff could not proceed with takings clause challenge to zoning board action without first seeking a variance from administrative entity).

1. State Governments

Section 1983 creates liability for every "person" operating "under color of" various laws (statutes, ordinances, and the like) of "any State or Territory." The legislative history of the statute makes plain that Congress did not intend to confine liability to natural persons (human beings). If one were to venture a guess as to what entity might count as a "person" under the statute, one might say "any State" or "any Territory." And that would be wrong. Why? As in many instances with the "person" requirement, the explanation derives from the Eleventh Amendment.

As explained in Chapter 13, the Supreme Court held in *Quern v. Jordan*, 440 U.S. 332 (1979), that Congress did not create an exception to the Eleventh Amendment bar to suits against states when it passed §1983. The *Quern v. Jordan* Court reasoned that when Congress creates an exception to the Eleventh Amendment, it must do so in unmistakably clear language, a standard Congress failed to satisfy in §1983. Thus, the question of whether a state is a "person" for the purposes of the statute is irrelevant for federal court suits because the Eleventh Amendment would disqualify the suits anyway.

But the Eleventh Amendment speaks only in terms of "[t]he Judicial power of the United States," and thus does not explicitly govern in state court. Since state courts can hear §1983 suits, the question remained whether state governments could be "persons" under the statute. Finally, the Supreme Court decided in *Will v. Michigan Dep't of State Police*, 491 U.S. 58 (1989), that states are not persons for §1983 purposes. The *Will* Court's reasoning was intertwined with *Quern v. Jordan* and the Eleventh Amendment. Noting that *Quern v. Jordan* had failed to find an explicit intent by Congress to override the Eleventh Amendment, the *Will* Court concluded that it likewise could not find that Congress "intended to disregard the well-established immunity of a State from being sued without its consent." Id. at 67. Following its decision in *Will v. Michigan Dep't of State Police*, the Supreme Court ruled that Congress's inclusion of territories in §1983 did not make them directly liable, but rather meant they should be treated as states. Thus, in light of its ruling in *Will*, the Court also ruled that territories are not persons for the purpose of the statute.[6]

2. Municipalities

Recall from the discussion of *Monroe v. Pape* that Justice Frankfurter lost the battle to confine §1983 liability to instances where officials acted pursuant to an explicit law, custom, or policy of the government they represent.

---

6. *See Ngiraingas v. Sanchez*, 495 U.S. 182 (1990).

Municipality liability under §1983 is one context where this position has prevailed. And, indeed, it is an important context. Municipalities, which include cities, counties, and other local governments, provide the bulk of human services in U.S. society. As the providers of such services as education, fire and police protection, and social safety net programs, municipalities interact frequently with citizens and are therefore in a position to violate citizens' rights.

Reversing its earlier position that municipalities were not persons for the purposes of §1983,[7] the Supreme Court ruled in *Monell v. Dep't of Soc. Servs.*, 436 U.S. 658 (1978), that plaintiffs may bring §1983 suits against local governments for damages, or declaratory or injunctive relief, for an action taken pursuant to a policy or custom of the municipality. Specifically, the Court stated that local governments could be sued for actions that implement or execute "a policy statement, ordinance, regulation, or decision officially adopted and promulgated by that body's officers" or that occur "pursuant to governmental 'custom' even though such a custom has not received formal approval through the body's official decisionmaking channels." *Id.* at 690-691.[8]

In limiting liability to action taken pursuant to a custom or policy, the Court eliminated a specific type of liability: liability for the random acts of officials. Had the Court intended to include such unauthorized actions within §1983's scope, it would have adopted what is known in tort law as vicarious liability or respondeat superior liability, that is, liability borne by an employer simply because the employer employs a tortfeasor. Thus, the Court explained that liability for the municipal government is present only when the official's "execution of a government's policy or custom" is the source of the plaintiff's injury. *Id.* at 694.

Example 14-5

One afternoon, the head of the license and inspections division in a large city stopped at a bar to ascertain whether the bar was complying with the local code. Finding a violation, the official told the bar owner she would forgive the violation if the owner gave her a year's worth of free drinks as a "gratuity." The bar owner capitulated, and the official immediately began to enjoy the gratuity, downing several drinks. While intoxicated, the official drove her city-owned car into oncoming traffic and struck a car driven by

---

7. This earlier ruling actually appeared in *Monroe v. Pape.*
8. As explained below, §1983 liability is available against municipal officers for prospective (injunctive and declaratory) relief. For that reason, allowing §1983 liability against municipalities for such relief makes little practical difference to a plaintiff trying to remedy a wrong. What is significant, however, is that since immunity doctrines do not shield municipalities, *Monell* effectively authorizes suits against municipalities for damages, a remedy that is unavailable in actions against municipal officers. LARRY W. YACKLE, FEDERAL COURTS 415 (2d ed. 2003) (explaining *Monell*'s significance).

Cassi. Cassi was badly injured and sued the city under §1983 for the damages she incurred as a result of the accident, claiming that the officials' actions violated her due process rights. The city moved to dismiss the suit for failure to state a cause of action. Should the court grant the motion?

Explanation

Yes, the court should probably grant the motion to dismiss the suit. This case does not appear to fall within the category of cases for which the *Monell* Court intended to create §1983 liability for municipalities. The type of wrong here appears to be a random bad act of an official, rather than an action taken pursuant to a law, custom, or policy. To hold the municipality liable under these circumstances would likely involve imposing vicarious liability, simply because the municipality employed a tortfeasor. As demonstrated below, Cassi is not wholly without a remedy: she can proceed against the license and inspections official in the official's personal capacity.

a. Ascertaining Law, Custom or Policies

Monell thus stands for the proposition that a §1983 plaintiff can get damages and other relief from a municipal government only if the plaintiff can show that the government created a law or endorsed or officially acquiesced in a custom or policy that violated the plaintiff's federal rights. If the law comes in the form of a legislative enactment, the analysis is generally straightforward, since the enactment speaks for itself. Moreover, the Supreme Court has said that "a single decision by . . . [a] properly constituted legislative body . . . constitutes an act of official government policy."[9]

The difficult job is identifying when a custom or policy exists in the absence of an official enactment. That process can entangle courts and litigants in a process of reviewing office manuals and tracing the chain of command in a local bureaucracy. In areas of doubt, state and local law controls the determination of who makes policy for the local government.[10] Moreover, liability can arise not only from recognized customs or policies, but also from certain circumstances where a municipality does not — but should — have a custom or policy.

b. Recognized Customs or Policies

In the absence of a legislative enactment that itself constitutes the challenged law, a custom or policy can exist in two circumstances: (1) where legislative authority that is delegated to a municipal agency or board results in a

---

9. *Pembaur v. City of Cincinnati*, 475 U.S. 469, 480 (1986).
10. *City of St. Louis v. Praprotnik*, 485 U.S. 112 (1988).

generalized action or (2) where individuals with final authority render an isolated decision that affects the plaintiff. The first circumstance is illustrated by Monell itself, where the Court held that regulations adopted by the city Department of Social Services and Board of Education requiring pregnant employees to take unpaid leaves and applied to specific individuals involved official policy.

The Supreme Court has encountered a greater challenge in mapping the parameters of the second circumstance. For example, in Pembaur v. City of Cincinnati, 475 U.S. 469 (1986), the Court held that a county could be liable for the single decision of a prosecutor authorizing law enforcement officers to make an unconstitutional entry into a doctor's clinic. By contrast, in City of St. Louis v. Praprotnik, 485 U.S. 112 (1988), a plurality of the Supreme Court refused to hold a city liable for alleged First Amendment violations that occurred when two senior supervisors dismissed a subordinate. The plurality applied state law to conclude that only the mayor and other select officials had policymaking authority over personnel decisions, but ruled that none of these policymakers had adopted a policy that caused the objectionable dismissal. Significantly, the Court concluded that the policymakers' delegation of discretion to take employment action to the supervisors did not allow for municipal liability for the supervisors' conduct.

In Jett v. Dallas Indep. Sch. Dist., 491 U.S. 701 (1989), a majority of the Supreme Court endorsed the reasoning of the Praprotnik plurality and outlined a procedure for deciding custom or policy questions concerning individual decisionmakers:

> (i) the judge should resolve first whether the municipal employee taking action has final decisionmaking authority, taking into account specific state and local laws as well as " 'custom or usage' having the force of law"; and
> (ii) the jury then decides whether the actual policymakers' decisions "caused the deprivation of rights at issue by policies which affirmatively command that [the deprivation] occur . . . or by acquiescence in a longstanding practice or custom which constitutes the 'standard operating procedure' of the local governmental entity."

Id. at 737, quoting City of St. Louis v. Praprotnik, 485 U.S. 112, 124 n.1 (1988).

Example 14-6

Spotted Owl Elementary School is in Lower Falls Township and is part of the Lower Falls School District. Students in the school proposed a design for their school tee-shirt that featured a spotted owl hanging by a noose. The children designed the tee-shirt to protest the potential extinction of their school mascot. The school principal refused to permit this design to be used, ruling that the design could not appear on the official school tee-shirt and that students were forbidden from wearing it. The principal explained that the tee-shirt conveyed a potentially violent message, contrary to the school's commitment to civility and morality.

In response to the principal's decision, the students sued the township of Lower Falls for damages resulting from this invasion of their First Amendment rights. They cited two theories for why the principal's actions represented a custom or policy of the township of Lower Falls. First, in explaining that the design could not be used, the principal pointed to the Spotted Owl Elementary School dress code, a written document stating that students were forbidden from wearing clothes bearing messages of violence. Next, they argued that the principal is the final decisionmaker on discipline issues for the school.

Research reveals that this is the first problem involving student free speech rights in the Lower Falls School District. The Lower Falls School District is run by a seven-member school board, elected by the township citizens. Because the state where Lower Falls is located provides extensive funding to the school district, however, the state department of education exerts significant influence over school district operations. Nevertheless, the Lower Falls School Board selects the Superintendent of Schools, who serves at the grace of the board. The superintendent exercises authority to hire and to fire school principals throughout the district.

The school board has promulgated a set of regulations, which include the following:

> Principals of schools are the responsible administrative heads of their respective schools and are charged with supervision and discipline thereof. They shall establish and enforce such regulations as they deem necessary, so long as the regulations are not contrary to the Rules of the School Board, the Uniform School District Disciplinary Code, or the rulings of the Superintendent of Schools.

Research also shows that the principal created the dress code pursuant to this regulation, which is unique to the Spotted Owl Elementary School in the Lower Falls School District.

Based on this research, what type of arguments might the township of Lower Falls make in order to avoid the conclusion that the principal's decision reflected a custom or policy attributable to the township?

Explanation

The plaintiffs are making an attack on two fronts, and the township needs to respond accordingly. The plaintiffs' attack is based on arguments establishing two separate customs or policies: (1) the written dress code and (2) the principal's decision to forbid the tee-shirt.

As to the dress code, the township should argue that the dress code is subject to higher levels of authority — including the rules of the Board of Education, the Uniform School District Disciplinary Code, and the superintendent's ruling. Therefore, the township could argue that the written dress code is a far cry from the official codification of delegated authority at issue in *Monell*, where the agencies involved promulgated rules providing the governing standards for handling pregnant workers.

This same approach will be useful to the township in arguing that the principal's decision is not a custom or policy. The township should assert that the first prong of the *Jett v. Dallas Indep. Sch. Dist.* test is not satisfied because the principal is not a final decisionmaker. In so arguing, the township can point to the school district's hierarchical structure, which suggests that the superintendent maintains complete control over the principal. Moreover, the school board's regulation makes clear that the superintendent can veto any decisions of the principal.

The township can further argue that the plaintiffs cannot resolve the municipal liability problem by focusing their arguments on the superintendent. Even assuming that the superintendent is the final decision-maker, the plaintiffs' case stumbles on the second prong of the *Jett v. Dallas Indep. Sch. Dist.* test. The plaintiffs would not be able to establish that the superintendent "caused the deprivation of rights at issue," since the facts show neither that the principal was acting pursuant to the superintendent's policy nor that the superintendent acquiesced in "a longstanding practice or custom which constitutes the 'standard operating procedure.'" *Jett*, 491 U.S. at 737. As the facts suggest, this is the first problem dealing with student speech rights in the history of the school district.

By arguing on both fronts, the township is likely to encounter success in avoiding municipal liability. *See Brandt v. Board of Education of City of Chicago*, 420 F. Supp. 2d 921 (N.D. Ill. 2006) (finding no municipal liability arising from principal's actions within similar school district structure). As a backup point of attack, plaintiffs can also investigate whether the school district administration is properly described as a municipal entity. Because the school district administration is entwined with the state, the township may be able to argue that the action here is attributable to the state, in which case liability would be unavailable. Precedent for such an argument appears in *McMillian v. Monroe County, Alabama*, 520 U.S. 781 (1997), in which the Court held that a county sheriff could not be a final decisionmaker for the local government because he was a state official.

c. Failure to Act

Perhaps no issue has attracted more § 1983 litigation than the question of when liability should attach for local governments who fail to provide a custom or policy in circumstances where prudence calls for one. Many of the cases have involved plaintiffs who claimed that law enforcement personnel received inadequate training. The Supreme Court outlined the general approach for analyzing "failure to train" cases in *City of Canton, Ohio v. Harris*, 489 U.S. 378

(1989). The *City of Canton* Court held that in order to demonstrate a policy of inadequate training, the plaintiff must prove that the local government acted with deliberate indifference. The Court also insisted that for liability to attach, the injury must have been caused by the inadequacy of the training program itself, not simply by the individual officer's mistake or indifference.

In a subsequent decision, the Supreme Court refined the causation requirement even further. In *Board of the County Comm'rs v. Brown*, 520 U.S. 397 (1997), the Court ruled that the plaintiff must establish that the municipality's deliberate indifference led to the risk that the particular injury suffered by the plaintiff would occur. By its own description, the Court required a "rigorous standard[] of culpability and causation" for the case, which involved a claim that a municipality had not adequately screened a police officer who had violent propensities. *Id.* at 405. Explaining that a single instance of inadequate screening was not sufficient for liability, the Court added that liability would depend on a "finding that [the] officer was highly likely to inflict the *particular* injury suffered by the plaintiff." *Id.* at 412 (emphasis in original).

Example 14-7

Police officers employed by the Miami Police Department conducted a raid using the department's canine unit. During the raid, one of the police officers lost control of a police dog, which inflicted permanent injury on Sally Suspect. Sally filed a §1983 action against Miami, seeking money damages. The sole basis for relief is Sally's claim that the city failed to adequately train its officers to control police dogs during raids. After discovery, Sally learned that the dog that attacked her suffered from a genetic condition causing the dog to behave violently and erratically, and to attack without prior notice of violent potential. Sally's research shows that an easily administered saliva test would have identified the genetic condition. This particular dog had never shown erratic behavior before.

The city of Miami has moved to dismiss the suit, arguing that it is not a "person" for the purposes of the §1983 liability. Should the court dismiss the suit?

Explanation

The Court should dismiss the case. Although one might be able to establish that the Miami Police Department was negligent in failing to detect the dog's genetic condition or to adequately control the dog, their failure to do so does not likely amount to deliberate indifference.

One might argue that the hostile settings in which police use dogs suggest a need for training. After all, police dogs are selected and trained to be loyal to their handlers, who are often under physical threat during raids. But the facts do not suggest that lack of training was the precise cause of the injury here. The rigorous standard of the case law likely requires a more concrete and particularized causation analysis linking the injury to the precise failure on the part of the municipality. Here, Sally's injury was caused by the failure by police to ascertain that this particular dog had a genetic defect linked to unpredictable, violent behavior. Because the facts establish that the dog had not exhibited erratic behavior before and include no reports of other dogs with genetic conditions causing problems in police canine units, the municipality could argue that it lacked notice of the need for testing and therefore could not have acted with "deliberate indifference." Accordingly, Sally will likely fail in her attempt to establish municipal liability. As the Brown Court said, a single instance of inadequate screening is not sufficient for liability.

Example 14-8

Tanya was seventy-one years old when she was found guilty of embezzling and sentenced to three years in the Sussex County prison. When she surrendered at prison, she explained to the intake physician that she had suffered several bouts of congestive heart failure. Ten days later, her heart condition worsened. Tanya was visited by nurses, who took her vital signs. The information recorded by the nurses documented that Tanya suffered from a severe and worsening medical condition. Three months later, without ever being seen by a physician, Tanya died.

Tanya's spouse brought a §1983 suit on her behalf against the county, arguing that the medical staff at the Sussex County prison acted improperly in failing to get her proper medical care. According to the complaint, an autopsy revealed that Tanya would have likely survived if she had received proper medications prescribed by a physician. Tanya's spouse, however, learned during discovery that doctors rarely, if ever, visit patients at the prison and that the warden has been heard to say that prisoners are "cheaper to feed when they are dead."

Sussex County moved to dismiss the case before trial, pointing to a prison policy stating that nurses should send for a physician if a patient's medical condition appears to be "serious." According to the county, this policy demonstrated that the county had procedures in place to ensure the welfare of its prisoners. Moreover, the county argued, the nurses who attended Tanya were trained professionals with valid nursing certificates, and Tanya's spouse could not show that other deaths at the prison occurred under similar circumstances. Based on these arguments, should the court grant the motion to dismiss?

Explanation

No, the court should probably not grant the motion. Tanya's spouse may be able to make a case for deliberate indifference, even though the facts do not suggest that the prison experienced a pattern of deaths under this type of medical circumstance. The *Board of County Comm'rs v. Brown* Court explained that a plaintiff might succeed in establishing a "failure to train" claim without demonstrating a pattern of violations where "a violation of federal rights may be a highly predictable consequence of a failure to equip law enforcement officers with specific tools to handle recurring situations." 520 U.S. at 409.

The county may argue that the nursing certificates constitute "specific tools to handle recurring situations." While helpful, the certificates alone do not insulate the county from liability. Although the nurses' training may inform them of circumstances calling for aggressive medical treatment, they nonetheless may not act on their knowledge if the prison employs insufficient doctors or practices an ethic of medical neglect. The warden's comment suggests that either or both of those conditions may exist in this circumstance. If that is the case, then the formal policy of sending for physicians to treat serious conditions cannot save the county from liability, since the officials either cannot or will not apply the policy.

Although a close call, this is the type of case in which a plaintiff might convince a jury that the defendant acted with deliberate indifference. Accordingly, a court would likely allow the case to proceed to trial. *See Long v. County of Los Angeles*, 442 F.3d 1178 (9th Cir. 2006) (denying summary judgment motion in case of medical neglect causing prisoner's death).

3. Individual Officers

In mapping circumstances under which state, territorial, and municipal officials are "persons" in §1983 suits, one must distinguish between "official capacity" actions and "individual capacity" actions. As explored in detail in Chapter 13, the distinction turns largely on which entity is expected to satisfy the judgment.[11]

For "official capacity" actions, the plaintiff may name the official as a defendant, but the government for whom the official works will actually satisfy the judgment. Satisfying the judgment can involve (1) paying damages if the judgment is a damages judgment or (2) financing compliance with prospective relief if the judgment is a declaratory judgment or an injunction. If the plaintiff chooses to sue an official in her individual capacity, the plaintiff proceeds as she would in any other private tort action.

---

11. Chapter 13 also reviews approaches to distinguishing between "official capacity" and "personal capacity" suits.

In such a case, the plaintiff may expect to have her judgment satisfied if she can successfully navigate common law immunity doctrines and indemnification procedures protecting the officials. Common law immunity doctrines are reviewed later in this chapter, as well as in Chapter 13.

Indemnification procedures are voluntarily provided by governmental entities to employees to pay for judgments against the employee. As a result of indemnification, a governmental entity that has successfully avoided direct liability for a wrong done "under color of" the government's authority may nonetheless pay the entire cost of a §1983 judgment. Since the indemnification process is voluntary, however, neither governmental entities nor employees may claim that indemnity is a shield against liability. For plaintiffs, indemnification can provide a bureaucratic barrier to satisfying a judgment. Indemnification is also discussed in detail in Chapter 13.

a. State Officers

In *Will v. Michigan Dep't of State Police*, 491 U.S. 58 (1989), the Supreme Court decided that states are not "persons" for the purposes of §1983 and that §1983 plaintiffs cannot sue state officials in their official capacity for damages. The Court reasoned that "a suit against a state official in his or her official capacity is not a suit against the official but rather is a suit against the official's office. . . . As such, it is no different from a suit against the State itself." *Id.* at 71 (citation omitted). Citing the Eleventh Amendment decision in *Ex parte Young*, 209 U.S. 123 (1908), the *Will* Court made an important modification to this prohibition: state officials were persons for the purposes of §1983 when sued in their official capacity for prospective relief. Thus, the Eleventh Amendment once again explains the Court's distinctions in defining a "person" for §1983 purposes. Using the *Ex parte Young* fiction, the §1983 plaintiff can evade the §1983 limitation preventing the plaintiff from formally naming the state as a defendant.

The Eleventh Amendment does not regulate suits against state officers in their personal capacity, since these suits seek personal liability against the officers. "Personal capacity" suits are, however, subject to defenses based on immunity doctrines, discussed below, and indemnification procedures.

Example 14-9

The state of Arkansas passed a statute making English the official language of the state. Citizens filed suit challenging the law on First Amendment grounds. They sought an injunction against the enforcement of this statute. The plaintiffs named as defendants the state of Arkansas and several state officials responsible for enforcing the statute. The complaint stated that the individual defendants were being sued in their official capacity. The defendants argued that the suit should be dismissed because they were not persons under §1983. Are the defendants correct?

Explanation

The defendants are correct that §1983 creates no remedy against the state itself. The court should dismiss the suit against the state. The §1983 action may be sustained, however, against the state officials, since the plaintiffs are suing them in their official capacity and request only prospective relief.

b. Municipal Officers

The §1983 rules for municipal officers do not parallel those for state officers. The Supreme Court ruled in *Monell v. Dep't of Soc. Servs.* that municipal officers sued in their official capacity are persons for the purposes of §1983 in those cases where a municipality could be sued in its own name. *Monell* allowed plaintiffs to sue local governments for damages, declaratory judgments, or injunction relief for an action taken pursuant to a policy or custom of the municipality. Accordingly, this standard applies to suits against municipal officials sued in their official capacity. As is the case for state officials, suits against municipal officials in their personal capacity are subject to immunity doctrines, which are discussed below, as well as indemnification procedures. Although officials may be subject to money damages for actions brought against them in their official capacity, indemnification is not necessary because the very definition of an "official capacity" suit requires that municipal funds satisfy the judgment.

Example 14-10

Recall the facts of Example 14-6, regarding the Spotted Owl Elementary School in a township called Lower Falls. In that example, students created a controversial design for the school tee-shirt, which the principal forbid them from using. In Example 14-6, plaintiffs sued the township of Lower Falls for damages resulting from this invasion of their First Amendment rights. Now assume that, rather than naming the township of Lower Falls as defendant, the plaintiffs sued the superintendent of schools and the principal in their official capacity, raising the same claims. Will the plaintiffs be any more successful in making a §1983 case against these defendants than they were in their suit naming only the township of Lower Falls as defendant?

Explanation

No, the plaintiffs are not likely to encounter any more success suing these individual defendants in their official capacity. *Monell* made clear that the same standards apply to "official capacity" suits against individual defendants as apply to suits against municipalities themselves. Thus, as in Example 14-6, the plaintiffs will encounter difficulties linking their constitutional injury to the action of a final decisionmaker.

Plaintiffs may be tempted to sue the individual defendants in their "individual" or "personal" capacities. If plaintiffs do so, the immunity doctrines provide a significant obstacle. A discussion of these doctrines follows.

Entity	Barrier to Being a §1983 "Person"	Federal Immunity Doctrine	Indemnity Procedures	Remedy Available	
				Prospec-tive	Retro-spective
State	Absolute barrier: no liability	Eleventh Amendment	N/A	No	No
Municipality	Officials must be acting pursuant to law, custom, or policy	No	N/A	Yes	Yes
State officers:					
Official capacity	Prospective relief only	N/A	N/A	Yes	No
Personal capacity	No barrier	Qualified and absolute immunity	Maybe	Yes	Yes
Municipal officers:					
Official capacity	Officials must be acting pursuant to law, custom, or policy	N/A	N/A	Yes	Yes
Personal capacity	No barrier	Qualified and absolute immunity	Maybe	Yes	Yes

Figure 14-1. The §1983 "Person" Requirement's Interaction with Other Doctrines.

4. Immunity Doctrines

For governmental entities such as states and local governments, state and local sovereign immunity principles may provide protection from suit in state courts. But in federal court, it is federal law—embodied primarily in the

Eleventh Amendment and case law governing it — that governs the entities' immunity. Significantly, the Eleventh Amendment does not protect local governments, and the Supreme Court refused to recognize immunities for municipalities.[12] Since municipalities are exposed to damage judgments as "persons" under §1983, the Supreme Court's decision not to grant them immunity protection renders them accessible to plaintiffs seeking civil rights remedies. See Figure 14-1 for a summary of immunity protection for various entities.

The United States Supreme Court created the immunity doctrines protecting officials by federal common law. For state and municipal officers, official immunity doctrine is largely the same.[13]

The decision of whether to grant immunity involves a delicate balance. On one hand, imposing personal liability can help deter violations of federal rights and provide a remedy for injury. Injured parties might otherwise receive no remedy since government entities are shielded by their own forms of immunity. On the other hand, personal liability can deter talented individuals from entering government service, thereby interfering with the ability of state and local governmental units to meet citizens' needs. Fairness concerns also come into play where the official caused injury while acting in good faith. Finally, case law expresses concern with officials being required to expend energy and expense in defending lawsuits, which constitutes an expenditure of resources borne by "society as a whole" through indemnification and the "diversion of official energy from pressing public issues."[14] The case law seeks to accommodate these competing values.

Immunity doctrines are divided into two categories: absolute immunity and qualified immunity. Absolute immunity is limited to certain officials. The Supreme Court has been "quite sparing"[15] in recognizing absolute immunity in the §1983 context; to read immunity broadly would undermine the purpose of the statute. Most officials enjoy qualified immunity.

a. Absolute Immunity

The Supreme Court's approach to absolute immunity focuses on an official's function rather than the official's title. The Court has recognized absolute immunity for individuals performing judicial and legislative functions.[16] In addition, the Court has recognized absolute immunity for police officers and prosecutors performing certain activities. Police officers enjoy absolute

---

12. See Owen v. City of Independence, 445 U.S. 622 (1980).
13. The doctrines are also largely the same for federal officials accused of misconduct in the course of their employment.
14. Harlow v. Fitzgerald, 457 U.S. 800, 814 (1982).
15. Forrester v. White, 484 U.S. 219, 224 (1988).
16. See, e.g., Stump v. Sparkman, 435 U.S. 349 (1978) (judicial immunity); Tenney v. Brandhove, 341 U.S. 367 (1951) (legislative immunity). The Court has recognized absolute immunity for federal counterparts in the judiciary and legislature as well as for the President of the United States for acts done while carrying out the presidency. Nixon v. Fitzgerald, 457 U.S. 731 (1982) (presidential immunity).

immunity for testimony they provide as witnesses, and prosecutors are absolutely immune when performing a variety of functions, most of which take place in court.

For judges, absolute immunity extends neither to judicial acts that are clearly outside the judge's jurisdiction nor to nonjudicial tasks. For example, if a judge is accused of a constitutional violation in hiring or firing an individual employee, that act is administrative, not judicial, and would not be subject to absolute immunity. Similarly, for legislators, absolute immunity shrouds acts that are central to deliberation and communication activities among legislature members, but not other matters, such as issuing press releases.

Prosecutorial immunity is among the most complicated of the absolute immunity categories. In a series of cases, the Supreme Court has restricted the reach of prosecutors' absolute immunity, which is designed to prevent suits by resentful criminal defendants from clogging the courts and to ensure that prosecutors are not discouraged from introducing relevant evidence and pursuing meritorious cases. Recognizing that these concerns focus on the integrity of the judicial process, the Supreme Court held that absolute immunity was inapplicable to a prosecutor's out-of-court acts, such as providing advice to police, gathering evidence, and making statements to the media.[17]

Example 14-11

Mia was serving a sentence in a detention facility for drug offenses when police found out that she might have been involved in a homicide. They consulted the county prosecutor, who told them that they could question Mia at the institution without notifying her family, asking her if she wanted a lawyer, or advising her of her Fifth Amendment right against self-incrimination. In accordance with this advice, the police officers interviewed Mia and obtained a confession from her.

Mia later filed a §1983 suit against the county prosecutor in her personal capacity, seeking damages resulting from the police officers' interview and confession. The prosecutor claimed that she was absolutely immune from suit. Is the prosecutor correct?

Explanation

No, the prosecutor is not correct that she is absolutely immune from suit. The prosecutor is correct that immunity is relevant in this case because Mia is suing her in her personal capacity, but absolute immunity is not available. Mia is suing the prosecutor for legal advice the prosecutor provided to police investigators, an activity for which the prosecutor enjoys only qualified immunity. See Burns v. Reed, 500 U.S. 478, 496 (1991) (holding that absolute

---

17. Buckley v. Fitzsimmons, 509 U.S. 259 (1993); Burns v. Reed, 500 U.S. 478 (1991).

immunity does not cover the prosecutorial function of giving advice to police). In *Burns v. Reed*, the Court determined that giving advice to police is not a prosecutorial function closely associated with the core purpose of absolute immunity: protecting the judicial process from "the harassment and intimidation associated with litigation." *Id*. at 494.

b. Qualified Immunity

To officers not performing functions entitled to absolute immunity, qualified immunity is available if the officers are sued in their personal capacity. Qualified immunity is available in damages actions only, not in suits for prospective relief. Qualified immunity most commonly arises in suits against executive officials, which include a range of government employees exercising various degrees of power.

The leading case outlining qualified immunity is *Harlow v. Fitzgerald*, 457 U.S. 800 (1982). The standard set forth in *Harlow* reflects the Court's attempt to balance the interest of the private citizen in receiving compensation for a harm done and the governmental concern that officials be able to effectively serve the public interest without being unfairly and unnecessarily burdened by litigation and liability. To these ends, the *Harlow* Court ruled that qualified immunity depends on two conditions: (1) whether an officer's challenged conduct occurred while the officer was exercising a discretionary function and (2) whether the challenged conduct is "objectively" reasonable. Qualified immunity shields officers performing discretionary functions "insofar as their conduct does not violate clearly established statutory or constitutional rights of which a reasonable person would have known." *Id*. at 818. Thus, the officer does not bear liability if the "duties legitimately require[d] action in which clearly established rights are not implicated." *Id*. at 819. Finally, *Harlow* recognizes an exception allowing qualified immunity for an officer who violates clearly established law but "claims extraordinary circumstances and can prove that he neither knew nor should have known of the relevant legal standard." *Id*.

Given the uncertainty surrounding statutory interpretation and the common law process for developing constitutional principles, the decision of whether a statutory or constitutional right is "clearly established" is not free from doubt. Over a series of cases, the Supreme Court has refined the inquiry for ascertaining whether a constitutional right is clearly established. First, the Court has determined that a right can be clearly established by controlling authority in the jurisdiction where the conduct occurred or by "a consensus of cases of persuasive authority such that a reasonable officer could not have believed that his actions were lawful."[18] As to the factual similarity between the existing case authority and the context of the

---

18. *Wilson v. Layne*, 526 U.S. 603, 617 (1999).

challenged conduct, the Supreme Court rejected the requirement that the precedent present "materially similar" facts.[19] Precedent need not specify that the challenged conduct was unlawful, but must provide the officer with "fair warning." In some cases, "a general constitutional rule already identified in the decisional law [applies] with obvious clarity to the specific conduct in question," making qualified immunity unavailable even though the conduct has not been previously held unlawful. *Hope*, 536 U.S. at 741.

Example 14-12

Recall the facts of Example 14-6, regarding the Spotted Owl Elementary School in a township called Lower Falls. In that example plaintiffs sued the township of Lower Falls for damages resulting from the invasion of their First Amendment rights, and in Example 14-10 the plaintiffs chose instead to sue the Superintendent of Schools and the principal in their official capacity. Now assume that plaintiffs raised the same claim for damages but sued only the principal in her *personal* capacity. The principal therefore argued that she was immune from liability.

To evaluate the principal's qualified immunity defense, the court must consider First Amendment precedent concerning student speech and expressive conduct. Under this precedent, the First Amendment constrains government from prescribing speech and expressive conduct, a category of protection that generally encompasses tee-shirt messages. Moreover, the Supreme Court has declared that students enjoy First Amendment protections, stating that "[i]t can hardly be argued that . . . students . . . shed their constitutional rights to freedom of speech or expression at the schoolhouse gate." *Tinker v. Des Moines Indep. Cmty. Sch. Dist.*, 393 U.S. 503, 506 (1969). Since the *Tinker* case, the Court has shown solicitude to the challenges of school officials seeking to maintain order in the school, to protect the rights of all students, and to promote a strong educational mission.[20]

Indeed, subsequent Supreme Court cases render less certain the right articulated in *Tinker*. In particular, the Supreme Court in *Hazelwood Sch. Dist. v. Kuhlmeier*, 484 U.S. 260 (1988), gave school districts greater latitude in suppressing expressive conduct. *Kuhlmeier* narrowed the First Amendment protection where one might reasonably perceive that the school actually endorsed the speech or conduct. Under those circumstances, school policy may restrict protected speech or conduct, if the school's actions are reasonably related to a legitimate pedagogical concern.

In light of *Tinker* and *Hazelwood*, will the principal likely succeed in the argument that she is immune from liability?

---

19. *Hope v. Pelzer*, 536 U.S. 730, 741 (2002).
20. *Hazelwood Sch. Dist. v. Kuhlmeier*, 484 U.S. 260 (1988). *See, e.g., Bethel Sch. Dist. No. 403 v. Fraser*, 478 U.S. 675 (1986).

Explanation

Yes, the principal is likely to succeed with this argument. To do so, however, she will have to establish qualified immunity, since she does not perform the type of governmental function protected by absolute immunity. The principal must raise qualified immunity as an affirmative defense. That way, the court may dispose of the defense at the threshold of litigation, possibly saving the principal the cost and hassle of further litigation.

The Supreme Court has outlined a two-step analysis for qualified immunity. First, the court must evaluate whether plaintiff's allegations, taken in the light most favorable to the plaintiff, include a meritorious federal rights violation. This allows the court to decide whether to dismiss the complaint without further proceedings. If the facts establish the violation of a federal right, the court must then determine whether that right was clearly established at the time of the conduct.[21]

As already noted, the court must consider First Amendment precedent concerning student speech and expressive conduct in order to evaluate the precedent. The court might begin its analysis with *Tinker v. Des Moines Indep. Cmty. Sch. Dist.*, acknowledging that students might enjoy First Amendment protection for messages on tee-shirts created as part of a school program and worn to school. The court might also note the countervailing precedent favoring school officials, and evaluate whether safety or educational concerns supported the principal's decision.[22] Nevertheless, taking the complaint in the light most favorable to the plaintiff, the court may not make any inferences about these matters.

Starting with the *Tinker* case, the court might note that *Tinker* recognized First Amendment protection for students wishing to wear armbands to protest the Vietnam War. The dead owl on the tee-shirt in this case is analogous: a viewer could interpret the image as a political message concerning the environment. Evaluating the complaint in favor of the plaintiff, the court could therefore easily conclude that the general principle of *Tinker* supports a First Amendment violation in this example.

Given the presence of a potentially meritorious First Amendment claim, the next step is to evaluate whether the elementary students had a clearly established right to adopt and wear the tee-shirts at the time that the principal issued her ruling preventing them from wearing the shirts. Were *Tinker* the only relevant precedent, the court might easily conclude that the students had a clearly established federal right to wear

---

21. See, e.g., *Saucier v. Katz*, 533 U.S. 194, 201 (2001) (outlining inquiry).
22. *Hazelwood Sch. Dist. v. Kuhlmeier*, 484 U.S. 260 (1988). See, e.g., *Bethel Sch. Dist. No. 403 v. Fraser*, 478 U.S. 675 (1986).

the shirts. The analytical connection is close between the political message conveyed by black armbands and the political message conveyed by a depiction of the dead member of an endangered species. Thus, the *Tinker* case gave the principal fair warning of the constitutional problem with her decision.

But the subsequent Supreme Court decision in *Hazelwood Sch. Dist. v. Kuhlmeier* undermines the conclusion that the principal's actions were constitutionally problematic. Indeed, *Kuhlmeier* narrowed the First Amendment protection in a context similar to this example: where one might reasonably perceive that the school actually endorsed the speech or conduct.

Kuhlmeier allowed school policy to restrict protected speech or conduct if the school's actions are reasonably related to a legitimate pedagogical concern. In this example, a factfinder might doubt whether the principal has articulated a legitimate pedagogical concern for suppressing the tee-shirt design. Specifically, the factfinder might be dubious as to whether the tee-shirt design truly undercuts the school's mission of promoting civility and morality. Nevertheless, the relationship between the design and the school's mission is sufficiently debatable to render uncertain the illegality of the principal's conduct. In other words, a court is likely to conclude that the Spotted Owl Elementary students' right to wear the tee-shirts was not clearly established at the time the principal made her decision. For that reason, the principal is entitled to qualified immunity, and the case should be dismissed. *See Brandt v. Board of Education of the City of Chicago*, 420 F. Supp. 2d 921 (N.D. Ill. 2006) (finding that qualified immunity should protect a principal under similar circumstances).

Example 14-13

Recall Example 14-11, where a prosecutor advised police officers that they could question Mia, a prisoner in a detention facility, without notifying Mia's family, asking her if she wanted a lawyer, or advising her of her Fifth Amendment right against self-incrimination. In accordance with this advice, the police officers interviewed Mia and obtained a confession from her. Now assume that, rather than suing the county prosecutor, Mia sued the police officers who conducted the interview under §1983 in their personal capacity. The police officers moved to dismiss the action, claiming that they relied on the advice of counsel that was grounded in the law and for that reason are entitled to immunity. Is it clear that the court should accept this argument?

Explanation

No, it is not clear that the court should accept this argument. First, the police officers are not entitled to absolute immunity, only qualified immunity. Second, the interview violated clearly established law requiring the officers to advise Mia of her right to counsel and her right against self-incrimination, suggesting that qualified immunity is unavailable.

The police officers therefore pursue their only hope of avoiding liability with their "reliance on counsel" defense. According to some interpretations, *Harlow v. Fitzgerald* recognized the possibility for such a defense when the Supreme Court stated that an exception to the general qualified immunity test existed "if the official pleading the defense claims extraordinary circumstances and can prove that he neither knew nor should have known of the relevant legal standard." 457 U.S. at 819. This exception is sometimes referred to as the "good faith" defense. Reliance on legal advice can be a factor in deciding whether the "good faith" defense is applicable[23] but does not provide an indisputable shield against liability.[24] In evaluating whether the defense should prevail, lower courts have held that courts should scrutinize the circumstances of the advice, ensuring that the lawyer received a full factual disclosure and carefully considered all relevant factors before giving the advice.[25] The facts here lack the type of detail necessary to satisfy this standard.

Perhaps even more significant, the law governing *Miranda* warnings for suspects in custody is so well established that the officers would have a difficult time defending the reasonableness of their decision to interview Mia. *See, e.g., Walters v. Grossheim*, 990 F.2d 381, 384 (8th Cir. 1993) (refusing qualified immunity where officials took counsel's advice not to follow final court order, because a reasonably competent official should know not to disobey such an order). An additional "yellow flag" is raised in this case because the "counsel" providing the advice is a prosecutor, who generally enjoys greater protection from immunity compared with other officials. Where, as here, the officer claiming qualified immunity is relying on consultation with a prosecutor, the courts may be suspicious that the "consultation with counsel" took place only for the purpose of whitewashing or insulating obviously illegal conduct. (Courts are also suspicious of attempts to shroud official misconduct from scrutiny by operation of the attorney-client privilege.) For all these reasons, the officers here will likely not succeed in convincing the court to afford them qualified immunity.

---

23. *See, e.g, Crowe v. Lucas*, 595 F.2d 985, 992 (5th Cir. 1979) (citing reliance on counsel as a factor shielding defendant from §1983 liability).
24. *See, e.g., Watertown Equip. Co. v. Norwest Bank Watertown, N.A.*, 830 F.2d 1487, 1495 (8th Cir. 1987) (stating that official does not satisfy burden of acting reasonably simply by relying on counsel).
25. *See, e.g., Tanner v. Hardy*, 764 F.2d 1024, 1027 (4th Cir. 1985).

E. "DEPRIVATION OF ANY RIGHTS, PRIVILEGES, OR IMMUNITIES SECURED BY THE CONSTITUTION AND LAWS"

As a "cause of action" statute, §1983 is merely a vehicle for enforcing rights. One must therefore identify which rights one might enforce when using §1983. The statute itself says that it creates liability for a "deprivation of any rights, privileges, or immunities secured by the Constitution and laws" of the United States. This language has spawned two areas of litigation:

1. *Federal statutory wrongs.* The statute's reference to a deprivation of rights protected by "laws" of the United States suggests laws other than constitutional law, such as federal statutes. Which federal statutes may a plaintiff enforce using the vehicle of §1983?

2. *Constitutional wrongs.* The reference to the "Constitution" of the United States suggests that the statute provides plaintiffs with a remedy if they can convince a court that a state or local official has violated a provision of the Constitution, which has its own force separate from §1983. This is an unremarkable observation illustrated in the materials reviewed thus far in this chapter. In interpreting §1983, the Supreme Court has been attentive to policing the relationship between constitutional law and state tort law.[26] What limitations has the Court created in this area?

1. Federal Statutes

When Congress decides to regulate in a particular area, it creates a standard of conduct: a rule as to how entities should or should not act. For example, Congress might decide to regulate the safety of airplane design. Once Congress settles on what that rule should be, it must also decide how that rule should be enforced. It can, for example, provide for an administrative scheme for enforcement. In that case, an administrative agency might establish penalties for failure to follow principles of proper airplane design. Or Congress can choose to authorize a private civil cause of action to help enforce the rule. A private civil cause of action would allow a private person injured by the defendant's failure to comply with airplane design principles to bring a civil lawsuit against the defendant. If the plaintiff sought damages, the damages judgment (and the threat of future ones) would deter the

---

26. An important body of academic literature explores this issue. *See, e.g.,* Christina B. Whitman, *Government Responsibility for Constitutional Torts,* 85 MICH. L. REV. 225 (1986).

defendant from using the unsafe design. If the plaintiff sought an injunction, that remedy would inspire greater compliance with the law as well.

Pursuing her own self-interest, the plaintiff thus receives a remedy for a wrong done, but she also helps the public good by maintaining an incentive for the defendant to comply with laws governing airplane design. The private cause of action thereby ensures that Congress's standards for airplane design actually influence conduct and achieve the safe conditions that Congress sought.

Sometimes Congress does not expressly provide for a private cause of action, but an injured party would nonetheless like to bring one. In instances where the wrongdoer is a governmental actor, §1983 provides a tempting alternative: the plaintiff may look to §1983 for the cause of action to enforce a standard of conduct articulated by Congress. At one time, the Supreme Court readily indulged this temptation. For example, in Maine v. Thiboutot, 448 U.S. 1 (1980), the Court allowed the plaintiffs to use §1983 as a vehicle to sue the state of Maine and its officers in state court for violations of the federal statutes governing welfare benefit calculations.

The approach in Maine v. Thiboutot promised to be a handy tool for allowing private lawsuits to enforce many federal rights that Congress created. Part of its appeal arose from the obstacles that plaintiffs had encountered in convincing federal courts to infer private civil causes of actions from statutory schemes in the absence of §1983. The Supreme Court had created a restrictive approach to creating what it termed "implied rights of action" from congressional enactments, and Maine v. Thiboutot offered an "end run" around these restrictions.

But in several decisions, the Supreme Court has withdrawn from its position in Maine v. Thiboutot. In fact, soon after Maine v. Thiboutot, the Court ruled it inappropriate to allow plaintiffs to use the §1983 cause of action not only where Congress had expressly precluded §1983 actions, but also where Congress had implicitly done so by creating a comprehensive scheme of express remedies. For example, in Middlesex County Sewerage Auth. v. National Sea Clammers Ass'n, 453 U.S. 1 (1981), the Court refused to allow the litigant to use §1983 to circumvent procedural requirements in a "comprehensive enforcement scheme" contained in congressional legislation. Thus, the plaintiffs in Sea Clammers were not able to use §1983 as a vehicle for suit where they had failed to comply with certification standards in federal environmental protection statutes.

Further restricting the Maine v. Thiboutot approach, the Supreme Court has added the requirement that, for a statutory standard to be enforceable through §1983, the standard must impose on states a binding obligation.[27] In one case, the Court determined that Congress created no binding

---

27. See, e.g., Wilder v. Va. Hosp. Ass'n, 496 U.S. 498 (1990); Golden State Transit Corp. v. City of L.A., 493 U.S. 103 (1989).

obligation because it gave states latitude to develop plans to enforce standards.[28] In another, the Court ruled that to create an enforceable right, Congress must have written the statutory provision in "mandatory rather than precatory terms."[29]

In perhaps its most restrictive opinion from this line of cases, the Supreme Court held in *Gonzaga Univ. v. Doe*, 536 U.S. 273 (2002), that Congress did not allow a private cause of action under the Family Educational Rights and Privacy Act, a statute Congress passed pursuant to its spending power. In strong language, the Supreme Court stated that "[w]e now reject the notion that our cases permit anything short of an unambiguously conferred right to support a cause of action brought under §1983." 536 U.S. at 283. The Court emphasized that Congress must " 'speak[] with a clear voice' and manifest[] an 'unambiguous' intent." *Id.* at 280 (quoting *Pennhurst State Sch. & Hosp. v. Halderman*, 451 U.S. 1, 17 (1981)).

Significantly, the *Gonzaga* Court also yoked the availability of §1983 to the question of whether Congress had created new rights in a statute that were enforceable through a private right of action implied from the statute itself (rather than through the vehicle of §1983). Thus the apparent demise of the *Maine v. Thiboutot* "end run": the Court made clear that its restrictive approach to inferring implied causes of action from statutes should also apply where plaintiffs seek to use §1983 to enforce standards of conduct from another statute. Finally, the *Gonzaga* case rested its decision in part on the source of congressional power to enact the Family Educational Rights and Privacy Act: the spending clause. The Court suggested that Congress has special enforcement leverage in the spending clause context by being able to cut off funds to recipient institutions, thereby rendering unnecessary a private enforcement mechanism through §1983.

Example 14-14

Congress passed the National Bank Act (NBA) to facilitate a national banking system. Wanda's Bank is a nationally chartered bank that brought a §1983 suit against a state banking commissioner, seeking to prevent enforcement of state banking laws on the ground that these state laws are preempted by the National Bank Act. Under the National Bank Act, national banks are federal instrumentalities. The enforcement mechanisms of the act allow the federal office of the Comptroller of the Currency to ensure a proper balance of power between state and federal regulation of the banking system. The banking commissioner argued that Wanda's Bank could not bring this suit because the National Bank Act is not a federal "law" under §1983, which Congress intended to be enforced through a civil lawsuit brought by a private entity such as Wanda's Bank. Is the banking commissioner correct?

---

28. *Suter v. Artist M.*, 503 U.S. 347 (1992).
29. *Blessing v. Freestone*, 520 U.S. 329, 341 (1997).

Explanation

Yes, the banking commissioner is correct. Wanda's Bank can point to nothing in the National Bank Act suggesting that Congress created a binding right enforceable in a civil action by a regulated national bank. The National Bank Act's regulatory focus concerns the allocation of regulatory banking authority between the state and federal governments, and not the empowerment of regulated entities. Moreover, the National Bank Act does not speak in terms of the "rights" of regulated entities. Thus, the National Bank Act fails to establish an "unambiguously conferred right" as required in *Gonzaga*. *See Wachovia Bank, N.A. v. Burke*, 414 F.3d 305 (2d Cir. 2005) (reaching same conclusion about the NBA and §1983).

Example 14-15

Congress passed a statute entitled the Help America Vote Act (HAVA), which provides as follows:

> If an individual declares that such individual is a registered voter in the jurisdiction in which the individual desires to vote and that the individual is eligible to vote in an election for Federal office, but the name of the individual does not appear on the official list of eligible voters for the polling place or an election official asserts that the individual is not eligible to vote, such individual shall be permitted to cast a provisional ballot. . . .

42 U.S.C. §15482(a). In another part of the statute, Congress specified the actions election officials should take in handling provisional ballots and provided that election officials must post information at polling places "on the right of an individual to cast a provisional ballot." 42 U.S.C. §15482(b)(2). The Help America Vote Act specifies two modes of enforcement: the U.S. Attorney General may bring an action to enforce specific provisions under the act and the states may establish administrative procedures to receive voter complaints. May private citizens who are not permitted to cast a provisional ballot bring a §1983 action against the officials who prevented them from doing so?

Explanation

Though one can marshal arguments on both sides, the answer is probably yes: a private citizen may bring a §1983 action to enforce the Help America Vote Act.

Perhaps the most significant barrier to allowing the §1983 action is the existence of other methods of enforcement in the Help America Vote Act: the provision for a U.S. Attorney General enforcement action and state administrative proceedings. This implicates the concern introduced in

Middlesex County Sewerage Auth. v. National Sea Clammers Ass'n: a complex enforcement scheme and the possible existence of statutory requirements that might be undermined by allowing a §1983 remedy. Lower courts have analyzed this barrier by evaluating whether the explicit remedial devices foreclose private enforcement of the statute using §1983. Applying this standard to the Help America Vote Act, courts have determined that the act's enforcement mechanisms do not foreclose private enforcement. According to these lower courts, the enforcement mechanisms in the act do not constitute the type of elaborate procedures that the Supreme Court has held to displace private civil actions.[30] Moreover, as one court observed, the Help America Vote Act contains "no indication . . . that the state administrative complaint process, which would relegate the plaintiffs to the unenviable task of asking the secretary of state to overturn her own directives, was meant to replace a private right that is enforceable pursuant to Section 1983." *Bay County Democratic Party v. Land*, 347 F. Supp. 2d 404, 427 (E.D. Mich. 2004).

Satisfaction of the *Sea Clammers* concern with preserving a statute's complex enforcement scheme does not end the analysis. Nonetheless, other strong arguments do suggest that a plaintiff may bring a §1983 action for a violation of the Help America Vote Act. Two features of the act suggest that a plaintiff wishing to use §1983 might establish the high threshold enunciated in *Gonzaga*. First, the Help America Vote Act uses language that is "mandatory rather than precatory." The statute speaks in terms of a binding obligation on the polling officials, requiring them to take specific action in allowing the voters to cast provisional ballots and in processing those ballots. The statute repeatedly uses the word "shall" in referring to action that the state must take, thereby expressing a congressional command, not simply a preference. Moreover, because the statute provides detailed, specific requirements, a court may easily ascertain what is needed to enforce the standards provided. Even where a statute is mandatory and possesses detailed requirements, a §1983 action may still not be appropriate because the congressional standard focuses on institutions generally or on the state, but not on the individual §1983 plaintiff. But that is not the case here.

---

30. *See, e.g., Sandusky County Democratic Party v. Blackwell*, 387 F.3d 565, 572-573 (6th Cir. 2004) (finding that HAVA does not preclude individual enforcement of right to cast provisional ballot); *Logan v. Belangia*, No. 6:06-1417-HMH-WMC, 2006 WL 1967307, at *3 (D.S.C. July 12, 2006) (stating that "most commentators and lower federal courts have concluded that private rights of action exist under the . . . Help America Vote Act"); *Fla. Democratic Party v. Hood*, 342 F. Supp. 2d 1073, 1077-1078 (N.D. Fla. 2004) (finding privately enforceable federal right under HAVA to cast provisional ballot); *Bay County Democratic Party v. Land*, 347 F. Supp. 2d 404, 424-427 (E.D. Mich. 2004) (finding that HAVA creates the privately enforceable right to cast provisional ballot). But *see Taylor v. Onorato*, 428 F. Supp. 2d 384, 386-387 (W.D. Pa. 2006) (finding that under provision of HAVA regulating voting machines, Congress did not create any federal rights privately enforceable under §1983); *Dorsey v. Barber*, No. 5:04-CV-2151, 2005 U.S. Dist. LEXIS 32865, at *26 (N.D. Ohio Sept. 9, 2005) (agreeing that HAVA allows for private enforcement of provisional ballots grievances but not for HAVA College Program provision).

The statute repeatedly mentions the individual voter and even speaks in terms of the "right" of an individual to cast a vote. For all these reasons, the balance of arguments favor allowing private citizens to bring §1983 actions to enforce the Help America Vote Act.

2. Constitutional Claims

Section 1983 allows plaintiffs to seek remedies for state and local violations of the "Constitution," and the statute is generally available for that purpose. In interpreting the reach of constitutional liability, however, the Supreme Court has recognized that many constitutional wrongs can be characterized as torts under existing state tort law. Accordingly, in the process of interpreting the reach of constitutional liability, the Court has been mindful of Justice Frankfurter's preference expressed in *Monroe v. Pape* to confine §1983 to instances where state remedies, such as state tort law, are unavailable. In fact, for the purpose of authorizing claims under the due process clause of the Fourteenth Amendment, Justice Frankfurter's position has largely prevailed: the Court recognizes a federal right only where it is needed to supplement existing state remedies. Contrary to other contexts where Justice Frankfurter's view has been debated, the Court's restrictions in this context are not confined to interpreting the scope of §1983. Rather, the Court imposes its restrictions on the reach of Fourteenth Amendment protections themselves. Combined with §1983, however, the Fourteenth Amendment restrictions produce the same result as would occur if the court were interpreting the words of §1983 directly: a plaintiff cannot recover from injury resulting from random and unauthorized acts of officials.

As in other areas touching §1983, the Supreme Court has used prisoners' claims as a vehicle for restricting liability in this area. First, in *Parratt v. Taylor*, 451 U.S. 527 (1981), the Court rejected the prisoner's procedural due process claim to recover the value of a hobby kit that prison officials negligently lost. The Court ruled that an allegation of negligence was sufficient to constitute a "deprivation" under the due process clause. Nonetheless, noting that the alleged official conduct was "random and unauthorized," the court observed that the only process that the officials could meaningfully have provided would have occurred after the prisoner was deprived of the property. The term of art for this is "postdeprivation process," which is contrasted with the "predeprivation" process that would occur before the officials lost the property.

Postdeprivation process, the *Parratt v. Taylor* Court observed, was provided by adequate state tort remedies, and the Constitution's due process clause does not require more. Translated into the terms of Justice Frankfurter's approach to §1983, this holding meant that state law was all that was required to redress the injury, and a federal remedy was not needed as a supplement.

Adding another obstacle, the Court held in two cases after *Parratt v. Taylor* that prisoners could not invoke the due process clause to recover for the negligent acts of officials.[31] Ruling that a due process claim requires proof of an intentional deprivation, the Court rejected that portion of *Parratt v. Taylor* allowing recovery for an official's negligent act. The Court explained that "[n]ot only does the word 'deprive' in the Due Process Clause connote more than a negligent act, but we should not 'open the federal courts to lawsuits where there has been no affirmative abuse of power.'" *Daniels v. Williams*, 474 U.S. 327, 330 (1986) (quoting *Parratt*, 451 U.S. at 548-549).

The Supreme Court declined the opportunity to expand *Parratt v. Taylor* beyond procedural due process claims in *Zinermon v. Burch*, 494 U.S. 113 (1990). Although *Zinermon* held that the *Parratt v. Taylor* restriction applies to deprivations of liberty as well as property, the Court established that the restriction does not apply to substantive constitutional guarantees (including rights rooted in substantive due process). In contrast to substantive claims, procedural due process claims are focused on procedure itself, thus making relevant the adequacy of state procedures in evaluating whether a violation of procedural rights occurred. The Court explained that the violations for substantive guarantees became complete at the time of the violation itself, a fact that could not be changed by the state's postdeprivation process.

Example 14-16

Aretha was an assistant to the county sheriff. After the sheriff was defeated in an election, the new sheriff fired her. She then brought suit against the new sheriff, arguing that the new sheriff failed to provide her the pretermination hearing required by state law and thereby violated her procedural due process rights. State procedures were available to allow her reinstatement and receipt of back pay. The new sheriff argued that the claim was barred by *Parratt v. Taylor*. Is the new sheriff correct?

Explanation

Although Aretha's claim clears the "intention" hurdle for due process claims, the new sheriff is correct that *Parratt v. Taylor* bars Aretha's claim. Each of the elements of *Parratt v. Taylor* is satisfied:

- Aretha's claim is a procedural due process claim.
- Aretha is seeking a postdeprivation federal remedy for a random and unauthorized act of the sheriff. The sheriff's act is random and

---

31. *Daniels v. Williams*, 474 U.S. 327 (1986); *Davidson v. Cannon*, 474 U.S. 344 (1986).

unauthorized because the sheriff did not follow state procedures in firing her.

- The officials who are responsible for administering the personnel system could not have anticipated the sheriff's unlawful act and therefore could not have known that they could provide a predeprivation hearing.
- State law provides for reinstatement and restitution of back pay, which allows for full relief for the harm done.

See Hadfield v. McDonough, 407 F.3d 11 (1st Cir. 2005) (dismissing procedural due process claim based on sheriff's failure to arrange for hearing before firing plaintiff). The result of *Parratt v. Taylor's* bar relegates Aretha to state court remedies. That result, it turns out, is not lost on the Supreme Court, which frequently alludes to trusting state court process in the *Parratt v. Taylor* line of cases. Thus, the parity debate — competing views on state courts' ability to provide fair justice — enters §1983 analysis yet again.

Example 14-17

Irena was a litigant in a child custody case. As part of the litigation, the Clerk of the County Court charged her a large fee for a filing. According to a state statute, the Clerk of the County Court has final discretion to set fees so long as the fees are below a specific ceiling. The fees charged to Irena were above that ceiling. Apparently the Clerk had systematically charged excessive fees to litigants for several years. Irena argued that the high fees impaired her access to court and that the clerk therefore denied her procedural due process rights. The clerk argued that *Parratt v. Taylor* barred this claim. Is the clerk correct?

Explanation

No, the clerk is not correct. Irena can likely overcome the *Parratt v. Taylor* barrier. The clerk has final decisionmaking authority for fees and has been exercising the authority in a manner that lied outside the statutory parameters for several years. Accordingly, the clerk's actions do not qualify as a "random and unauthorized act" for the purposes of *Parratt v. Taylor*. Indeed, the facts here suggest that the clerk would satisfy the "custom or policy" requirement, so as to be classified as a "person" for the purposes of municipal liability under §1983. Courts have noted that employee "actions in accordance with an 'official policy' . . . can hardly be labeled 'random and unauthorized.'" *Brooks v. George County*, 84 F.3d 157, 165 (5th Cir. 1996) (quoting *Wilson v. Civil Town of Clayton, Indiana*, 839 F.2d 375, 380 (7th Cir. 1988)). This connection between the "person" requirement of *Monell v. Dep't of Soc. Services* and the *Parratt v. Taylor* requirement for a due process cause of action illustrates one lesson from this chapter: the persistence of Justice Frankfurter's preference for restraining federal intervention to instances where the state is endorsing or acquiescing in wrongdoing (see Figure 14-2).

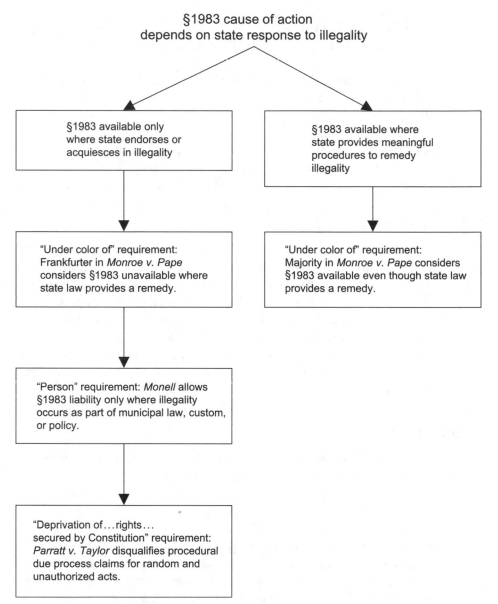

Figure 14-2. Justice Frankfurter's View of §1983 Is Manifest in Several Parts of the Statue.

F. "[A]CTION AT LAW, SUIT IN EQUITY, OR OTHER PROPER PROCEEDING FOR REDRESS"

One way of analyzing §1983 case law from the last several decades is to regard each snippet of statutory language as an opportunity for the Supreme Court to render §1983 less attractive to potential plaintiffs and thereby reduce the flood of §1983 actions clogging the federal court docket. The Supreme Court's interpretation of the remedy language in §1983 is consistent with this view. Perhaps the most significant remedies decision occurred when the Court grappled with the following question: can damages be awarded in §1983 actions on the basis of the inherent value of constitutional or statutory rights? The Court's answer was no. Because the "bottom line" of what a lawsuit might yield is relevant to any plaintiff (and her attorney) in evaluating whether to file a lawsuit, the Supreme Court's remedies decisions have the potential to make a significant impact on the volume of §1983 litigation.

In *Carey v. Piphus*, 435 U.S. 247 (1978), the Supreme Court evaluated the appropriate damages for students denied procedural due process when a principal summarily suspended them. Although the facts made clear that the students' constitutional rights were violated, the Supreme Court concluded that, without specific proof of actual injury suffered, the students could each recover only one dollar in nominal damages. The plaintiffs had urged the Court to apply a well-known tort law doctrine known as presumed damages, which allows a plaintiff to recover substantial damages in circumstances where the gravity of a legal violation is significant and the harm suffered is likely but is difficult to prove. Although the Court stopped short of an all-out prohibition against presumed damages, its reasoning makes it difficult for a court to properly justify using them in a §1983 action. *See Memphis Community Sch. Dist. v. Stachura*, 477 U.S. 299, 310-311 (1986) (stating that, after *Carey*, "[w]hen a plaintiff seeks compensation for an injury that is likely to have occurred but difficult to establish, some form of presumed damages may possibly be appropriate").

At first blush, the Court's insistence on proof of actual injury in a §1983 case may seem the only defensible position. After all, §1983 provides a vehicle for private civil actions, and an overarching purpose of private civil actions is to provide plaintiffs with compensation for injury. If plaintiffs cannot produce evidence of injury, why should they recover anything? The provision for nominal damages in procedural due process cases sends a message that the defendant committed a culpable wrong. Anything more than nominal damages is appropriate only to compensate for harm that the plaintiff actually suffered. Moreover, punitive damages are available for malicious deprivations of rights.

Observations about the realities of civil litigation as well as the importance of federal constitutional and statutory guarantees suggest countervailing arguments to *Carey*'s position. First, although the Supreme Court has authorized punitive damages against officials in §1983 actions, such damages are available only against officials (not governmental entities) and only in the most egregious cases. *See Smith v. Wade*, 461 U.S. 30, 56 (1983) (holding punitive damages are available when an official's "conduct is shown to be motivated by evil motive or intent, or when it involves reckless or callous indifference to the federally protected rights of others").

More important, the Court's limitation on compensatory damages can have a profound effect. If a plaintiff had proof of concrete damages, such as lost wages or medical bills, she would no doubt introduce them at trial. But their absence does not necessarily imply that the plaintiff avoided significant suffering as a result of a constitutional violation; the plaintiff may have suffered indignities or emotional pain that is profound yet extremely difficult to prove within the parameters of traditional civil litigation. Moreover, the focus on precisely what the plaintiff can prove fails to account for the damage to society when constitutional and statutory guarantees are violated. As such, the rule ignores the regulatory purposes of §1983.

Procedural due process is key to citizens' trust in democracy, legal order, and the inherent fairness of government. If trust fails, so does citizens' investment in social good, and their commitment to the rule of law may soon follow. Where an official violates a citizen's procedural rights, the damage reverberates beyond the particular plaintiff harmed. Indeed, the *Carey* Court acknowledged as much by allowing nominal damages: "Because the right to procedural due process is 'absolute' . . . and because of the importance to organized society that procedural due process be observed, . . . the denial of procedural due process should be actionable for nominal damages without proof of actual injury." 435 U.S. at 266.

By allowing only a one-dollar damage award in the absence of proof of actual injury, the Supreme Court appeared to give more weight to the operation of the federal judicial system than to the protection of federal rights. Although symbolically significant, a one-dollar damage award has no financial "sting." Accordingly, the absence of significant presumed damages substantially reduces §1983's effectiveness in deterring state and local violations of federal law.

The Supreme Court has expanded *Carey*'s restriction on damages in *Memphis Community Sch. Dist. v. Stachura*, which concerned an alleged First Amendment violation. The Court applied *Carey*'s actual damage requirement to the case, resolving uncertainty about whether *Carey* applied outside the procedural due process context. The Court stated its holding as follows: "damages based on the abstract 'value' or 'importance' of constitutional rights are not a permissible element of compensatory damages" in §1983 cases. 477 U.S. at 310.

Example 14-18

Frederick was a state police officer who wished to avail himself of a thirty-day leave to nurture his newborn child under the federal Family Medical Leave Act. His supervisor denied the request for leave. In denying the request, the supervisor said Frederick could get leave only if "he taught himself how to breastfeed or if he put his wife in a coma so that no one else would be available to take care of the child." After the child was born, the supervisor assigned Frederick to another county, requiring him to spend long absences from home during the first month of the child's life.

Frederick filed a §1983 action, seeking damages for this violation. The district court ruled that the supervisor's denial of leave did violate the Family Medical Leave Act, but that the conduct was not sufficiently egregious to merit punitive damages. The court did rule that Frederick may try to prove compensatory damages, and set the matter for trial on that issue. Frederick's only injury was the extreme emotional distress he experienced in withstanding these abusive comments, in being denied his rightful leave under federal law, and in missing the first part of his child's life. How can Frederick meet the standard for proving actual damages from *Carey v. Piphus* and *Memphis Community Sch. Dist. v. Stachura*?

Explanation

If Frederick suffered his pain in silence and demonstrated no outward manifestations, he may have a difficult time showing actual injury, and the wrong done to him may be remedied only with a nominal $1.00 verdict. A factfinder is likely to view a victim's own testimony alone as self-serving and of limited use. Indeed, the factfinder may need a point of reference for evaluating the victim's credibility as well as the intensity of the suffering. Even if the victim is trustworthy, the victim may lack perspective on the gravity of the emotional injury. The type of proof mentioned in case law — other than the victim's testimony — that can help establish actual injury includes

- Medical attention resulting from the emotional distress
- Psychiatric or psychological treatment
- Antisocial behavior
- Refusal to participate in usual activities
- Contemporaneous statements to others that corroborate plaintiff's testimony
- Physical injuries suffered as a result of the emotional distress

See, e.g., *Price v. City of Charlotte*, 93 F.3d 1241 (4th Cir. 1996). One difficulty with the law's preference for outward manifestations of emotional distress, however, is that it encourages "whining" as well as the potential for medical fraud.

Some courts have also required a nexus between the defendant's misconduct and the emotional distress to support the claimed injury. For example, in this fact pattern, Frederick would have to draw a connection between the supervisor's violation and the distress for which he seeks compensation. The law guarantees Frederick only thirty days of leave after the child's birth, thus circumscribing the time period in which the root cause of the distress transpired. Frederick would need to establish that whatever distress he experienced after that thirty-day point was attributable to the supervisor's earlier illegal actions. Frederick will likely encounter difficulty establishing that causal connection. *See Knussman v. Maryland*, 272 F.3d 625, 640-643 (4th Cir. 2001) (granting a new trial on damages where the police officer denied "nurturing leave" failed to establish nexus between emotional injury and actual violation).

Through interpretation of the various components of §1983's language, the Supreme Court has created a maze of hurdles for a potential civil rights plaintiff. Compounding this burden are the immunity doctrines for governmental entities and government officials. After *Carey v. Piphus* and *Memphis Community Sch. Dist. v. Stachura*, a plaintiff may successfully navigate this gauntlet of hurdles only to discover that her injuries are not sufficiently provable or concrete to establish significant damages. Enforcement of federal law may suffer as a consequence, since litigants lack a financial incentive to litigate constitutional harm. From this perspective, *Carey v. Piphus* and *Memphis Community Sch. Dist. v. Stachura* restrain federal courts from playing a role many deem key to our governmental system: declaring broad norms and transforming constitutional values into meaningful restraints on government conduct. On the other hand, the "proof of actual damages" rule discourages frivolous cases from cluttering the federal court docket and binds the federal judiciary to an alternative role: providing individual justice to individual litigants with discrete injuries. These competing views on *Carey v. Piphus* and *Memphis Community Sch. Dist. v. Stachura* are thus symbolic of the larger debate over the appropriate role and potency of the §1983 remedy.

G. THE PARALLEL CAUSE OF ACTION AGAINST FEDERAL OFFICERS: *BIVENS V. SIX UNKNOWN NAMED AGENTS OF FEDERAL BUREAU OF NARCOTICS*

An important limitation of the §1983 cause of action is its focus on wrongs committed by state and local governments and officials: §1983 does not authorize suits alleging wrongs by federal officials. A litigant wishing to pursue a civil remedy against federal officials for violations of federal rights must instead find a federal statute that could authorize the specific suit, or must invoke an implied cause of action, such as that identified in *Bivens v. Six Unknown Named Agents of Federal Bureau of Narcotics*, 403 U.S. 388 (1971). A "*Bivens* action" is often viewed as the federal-official counterpart of a §1983 action, used by plaintiffs complaining that a federal official violated their rights protected by the U.S. Constitution.

Under the theory that the rights enunciated in the Constitution deserve a remedy to make them meaningful, the *Bivens* Court held that an injured plaintiff may seek money damages against individual federal officers for alleged violations of the plaintiff's Fourth Amendment rights. The United States Supreme Court as well as lower federal courts have expanded the *Bivens* holding to other portions of the Constitution.

Despite the initial expansion of *Bivens* actions, the Supreme Court has recently sought to confine those actions to circumstances already identified. The Court has emphasized that *Bivens* suits are not available (1) where Congress created a "remedy which it explicitly declared to be a *substitute* for recovery directly under the Constitution and viewed as equally effective" or (2) where " 'special factors' " suggest that a court should hesitate to infer a cause of action even though Congress has not created a remedy.[32] Recognizing that *Bivens* identified a cause of action against *individual officers*, the Supreme Court has also established that a plaintiff may not bring a *Bivens* action against a federal agency.

---

32. *Carlson v. Green*, 446 U.S. 14, 18-19 (1980) (emphasis in original) (quoting *Bivens*, 403 U.S. at 396).

Federal Courts as Lawmakers

VII

The final federal court function reviewed in this volume is perhaps the most controversial: lawmaking. The controversy arises because federal court lawmaking implicates both broad categories of governmental constraints on federal courts: separation of powers and federalism.

Federal court lawmaking triggers separation of powers principles because it involves federal courts in an enterprise thought to be the province of Congress. As every civics students is taught, legislatures "make the law" and courts "apply the law." In practice, of course, the division of labor does not divide so neatly. Yet when a judge creates broad legal principles of general applicability, alarm bells sound: many would argue that the policy decisions necessary to fashion those general principles should be made by democratically elected representatives rather than by appointed, life-tenured federal judges.

Then there's concern with federal courts usurping state prerogatives by making law in areas where state law could govern. It's not so much that federal court lawmaking is always invading areas of exclusive state domain, illegitimately creating legal principles where only state law has that prerogative. Rather, in most instances, the worry is that federal court lawmaking may incrementally displace state lawmaking power in areas that both federal and state governments may legitimately regulate. To the extent that our system tolerates routine federal court lawmaking, state power will diminish considerably over time — a result inconsistent with the assumptions underlying our federalist form of government.

Finally, mistrust of federal court lawmaking also springs from the intersection of separation of powers and federalism. Motivating this particular mistrust is the notion that the states knowingly joined the union (i.e., ratified the Constitution) under the assumption that the federal government might create laws and that those laws would displace state laws under the supremacy clause. But the states agreed that would happen (and they would thereby lose power) only under certain circumstances. Those circumstances are outlined in the Constitution's Article I, which lists the different subject areas over which the U.S. Congress has lawmaking authority. The Constitution put the states on notice that federal judicial power would exist, but only to the extent that it was used to resolve certain cases or controversies. In other words, the argument goes, states did not give up lawmaking power to federal *Courts*, only to the federal *Congress*. Presumably, the states would be more comfortable with ceding power to Congress, which is staffed by representatives elected by citizens of the states,[1] than with ceding lawmaking power to appointed federal judges.

Example 1

A federal district court in Boise, Idaho, was adjudicating a lawsuit regarding fertilizer runoff into the Delaware Bay. The judge decided that the farming methods that Delaware and New Jersey farmers were using were exacerbating the ecology problems in the bay, causing additional imbalance with connected inland waterways. As part of the lawsuit, the judge issued an opinion containing an extensive list of requirements that Delaware and New Jersey farmers must satisfy to remedy the fertilizer runoff problem. Are there any governmental or structural problems with the federal judge enunciating these requirements in the opinion?

Explanation

The judge might be intruding on Congress's powers to regulate waterways and interstate commerce. This is a separation of powers problem. The judge might be intruding on the powers of the states, which generally enjoy wide latitude regulating agriculture. This is a federalism problem. The states may be willing to cede some control over agriculture, so long as the rules that the federal government creates derive from careful information gathering, study, and debate. Since the requirements here resulted from judicial fiat

---

1. Actually, at the time of the original ratification and before the Seventeenth Amendment, the state legislatures selected representatives in the Senate, giving state governments even greater control of the Congress.

rather than the legislative process, the state's conditions for ceding control are therefore not met. That is a problem stemming from the intersection of federalism and separation of powers concerns. Moreover, the states of Delaware and New Jersey may bring special expertise to bear on the problem. The people of those states may believe themselves entitled to control or direct influence over the regulation, since they are the people who will be most affected by the regulations. Here, a federal judge in a distant state — Idaho — has come up with rules that affect their lives, without entertaining their concerns. Again, that is a problem derived from both separation of powers and federalism.

More information is needed before one can finally condemn the judge's actions. What type of subject matter jurisdiction was the federal court exercising? Did a federal legislative scheme provide the outlines for the judge's ruling? Does the fertilizer runoff problem implicate overpowering federal interest? Chapters in this part will explore how these questions bear on the legitimacy of that federal judge's decision to enunciate rules regulating the farming methods.

Through the twisted course of history, issues regarding federal lawmaking power are manifest in two areas: the doctrine of *Erie Railroad Co. v. Tompkins*, 304 U.S. 64 (1938), and principles governing federal common law. Both areas exhibit these overlapping federalism and separation of powers themes. This part covers both, starting with Chapter 15, on the *Erie* doctrine, and continuing with Chapter 16, which covers general principles of federal common law.

CHAPTER 15

The *Erie* Mandate

Erie Railroad Co. v. Tompkins, 304 U.S. 64 (1938), created a rich universe of jurisprudential thought, including deep analysis of the nature of law itself. As part of the more restrictive world of federal court jurisdiction, the *Erie* doctrine is also usefully viewed from a narrower perspective. With the goal of "cutting to the bone" of what *Erie* means for the day-to-day operations of federal courts, this chapter will explore the doctrine in terms of federal court functioning: specifically, what does the *Erie* doctrine say about the appropriate scope of federal lawmaking, and what are the obligations of federal courts in honoring state laws? The answers to these questions depend upon an interplay between the themes of federalism and separation of powers.

At bottom, *Erie* provides tools for answering a "choice of law" question: should a federal court apply state or federal law to resolve a particular legal issue? This problem arises from the mosaic of governmental powers we call the United States, where the federal government on one hand and state governments on the other hand compete to govern the lives of citizens. In deciding which law should govern a particular question, a federal court generally should start with the choice between state and federal law. If federal law is the answer, the court has completed the "choice of law" inquiry. The *Erie* doctrine governs that choice between state and federal law. Although some thinkers maintain that the term "*Erie* doctrine" applies only to instances where the federal law is court-made law, this chapter also uses that term for the "choice of law" issue where federal rules of civil procedure or federal statutes are involved.

In developing the functional approach to Erie, this chapter first reviews the constitutional background for the decision as well as the statute that Erie interpreted, the Rules of Decision Act. Next, the chapter explores the Erie decision itself and its aftermath. It then outlines how to perform the Erie "choice of law" analysis under current law. This exposition is organized according to the type of federal law involved in the choice: federal court-made law, Federal Rules of Civil Procedure, or a federal statute. Finally, the chapter reviews what a federal court should do when it determines that state law should govern a particular legal issue, but needs to choose among competing state laws.

A. THE CONSTITUTIONAL SCHEME AND THE RULES OF DECISION ACT

As outlined at the beginning of this part, the Erie doctrine concerns the legitimacy of federal court lawmaking, a function regulated by the Constitution itself. The Constitution, of course, creates a federal government of limited power. As is reinforced by the Tenth Amendment to the Constitution, those powers not delegated to the federal government (or prohibited by the Constitution to the states) "are reserved to the States respectively, or to the people" U.S. CONST. amend. X. In Article I, §8, the Constitution lists a number of subject areas for legislative powers, which may be expanded as is "necessary and proper." The Constitution gave the judiciary only the power to resolve cases or controversies. Those cases or controversies — listed in Article III — include fights arising under federal law, which encompasses laws created pursuant to Congress's powers in Article I, §8. But the Article III cases and controversies also include lawsuits not arising under federal law at all, but rather involving certain classes of litigants. Among the lawsuits listed in Article III are diversity cases, which by definition do not arise under federal law. Where, for example, a citizen of New Hampshire sues a citizen of Maine for a violation of federal employment discrimination laws, the suit is a "federal question" case, and a federal court has subject matter jurisdiction on that basis. The diversity of citizenship between the plaintiff and the defendant is irrelevant.

If, on the other hand, their dispute is a "bread and butter" tort case with an amount in controversy in excess of $75,000, then it likely comes into federal court on the basis of "diversity of citizenship" jurisdiction. In that event, the question becomes: what law applies to the various aspects of the case? As it turns out, the first Congress, which created lower federal courts, also provided guidance on what law the courts should apply. Specifically, the Judiciary Act of 1789 contained a provision known as the Rules of Decision Act, which provides,

> The laws of the several states, except were the Constitution or treaties of the United States or Acts of Congress otherwise require or provide, shall be regarded as rules of decision in civil actions in the courts of the United States, in cases where they apply.

28 U.S.C. §1652. This language seems to include at least two instructions:

1. In cases where the federal Constitution, treaties, or statutes of the United States "require or provide," federal courts should apply them.
2. If instruction 1 is not applicable, then "[t]he laws of the several states" should be the "rules of decision" in the federal court cases where they are relevant.

For federal question cases, the Rules of Decision Act mandate is clear: apply the federal Constitution, statutes, or treaties. For "diversity of citizenship" cases, however, two questions about the Rules of Decision Act immediately present themselves: What are the "laws of the several States"? What are "rules of decision"? The Supreme Court answered the first question in the 1842 decision *Swift v. Tyson*, 41 U.S. 1, but it took a series of cases after the *Erie* decision itself before the Court truly wrestled with the second question.

In *Swift v. Tyson*, the Court interpreted the statutory phrase "laws of the several States" to include only state statutes and certain established local usages in the state (concerning specific matters such as land). The Court did not read the statutory phrase to include state court decisions about matters of general concern, such as basic principles of tort and contract. In the Court's view, state court decisions on these topics were the product of the same judicial thought process as federal decisions, and thus were entitled to no greater weight. *Swift v. Tyson* concluded therefore that federal courts exercising diversity jurisdiction were free to fashion their own principles of general common law.

Example 15-1

Lena is a citizen of South Carolina, and Carol is a citizen of Georgia. Lena entered into a sales contract with Carol to sell oranges in the state of Georgia for $100,000. Carol breached the contract, and Lena sued her in federal district court. Carol argued that the contract was invalid and therefore unenforceable. No state statute appeared to govern the question of the validity of the contract. Under *Swift v. Tyson*, what law would have governed the validity question?

Explanation

Under *Swift v. Tyson*, the federal district court would have been able to apply its own view of appropriate general principles of contract law to govern this dispute. The case is in federal court by virtue of diversity of citizenship. No federal statute, constitutional provision, or treaty appears to be on point. Nor do any state statutes govern the matter. *Swift v. Tyson* suggested that state common law decisions on local concerns should govern diversity actions, and courts had a difficult time mapping the line between "local concerns" and "general concerns." Principles governing commercial transactions such as those here, however, are clearly "general concerns." Thus, the federal court would not have been required to apply state common law.

Scholars often describe *Swift v. Tyson* as a creature of the jurisprudence of its times, when courts were viewed as instruments working to discover "true" principles of law. Whatever can be said for the theoretical underpinnings of *Swift v. Tyson*, however, the lawmaking license it gave federal courts created social tensions, clashes between state and federal power, and inconsistent results in state and federal courts.

B. THE *ERIE* DECISION

Erie Railroad Co. v. Tompkins reacted decisively to *Swift v. Tyson*'s problems. The *Erie* case arose from an accident where Tompkins was hit while walking along train tracks by a protrusion from a passing train. During Tompkins's federal diversity action against the railroad, the question arose as to what duty of care the railroad owed him. State law on the issue suggested that Tompkins would lose, and federal law on the issue suggested that he would win. The Supreme Court took the case to evaluate whether federal law could govern the "standard of care" issue and decided that it could not. In the process of rendering that holding, the Court overruled *Swift v. Tyson*.

The *Erie* Court proposed three separate bases for overruling *Swift v. Tyson*, which the opinion conveniently labeled as paragraphs beginning with First, Second, and Third.

First: The first basis concerned *Swift v. Tyson*'s interpretation of the Rules of Decision Act. Based on historical evidence that had been recently discovered, the *Erie* Court concluded that *Swift v. Tyson* erred in reading "laws of the several states" to exclude general decisional law of state courts.

Second: As its second reason, the Court concluded that *Swift v. Tyson* created unsound social policy. The decision allowed those with access to federal court to benefit from a different set of common law rules. In so doing, the decision "introduced grave discrimination . . . [and] made rights enjoyed . . . vary according to whether enforcement was sought in the state or in the federal court." 304 U.S. at 74-75. "Thus," the Court concluded, "the doctrine rendered impossible equal protection of the law." *Id.* at 75.

Courts and scholars generally agree that the *Erie* Court did not mean to suggest that *Swift v. Tyson* lawmaking violated the Constitution's equal protection clause. Rather, the understanding is that the Court condemned *Swift v. Tyson* for promoting different treatment for similarly situated litigants with similar legal problems. Indeed, the *Erie* Court observed that litigants with similar disputes could receive different resolutions if, by happenstance, one litigant had an opponent who was a citizen of a different state and was therefore able to litigate in federal court. That, the Court suggested, is not the brand of evenhanded justice that is dispensed in this country.

Third: Finally, and most baffling for courts, students, and scholars, the *Erie* Court declared that *Swift v. Tyson* was unconstitutional. Although oblique, the constitutional basis for the decision presents an important statement on the nature of our federalist system. Specifically, the Court first declared, "There is no federal general common law." 304 U.S. at 78. (The word "general" in this sentence is very important since, as explained in the next chapter, federal courts indeed make common law in specific areas all the time.) The Court explained further, "Congress has no power to declare substantive rules of common law applicable in a State, whether they be local in their nature or "general," be they commercial law or part of the law of torts. And no clause in the Constitution purports to confer such a power upon the federal courts." *Id.*

The *Erie* Court never cited the precise basis in the Constitution for its holding that the lawmaking license that federal courts enjoyed under *Swift v. Tyson* was an improper usurpation of state power. Obviously, though, the structural assumptions about the federal government's limited power, which are reflected in the Tenth Amendment, inspired the constitutional ruling.

In sum, the three numbered paragraphs presented the following foundations for the *Erie* decision:

1. FIRST: In cases where no federal statute, constitutional provision, or treaty governs, the Rules of Decision Act requires federal courts to apply state court-made law as well as state statutory law.
2. SECOND: Policy considerations in our system of federalism require that litigants not receive a different result in federal court than they would receive in state court.
3. THIRD: The U.S. Constitution prohibits federal courts from making general federal common law.

C. THE AFTERMATH OF *ERIE*: CHARTING THE LINE BETWEEN SUBSTANCE AND PROCEDURE

1. The Impulse to Apply Federal Procedural Law

While the mandate of *Erie* was unequivocal, lower federal courts never stopped trying to apply their own legal principles to some questions. In particular, the federal courts created law for matters that they perceived to be procedural — and applied those procedural laws even in actions based on diversity of citizenship. What possessed them to believe they had the power to do that? Did not *Erie* say that it was contrary to the Rules of Decision Act, bad social policy, and unconstitutional for federal courts to create their own law?

While no Supreme Court opinion lays out the precise reasoning, the answer seems to lie in the nature of procedural law. Procedural law, it turns out, has a unique relationship with the three bases for the *Erie* decision.

First: The Rules of Decision Act says that state law should govern precisely that: rules of decision. One might define these as substantive rules that bear on the actual outcome of a court decision. Procedural rules regulate the process of litigation and court operation, but are not fashioned to guide the court to reach one decision or the other. Thus, procedural rules may not be "rules of decision."

Second: Because procedural rules are not meant to channel a court toward one disposition or another, application of federal procedural rules in a diversity action might not promote the type of inequality that *Erie* condemned. True procedural rules stay in the background. They are akin to infrastructure, keeping the machinery of justice in good working order but providing no great concern to the litigants (unless, of course, the judicial system "breaks" for lack of proper maintenance).

Thus, the application of federal procedural law in a diversity action enhances fairness, accuracy, and efficiency in federal courts. It is *good* social policy, not bad. Federal courts understand what is best for running a smooth and accurate litigation system in federal courts. Federal judges and support staff are able to apply procedural rules with more alacrity than they can state rules because they know the federal rules better. Moreover, federal rules "fit" better with other components of federal court business than do state procedural rules. Finally, lack of uniformity between the justice dispensed in federal and state courts should not occur if federal procedure controls all cases: procedural rules control the manner of litigation, but not the actual "bottom line" of a case.

Third: The constitutional basis of *Erie* condemned *Swift v. Tyson* for inviting federal courts to exercise power they did not have. Yet federal procedural rules control the operation of federal courts—a matter that the federal government obviously has the authority to regulate. If one wants to get specific, Article III of the Constitution not only creates the "federal judicial power" but also gives Congress the prerogative of creating lower federal courts. The greater power surely includes the lesser: a court's power to exist and adjudicate cases includes the power to enunciate the logistics for doing that job. Put differently, the states already ceded control over federal court procedure, so they should not be able to complain when federal courts exert some influence over the day-to-day operation of their own affairs.

Example 15-2

Assume that a federal district court in a small town in New Mexico has a court-made rule that litigants can file hard copies of papers only if the papers are printed in a particular type and size of font (Times Roman 12-point font). The state court in the same town has a rule requiring that hard copies of papers must be filed in an entirely different font type and font size. The purpose of the font requirement in federal court is to enable quick review of case files, so that the judge and courthouse personnel can readily distinguish litigant filings from court-generated paperwork, for which the court uses a distinct font.

The district court has been requiring all litigants—even those in diversity cases—to make all filings in Times Roman 12-point font. Lana Litigant recently argued that the district court is contravening the three bases of *Erie* by requiring litigants in diversity actions to file their hard copies in this font. Does *Erie* require the district court to accept this argument and change its font requirements for diversity actions?

Explanation

No, the district court is not required to accept Lana's argument. The uniform font requirement does not contravene the three bases of *Erie*.

First, if one were to imagine a rule that did not fall within the description "rules of decision," it would be a rule governing font or typeface. One would be hard-pressed to imagine a law more mundane and less consequential to the actual decision in the case.

Second, the font rule does not reflect bad policy. The rule should not implicate unfairness, inequality, or disparate results. In fact, the court is acting with good sense in applying a uniform font requirement to all filings: the district court clerk's office no doubt has systems created for paper handling, and having two font requirements for litigant filings may require a duplicate processing system. If nothing else, the district court personnel are conditioned to look for a particular font when working with litigant filings, and allowing a different font might cause mistakes and foster inefficiency.

Third, a rule that mandates a particular font is not unconstitutional. The font rule is a logical incident of running a federal court system. The rule concerns matters well within the federal domain, far from sensitive matters of state control. Allowing federal courts to fashion their own procedural rules does not threaten to diminish state sovereignty by the incremental, yet boundless, growth of federal law.

2. *Guaranty Trust Co. v. York*: Outcome Determination

Why would a litigant such as Lana in Example 15-2 argue that the state rule must govern in federal court? Sheer mischief? Possibly, but litigation is so expensive and the sanctions for mischievous litigation tactics so severe that an ethical, reasonable explanation is more likely. One explanation points to a possible mistake — Lana tried to file a crucial motion in the wrong font, and the federal court clerk's office rejected it. Perhaps the due date for the filing has passed and Lana is using an *Erie* argument to ensure that the district court will allow a filing *nunc pro tunc* (a late filing).

Assume that the district court will not allow Lana to file the crucial filing late: what was once an apparently inconsequential rule now determines the outcome of the case. Such was the type of situation presented to the Court in *Guaranty Trust Co. v. York*, 326 U.S. 99 (1945), where the Court held that a district court must apply state statute of limitations in a diversity action. The Court condemned application of a more forgiving federal rule because the federal rule would have produced a different outcome for the litigation. This concern with the outcome of litigation sprung from *Erie*'s second foundation: the Court attempted to fashion a test that ensured evenhanded justice.

Lower courts found this "outcome determination" test quite handy. The problem, however, is that, as applied by the lower courts, the test nearly always pointed to state law (and accordingly turned out to be no test at all). Litigants would bring an *Erie* "choice of law" problem to the district court for decision only if they really cared about the issue — and, like Lana, they only really cared about the decision if it affected whether they won or lost.

3. *Byrd v. Blue Ridge Rural Electric Cooperative*: A Balancing Test?

Thus, the outcome determination test was overbroad in application. So the Court tried to reformulate the *Erie* inquiry in *Byrd v. Blue Ridge Rural Elec. Coop., Inc.* 356 U.S. 525 (1958). Apparently focusing on *Erie*'s constitutional foundation (the third foundation), the *Byrd* Court stated that federal courts must apply a state rule if it is "bound up" with "state-created rights and obligations." 356 U.S. at 535. Yet also apparently recognizing some flexibility in *Erie*'s policy basis (the second foundation), the Court found room for integrating federal interests into the analysis. According to *Byrd*, federal law could reflect such strong "affirmative countervailing considerations" as to counsel a court to apply the federal law in the face of a contrary state rule. *Id.* at 537. Presumably the Constitution would allow federal law to apply in cases where necessary to preserve the "independent [federal] system for administering justice to litigants who properly invoke its jurisdiction." *Id.*

Lower courts interpreted this language as authorizing a balancing test. Debate has surrounded precisely how a court should balance the federal interest against other concerns. Lower courts concocted myriad approaches, most of which involved balancing the importance of the state rule against the importance of the federal rule relevant to a particular case.

Several courts and many scholars have suggested that the Supreme Court disavowed *Byrd* balancing in its decision in *Hanna v. Plumer*, 380 U.S. 460, 468 n.9 (1965) (suggesting that the lower court erred in evaluating how "important" a rule was to the state). But *Hanna* did not explictly disapprove *Byrd*, and lower federal courts continue to find *Byrd* balancing useful to this day. Even more significant, the Supreme Court in a subsequent decision, *Gasperini v. Center for Humanities, Inc.*, 518 U.S. 415 (1996), suggested that district courts should consider the strength of federal interests. In fact, the *Gasperini* Court criticized the lower court in that case for failing to "attend to '[a]n essential characteristic of [the federal court] system'" in choosing between state and federal law. 518 U.S. at 431 (quoting *Byrd*, 356 U.S. at 537).

The essential federal characteristic in *Byrd* and *Gasperini* is indeed an important one, grounded in tradition as well as in the Constitution itself: the extensive practice of using jury trials in federal court civil actions. But neither decision suggested that its approach was limited to jury trial issues or the particular context of the case. Accordingly, as judged by the work of the lower courts, scholars, and the Supreme Court in *Byrd* and *Gasperini*, one may legitimately integrate the federal interest in application of federal law into the analysis of whether a federal court-made rule should govern in a diversity action.

Although refined in subsequent cases, *Hanna v. Plumer* is still considered the definitive word on current *Erie* analysis. One of *Hanna*'s most helpful contributions is clarifying that the *Erie* analysis differs according to whether the federal law is court-made law or a federal rule promulgated under the Rules Enabling Act (such as a Federal Rule of Civil Procedure). If the federal law is court made, then the choice between state and federal law is governed by the Rules of Decision Act. By contrast, where the federal law is a Federal Rule promulgated under the Rules Enabling Act, then that statute controls the "choice of law" analysis.

D. A RULES OF DECISION ACT CASE: THE CHOICE BETWEEN STATE LAW AND FEDERAL COURT-MADE LAW

The *Hanna* dispute concerned whether to apply state law or a Federal Rule of Civil Procedure. Thus, the Court's discussion of the appropriate analysis for court-made law was actually dictum. Nevertheless, the Supreme Court in subsequent cases as well as lower courts have treated the discussion as controlling law. *Hanna* therefore provides the definitive test for federal courts undertaking the *Erie* analysis in a Rules of Decision Act case.

Hanna said that when a federal court is confronted with a clash between state and federal law, it may apply federal law only if doing so conforms with the twin aims of *Erie*: avoidance of forum shopping and encouragement of equitable distribution of law. Both aims appear to be tied to the second basis of *Erie*, focusing on sound social policy. Specifically, the Court explained that the aims reflected the *Erie* Court's "realization that it would be unfair for the character or result of a litigation materially to differ because the suit had been brought in a federal court." 380 U.S. at 467.

Hanna recognized that "*every* procedural variation is 'outcome determinative'" at the point when the parties start to spar over the choice between state and federal law. *Id.* at 468. Thus, the Court explained, in applying the twin aims of *Erie*, the district court should ask whether the difference between state and federal law would have inspired the plaintiff to choose federal court over state court. Consequently, the issue of whether the state or federal rule affects the outcome of the case is relevant, but only from the point of view of a plaintiff deciding where to file the lawsuit. Accordingly, in applying the forum-shopping aim of *Erie*, the district court should consider the point in litigation preceding the plaintiff's filing the complaint. If the plaintiff would choose federal court because federal law applies to a particular issue, then the federal court should apply *state* law to the issue.

The perspective of a plaintiff choosing where to file a lawsuit also sheds light on the "inequitable distribution of law" aim mentioned in *Hanna*. That aim is focused on whether application of federal law "alters the mode of enforcement of state-created rights in a fashion sufficiently 'substantial' to raise" the kind of inequality concerns inspiring *Erie*'s social policy basis. 380 U.S. at 469. Thus, just as the difference between state and federal law must be a "big enough deal" to influence the plaintiff's calculus at the point when she chooses where to file a lawsuit, the difference must also be a "big enough deal" to raise concerns with uniform and fair law administration.

Example 15-3

Edith entered a contract with Fiona and later concluded that she was defrauded by Fiona. No federal law governed the contract, but the suit fell within the parameters for "diversity of citizenship" jurisdiction. Edith is from a different state than Fiona, and the amount in controversy is in excess of $75,000. But the amount by which the controversy actually exceeds $75,000 depends on how the court calculates damages. Assume research reveals that federal courts have devised a "benefit of the bargain" measure for fraud damages and that the relevant state law uses an "out-of-pocket" measure for fraud damages. As applied to Edith and Fiona's dispute, the "benefit of the bargain" measure would yield greater damages. Edith is "out-of-pocket" approximately $80,000, which she spent in reliance on the alleged fraud. Had the subject matter of the contract been as Fiona represented, however, Edith could have expected a $240,000 gain. Thus, $240,000 represents the "benefit of the bargain."

Edith filed suit in federal court, and the case is set for trial. The parties are now fighting over what law will govern the measure of damages. What should the district court do?

Explanation

The district court should apply *Hanna*'s Rules of Decision Act analysis and conclude that state law should govern. The Rules of Decision Act analysis applies because the federal law on fraud damages is court made. According to that analysis, the federal court should ask whether application of federal law would implicate either of the twin aims of *Erie*: discouragement of forum shopping and avoidance of inequitable administration of the laws.

As applied here, both aims are implicated. The "benefit of the bargain" measure yields three times the amount of damages as the "out-of-pocket" measure. Edith therefore has a strong, tangible reason to prefer federal court over state court. Significantly, she would have been able to ascertain the difference between state and federal law in this case before she filed suit. For these reasons, one can say that the fraud damages formula is the type of rule that would have influenced the choice of forum. Moreover, the damages formula implicates how the law of fraud is enforced. With the "benefit of the bargain" formula, federal courts have made a judgment that the tort is sufficiently serious to justify a higher measure of damages than the state courts were willing to provide. Accordingly, in the words of *Hanna*, the damages calculation implicates "the mode of enforcement of state-created rights." 380 U.S. at 469. Cf. *Gasperini v. Center for Humanities, Inc.*, 518 U.S. 415, 437 (1996) (approving lower court's decision that state law governs allowable damages). Since the difference between the two measures in this case is so large, one can easily conclude that the difference is sufficiently "substantial" to raise concern with equitable administration of state and federal laws.

This example's clash with *both* aims of *Erie* is no surprise. In applying the twin aims, one can expect that a federal law triggering one *Erie* aim will also trigger the other aim. Indeed, some commentators have suggested that the two aims are essentially the same — tied to the same principles of fair judicial administration.

Example 15-4

A group of plaintiffs filed a diversity suit in the United States District Court for the Northern District of Florida seeking damages resulting when a cruise ship sank in the Atlantic Ocean. The ship was registered to a company from New York and the captain and crew were all New York citizens, but most of the passengers were from Florida. The plaintiffs' theory of liability for the suit is negligence. The plaintiffs researched this cause of action before filing suit and determined that all state laws in the United States have the same rules governing the application of negligence principles as well as the available damages in this case.

The defendant, which is the New York company that owned the ship, moved to dismiss the suit under the doctrine of forum non conveniens. Under federal forum non conveniens law, it is difficult to predict whether the federal district court should dismiss the suit. Florida forum non conveniens law, however, is set forth in a straightforward Florida Supreme Court decision and is favorable to the defendant's desire to have the suit dismissed. The defendant argues that Florida law should govern. Should the Florida federal district court apply Florida law or federal law to the question of whether to dismiss the suit pursuant to the doctrine of forum non conveniens?

Explanation

The weight of lower court authority as well as the circumstances of this case suggest that the district court should apply federal forum non conveniens doctrine.[2] Forum non conveniens is a tool that a defendant can use to veto a plaintiff's choice of forum. A court may grant a motion to dismiss a suit pursuant to the forum non conveniens doctrine if, in its judgment, the interests of the parties and the public suggest that fairness and efficiency would be better served if the dispute were adjudicated elsewhere. Under federal law, forum non conveniens doctrine is a court-made doctrine, so *Hanna*'s Rules of Decision Act analysis applies.

The question of whether state or federal law should govern the disposition of this forum non conveniens motion is not clear-cut. The

---

2. The United States Supreme Court explicitly left open the question of whether state or federal forum non conveniens law governs in a diversity action in *Piper Aircraft Co. v. Reyno*, 454 U.S. 235, 249 n.13 (1981).

forum non conveniens doctrine controls the forum of the litigation—which can, of course, have a significant effect on the procedural rules applied to the suit and the convenience of the parties. Presumably, the plaintiffs chose federal court in Florida for these reasons. But did the plaintiffs rule out federal court because of the possibility that the federal court might apply federal forum non conveniens law? Unlikely.

To begin with, the plaintiffs are most concerned about the success of their cause of action and their attempt to obtain significant damages. According to the research, the laws governing these matters would be uniform in all courts in the United States. This uniformity suggests that the actual location of the litigation is less important than it is in many cases. Second, even if the plaintiffs have a strong preference for the federal court in Florida, the facts do not establish that they would clearly retain that forum if the court applied federal, rather than state, forum non conveniens law. Accordingly, one would likely not conclude that the district court would encourage forum shopping by applying federal forum non conveniens law.

Nor would application of federal forum non conveniens law likely lead to the inequitable administration of the laws. The forum where a lawsuit is adjudicated influences the "mode of enforc[ing] . . . state-created rights," and the defendants appear to believe that they would benefit from adjudicating the lawsuit in some place other than Florida federal court. What is not established, however, is whether state forum non conveniens law is so much more preferable to the defendant's goal of litigating elsewhere than federal forum non conveniens law.

Under some interpretations of *Hanna*, the analysis would end there: a federal court may apply federal forum non conveniens law because to do so would not implicate the twin aims of *Erie*. As noted above, however, a court might supplement the analysis by considering the federal interest in applying federal law as authorized by the pre-*Hanna* decision in *Byrd v. Blue Rural Ridge Elec. Coop., Inc.* and *Gasperini v. Center for Humanities*. Using this analysis, the federal courts apply federal law if a strong federal interest favors doing so.

In the context of the choice between state and federal forum non conveniens law, federal courts have routinely relied on the federal interest in applying federal law. The types of federal polices invoked include the federal courts' interest in self-regulation, administrative independence, and a uniform set of national venue rules. For cases with international elements, federal courts evaluating whether to apply state or federal forum non conveniens law have also cited the federal interest in regulating foreign relations and in providing a domestic forum for plaintiffs who are United States citizens. *See, e.g., Esfeld v. Costa Crociere, S.P.A.*, 289 F.3d 1300, 1311-1314 (11th Cir. 2002); *Monegro v. Rosa*, 211 F.3d 509, 511-512 (9th Cir. 2000). Thus, even in cases where the *Hanna* twin aims point more definitively to state law than in this example, a federal court may be justified in applying federal forum non conveniens law.

E. A RULES ENABLING ACT CASE: THE CHOICE BETWEEN STATE LAW AND A FEDERAL RULE OF CIVIL PROCEDURE

1. *Hanna*'s Rules Enabling Act Test

As noted above, *Hanna* concerned a clash between a state law and a Federal Rule of Civil Procedure. Accordingly, to dispose of the case, the Court needed to clarify how to analyze the "choice of law" question where the federal law was promulgated under the Rules Enabling Act.

In the Rules Enabling Act, 28 U.S.C. §2072, Congress delegates to the Supreme Court of the United States its authority to promulgate "rules of practice and procedure" for federal courts. Aside from the Federal Rules of Civil Procedure, the Rules Enabling Act also authorizes the Supreme Court to create other procedural rules, such as the Federal Rules of Appellate Procedure. Nevertheless, the second sentence of the act, §2072(b), restricts the power delegated to the Supreme Court. That sentence mandates that rules promulgated under its authority "shall not abridge, enlarge or modify any substantive right."

In setting forth the "choice of law" test to use in a Rules Enabling Act case, the *Hanna* Court "tipped its hat" to the third basis of the *Erie* decision: the Constitution. The Court explained that in order for a Federal Rule of Civil Procedure to be valid, it must be constitutional. This means that Congress must possess the power to create such a rule under the Constitution. The test for this constitutional inquiry, however, is easy to satisfy. Congress's power to create lower federal courts in Article III includes the power, augmented by Article I's "necessary and proper" clause, to create rules of practice and procedure in those courts. To fall within these constitutional powers, these rules must be "rationally capable of classification" as procedural. *Hanna*, 380 U.S. at 472.

The *Hanna* Court also explained that to govern in federal court, a Federal Rule of Civil Procedure must be consistent with the Rules Enabling Act's constraints. Specifically, the rule must not violate the admonition in the Rules Enabling Act's second sentence, providing that the rules "shall not abridge, enlarge or modify any substantive right." Thus, the federal court must ask whether the rule regulates procedure, defined as the judicial process for enforcing rights, rather than the rights themselves.

While not explicit about it, *Hanna*'s decision regarding the Federal Rules of Civil Procedure also accommodated the first basis of *Erie*: the Rules of Decision Act. The Rules of Decision Act provides that state law should govern unless a federal statute, constitutional provision, or treaty provides otherwise. The Rules Enabling Act is just such a federal statute, which the Rules of Decision Act exempts from its mandate. Accordingly, the Rules of

Decision Act provides no obstacle to the mandate of the Rules Enabling Act requiring Federal Rules of Civil Procedure to govern in federal court. Thus, *Hanna* demonstrated that the Rules of Decision Act does not provide the governing statute where a federal court determines that a Federal Rule of Civil Procedure displaces a state law, is a valid exercise of Congress's power, and is within the scope of the Rules Enabling Act.

Example 15-5

Horace filed a complaint in federal court against Ernest, invoking the federal court's "diversity of citizenship" jurisdiction. Ernest wished to defend by filing an answer, which included a defense that the complaint should be dismissed for improper service of process. Under the rules of the state where the district court sits, this defense must be raised only by motion. Federal Rule of Civil Procedure 12 allows a defendant to raise the defense of improper service of process by motion or in a responsive pleading such as a complaint. Which rule should the district court apply?

Explanation

The district court should apply Federal Rule of Civil Procedure 12. All Federal Rules of Civil Procedure are presumptively valid and should be applied unless they are unconstitutional or outside the scope of the Rules Enabling Act. Rule 12 easily satisfies both conditions, which focus on whether the rule possesses a procedural quality. As to the Rules Enabling Act test, one can say that the rule regulates only what litigants do. As such, the rule influences only what happens in court (not out of court) and therefore does not abridge, enlarge, or modify any substantive right. The constitutional test is even easier, characterized by Justice Harlan in his *Hanna* concurrence as a test that looks to whether the rule is "arguably procedural." Accordingly, the state rule must yield to Federal Rule 12.

2. Analysis of Conflict Between a State and Federal Rule

In a series of cases after *Hanna*, the Supreme Court reaffirmed its deferential approach to evaluating the validity of Federal Rules of Civil Procedure. The Court, however, showed a tendency to read rules promulgated under the Rules Enabling Act narrowly so as to avoid a conflict with state law, thereby allowing both the Federal Rule and state law to regulate. Thus, for example, in *Walker v. Armco Steel Corp.*, 446 U.S. 740, 749 (1980), the Supreme Court stated that the state law must yield only if it directly conflicts with the Federal Rule. Likewise, in *Semtek Int'l Inc. v. Lockheed Martin Corp.*, 531 U.S. 497 (2001), the Court interpreted the Federal Rule of Civil Procedure in such a way as to avoid a difficult power clash between state and federal law.

Example 15-6

Assume that the Mississippi legislature enacted a statute imposing an "affirmance penalty on certain litigants who file appeals in the Mississippi court system." By its terms, the statute applies when a defendant unsuccessfully appeals the judgment of a Mississippi trial court. If the judgment is affirmed on appeal, the statute requires that the defendant pay to the opposing party a penalty equal to 15 percent of the judgment. The Mississippi statute is mandatory: the appellate court must impose the penalty if it affirms the judgment without modification. Mississippi courts have declared that the affirmance penalty has many purposes: to penalize and discourage frivolous appeals, to penalize and discourage appeals filed for the purposes of delay, and to provide compensation to plaintiffs who suffer the ordeal of defending judgment on appeal.

Following an accident on her bike, Madeline Motorcycle brought an action against another driver, Harriet Harley, in federal district court in Mississippi. Subject matter jurisdiction for Madeline's suit was premised on the parties' diversity of citizenship. After trial, judgment was entered in favor of Madeline. Harriet appealed the judgment, which the Court of Appeals for the Fifth Circuit affirmed without modification.

Madeline filed a motion in the Court of Appeals requesting that the court apply Mississippi's 15 percent affirmance penalty. In defending the motion, Harriet called the court's attention to Federal Rule of Appellate Procedure 38. This rule, which is titled Frivolous Appeal — Damages and Costs, provides, "If a court of appeals determines that an appeal is frivolous, it may, after a separately filed motion or notice from the court and reasonable opportunity to respond, award just damages and single or double costs to the appellee." Should the court of appeals grant Madeline's motion under the Mississippi statute?

Explanation

No, the court of appeals should probably not grant Madeline's motion under the statute. The answer is not straightforward, however, because it depends on whether the federal rule clashes with the state statute. One can make arguments on both sides of that issue. On one hand, the existing law supports not finding a clash. One should start the interpretation process with the orientation of avoiding a conflict: the Supreme Court has shown a tendency to read Federal Rules narrowly to avoid displacing state law. To that end, one might try to argue that the federal court could grant Madeline's motion and use Federal Rule of Appellate Procedure 38 as a supplement to the Mississippi statute. The idea is that the state statute applies in order to fill the myriad purposes for which it is designed, one of which is also the goal of Federal Rule 38: regulating frivolous appeals. The court can then in its discretion add further regulation with Federal Rule 38, if the appeal is particularly frivolous.

The problem with using the state and federal laws in tandem is that they take different approaches to the same problem. They have the same "sphere of operation" but regulate that sphere with disparate policy judgments. *See Burlington Northern R. Co. v. Woods*, 480 U.S. 1, 7 (1987) (identifying the inquiry as whether a Federal Rule "occupies [the state law's] field of operation"). State law takes into account problems that Rule 38 does not reckon with, such as compensating winning plaintiffs and avoiding delay. To regulate that problem, state law makes the judgment that a mandatory rule is needed.

Federal law, however, is much more modest. First, the law chooses to regulate the decisionmaking behind appeals only in the most egregious cases. Rule 38 anticipates that no penalty or sanction will apply *unless* the appeal is deemed frivolous. Second, the law grants discretionary power to the court to determine, given the specific equities of the case, whether a drastic approach such as a penalty is appropriate. If a court deems a penalty apt, the court can calibrate the penalty appropriately under the circumstances, and is not bound to a fixed rate as in the Mississippi statute.

The decision to implement this modest approach in the federal rule likely reflects the drafters' decision to avoid the more sweeping approach of the state statute. As demonstrated by Federal Rule of Civil Procedure 11, the drafters of the Federal Rules take seriously the risk that sanctions for lawyering that pushes the law beyond well-settled boundaries may stifle the creative legal thinking necessary to the development of the common law. The drafters' approach in Rule 38 appears to balance the risk of suppressing creativity with the need for efficiency in the appeals process. Only where efficiency is directly challenged by frivolity does the court have any latitude to impose a sanction. The drafters envisioned a case-by-case analysis of whether sanctions were necessary, not a "blunt" sanction. Indeed, under this reading of the federal rule, a large fixed sanction such as in the Mississippi statute is not even within the federal court's discretion. Thus, using Rule 38 as a supplement to the Mississippi statute would actually exacerbate the clash, rather than resolving it.

Because Federal Rule 38 and the Mississippi statute conflict, one must undertake an *Erie* analysis to determine which law to apply. Federal Rules of Appellate Procedure are promulgated under the Rules Enabling Act, and a Rule should apply if it is (1) within the scope of the Rules Enabling Act and (2) a constitutional exercise of Congress's power. In applying these tests, the court should treat Rule 38 as presumptively valid.

Rule 38 is within the scope of the Rules Enabling Act because it does not abridge, enlarge, or modify any substantive right, as the Supreme Court has applied that standard. A rule passes that test if it regulates the judicial process for enforcing rights, rather than the rights themselves. Rule 38 focuses on

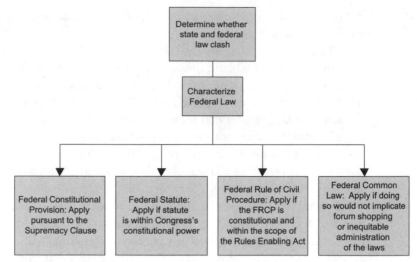

Figure 15-1. Choosing Between State and Federal Law

conduct and decisions that take place in court, concentrating on litigants' decisions to take a frivolous appeal. As such, the Rule does not regulate primary, out-of-court conduct for which the law assigns rights and responsibilities.

For these same reasons, Rule 38 is constitutional. The Rule is "rationally capable" of being labeled a rule of procedure because it regulates the appeal process. Thus, Congress possessed power under the Constitution to promulgate Rule 38, and the Rule therefore passes *Hanna*'s constitutional test.

F. A STATUTORY CASE: THE CHOICE BETWEEN STATE LAW AND A FEDERAL STATUTE

The final type of federal law that the Supreme Court has channeled through its *Erie* jurisprudence is federal statutes. Initially, viewing the choice between a federal statute and state law through the lens of *Erie* seems unnecessary. The Supreme Court has already developed a body of general preemption principles for evaluating whether federal statutes may displace state laws. Nevertheless, the statutory decisions from the *Erie* cases provide a useful spin on the general preemption cases. The *Erie* statutory approach is consistent with general preemption principles, yet suggests a specialized analysis for procedural statutes.

The Constitution's supremacy clause provides that acts of Congress, if valid, should apply in the face of conflicting state laws (see Figure 15-1). In *Stewart Org., Inc. v. Ricoh Corp.*, 487 U.S. 22 (1988), the Court explained that, for federal statutes, a court evaluates whether the statute is constitutional by the same constitutional test enunciated for rules promulgated under the Rules Enabling Act. Quoting *Hanna v. Plumer*, 380 U.S. 460, 472 (1965), the *Stewart* Court explained that the constitutional authority of Congress to enact procedural statutes comes from " 'the constitutional provision for a federal court system,' " which includes " 'power to make rules governing the practice and pleading in those courts, which in turn includes a power to regulate matters which, though falling within the uncertain area between substance and procedure, are rationally capable of classification as either.' " 487 U.S. at 32. In *Stewart*, the Court advised that the same deference required in evaluating Federal Rules of Civil Procedure is called for in evaluating the constitutional legitimacy of statutes.

Since the constitutional test is so easy to satisfy, the more significant question is often the threshold issue of whether a federal statute conflicts with state law. Unlike rules promulgated under the Rules Enabling Act, which represent acts of power delegated from Congress to the Supreme Court, statutes are a direct product of Congress. Perhaps for that reason, the *Stewart* Court appeared more deferential to statutes than to Federal Rules, and inclined to authorize a broader reading of federal statutes than for rules promulgated under the Rules Enabling Act. Specifically, *Stewart* explained that a court need not require exact overlap between a federal statute and a state law before finding a conflict. To find a conflict, a court need not determine that the two provisions are "perfectly coextensive and equally applicable" to the legal issue at hand; "rather," *Stewart* continued, "at least where the applicability of a federal statute is at issue," the relevant inquiry is whether the statute is "sufficiently broad to cover the point in dispute." 487 U.S. at 27 n.4.

Example 15-7

Joanne filed a diversity suit in federal court concerning qualifications for athletes at Inner City University. The federal district judge to whom the case was assigned was a graduate of Inner City University and is on the board of trustees there. Joanne wanted to disqualify the judge. Her opponent, Inner City University, liked the assignment and therefore wanted the judge to stay on the case. Joanne argued that the relevant standard for disqualification was set forth in 28 U.S.C. §455(a), stating that a judge shall disqualify herself "in any proceeding in which [her] impartiality might reasonably be questioned." Inner City University argued that the relevant standard was set forth in the code in the state where the district judge sits. That state code provision reads, "A judge shall disqualify himself only if it is shown by clear and convincing evidence that the judge has a direct conflict of interest involving a party." Which standard should apply?

Explanation

The standard from the federal statute should apply. In coming to this conclusion, one should first ask whether the state standard and the federal statute conflict. As *Stewart* explained, a federal statute should apply if it is broad enough to control the issue. That appears to be the case here: the "issue" is the standard for judicial disqualification. The federal statute, §455(a), provides the circumstances under which a judge should disqualify herself. One might try to make subtle arguments about how the state and federal standards might be harmonized, but *Stewart* made clear that "[i]f Congress intended to reach the issue before the district court, and if it enacted its intention into law in a matter that abides with the Constitution, that is the end of the matter." 487 U.S. at 27.

The statute here "abides with the Constitution." Regulation of the circumstances under which a federal judge should preside over a case falls among matters relating to the operation of federal courts, a subject matter well within Congress's power over practice and procedure in the federal judicial system. In fact, the disqualification standard is so central to federal court operation that allowing state regulation is arguably inconsistent with the Constitution's vision of an independent federal judiciary.

G. CHOOSING AMONG STATE LAWS: *KLAXON V. STENTOR*

The choice between state and federal law is a *vertical* "choice of law" problem. Because the federal government enjoys the advantage of the supremacy clause, federal law enjoys the status of higher law. Once a federal court determines, however, that state law should govern a particular issue, the court must often choose among several potentially applicable laws from different states. Because state laws enjoy equal prestige in our system of justice, the choice among state law is a *horizontal* "choice of law" problem.

Horizontal "choice of law" problems have bedeviled courts and commentators for millennia. Because the relevant sources of law — by definition — enjoy equal power and dignity in a horizontal setting, no ready tiebreaker is available for determining which of the competing laws "wins." Given the intractable nature of the horizontal "choice of law" problem, many different methodologies compete for guiding the choice. Throughout the United States, state courts use more than five discrete "choice of law" methodologies in evaluating which of several state laws should apply to a given legal issue. Thus, once a federal court applying *Erie* analysis decides that state law should govern a legal issue, it must choose among these various methodologies in deciding which state law should govern.

Uncharacteristically in this area of federal courts law, the Supreme Court has provided direct, unwavering guidance on the question of what "choice of law" methodology to use. In *Klaxon Co. v. Stentor Elec. Mfg. Co.*, 313 U.S. 487 (1941), the Court directed that federal courts sitting in diversity must apply the "choice of law" rules of the forum state in which they sit. The rationale for this directive is straightforward: to the extent that justice and practicality allow, the federal district court should make the proceedings mirror those that would have occurred in state court in the absence of "diversity of citizenship" jurisdiction. While subject to criticism, *Klaxon* remains good law, and was reaffirmed by the United States Supreme Court in 1975.[3] See Figure 15-2.

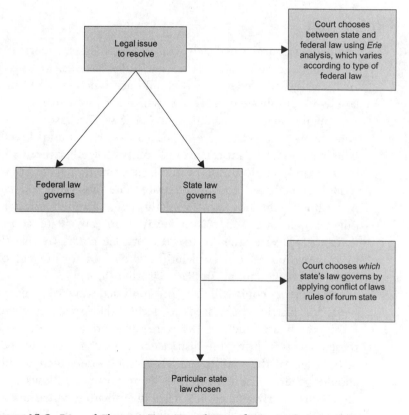

Figure 15-2. Erie and Klaxon: A Two-Tier Choice of Law Analysis

---

3. *Day & Zimmermann, Inc. v. Challoner*, 423 U.S. 3, 4 (1975).

Example 15-8

Mandy sued James in federal court in Pennsylvania for damages that Mandy incurred when she was a passenger in James's car. Mandy asserted that James was negligent in his driving. The basis of the suit was diversity of citizenship, and James's car was insured in Pennsylvania. Mandy is from Delaware, James is from Pennsylvania, and the accident occurred in Pennsylvania. James defended the action by pointing to a guest statute in Delaware, which shielded him from liability to any guest riding in his car. Neither Pennsylvania nor federal law has any such guest statute or other shield for liability that would prevent Mandy from recovering if she proved James's negligence. The only arguably relevant federal law is court made.

Mandy therefore argued that either Pennsylvania law or federal law should govern the issue of whether James enjoys a shield from liability. How should the district court analyze this argument?

Explanation

The district court should start with an *Erie* analysis. Federal law, if any, on the issue is court made. Thus, the Rules of Decision Act controls the analysis, and the federal court should ask whether application of federal law would implicate one of *Erie*'s twin aims: avoidance of forum shopping and inequitable administration of the laws. Because the particular legal issue here goes to the core of the parties' rights and directly influences whether the defendant can avoid liability altogether, both aims are implicated. Mandy could foresee at the time of bringing the litigation that she would immediately lose if Delaware state law governed James's rights. Accordingly, she hopes to avoid the guest statute's effect by filing suit outside Delaware and staying away from any state court that might defer to Delaware law. For that reason, one could say that the difference in laws would affect the plaintiff's choice of forum and could lead to disparate results among similarly situated litigants.

The district court will therefore apply state law to the liability question. Next, the district court needs to decide which state's law should govern. Likely candidates include Delaware law and Pennsylvania law. Because these two laws differ, the district court needs to look to the "conflict of laws" rules of the state where it sits to choose which of these two laws should govern. The forum state, Pennsylvania, follows its own hybrid approach to horizontal choice of law in evaluating which among competing states has the greatest interest in applying its own law. The district court will use this analysis to evaluate the interests of Delaware and Pennsylvania. The precise details of this analysis are beyond the scope of the discipline of federal courts. In short, however, the court is likely to decide that Pennsylvania has the greatest interest in applying its law because Pennsylvania is James's domicile as well as the location of the accident and the car insurer.

16

CHAPTER

Federal Common Law

The study of federal common law principles investigates when federal courts may legitimately make law, and it is closely connected to the doctrine of *Erie Railroad Co. v. Tompkins*, 304 U.S. 64 (1938). *Erie* presents a vertical "choice of law" problem, with federal law granted a higher status by virtue of the supremacy clause. The area of federal common law similarly presents a vertical "choice of law" problem. The question of whether a federal court should make federal common law arises only where no federal constitutional provision, statute, treaty, or regulation governs a particular issue. If the court decides that it cannot or should not create federal law to govern a particular issue, then state law would fill the void. Thus, the question of whether to create federal common law essentially presents a choice between state and federal law.

Characterizing the decision of whether to create federal common law as a vertical "choice of law" problem helps to illustrate its federalism implications. But separation of powers issues also weigh heavily in federal common law doctrine. As case law has developed, these separation of powers issues have informed federal common law principles more than the *Erie* doctrine, where a federal court is reckoning with the "choice of law" problem in the specific context of a particular diversity case in federal court. Most federal common law applies in both state and federal court, regardless of jurisdictional basis, and governs throughout the United States (subject, of course, to

443

the supervisory power of the United States Supreme Court).[1] For this reason, federal common law has much greater potential than *Erie* to invade the province of Congress.

Thus, federal common law is deeply connected to both federalism and separation of powers concerns and thus, like the *Erie* doctrine, is subject to constitutional constraints. Neither courts nor scholars have developed a uniform, generally accepted constitutional theory for federal common law, but rough guidelines exist that help give federal common law doctrine some coherence. These guidelines are depicted in Figure 16-1. Although all case law does not fit neatly into one of the four quadrants in Figure 16-1, the quadrants are useful constructs for exploring federalism and separation of powers constraints on federal common law.

On one hand, many thinkers maintain that areas of exclusive state control exist where no federal regulation is allowed by federal common law or federal statute. This area is labeled Quadrant 1 in Figure 16-1. On the other hand is a parallel domain of exclusive federal control (Quadrant 4). In this exclusive federal domain, federal common law is deemed necessary to protect federal interests because Congress has not acted.

Next are areas of shared state and federal power and influence (Quadrants 2 and 3). If Congress has acted in those areas, federal courts may make law to supplement what Congress has done (Quadrant 3). If, however, Congress has not acted, then federal courts may not make common law, because to do so would be to displace an opportunity for state law to govern. Presumably, it was in this context that the legal question at issue in the *Erie* decision was located. *Erie* concerned the duty of care that railroads owe to individuals walking along the railroads' tracks. This is surely a matter that Congress could have regulated as part of its Article I power to regulate interstate commerce. But Congress had not done so, and *Erie* made clear that the federal courts could not make law in its place. It was in this context — which falls within Quadrant 2 — that the Supreme Court in *Erie* said that federal courts may not make "general federal common law."

The area of federal courts doctrine known as federal common law can sometimes be difficult to distinguish from constitutional interpretation. Since interpreting the Constitution is deemed the judiciary's province, one might reasonably describe judicial analysis and description of constitutional provisions as "court-made law" or "common law." These judicial decisions contrast with federal common law, however, because the legal standard for conduct itself comes from the Constitution, not from the conscience of the court. Likewise, when a court interprets a standard enunciated in a federal statute, the judicial gloss on the statute's

---

1. One of the areas of federal common law — federal procedural law — does not generally apply in state court. Chapter 15 discusses federal common law governing matters of the procedure in the context of the *Erie* doctrine.

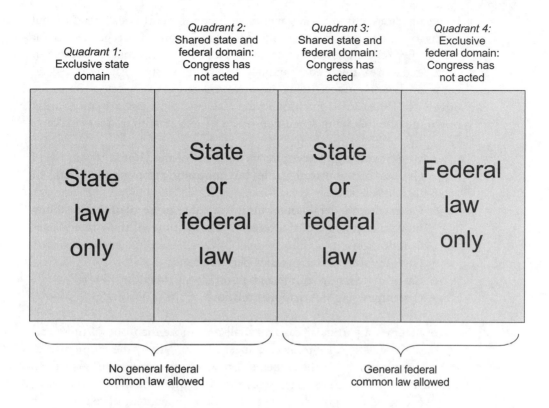

Federal Common Law Through the Prism of Federalism and
Separation of Powers

Figure 16-1.

meaning is not federal common law, but simply statutory interpretation. Sometimes, of course, the line between interpreting a preexisting standard and judicially creating a new standard is difficult to discern. One helpful distinction appearing in case law and commentary describes a new legal standard as one creating a "primary right or obligation."

As illustrated in Figure 16-1, federal courts' power to make federal common law is limited to Quadrant 3 and Quadrant 4. Lawmaking in Quadrant 3 is sometimes called interstitial lawmaking; here, federal courts make common law to fill gaps left by Congress in statutory schemes. The courts making law in these areas are filling the "interstices" between statutory provisions. This is by far the most common quadrant for federal common lawmaking. Federal common lawmaking in Quadrant 4 is rarer.

Sometimes in Quadrant 3, the Supreme Court allows federal lawmaking on the strength of congressional intention. In such cases, Congress's goals in a statute are so clear that the Court deems lawmaking appropriate to fill a gap that Congress would have filled had it been confronted with the particular case being adjudicated. In other instances, the Supreme Court has allowed federal courts to make common law on a topic where Congress has regulated, but it has justified regulation not simply on the basis of congressional purpose, but because the area involved "uniquely federal interests" that need federal common law to protect them. *Banco Nacional de Cuba v. Sabbatino*, 376 U.S. 398, 426 (1964). As is manifest in the case law, these circumstances break down into the following specific instances of federal common law making:

- Cases involving the proprietary interests of the United States
- Cases involving private parties but implicating important concerns of the United States
- Cases where federal courts imply a private cause of action enabling individuals to sue federal officials for violations of the United States Constitution
- Cases involving controversies between states
- Cases involving maritime and admiralty jurisdiction
- Cases involving international relations

Sometimes a particular case may fall into more than one of these categories. These categories reflect no special logic; rather, the entire area of federal common law has developed in a random, ad hoc manner. As federal courts have confronted cases that they believe require federal common law, they have added categories to the list. Within the context of existing case law, particularly important and complicated categories of federal common law are the first two listed above: cases involving the proprietary interests of the United States and cases involving private parties but nonetheless concerning important federal interests. These two categories provide the focus for this chapter.

A. CASES CONCERNING FEDERAL PROPRIETARY INTERESTS

1. General Principles

The United States' proprietary interest is a classic trigger inspiring federal courts to create common law. Generally, a proprietary interest is a right or obligation relating to property ownership or contract. The Supreme Court has decided that the United States has a proprietary interest requiring federal common law protection in a wide range of cases, sometimes considerably expanding the notion of "proprietary" beyond its plain-language meaning. Cases in which the Supreme Court has recognized a proprietary interest of the United States requiring federal common law include those concerning (1) commercial paper that the United States issues or holds,[2] (2) title to land,[3] (3) the right to bring tort actions,[4] and (4) rights under certain contracts.[5]

But the Supreme Court has not created federal common law in every case in which federal propriety interests are involved; instead, the Court has required the presence of "uniquely federal interests."[6] One of the Court's first commercial paper decisions in this area, *Clearfield Trust Co. v. United States*, 318 U.S. 363 (1943), is instructive. In *Clearfield Trust*, a government check had been forged and deposited in a bank, Clearfield Trust. After several years, the government realized that the check was forged and filed suit to have Clearfield Trust reimburse the government for the check, as required by principles of commercial paper law. Clearfield Trust said the action was time barred, pointing to the forum state's statute of limitations. The Supreme Court rejected this assertion, ruling that federal law should govern whether the action was time barred. As the source of this federal law, the Court used commercial law created by a federal judge during the "golden age" of federal common law before *Erie Railroad Co. v. Tompkins*, 304 U.S. 64 (1938).

To justify its reliance on federal common law, the *Clearfield Trust* Court explained that the United States government needs a national, uniform body of law to govern the vast amounts of commercial paper it issues. Suggesting that expediency alone does not justify federal common law, the Court observed that the United States government issued commercial paper pursuant to the federal authority grounded in the Constitution and federal statutes. Given this established federal foundation for the government's actions, the federal interest in uniform regulation justified federal rules governing the right to enforce commercial paper issued by the United States.

Example 16-1

The state of Florida experienced a natural disaster, and the federal government provided assistance pursuant to a congressional statute, the Disaster

---

2. *Clearfield Trust Co. v. United States*, 318 U.S. 363 (1943) (creating law to govern United States suit to recover forged government check).
3. *See, e.g., Wilson v. Omaha Indian Tribe*, 442 U.S. 653 (1979) (holding that federal law determines effect of stream's course changes on property in which the United States is a riparian owner); *United States v. Little Lake Misere Land Co.*, 412 U.S. 580 (1973) (determining that federal law governs land acquisition for public uses pursuant to a land contract).
4. *United States v. Standard Oil Co. of Cal.*, 332 U.S. 301 (1947) (holding that federal law should govern suit by United States to recover for injured military personnel's expenses).
5. *See, e.g., United States v. Texas*, 507 U.S. 529 (1993) (upholding common law right of United States to collect pre-judgment interest on debts owed by states).
6. *Boyle v. United Techs. Corp.*, 487 U.S. 500, 504-06 (1988).

Relief Act. In particular, the federal government gave Florida a large number of mobile homes that would be "placed on a site provided by the State, without charge to the United States." The state was unable to prepare the home sites. Thus, the Army Corps of Engineers performed the work for the state of Florida, pursuant to a contract in which Florida promised to pay for the home site preparation. Florida, however, failed to pay the United States under the contract.

The United States brought suit against the state, seeking to recover under the contract. The parties agreed that federal law governed whether to enforce the contract. The district court granted summary judgment on the issue of payment under the contract, ruling that Florida owed the money due under the contract. The United States next argued that it was entitled to pre-judgment interest on those payments. Florida fought this assertion, noting that pre-judgment interest would not be allowed under state law. The United States contends that federal common law, not state law, should govern the question of whether it is entitled to that interest. Should the district court accept the United States' contention?

Explanation

Yes, the district court should create federal common law. The question of whether pre-judgment interest is due requires a court's equitable judgment, balancing principles of fairness and incorporating particular circumstances of the case. Several qualities about this example suggest that a unique federal interest is involved, justifying the use of federal law in calculating this balance. First, the example involves a right of the United States to monies due under a contract, a subject area reasonably characterized as "proprietary." Second, the example requires evaluating the rights of two sovereigns: the federal government and the state government. Because this process involves the federalist system maintained under the United States Constitution, federal law is best designed to accommodate the roles of both governments in the federalist system. Third, Congress stated its view on those roles in the Disaster Relief Act, expressing a policy of apportioning responsibility for disaster relief between the state and federal governments. Congress suggested that the United States should not bear any financial burden concerning home site preparation, and federal common law can incorporate that preference in establishing the calculus for pre-judgment interest in this case. Requiring pre-judgment interest ensures that the United States receives full compensation for assisting with home site preparation, a result consistent with the resource allocation decisions in the Disaster Relief Act. *See West Virginia v. United States*, 479 U.S. 305 (1987) (applying federal common law to govern the availability of pre-judgment interest in Disaster Relief Act dispute).

A tricky part of federal common law is identifying the factors alerting a court to use federal power, not state power, to regulate a particular legal standard. When is the federal interest unique and sufficiently important to call for creating and applying federal common law? One approach is to look at the subject areas where the Supreme Court has identified federal common law in the past. If the case falls within one of those areas, federal common law is likely appropriate. Another approach is to look for reasons that — in light of separation of powers and federalism — federal court lawmaking might be justified in that particular context.

Applying the latter approach in this example, one might observe that the dispute arises in an area marked by both the United States Constitution (allocation of authority between federal and state governments) and by a federal statute (the Disaster Relief Act). These constitutional and statutory provisions are not the actual source of the legal standard governing pre-judgment interest. Rather, federal court-made law is the source of the standard, with the Constitution and the Disaster Relief Act providing background guidance and shrouding the court's lawmaking with legitimacy. The act of federal common law–making in this context does not constitute an assault on federalism because the states ceded ultimate control when they ratified the Constitution over matters concerning federal-state governmental relations and gave Congress the authority to pass legislation such as the Disaster Relief Act. Moreover, federal common law making steers clear of problems with separation of powers because Congress has expressed policy judgments in the Disaster Relief Act, which can guide the court in fashioning a pre-judgment interest ruling in this case.

2. The Content of Federal Law

The question of whether to apply federal common law does not require an all-or-nothing decision. Just because a court decides that federal common law should govern a particular area does not mean that federal principles and standards control the *content* of the federal common law. The court may deem it more appropriate to borrow state law concepts and incorporate them into the federal common law.

In a series of cases culminating with *United States v. Kimbell Foods, Inc.,* 440 U.S. 715 (1979), the Supreme Court explored the possibility of using state law to direct the content of federal common law. In *Kimbell Foods,* the Court expounded a balancing test for considering the content of federal common law. On one side of the balance are concerns with uniformity and avoiding obstacles to fulfilling the potential of regulatory programs. The Court explained that "federal programs . . . 'by [] nature . . . must be uniform in character throughout the Nation'" and possess "specific objectives" that would be frustrated by state law principles." 440 U.S. at 728-729 (quoting *United States v. Yazell*, 382 U.S. 341, 354 (1966)). On the other hand, uniformity may not be necessary in certain contexts, and "application of a federal rule [might] disrupt commercial relationships predicated on state law." Id. at 729.

Example 16-2

Consider the facts of Example 16-1, regarding money owed by Florida to the United States for home site development work. Once the court determines that federal common law should govern the pre-judgment interest question, the court should consider the second step of the inquiry: what should be the content of federal common law? Should the court incorporate state law into the content of federal common law governing pre-judgment interest?

Explanation

No, the court should not incorporate state law on this question. First, the pre-judgment interest question arises as part of a federal program in which Congress has tried to develop a uniform approach toward helping the states with the consequences of disasters. Allowing state law to govern whether the United States should receive pre-judgment interest injects inequality into the process of awarding aid to state governments: some state governments will have to pay pre-judgment interest and some will not. The different treatment will result not from considering equities unique to each case, but from the fortuity of different states' laws. Moreover, since disasters are sporadic and unpredictable events, this is not an area where the application of pure federal principles would disrupt routine matters and fixed relationships that are ordinarily governed by an established state law scheme. See *West Virginia v. United States*, 479 U.S. 305 (1987) (applying federal law, not state law, to determine the content of federal common law on the issue of pre-judgment interest in Disaster Relief Act dispute).

Example 16-3

Three women owned a corporation known as the Sham Corp., which ran an apartment building with a mortgage held by the United States Department of Housing and Urban Development (HUD). The mortgage was granted as part of HUD's national lending program, and Sham Corp. signed a standard "Regulatory Agreement" with HUD specifying the terms of payment under the mortgage.

The United States brought suit against the three owners of Sham Corp., alleging that they were in default under the mortgage (in violation of the Regulatory Agreement). The United States sought to have the three women satisfy the indebtedness, alleging they were "alter egos" of Sham Corp. According to the United States, Sham Corp. was inadequately capitalized and was not run according to the usual formal rules of corporate structure and operations. For that reason, the court decided it should "pierce the corporate veil" and impose liability on the three owners. The United States asked the federal court to apply federal common law, which has a different "alter ego" standard than applicable state law. Federal law is less protective of the individuals than state law, making it more likely that the court would pierce the corporate veil. Should the district court apply federal common law? If so, what should be the content of the federal common law?

Explanation

Yes, the district court should apply federal common law. The option of piercing the corporate veil arises in the context of a federal regulatory scheme regarding a national program, and the United States government's rights under that program are implicated. Thus, not only does the United States' proprietary interest hang in the balance, but Congress has already acted to create standards in the general subject area.

The next question, then, is whether the court should borrow from state law to provide content to the federal common law. The three crucial factors for courts to balance are (1) the possibility of frustrating objectives of the federal program, (2) a need for national uniformity, and (3) the possibility that federal law would disrupt commercial relationships protected by existing state law. As for the first factor, a possibility may exist that state law provides too much protection to the individual women, undermining the national lending program by allowing the women to escape payments that would help keep the program financially secure. Moreover, because the HUD mortgages come from a single source and are supported by a standard Regulatory Agreement, the federal program appears to be premised on providing borrowers with credit on uniform terms. Finally, because HUD is a federal entity, the relationship between Sham Corp. and HUD is not necessarily established and protected under state commercial law. Sometimes the federal government's business dealings affect relationships between private entities, but no facts suggest that this is the case here. Thus, all three factors suggest that federal law, not state law, should determine the content of federal common law in this example. *See United States v. Golden Acres, Inc.*, 702 F. Supp. 1097, 1103-1104 (D. Del. 1988) (deciding that federal law should provide the content of federal common law governing whether to pierce the corporate veil in a HUD mortgage transaction).

Although the court will likely conclude that Sham Corp. and HUD's relationship is not necessarily protected under state commercial law, the court may, upon reflection, identify some state law-protected commercial relationships that may be affected by a decision piercing the corporate veil in this example. The court may also decide that state and federal law are not so different as to threaten uniformity in administering the loan program. If that is the case, the court is free to integrate state law to the extent desirable, if only to consult state cases for guidance. *Id.* at 1104 (observing that state and federal law regarding corporate alter egos are similar, but that federal law is "simply broader"). In other words, a decision that federal standards generally should provide the content of federal common law questions does not brand state law as entirely off limits.

B. CASES BETWEEN PRIVATE PARTIES IMPLICATING FEDERAL INTERESTS

As shown previously, the Supreme Court has willingly endorsed federal common law in a number of contexts involving federal proprietary interests where the United States (or a United States officer) was a party to the suit. The Court has been much less willing to create common law (or endorse its use) where federal proprietary interests are implicated but the suit is between private parties. Thus, the Court rejected federal common law claims in a suit by private parties to recover for conversion of United States bonds[7] and to recover as beneficiaries to a contract involving the Federal Aviation Administration.[8] Perhaps even more significantly, the Court refused to apply federal common law in a suit by the Federal Deposit Insurance Corporation against a bank officer for breach of fiduciary duty. The Court reasoned that the case involved predominantly private interests because the Federal Deposit Insurance Corporation sued to enforce the bank's rights, not its own.[9]

In stark contrast to these cases, the Supreme Court did create federal common law in a case concerning a private entity's liability in a state tort suit brought by relatives of a dead Marine Corps member. In *Boyle v. United Technologies Corp.*, 187 U.S. 500 (1988), a private entity had produced a helicopter under contract with the federal government. Plaintiffs alleged that the helicopter contained a design defect that allegedly caused the serviceman's death. The Supreme Court justified the application of federal

---

7. *Bank of America Nat'l Trust & Savings Ass'n v. Parnell*, 352 U.S. 29, 33 (1956).
8. *Miree v. DeKalb County, Ga*, 433 U.S. 25 (1977).
9. *O'Melveny & Myers v. Fed. Deposit Ins. Corp.*, 512 U.S. 79, 84-87 (1994). The *O'Melveny & Myers* Court reasoned that since the Federal Deposit Insurance Corporation was suing to enforce the bank's rights, the case did not involve the rights of the United States in a national program. The Court also noted the parties' failure to identify significant differences between state and federal law.

common law defense shielding the government contractor from liability by invoking two federal interests that spilled over into the private suit. First, the federal government has an interest in cost control in procuring military hardware; if contractors are held liable, the Court reasoned, the contractors would pass litigation costs on to the United States in the form of higher contract prices. The second justification was an exception to the Federal Tort Claims Act known as the discretionary function exception. Under this exception, claimants may not recover tort damages against the United States for actions of the United States made in the exercise of discretion. The Court reasoned that the contractor's designs were discretionary and therefore entitled to the same protection as would apply if the government designed the equipment itself.

Boyle is remarkable for a number of reasons. The first reason is the Court's readiness to extend the prerogative of federal common law to a private entity. Second, the Court framed the federal common law inquiry as a form of preemption: the need for uniform federal law to protect military contractors was so strong that it displaced state law. Third, the decision has significant separation of powers ramifications. Justice Brennan's dissent reviewed failed attempts by military contractors to lobby Congress to create a military contractor defense legislatively, yet the Supreme Court implemented the defense by judicial decision. Therefore, *Boyle* is a testament to the strength of the Supreme Court's conviction concerning the importance of uniform federal law governing military matters — at least where significant federal financial exposure is threatened.

Under *Boyle*, such military matters apparently fall into the area of exclusive federal domain, illustrated in Figure 16-1 as Quadrant 4. Quadrant 4 includes circumstances where Congress has not acted but where federal common law is necessary to protect federal interests. In *Boyle*, state law had attempted to regulate the controversy by providing for tort liability, but the Supreme Court preempted that law with the government contractor defense. The federal interest was so strong as to displace state law and call for federal lawmaking even in the absence of congressional action.

Example 16-4

Sam and Sally Service were married in 1985 and settled in their home state of California. It soon became apparent that their marriage would not be a happy one. Nevertheless, they remained married and continued to pool their financial resources until Sam's death in 2005.

Sam had enlisted in the military two years after their marriage. At the time he enlisted, he became eligible for a life insurance policy issued pursuant to the National Service Life Insurance Act. Because he felt no warmth or responsibility toward Sally, Sam designated his mother as the policy beneficiary. Pursuant to the National Service Life Insurance Act, the federal government paid most of the premium on Sam's policy. A very small percentage of the premium was paid through a deduction from Sam's paycheck every month. The National Service Life Insurance Act provides that premiums would be waived during any period of disability. The act further provides that "[n]o one shall have a vested right" in any proceeds under the policy.

Sam died while serving in active duty. After his death, the federal government transferred the insurance policy proceeds to Sam's mother as the policy's beneficiary. Shocked to learn that she was not the beneficiary under the policy, Sally brought an action in state court against Sam's mother. Sally's suit seeks an order requiring Sam's mother to disgorge one-half of the policy proceeds. Sally argues that the community property laws of California entitle her to half of the policy proceeds because the policy premiums were paid with marital property — Sam's salary. The National Service Life Insurance Act says nothing directly on this issue.

Should California or federal law govern the dispute? If federal law governs, what should be its content?

Explanation

Federal law, not California law, should govern this dispute. The pendency of the suit in state court does not affect this result. Like a federal court, the state court will have the obligation of ascertaining and applying federal common law.

The benefits provided to military personnel include life insurance coverage. Clearly, the military has tried to make this an attractive employment benefit, including inexpensive subsidized premiums that are waived during any disability. Part of the benefit's appeal includes the freedom that service personnel enjoy in choosing their beneficiary. By stating that "[n]o one shall have a vested right" in the policy proceeds, Congress has made a judgment to allow personnel to circumvent other requirements (such as state laws) that might constrain them. Although Congress does not provide that the National Life Insurance Act displaces state law, Congress's negation of vested rights suggests that it does not intend these policies to provide an area for state regulation. Acknowledging this cue, as well as *Boyle*'s emphasis on the importance of a federal interest in the military, the state court should conclude that this is an area for federal common law.

Although *Boyle* guides the disposition of this example, the example does not present a circumstance (such as in *Boyle*) represented by Quadrant 4 in Figure 16-1. Rather, the example falls within Quadrant 3. First, state law generally governs insurance contracts and administration of decedent's estates. Issues concerning who receives policy proceeds following an insured's death likely fall within the shared state and federal domain, even if the insured has a military connection. Moreover, this example does not fall within Quadrant 4 also because Congress has acted in passing legislation on the subject matter of the dispute. Thus, the court would be engaged in interstitial lawmaking, filling gaps left by Congress in the National Life Insurance Act.

The final question concerns what the content of federal common law should be. Given that lack of uniformity is rarely tolerated in the military setting, the state court should conclude that the content of federal common law should be federal law, not state law. In applying federal law, the state court should fashion a federal rule that is consistent with Congress's objective of providing service personnel with a liberal and generous benefit. *See Wissner v. Wissner*, 338 U.S. 655, 656-660 (1950) (holding that federal law, not state community property law, controlled the estranged wife's entitlement to husband's federal life insurance benefits). *See also Ridgway v. Ridgway*, 454 U.S. 46 (1981) (holding that serviceman's beneficiary designation under federal life insurance policy prevailed over state law constructive trust imposed on policy proceeds). Here, if the state court were to incorporate California's community property laws into federal common law, the court might frustrate Congress's objectives in the National Life Insurance Act.

Example 16-5

The United States entered into a lease contract with Breaching Corporation. Gregory was not a party to the contract, but was a third-party beneficiary because he stood to benefit significantly from the lease. Breaching Corporation broke the lease agreement, and Gregory sued Breaching Corporation only. Breaching Corporation argues that federal common law should govern the dispute. Should the court accept this argument?

Explanation

No, the court should not accept this argument. The only fact vaguely suggesting that this is a federal common law case is the presence of the United States as a party to the contract. But that alone is not enough to render the case appropriate for federal common law. The facts do not suggest that the litigation will concern liability of the United States or responsibilities of the United States under the contract. As the Supreme Court observed in *Miree v. DeKalb County, Ga.*, 433 U.S. 25 (1977), where a case would result in no direct effect on the United States or the United States treasury, the court should not apply federal common law. *See also Charest v. Olin Corp.*, 542 F. Supp. 771 (N.D. Ala. 1982) (holding state law, not federal law, governs private action by third-party beneficiary to contract for which United States is a party).

Example 16-6

Generous Corporation is a fledgling company that is struggling to make a profit, yet is committed to providing a generous benefits package to its employees. To that end, Generous Corporation has made monthly contributions to its employee benefit plan for the past five years. It has now discovered that it overpaid its contributions during that period and has requested that the plan manager, Stingy Funds, Inc., refund the overpayment. Stingy Funds refused to do so. Although employee benefit plans are extensively regulated by a federal statute known as the Employee Retirement Income Security Act (ERISA), no statutory provision provides a vehicle for Generous Corporation to recover the overpayment. ERISA provides that, except in limited instances, the statute "shall supersede any and all State laws in so far as they may now or hereinafter relate to any employee benefit plan."

Undaunted by this provision, Generous Corporation filed an action against Stingy Funds for restitution of the money. Generous Corporation argued that the court should apply federal common law principles of restitution, requiring Stingy Funds to disgorge the amount of the overpayment.

Should the court accept Generous Corporation's suggestion to apply a federal common law of restitution? If so, should state or federal law provide the content of this federal common law?

Explanation

Yes, the court should accept the suggestion of Generous Corporation. First, the facts appear to present a classic case for restitution: a benefit was mistakenly conferred to an entity, and the entity had no right to the benefit. Yet no tort, contract, or other formal cause of action provides a mechanism to require the entity to disgorge the benefit wrongfully conferred. Restitution supplies a mechanism to fill a void in the legal remedies, providing justice to the victim of the mistake. In fact, a state law theory of restitution might fit the facts here. The problem with a state law restitution theory, however, is that ERISA has such a wide preemptive reach that it arguably leaves no room for the operation of such a state law remedy. Thus, if common law is to fill the void, it must be federal common law.

Several factors suggest that a court would act appropriately in creating federal common law in this instance. Given ERISA's broad preemptive sweep, the creation of federal common law to fill a gap in the scheme would likely not displace state law. For that reason, the court need not worry about improper federalism implications. Moreover, granting the common law right to restitution is compatible with Congress's intent in creating ERISA, thus avoiding separation of powers concerns as well. Creating federal law to govern Generous Corporation's problem is consistent with Congress's policy of complete federal control of all facets of employee pension plans. Perhaps even more important, recognizing the federal restitution claim furthers the policy of ensuring pension benefits for employees. Allowing the restitution encourages small and struggling employers such as Generous Corporation to provide benefit plans to their employees by reducing the risk of unjustified loss. *See Jamail, Inc. v. Carpenters District Council*, 954 F.2d 299, 302-306 (5th Cir. 1992) (recognizing federal common law action for restitution of overpayment of contributions to employee benefit plans).

On the issue of the content of federal common law, Congress's overriding intent to create uniform rules for pension plans suggests that the court should not borrow state law to provide the full content of federal common law. Noncritical adoption of state law could interfere with the complex statutory scheme Congress established in ERISA. That does not mean, however, that state law regarding restitution cannot inform the development of federal law principles, so long as the state law principles are modified appropriately to ensure they do not clash with ERISA's particular requirements.

C. CASES WHERE NECESSITY, EXPEDIENCY, OR JUSTICE REQUIRE FEDERAL COMMON LAW

In adjudicating rights of real persons in real situations, federal courts often encounter situations where other lawmaking bodies—such as state lawmakers, the United States Congress, and the United States executive branch—have not provided legal rules to dispose of the case. To get the job of adjudication done, therefore, federal courts must make law. Sometimes the impulse to make federal common law comes from necessity or expediency, such as when federal courts fashion procedural law to govern the process of adjudicating rights.[10] Other times, federal courts may make law out of a sense of justice.

Two examples of interstitial lawmaking illustrate this impulse to do justice. First, federal courts make law where they infer a private right of action to enforce the standards in a statutory scheme. In these cases, Congress has created a legal requirement but has failed to establish a cause of action for private parties to enforce that requirement in a civil suit. Divining Congress's intent, the federal court will infer this cause of action from the statutory scheme to ensure an effective remedy for a wrong done. In a related context, the Supreme Court has authorized lower courts to look to

---

10. Chapter 15 discusses common law governing matters of procedure in the context of the *Erie* doctrine.

norms of international customary law in recognizing causes of action under the Alien Tort Statute and in identifying legal standards enforced through those causes of action. *Sosa v. Alvarez-Machain*, 542 U.S. 692 (2004). The impetus behind this decision was ensuring that the Alien Tort Statute had the practical effect of providing an appropriate remedy for harms suffered.

These instances of federal court lawmaking cannot be organized neatly into a grand theory of legitimate areas of federal common law. Such is the ad hoc nature of the jurisprudence concerning federal courts' job description. The tools for analyzing federal common law issues — and anticipating when a federal court might find common law making appropriate — are thus the same as those useful in other areas of federal courts law: governmental theories pertaining to federalism and separation of powers, the ability to marshal arguments on both sides of an issue, healthy skepticism, and, of course, a sense of humor.

Table of Cases

Index